DOCUMENTS ON BRITISH FOREIGN POLICY
1919–1939

EDITED BY

W. N. MEDLICOTT, M.A., D.Lit., D.Litt.

Emeritus Professor of International History, University of London

DOUGLAS DAKIN, M.A., Ph.D.

Professor of History, Birkbeck College, University of London

AND

M. E. LAMBERT, M.A.

SERIES IA

Volume IV

LONDON
HER MAJESTY'S STATIONERY OFFICE
1971

© *Crown copyright 1971*

Published by

HER MAJESTY'S STATIONERY OFFICE

To be purchased from
49 High Holborn, London WC1V 6HB
13a Castle Street, Edinburgh EH2 3AR
109 St Mary Street, Cardiff CF1 1JW
Brazennose Street, Manchester M60 8AS
50 Fairfax Street, Bristol BS1 3DE
258 Broad Street, Birmingham B1 2HE
80 Chichester Street, Belfast BT1 4JY
or through booksellers

SBN 11 591786 1*

PRINTED IN ENGLAND
FOR HER MAJESTY'S STATIONERY OFFICE
BY VIVIAN RIDLER AT THE UNIVERSITY PRESS, OXFORD

DOCUMENTS ON BRITISH FOREIGN POLICY
1919–1939

Series IA, Volume IV

European and Security Questions
1927–1928

PREFACE

In sequel to Volume III this volume illustrates British policy on European and security questions from September 6, 1927, until April 13, 1928, when the American draft treaty for the renunciation of war was formally presented to His Majesty's Government. As in Volume III European questions, centring on problems relating to Germany, are treated in the first two chapters, while papers on Anglo-American relations and naval disarmament are printed in the following two chapters. Correspondence on the proposed treaty for the renunciation of war naturally falls into these latter chapters, and it has seemed appropriate to vary the arrangement adopted for Volume III and include here the documentation on the consideration of security by the Preparatory Commission for the Disarmament Conference.

The main problems concerning Germany in the period covered in this volume related to reparations and the occupation of the Rhineland ('the iron curtain between Germany and France': document No. 141) rather than to disarmament, where little work remained for the military experts in Berlin. In September 1927 Sir Austen Chamberlain supported M. Briand, the French Minister for Foreign Affairs, in refusing at that time to discuss the evacuation of the Rhineland with their German colleague, Dr. Stresemann (document No. 8). In the interests of Anglo-German relations, Sir Ronald Lindsay, H.M. Ambassador at Berlin, agreed with Sir A. Chamberlain in wishing to terminate the occupation, but he considered it had a value in its relation to the acceptance of a definitive scheme of reparation payments (document No. 180).

The continuing ability of Germany to pay the reparation annuities stipulated in the Dawes Plan of 1924 obviously depended on her maintaining a satisfactory financial position. Doubts on this score were expressed by Mr. Parker Gilbert, Agent General for Reparation Payments, notably in his letter of October 20, 1927, to the German Minister of Finance, Dr. Köhler. Mr. Gilbert criticized Germany's budgetary practice and considered her foreign borrowing excessive. Generally similar doubts were felt by Mr. E. Rowe-Dutton, Financial Adviser to H.M. Embassy at Berlin, who considered the prospect for 1929 was 'depressing'. The conclusion drawn in the Foreign Office on February 9, 1928, by Mr. J. V. Perowne of the Central Department was that 'if Mr. Rowe-Dutton's view is correct, as there seems no reason to doubt, that the German budget, though balanced, is really top-heavy and that the prosperity of 1927 was due to the influx of foreign loans, there appears to be little chance of Germany being able to provide the necessary financial solatium in return for which, plus some form of control, the French have indicated that they are ready to leave the Rhine' (document No. 137).

Mr. Parker Gilbert also suggested that the total of Germany's liability to reparation payments, on which the Dawes Committee had not ruled, should be fixed. This raised the question of the continuing validity, accepted by the French Government, of the decision by the Reparation Commission in 1921 that Germany should pay 132 milliard gold marks. For His Majesty's Government the fixation of the German liability was further connected with the question of war debts, on which British policy had been set out in the Balfour Note of August 1922. In this note His Majesty's Government had informed their debtors that they would not demand from them more than they themselves had to pay their creditors, notably the United States. This connexion between reparations and war debts was not accepted by Mr. Mellon, Secretary of the U.S. Treasury. The British view was, therefore, that so long as the required payments continued, it was inadvisable to raise the question of Germany's total liability until after the new American President had been installed in March 1929; if discussion was unavoidable a new Dawes Committee should consider the question (document No. 176).

Difficulties about the Rhineland and reparations did not prevent wide-ranging discussion of European problems on December 12, 1927, between Sir A. Chamberlain and Dr. Stresemann, who remarked frankly that 'the Danzig corridor also presented an insuperable difficulty for Germany. Germany could never admit that East Prussia should permanently remain "a colony"' (document No. 91). He hoped, however, that it might be possible to do business directly with Marshal Pilsudski, Polish President of the Council, notably on commercial matters. This reference reflected the importance of German trading interests in Poland. Their jealousy of potential rivalry from Great Britain was reported by Mr. R. A. Leeper, H.M. Chargé d'Affaires at Warsaw. He regretted British failure to develop commercial opportunities in Poland, and considered that 'the political stability of Poland is of real political importance to us. It not only keeps the balance in Europe, but it keeps Bolshevism at bay' (document No. 102).

In the Polish view, wrote Mr. Leeper on December 13, 1927, there was no reason to be 'alarmed by Russian Bolshevism as a real social danger' or to be over-impressed by the danger of Russian nationalism (document No. 93). In the light of the reduction of available information since the rupture of Anglo-Soviet relations in May 1927 opinions in this neighbour of the U.S.S.R. were of interest but Polish views of Soviet weakness were not shared in the Foreign Office. British policy remained to abstain from any interference in Soviet internal affairs, or from any anti-Soviet bloc, and Sir A. Chamberlain noted that if there were any 'fissiparous tendency in Russia, it would I am convinced be killed by any external interference' (letter to Sir W. Erskine, H.M. Minister at Warsaw, January 26, 1928, document No. 123). In a conversation with the Soviet Vice-Commissar for Foreign Affairs at Geneva on December 5, 1927, Sir A. Chamberlain stated in reply to an inquiry from M. Litvinov, that 'His Majesty's Government had had to complain of the interference of the Soviet Government in the domestic affairs of Great Britain and of the constant hostility of Russian agencies throughout the world to the British Empire. What His Majesty's Government required for the resumption of relations was proof that these obnoxious activities had ceased' (document No. 82).

In their conversation on December 12, 1927, Sir A. Chamberlain and Dr. Stresemann also discussed Italian policy. Franco-Italian rivalry in the Balkans had recently assumed a sharper form with the signature on November 11 and 22 respectively of treaties between France and the Serb-Croat-Slovene State and between Italy and Albania. Neither treaty had been welcomed by Sir A. Chamberlain, who continued to use his influence in favour of a better understanding between France and Italy while avoiding active mediation. At the same time Sir R. Lindsay was instructed to watch for signs of Italy's seeking German support, though it was not thought likely that this would be forthcoming so long as Franco-German relations remained satisfactory. This British anticipation appeared to be confirmed by Dr. Stresemann's saying to Sir A. Chamberlain that 'if Germany, Great Britain and France remained united, we could oblige Signor Mussolini to keep the peace' (document No. 91). Evidence reaching the Foreign Office appeared to indicate that there was Italian involvement in the smuggling of arms to Hungary early in 1928 and in the activities of the Macedonian Revolutionary Organization. Both Sir A. Chamberlain and Sir Ronald Graham, H.M. Ambassador at Rome, continued to believe that the policy of encouraging a Franco-Italian *rapprochement* should be pursued, despite an unpromising beginning in January 1928 to conversations between Signor Mussolini and the new French Ambassador at Rome.

Developments with a significance lying yet further in the future in the field of European integration were not ignored in the Foreign Office, though on the available evidence their short-term possibilities seemed of more consequence. In a memorandum of September 8, 1927, Mr. M. Huxley of the Central Department argued that, despite disadvantages, it would be in long-term British interests to 'try to strengthen the Pan-European movement', but he did not suggest any active support for it (document No. 4). An unofficial French warning in March 1928 that growing Franco-German industrial co-operation might lead to political co-operation which would result in the isolation of Great Britain was considered, but was regarded as an attempt 'to frighten us with the bogey of isolation, but it may well be that this isolation, if it materialises, will be more dangerous to France than to Great Britain' (memorandum of March 20, 1928, by Mr. O. G. Sargent, Head of the Central Department, document No. 167).

The documents in Chapters I and II thus illustrate a rather ominous period when the goodwill generated by the co-operation achieved at Locarno by the four great Powers of Western Europe was tending to become a diminishing asset while the fundamental problems of their relations with each other and with the U.S.S.R. remained unresolved.

Chapters III and IV relate to the consideration of other unsolved problems in the field of security, and in particular Anglo-American naval rivalry and the search for a watertight system of security by the League of

Nations, through its organ the Preparatory Commission for the Disarmament Conference.

The heart of the problem for the League of Nations was to decide whether disarmament or the establishment of a system of security should have priority. Whereas in the spring of 1927 the Preparatory Commission had failed to solve the concrete problems of disarmament, in September the Assembly of the League of Nations decided that it should pursue the question of security. This change of priority inevitably raised for Germany the question of her state of restricted armament as compared with other Powers, and for H.M. Government their previous rejection of a system of general security and compulsory arbitration in the Geneva Protocol of 1924. The prospects for the new Committee on Arbitration and Security of the Preparatory Commission were gloomily analysed on October 26, 1927, by Mr. Cadogan, an Assistant to the British Delegate to the League of Nations, who saw no way out of the dilemma while the current feeling of insecurity prevailed in Europe (document No. 219). The documents relating to the Committee printed in Chapters III and IV show that in spite of goodwill and hard work on the part of delegates, whose deliberations were complicated by the need to consider a scheme for universal disarmament sponsored by the Soviet Government, it could produce only paper solutions unbacked by any confidence in governments.

Mutual distrust also threatened Anglo-American relations since the tripartite conference at Geneva in the summer of 1927 had revealed how deep were feelings on both sides of the Atlantic on naval questions. Within His Majesty's Government much consideration was given to the basis of the British position on the laws of war at sea in the light of the unpleasant realization that the failure of the Geneva Conference was an indication that the possibility of a war between the two countries arising from a dispute about rights of blockade could not be excluded. By April 1928 it appeared that the best course would be to discuss this question with the American Government when the new Administration due to take office in March 1929 was ready.

Meanwhile in their desire to break the deadlock on naval disarmament which was preventing economies in naval spending, His Majesty's Government held further discussions with the French Government. Talks between naval representatives in November 1927 indicated that French opposition to British insistence on naval limitation by classes rather than by total tonnage might be less rigid. Sir A. Chamberlain therefore put before M. Briand on March 9, 1928, revised proposals for naval limitation in six classes, indicating that if he could point to a French concession here, British public opinion might acquiesce in his yielding to French insistence that military reserves should not be limited. He added that he did not wish to be driven to vote against France with Germany and still less with the U.S.S.R. on the latter point (documents Nos. 304 and 306).

On the American side a new move to forward the peaceful settlement of disputes was made by Mr. Kellogg, the American Secretary of State, when he suggested to the French Government on December 28, 1927, a draft treaty for the renunciation of war in elaboration of the proposal originally made by M. Briand in the previous April. The draft treaty was not formally laid before His Majesty's and other interested Governments until April 13, 1928, but it was discussed by Mr. Kellogg with Sir Esme Howard, H.M. Ambassador at Washington. Sir A. Chamberlain's reaction was to doubt whether 'there is any reality behind Kellogg's move' (letter to Sir E. Howard, February 13, 1928, document No. 275). At the same time he feared the effects of agreeing to submit all disputes to arbitration, including possibly those arising out of any future British exercise of belligerent rights at sea. Nevertheless, he recognised that there were 'many disadvantages in doing anything which Mr. Kellogg may regard as a rebuff' and hoped that Sir E. Howard could 'inspire him with caution without throwing doubt on our goodwill' (*ibid.*).

In compiling this volume the Editor has used the private papers of Sir Austen Chamberlain and Sir Orme Sargent, filed as F.O. 800, volumes 261–2 and 275 respectively.

The conditions under which the Editors accepted the task of producing this Collection, namely, access to all papers in the Foreign Office archives and freedom in the selection and arrangement of documents, continue to be fulfilled. The explanation in the preface to Volume I of archival difficulties and of editorial expedients employed to minimize them applies also, however, to the present volume. Where the Confidential Print only is preserved in the main file an asterisk is added after the heading (e.g. document No. 24).

I should like to thank the Head of the Library and Records Department of the Foreign and Commonwealth Office, Mr. B. Cheeseman, O.B.E., and his staff for their indispensable assistance. I should also like to thank Mrs. Marilynne Morgan, B.A., whose help in all stages of the preparation of the volume has been invaluable.

M. E. LAMBERT

January 1971

CONTENTS

CHAPTER SUMMARIES

CHAPTER I

European, including German, questions: signature of treaties between France and the Serb-Croat-Slovene State and between Italy and Albania

September 6–December 31, 1927

xxi

CHAPTER II

Correspondence on European Questions
January 3–April 13, 1928

xxiii

British policy on disarmament following the Tripartite Naval Conference at Geneva

September 6–December 29, 1927

CHAPTER IV

The American proposal for the Renunciation of War: discussions at Geneva on Security

December 30, 1927–April 13, 1928

European, including German, questions: signature of treaties between France and the Serb-Croat-Slovene State and between Italy and Albania

September 6–December 31, 1927

No. 1

Sir A. Chamberlain (Geneva) to Sir W. Tyrrell[1] (Received September 9)
No. 7 L.N.A. [C 7489/4815/90]

GENEVA, *September 6, 1927*

Sir,

Monsieur Marinkovitch[2] asked me to receive him yesterday. He expressed his thanks for the part taken by His Majesty's Government in the settlement of the difficulty which had recently arisen between Yugoslavia and Albania, or rather, as he said, Italy,[3] and expressed the hope that I would continue to use my good offices with the Italian Government in order to promote an understanding. The conversations between Monsieur Rakic[4] and Signor Mussolini[5] had made no progress and he was afraid that when they were renewed they might lead to serious difficulties. It was his intention to begin them by a reference to the past when the relations between Yugoslavia and Italy were on a perfectly satisfactory footing, and to invite the Italian Government to examine all that had passed since then with a view to discovering and removing the misunderstandings or grievances which had caused the present unsatisfactory change; but he was afraid that when they came to the Treaty of Tirana[6] there might be difficulties. That Treaty was ambiguously worded. It might be perfectly innocent and a simple explanation might remove all cause for trouble. If, however, it was to be interpreted as the assertion of a right by the Italians to land troops in Albania to put down a local movement,

---

[1] Sir W. Tyrrell, Permanent Under Secretary of State for Foreign Affairs, was in charge of the Foreign Office during the absence of Sir A. Chamberlain, who was attending the meetings of the Council and Assembly of the League of Nations at Geneva (see Cmd. 3009 and 3008 of 1928 for reports thereon). Sir A. Chamberlain subsequently went on a cruise in the Mediterranean, visiting Paris on October 7–9 on his way back to London where he arrived on October 10.

[2] Serb-Croat-Slovene Minister for Foreign Affairs.

[3] See Volume III, Chapters I and II, *passim.*

[4] Serb-Croat-Slovene Minister at Rome.

[5] Head of the Italian Government and Italian Minister for Foreign Affairs.

[6] The Italian–Albanian treaty of November 27, 1926, is printed in *British and Foreign State Papers*, vol. 125, pp. 5–6.

that was a thing to which Yugoslavia could never consent and in that case the situation would be very grave.

2. In reply, I remarked that I understood from what Monsieur Rakic had said to Sir Ronald Graham[7] that he had been well satisfied with his first conversation with Signor Mussolini, that Signor Mussolini had met him in a very friendly spirit and had invited him to renew their intercourse whenever he chose.[8] If, therefore, further conversations had not taken place, it was, I presumed, because Monsieur Rakic thought that agreement would be more likely to be reached if time was given for the feelings roused by recent events to subside and for a calmer atmosphere to prevail. As to the course which he proposed to give to the conversations, it seemed to me that his decision was wise and that, if they were conducted in this way, the Treaty of Tirana would appear in its proper place in a series of subjects which required to be explained and settled, instead of as an isolated incident blocking the path at the very commencement of the negotiations.

3. I then repeated to Monsieur Marinkovitch, what I have so often had occasion to say to the Yugoslav representatives in London or here, as to my conviction that a perfectly satisfactory solution might easily have been obtained at the first moment if it had been quietly sought in a friendly spirit, but that Monsieur Nincic's resignation,[9] the manner of it and the reasons given for it, together with the press campaign in Yugoslavia, had singularly complicated the affair. Further, Monsieur Marinkovitch must remember what the recent history of Albania had been. The revolution which overthrew Fan Noli[10] and made Ahmed Zogu President had started from Yugoslav soil with, as I was convinced, the connivance if not the active support of the then Yugoslav Government. Obtaining power in this way, suspected as Ahmed Zogu therefore naturally was of having come under engagements to the Yugoslav Government to lean upon that country and to give a Yugoslav direction to his policy, it was natural that he should feel that the danger which menaced him was from the Italian side, and that as a consequence he should at once devote himself to securing the friendship of Italy. Then came his need of money, his failure to obtain it in Yugoslavia and his improvident financial bargain with the Italian Bank.[11]

4. I next turned to the events of last autumn—again a revolution, this time unsuccessful but starting like the other from Yugoslav territory,[12] though I did not suggest that on this occasion there had been any connivance on the part of the Yugoslav Government. The result of this was, in the first place, to expose the Albanian Government to great expense, and therefore to make

[7] H.M. Ambassador at Rome.　　　　　　　　　　[8] See Volume III, No. 254.

[9] M. Ninchitch had been Serb-Croat-Slovene Minister for Foreign Affairs, December 1921–December 1926. For his resignation see Volume II, No. 328, note 7.

[10] Bishop Fan Noli had been President of Albania, June–December 1924.

[11] In February–March 1925 the Albanian Minister of Finance had negotiated with an Italian financial group a concession giving it the right to establish a national bank of issue in Albania. The group was also to float a loan of 50 million gold francs, and to form a development corporation, for public works in Albania.

[12] See Volume II, No. 312.

them more than ever dependent upon the financial aid which they might get from Italian sources. For this reason alone Yugoslavia would have had the greatest interest in preventing the movement. The second result of the insurrection had been to frighten Ahmed Zogu and produce the Treaty of Tirana. At this point I observed that Signor Mussolini had first spoken to me about Albania at the time of my visit to Rome for the Council meeting of December 1924. Monsieur Nincic was then in Rome. Both these statesmen had informed me that they were negotiating an *accord* and, as I was leaving Rome, the Secretary General of the Italian Foreign Office had informed me that the negotiations had been successful and that a pact had been signed.[13] Signor Mussolini had at that time told me that he had no designs on the independence or integrity of Albania, and when I met him last September at Leghorn, in the course of a long conversation in which we reviewed all matters of common interest, he had repeated this declaration to me the good faith of which I did not doubt, and had added that he was at any time ready to give an assurance to that effect in treaty form.[14] That was all that I had known of the Treaty of Tirana until, on the eve of its publication and just as I was leaving for Geneva for another Council meeting, the Italian Ambassador had informed me that a treaty had been signed with Albania and would be shortly published.[12] The actual terms of the treaty became known to me only after I reached Geneva. At the time at which Signor Mussolini had spoken to me at Leghorn, I had gathered, rightly or wrongly, that the treaty which he had in mind would be one with Yugoslavia. Either this was not his intention at the time, or he had subsequently changed it and he had made his treaty with Albania but, according to my information, it was the insurrectionary movement of last year which had precipitated its signature, Ahmed Zogu, who had previously been hanging back, having then pressed for its immediate conclusion and, as I presumed Monsieur Marinkovitch knew, insisted upon the insertion of the very phrase to which the Yugoslav Government took exception and which had not been in the original Italian draft.

5. I here added that His Majesty's Government had no direct interest in this question. Such interest as it had for us arose solely from our general desire for the preservation of peace and the maintenance of the integrity and independence of a state member of the League of Nations; but for myself, I still saw no reason to doubt the declarations as to the standpoint and intentions of Italy which Signor Mussolini had volunteered to me. I could, of course, take no responsibility for the policy of the Italian Government and give no guarantee of their intentions, but in my own mind I was convinced that Signor Mussolini did desire to preserve the integrity of Albania and that he did not contemplate any act of aggression. It was obvious that he had need of peace to consolidate the position in Italy and to develop the great measures of reform which he had undertaken, nor could I hear of any sign of preparation for a military undertaking; but, having regard to the history of the case

[13] Cf. *I Documenti Diplomatici Italiani*, Settima Serie, vol. iii, p. 369, note 2.
[14] See Volume II, Nos. 235 and 255.

as I had recited it, Monsieur Marinkovitch must not be surprised if Signor Mussolini required to be assured that, whilst abstaining from intervention himself, he would not be exposed to seeing Ahmed Zogu's administration overthrown from another side merely because Ahmed Zogu pursued a policy friendly to Italy.

6. In reply, Monsieur Marinkovitch said that he did not in the least complain that the Rome conversations had not yet been resumed. He entirely agreed that it was better to wait for a calmer atmosphere. Neither did he complain because Albania cultivated friendly relations with Italy. As regards the history of the case, he would ask my permission to put it in what he thought was its true light. He had been Minister of Foreign Affairs at the time when Fan Noli was expelled. Fan Noli's administration was a Bolshevik administration acting under the influence of the Soviet Government. It was a principle of Yugoslav policy that they could not allow a non-Balkan power to establish itself in the Balkans. He admitted, therefore, that he had given a large liberty of action to Ahmed Zogu, for, had Soviet influence affirmed itself in Albania, that would have been a situation which Yugoslavia could not have tolerated and Yugoslavia would herself have been obliged to intervene by armies. As to the later movement, the Yugoslav Government had perhaps not exercised a sufficiently strict control over the Albanian emigrants, but Yugoslavia herself had a large Albanian population living on the frontier in poverty and distress and only too ready to take a part in any disturbances. The physical features of the frontier made it extremely difficult to control and it was for this very reason that he desired close cooperation between the two governments in order to prevent violations of it.

7. I spoke very seriously to Monsieur Marinkovitch about his avowal that he would have interfered with the internal affairs of Albania if he thought that Bolshevik influences were prevailing. I replied that any such step must have the gravest consequences and that he certainly could not expect that Signor Mussolini would tolerate such an intervention. Apart from the obligations of Yugoslavia as a signatory to the Covenant, to which I begged his serious attention, I observed that such action would be a direct provocation to Italian intervention.

8. As regards the present situation, I repeated that no doubt there would be great difficulties to be overcome in the negotiations, difficulties which arose from or were aggravated by the recent course of events as described by me. It was for Monsieur Marinkovitch to consider how he could give Signor Mussolini the necessary assurances as to the intentions of Yugoslavia. For my part, I had intervened most reluctantly in the affair and had only offered advice to the Yugoslav Government when expressly and repeatedly pressed to do so by them. My efforts had been directed to making direct negotiations between the two parties possible. The good relations existing between the British and Italian Governments, as well as the very friendly personal relations between Signor Mussolini and myself, had perhaps enabled me to be of some service in this respect, but I did not direct Italian policy, I could not be held responsible for it and any intervention of that kind could obviously be

4

employed only on rare and carefully chosen occasions. It was now for the Yugoslav Government, when they resumed the negotiations, to find the solution of the difficulties which had arisen. I had not the pleasure of knowing Monsieur Rakic, but from all I had heard he was a very skilful diplomat and I hoped that he would achieve success.

9. The arrival of another visitor brought the conversation to a close, but Monsieur Marinkovitch repeated as his parting words his thanks for what I had done and his hope that, as our relations with Yugoslavia were equally friendly, he might still receive our assistance in future.[15]

I have, &c.,
Austen Chamberlain

[15] A copy of this despatch was transmitted to Belgrade in Foreign Office despatch No. 475 of September 12.

No. 2

Sir R. Lindsay[1] *(Berlin) to Sir A. Chamberlain (Received September 13)*
No. 532 [N 4326/309/38]

BERLIN, September 7, 1927

Sir,

In the course of conversation to-day with Herr Köpke,[2] who is in charge of the Foreign Office in the absence at Geneva of Dr. Stresemann and Herr von Schubert,[3] he informed me that he had just received a visit from M. Brodowsky, the Soviet Chargé d'Affaires, who had enquired anxiously about the Polish proposal for a non-aggression pact,[4] and had thought it necessary too to imply some suspicion of the German attitude in the matter. Herr Köpke replied that he knew no more about it than what he had read in the papers, but that it seemed to him that the Poles had rather clumsily sprung a surprise on a completely unprepared assembly. But how, he asked, were the Russo-Polish negotiations on this subject progressing.[5] M. Brodowsky had answered that these negotiations had not been broken off—indeed they were continuing, but they were making no progress, and 'Germany need feel no anxiety'.

2. M. Brodowsky then passed to the usual theme of Great Britain and her machinations and inveighed against British 'naval and air manoeuvres' in the Baltic. He complained that the Air Minister had visited Berlin just at this moment and thought it significant. Herr Köpke ridiculed all this. There

[1] H.M. Ambassador at Berlin.
[2] Ministerial Director of the Western European Department of the German Ministry of Foreign Affairs.
[3] Respectively German Minister for Foreign Affairs and State Secretary in the German Ministry of Foreign Affairs.
[4] See Volume III, Nos. 327–8, and below, Nos. 202–3.
[5] For a statement on these negotiations by M. Rykov, Chairman of the Council of People's Commissars, on April 18, 1927, see Jane Degras, *Soviet Documents on Foreign Policy* (London, 1951 f.), vol. ii, pp. 190–1.

were, he said, only three or four submarines and three or four sea planes; they had cruized [*sic*] in the Baltic in even greater force in previous years, had made friends in German stations, and were well known throughout these waters. As to the Air Minister, it was only Sir Sefton Brancker[6] who had discussed some questions of commercial aviation on a short visit to Berlin. Why, asked Herr Köpke, was the Soviet Government always making this ridiculous fuss and always talking about imminent war? Whereupon M. Brodowsky had admitted that the frantic excursions and alarms of his Government were indeed exaggerated, but the Russian people were so apathetic, so 'nitchevo-[7] ish' that it was found necessary to stimulate them constantly, to keep them prepared for war, and so to avert the danger of war. Herr Köpke had replied that there was in Germany a certain amount of useful capital seeking investment in Russia; had it not occurred to the Soviet Government that all this agitation must have the effect of frightening the German Banker and forcing him to keep his capital at home? M. Brodowsky answered that Moscow was perfectly alive to this, but had calculated that what the Soviet could lose through the timidity of foreign finance was only one eighth of what they would lose if a war were to break out, and they therefore quite deliberately preferred their present course of policy.

3. I only report these extraordinarily foolish vapourings because Dr. Stresemann informed me a little while ago that M. Brodowsky is the brains and the principal influence in the Soviet Embassy here. M. Krestinsky, the Soviet Ambassador here, he said, never comes to the German Foreign Office without bringing Brodowsky with him, nominally as interpreter, but really to take an important part in any discussion that may be forward.

I have, &c.,

E. M. B. Ingram[8]

For the Ambassador

[6] Air Vice-Marshal Sir Sefton Brancker, Director of Civil Aviation in the Air Ministry.
[7] Not anything.
[8] First Secretary in H.M. Embassy at Berlin.

No. 3

Mr. Wingfield (Rome)[1] *to Sir A. Chamberlain (Received September 12)*
No. 681 [C 7563/80/22]

ROME, *September 8, 1927*

Sir,

Signor Mussolini loses no opportunity of preaching the doctrine of large families and of denouncing 'neo-malthusian' doctrines and practices. In his speech, a summary of which formed an enclosure to Sir R. Graham's despatch No. 412[2] of May 27th last, he declared that the new tax on bachelors was not

[1] Counsellor in charge of H.M. Embassy at Rome in the absence on leave of Sir R. Graham.
[2] Not printed. Signor Mussolini's speech under reference was delivered to the Chamber of Deputies on May 26.

a mere device to raise revenue. It was imposed for 'demographic' reasons and might be followed by a tax on childless marriages. The 'demographic' power of a nation was a most important factor in its political standing and consequently in its economic and moral situation. The inhabitants of Italy were only forty millions compared with ninety millions of Germans and two hundred millions of Slavs. If Italy was to count for anything in this world, she should enter the second half of this century with a population of sixty millions. A falling off in the birth-rate meant national decadence. Urban industrialism and small agricultural holdings alike led to sterility, as did the moral depravity of the so-called upper classes. He was therefore only in favour of healthy industries, such as those which gave employment in agriculture or on the sea.

2. But not content with efforts to increase the birth-rate in Italy, the Fascist Government, as reported in my despatch No. 623[3] of the 18th ultimo, have taken steps to restrict emigration from this country on the ground that it deprives Italy of the services as soldiers and workers of the sons whom she has nourished and educated.

3. It is clear therefore that Signor Mussolini is doing everything possible to increase the numbers of the inhabitants of Italy, whilst, on the other hand, the press continues to proclaim that the pressure of an increasing population, in a country whose natural resources are not sufficiently rich to support them, makes it necessary for Italy to obtain colonial territories, which will furnish her with raw materials, whilst permitting the emigration of her sons without the loss of their energies and intelligence to the mother-country. On this ground is founded the claim that Italy should have a Colonial Mandate allocated to her, if one should fall vacant (cf. Sir R. Graham's despatch No. 358[4] of May 6th last); and Signor Mussolini himself referred to this need for overseas outlets in conversation with a correspondent of the 'Chicago Tribune', as reported in Sir R. Graham's despatch No. 1013[5] of November 26th, 1926.

4. In his despatch No. 511[6] of June 24th, 1926, Sir R. Graham expressed the opinion that Italy, owing to her population problem, had a real case for obtaining an area for overseas expansion; but that the recognition of the existence of such a claim did not bring any nearer the solution of the problems involved.

5. In these circumstances the World Population Conference at Geneva has naturally aroused very considerable interest in the Italian press, and I beg leave to transmit to you herewith a summary[5] of the comments which have appeared in the principal newspapers of this country. You will notice that in them there is no suggestion that the writers perceive that there is any

[3] Not printed. This despatch transmitted a translation of an official communiqué published in the *Tribuna* of August 2, 1927.

[4] Not printed. This despatch reported on reactions in the Italian press to recent suggestions in the British press that H.M. Government should hand over to the Italian Government the mandates for Palestine and Mesopotamia.

[5] Not printed.   [6] See Volume I, No. 488, note 2.

inconsistency in the two theses:—(a) that Italy is already over-populated and therefore has a claim that her neighbours should provide her with more territory; and (b) that, in order to hold her own with other Powers, Italy must actively bestir herself to increase her population as much as possible. The opposition to any adoption of methods of birth-control, which is voiced in some of these articles, is doubtless to some extent due to religious scruples, but there is little doubt that its violence is inspired rather by nationalistic impulses and the desire to ensure the expansion of Italy in the future at the expense of less prolific races.

I have, &c.,
CHARLES WINGFIELD

No. 4

Memorandum by Mr. Huxley[1]
[*C 7348/7348/62*]

FOREIGN OFFICE, September 8, 1927

Having now read for the first time the despatches and minutes in File 10417/62 of 1926,[2] I find it a little difficult to understand how far we are prepared to go in support of Count Coudenhove-Kalergi and his Pan-Europa Society.[3]

His ideas have been stigmatized as ludicrous and unpractical, and I feel that I run a grave risk of being classed among the 'long-haired idealists', with whom, according to yesterday's 'Evening Standard', the Foreign Office is filled, if I venture to support them.

Nevertheless I remain convinced that the Pan-European idea is a coming force—if not *the* coming force—in Europe; and I think most people in this country would be astonished to learn with what frequency it crops up in European speech and writing. A minor instance was the occasion which I mentioned in my notes on a visit to Germany last May (see Flag A).[4] It is true that the speaker was a professed pacifist, but her remarks evidently appealed to widely differing sections of the audience.

It is sufficiently obvious what forces in Europe are working in favour of Count Coudenhove-Kalergi, and what against: in any case they cannot be surveyed in this minute. The question is, what our attitude should be. From

[1] A member of the Central Department of the Foreign Office.

[2] Not printed.

[3] The Pan-European Union was founded by Count Richard Coudenhove-Kalergi, an Austrian writer, in 1923; for an account of his movement see R. Coudenhove-Kalergi, *Crusade for Pan-Europe* (New York, 1943). On September 1, 1927, he transmitted to Sir A. Chamberlain a manifesto for a Pan-European Locarno Conference and requested his opinion on a proposed 'extension of the Locarno Treaty on Pan-European lines'. (The treaty of mutual guarantee and other agreements concluded at Locarno on October 16, 1925, are printed in Cmd. 2525 of 1925.)

[4] No reference was given to Flag A, but the notes were probably those recorded in the minute cited in Volume III, No. 176, note 4.

one point of view, a pronouncement in his favour has received the approval of the Secretary of State in the draft in C.6180/1323/18.[5] From another point of view, viz. the economic, the minutes in C.10417/10417/62/1926[2] appear to indicate that we should oppose him. On the other hand, it will be noted that while Lord Chilston[6] in his despatch in that paper[7] states that he 'has found some difficulty in taking Count Coudenhove's proposals seriously', and that he 'will not attempt to lay before the Secretary of State what seem to him decisive reasons why such a' (Pan-European) 'combination might well prove detrimental to British interests—not so much from military and political as from economic grounds', after hearing Count Coudenhove-Kalergi speak at the 'Pan-European Congress' of last year and reading his books, Lord Chilston when writing his despatch in C.10831/10417/62[8] had so far changed his views as to state that 'Sooner or later the whole question may deserve impartial consideration from the point of view alike of British and world interests. Certainly if Count Coudenhove and his adherents prove wizards enough to allay the fury of nationalism and of protectionism which is preventing the progress of Central and Eastern Europe, he may do a service to European peace and to British trade which may outweigh many other disadvantages of his plan from a British point of view.'

I have ventured to express a similar opinion in my minute on C.6644/33/18.[9] 'Qui veut la fin veut les moyens.' If we consider that in the long run the elimination of war on the European continent is a major British interest, and that it ought to be allowed to outweigh those minor British interests, to the detriment of which a permanent settlement between the European rivals might react, then we should evidently try to strengthen the Pan-European movement.

What action on our part is best calculated to do so, is a different question. So far as the present request is concerned, I should be inclined to reply on the lines that, as Count Coudenhove-Kalergi himself recognises (vide his books, passim, and also paragraph 6 of Lord Chilston's despatch in C.10831/10417/62/1926),[8] Great Britain has undertaken tasks in and developed bonds

[5] The reference was to the draft, initialled by Sir A. Chamberlain on August 10, of the letter of August 13 about the German colonial question from Sir V. Wellesley, Deputy Under Secretary of State for Foreign Affairs, to Mr. Ormsby Gore, Parliamentary Under-Secretary of State for Colonial Affairs, of which an extract is printed in Volume III, No. 274, note 7. Sir A. Chamberlain minuted in the margin against this reference: 'Oh no! I did not so intend it & I do not think that it will bear that construction. A.C. 10.10.'

[6] H.M. Minister at Vienna.

[7] Vienna despatch No. 250 of September 22, 1926, is not printed.

[8] Vienna despatch No. 260 of October 6, 1926, is not printed.

[9] With reference to an extract from the *Débats* of August 7, 1927, on the subject of a Franco–German alliance, transmitted in Paris covering despatch No. 1712 (not preserved in Foreign Office archives), Mr. Huxley minuted on August 10: 'It is arguable that a Pan-European Union or any permanent settlement between the various European rivals would work out to our detriment: . . . if once the desirability of such a permanent settlement is admitted, one must also admit the desirability of the Franco–German rapprochement on which that settlement depends, even though some British interests may suffer as the price of its attainment.'

with extra-European territories which render her inclusion in the Pan-European Union an impossibility. Neither, for similar reasons, can she take upon herself, in 'an extension of the Locarno Treaty on Pan-European lines', any extension of her commitments as guarantor in the original Locarno Treaty. But the promoters of the Pan-European movement may rely on the benevolent co-operation of H.M. Government in the furtherance of their ideals, to which those of the British Empire, so far from being opposed, are but complementary.[10]

M. H. HUXLEY

[10] Mr. Sargent, head of the Central Department of the Foreign Office, stated in particular in a minute of September 8: 'The Pan-European movement may be a coming force as Mr. Huxley suggests, but for the present it is not a matter of practical politics and it would be waste of time to try to formulate a definite and consistent policy with regard to it.'

Sir A. Chamberlain minuted on October 10: 'I differ entirely from Count C-K's appreciation of the present position & results of the Locarno treaties. They are doing their work. I am not clear what he means by his Pan European Locarno. It seems however to imply compulsory arbitration in all cases & unlimited obligations to the victim of any aggression. Before it was finally drafted, it would be the [Geneva] Protocol [see No. 92, note 4] again. We can't touch it & it will probably be sufficient to put in a caveat about his desponding remarks on the present situation & to refer him to my speech at Geneva explaining the attitude & policy of H.M.G. [See No. 5, note 3.] A.C. 10.10.'

Further action in regard to Count Coudenhove-Kalergi's manifesto was suspended.

No. 5

Sir A. Chamberlain (Geneva) to Sir W. Tyrrell (Received September 15)
No. 18 L.N.A. [W 8755/788/98]

GENEVA, September 12, 1927

Sir,

Signor Grandi,[1] who arrived in Geneva on Saturday[2] morning and is leaving for Rome this evening, called upon me to-day and we had a lengthy and interesting conversation which in one point at least is of great importance. After delivering a very friendly personal message from Signor Mussolini, in the course of which he said it was primarily for the purpose of a meeting with me that Signor Mussolini had sent him to Geneva, Signor Grandi spoke of the last week's debates in the Assembly and, in particular, of the speech which I made on Saturday afternoon.[3] This gave me an opportunity to explain my views of the League in terms of a sober but hopeful realism. I said that I distrusted as much as Signor Scialoja,[4] whose observations made on Friday you will doubtless have observed, the exaggerated pretensions and hopes to which expression was given in some quarters, and that I thought them

[1] Under-Secretary of State in the Italian Ministry of Foreign Affairs.

[2] September 10, 1927.

[3] See *League of Nations Official Journal: Special Supplement No. 54, Records of the Eighth Ordinary Session of the Assembly, Plenary Meetings* (Geneva, 1927), pp. 95–99.

[4] Italian delegate to the League of Nations. For his speech see *ibid.*, pp. 84–86.

injurious and even dangerous to the League's success. On the other hand, it would be an immense political blunder to under-rate what the League had already achieved in creating, quite apart from sanctions and treaties, an international tribunal whose moral judgment no Power could afford to neglect in the conduct of its policy, since a defiance of that judgment—an act of aggression condemned by it—would leave, as Monsieur Briand[5] had said, even a victorious aggressor branded on the forehead and a pariah in the society of nations. In thus speaking, I desired once again to present the League to Signor Mussolini in that realistic aspect which most readily appeals to him and which was most likely to influence his policy and conduct should Italy become engaged in any serious international trouble.

2. Signor Grandi remarked that the League was in short *a fact*, that he could assure me that Signor Mussolini recognised its importance and that he hoped to cooperate more and more with it. Would he, asked Signor Grandi, send a man like Signor Scialoja to represent him here if that were not the case? Would Signor Scialoja himself, who had participated in the discussions on the drafting of the Covenant and who was so deeply devoted to the idea and aims of the League, consent to be Italy's representative on any other condition? I must not be misled either by articles in the Italian press or by violently expressed speeches. As a result of their internal struggle, Italians had come to use the language of war on almost every occasion. Thus, if there were a shortage of corn, it became at once 'the corn war'; but, though Signor Mussolini had to allow a great latitude for the expression of the views of the extremer sections of Fascist opinion and though, when addressing a crowd, he had to use the language which the crowd understood, I should observe that he spoke quite differently in the Senate which he recognised as a serious body, and I might be assured that he was quietly working in the sense which I desired. Signor Grandi had himself brought with him to Geneva a number of young Fascists belonging to the extreme section of opinion, and the result of the debate had been to convert them into ardent 'Leaguers'.

3. Passing from this subject, Signor Grandi spoke briefly of the relations between France and Italy and of the Tangier negotiations.[6] Then he passed to Albania, and it was because I felt that the interview could not end without a discussion on Italo–Yugoslav relations that I had laid so much stress at its opening upon the importance of the League and the very real influence and authority which it had already acquired. Signor Grandi said that, acting upon the suggestions—or to use his own words, '*les conseils*'—that I had given,[7] Signor Mussolini had used all his influence to induce Ahmed Zogu to pay more attention to the conditions in the north, to improve his administration,

[5] French Minister for Foreign Affairs.

[6] The reference was to the Franco–Spanish conversations held, with the agreement of the British and Italian Governments, between February and August 1927, following Spain's putting forward of a claim for the incorporation of Tangier into the Spanish Zone of Morocco contrary to the provisions of the Convention of December 18, 1923, on the Organization of the Statute of the Tangier Zone, printed in Cmd. 2203 of 1924: see Volume III, appendix, paragraphs 31–33, and Nos. 201 and 276; see also *Survey of International Affairs 1929*, pp. 189–201.   [7] Cf. Volume III, No. 239, note 1.

and to adopt a more conciliatory policy. It was indeed on Signor Mussolini's advice that Ahmed Zogu had recalled some of the exiles and had undertaken his northern tour, and he repeated on Signor Mussolini's behalf that he had no aggressive designs, that he had no desire to occupy Albanian territory and that he had definitely refused a proposal made by Monsieur Nincic for the division of Albania between Italy and Jugoslavia.

4. I replied that I was very glad that he had mentioned this subject, for I must confess that it was one which had been giving me a great deal of anxiety and seemed to me perhaps the most dangerous at this moment. I then told him what I had said to Signor Scialoja and repeated to the Yugoslav Minister last June, namely that, whilst in Rome they were under the impression that Yugoslavia was suffering from swelled head, she was in fact a victim of the complex of inferiority, and that, if the Yugoslav Government and people could only arrive at a just appreciation of the new position which the war had created for them, they would cease to entertain unfounded fears and would have avoided some follies which they had committed. Signor Grandi seemed surprised but interested by my diagnosis of the Serbian malady. I continued that I had throughout used such influence as I possessed to urge moderation and caution upon the Government of Belgrade and I might add that Monsieur Briand, who naturally had in that quarter a greater influence than I could pretend to wield, had to my knowledge consistently taken the same course. The Yugoslav Government had indeed at times sought my advice, but they came to me still more to plead for the use of the influence which they supposed me to possess in Rome. I had, therefore, taken pains to make it clear to them that I did not direct Italian policy and could take no responsibility for it. I had been willing to use my good offices to help to smoothe away the preliminary difficulties which obstructed the opening of direct negotiations. Monsieur Rakic was now in touch with Signor Mussolini and the settlement must now be made direct between them. Only one thing would I add. I would beg the Italian Government not to exclude in advance the idea of themselves bringing the question before the Council of the League if any untoward event should happen. I recalled what I had said as to the position and influence of the League at the opening of our conversation. I said that I need not dwell upon the effect that would be produced upon this assembly of the nations if Italy seemed to be guilty of any act of aggression without having exhausted the means of conciliation that were open, and I reminded Signor Grandi that certain of the powers had come under engagements to Italy which even placed her to some extent in a privileged position for such an appeal to the League.

5. Signor Grandi asked me to repeat what I had said, and then replied that all this was fully recognised by Signor Mussolini. He intended to pursue increasingly a League policy and, though, with all that I have had to do since this conversation was held only a few hours ago, I cannot now recall his exact words, he expressed himself in such terms as constituted to my mind at the moment an assurance that if trouble did arise Italy would appeal to the League.

6. I told Signor Grandi that what he had said had greatly reassured me. I begged him to express to Signor Mussolini the pleasure with which I had heard the statement of his policy and to say once again how much importance I attached to the cordial cooperation of our two governments which I was glad to think was facilitated by our personal relations.[8]

7. Proceeding from this interview direct to the Assembly, I met Monsieur Briand in the lobby. I told him, speaking most confidentially, that I had just had a most satisfactory conversation with Signor Grandi, particularly in regard to Albania, and I said that it left upon my mind the assurance that, in case of a really serious incident, Italy intended to appeal to the League and to call upon us to implement the engagements which France and England had undertaken. Monsieur Briand replied that this was indeed most satisfactory, and that he was delighted to hear it. On his part he had just had an interview with Monsieur Marinkovitch, in which he had urged him in the strongest terms to ratify the Nettuno Conventions,[9] adding that without that he could not hope to come to a satisfactory arrangement with Italy, and Monsieur Marinkovitch had, in fact, promised him that this should be done.[10]

8. 'There is many a slip twixt the cup and the lip', but if the respective assurances given by Signor Grandi to me and by Monsieur Marinkovitch to Monsieur Briand can be relied upon, we may, I think, hope that the Albanian imbroglio will find a peaceful solution and will not become the occasion of a new war.

I am, &c.,

AUSTEN CHAMBERLAIN

[8] For an account by Signor Grandi of this conversation dated September 13, 1927, see *I Documenti Diplomatici Italiani*, Settima Serie, vol. v, Nos. 413–15.

[9] These technical conventions of July 20, 1925, between Italy and the Serb-Croat-Slovene State dealt especially with Fiume, Zara, and Dalmatia and are printed in *League of Nations Treaty Series*, vol. lxxxiii, pp. 33–303.

[10] In Belgrade despatch No. 358 of September 15, Mr. Kennard, H.M. Minister in Belgrade, reported in particular that M. Marinkovitch had informed him that he had 'expressed to M. Briand the view that it would be advisable to conclude the Franco–Jugoslav pact [see Volume III, No. 304, and below, No. 41, note 3, and No. 62] shortly, but the latter had preferred not to do so at present and had expressed himself philosophically as regards Italian encroachments in Albania which he regarded to a great extent as bluff'.

No. 6

Sir W. Max Muller[1] *(Warsaw) to Sir A. Chamberlain (Received September 19)*
No. 409 [N 4427/22/55]

WARSAW, *September 13, 1927*

Sir,

I have the honour to report, with reference to my despatch No. 82[2] of 24th February, that during a recent visit to Katowice, Mr. Kimens, the Commercial Secretary to this Legation, had two long conversations with Baron

[1] H.M. Minister at Warsaw.   [2] Not printed.

Grünau, the German Consul-General, who, after observing that he was speaking privately, launched out into a lengthy tirade regarding Polish–German relations in Polish Upper Silesia.

2. He began by saying that relations between the Germans and the Poles in Polish Upper Silesia had, during the two and a half years that he had been in Katowice, become, if anything, more strained, and that he attributed the deterioration of the situation which had become more particularly noticeable during the last year, to the intransigent attitude and anti-German policy adopted by the present Voivode,[3] Dr. Grazynski, who, he declared, was in the hands of the insurgents[4] and disregarded the instructions of the central authorities.

3. He referred more particularly to the school question,[5] to the frequent demands by the authorities for dismissals of German directors and employees in industrial undertakings, accompanied in some cases by threats that in the event of the non-fulfilment of these directions, the companies would receive no Government orders. In connection with this latter point he laid emphasis on the dismissal of Herr Pietsche of the Vereinigte König and Laure-hütte, whose case has still to be decided by the Mixed Commission at Beuthen, and to that of Herr Schulz of the Henckel von Donnersmarck Beuthen Estates, Limited. (As will be seen from my despatch no. 407[6] of even date, Baron Grünau was in no way justified in quoting Herr Schulz's case in support of his thesis.)

4. Baron Grünau went on to say that the present state of affairs had fully confirmed the German thesis that the partition of Upper Silesia would lead to endless difficulties and could never assure peace and quiet, the development of trade and the equitable treatment of the German minority, though he was forced to admit that industrially the position was now better than he had anticipated several months ago after the termination of the coal strike in the United Kingdom.[7] He declared that, until Polish Upper Silesia and the Corridor had been returned to Germany, good relations between Poland and Germany were out of the question, and until then there would be no peace in Europe, as the German nation would in no circumstances reconcile itself to the idea of the permanent detachment of these territories from the German State.

5. In spite of Baron Grünau's assurance that he was speaking in a purely private capacity, Mr. Kimens gained the impression that he was voicing the opinion of his Government and of the German nation, and in conversations which Mr. Kimens subsequently had with German business men in Katowice

[3] Provincial Governor.

[4] i.e. *Związek Powstańców Śląskich*, the Union of Silesian Insurgents, dating from the time of the plebiscite in March 1921: cf. First Series, Volume XVI.

[5] For consideration by the Council of the League of Nations of reports on the question of German minority schools in Polish Upper Silesia on March 8 and 12, 1927, see *League of Nations Official Journal*, April 1927, pp. 376–7, 400–3, 474–505, and 592–3.

[6] Not printed. This despatch stated that the initiative in the retirement of Herr Schulz as Managing Director had not been taken by the Polish Government but by the company.

[7] In November 1926.

the opinion was freely expressed that Germany was looking upon the present state of affairs in that part of the world as merely temporary.

6. As I had the honour to observe in my despatch under reference, the views of Baron Grünau are in my opinion largely coloured by his own wishes; nor am I disposed to find in any of his strictures upon the Polish regime in Upper Silesia anything which would move me to revise the opinion I then expressed that there is no sufficient reason why, when once the painful process of readjustment has been overcome, the new frontiers should not prove as workable as the old.[8]

7. I am sending a copy of this despatch to his Majesty's Chargé d'Affaires at Berlin.

I have, &c.,
W. G. Max Muller

[8] Mr. Collier of the Northern Department of the Foreign Office minuted on this despatch on September 19: 'Whatever the cause—I think for myself that it is mainly, but not wholly, the personality of the Voivode—the fact remains that Polish–German relations in Upper Silesia have not improved, & are not likely to improve in the near future. From N 4426/22/55 [Warsaw despatch No. 408: not printed], it appears that the Polish Government themselves approve the policy of the "Union of Insurgents". If this is their fixed policy, I think it can safely be said that the situation will *never* improve.'

No. 7

Letter from Sir W. Tyrrell to Sir R. Graham

[C 7410/25/90]

FOREIGN OFFICE, *September 13, 1927*

My dear Ronald,

I must apologise for writing to you on official matters while you are on leave, but we have received a despatch from Leeper[1] at Durazzo, copy of which I enclose,[2] in which he raises a rather important question in connection with our attitude towards Italian activity in Albania. I also enclose a copy of a private letter[3] he has written to Sargent on the same subject in which he develops his views more fully. Leeper, basing himself on the assumption that it is our policy to acquiesce in Italian predominance in Albania, suggests in short that we should be more likely to avoid future trouble if we went one better than this and took it upon ourselves to prompt the Italians as to the methods they should employ in order to set Albania really on her feet.

From the point of view of British as distinct from Albanian interests, the chief objection of course lies in the fact that to initiate discussions with Signor Mussolini on the basis suggested by Leeper, would constitute a new departure and as such would probably be interpreted by Signor Mussolini as an

[1] Mr. R. A. Leeper was in charge of H.M. Legation at Durazzo from July 31 to October 5, 1927, during the absence of H.M. Minister, Mr. Seeds.

[2] Durazzo despatch No. 118 of August 22 is not printed: see Volume III, No. 302, note 2.

[3] See Volume III, No. 302.

abandonment by His Majesty's Government of the claims and rights which they have so far asserted in regard to Albania.

You will recollect that in August 1926, in reply to a somewhat offensive protest by Signor Mussolini against the alleged policy of intervention of His Majesty's Government in Albania to the detriment of Italian interests, we wrote as follows:—

'His Majesty's Government have themselves no special interest in Albania, and have no desire to obstruct legitimate Italian expansion in that country. In the resolution of the 9th November, 1921,[4] moreover, they have recognised the special interests of Italy in the maintenance of the integrity of the country. Whilst His Majesty's Government have never suggested that Italy should not exercise there the influence to which her importance and her proximity entitle her, they have consistently declined to admit, as is made clear by the circumstances in which the resolution was drawn up and by the text as finally signed, that any Power should enjoy there an exclusive influence. The position of Italy in respect of Albania owing to geographical and economic considerations, must necessarily be of a very special kind, but the resolution cannot be interpreted as conferring upon any Power any exclusive right of influence or intervention in normal times, as apart from those special circumstances of foreign invasion or other event involving a threat to Albanian integrity. Such remains and must remain the consistent policy of His Majesty's Government, not from any selfish motive, but from the conviction that such a claim by any Power would be viewed with suspicion by third parties and might lead, however baseless the suspicion, to a situation not unlikely to endanger peace.'[5] This statement clearly lays down the principle that His Majesty's Government do not recognise the exclusive influence or right of intervention of Italy in Albania.

This spring as you know a further exchange of notes took place with Signor Mussolini in connection with our efforts to ease the strained relations between Italy and Jugoslavia caused by the Treaty of Tirana.[6] In this exchange of notes Signor Mussolini apparently claimed the right to protect and defend any régime in Albania friendly to Italy, even against internal opposition. The question was carefully considered at the time as to whether we should do well to dispute this claim of Signor Mussolini's which practically amounted to a claim to control the internal administration of Albania and was therefore in direct conflict with our declaration of the preceding August. As, however, in practice there was no alternative to Ahmed's Government and the collapse of this Government would, more than anything else, endanger the independence of Albania, and as the Italian Government's policy was to support this Government, it was finally decided that we would do no good and might be doing a lot of harm by taking up Signor Mussolini's challenge. We accordingly said nothing in reply on this point and may be held therefore to have tacitly acquiesced in the claim.

[4] This declaration by the Conference of Ambassadors is printed in *League of Nations Treaty Series*, vol. xii, p. 383.

[5] See Volume II, No. 157.   [6] See Volume III, Nos. 105, 162, and 183.

Leeper's present proposal would be tantamount to taking now the further step of openly acknowledging to Signor Mussolini that we are prepared to recognise the claim which he put forward in the spring and that we have abandoned our counter-claim of last year when we denied that any one Power should enjoy exclusive right of influence or intervention in Albania.

If we could be reasonably sure that by taking this further step we should be ensuring peace in Albania, and what is more important, peace between Italy and Jugoslavia, there would no doubt, be a great deal to be said in favour of our sacrificing some of our local British prestige and influence in order to attain such a laudable object. But it seems to us more than doubtful whether our sacrifices would in practice produce the immediate result, as Leeper anticipates, of strengthening the Government of Albania and improving the condition of the country. It can by no means be taken for granted that the likelihood of trouble will be much diminished by any advice we may offer to the Italians. Even if the Italians do not resent advice on such a delicate subject as the unsuitability of their methods in Albania, it is highly problematical whether they have the administrative and diplomatic talent capable of instituting a Cromer régime[7] there. Incidentally, to offer such advice to the Italians might quite possibly lead them to reply that they should be granted a mandate or at least some permanency of tenure if they are to invest money and brains in the task of civilising the country. Far from making matters better this would precipitate trouble.

The main ultimate object of our Albanian policy is, of course, to prevent its becoming the cause of war between Italy and Jugoslavia, and it would be difficult to justify a change in our policy unless we were sure that by doing so we were more likely to attain this object than at present. Leeper in his letter does not discuss this aspect of the question, but my own impression is that his proposal might very easily have the opposite effect to the one which we are aiming at. For cannot it be convincingly argued that if we adopt the policy of giving Italy a free hand in Albania and are known to be urging her to take the administration of the country firmly in hand, the result would be that Jugoslavia's suspicions and fears would be proportionately increased and that she would be all the more tempted to try her luck in dispossessing Italy of her foothold in the Balkans before it was too late? Even if there was no tangible change in the relations between Italy and Albania, the mere fact that Jugoslavia had reason to suppose that we had abandoned the principle of an independent Albania, and had recognised the need of some sort of Italian protectorate or mandate, might very well precipitate the crisis which we wish to prevent.

However we have not made up our minds yet and before doing so we think it well to consult you and Seeds. But at present I am inclined to think that it is best on the whole to carry on along existing lines, even though they may be unsatisfactory, since the alternatives seem still less satisfactory. On the other hand, no harm can come from an occasional hint to Signor Mussolini when

[7] The reference was to the term of office in Egypt of Lord Cromer (1841–1917), Agent and Consul-General 1883–1907.

specific questions arise, as for instance your hint some six weeks ago[8] which led to Ahmed's visit of pacification to the North. Such occasional hints are not open to the objections of the wholesale advice advocated by Leeper.[9]

Yours ever
W. TYRRELL

[8] The reference is uncertain: cf. however, No. 5, note 7.

[9] In his letter of September 20 in reply Sir R. Graham expressed general agreement with Sir W. Tyrrell. In a minute of September 26 Mr. Sargent stated that Mr. Seeds also agreed. On September 30 Mr. Sargent stated in a letter to Mr. Leeper, in which copies of the correspondence between Sir W. Tyrrell and Sir R. Graham were enclosed: 'In all the circumstances we have decided, as you will see, that it is better to carry on along the lines we have followed hitherto in Albania rather than to adopt a policy which would involve avowed approval of Italian predominance there. You will notice, however, that the idea of giving occasional hints to Signor Mussolini on specific questions has been endorsed and I think myself that by this means we are more likely to influence Italian policy than by any other.'

No. 8

Sir A. Chamberlain (Geneva) to Sir W. Tyrrell (Received September 16)
No. 31 L.N.A. [C 7654/5294/18]

GENEVA, September 14, 1927

The British delegate to the League of Nations presents his compliments, and has the honour to transmit copies of a memorandum recording a conversation with M. Briand, and of [*sic*] a conversation between the Locarno Powers on the 14th September.

ENCLOSURE IN No. 8

Memorandum by Sir A. Chamberlain of a conversation with Monsieur Briand, for use by the Foreign Office as required.

GENEVA, September 14, 1927

1. Monsieur Briand called upon me this morning. In consequence of a desire expressed to him by Dr. Stresemann that the Locarno Powers might meet together during our presence in Geneva, Monsieur Briand had pointed out to him that, in view of the suspicions to which these meetings gave rise and the criticism made on them in the Assembly, such a meeting would perhaps not be very opportune. Nevertheless, he would not decline it.

2. I replied that neither would I, but I would make it a condition that on this occasion Dr. Stresemann should openly take the responsibility of calling the meeting and should convoke us in his own room; but it subsequently occurred to us that we should all be lunching to-day with the President of the Council[1] and that perhaps it might be possible for the Locarno Powers to hold their conversation in a corner of the room after luncheon, when

[1] i.e. M. Villegas, President of the 47th Session of the Council of the League of Nations and Chilean delegate at Geneva.

their conversation would have an accidental rather than a premeditated appearance.

3. Monsieur Briand then went on to say that, doubtless, Dr. Stresemann urged on by his Nationalists desired to raise the question of the evacuation of the Rhineland. That was an obvious impossibility at the present time and he deprecated any discussion of it.

4. I told Monsieur Briand that I entirely agreed. It was my hope that sooner or later we should find it possible to withdraw the troops before the dates named in the treaty,[2] but a discussion at this moment could serve no useful purpose. On the contrary, this was one of those questions which ought never to be discussed until the moment had come when a solution was within sight. To keep on raising the question as long as the answer could only be in the negative was to adjourn still further any prospect of action.

5. Our conversation turned in succession to the relations of Italy and Jugoslavia, to the policy of Poland and to the Paris negotiations about Tangier. I find that Signor Grandi told Monsieur Briand as well as me[3] of the presence of a certain number of young Fascists at the present Assembly, and he explained that this was part of a course of education which Signor Mussolini was giving to them in order that they might become aware of the realities of the League.

6. Monsieur Briand repeated that he had advised Monsieur Marinkovitch to ratify the Nettuno conventions, but on this occasion he did not go so far as to say that the Jugoslav Minister had given a promise to do so. He more cautiously stated that he seemed to Monsieur Briand to have that intention.

7. Finally we reached Tangier *à propos* of the short holiday which it is my hope to take.[4] I took the opportunity to press Monsieur Briand to take the negotiations more into his own hands and to conduct them directly with Señor Quiñones de Leon instead of leaving them to the negotiators who have hitherto had charge of them, and I urged upon Monsieur Briand that France could afford to make larger concessions in the matter of the gendarmerie than she had hitherto indicated.

[2] According to article 429 of the Treaty of Versailles, the occupied German territories were divided into three zones centred on Cologne, Coblenz, and Mainz: these zones were to be evacuated at the expiration of five, ten, and fifteen years respectively from the coming into force of the treaty (January 10, 1920), provided that the conditions of the treaty had been faithfully carried out by Germany. For documentation regarding the evacuation of Cologne, see Volume I, Chapters I–II, *passim*.

[3] See No. 5.

[4] General Primo de Rivera, President of the Spanish Council of Ministers and Minister for Foreign Affairs, sent a message to Sir A. Chamberlain through Señor Quiñones de Leon, Spanish Ambassador at Paris, expressing the hope that a meeting might be arranged if Sir Austen were in Spanish waters. General Primo de Rivera dined with Sir A. Chamberlain on the yacht Dolphin on September 30. Sir A. Chamberlain recorded the most important parts of the conversation, respecting hopes for Spain's resuming active co-operation in the work of the League of Nations and respecting the negotations on Tangier, in his despatch No. 466 to Madrid of October 10, not printed. For the gist of this conversation see Sir A. Chamberlain's statement of November 14 printed in *Parl. Debs.*, *5th ser.*, *H. of C.*, vol. 210, cols. 638–9; see also *The Times*, October 8, 1927, p. 10.

8. Monsieur Briand replied that it was his intention to take this matter in hand himself, that he was studying the concessions which could be made and he hoped to put forward proposals which would give satisfaction to Spanish *amour propre* and afford her a protection against those alleged abuses of the neutrality of Tangier which she represented as her principal grievance. At the same time he urged that at the right moment I might usefully say a word in Madrid, counselling the Spanish Government to be conciliatory and reasonable. He remarked that my last intervention in that quarter had had the happiest results.[5]

9. Since dictating the above, Monsieur Villegas' luncheon has taken place. Towards the close of it, Dr. Stresemann, Monsieur Briand, Signor Scialoja and I drew apart.

10. Dr. Stresemann explained that he wished to mention the question of the evacuation of the Rhineland. Monsieur Briand at once stated that he was unable to discuss this question. He had indeed been expressly forbidden by the Council of Ministers in Paris to enter into any such discussion. The allies had made the reduction in the troops of occupation for which Dr. Stresemann had asked at the last meeting of the Council.[6] For the present, nothing more could be done, and, apart from the express prohibition which he must obey, the moment was most inopportune for opening this question.

11. Dr. Stresemann then explained that he did not wish to raise the question of the evacuation itself at this moment, but that the German Cabinet on his return intended to consider what would be the proper moment for raising it and he had therefore wished to ascertain our point of view in order to equip himself for that discussion. To the Germans the reasons for evacuation were twofold: first, there were the Treaties of Locarno, which guaranteed security and therefore made the continuation of the occupation unnecessary; secondly, there was Article 431 of the Treaty of Versailles.

12. Monsieur Briand replied that the Treaties of Locarno had nothing to do with the question. As regards Article 431, the German Government had referred to it in one of the Notes which preceded the meeting at Locarno, and he had replied in writing, on behalf of the French Government, that nothing which might be done at Locarno could deprive the Germans of any rights which they enjoyed under the Treaty of Versailles.[7] The only question was—

---

[5] The reference would appear to be to Sir A. Chamberlain's proposal for Anglo–Franco–Italian–Spanish conversations on Tangier: see Volume III, No. 276.

[6] See Volume III, Nos. 234, 241, and 244 for requests by Dr. Stresemann. M. Briand's note of September 5 to Dr. Stresemann on behalf of the Belgian, British, French, Italian, and Japanese Governments regarding the reduction of the forces of occupation to 60,000 men is printed *ibid.*, as the enclosure in No. 331.

[7] Mr. Huxley minuted on September 19 that the relevant passages in the correspondence of 1925 referred to by M. Briand were (i) the last paragraph of section III of the French note of June 16, 1925, to the German Government (Cmd. 2435 of 1925, p. 50); (ii) the second paragraph of section I of the German note of July 20 (Cmd. 2468 of 1925, pp. 6–7); (iii) the fifth paragraph of section I of the French note of August 24 (printed in *The Times*, August 27, 1925, p. 9). For a fuller statement of the British view referred to by Sir A. Chamberlain in paragraph 13 below, Mr. Huxley drew attention to the despatches printed in Volume II as Nos. 93 and 153.

was this the moment to exercise their right to appeal to the Article in question, and in this matter, though he was transgressing instructions in entering into such a conversation at all and could speak only quite unofficially, he would beg Dr. Stresemann to wait for a time when his hopes might be realisable. France and Germany were alike entering upon an electoral period; no moment could be worse for opening such a discussion, but he repeated that no-one disputed the validity of Article 431 or the right of Germany to appeal to it whenever she chose. He added, however, with reference to Thoiry,[8] that the right to evacuation was conditional on the fulfilment of obligations; that already a section of German opinion was demanding it unconditionally, whilst as a natural consequence French opinion was beginning to assert itself strongly in the opposite sense. This was another reason for not raising the question now. Let Dr. Stresemann wait for the moment when he could offer some such inducements as they had had in view at Thoiry. Dr. Stresemann said that he did not desire to push the matter any further at the moment. He was well satisfied with the assurance of Monsieur Briand that the German right to appeal to the Article was recognised. There had been some people in Germany who had contended that it was denied by the Allies, and that not to raise the subject with us during our present meeting at Geneva would be to recognise that the Article no longer had any force.

13. I associated myself with what Monsieur Briand had said as to the validity of the Article, but I said that I would permit myself to add something which Monsieur Briand had not said, and which perhaps would even have the air of taking away some part of what he had said. If Dr. Stresemann looked carefully at the terms of the Article, he would see that they gave him very little foundation for a claim of right to the evacuation of the Rhineland. The right was subordinated to the condition of the fulfilment of obligations which, in fact, were of such a nature that Germany, with the best will in the world, could not execute them within the period fixed. I did not say this because I wanted to prolong the occupation to its utmost limit. On the contrary, I thought it would be a misfortune for our future relations if we had not been able to withdraw before the time limit expired, but it was an additional argument for not raising the question until the state of public opinion in the countries affected made agreement possible.

14. Signor Scialoja, who had hitherto been silent, supported this view. In prevision of the character of the discussion, I had copied out a sentence from the recently published life of Cavour by Monsieur Maurice Paléologue,[9] and

[8] M. Briand and Dr. Stresemann had met at Thoiry on September 17, 1926: for records of this conversation by Dr. Stresemann and Professor Hesnard of the French Embassy at Berlin see respectively, *Akten zur deutschen auswärtigen Politik 1918–1945*, Series B, vol. i, part 2 (Göttingen, 1968), Nos. 88 and 94–5 (cf. *Gustav Stresemann: His Diaries, Letters, and Papers*—ed. and trans. by Eric Sutton: London, 1935 f.—vol. iii, pp. 17–26), and Georges Suarez, *Briand: Sa Vie—Son Œuvre* (Paris, 1938), vol. vi, pp. 218–27, *passim*. See also Volume II, Chapter II, *passim*.

[9] M. Paléologue, a former French Ambassador to Russia, had been Secretary-General of the French Ministry of Foreign Affairs in 1920. His biography of Count Cavour (1810–61), Prime Minister of Piedmont 1852–61, appeared in 1926.

I commended it to Dr. Stresemann's attention. It ran:—'Le génie pratique de Cavour ne lui permet de s'interésser aux idées qu'à partir de l'instant où elles deviennent réalisables.' Signor Scialoja remarked that as an Italian he could not do better than follow Cavour. Monsieur Briand observed that this exactly expressed his thought and Dr. Stresemann carried away my paper presumably for the edification of his ministerial colleagues.

15. Our conversation then turned, in what precise connection I cannot say, to Monsieur Poincaré.[10] Monsieur Briand said that there had already been a considerable change in his attitude, but that he must be given time for his evolution. Indeed, Monsieur Poincaré himself had said as much to Monsieur Briand, and then Monsieur Briand added: 'You must remember the difficulties of his position. Il est lorrain et il a à côté de lui au Conseil un autre lorrain—Monsieur Marin[11]—qui est plus lorrain que lui. Maintenant, Monsieur Poincaré se vante d'être lorrain et il ne peut supporter qu'un autre le soit plus que lui.' Encouraged by the frankness with which we were speaking, I asked Dr. Stresemann whether I had ever told him what a Frenchman had said to me about Monsieur Poincaré at the moment when, under his presidency of the Council, relations between France and England had been most difficult?[12] This Frenchman had observed to me that Monsieur Poincaré 'est lorrain et qui dit lorrain dit moitié allemand'. This story, I said, I ventured to repeat because it illustrated what to us seemed to be the attitude of so large a section of German opinion. The very faults with which they reproached Monsieur Poincaré appear to be reproduced in many of the speeches and articles which come to us from the German side of the frontier, and it was precisely this attitude of so large a part of German opinion which rendered our progress so difficult. My criticism did not, of course, in any way apply to Dr. Stresemann himself, whose policy had raised Germany to her present position and brought us all into our actual relations. I only mentioned it because it was the failure of others to follow his example which impeded his policy and delayed our progress.

16. You will observe that the 'secret conclaves' of Geneva permit of an extraordinarily frank and friendly discussion of even the most delicate points.

(For the Secretary of State)
WALTER ROBERTS[13]

[10] President of the French Council of Ministers.
[11] French Minister of Pensions.
[12] The reference was to the Franco–Belgian occupation of the Ruhr (1923–5) initiated during M. Poincaré's previous tenure of office (1922–4).
[13] An assistant to the British delegate to the League of Nations.

No. 9

Sir W. Tyrrell to Mr. Ingram (Berlin)
No. 1166 [C 7604/7485/18]

FOREIGN OFFICE, September 14, 1927

Sir,

I have received your telegrams Nos. 86 and 87[1] of the 12th instant, recommending a reversal of the decision taken by the British military authorities in the Rhineland, with the concurrence of the Rhineland High Commission, not to permit the attendance of a number of German officers at a meeting of the German 'Scientific Society for Aeronautics' which is to be held at Wiesbaden on the 16th instant.

2. The considerations adduced in these telegrams in support of your recommendation do not, as you will already have learnt from my telegram No. 98[1] of the 14th instant, appear to me sufficiently cogent to outweigh the disadvantages of such a course, nor can they be regarded as valid in themselves.

3. In the first place, the organisers of this meeting must be prepared to pay the penalty of their failure to notify either the Rhineland High Commission or even the German authorities in the Rhineland of their choice of Wiesbaden as its *venue*, a choice which may, as you state, be attributable to sheer tactlessness, but which may equally well, as there is some reason to believe, have been made with the design of obtaining from the more lenient British military authorities permission for a demonstration which would certainly not have been allowed by the authorities elsewhere in the occupied territory. The German Government may, in fact, regard it as fortunate that the Rhineland High Commission did not forbid the meeting altogether, especially since, according to paragraph 4 of Colonel Ryan's[2] despatch No. 131[3] of the 10th instant, copy of which has already been sent to you direct, the Military Authorities of Occupation only refrained from pressing for this action in view of the refusal of the British military authorities to allow German officers to attend.

4. Permission for the meeting having nevertheless been granted, the German authorities are, it seems, of the opinion, which you apparently share, that because officers of the Reichswehr have made a practice of attending such meetings in unoccupied territory, therefore they have a right to attend this meeting in occupied territory. Apart from the occasion of the Hendon Air Pageant,[4] which was indeed visited by certain German officers but, I would point out, without invitation from His Majesty's Government and without the previous knowledge of the Foreign Office, His Majesty's

[1] Not printed.

[2] Colonel R. S. Ryan, Acting British High Commissioner on the Inter-Allied Rhineland High Commission during the absence of the Earl of Erroll on sick leave.

[3] Not preserved in Foreign Office archives. According to the docket this despatch was in the sense here indicated.

[4] The reference was to the Royal Air Force Display held on July 2, 1927.

Government have hitherto been unaware that such a practice existed. The present disclosure of its existence affords, as you have observed, evidence of an interest in aeronautics among members of the Reichswehr which may well be regarded in ex-Allied countries with considerable disquiet, and the necessity of protesting against it may require serious consideration: but no deduction would be less justified than that, a possibly illegal precedent having, unknown to His Majesty's Government, been set on the occasion of previous meetings of this particular Society in unoccupied territory, His Majesty's Government are therefore bound by this precedent when it is a question of officers wishing to attend a meeting which the Society elects to hold in occupied territory.

5. The statement that no subject of a military nature will be discussed at the meeting might well be adduced in favour of allowing the meeting itself to be held; but it is not germane to the question of giving German officers permission to attend it, this latter question being solely dependent on whether such attendance is or is not in conformity with the spirit of the Treaty of Versailles and of the Air Agreement of May 1926.[5] Now, according to section V of Pièce C, annexed to that Agreement, wherein are defined the circumstances in which certain officers, up to an eventual total of 36, may be given an exceptional authorisation to fly their own sporting aeroplanes, the German Government ought not to have granted such an authorisation, in the twenty months which have elapsed since the 1st January, 1926, to more than 10 officers. There is nothing in the present correspondence to show that the officers who are now applying for permission to attend the meeting are in fact the 10 officers to whom such authorisation may have been granted; but even if these are the 10 officers in question, it is clear that the Reichswehr authorities are specifically forbidden in the same section to give such officers 'congés spéciaux' for the purpose of indulging their aeronautical tastes. It appears from the first of the points raised in your telegram No. 86 that this is precisely what the Reichswehr Ministry have done in the present instance. So far, therefore, from the considerations adduced by the Air Attaché to His Majesty's Embassy militating in favour of a reversal of the decision taken by the British authorities in the Rhineland, they only serve to confirm my opinion that this decision should be upheld.

6. As for the possibility that, by maintaining our refusal to satisfy in the present instance the desires of the Reichswehr Ministry, the Aeronautical Section of the Transport Ministry and the Council of the 'Scientific Society for Aeronautics', we may arouse such resentment among the Nationalist members of these bodies as to increase the difficulties of Herr Stresemann in dealing with his Nationalist colleagues in the German Government, I would remind you that we would run the much more serious risk of gratuitously

[5] For the documents comprising the agreement on aerial navigation between the German Government and the Belgian, British, French, Italian, and Japanese Governments with a view to the application of article 198 of the Treaty of Versailles, see *League of Nations Treaty Series*, vol. lviii, pp. 332–74, and G. F. de Martens, *Nouveau Recueil Général de Traités*, Troisième Série (Leipzig, 1900), vol. 16, pp. 895–6.

antagonising French opinion if we were to reverse at the eleventh hour, with the minimum of apparent justification, a decision taken by our own military authorities and approved by the Rhineland High Commission, on a subject with regard to which the French are rightly or wrongly particularly sensitive. If it is a question of choosing between these two risks, His Majesty's Government prefer the lesser of the two and must be prepared on this occasion to risk the possibility of 'weakening' Herr Stresemann.

7. Apart from this, there remains the offensive manner in which the German Government have raised this question. I am glad to note that you yourself in the first instance resented and resisted the method adopted by the officials of the German Ministry for Foreign Affairs, in endeavouring to obtain a favourable solution of this question as the price of their consent to a request on the part of His Majesty's Government, the granting of which was a matter of the merest courtesy, and which related to another question not even remotely connected with that to which this despatch refers.[6] You will readily understand that similarly this sort of procedure is not calculated to produce a favourable impression on His Majesty's Government nor to predispose them to go out of their way subsequently to make a gratuitous concession to the German Government.

8. Lastly, you observe that if the decision of the military authorities is maintained, the Air Attaché in Berlin considers that he will be considerably hampered in his efforts to gain the confidence of those circles where his work invariably lies. I regret that this should be the case, but it is clearly impossible for His Majesty's Government to refrain from dealing with this question on its merits merely in order to assist the Air Attaché in the exercise of his duties.

9. Since the foregoing paragraphs were drafted, I have received Coblenz telegram No. 19[7] of the 13th instant, the contents of which can but be regarded as a decisive endorsement of the decision which has already been taken.[8]

I am, &c.,

(For the Secretary of State)
Orme Sargent

[6] Mr. Ingram had reported in Berlin telegram No. 80 of September 9 that he had been informed by the Ministry of Foreign Affairs that there would have been no difficulty in acceding to a British request that a team from the Royal Air Force should be permitted to go in uniform to Königsberg via Danzig to repair the wreck of the British flying boat *Valkyrie* if the British authorities had given permission for ten German officers to attend the meeting at Wiesbaden.

[7] Not printed. This telegram explained why the Inter-Allied Rhineland High Commission and the military authorities of the occupying powers would have 'strong objection' to reversing the decision referred to in paragraph 1 above.

[8] On September 15, Mr. Selby, Private Secretary to Sir A. Chamberlain, recorded that he had acted on instructions from Sir Austen to tell Herr von Schubert that 'the tactlessness of these people is inexplicable—unless indeed Prince Henry [of Prussia] & his Society are deliberately working to obstruct & if possible destroy Dr. Stresemann's policy. They do everything they can to arouse the suspicions of the French & to strengthen the reactionary elements in France. Incidentally they annoy every Englishman concerned in the matter. No sane man, who did not desire to provoke a row, would have chosen Wiesbaden for this

purpose during the occupation, & above all at the moment that we are making our respective reductions in the troops of occupation—still less would they have done it without consulting the Com[missio]n.' Mr. Selby stated that 'Herr von Schubert explained that he knew nothing of the matter and admitted at once the justice of Sir Austen Chamberlain's representations. It was really foolish in the extreme for the Society to have selected Wiesbaden as a place of meeting. He said that he would at once look into the matter.'

On the same day Mr. Ingram reported in Berlin despatch No. 549 that he had informed the German Ministry of Foreign Affairs of the decision in Foreign Office telegram No. 98 to Berlin (see paragraph 2 above).

No. 10

Letter from Mr. Selby (Geneva) to Mr. Sargent
[C 7681/2050/18]

GENEVA, *September 15, 1927*

My dear Sargent,

I enclose a copy of the note which is to be addressed by Monsieur Briand to Dr. Stresemann. You will observe that no mention is made of the Belgian forces. The Belgians have not yet got the information, but the French did not wish to delay the communication to Stresemann on that account.

What the Germans are really interested in is to know the places, barracks and billets which will be vacated as a result of the British reductions. We have hesitated to commit ourselves to details on the War Office telegrams.[1] I have told Schubert that we would let the Embassy in Berlin know in due course exactly what evacuations would take place. Could you prepare some such statement in consultation with the War Office and communicate it to the Embassy in Berlin, as soon as you have got the information, for communication to the German Government.[2]

Yours ever
W. S.

ENCLOSURE 1 IN No. 10

Letter from Mr. Selby (Geneva) to M. Massigli[3]

GENEVA, *September 15, 1927*

My dear Massigli,

To confirm what I told you this morning, the Secretary of State concurs in the draft note to be despatched by Monsieur Briand to Dr. Stresemann in regard to the reduction of troops in the Rhineland which we discussed yesterday.[4]

I understand that the Belgians will furnish their information to the Germans later.

Yours very sincerely,
W. SELBY

[1] Not printed.
[2] Mr. Sargent sent a summary of this letter together with a copy of enclosure 2 below to Colonel McGrath of the General Staff at the War Office on September 19. No reply has been traced in Foreign Office archives.
[3] Secretary-General of the Conference of Ambassadors.
[4] No record of this conversation has been traced in Foreign Office archives.

Copie

La réduction à 60,000 hommes des effectifs d'occupation de Rhénanie, dans les conditions rappelées par la lettre que M. Briand a adressée le 5 septembre à M. Stresemann au nom des Gouvernements belge, britannique, français, italien et japonais,[5] aura les conséquences suivantes:

1° / Dans la zone britannique, il sera procédé au retrait d'un bataillon et à diverses compressions d'effectifs;

2° / Dans la zone française seront retirés un Etat-Major de Corps d'Armée, un Etat-Major de division, un état-major d'infanterie divisionnaire, deux états-majors de demi-brigade de chasseurs mitrailleurs, six bataillons de chasseurs mitrailleurs, un bataillon et une compagnie du génie et un groupe d'aviation, ainsi que des détachements de divers services.

Les remaniements qui résulteront de ces suppressions pour le groupement de l'armée française entraîneront la disparition de la garnison de Diez, actuellement composée d'un état-major et de deux bataillons d'infanterie. En outre, les garnisons de Duren, Euskirchen, Coblence, Trèves, Kreuznach, Worms et Germersheim, ainsi qu'une garnison du Palatinat qui n'est point encore déterminée, seront réduites.

3° / Les renseignements relatifs aux mesures qui seront prises dans la zone belge seront donnés ultérieurement.

Les différentes opérations visées aux paragraphes 1 et 2 ci-dessus seront effectuées dans le courant du mois d'octobre; elles auront comme suite la remise à la disposition des autorités et des populations d'un nombre de locaux et de logements qu'il n'est pas encore possible d'évaluer exactement mais qui sera certainement très appréciable, en raison notamment de la suppression d'états-majors et de services importants.

GENEVA, *le 15 septembre 1927.*

[5] See Volume III, enclosure in No. 331.

No. 11

Sir A. Chamberlain (Geneva) to Sir W. Tyrrell (Received September 20)
No. 41 L.N.A. [C 7748/304/18]

GENEVA, *September 16, 1927*

Sir,

Dr. Stresemann having expressed a desire for another conversation with me before I left, I called upon him to-day at his hotel. I first asked him to use whatever influence he thought he might properly employ to persuade the Hungarian Government to accept the proposals of the Committee of Three over which I preside.[1]

[1] For consideration in 1927 by the Council of the League of Nations of the jurisdiction of the Mixed Roumano–Hungarian Arbitral Tribunal in respect of cases in connexion with the immovable property in territories transferred to Roumania under the Treaty of Trianon of persons opting for Hungarian nationality, see *League of Nations Official Journal*, April 1927, pp. 350–72, July 1927, p. 790, and October 1927, pp. 1379–1414. The Committee of Three

2. Dr. Stresemann had not yet read the report of my committee, but he sent for it and read it in my presence. I offered some explanations, and he appeared well satisfied of its impartiality and wisdom. He told me that he should press its acceptance upon the Hungarians and tell them that the German Delegation felt bound by the unanimous opinion of the jurists of whom Herr Gaus[2] was one.

3. For some reason which I do not quite fathom, the German Delegation have been interesting themselves particularly in the position of the Chinese representative here, and Dr. Stresemann again spoke to me upon this subject. He had, of course, had a report from Herr von Schubert of a conversation which that gentleman had held with Mr. Selby,[3] and there was nothing for me to do but to amplify and confirm what Mr. Selby had already said.

4. Dr. Stresemann then enquired whether there was anything new in our relations with Russia, and I replied in the negative. He said that Chicherin[4] continued to tell him that we were preparing for war and that war would come in the spring, and he added laughingly that he could not sufficiently congratulate himself that he had not formed one of the German party at Talloires on Sunday last when the Prime Minister and I lunched together there.[5] The fact that the Prime Minister had spoken for a minute with Herr von Schubert had already given rise to comment enough and, had he himself also been present, Chicherin would have believed that a secret treaty had been signed by the Prime Minister and himself.

5. Finally, Dr. Stresemann asked to refer once again to the Rhineland occupation. Monsieur Briand, he said, had sent for a member of the German party and told him that he could not do anything further in that matter as long as the Nationalists were included in the German Government. This, Dr. Stresemann observed, showed a complete misapprehension of the position. Monsieur Briand had said that he had faith in Dr. Stresemann, but Dr. Stresemann's feet were chained by his Nationalist colleagues. This was the exact opposite of the facts. The people who were chained were the Nationalists who, by

to consider the question was composed of Sir A. Chamberlain, M. Villegas, and the Japanese delegate to the League of Nations, Viscount Ishii (later Mr. Sato) (*v. op. cit.,* April 1927, p. 372). For their report to the Council of the League of Nations on September 17, 1927, *v. op. cit.,* October 1927, pp. 1379–83. Consideration of the question by the Council in December 1927 was deferred owing to the illness of M. Titulesco, the Roumanian Minister for Foreign Affairs: *v. op. cit.,* February 1928, pp. 110–12. (The Hungarian peace treaty of Trianon of June 4, 1920, is printed in *British and Foreign State Papers,* vol. 113, pp. 486–645.)

[2] Dr. Gaus, Legal Adviser to the German Ministry of Foreign Affairs, was evidently one of the eminent legal authorities consulted by the Committee of Three.

[3] Geneva covering despatch No. 37 L.N.A. of September 16 (not preserved in Foreign Office archives) transmitted a copy of a memorandum by Mr. Selby of September 15, not printed, recording a conversation he had had that morning with M. Ouang, who had said that he hoped Sir A. Chamberlain 'would always understand' that Sir Austen 'could rely on his support and friendship on the Council'.

[4] Soviet People's Commissar for Foreign Affairs.

[5] Sir A. Chamberlain had met Mr. Baldwin, who was on holiday at Aix-les-Bains from August 29 to September 26, on September 11 at Talloires on Lake Annecy: cf. No. 215, below.

joining the government, were obliged to take responsibility for and associate themselves with the Locarno policy and unable to continue the *intransigeant* attitude which they had adopted in 1920, 1921 and 1922. Just as it was an advantage that Monsieur Poincaré should be associated with Monsieur Briand and therefore obliged to assume responsibility for his policy, so was it equally advantageous that the Nationalists should be in the German Government and not free to adopt the attitude of violent opposition which their previous irresponsibility had made possible, and after all, he concluded, he had no-one as extreme in his Cabinet as Monsieur Marin, and indeed by now there was no difference in the German Delegation, and Professor Hoetzsch[6] was as strong a supporter of the League and Locarno policy as Dr. Breitscheid.[7] Monsieur Briand had, however, told his interlocutor that I shared his point of view. Was it possible, asked Dr. Stresemann, that I so misinterpreted the situation?

6. I replied that Monsieur Briand had no authority from me for any such statement, that indeed I recognised that the election of President Hindenberg [*sic*],[8] which I had at first dreaded, had turned out to be very favourable to our policy, and I quite understood the advantages which Dr. Stresemann found in making the Nationalists take responsibility for the policy that he was pursuing.

7. Dr. Stresemann then added that the coalition of parties in Germany was, in fact, determined by domestic politics. The agrarians and the industrialists both needed protection and, in consequence, must work together. Their daily cares and interests influenced the relations of parties more than the wider questions of foreign policy, and they were both content to let him have his own way in the sphere of international relations provided that they could maintain what they considered a sufficient measure of protection for agricultural and industrial production.

I am, &c.,
Austen Chamberlain

[6] Professor Otto Hoetzsch was a German National Peoples Party deputy in the Reichstag.

[7] Dr. Breitscheid was a Social Democratic deputy in the Reichstag.

[8] Field-Marshal Paul von Hindenburg had been elected German President in April 1925.

No. 12

Mr. Ingram (Berlin) to Sir A. Chamberlain
(Received September 19, 4.40 p.m.)

No. 90 Telegraphic [*C 7737/1160/18*]

Important   BERLIN, *September 19, 1927, 3.10 p.m.*

Points in the President of Reich's speech yesterday at opening of Tannenberg memorial[1] were following:

A. 'Every section of the German people repudiates unanimously the

[1] For the text of President von Hindenburg's speech on the occasion of the inauguration of the memorial to the Battle of Tannenberg, August 26–30, 1914, see *The Times* of September 19, 1927, p. 12.

impeachment that Germany was responsible for this the greatest of all wars.'

B. 'Germany is at all times ready to establish this before impartial judges.' Text follows by bag.[2]

[2] Berlin despatch No. 554 of September 20 is not printed. Mr. Sargent minuted on the present telegram on September 21: 'President Hindenburg's pronouncement is the culminating point of an unofficial campaign which has been gathering force for a long time past.... It is devoutly to be hoped that on the present occasion it will be equally possible to allow sleeping dogs to lie. It seems highly improbable that the Hindenburg pronouncement will be followed up by any sort of communication from the German Government on this subject. I think we can count on Dr. Stresemann to prevent any such folly.'

In a letter to Mr. Sargent of September 23, Mr. Ingram reported that he had heard 'from a very confidential source' that the whole affair was 'in its origins a party manoeuvre'. The President had refused to act without the consent of the Departments concerned, all of whom had agreed to the text save the Ministry of Foreign Affairs: Dr. Stresemann had, however, apparently consented.

No. 13

Mr. Ingram (Berlin) to Sir A. Chamberlain (Received September 26)
No. 561 [C 7901/3636/18]

BERLIN, *September 22, 1927*

Sir,

I have the honour to transmit to you herewith a copy of a despatch which the Naval Attaché at this Embassy is addressing to the Director of Naval Intelligence at the Admiralty regarding the armament of new German 10,000 ton battleships.

2. As the question seemed to be one for discussion by the Conference of Ambassadors and not for decision by any of the Powers separately, I instructed Commander Nash to say nothing to the Marineleitung[1] which would lead them to expect an isolated expression of opinion from His Majesty's Government and merely to send Captain Canaris a simple acknowledgment of his letter of the 6th instant.[2] I also urged him to endeavour to induce his French and Italian colleagues to exercise a similar caution in dealing with the question.

I have, &c.,
E. M. B. INGRAM

ENCLOSURE 1 IN No. 13
Commander Nash (Berlin) to Admiralty

Confidential   BERLIN, *September 22, 1927*

Sir,

I have the honour to inform you that on the day before proceeding on my visit to the Baltic States I was asked by the Marineleitung if I would visit them in order to discuss a certain question.

[1] Naval Command Staff.

[2] Printed in translation as enclosure 2 below. The original German text is untraced in Foreign Office archives. Captain Canaris was in the Fleet Department of the Marineleitung.

30

2. In an interview with two members of the staff, I was informed that although they were not thinking of replacing their old battleships in the near future they were nevertheless naturally investigating various designs of ships and the possible composition of armament which could be put into a vessel of 10,000 tons.

3. They pointed out that as they were limited to this tonnage, they naturally desired to utilise guns of the largest size possible, and they hoped that by reducing the weight of the machinery as much as possible, by the installation of motor engines and in other ways, they could arm them with six 30·5 cm (12-inch) guns.

4. In this connection, however, they were not clear on referring to 'Table "B" Annual Replacements of Guns' (drawn up by the Naval Inter-Allied Commission of Control) as to whether they were allowed to put 30·5 cm guns into their ships, or whether this table limited them to 28 cm guns. They therefore asked me if I would ascertain the view of the British Admiralty on the subject.

5. I observed that, if it were finally the opinion of the other Nations that they could arm their replaced battleships with 30·5 cm guns, an alteration to Table 'B' would apparently be necessary, as it is fairly obvious from the number of guns allowed by this table that 30·5 cm guns were only intended for Coastal fortifications. They replied in the sense that Table 'B' had already been modified once, viz. in 1923 when the size of the armament of their cruisers was raised from 10·5 cm to 15 cm.

6. I further added that in my opinion the question was one which would finally have to be dealt with by the League of Nations, and that I therefore presumed that they would communicate with the other Naval Attachés concerned on this subject; stating that I could only comply with their request on this assumption. I have since been informed that they have communicated with the French and Italian Naval Attachés.

7. The Marineleitung has since communicated with me officially on the subject, and I enclose a copy of their letter, together with a translation.

I have, &c.,

G. S. F. NASH

ENCLOSURE 2 IN No. 13

Captain Canaris to Commander Nash (Berlin)

Translation   BERLIN, *September 6, 1927*

Dear Captain,

With reference to our verbal conversation of to-day relative to the question of the armament for the 10,000 tons replacement ship allowed by the Treaty of Versailles, I would be very grateful if you would ascertain and inform us of the opinion of the British Admiralty in regard to whether an armament of 6–30·5 cm can be regarded as permissible for the replacement ships under the terms of Table 'B' laid down by the N[aval] I[nter-] A[llied] C[ommission of Control] for the armament of the German Navy, or whether we must be satisfied with an armament of only 6–28 cm.

Yours sincerely,
CANARIS

No. 14

Letter from Mr. Preston[1] (Turin) to Mr. Gascoigne[2]

[*N 4550/9/38*]

TURIN, *September 22, 1927*

Dear Gascoigne,

Although perhaps out of my province now, I thought the gist of the following conversation I had yesterday with a German acquaintance of mine on Soviet business conditions since the break would not be without interest.

In his statement my friend, who used to represent a British firm in Leningrad, quotes very largely a man called Begge whom we both personally knew formerly in Leningrad, and who is at present head of the Soviet Torgpredstvo[3] in Berlin.

It would seem that about May last German industrialists (including my friend) were advised by British banks that the discounting for them of Soviet Bills would be discontinued. To-day as a result of the cessation by the British banks of this kind of business the discount rate for Soviet Bills in Germany has increased from 9%—last May—to 28%. This is a great obstruction to Soviet foreign trade and as German banks cannot hope to cope with the business formerly done by similar British institutions Soviet foreign trade is diminishing in consequence.

Similarly, as a result of the break, the aggregate of Soviet foreign trade is decreasing in volume to the extent that trade has been abandoned with Britain.

Speaking about Soviet Russia as a German market, my friend said that although the difficulties were very great, some business was done, particularly in steel, high speed and tool, but that with the British banks action in discontinuing to discount Soviet bills even this trade would probably decline. The trade with Soviet Russia was actually less than 2% of the total German foreign trade. On the other hand the investment of German capital in Russia had been a hopeless failure to which fact the Mologoless timber concession failure[4] amply testified. My friend added that it was politics more than economics that kept the Germans in Russia, by which he implied that Germany would have to keep in Russia as long as other countries did so.

I then asked my friend whether he intended to return to Russia. His reply was that although he and his company had done very well in their trans-

---

[1] Mr. Preston, H.M. Acting Consul at Turin, had served as H.M. Consul at Leningrad from November 1922 to June 3, 1927, when he left the U.S.S.R. following the rupture of Anglo–Soviet relations.

[2] A member of the Northern Department of the Foreign Office.

[3] *Torgovoe predstavitelstvo*, trade delegation.

[4] Cf. Volume III, No. 144, enclosure, and No. 205, enclosure.

actions with the Leningrad trusts nothing would induce him to return. He was in constant touch with the development of events in that country and he had no information to hand that would justify the belief that any change was possible or likely, as it seemed in his lifetime.[5] He had decided, more especially as he had had a nervous breakdown since he left Russia which kept him away from work a whole year, 'to put three crosses on Soviet Russia', which being interpreted into terrestrial language means 'wipe it out of his memory'.

Yours ever,
T. H. PRESTON

[5] Mr. Preston noted at foot with reference to this passage: 'Perhaps this is rather too pessimistic.'

No. 15

Viscount Chilston (Vienna) to Sir A. Chamberlain (Received October 4)
No. 214 [C 8087/55/3]

VIENNA, *September 29, 1927*

Sir,

With reference to your Despatch No. 282[1] (C 7436/55/3) of the 15th instant I have the honour to report that my French colleague in conversation yesterday told me that he was going to write to his Government about the desirability of bringing the work of the Organ of Liquidation[2] to an end as soon as possible. He himself felt very strongly that this would help to make the Austrians realise their independence and the necessity of looking after their affairs themselves. He said he understood that there was now very little left unfulfilled of the disarmament obligations undertaken by the Austrian Government in July of last year,[3] and he hinted at the possibility that perhaps if the Austrian Government were to give an undertaking that within a certain period everything would be completed the Commission might meanwhile be withdrawn. M. de Chambrun added that he believed that feeling was now running much higher with regard to the continued presence of the Organ here while Germany and Hungary had already been relieved of their Organs of Control; and that he rather expected a Press campaign would be started.

[1] This covering despatch is not preserved in Foreign Office archives. It transmitted copies of: (i) a letter from the War Office of September 6 enclosing a copy of a letter from Colonel McGrath dated September 2, together with enclosures, regarding the dissolution of the Municipal Guard in Vienna; (ii) the reply from Mr. Sargent dated September 13, in which it was suggested that the question be held in abeyance until the Allied Military Committee of Versailles had had an opportunity to examine the whole question of Austrian disarmament. Cf. Volume III, No. 295.

[2] On February 20, 1921, the Inter-Allied Military Commission of Control, which had been set up by articles 149–55 of the Treaty of Saint Germain, signed by Austria and her former enemies on September 10, 1919 (printed in *British and Foreign State Papers*, vol. 112, pp. 317–498), had been withdrawn from Austria and an Organ of Liquidation constituted to clear up outstanding matters.

[3] The procès-verbal of July 30, 1926, recording agreement regarding the completion of Austria's disarmament obligations is printed in Volume II as the enclosure in No. 119.

2. I said that I would speak to Colonel Salter[4] as to how far off fulfilment the various obligations were, and what was the actual position, but I fancied there were still a large number of machines to be dispersed, in fact that little had yet been done in that respect, although with regard to destruction the Organ was now pretty well satisfied. As to the idea of another undertaking by the Government I did not see that, if we really desired to see the complete fulfilment of all the conditions, we should attain that result. The undertakings given in the Protocol of July 1926[3] ought to have been fulfilled long ago and I had little doubt that once the Commission was withdrawn nothing further would be done by the Austrians towards destruction or dispersal of the machines, prevention of manufacture, or even the proper completion of the remaining section of the Single State Factory.[5] At the same time I entirely agreed with him that we wished to terminate the liquidation as soon as possible and I knew that my Government had always been of that opinion. The Powers had always been very lenient towards the Austrians in these matters, for internal political reasons, and had given them concessions and plenty of time. The Austrian Government had until recently shown a lamentable disregard of their obligations, in fact had never done anything except under constant pressure. As to feeling in Austria against the presence of the Organ I was surprised that this should be at all strong, since most Austrians until now had appeared to be singularly indifferent and in general rather to be ignorant of the presence of the Control. If there should be any campaign or protest the answer was obviously that it was in the power of the Austrian Government themselves to bring about that end, which the Powers also desired.

3. I understand from Colonel Salter that there is still a good deal which according to the terms of the Protocol is yet to be done, except in regard to destruction. From the general political point of view, apart from the military or technical aspects and that of the due fulfilment of the Clauses of the Peace Treaty, the question appears to me to be whether the carrying out of the remaining disarmament conditions is of sufficient importance as against the desirability of freeing Austria, like Germany and Hungary, of all further Control. Austria, although she may and does still possess rifles and a few armament machines and a few potential manufacturing buildings, cannot of herself be held to constitute a menace to any country in a military sense. On the other hand she could, if entirely free, become again a powerful centre of munition making and export, and there is no doubt that, as soon as the Control is withdrawn, the armament firms will begin to manufacture and export. Hence the importance of the destruction or dispersal of all 'special machines'.

4. As to the finding and taking over of rifles which are still known to exist in various places, it becomes more and more difficult, as far as I understand, for the Organ to get any satisfaction. I am told that there are, for instance,

[4] British representative on the Organ of Liquidation in Vienna.
[5] Article 132 of the Treaty of Saint Germain stipulated that the manufacture of war material in Austria must be confined to a single State factory.

7,000 army rifles in a Socialist Arbeiterheim[6] on the outskirts of Vienna, but that in view of the embittered feeling between the Socialists and the Government the latter hesitates to provide the necessary authority and facility for securing them. One must also consider that it is not only the Socialist Republikanische Schutzbund[7] which seems to be able to lay its hands upon certain stores of arms but that the various provincial anti-Socialist bodies, although mainly supplied with sporting rifles, have also some concealed stores of army rifles. These associations, as I reported in a recent Despatch,[8] are now strenuously exerting themselves to recruit and consolidate the so-called 'Heimatwehr'[9] for internal political purposes.

5. These unauthorised formations are, according to the Decrees which Dr. Seipel[10] caused to be issued, to perform no military exercises and to have no connection with the Ministry of War. As to the latter point it may be the case that they have none, but there is no doubt that they are attempting to give themselves such military training as may enable them to mobilise against any Socialist dangers. The existence of all these bodies, while contrary to the Peace Treaty, is hardly a danger internationally; the chief danger lying in them is in the internal troubles which would be caused by any clash between them; and any serious internal troubles might to a certain extent produce outside complications. For the present probably all that the 'Heimwehren' hope to do is to act as a powerful menace against future Socialist or Communist agitations. It is indeed generally believed among the upper and middle classes that it was this menace which checkmated the Socialists last July in Vienna[11] and will act as a powerful deterrent in future.

6. As to the 'Municipal Watch' which is the subject of the enclosures in your Despatch No. 282, it is natural that the Allied Military Committee and the Organ of Liquidation, from the point of view of the military clauses of the Peace Treaty, should regard this as another unauthorised body or an unauthorised addition to the police forces, and should demand its disbandment. They are armed with pistols; but their functions can hardly be likened to those of the police. Looking at the matter from a larger aspect they cannot be regarded as a danger to Vienna, and moreover, if as is generally admitted, the far larger semi-military body the Republikanische Schutzbund cannot be disbanded (and the same may be said of the provincial 'Heimwehren') then it does not seem reasonable to press for the disbandment of the body of one thousand men, who were allowed by the Government to continue for the present in order to save the face of the Social Democrat leaders to tide over the present difficulties and to make it possible for Dr. Seipel to carry on without bringing matters too much to a head with the Socialists, in any case to give him some delay. It is, I am convinced, impossible for any Government in present circumstances to take any steps towards disbanding or

---

[6] Workers' Home.   [7] Republican Defence Union.
[8] Vienna despatch No. 212 of September 21 is not printed.   [9] Home guard.
[10] Dr. Seipel was Austrian Chancellor and retained charge of home and foreign affairs.
[11] For a brief account of the riots in Vienna on July 15–16, 1927, see *Survey of International Affairs 1927*, pp. 217–18.

disarming all these associations to which I have referred. If it were forced, by some special means of pressure, to take steps in such a direction, that which it is desired to avoid might actually be produced, i.e. serious internal conflicts.

7. It is to be hoped that the report of the Organ of Liquidation on the present state of affairs with regard to the completion of the remaining disarmament work will be presented with the least possible delay, and that then a definite decision may be taken as to the withdrawal of the Organ.

I have, &c.,

CHILSTON

No. 16

Memorandum by Mr. Huxley[1]

[C 5711/374/18]

FOREIGN OFFICE, *September 30, 1927*

This correspondence is incomprehensible without a knowledge of the earlier history of the Reparation Recovery Act[2] and of the considerations which have led to the adoption of the present method of collecting the levy imposed by that Act on German exports to this country. An attempt has been made to explain these matters in the memorandum in C.7455,[3] the compilation of which, together with the necessity for summarizing the correspondence has unduly delayed its submission.

The main features of the correspondence itself are as follows: Early this year the Reserve Fund mentioned in paragraph 41 of the attached memorandum C.7455[4] began to fall very low, and when the attention of the responsible German authorities was drawn to the matter by Mr. Finlayson,[5] their attitude appeared unsatisfactory.

---

[1] This memorandum was written in connexion with the letter of June 21 to Mr. Leith-Ross, Deputy Controller of Finance in H.M. Treasury, from Mr. Parker Gilbert, Agent General for Reparation Payments by Germany under the Dawes Plan, referred to in the final paragraph below. General Charles Dawes, an American citizen, had been chairman of the Committee of Experts appointed by the Reparation Commission on November 30, 1923,'to consider the means of balancing the budget and the measures to be taken to stabilise the currency of Germany'. The committee submitted its plan to the Reparation Commission on April 9, 1924 (see Cmd. 2105 of 1924). A draft agreement for carrying into effect the plan for the discharge of the reparation obligations of Germany proposed by the Committee of Experts was formally adopted and signed by the Reparation Commission and the German Government on August 9, 1924 (see Cmd. 2270 of 1924). The Dawes Plan was finally put into effect and the Agreement of August 9, 1924, completed by the London Agreements of August 30, 1924, between the Allied Governments and Germany (see Cmd. 2259 of 1924).

[2] The German Reparation (Recovery) Act (11 & 12 Geo. 5, c. 5) of March 24, 1921, is printed in *British and Foreign State Papers*, vol. 114, pp. 26–29.

[3] Not printed. This memorandum by Mr. Huxley, dated September 8, outlined developments in connexion with the Reparation Recovery Act since January 1921.

[4] Mr. Huxley stated in this paragraph that as a measure of precaution against any deficiency in the sterling receipts of the German Reichsbank a special reserve fund, consisting of sterling equivalent to 10 million marks (£500,000), had been established in 1925.

[5] Financial Adviser to H.M. Embassy at Berlin.

This circumstance was the occasion of a letter which Mr. Leith Ross of the Treasury addressed to Mr. Finlayson on April 27th (C.5369),[6] in which he indicated the probable cause of the falling off in the Reserve Fund, namely, that during 1926 German exports to Great Britain had been abnormally large owing to the coal stoppage and that it had therefore not been necessary, in order to cover the British Reparation quota, to take nearly 26 per cent. of the sterling obtained in exchange for those exports. Presumably therefore the German Government had ceased to exert any pressure on the 800 exporters to surrender their sterling. The moment had, however, arrived for reversion to a stricter procedure so that the Reserve Fund might be built up again: otherwise H.M. Government would be compelled to suggest some new arrangement, such as an increase in the percentage surrendered by the said 800 exporters above the 30% laid down in the agreement of April 1925.[7]

Furthermore, Mr. Leith Ross foresaw the approach of a time when we might no longer be able to absorb the whole of our Reparation quota through the Recovery Act machinery as at present applied: since, while the maximum obtainable thereby (26 per cent. of all German exports to this country) had sunk to about £1,300,000 a month during the first quarter of 1927, our regular monthly allocation under the Dawes scheme, which had averaged about £830,000 during 1926, had already passed the million level, and would be increased to £1,175,000 after September 1927. Besides this regular monthly allocation, certain other payments would have to be absorbed, such as our share, amounting to over £1 million in August 1927 and over £1½ million in April and again in August 1928, of the payments on the Industrial Debentures. While therefore the German exports to this country were then, in April 1927, sufficiently large to enable us to absorb the whole of our Reparation quota through the 26%, the margin was about to become dangerously narrow, and a serious shortage would occur if those exports fell back to the average of 1925, the last normal year. Moreover, even if they maintained their existing level, any payments outside the regular monthly allocation would begin to accumulate in the shape of a credit balance unless, of course, they were to form the subject of a cash transfer.

There were, Mr. Leith Ross considered, two ways of combating the danger which he thus anticipated:

(a) by increasing the rate of the Recovery Act levy above 26%, or
(b) by maintaining the rate at 26%, but basing it on exports from Germany to the whole British Empire, instead of on exports to the United Kingdom only.

During the last four years, exports to India and the Dominions amounted to about 40% of the exports to the United Kingdom (the greater part being to India), and the result of basing the levy on exports to the whole Empire would thus be probably about the same as that of increasing the rate on

---

[6] This letter is not printed.
[7] The reference was to the agreement of April 3, 1925, between Great Britain and Germany for amending the method of administering the German Reparation (Recovery) Act, printed in Cmd. 2384 of 1925.

exports to the United Kingdom from 26 to 36%. It would clearly be equitable to base the levy on exports to the whole Empire, as the whole Empire shares in the proceeds.

On May 16th Mr. Finlayson wrote to Mr. Leith Ross[6] informing him that he had discussed the above-mentioned points with the Agent-General. Mr. Gilbert did not consider that the decline in the Reserve Fund was due to any omission on the part of the German Government, who, he understood, had recently issued a severe warning to the German exporters; but he agreed to address the competent German official and to urge on him the necessity of maintaining the fund at the arranged level.

As for Mr. Leith Ross's two proposals for increasing our power of absorbing reparations through the Reparation Recovery Act machinery, Mr. Gilbert was dead against any increase in the rate of the levy, amongst other reasons because all the arrangements that had been made were based on the assumption that it would remain at 26%; though he admitted that 'there was no legal doubt that the levy *could* be screwed up to a maximum of 50%'. The second proposal, for extending the scope of the levy so as to cover German exports to the whole Empire, Mr. Gilbert liked somewhat better; but he feared that if such a scheme were proposed to the Germans they would reply (1) that the distribution of Great Britain's share in the annuity was purely a matter of British internal administration, in which they were not interested, and (2) that, before any such proposal could even be discussed, the German Government would first like to obtain certain trade concessions in the form of commercial treaties with the component parts of the Empire. In fact, Mr. Gilbert would prefer to abide by present arrangements. Nor could he undertake to pay us cash for the residue, if the Reparation Recovery Act machinery failed to absorb our quota.[8]

On May 18th Mr. Goodchild of the British Delegation to the Reparation Commission, wrote to Mr. Leith Ross[6] stating that he had discussed with Mr. Fraser, the Agent-General's representative at Paris, the question of the absorption by the various creditor Powers of the reparation quotas due to them. Obviously, if the Agent-General were to find himself in a chronic state of holding large mark balances which those Powers had failed to utilize, an opening would be given to opponents of the Dawes Plan to say that the Allies had bitten off more than they could chew, and that the annuities ought to be revised so as to correspond to the Allies' power of absorption. There was reason to think that Dr. Schacht, President of the Reichsbank, had been working to that end, and in these circumstances Mr. Gilbert was very anxious that the creditor Powers should make a real effort to cover their shares by deliveries in kind to the extent to which they could not be met by cash transfers. The other Allies were going to ginger up their programmes for

[8] Mr. Perowne, a member of the Central Department of the Foreign Office, here noted in the margin: 'This does not quite convey the sense of Mr. Parker Gilbert's remarks; he merely said he could not give an undertaking to pay cash, tho' he admitted that that would be the simplest plan—see p. 3. of Mr. Finlayson's letter of May 16th in C5369 J.V.P. 30/9'.

deliveries in kind (it will be seen from C.7344/120/18[9] that the French have successfully done this), and Mr. Fraser asked what H.M. Government intended to do about it. To all appearances, the cash transfer of 100 million marks which was due to take place in August (this has since been effected) would still leave H.M. Government with a surplus credit of some 32·5 million gold marks at the beginning of the next Dawes year, which the prospective increase of the Annuity to 1,750 million marks would make it difficult to overtake.

Mr. Goodchild had then referred to Mr. Leith Ross's two proposals (a) of increasing the Recovery Act levy in respect of exports to Great Britain to 35 or 40%, (b) of charging the percentage at its present rate to the whole of the British Empire. Mr. Fraser stated that he had sounded Mr. Gilbert on these points but had failed to smoke him out. His general impression was that Gilbert and the Transfer Committee[10] would be hostile to an increase in the rate of the levy, largely from dislike of the precedent which it would set for other Allied Powers, such as France. While Mr. Gilbert might not view with much favour the other proposal, for broadening the base of the levy, Mr. Fraser thought that it was in itself defensible; and if H.M. Government proposed to take such a step, now was probably the favourable moment. Mr. Goodchild's opinion was that an immediate initiative might be taken.

On receipt of this letter Mr. Leith Ross wrote to Mr. Parker Gilbert the letter of May 26th (C.5369: Flag A),[11] which should be read in full. Before this letter was actually despatched he had received Reparation Commission Annex 3153 A (C.4445/309/18)[12] in Schedule III of which is shown the programme for June, July and August 1927. 56,091,660·61 Reichsmarks are shown as available for the British Reparation Recovery Act, but, according to a footnote, 'subject to the limitations of the 26% levy on German exports to Great Britain'. He accordingly instructed the British delegate to make, at the Reparation Commission's meeting on May 28th, the statement which

[9] i.e. Paris covering despatch No. 1881 of September 3 (not preserved in Foreign Office archives) and the enclosed extract from Le Temps of September 4, 1927, containing the text of a statement by the French Ministry of Finance on the satisfactory nature of the third Dawes year (1926–7) from the French point of view.

[10] i.e. the committee under the presidency of Mr. Parker Gilbert charged with controlling the transfer of money collected under the Dawes Plan to the creditor Powers.

[11] Not printed. Mr. Leith-Ross referred to Mr. Gilbert's conversation with Mr. Finlayson on May 16 and requested his support in obtaining the agreement of the Transfer Committee to the increase of the rate of the levy under the Reparation (Recovery) Act to 35% or 40% to avoid the accumulation by His Majesty's Government of a credit balance which could not be absorbed. In a postscript Mr. Leith-Ross referred to the letter of May 13 from Mr. Gilbert to the Secretary-General of the Reparation Commission (circulated as Reparation Commission Annex 3153A) which is cited below and which transmitted three schedules relating to payments under the Dawes Plan from June to August 1927. Mr. Leith-Ross referred in particular to the footnote on Schedule III cited below and stated that the proviso therein made it necessary for the British Delegate to the Reparation Commission, Lord Blanesburgh, 'to put in a reserve about our right to increase the levy, but it will be in quite general terms and I shall await your considered views both on the acceptability of the proposal and on the question of the best time to put it forward'.

[12] i.e. Mr. Gilbert's letter of May 13: see note 11 above. The copy entered on this file is not preserved in Foreign Office archives.

forms the first enclosure to C.5609[13] and is mentioned at the conclusion of the above-mentioned letter to Mr. Parker Gilbert. This statement made it clear that H.M. Government did not regard the rate of the levy as being fixed for all time at 26%; and that while the necessary arrangements for any increase in the levy would have to be concerted with the Transfer Committee and with the German Government, H.M. Government trusted that they might rely on the co-operation of the Agent-General in negotiations to this end if the point arose, the more so as he had drawn attention (in his letter of May 13th: Annex 3153 A: C.4445) to the importance of all the creditor Powers, 'and particularly those specially interested in deliveries in kind, devoting their best efforts to the current utilization of their respective shares'. To the words 'deliveries in kind' Lord Blanesburgh's statement added a gloss, to the effect that this term 'of course covered the Reparation Recovery levy'. Mr. Parker Gilbert, in a letter which he addressed to the Reparation Commission on June 15th (Annex 3185 A: C.5398, also 2nd enclosure in C.5609)[13] drew attention to this gloss and rejected the implication to which it gave rise, declaring that 'he had no intention of expressing any opinion whatsoever on the question of increased levies under the Reparation Recovery Act'. He also referred to the assurance given by H.M. Government in March 1925 to the effect that 'the present rate of 26 per cent. in force under the Reparation Recovery Act would not be increased without the previous agreement of the Transfer Committee' (see paragraph 33 of memorandum in C.7455[3]).

Mr. Parker Gilbert's letter came before the Reparation Commission at its meeting on June 25th, when Lord Blanesburgh stated that he entirely accepted Mr. Gilbert's explanation of the meaning of his letter of May 13th and of the footnote to Schedule III enclosed therein, adding that 'there was no more intention of intimating any arbitrary alteration in the rate of the levy without the concurrence of the Transfer Committee than there could have been on the part of the Agent-General, acting on behalf of the Transfer Committee, to intimate in advance any objection to an alteration in the rate of the levy irrespective of the merits or necessities of the case when the question should arise'.

Meanwhile, Mr. Parker Gilbert had replied to Mr. Leith Ross' letter of May 26th[11] in the letter within,[14] which should also be read in full. Since this

[13] C.5609/374/18 (not printed) comprised Report No. 615 of June 27 from Mr. Goodchild to the Treasury enclosing: (1) item No. 3506 from Reparation Commission minutes No. 505 of May 28, namely a statement by Lord Blanesburgh as indicated below; (2) a letter of June 15, of which the gist is indicated below, from Mr. Gilbert to the Secretary-General of the Reparation Commission, circulated as Annex 3185A; (3) Reparation Commission Annex 3153A (see note 11 above); (4) a note of May 21 by the Secretary-General of the Reparation Commission, circulated as Annex 3153B, which submitted to the Commission the schedules appended to Annex 3153A. Mr. Goodchild's covering report referred in particular to Lord Blanesburgh's statement of June 25, in regard to which an extract from Mr. Goodchild's report is cited below.

[14] Not printed. A copy of this letter of June 21 was transmitted by Mr. Ingram in a letter of June 29 (not preserved in Foreign Office archives). In his letter Mr. Parker Gilbert argued in particular that there was no practical necessity for an increased levy under the Reparation (Recovery) Act and that any such proposal would raise most serious issues for the

was received we have heard nothing more either from Berlin or from the Treasury, and it may therefore be desirable, in sending to the latter the memorandum in C.7455 for their observations, to ask them how the general question now stands. A draft in this sense is submitted herewith.[15]

M. H. HUXLEY

p.p. J. V. PEROWNE

Transfer Committee and from the standpoint of the operation of the Dawes Plan as a whole.

[15] Mr. Sargent's ensuing letter of October 4 to the Treasury is not printed. In a letter of November 5 in reply the Treasury stated in particular that the Lords Commissioners of H.M. Treasury had 'intimated to the Agent-General that They are willing to leave in abeyance any question of a change in the existing procedure, until an undrawn surplus has actually accumulated; but that, if and when this occurs, it will be necessary for Them to ask the Transfer Committee to agree to an increase in the rate of 26%, or, alternatively, to arrange that the rate while remaining at 26%, should be based on imports from Germany to the whole of the British Empire. In order to effect either of these changes, it will be necessary to obtain the consent of the Transfer Committee and also to arrange with the German Government that the Declaration given by German exporters shall be modified to fit in with the new scheme. Mr. Gilbert apparently considers that it would also be desirable to obtain the approval of the Reparation Commission and, although Their Lordships do not consider that, strictly speaking, this is the case, They do not propose to raise any objection to submitting the matter to the Reparation Commission, if Mr. Gilbert so desires.'

No. 17

Memorandum by Mr. Headlam-Morley[1]

[C 8107/1160/18]

FOREIGN OFFICE, *October 4, 1927*

I have only just had an opportunity of seeing the files dealing with Hindenburg's speech at Tannenburg [Tannenberg] and should like to take the opportunity of making one or two observations.

Surprise has naturally been expressed that he appears to repudiate all responsibility on the part of Germany for the outbreak of war and asserts that Germany 'went to war for the preservation of our independence against a host of enemies'. To us this naturally appears absurd, so absurd as to be almost inexplicable. It is, however, in accordance with the theory which has during recent years been worked up with great persistency by German writers who represent that the fundamental cause of the war was the aggressive military preparations being made by France, and especially by Russia in agreement with France, which when they had been completed—that is by 1916—would have become a great danger to Germany. With this they would associate the very active and aggressive diplomatic campaign which in the spring of 1914 had been carried on by Russia in the Balkans (a campaign which the French supported, but with which Sir Edward Grey[2] refused to

[1] Historical Adviser to the Secretary of State for Foreign Affairs.

[2] Sir E. Grey, later Viscount Grey of Fallodon, was Secretary of State for Foreign Affairs, 1905–16.

associate himself and of which he probably disapproved), and also the agitation, which was really very dangerous, spreading discontent and disloyalty not only in Bosnia and Herzegovina, but also in Croatia. There is no doubt that this combination did really cause genuine apprehension at Berlin. Ever since the Treaty of Bucarest[3] the German Government had begun to feel that it was on the defensive, that the reins of power were slipping out of its hands. It is I think true that they were beginning to be rather frightened. When then Hindenburg says 'Neither envy, hatred nor thirst for conquest caused us to take up arms' there is a point of view from which this is true, and if a German were asked why they took up arms, the right answer would be Fear. And a German apologist would then proceed to point out that this fear was the real explanation of the diplomatic action in July 1914; he could do this without in the least defending the diplomatic blundering of the German Government which in reality few Germans would defend. But he would say it was blundering, not criminal perversity, and the explanation must be found in the difficult situation in which the German Government was, a situation which was not understood at the time here, though Sir Edward Goschen[4] went very near to a correct interpretation.

This merely is an attempt at explanation; of more importance is the question which is discussed in many of the minutes[5] as to whether it is desirable that any action should be taken here in regard to the whole matter.

I entirely agree with the view expressed, that we should like to relegate the whole matter to the historians, that is, to regard it as a question on which official or semi-official pronouncements are out of place. As the Secretary of State has pointed out, English and Germans would never come to a real agreement upon the matter, but if it were relegated to historians, then the continuance of the difference would not affect official relations and would not be incompatible with friendly relations between the two nations.

This is the situation in which we want to get. So far, I am in agreement with what has been written. My difficulty is that I do not see how we can get into this position without some pronouncement from our side. After all we are in a false position in maintaining this view that the whole matter is not one for official pronouncement so long as it is dealt with in the text of the treaty[6] and so long as there remains on record a fully official declaration dealing with the matter. I should therefore like to see a real effort made for devising some means for getting out of the false position in which we are. But this can only be done by some kind of *official* declaration withdrawing the official formulation of the charge. Without this any statement to the effect that we did not agree with the modern German interpretation of the historical point would be worse than useless. The essence of the whole thing would be (1) that we withdrew the charge as *officially* made, or at the least declared that

---

[3] The treaty of peace between Bulgaria and Greece, Montenegro, Roumania, and Serbia, signed at Bucharest on July 28/August 10, 1913, is printed with annexed documents in *British and Foreign State Papers*, vol. 107, pp. 658–73.

[4] H.M. Ambassador at Berlin, 1908–14.   [5] Not printed.

[6] See article 231 of the Treaty of Versailles.

we no longer held Germany to be bound by the forced assent in the treaty; (2) that in doing this, we did not mean that we accepted the view on the historical point now commonly held in Germany, but only wished to establish a situation in which the free discussion of the matter should be regarded as outside official action.

I quite recognise the difficulties and that it might prove impossible to find a suitable form of words, and the greatest of the difficulties would be the question of France. There are obvious objections to acting alone—though M. Poincaré has often done so—and I am not hopeful of getting any agreed form of words which would produce the right effect and yet be accepted by the French. If any statement were made by the Secretary of State, I venture however to suggest that in order to give it sufficient weight, it should be made either in Parliament or in a despatch; the whole object would be so to speak to close the controversy and a speech which would put any statement made by him on a line with those made by M. Poincaré—for instance, a speech at the opening of a war memorial—could not have this effect.

One other matter. It would be absolutely essential that anything said about the origin of the war should be completely dissociated from questions as to the conduct of the war; M. Poincaré is always talking of the two things in the same breath.[7]

J. W. H. M.

[7] On October 6 Sir W. Tyrrell minuted in agreement with a minute of October 5 in which Mr. Sargent referred to hopes that responsible statesmen and the responsible press in the countries concerned would avoid agitating the question of war guilt more than necessary. Mr. Sargent stated in particular: 'The comparative moderation displayed in dealing with the Tannenberg speech both in Germany and France is of good augury in this respect. But as in all cases where German mentality is concerned, there is always a danger that if moderation displayed by France and Great Britain takes the form of silence, the average German, interpreting it as a confession of weakness, will at once reinforce his demand for an immediate judicial enquiry. It is this fact which may still make it necessary that H.M. Government, far from adopting Mr. Headlam Morley's proposal, should on the contrary reassert the Treaty declaration so as to prevent the Germans from developing their present campaign on such lines as will before long result in a definite accusation that the Allies were *alone and entirely* responsible for the war. The extension of this campaign to America, as shown in C.8060 [these press extracts from the British Library of Information in New York on President von Hindenburg's speech are not printed], is not an encouraging symptom.'

No. 18

Sir E. Howard[1] *(Washington) to Sir A. Chamberlain (Received October 17)*
No. 1757 [C 8394/1498/18]

WASHINGTON, *October 5, 1927*

Sir,

With reference to my despatch No. 1629[2] of the 2nd ultimo regarding the reported intention of the French Government to float a loan on the American market for the purpose of refunding certain obligations incurred in 1920, I

[1] H.M. Ambassador at Washington.   [2] Not preserved in Foreign Office archives.

have the honour to quote the following interesting extract from the 'U.S. Daily' of the 27th September purporting to reproduce an oral statement made by an official of the State Department regarding the attitude of that Department and of the United States Government generally towards the placing of foreign loans here:—

'The Government's attitude toward the placing of foreign loans remains unchanged, according to an oral statement by the Department of State on September 26. This explanation was given in answer to inquiries regarding the proposal to make a private loan of $30,000,000 to Prussia for the development of harbors and agricultural lands.[3]

'The Department is still considering the matter and has asked for more information regarding it, it was stated.

'In outlining the general policy of the Department regarding the approval or disapproval of foreign loans on which American bankers seek advice, it was explained that only two kinds of loans are disapproved by the Department.

'These were stated to be: First, loans to countries which have not completed funding arrangements for their war debts to the United States.

'Second, loans to monopoly organizations held to be prejudicial to the best interests of the United States.

'In the instance of the German-French Potash loan, the Department withheld its approval, as also in the case of the Brazil coffee valorization loan, it was explained.

'The Department of State, it was stated, has adopted no definite policy regarding loans for the purpose of buying munitions or creating armaments, although the Secretary of Commerce, Herbert Hoover, advocated, at the Third Pan American Commercial Conference, the barring of all loans for unproductive purposes, while President Coolidge has favored the disapproval of loans to countries for the purpose of building competitive armaments.'

2. From the foregoing statement it might not unreasonably be inferred that the State Department were quite sincere in their earlier declaration to the effect that they had no information whatever regarding the proposed French refunding operation and that inference is strengthened by a statement recently made to a member of my staff by the Financial Attaché of the French Embassy, who said, in effect, that the newspaper reporters have distorted the remarks made by the French Ambassador when he returned to the United States on the 30th August. Mr. Lacour-Gayet gave it to be understood that no communications had previously taken place between the French Embassy and the State Department. However, the Ambassador's remarks, distorted or not, have done no harm to the interests of his country. They served to call public attention to the improved financial situation of the French Government

[3] For a report on a conversation between Mr. Castle, Assistant Secretary of State in the State Department, and the German Chargé d'Affaires in Washington on September 26, see *Papers relating to the Foreign Relations of the United States 1927*, vol. ii, pp. 728–9.

and, if the latter should really desire, as they probably will, to convert the 8% loan of 1920 into a new loan bearing interest at 6%, the United States Government will find it hard to refuse their covering sanction to the operation.

3. As regards the proposed private loan to Prussia which forms the immediate subject of the oral statement quoted above, yesterday's Journal of Commerce points out that if the State Department continue, as they are now doing, to withhold the usual statement that this loan is in accordance with public policy, it will practically block the way to its flotation. The Journal of Commerce furthermore alleges that the present hesitation of the State Department to approve the loan is due to the attitude of the Federal Reserve Bank of New York, who are desirous of halting the flow of dollars into Germany which merely go to pay reparations to the Allies. The standpoint of the Federal Reserve Bank results, it is stated, from representations which Dr. Schacht, head of the Reichsbank, made to them at the Conference of central bank heads held at New York last summer. Dr. Schacht then stated that whilst Germany was in need of working capital, the flotation of loans in the United States merely went to pay reparations[4] and actually resulted in Germany's incurring obligations abroad without any corresponding return for herself. He suggested as an alternative arrangement to the present system that the proceeds of the sale of German bonds here be specially earmarked, and made unavailable for retransfer abroad by the agent general of reparations to the Allies.[5] In this way, he pointed out, Germany would secure the working capital still sorely needed to permit her to further restore her industries, while assurance would be given that this money would not pass through Germany as through a sieve, leaving the country with another foreign debt to pay in the future, while giving her no present aid. Lastly he urged that the sale of further dollar bonds in this country should be halted. In this way, he said, the real test of the workability of the Dawes plan could be had immediately, and thus there would not be a postponement of the day of reckoning, when the ultimate ability of Germany to pay reparations must be decided once and for all.

4. The assumption of the Journal of Commerce that the attitude of the State Department constitutes the chief obstacle to the flotation of the Prussian loan is not borne out by articles on the subject in other sections of the press, from which it would appear that the main source of opposition emanates from Government quarters in Berlin.

5. In this connection today's Journal of Commerce reports that the Reichsbank has decided to raise its discount rate from 6 to 7 per cent and argues that this decision reflects a stringency of capital in Germany, and shews that

---

[4] A marginal note by Mr. Sargent here read: 'I find it hard to believe that Dr. S. gave his argument such a tendentious form.'

[5] A marginal note by Mr. Perowne here read: 'The Treasury say this is prima facie meaningless but that if it is some scheme for credits & the export trade from Germany or some such scheme, as seems likely, it w[oul]d be a "manoeuvre" in the sense of the Experts plan. They promise comments later. (See p. 112 [Annex 6, paragraph 8] of the Experts plan.) J.V.P.'

the authorities concerned, after calling a halt in the Prussian loan negotiations, are now making a further effort to bring to the surface the claim that the Dawes plan payments are causing a dangerous loss of liquid capital to Germany.

6. The close interest with which the trend of economic events in Germany is now being followed here is no doubt symptomatic of the fact that these events are rapidly developing towards a crisis in the operation of the Dawes plan and of reparation transfer payments which will in turn affect the position of United States investors in German industrial and state securities.

7. Today's Journal of Commerce, it should be added, also draws attention to the fact that the question of approving the loan to Prussia constitutes a test case upon the outcome of which will depend all future action as regards the flotation of German state and municipal loans now in contemplation amounting to some $200,000,000. So far as concerns the payment of interest and principal on German loans already floated in the American market, the Journal of Commerce believes that the position is well secured; alleging that virtual assurances have been received that even in the event of Germany's inability to continue reparation transfers under the Dawes plan, the Reichsbank will sell foreign exchange for this purpose as far as possible and if necessary permit gold exports on a large scale.

I have, &c.,
ESME HOWARD

No. 19

Sir A. Chamberlain to Sir W. Max Muller (Warsaw)
No. 482 [N 4783/61/59]

FOREIGN OFFICE, *October 11, 1927*

Sir,

Whilst I was at Geneva I received several messages from M. Zaleski,[1] expressing his earnest hope that he would be able to come to Geneva while I was still there, and when that became evidently impossible he instructed M. Skirmunt,[2] who was at Aix, to visit me at Geneva and to express the hope that I would give him the opportunity of a meeting either on the Riviera, whither he was going for his convalescence, or in Paris, to which place he would return from the Riviera for the special purpose of the meeting. As a matter of fact he arrived in Paris last Saturday,[3] and he called upon me at the British Embassy on Sunday morning. He said that the subject on which he particularly wished to speak to me was the relations between Poland and Lithuania. Even that morning there had appeared in the Paris papers a message from Berlin speaking of the renewed tension between the two countries and the situation gave him considerable anxiety.

---

[1] Polish Minister for Foreign Affairs.
[3] October 8, 1927.

[2] Polish Minister in London.

At this point he said that he thought it would perhaps be best that he should communicate to me a letter which Marshal Pilsudski[4] had addressed to him and of which he had prepared an English translation which he was good enough to leave with me, and of which I am therefore able to enclose a copy. As I read this letter I allowed my face to show the feelings with which it inspired me, and M. Zaleski then asked my permission to offer a commentary upon it. The Lithuanian Government had recently deprived of their functions on the pretext of their failure to pass an examination seventy Polish teachers in Polish schools in Lithuania. It was true that the Lithuanian Government said that they had at the same time cashiered 200 Lithuanian teachers on the same grounds; M. Zaleski did not know what proportion these 200 were of the whole body of Lithuanian teachers; but the seventy Polish teachers were the whole of the Polish teachers. Moreover, these Poles taught in private schools privately maintained. In Poland itself, there were 70,000 Lithuanians scattered in different places, but mainly concentrated in the corner of the country adjacent to Germany. These Lithuanians were provided with public schools at the expense of the Polish State, and since Poland could not provide Polish teachers who spoke the Lithuanian language, they had actually encouraged Lithuanians from Lithuania to teach in these schools. As a further sign of their goodwill, in spite of the fact that Lithuania continued to maintain a technical state of war with Poland,[5] the frontier had been opened on several occasions when ceremonies of particular interest to Lithuanians were being celebrated at Vilna or elsewhere in Polish territory. The Polish Government had thus done everything they could to ameliorate Polish–Lithuanian relations and, if at first they had asked for larger concessions such as consular representation, they had now reduced their demands to the single claim that the Lithuanian Government should issue a declaration of a state of peace. It might be even a unilateral declaration without the signature of any treaty.

At this point M. Zaleski said that the Administration of M. Waldemarass[6] was a good one. He thought that it had been well intentioned, but M. Waldemarass had over-estimated his strength and he had now found himself obliged to form a coalition with the Christian Democratic party, which was more under German influence and less well disposed to Poland. They had actually under discussion a Constitution in which it was proposed to declare as part of the Constitution that Vilna was the capital of the Lithuanian State.

[4] Marshal Josef Pilsudski was Polish President of the Council and Minister for War. (Marshal Pilsudski had also been Provisional President, November 1918 to December 1922.)

[5] For the background of Polish–Lithuanian relations in connexion with the occupation of Vilna in October 1920 by a Polish force under General Zeligowski, an independent Polish Commander, see First Series, Volume XI, Chapter II, *passim*; cf. also *Survey of International Affairs 1927*, pp. 235–47. On March 15, 1923, the Conference of Ambassadors had agreed to a definition of the eastern frontiers of Poland: see *British and Foreign State Papers*, vol. 118, pp. 960–3.

[6] Professor Voldemaras was Lithuanian Prime Minister and Minister for Foreign Affairs.

These constant provocations were a real danger. It was impossible for the Polish Government not to take reprisals. Public opinion would not allow them to continue the privileges of Lithuanian children in Polish schools, whilst the Polish schools in Lithuania were closed by the expulsion of the teachers. He was convinced that the President did not wish to embark upon a policy of force, but if driven to it he would not hesitate, and M. Zaleski himself could not but feel that Lithuania was encouraged to maintain this uncompromising and hostile attitude by a feeling that the Great Powers took no interest in the matter, and that the League would protect them against Poland. He desired, therefore, to urge that France and Great Britain should use their influence to secure the immediate demand of Poland, namely the declaration of the state of peace, and he insisted that this was not a mere formality. There were Lithuanians who desired good relations with Poland, but as long as Lithuania was technically at war it would be an act of high treason in them to give expression to their views. Failure to declare peace, therefore, prevented the play of forces which would otherwise assist in improving the situation.

When M. Zaleski had finished his exposition of the Polish case, I told him that I had now been away from home for six weeks and was not cognisant of the latest developments. M. Waldemarass had not spoken to me on the subject last month, but I had at a previous meeting taken the opportunity to impress upon him the necessity of improving the relations of Lithuania with her neighbours. I was impressed with what M. Zaleski had told me, and I would certainly study the question as soon as possible after my return, but having said so much he must allow me to speak quite frankly about the marshal's letter which he had permitted me to peruse. I could do so with the more freedom as I felt myself entitled to claim that I had been of some service to Poland in the Locarno negotiations and had proved myself a sympathetic friend to his country. Now I must plainly declare that any attempt by Poland to secure satisfaction from Lithuania by force would turn the whole of my countrymen against her. Rightly or wrongly—it did not matter—Poland was considered in many quarters as a rather restless Power and as a source of danger to the peace of Europe. The Polish Government more than any other needed to pursue a policy of the greatest patience and moderation. The episode of Vilna had not been forgotten and though the result had been sanctioned by the Ambassadors' Conference and was binding upon us, it had not been wholly forgiven. If now any act of the Polish Government gave rise to a new disturbance, the immediate consequences would be grave. What the action of the League might be I could not say, but it might have serious consequences for his country. The days for a Corfu adventure[7] had gone by and he would be as well aware as I of the perils which his country would run. But even more serious for Poland would be the results on the day if it ever came when she was in serious danger and when the support of the League and the sympathy of other Powers would be of the utmost consequence to her. I

[7] For this incident of 1923 between Greece and Italy, cf. *League of Nations Official Journal*, November 1923, *passim*, and April 1924, pp. 523–7.

begged him to represent to Marshal Pilsudski in the strongest terms my opinion of the fatal character of any such forcible action as that hinted at in his letter.

M. Zaleski obviously shared my views and I think my expression of them was not unwelcome to him. He said that he would convey them to the marshal. In the meantime he only ventured again to insist that it was the sense of the protection afforded by the League which alone encouraged the Lithuanians to pursue their hostile policy. I repeated my promise to examine the question as soon as I returned to London.

M. Zaleski then turned to events at Geneva and in particular to the circumstances surrounding the origin and course of the Polish resolution.[8] I said that I was very glad that he had mentioned this subject, not indeed that it was necessary to offer any explanations as to the past, but because I was glad to have the opportunity of expressing to himself what I had already said to M. Sokal[9] and M. Skirmunt about the Polish attitude to the question of security in general. We had an English proverb which emphasised the folly of 'crying stinking fish'. The Poles were in fact in possession of very valuable guarantees. It appeared to me that they committed a mistake when, by language or action, they seemed to undervalue or cast doubt upon the securities which they already possessed. I would urge that it would be far wiser to take a leaf out of M. Briand's book and to call the world to witness what engagements Germany and Poland had already undertaken towards one another for the settlement of disputes by arbitration and the maintenance of peace. I had myself supplied M. Skirmunt with an extract from a speech made by Dr. Stresemann in the month of May last in Germany.[10] I had actually obtained this quotation from the German delegation at Geneva and had at one time intended myself to use it in the course of my own speech there. If I were a Polish Minister, I would watch these utterances of Dr. Stresemann. I would pigeon-hole them and from time to time when a doubt arose I would take the world to witness that the German Foreign Minister had declared that the value of the treaties of Locarno rested not only on the relations established with Germany's neighbours on the west, but on the fact that by their arbitration treaty with Poland[11] they had rendered impossible the resort to war for the solution of any difficulties which might arise between them, and I should repeat this declaration for myself and for my own country and thus give to it all the publicity and all the solemnity within my power.

I may add that I had already expressed to M. Briand my intention to speak in this sense to M. Zaleski and that M. Briand had told me that he had given the same advice to M. Sokal at Geneva and would repeat it to

[8] See No. 2, note 4.

[9] See Volume III, No. 328, for Sir A. Chamberlain's conversation with the Polish delegate at Geneva.

[10] See enclosure 2 below for an extract from Dr. Stresemann's speech at Oeynhausen on May 8: for a report on this speech see *The Times*, May 10, 1927, p. 16.

[11] Printed as annex D to the Final Protocol of the Locarno Conference in Cmd. 2525, pp. 35–45.

M. Zaleski in Paris. M. Briand had at the same time invited me once again to urge moderation upon M. Zaleski.

I am, &c.,
Austen Chamberlain

Enclosure 1 in No. 19

Letter from Marshal Pilsudski to M. Zaleski

Druskieniki, *September 13, 1927*

My dear Minister,

After my conversation with Mr. Knoll[12] I decided to formulate my views on the Lithuanian question in order that you could take them in consideration.

I had to deal with it since 1918. Many times I nearly took the decision of solving it by force. Knowing well the country, with its customs and the character of the Lithuanian race (of which I am a descendant myself), I know that even the smallest change of opinion takes there a very long time. When spirits are high the voice of reason cannot make itself heard.

Especially during the period when I had in my hands the means of war my temptations were great. I took, then, the decision of leaving the situation to develop on evolutionary and peaceful lines, and I had to regret it often afterwards and now. I so decided because I did not wish to create the tradition of bloodshed between two nations so closely connected in history.

If I begin to hesitate again, and if I am putting the question nearly on the edge of the sword (as I did in the beginning of this year), I do it because I foresee a gradual growth of difficulties in the general situation of Eastern Europe, and because I see that the internal situation of Lithuania is not stabilised, so that many an important decision must be taken there not on its merits but for reasons of internal politics, the Government looking for foreign successes in order to strengthen their own prestige.

We have now a typical example of such a case in the school question. You will agree with me as to the impression it must create on the Poles of Lithuania, who will see their children taught in a foreign language. When the Poles of Lithuania were expropriated, and from rich landlords changed into poor beggars, I did not say a word, but now, when questions of national tradition are at stake, I shall not remain indifferent, and I shall react, perhaps even stronger than the gentlemen from Kowno imagine. According to my information, we must ascribe this state of things to M. Waldemarass's megalomania.

I must inform you that immediately after my return I shall organise reprisals.

Yours, &c.[13]

Enclosure 2 in No. 19

Extract from Speech of German Foreign Minister, May 8, 1927

As regards the discussions on the question of an Eastern Locarno, I would observe that our relations with our eastern neighbours, in particular with

---

[12] Polish Minister at Rome.   [13] Signature lacking from filed copy.

Poland, are regulated by the agreements which were reached at Locarno. These agreements are often made to refer only to our relations with France and Belgium. The total value of these agreements consists, on the one hand, in their binding obligations towards our western neighbours, and, on the other hand, in the arbitral agreement concluded with Poland, which guarantees a peaceful settlement in all cases of dispute between the two countries.

The new Government, on its formation, found this situation in existence, and has emphasised its particular importance by repeated expressions of its recognition of existing treaties. Our relations with Poland result, therefore, from the situation thus created.

No. 20

Record by Sir A. Chamberlain of a conversation with M. Briand
[*C 8387/304/18*]

FOREIGN OFFICE, *October 13, 1927*

In the course of my conversation with Monsieur Briand at the Quai d'Orsay[1] on Friday last,[2] I told him that I was preoccupied with two questions, one more immediate, the other more remote. The former of these preoccupations related to the divergences of view between the French and British Governments on the subject of disarmament, which might be renewed and emphasised when the Preparatory Commission met again in November unless we had previously come to some agreement. Monsieur Briand rather lightly waived [*sic*] the subject on one side as one which could not present serious difficulties. I did not pursue it.

The second subject of which I spoke was the Rhineland occupation. I remarked that time was passing, that we were not so very far away from the date on which the second zone must be released and even the final date fixed for total evacuation was only a few years distant. I was most anxious that we should not exceed the dates named by the Treaty[3] and indeed that we should if possible anticipate them, but I knew that, whenever the question arose in a practical form, I should be told that the new French defences were not ready and that the occupation must, therefore, continue. Monsieur Briand would understand what insuperable difficulties any such reply by the French Government would create for the friends of France in England. I would beg him, therefore, to use his influence with the French Government to get on with the defence of the new frontier as rapidly as possible.

Monsieur Briand replied that he was entirely of my opinion, that it was indeed the failure of the military authorities in this respect which had enabled him to exact from them concessions in some other matters. He had insisted upon a meeting of the Conseil Supérieur de la Guerre and he had asked them what they supposed would be the effect upon French opinion if it became known that, eight years after the signature of peace, the fortifications of

[1] The French Ministry of Foreign Affairs.   [2] October 7, 1927.
[3] Of Versailles.

Strasburg and Metz still faced towards France and were useless for purposes of defence against Germany. He told them that he well knew the explanation. They had been hoping that, by hook or by crook, they could succeed in prolonging the occupation, to which he had replied: 'As to that, NO. That is not the Treaty and it is impossible.' He had insisted, therefore, that the new defences should be taken in hand at once and with his usual optimism expressed the hope that the work would be done in a couple of years or so. In any case, he said, he would like to terminate the occupation at least a year in advance of the Treaty dates. As regards the second zone, he observed that it had in fact no military consequence, though of course the evacuation of the third zone was a far more serious matter.

I informed Lord Crewe[4] verbally of this conversation. He expressed some doubt (which I share) as to whether Monsieur Briand had consulted his colleagues or was speaking for anyone but himself.

A. C.

[4] H.M. Ambassador at Paris.

No. 21

Sir A. Chamberlain to the Marquess of Crewe (Paris)[1]
No. 2574 [C 8165/2050/18]

FOREIGN OFFICE, *October 13, 1927*

My Lord Marquess,

You are aware from the correspondence terminating with my despatch No. 2298 of the 9th September[2] last that the British, French and Belgian Governments recently decided to implement the promise contained in the letter from the Conference of Ambassadors of the 11th [14th] November, 1925,[3] regarding a reduction in the strength of the forces of occupation in the Rhineland, by withdrawing 10,000 men from those areas and by fixing at 60,000 the future maximum strength of those armies. At the same time the three Governments agreed among themselves as to the reductions which it would be necessary to make in each army in order to give effect to that decision. Henceforward the British, French and Belgian armies in the Rhineland would number 6,250, 48,450 and 5,300, respectively.

2. The German Government were informed of the Allied decision by the words contained in the third paragraph of the note addressed by M. Briand to Herr Stresemann at Geneva on the 5th September last (a copy of which was enclosed in my despatch referred to above): 'les Puissances participant à l'occupation se sont entendues . . .[4] pour fixer . . .[4] à 60,000 hommes l'effectif, dans des circonstances normales, des armées de Rhénanie.'

[1] *Note on filed copy*: 'Similar despatch sent to Brussels *mutatis mutandis*' as No. 628.

[2] This despatch (not preserved in Foreign Office archives) transmitted a copy of Volume III, No. 331, enclosure.

[3] This letter to the German Ambassador at Paris is printed as item No. 3 in Cmd. 2527 of 1925.

[4] Punctuation as in original quotation.

3. I have given the interpretation of this passage from M. Briand's note my careful consideration. In this connection, my attention was drawn to the possibility that the total number laid down in the note for the occupying troops might be slightly exceeded during the period of replacement when the in-going and out-going drafts overlap.

4. In the case of the British and Belgian forces this excess might amount to no more than 200 or 300 men, yet a proportionate excess in the French forces would amount to as much as 2,000 men, so that, in practice, the total of the Allied troops in the Rhineland might periodically reach the figure of 63,000. It is clear that a fluctuation of such magnitude, however temporary, would go a long way towards stultifying the undertaking that in future the total number of the Allied troops would not exceed 60,000 men.

5. I am strongly of the opinion that the figure of 60,000 must be regarded as an absolute maximum, and that the expression 'dans des circonstances normales' cannot be interpreted to mean that this maximum figure may be exceeded periodically at the time when the in-going and out-going drafts overlap. In this connection I transmit to your Lordship herewith a copy of a letter from the War Office with enclosure, from which it will be seen that the General Officer Commanding British Army of the Rhine has been given specific instructions that on no account must the total strength of the troops under his command ever exceed 6,250, all ranks.[5]

6. I request that you will inform the French Government that His Majesty's Government's interpretation of the undertaking given at Geneva is as set forth in the first sentence of the preceding paragraph.[6]

I am, &c.,

(For the S[ecretary] of S[tate])

ORME SARGENT

[5] This letter of September 3 with enclosed table setting out in detail the maximum strength of the British Army of the Rhine is not printed.

[6] Lord Crewe and Sir G. Grahame, H.M. Ambassador at Brussels, acted on these instructions in notes of October 17 to the French Ministry of Foreign Affairs and M. Vandervelde, Belgian Minister for Foreign Affairs, respectively. In notes of November 11 (transmitted in Paris despatch No. 2257 of the same day) and December 1 (transmitted in Brussels despatch No. 942 of the same day) the French and Belgian Governments respectively signified their agreement with His Majesty's Government's definition and undertook that the stipulated strength of their armies should not be exceeded except in quite exceptional circumstances.

No. 22

Memorandum by Mr. Perowne

[C 8394/1498/18]

FOREIGN OFFICE, *October 18, 1927*

Prussian Loan.[1]

This is very interesting, but still rather obscure. The State Department are 'asking for more information' and the hitch is ascribed to various causes—the

[1] See No. 18.

objection entertained by the Administration to 'unproductive' loans, the machinations of Dr. Schacht with a view to provoking a crisis in the **Repara-tion** situation, the attitude of the authorities in Berlin dictated by similar 'revisionary' motives. Under all this lies the great question affecting the whole future of Reparations of how far the apparent prosperity of Germany is real. To the eye that prosperity seems plain enough: the evidence greets the traveller on every hand; but it may only too probably have been achieved by the in-curring of foreign obligations (to an extent which it may prove impossible to meet) for the purpose, as the Germans and their friends are fond of saying, of paying the Annuities. The Annuities may have been *financed* by the flow into Germany of foreign funds realised by loans raised abroad, but the money has not been spent (or raised for that matter) for that purpose. Ambitious muni-cipal schemes, museums, operas, flying subsidies have benefited, and one really begins to wonder (with other far more qualified observers) what will happen when the day of reckoning or *a* day of reckoning comes, and how near it is, or may be brought by some longsighted persons like Dr. Schacht. I cannot avoid the impression that Dr. Schacht is up to something. Both he and the Agent-General object publicly to the further extension of Germany's foreign indebtedness, but for different reasons. Mr. Parker Gilbert objects because the transfer of the service of such loans raises the question of the Transfer priority of the Dawes Annuity and because the incurring of such loans[2] may lead to severe economic depression and hence injure Germany's capacity to make reparation payments. As a good German Dr. Schacht is doubtless moved by the severe economic depression consideration, but even more, as a protagonist —under the rose—of revision (all Germans are revisionists at heart), by the consideration that the raising of such foreign loans assists[3] enormously to get the annuity safely across the exchange into Allied pockets. There are plenty of 'revisionists' about outside Germany, particularly among the American bankers. I cannot pretend to suggest what precise scheme the revisionists are following; but I venture to think that the Treasury are a little light hearted over all this. Mr. Parker Gilbert is certainly uneasy: Dr. Schacht has got him guessing and wondering whether the powers of the Transfer Committee are going to be adequate if it comes to an open struggle (i.e. if all these intrigues can be proved and shewn to be 'concerted manœuvres' in the sense of the Experts' Report: see page 112 of attached volume).[4]

Dr. Schacht is a realist in politics and finance whereas Mr. Parker Gilbert is far more the technician, lacking general experience of affairs outside his

---

[2] A marginal note by Mr. Sargent who here added the words 'if not really productive' here read: 'economically they are only justified if they help to increase the German export trade & this they are certainly not doing. According to Mr. Finlayson they are being largely used to cater for the artificial internal "boom" now in progress in Germany. O.G.S.'

[3] A marginal note by Mr. Sargent here read: 'If the proceeds of the loans are used, as alleged by Dr. Schacht, to pay the Dawes annuities, they cannot be used as well to finance unproductive internal "booms", as alleged by Mr. Finlayson & also presumably by Mr. Gilbert. We are here face to face with a fundamental disagreement as to the real use to which these loans are being put. O.G.S.'

[4] See No. 18, note 5.

own province, nor indeed concerned with them, his horizon being conditioned by his youth and nationality, and his present attitude is one rather of bewilderment.

But it is impossible to offer observations of the slightest value without more information on the subject not only of the immediate matter in hand but also of the economic situation in Germany. Mr. Finlayson's latest memorandums[5] have usually set out to prove that in spite of the internal boom the trade balance is passive and that the outlook is not hopeful, and that living by expedients is in sight. But there are so many cross currents that Mr. Finlayson gets tempted away from his main thesis and the unhappy student gets left without a guide.

Incidentally, if the situation is as pregnant with important eventualities as it seems to be, is this the moment, as the Treasury propose, to replace Mr. Finlayson at Berlin where he knows all the officials intimately and has proper sources of information which would be invaluable to H.M. Government but by which his successor cannot hope to profit?

See also the press cuttings in C.7969.[6]

But before we go any further I think we should have the observations of both Treasury and Berlin, not only about the Prussian loan but also about the revisionists and their policy and general prospects about the future of reparations.

Q[uer]y copy Berlin and Treasury for observations, informing each, and B[oard] of T[rade] for information.[7]

J. V. PEROWNE

[5] Not printed.
[6] Not preserved in Foreign Office archives. According to the docket, these extracts reported that the news that the United States State Department might veto the loan had given rise to misgivings in Prussian financial circles: see *The Times*, September 28, 1927, p. 13.
[7] Copies of No. 18 were transmitted to Berlin, as Foreign Office despatch No. 1301, to the Treasury and the Board of Trade on October 20, and to Paris as Foreign Office despatch No. 2639 on October 21.

No. 23

Sir R. Lindsay (Berlin) to Sir A. Chamberlain (Received October 24)
No. 631 [N 4990/227/59]

BERLIN, *October 21, 1927*

Sir,

I asked Dr. Stresemann yesterday if he felt any anxiety about Lithuania and my question provoked from him something of an outburst. Lithuania he said was identical with M. Waldemaras and M. Waldemaras was perfectly impossible. In a conversation at Geneva this person had opened by saying that several of the questions pending between his country and Germany were not susceptible of a peaceful solution. This impertinent nonsense from a man who presumably must be a German of some sort, who had been a Ukrainian, was now a Lithuanian and might to-morrow be a Russian, and who had quarrelled with almost every Government with whom he had relations, had roused his utmost indignation; but he had remembered, he said, that the existence of Lithuania was a necessity for Germany, who could not allow Poland to push up to the sea between her and Russia, so he had merely decided that at any further interview he might have to have with M. Waldemaras he would see that Herr von Schubert should also be present to help him to exert self-restraint. He had complained to M. Waldemaras that the exequatur of the German Consul General for Memel had been refused with no reason assigned, and the answer had been that there was no Consular Convention with Lithuania; then that the relationship between the Consulate General at Memel and the Legation at Kovno had not been determined; and finally that the Consul General's Christian name had not been given. When discussing wider questions concerning Memel affairs M. Waldemaras had insisted on ignoring altogether the existence of the Memel Statute[1] and talking of some fancied parallel in the relations between the Reich and its component States. There was a provision in the Statute that certain officials at Memel should have a knowledge of Lithuanian and this had in practice been interpreted in such a way that a railway pointsman in the district was required to pass an examination in which *inter alia* he had to write an essay in Lithuanian on Dürer's engraving of the Knight, the Devil and Death. Yes, indeed, Lithuania was difficult to have dealings with; he admitted that Statesmen could hardly be come by in such a country, but could it not at least produce a peasant with some common sense? M. Cielens, the Latvian Minister for Foreign Affairs, had approached him at Geneva with the suggestion that a kind of Baltic Locarno might be contemplated between the four Baltic States under the guarantee of Germany, Russia, France and Great Britain, and that if the two latter were to refuse the commitment then they might yet proceed with the signature of the two former alone. Dr. Stresemann had answered that he must think it over before he could accept any such principle, but, as an immediate practical point he had asked how Lithuania was to be brought to accept this or any other idea; whereupon M. Cielens had at once concurred and said that it was useless to contemplate the scheme seriously until M. Waldemaras was off the stage. Dr Stresemann had his apprehensions too about the relations with Poland. There too Marshal Pilsudski was a dictator but though his power was still absolute the parties which support him had, he said, crumbled away under him so that his position was not really secure and the international situation was one of some danger. The latest quarrel between Lithuania and Poland was now referred to the League[2] and would come up in December, he regretted this because he feared the

---

[1] i.e. annex 1 to the Convention of May 8, 1924, between the British Empire, France, Italy, Japan, and Lithuania respecting the Memel Territory, printed in *British and Foreign State Papers*, vol. 119, pp. 502–15.

[2] Cf. No. 19. The Lithuanian Government had appealed to the Council of the League of Nations on October 15 under Article 11 of the Covenant: cf. the statement made to the Council by M. Voldemaras on December 7 printed in *League of Nations Official Journal*, February 1928, pp. 144–7.

Council might be unable to find a solution and would be in a position of rather undignified impotence. He would have preferred in this case and in the case of the Hungarian Roumanian quarrel,[3] that some settlement should be found out of court before the meeting, but he made no suggestions as to how this consummation might be brought about.

I have, &c.,
R. C. LINDSAY

³ Cf. No. 11, note 1.

No. 24

Sir R. Lindsay (Berlin) to Sir A. Chamberlain (Received October 28)
No. 640 [C 8708/857/18][*1]

BERLIN, *October 24, 1927*

Sir,

I have read with interest Sir E. Howard's despatch No. 1757[2] of the 5th October dealing, in part, with the recently-issued Prussian 6 per cent. Loan.

2. I travelled from New York to England on the 5th October with the London agent of Harris Forbes and Co., the firm issuing this Prussian Loan. He told me that his firm had obtained the approval of the State Department and of the Beratungsstelle[3] in Berlin, and that then, when they had signed their contract with the Prussian Government, Mr. Parker Gilbert had intervened with the demand, accompanied by threats, that the prospectus must include specific mention of the Dawes plan and of article 248 of the Versailles Treaty. The agent expressed himself with some indignation on the subject of Mr. Gilbert's action. Mr. Gilbert tells me here that Harris Forbes did indeed get the approval of the State Department and the Beratungsstelle, but that they got it by the old trick of assuring each simultaneously that the other had already agreed. He himself had been away and only heard of the transaction just in time to intervene, with the result that Harris Forbes spent a fortnight or three weeks in the air with a 30-million-dollar liability hanging over them. Mr. Gilbert was not at all pleased with the behaviour of the firm —so far at least as concerns the getting of the approvals of Berlin and Washington. Finally, I may mention that I saw Governor Strong of the Federal Reserve Board in New York about 26th September. We were not discussing the Prussian Loan, but talking generally about German borrowing, and he told me with some emphasis that if dollar loans to Germany were to be stopped or checked it was only in Berlin and it was not in America that useful action could be taken. From the foregoing and from the statements reproduced in Sir E. Howard's despatch, I think it may be inferred that, except those directly interested in the issue, everyone looked askance at the Prussian Loan, but only Mr. Gilbert was able or willing to take any action against it.

¹ Throughout this volume an asterisk after the file number denotes that the document has been printed from Confidential Print, being the only text preserved: see Preface, p. ix.
² No. 18.   ³ Foreign Loans Control Committee.

3. In my conversation with Mr. Gilbert on the 21st instant I asked him whether he thought it wise to make such a point of article 248, and to attack so strongly German borrowing, which seemed to me to be only a part of the evil from which Germany is at present suffering. He replied admitting in substance that article 248, when applied to transfers, might prove something of a broken reed (for a discussion of this point, see Mr. Finlayson's note 'German Government's Policy regarding Foreign Loans', forwarded under cover of my despatch No. 639[4] of the 24th October), but he had to insist on it because, if he did not, he would merely 'be clearing the decks for those issuing houses in America'. As to foreign loans in general, he thought some might, indeed, be properly required, but he attacked them because they were at present subserving and fostering the extravagance of all German public bodies. This, he said, was the main object of his attack, and he referred me to the remonstrance he had just addressed to the Reich Minister of Finance, a copy of which he had just handed to me, and which is transmitted to you in my despatch No. 637[5] of to-day. He expressed himself as deeply concerned as to the economic situation in Germany at the present moment, and apprehended that if matters pursue their present course a crisis would supervene within a very few months which would gravely imperil German credit.

4. I am not competent to explain or discuss the serious economic trouble in which Germany is involved at the present moment. It is fully exposed in Mr. Finlayson's technical reports to the Treasury, which are available in your department, in Mr. Gilbert's last two reports to the Reparation Commission, and in his two remonstrances of the 17th March[6] and the 20th October to the Reich Minister of Finance. Broadly speaking it is the simple old

[4] Not printed. In his memorandum of October 17 Mr. Finlayson discussed, in particular, difficulties in applying the provisions of article 248 of the Treaty of Versailles in the absence of any provisions in the Dawes Plan for the priority of transfer for reparation payments: cf. No. 53 below, § (3). Mr. Finlayson concluded his memorandum as follows: 'There is no doubt that the development of Germany's public finances, i.e., Reich, States and communes, gives rise to grave concern. The present policy, if continued, is bound to lead to catastrophe, for recent history shows that, as the revenues increase, so does public expenditure. The various administrative departments must be made to realise the utter necessity of limiting the outgoings, especially on social, cultural, hygienic and æsthetic ends. The communes, in particular, have not been able to cast off their inflation habits, and have contracted loans right and left for all and sundry requirements. Herein lies the root of the whole trouble. What then are the methods to be adopted to cure this unhealthy state of affairs? It would be inadequate to attack merely one side of the problem, viz., foreign loans; that would not cure the disease. For instance, suppose the communes were forbidden from taking up loans abroad and were forced to appeal to the home market. What would be the result? There would be a stringency which would be bound to force others in search of capital, private persons who would not be under the control of the Loans Council, to seek money abroad. In the end the effect would be the same, and Germany's foreign indebtedness would not be diminished. To pick out loans of public undertakings as the great evil is merely treating a symptom. The malady can only be cured by a reform in the public spending departments.'

[5] Not printed. The enclosed memorandum handed by Mr. Gilbert to Dr. Köhler on October 20 is printed in annex 1 to *Report of Agent General for Reparation Payments, December 10, 1927.*

[6] This letter is printed in *Report of Agent General for Reparation Payments, May 21, 1930* (Berlin, n.d.), pp. 363–7; see also Volume III, No. 48.

tale: that German public bodies, Reich, States and towns, so far from having forgotten the habits incurred in inflation days, are now 'splurging' money again in a dangerous fashion. It is on this point that Mr. Parker Gilbert has now squarely taken issue with the German Government, and it is clearly to the real interest of Germany that his advice should be accepted and saner financial methods adopted. Yet it is difficult to believe that Mr. Gilbert's views will prevail without a struggle. There is the difficulty of accepting the dictation of a foreigner; and the German Government is weak, as all its Republican predecessors have been, precariously balanced among the parties in the Reichstag, anxious to get popularity in the country, and willing to pay for it.

5. Mr. Gilbert can count confidently on French and British sympathy with his views if only on account of reparations, but the ex-Allied Governments cannot for obvious reasons actively intervene in support of him, and Germans will discount the opinions of the financial circles in Paris and London. They never expected anything else than that their ex-enemies should wish to draw the last drop of blood out of their suffering body. What will count in Germany is the view taken in America, whence the dollars have been flowing in such an agreeable volume. Doubtless the Federal Reserve Board and the United States Treasury will take the broad and sensible view, but I cannot help feeling some apprehension about New York. Except J. P. Morgan and Sons every bank in the Eastern United States seems to have indulged in German loans, an enormous further programme of lending is contemplated, and a serious fall in the value of the investments already made would be looked forward to with alarm. It appears important that American financial opinion should be correctly instructed as to what is happening to the finance of this country; yet the articles on the subject which have appeared recently in the London 'Times' have not hit the nail on the head and the remarks quoted by Sir E. Howard from the 'New York Journal of Commerce' are even wider of the mark. It may be a good thing if events here take such a course that the publication of Mr. Gilbert's memorandum of the 20th October becomes necessary.

6. I have addressed a copy of this despatch to His Majesty's Ambassador at Washington.

I have, &c.,

R. C. LINDSAY

No. 25

Memorandum by Sir A. Chamberlain on the Anglo-Portuguese Alliance[1]

C.P. 255 (27) [W 10048/4573/36]

FOREIGN OFFICE, *October 24, 1927*

The continued refusal of the Portuguese Government to give any redress in a series of cases in which British citizens have suffered grave injury in person

[1] Annexed to this memorandum were extracts from the Anglo-Portuguese treaties of alliance of June 16, 1373, May 9, 1386, January 29, 1642, July 20, 1654, April 28, 1660, June 23, 1661, May 16, 1703 (printed in *British and Foreign State Papers*, vol. 1, part i,

or in property and the long drawn-out dispute between the Government of the Union of South Africa and the Portuguese authorities in regard to the railway and port administration at Lourenco Marques, which recently culminated in a singularly offensive letter from the Portuguese Minister of the Colonies to General Hertzog,[2] led me to ask myself whether the time had not come to reconsider our treaty obligations to Portugal. I accordingly addressed an enquiry to Sir W. Tyrrell[3] and requested him to have the whole subject examined in the Foreign Office.

I now circulate for the consideration of the Cabinet the terms of my enquiry and the very able memorandum in which Mr. Villiers[4] has replied to it.

A. C.

Annex 1 to No. 25

Sir A. Chamberlain (Geneva) to Sir W. Tyrrell

GENEVA, September 18, 1927

The Portuguese Government claim our support on all manner of occasions on the ground of our alliance, e.g., for their candidature for the Council, and, at the other end of the world, for the defence of Macao, or again in India for the maintenance of the authority in British India of the Portuguese Patriarchate. I can see what we stand to lose by the Treaty of Windsor;[5] I am not clear what we gain. Please let this question be examined and a report submitted to me on my return.

Annex 2 to No. 25*

Memorandum by the Foreign Office, October 1927

The advantages which we derive from the Portuguese Alliance may be stated under three heads:—

1. *Portuguese assistance in time of war.*

The amount of reliance which can be placed on the Portuguese army and

---

pp. 462–506) and January 22, 1815 (printed *op. cit.*, vol. 2, pp. 348–55). Also annexed were (*a*) a memorandum of November 13, 1922, on 'Treaty Obligations of Great Britain towards Portugal, with Special Reference to Macao' which was on generally similar lines to paragraphs 33 and 35–36 of the appendix to Volume I of this series; (*b*) an extract from the despatch of February 19, 1873, from Earl Granville to H.M. Minister at Lisbon printed in G. P. Gooch and Harold Temperley, *British Documents on the Origins of the War 1898–1914* (London, 1926 f.), vol. i, p. 51; (*c*) an undated paper commenting on an appended variant text of the secret article of the treaty of June 23, 1661; (*d*) the Anglo-Portuguese Secret Declaration of October 14, 1899, printed *ibid.*, pp. 93–94.

[2] This letter of May 28, 1927, to the Prime Minister of the Union of South Africa is not printed. A copy was received in the Foreign Office on September 21 from the Dominions Office. The letter argued in particular that the railway between Lourenco Marques and the Transvaal operated to the detriment of Mozambique.

[3] The paper in annex 1 below was an extract from an unnumbered telegram from Geneva, not printed in full.

[4] Head of the Western, General and League of Nations Department of the Foreign Office. The annexed memorandum was a condensed version of a memorandum of September 29 by Mr. Villiers.

[5] This Anglo-Portuguese Treaty of November 16, 1904, is printed in *British and Foreign State Papers*, vol. 97, pp. 68–69.

navy, and the efficacy of their armed assistance are very little. In fact, the Portuguese troops in the late war were a positive danger and had to be sent home. Nevertheless, in both the wars which we have waged during the present century the Portuguese Alliance has been of real value to us. It was in virtue of the alliance that the Portuguese Government in 1899 agreed, in the Anglo-Portuguese Secret Declaration, that they would not allow arms and ammunition to be imported through their African Colonies into the Transvaal, and that they would not proclaim neutrality in the Boer War. In the Great War the Portuguese Government, besides handing over 20,000 otherwise unobtainable rifles and ammunition to the South African Government, and allowing us to have some of their artillery, seized the German ships at Lisbon and, most unwillingly, handed them over to us. At a time when ships were priceless these vessels were of incalculable use to us. Certainly neither of these contingencies were foreseen when the alliance was concluded. It is at least possible that similar unforeseen contingencies may arise in the future. Presumably, too, the knowledge that Portugal cannot be reckoned among potential enemies is of assistance to our naval and military authorities in drawing up schemes both for defence and attack.

2. *The grant to us and the denial to our enemies in time of war of the use of the Tagus and the Portuguese Atlantic islands as bases for warships, submarines and aircraft, and the undertaking of the Portuguese Government not to grant to foreigners concessions for coaling stations or cable landing rights in the Atlantic islands without consulting us previously.*

The removal of the German menace has greatly lessened the immediate strategic value of the alliance in the above respect. If in 1914 the Portuguese had been in alliance with the Germans, or had been neutral in the sense that the Swedes were neutral, our situation would have been rendered immeasurably more dangerous and difficult. It might, indeed, have nearly lost us the war. In the course of time another country may take the place held by Germany during the first two decades of this century, and the value of the islands as a base for aircraft and submarines operating against the ships on which we depend in time of war for our daily bread may be as great in the future as it was in 1914. Denunciation of the alliance with the possible result of throwing Portugal into the arms of a potential enemy would be a very serious step.

In a memorandum, dated December 1912, the Admiralty held that—

'If ever the alliance is terminated by action on either side, we should make it a cardinal point of our subsequent policy to see that no maritime State, such as France or Germany, replaces us, and thus obtains the right to use the Cape de Verdes, the Azores, or Portuguese Guinea, either as a sovereign Power or as an ally of Portugal. We should prevent at all costs the transfer of these particular possessions to any strong naval Power.'

The Foreign Office views on the Admiralty memorandum were as follows:—

'The Admiralty consider that we may safely give up the alliance provided Portugal remains independent and her Atlantic islands are not acquired by a maritime Power.

'But by what means other than the alliance is it suggested that this condition can be fulfilled? At the present moment there can be no question but that the alliance, and the alliance alone, stands in the way of the islands falling into other hands. It is the easiest thing in the world for Germany or France to pick a quarrel with Portugal that would lead to war, and then to attack and keep the islands. . . .[6] By deliberately giving up the alliance we should have lost the only *locus standi* enabling us to interpose and prevent such a consummation. There seems no other means of obtaining such a *locus standi*. We should be reduced to making a peremptory demand on Germany, without any legal justification of any kind, to keep her hands off territory from which we had openly withdrawn our protecting hand. This would be a most invidious policy to pursue, and one not likely to command popular support at the critical moment in this country.

'Even if we could secure a right of pre-emption over the islands—a most unlikely thing for any Portuguese Government to concede to us if we insist on repudiating the alliance—such pre-emptive rights would not legally stand against a conquest by a third Power.

'Under the existing arrangements, the alliance prevents any third Power from acquiring the Portuguese islands except by going to war with England and defeating her. Moreover, an appeal to the alliance has enabled us on several occasions to defeat German schemes of disguised designs in the way of coaling stations, wireless installations, and other similar enterprises in the islands, notably Madeira and Teneriffe.

'The conclusion appears to be that the conditions which the Admiralty consider essential to any arrangement for terminating the alliance could not be fulfilled except by maintaining it.'

In spite of the elimination for the time being of the German menace, the above contention remains sound.

The Portuguese undertaking not to allow foreigners to obtain a foothold in the islands in time of peace is not without value, but this value is lessened when, as happened within the last three months, the Portuguese Government 'forget' the obligation. They have granted cable landing rights in the Azores to the Italian Italca Company. We are making a formal protest.

3. *A certain measure of control over Portuguese foreign policy in its widest aspects and the support of the Portuguese Government in various cases where their interests are not concerned.*

The Portuguese cling desperately to the British Alliance. It is almost their sole claim to respectability and consideration. For this reason they are most unlikely to take any radical step or enter into serious political commitments without our consent.

Only a few months ago they consulted us before listening to Spanish advances. In the event, say, of Signor Mussolini endeavouring to form an anti-British Italo–Spanish *entente* or agreement, Portugal would certainly not

[6] Punctuation as in original quotation.

join. In international conferences where no Portuguese interests are at stake we can generally rely on Portuguese support. In the same order of things, the Portuguese representative on the Committee of Control at Tangier invariably votes with his British colleague. The King of Spain once called Portugal a British satellite. This, of course, is an exaggeration, but it contains a measure of truth.

Whereas we have held for many years and have informed the Portuguese Government that we consider ourselves entitled to judge the circumstances in which help may be given to or withheld from the Portuguese, the latter showed by their attitude on the outbreak of war that they consider themselves bound by the alliance. There is no reason to suppose that the Portuguese Government hold other views now, and the natural inference is that they will not of their own accord consent to release us from the obligations of the treaties. The question at once arises whether we can release ourselves without their consent. The answer appears to be in the negative.

Not one of the treaties contains any provisions or machinery for termination or denunciation. Indeed, the treaty of 1373 speaks of 'perpetual Friendships, Unions, Alliances, and Leagues'; the treaty of 1386 lays down that 'there shall be inviolate and endure for ever . . .[6] a solid, perpetual and real League'; the treaty of 1642 concludes, 'for ever a good, true and firm peace and amity'; and so on. In mediæval days and later a Perpetual Treaty of Alliance could always be terminated by a declaration of war. No such solution is possible in the present instance.

Oppenheim's standard work on 'International Law' states as follows[7]:—

'Although . . .[6] such treaties as are apparently intended or expressly contracted for the purpose of setting up an everlasting condition of things cannot in principle be dissolved by withdrawal of one of the parties, there is an exception to this rule. For it is an almost universally recognised fact that vital changes of circumstances may be of such a kind as to justify a party in demanding to be released from the obligations of an unnotifiable treaty. The vast majority of publicists, as well as the Governments of the civilised States, defend the principle *conventio omnis intelligitur rebus sic stantibus*,[8] and they agree, therefore, that all treaties are concluded under the tacit condition *rebus sic stantibus*. That this condition involves a large amount of danger cannot be denied, for it can be, and, indeed, frequently has been, abused for the purpose of hiding the violation of treaties behind the shield of law, and of covering shameful wrong with the mantle of righteousness. But all this cannot alter the fact that this exceptional condition is as necessary for international law and international intercourse as the very rule *pacta sunt servanda*.[9] When the existence, or the vital development of a State

[7] See L. Oppenheim, *International Law: A Treatise*, vol. i (Third Edition, London, 1920), p. 539.

[8] A term given to a tacit condition said to be implied in every treaty that, if by a vital change of circumstances an obligation stipulated in the treaty should imperil the existence of one of the parties, such party should have a right to demand to be released from the obligation concerned.   [9] Treaties must be observed.

stands in unavoidable conflict with its treaty obligations, the latter must give way, for self-preservation and development, in accordance with the growth and the vital requirements of the nation, are the primary duties of every State. No State would consent to any such treaty as would hinder it in the fulfilment of these primary duties. The consent of a State to a treaty presupposes a conviction that it is not fraught with danger to its existence and vital development. For this reason every treaty implies a condition that, if by an unforeseen change of circumstances an obligation stipulated in the treaty should imperil the existence or vital development of one of the parties, it should have a right to demand to be released from the obligation concerned. . . .[6]

'It is generally agreed that the clause, *rebus sic stantibus*, may only be resorted to in very exceptional circumstances, and that certainly not every change of circumstance justifies a State in making use of it. All agree that, although treaty obligations may, through a change of circumstances, become disagreeable, burdensome, and onerous, they must, nevertheless, be discharged. All agree, further, that a change of government, and even a change in the form of a State, such as the turning of a monarchy into a republic, and *vice versâ*, does not alone, and in itself, justify a State in resorting to the clause. On the other hand, all agree in regard to many cases in which it could justly be made use of. Thus, for example, if a State enters into a treaty of alliance for a certain period of time, and, if, before the expiration of the alliance, a change of circumstances occurs, so that now the alliance endangers the very existence of one of the contracting parties, all will agree that the clause, *rebus sic stantibus*, would justify that party in demanding to be released from the treaty of alliance.

'A certain amount of disagreement as to the cases in which the clause might, or might not, be justly applied will, of course, always remain as long as there is no international court which could decide each case. But the fact is remarkable that since the beginning of the 19th century only very few cases of the application of the clause have occurred. And there is no doubt that during the last century a conviction became more and more prevalent that the clause, *rebus sic stantibus*, ought not to give a State the right, immediately upon the happening of a vital change of circumstances, to declare itself free from the obligations of a treaty, but should only entitle it to claim to be released from them by the other party or parties to the treaty. Accordingly, when a State is of the opinion that the obligations of a treaty have, through a vital change of circumstances, become unbearable, it should first approach the other party or parties, and request them to abrogate the treaty. If such abrogation be refused a conflict arises between the treaty obligations and the right to be released from them, which, in the absence of an international court that could give judgment in the matter, cannot be settled juridically. It is only then that a State may perhaps be justified in declaring that it can no longer consider itself bound by those obligations.'

Has there been any 'vital change of circumstances' since in 1899, and again inferentially in 1904, we confirmed our obligation to 'defend and protect' the Portuguese Colonies? Can it be said that our 'existence' or our 'vital development' stand in unavoidable conflict with the obligations imposed by the treaties? Does the alliance 'endanger our very existence'? The answer in every case is in the negative. The defeat of Germany in the Great War is a change of circumstances certainly, but not within Oppenheim's meaning. The Portuguese Colonies are no worse administered now than they were in 1899 or previously. If we told the Portuguese Government that we intended to denounce the treaties, they would presumably reply by demanding arbitration. This we could not possibly refuse, and we should lose the case.[10]

[10] On November 17 Mr. Villiers sent a letter to Sir L. Carnegie, H.M. Ambassador at Lisbon, to inform him that the Cabinet had decided that it was 'undesirable to re-consider our treaty obligations with Portugal as set forth in the memorandum'. See *Parl. Debs.*, *5th ser.*, *H. of C.*, vol. 212, col. 385, for a statement of December 21 by Sir A. Chamberlain of His Majesty's Government's intention to maintain in force the Anglo-Portuguese Alliance. Sir L. Carnegie was instructed in Foreign Office despatch No. 501 to Lisbon of December 23 to inform the Portuguese Minister for Foreign Affairs of the substance of this statement, and reported the great satisfaction of the Portuguese Government in his despatch No. 12 of January 7, 1928.

No. 26

Letter from Sir W. Tyrrell to Sir R. Graham (Rome)
[*C 8414/4526/7*]

FOREIGN OFFICE, *October 24, 1927*

My dear Graham,

Upon reading your despatch No. 789[1] of October 14th in regard to the attitude of the Italian press towards the recent Bulgarian comitadji[2] outrages the Secretary of State's comment was that it was amazing that Signor Mussolini did not see what material these diatribes against Jugoslav action in Macedonia afforded to that section of foreign opinion which is only too ready to adopt the Austro-German view on Italian policy in the Italian

[1] Not printed. This despatch reported in particular that 'the conflict between Yugoslavia and Bulgaria, which has been brought about by the murder [on October 5] of General Kovachevitch [the officer in command of Serb-Croat-Slovene forces at Stip], is being watched with the keenest interest by the Italian press. . . . In the present crisis Italian sympathy, as expressed in the press, is almost entirely on the side of Bulgaria. . . . Press comments upon the situation betray a uniformity which points to official inspiration. . . . In a message from Rome to the "Secolo" (October 9) it was pointed out that the main cause of the occurrences on the Yugoslav-Bulgarian border lay in the "iniquitous and barbarous mutilation of Macedonia imposed by the peace-treaties which are, in certain zones, permanent causes of unrest and revolt". After denouncing the "inhuman policy of terror" pursued by Yugoslavia in Macedonia, the "Secolo" correspondent asked why was not the Macedonian problem tackled. Geneva, evidently, had no time to devote to such matters. The correspondent, finally, hinted at a possible connection between Moscow and the Macedonian revolutionaries.' For an account of recent developments in relations between Bulgaria and the Serb-Croat-Slovene State, the activities of the Macedonian Revolutionary Organisation and the assassination of General Kovachevitch see *Survey of International Affairs 1927*, pp. 210–16.

[2] A Turkish word meaning committee men and signifying guerillas or bandsmen.

Tyrol. 'One is almost tempted to ask' he says 'whether the "Secolo" article was not written by an Austrian for its usefulness as Austrian and pan-German propaganda.'

Do you think this aspect of the question has ever occurred to Mussolini? To us it seems obvious that once the permanence of the frontiers laid down by the peace treaties is allowed to be questioned, in whatever part of the world, we are opening the way for a most dangerous campaign on the part of all the ex-enemy powers. It is impossible to draw up ideal frontiers in the Balkans and least of all in regard to Macedonia, but we feel strongly that the existing frontiers laid down between Jugoslavia, Bulgaria and Greece are the best possible in the circumstances, and that the only way to secure peace in the Balkans is to insist on their absolutely final character. To allow discussion favouring their revision gives encouragement to all potential disturbers of the peace and most of all to the Macedonian Revolutionary Organisation. This body, in our view, has been fighting a losing battle for some time simply because public opinion is getting accustomed to the fact that there is no earthly prospect of Macedonian hopes being realised and because the peasantry in consequence are at last making up their minds to settle down peacefully under their present masters.

The position with regard to the Italian press of course is very different from that in any other country. We have had the pernicious Rothermere campaign for the revision of the Hungarian frontiers,[3] but as everybody knows, His Majesty's Government have little or no control over the British press. In Italy, however, where there is a strict censorship and no anti-government press at all, it does seem to us that the Fascist Government are playing with fire in allowing these loose discussions to go on upon a subject which, to our minds, it is the most important interest of all the ex-allied countries and especially Italy to treat as definitely closed.

You may have an opportunity of making this point to Signor Mussolini if you think fit, but of course we wish to leave you full discretion in the matter.

You will see from Kennard's despatch No. 391[4] of October 13th that that . . .[5] man Balugdić has been writing again in the Belgrade press attacking Italy, and the vicious circle thus continues. The Secretary of State has however told Kennard to point out if he thinks he can to Marinkovitch how dangerous this is. I mention this as you might, if you speak to Mussolini like to be able to tell him that we are very disgusted with the Serb press and are trying to induce them to recognise their folly.[6]

Yours ever

W. TYRRELL

[3] For an account of this campaign, opened by an article in the *Daily Mail* on June 21, 1927, by Lord Rothermere, chief proprietor of the *Daily Mail*, *Daily Mirror*, and London *Evening News*, see *op. cit.*, pp. 205–7.

[4] This covering despatch (not preserved in Foreign Office archives) transmitted a summary of an article in *Politika* of October 9 by M. Balougdjitch, Serb-Croat-Slovene Minister at Berlin and formerly at Rome, on recent Comitadji activities, together with a résumé of other press comments on the subject. [5] A personal reference is here omitted.

[6] Sir R. Graham replied on October 28 in a letter to Sir W. Tyrrell that he entirely agreed

and had spoken in the sense of Sir W. Tyrrell's letter to Signor Grandi on the previous day. Sir R. Graham added: 'I asked Grandi whether Rakic had been to the Ministry lately and whether there was any progress in the conversations with him? Grandi said that they had had an amicable talk about a week ago, but that he thought it was better not to hurry matters on, but to let feeling between the two countries gradually simmer down and reach a more normal footing. As, little by little, Yugoslav opinion came to recognise the sincerity and honesty of Italian policy in Albania, tension would subside. I fear this is an optimistic view.'

No. 27

Letter from Mr. Ingram (Berlin) to Mr. Sargent
[*N 5072/520/38*]

BERLIN, *October 25, 1927*

My dear Sargent,

I enclose herewith a copy of an interesting letter from Finlayson to Leith Ross upon the subject of German credits to Russia, together with some comments of our second commercial secretary on the same.

Yours ever

E. M. B. INGRAM

ENCLOSURE 1 IN No. 27

Letter from Mr. Finlayson (Berlin) to Mr. Leith-Ross (Treasury)

BERLIN, *October 6, 1927*

My dear Leith Ross,

I notice that the English newspapers (among others, the Daily Telegraph) are bringing up again the subject of German credits to Russia. Following my usual practice and, in accordance with your wish, expressed long ago, that I should keep an eye on Russian developments, I shall strive to set out what I understand to be the present state of affairs.

First of all, it is difficult either to refute or confirm the Daily Telegraph's statement that German firms have granted short-dated credits to Russia, in the form of twelve and eighteen month bills, to a total value of 400 million reichsmarks. So far as I am aware, there is no means available of arriving at any reliable estimate. The figure appears to me to be rather on the high side. It is, of course, true that, prior to the Anglo-Russian diplomatic conflict, many of these Russian bills found their way to the city for re-discount and the breaking-off of relations put an end to this practice. I never heard that this had any untoward repercussions here, although Ramsden of the F[ederation of] B[ritish] I[ndustries], when he was in Berlin last summer, hinted to me that the effect might likely be to put the Russians in a financial hole. But this, as I say, does not appear to have been the case, in spite of the fact that the number of bills floating around in Berlin must have materially increased for lack of an outside rediscount market.

As regards the Otto Wolff contract to deliver oil-pipes for the Baku mines, I am informed that the position is, that the proposed contract is for 20 million reichsmarks, to be given in the form of a credit of thirty months. The comment on this proposal which appeared in today's 'Börsen Courier' is:—'In authoritative circles there is [sic] already grave doubts whether, in view of the anxious financial situation in Soviet Russia, it is wise to extend such long credits at the present moment.'

By far the most important project is, of course, the proposed German–American deal in Russia. It would appear from available information at this end, that the plan has been thought out in the United States of America and that negotiations have been going on for over a year between American interested groups and the Russians with regard to the extension and reorganisation of the Jugostal works, a South-Russian steel undertaking in the neighbourhood of Kharkov (midway between Moscow and the Crimea, on the north frontier of the Ukraine). Now, the Germans have been most anxious to get into this deal and a syndicate, composed of Otto Wolff, the Vereinigte Stahlwerke and the Demag (Deutsche Maschinenfabrik A.G.) has apparently succeeded in getting its hand in. Under the terms of the scheme, the Jugostal works are going to be extended by five blast-furnaces and three rolling-mills, at a cost of forty million dollars.

It was of course to be expected that the Yanks were not prepared to let the Germans into the scheme 'pour leurs beaux yeux'. As a price, the Germans had to offer to take over three-quarters of the risk in return for the right of delivering all the material. Now, such an obligation viz. to put up 75% of forty million dollars, was apparently too much for the Syndicate and that is why it is now rumoured that an appeal is being made to the Reich for a 60% 'Ausfall-Garantie', such as was accorded in the three hundred million reichsmark credit to Russia.[1] The 'Börsen Courier' of today states that 'It is not correct that the German Government are prepared to undertake a 60% guarantee . . .[2] an application to that effect has not yet been made to the German Government. In view of the external political situation, of the Anglo–Russian conflict and of the current Franco-Russian negotiations[3] it must be regarded as absolutely unlikely that such a credit could be arranged at the present moment with the cooperation of the German Government'. These are very guarded terms and mean very little. The 'Magazin der Wirtschaft' (No. 40 of the 6th of October) maintains, on the other hand, that 'negotiations are apparently taking place in regard to a 60% guarantee but it is not yet settled whether and under what conditions it will be accorded'.

As regards the financing of the transaction the German Syndicate are in negotiation with Dillon, Read & Company, who are apparently prepared to put up the ten million dollars of their participation. It is a matter of great satisfaction here that Dillon, Read, have not been acting without the consent of the United States State Department, as this is regarded as a change in the American official attitude towards Russian business.

[1] Cf. Volume III, Nos. 158 and 180.   [2] Punctuation as in original quotation.
[3] For an account of Soviet–French relations 1925–7 see *Survey of International Affairs 1927*, pp. 278–95.

Finally, the scheme provides that the works will be carried out within two years, while the credit, with interest, is repayable in six years.

Yours sincerely,
H. C. F. FINLAYSON

ENCLOSURE 2 IN No. 27

Letter from Mr. Kavanagh (Berlin) to Mr. Ingram

BERLIN, *October 11, 1927*

Dear Ingram,

With reference to the attached letter of Finlayson, I have not sent home anything on the specific points dealt with, as I want to get some confirmation on points (2) and (3) from Herr Wolff.

As regards the 'Daily Telegraph's' statement that German firms have granted short-dated credits to Russia, I am very sceptical concerning the amount of 400 Million Reichsmarks quoted and should be inclined to place the sum at a much lower figure. I quite agree with Finlayson that there are no means available of arriving at any reliable estimate.

I have not yet reported the proposed German–American deal in Russia concerning the extension and reorganisation of the Jugostal works for the reason that from the recent press reports it is impossible to state how far the matter has actually progressed and I was waiting to obtain confirmation from Herr Otto Wolff on his return to Berlin. I see that the 'Frankfurter Zeitung' of the 7th October states that the 'Deutsche Volkw.'[4] asserts that the agreement was concluded some weeks ago between the American group, the Soviet Government and the German group and that only the attitude of the State Department in Washington and of the German Government remain to be defined. As, however, the scheme would appear to be impossible of achievement without the consent of the former and the co-operation of the latter, this report does not carry us much further.

Yours ever,
C. J. KAVANAGH

---

[4] Presumably the *Deutsche Volkswirt*, an economic and financial weekly paper.

No. 28

Sir R. Lindsay (Berlin) to Sir A. Chamberlain (Received October 31)
No. 648 [C 8796/857/18]

Confidential BERLIN, *October 27, 1927*

Sir,

I saw the Agent General for Reparations this evening and asked him if he could tell me anything about the events of the last few days in connection with his memorandum to the German Government. He thereupon gave me some interesting information.

2. As announced in the press, Mr Gilbert had had an interview with the Finance Minister. He had been received with kindness, with gratitude, with

effusion. Not one word of reproach! Dr Koehler said that the memorandum exactly indicated all the objects which the German Government were aiming at and most desired to attain, and it was therefore of great help. He carried on in this strain for three and a quarter hours, but Mr Gilbert attached no importance to this language. Dr Koehler, he said, is a fluent and agreeable talker but no financier. He can string words together by the hour without saying anything—and Mr Gilbert instanced the Minister's speech in committee reported in my despatch No. 646[1] of to-day's date. Talking with Dr Koehler, he said, would never do any good at all, and for business it would always be necessary to get to writing.

3. Mr Gilbert was rather put out by the effort now being made to spread it about that his memorandum had been asked for by the German Government. Of course he said there was absolutely no justification for this. He had indeed often talked with Dr Koehler, perhaps as often as once a week, and that might just enable the Minister to say that the memorandum was a link in a chain of previous communications, though that was going rather far. But what had roused him was a suggestion now being put about that it was he, Mr. Gilbert, who desired that the memorandum should be kept confidential. He had therefore just placed it formally on record in writing that he had no objection whatever to the publication of the memorandum. He had gone further and formally reserved to himself the right to publish the communications he might from time to time have to make to the German Government.

4. Mr. Gilbert told me he had just been to see Dr. Stresemann and had handed to him a copy of this letter. Dr. Stresemann, he told me, had said that there were certain passages in the memorandum which he was inclined to criticise, but that looking at it broadly he agreed with its general purport. He was at that moment going to attend a meeting of the Cabinet and he meant to support the views expressed by the Agent General. He meant to ask his colleagues how they could expect him, as Minister for Foreign Affairs, to say at Geneva that Germany's reparation burden was too heavy and that the Dawes Plan must be revised when there was in existence this indictment of their financial behaviour. On the question of publication Dr. Stresemann was all in favour of immediate action; if one has to plunge into cold water, he said, it is best to do so at once, and then get out again as quickly as possible. I expressed the view that it was high time for Dr. Stresemann to intervene in the Cabinet *qua* Minister for Foreign Affairs, as any considerable shock now to German credit would affect disastrously Germany's position as a Power. Mr. Gilbert said that Dr. Stresemann had been seriously thinking about it for some time, but he was in a difficult position. The two Ministers belonged to

---

[1] Not printed. This despatch transmitted relevant portions of Dr. Köhler's speech before the Reichstag budget committee on October 26 (see *The Times*, October 27, 1927, p. 11), and reported that, after delivering this speech, the Finance Minister went on to explain to the Committee *in camera* the origin of the Agent General's memorandum. Sir R. Lindsay stated in particular that Dr. Köhler pointed out again that the memorandum 'had been communicated to him by virtue of a previous agreement and as a link in the chain of discussions which had been going on for a long time. There was no cause for the anxiety which has arisen as a result of indiscretions in the press.'

one Government indeed but to two different parties; the ministries were perpetually at logger-heads with each other; and the Ministry of Finance was chaotically organized, in such a way as to make ministerial collaboration peculiarly difficult.

5. Mr. Parker Gilbert told me he had not seen Dr. Schacht for more than three weeks—indeed he had rather avoided seeing him while he was preparing to put in his memorandum. Dr. Schacht had only been shown the memorandum on October 27—five days after its delivery.[2] He had then sent a message to Mr. Gilbert to say that he entirely agreed with the views it expressed. He also added the admission that he had misjudged the situation last spring and that he would then have been well advised if he had raised the Bank rate at once instead of taking the measures he did take.

6. What was greatly concerning Mr. Gilbert was the question of publication. The German Government, in putting it about that the memorandum had been asked for by Dr Koehler, were trying to minimize its importance, to gain time in which public interest would die down, and so turn an awkward corner and have a free hand for such action as might seem suitable to them. To defeat this manoeuvre, Mr. Gilbert was half inclined to publish the memorandum himself, and was certainly anxious that it should be published. I said I thought the relations between himself and the German Government must in general be of an essentially confidential character. In his biennial reports he could say anything he liked, but if, except perhaps in very extraordinary circumstances he were to publish his communications to them without their consent he would be putting himself wrong with them. I agreed that the document ought to be published by the German Government. Now that its existence was known to the public, it would do more harm to German credit by being kept secret and so constituting a vague and unknown menace than if the worst were known at once. We both thought it likely that somehow or other the paper would see the light of day. Berlin is full of journalists longing to get it; and the German Ministries are full of politically minded officials, many of whom would be delighted to do the Government a bad turn. This was the end of our conversation.

7. The German Government are in a difficult position and are making every effort to keep Mr. Gilbert's memorandum secret. If it is published it will be extremely hard for them to pursue their policy and carry through the Reichstag the School Bill, the Officials Salary Bill, and the Compensation Law, all of which involve vast commitments. At the same time they are so deeply pledged to these projects—or at least to the first two of them, that to drop them is hardly possible. It is beginning to look to me as if, in accordance with the precedent observed for some years, we may have our Christmas in Berlin without any Government at all. If we are to have trouble, the sooner it comes the better. I suppose the publication of the memorandum might cause a flutter in German finance, but it would be all the sounder for it at base; and the position would then be all the clearer for the more serious

[2] The text here appears to be incorrect. Mr. Gilbert handed his memorandum to Dr. Köhler on October 20.

difficulties which may be due next autumn, when the reparation payments rise another step higher and when, be it noted, the American Presidential campaign will be in full blast.

I have, &c.,

R. C. LINDSAY

No. 29

Record by Sir W. Tyrrell of a conversation with the French Ambassador
[*N 5093/61/59*]

FOREIGN OFFICE, *October 28, 1927*

The French Ambassador called today and asked me for our views on the Lithuanian situation.

I told him that I had informed Sir Austen Chamberlain of the démarche at Kovno suggested by the French Government, which he had communicated to me on October 26th [*sic*].[1]

Sir Austen's view had been in favour of some such action by Great Britain, France and Italy, but since then information had reached him which had induced him to change his mind and think that such representations might no longer be useful. Sir Austen had heard that the President of the Council of the League of Nations proposed to give effect to the appeal made by Lithuania by appointing a sub-committee of the Council of the League, which was to consist of three members. M. Villegas, the President of the Council, proposed to invite a Dutchman to take the chair, and M. Briand and Dr. Stresemann to be members of this committee.

I expressed Sir Austen's earnest hope that M. Briand would see his way to accept this invitation and to attend in person, as he thought it was an occasion on which the authority of a Minister for Foreign Affairs was essential for the success of the deliberations. Moreover, he felt convinced that if M. Briand

---

[1] Sir W. Tyrrell had stated in particular in a record dated October 24 of a conversation that day with M. de Fleuriau that the latter had put forward proposals from his Government that 'the representatives of Great Britain, France and Italy at Kovno should take steps to obtain:

(1) A reciprocal recognition by the Polish and Lithuanian governments of their respective governments.

(2) A disavowal of the state of war by the Lithuanian government.

(3) A resumption of negotiations for the purpose of establishing economic and consular relations between the two countries.

(4) An admission of "reserves" with regard to what M. de Fleuriau presumed was the question of Vilna, as the telegram which had reached him was so corrupt that he was unable to state categorically that these reserves related to Vilna.

'I thanked the Ambassador for this communication and promised to let him have an answer as soon as possible.

'I explained to him the point of view of Sir Austen Chamberlain, which was that he was very anxious to take some action at Kovno which would enable the three governments eventually to restrain the Polish government from taking action themselves.

'His Excellency told me that this point of view was entirely shared by his government.'

accepted, Dr. Stresemann would follow suit. This would secure German co-operation, which was so essential for the solution of this vexed question.

I told M. de Fleuriau that, since his communication to me of October 26th [24th], a despatch had been received by the Secretary of State from His Majesty's Ambassador at Berlin, recording a conversation which he had had with Dr. Stresemann on the subject, and which went far to dissipate any suspicions we might have had as regards Dr. Stresemann's attitude and feelings with regard to Lithuania, and I proceeded to give the French Ambassador the substance of Sir Ronald Lindsay's despatch no. 631[2] of October 21st.

Finally, I told His Excellency that, in Sir Austen's opinion, the appeal to the League by Lithuania gave us an opportunity to strengthen the authority of the League, to which M. Briand attached as much importance as Sir Austen himself. This appeal by Lithuania was likely to prevent any ill-advised action by that state pending the hearing of its appeal.

As regards Poland, it seemed to the Secretary of State that she also would be well advised to appeal to the League, as it would enable her to give full publicity to the fact that, though Lithuania was a member of the League, she had declared herself to be at war with another member of the League—a fact which appeared to be but little known and appreciated by the general public. This ignorance was prejudicing the Polish case, and it would be to Polish interest to remove this prejudice.

Sir Austen was not prepared to suggest to Poland an appeal to the League, but he thought that M. Briand might be disposed to do so. If Poland decided to appeal, there would be no danger of Poland taking action independently of the League.

M. de Fleuriau told me that he thought Sir Austen's decision a wise one, and one that he would recommend to his government for favourable consideration.[3]

W. T.

[2] No. 23.
[3] Lord Crewe was informed of this conversation in Foreign Office despatch No. 2717 to Paris of November 2.

No. 30

Sir R. Lindsay (Berlin) to Sir A. Chamberlain (Received October 31)
No. 649 [C 8797/857/18]

BERLIN, *October 28, 1927*

Sir,

In continuation of my despatch No. 648[1] of yesterday respecting the Memorandum to the German Government of the Agent General for Reparations, I have the honour to report that I called to-day at the Ministry for Foreign Affairs on Dr Köpke on some other business, but also with the

[1] No. 28.

intention of discussing the latest phase of the Reparation questions. Dr Köpke is only third in rank in the Ministry, so that anything I said would be more or less unofficial in character. At the same time he is intelligent and he reports accurately to the Minister.

2. I said that without having seen Mr Gilbert's memorandum, I knew enough about the financial situation here to have a good idea of what its gist must be, and that I thought it high time that the Ministry for Foreign Affairs should take charge of this question and assert itself. Germany could not suffer a second shock to her credit and recover as quickly as she had from the first. Her position in the world would be irretrievably damaged. Dr Köpke said that this was entirely the view taken by Dr Stresemann and recently stoutly maintained by him, though at the cost of a considerable amount of tension with the Finance Ministry. The view of the Foreign Office as to Mr Gilbert's action was that it must not be regarded as anything hostile, but rather the contrary. Mr Gilbert was not to be looked on as a bailiff put in by creditors, but as a man whose duty it was to administer a scheme as well as possible until financial laws, as inexorable as the law of gravity itself, demonstrated the necessity for its revision. For this reason the Ministry had exerted itself to stop any press attacks against the Agent General, and I would have observed that they had succeeded pretty well.

3. On the question of publication I said to Dr. Köpke what I had said last night to Mr. Gilbert, that as the existence of the memorandum was known it had better be published at once rather than remain unknown and frighten foreign financiers. Dr. Köpke told me the Minister for Foreign Affairs shared this view in principle, but it appeared that this memorandum, which had been prepared on the suggestion of the Minister of Finance, was to be regarded more or less as an indication of Mr. Gilbert's regular report to the Reparations Commission and was to form the subject of discussion between Dr. Koehler and Mr. Gilbert before the Report was published. Immediate publication therefore could not be arranged until those discussions had taken place, as Dr. Koehler might have some criticisms to suggest and his claims to state them would be prejudiced.

4. This view is of course completely and diametrically opposed to that held by Mr. Gilbert himself. The foolish disingenuousness of it may be ascribed to Dr. Koehler, and I do not suppose that Dr. Stresemann himself has done more than accept the statements of his colleague. I myself did not care to tell Dr. Köpke the truth because I owe it to Mr. Gilbert to appear less well informed on these points than I really am; but I think I had better tell Mr. Gilbert of what passed.

5. Dr. Köpke told me that Dr. Stresemann wants to talk to me about the present phase of the Reparations Question, but will be out of town till Tuesday.[2] I shall arrange for an interview for that day with His Excellency.

I have, &c.,

R. C. LINDSAY

[2] November 1, 1927.

No. 31

Sir A. Chamberlain to Mr. Kennard (Belgrade)
No. 528 [C 8728/808/92]

FOREIGN OFFICE, *October 29, 1927*

Sir,

I observe from your despatch No. 399[1] of the 17th October last that when discussing with you the present conditions existing between the Serb-Croat-Slovene State and Italy, the Serb-Croat-Slovene Minister for Foreign Affairs stated that he had instructed the Serb-Croat-Slovene Minister at Rome not to ask for any further interview with Signor Mussolini for the present as he did not feel the moment to be propitious. I was already aware from the conversation I had with M. Marinkovitch last month at Geneva (see my despatch No. 475[2] of the 12th September) that this was his policy for the time being, but I am somewhat afraid lest it be not generally understood in Jugoslavia that this decision of M. Marinkovitch is the cause—and the only cause—of the interruption of the conversations which were started in Rome on the 26th [24th] June.[3] For instance, I was disagreeably struck by the remark made to you by the King, as reported in your despatch No. 396,[4] to the effect that the Jugoslav Minister in Rome had endeavoured without result to initiate frank conversations between the two Governments with a view to their returning to the basis of the Pact of Rome.[5] If this really represents His Majesty's view of the situation, I conclude that public opinion is equally misinformed, and that the interruption of the Rome conversations is generally attributed to the ill-will and obstructions of Signor Mussolini instead of to the cautious policy of M. Marinkovitch.

2. Quite apart from the danger in present circumstances of allowing such misrepresentations to take root, the absence of any improvement of relations between Rome and Belgrade since the June meeting is causing me some preoccupation. Jugoslav public opinion appears to be growing increasingly suspicious and nervous, and the fact that it is generally believed that Italy is at the back of the recent komitaji outrages gives us the measure of Jugoslavia's morbid susceptibility. In fact, far from the situation having improved, as M. Marinkovitch had hoped, through being allowed to drift for the last four months, it is evident that relations between Jugoslavia and Italy have, if anything, deteriorated, and that unless some steps are taken in the near future to create a better atmosphere, these relations may be expected to grow

---

[1] Not printed. In this report of his conversation on October 17 with M. Marinkovitch, Mr. Kennard stated in particular: 'in my conversations with the King [see below] and M. Marinković I have held out no hope that His Majesty's Government would again intervene in any way in the dispute between the Italian and S.C.S. Governments and this side of the matter has not been mentioned'.

[2] See No. 1, note 15.   [3] See Volume III, No. 254.

[4] Not printed. This despatch of October 15 reported on a conversation on the previous day between King Alexander and Mr. Kennard.

[5] The Italian-Serb-Croat-Slovene treaty of January 27, 1924, is printed with additional protocol in *British and Foreign State Papers*, vol. 120, pp. 683–4.

progressively worse. As stated above, when I discussed this very subject with M. Marinkovitch at Geneva, his Excellency informed me that he made no complaint that the conversations between M. Rakic and Signor Mussolini had not yet been resumed, because he considered that it would be better to wait for a calmer atmosphere before proceeding further with them. At that time I did not criticise this policy, but now, in view of subsequent developments, I am doubtful whether M. Marinkovitch is wise in still continuing to postpone these negotiations indefinitely. What I particularly fear is that if further time is wasted and no approach is made by the Serb-Croat-Slovene Government to the Italian Government, the relations between the two countries will reach so strained a state that it will be impossible to resume the conversations, or, at least if they are resumed, the Jugoslav Government will find that constantly repeated press polemics have produced their effect on Signor Mussolini, and that the latter is consequently no longer inclined to respond in the same friendly spirit as he displayed last summer.

3. I should be glad, therefore, if you would represent to M. Marinkovitch the dangers which I foresee in his delaying any longer the renewal of the conversations between M. Rakic and Signor Mussolini. There seems to be in some quarters a feeling that Signor Mussolini is himself averse from, or even obstructing, these conversations, but I can see no evidence for this. On the contrary, Signor Mussolini, in his conversation with M. Rakic of the 26th [24th] June, stated that he was ready to continue the discussions, and up to the present his offer still stands. In these circumstances it rests entirely with the Serb-Croat-Slovene Government to take the initiative of putting this offer to the test. If, therefore, it is permissible for me to advise M. Marinkovitch in this matter, I would suggest that before the situation has further deteriorated instructions should immediately be given to M. Rakic to ask for a further interview with Signor Mussolini in order that the general state of Serbo-Italian relations may be examined and remedies devised for the present causes of friction.

4. As I told M. Marinkovitch in my conversation with him on the 6th September, I consider that the course which he proposes that these conversations should follow is a wise one, and I am glad to think that he does not in any case intend to bring forward the question of the Treaty of Tirana in the first instance, but rather to invite the Italian Government to review all that has passed since the Pact of Rome in the hope of removing the misunderstandings and grievances which have caused the present unsatisfactory change in the relations between the two countries. But I would venture to remind him that the Serb-Croat-Slovene Government cannot expect a satisfactory solution of the existing difficulties unless they on their part are prepared to offer some concession to the Italian Government. I suggested to M. Marinkovitch at Geneva that it would be necessary for him to consider how he could give Signor Mussolini some assurances as to the intentions of Jugoslavia in respect of intervention in Albania. I would now add a further suggestion, and that is that he should undertake to ratify the Nettuno conventions without further delay. I am aware of the parliamentary difficulties

which the Serb-Croat-Slovene Government anticipate in obtaining the ratification of these conventions, but I am equally aware that the importance which the Italian Government attach to the fulfilment thereof is such that if the Serb-Croat-Slovene Government are not ready to show themselves accommodating in the matter of these conventions, it will be correspondingly difficult for Signor Mussolini to make advances on his side. I would add that I have been informed by M. Briand that, impressed by the same considerations, he had himself recently advised the Serb-Croat-Slovene Government to meet the wishes of the Italian Government in regard to these conventions.

5. In speaking to M. Marinkovitch on these lines, you should assure his Excellency that the advice which I venture to tender to him is only given after mature consideration and in the confident belief that it is in the imperative interest of Jugoslavia that the present state of friction which exists between that country and Italy should be removed at the earliest possible moment.[6]

6. A copy of this despatch has been sent to His Majesty's Ambassador at Rome, but I am not instructing Sir R. Graham to make any representations to Signor Mussolini on the matter as it appears to me that the first move should come from the Serb-Croat-Slovene Government.

I am, &c.,

(For the Secretary of State)

C. Howard Smith[7]

[6] Foreign Office despatch No. 2721 to Paris of November 2 instructed Lord Crewe to suggest to the French Government that the French Minister at Belgrade should receive instructions similar to those set out above. In Paris despatch No. 2227 of November 7 Lord Crewe reported a conversation with M. Berthelot, Secretary-General of the French Ministry of Foreign Affairs, on November 4, when he acted as instructed.

[7] A senior member of the Central Department of the Foreign Office.

No. 32

Mr. Kennard (Belgrade) to Sir A. Chamberlain (Received October 31, 1 p.m.)

No. 171 Telegraphic [C 8806/4490/92]

BELGRADE, *October 31, 1927, 12.15 p.m.*

Your despatch No. 512.[1]

French Minister[2] informs me that French Ambassador at Rome[3] has informed Signor Grandi that as Italian government have shown no inclination to enter into a tripartite agreement, Franco-Yugoslav pact will be signed shortly. Latter apparently accepted statement without comment.

[1] This despatch of October 15, not preserved in Foreign Office archives, probably transmitted to Belgrade a copy of Foreign Office despatch No. 2575 to Paris and 1245 to Rome (not preserved in Foreign Office archives). The docket of a minute by Mr. Howard Smith submitting the draft of this despatch described it as 'stating that the French Minister at Belgrade has informed His Majesty's Minister at Belgrade that while there is no question of signing [Franco-Yugoslav] pact at present, instructions have been sent to French Ambassador at Rome to inform Italian Government that its signature cannot be postponed indefinitely'.   [2] M. Dard.   [3] M. Besnard.

French Minister while not anxious to show me the text assures me that pact which will be registered with League of Nations is quite harmless in character and resembles arbitration agreement with Roumania of 1926.[4]

Addressed to Foreign Office No. 171; repeated to Rome.

[4] The convention between France and Roumania for the pacific settlement of disputes, signed on June 10, 1926, is printed in *League of Nations Treaty Series*, vol. lviii, pp. 233–43.

No. 33

Sir A. Chamberlain to the Marquess of Crewe (Paris)
No. 2746 [N 5196/61/59]

FOREIGN OFFICE, *November 4, 1927*

My Lord Marquess,

The French Ambassador spoke to me to-day about the Polish–Lithuanian dispute. His Excellency said that after his conversation with me the other day he had immediately brought to Monsieur Briand's notice the suggestion made by me that he, Monsieur Briand, should act as one of the members on the Committee which was about to be set up at Geneva to examine the question.[1]

Monsieur de Fleuriau had now received Monsieur Briand's reply, which was to the effect that the actual position was not quite that represented to him by me. According to Monsieur Briand's information, the Lithuanian Government have appealed to the League on the question of schools alone. The idea of a Committee of three was still in a tentative stage and would come up for decision at the next meeting of the Council. Therefore, the position was precisely the same as when Monsieur Briand made his suggestion that joint action should be taken at Kovno. He was still of opinion that the Powers should act there without waiting for the decision of the League.

I told the Ambassador that the position as described by Monsieur Briand was exactly the one which I had contemplated. I was afraid that I had perhaps not expressed myself sufficiently clearly and presumed too much on the Ambassador's knowledge of the practice of the League. I remained strongly of opinion that, in view of the jealousy of the Great Powers which had been shown at the last League Assembly and even by some members of the Council it would be very unwise for us to make a separate *démarche* at Kovno now that the Council had been formally seized of the question by Lithuania. The appeal to the Council was made under article 11[2] and its committee would, therefore, have full power to go into the whole question and to treat the Polish reprisals of which the Lithuanian Government complained as merely an incident in the larger issue of the maintenance by Lithuania of a state of war with Poland. Monsieur Briand, Dr. Stresemann and I had all thought it necessary in our speeches to the Assembly to make an effort to dispel the

[1] No record of the conversation in which Sir A. Chamberlain made this suggestion to M. de Fleuriau has been traced in Foreign Office archives: cf., however, No. 29.

[2] Of the Covenant of the League of Nations.

suspicion that the Great Powers sought to settle the business of the Council in private conversations, and to arrogate to themselves the rights of the Council. I should, of course, be reluctant at any time to refuse to cooperate with France, Germany and Italy in a step which they all thought desirable, but I could not believe that it would be wise for the Great Powers to take action which I felt would certainly revive the jealousies and suspicions of which I had spoken. I added that I did not desire to offer any advice to the Polish Government as to how they should conduct their case but if, as Monsieur Skirmunt had suggested to me,[3] the way in which the matter was presented by Lithuania was unfair to Poland, it was, of course, open to Poland to make her own independent appeal to the Council. Whether she did this or not, I repeated that since the Lithuanian appeal was made under article 11, it appeared to me to authorise and indeed require the Council to take up the larger question, and it seemed to me that Poland had every interest in getting such a public discussion, and that it was only through the combined influence of the Council and its committee, and under the pressure of a public opinion created and dictated by discussion before the Council, that there was any prospect of inducing the Lithuanian Government to adopt a correct attitude.[4]

I am, &c.,

AUSTEN CHAMBERLAIN

[3] In a conversation of November 1 recorded in Foreign Office despatch No. 520 to Warsaw of that date. Sir A. Chamberlain had spoken to M. Skirmunt on the same lines as to M. de Fleuriau as here recorded and had further read to him a considerable part of No. 23 in order to help remove Polish suspicions of German policy. Sir W. Max Muller subsequently reported to Sir A. Chamberlain in Warsaw telegram No. 93 of November 22 that M. Zaleski had stated on the previous day 'that he was acquainted with the reasons of your refusal to join in proposed démarche at Kovno but felt that they were based on a misconception of the real cause of the jealousy of great Powers shown at the last League Assembly. What the lesser Powers objected to was the tendency alleged or real of the great Powers to withdraw from the competence of the Council disputes in which they themselves were concerned; but they would have no objection to great Powers settling a dispute between two lesser Powers even if it had been submitted to the Council.'

[4] Foreign Office despatch No. 1385 to Berlin of November 11 referred to No. 23 and informed Sir R. Lindsay that Sir W. Tyrrell had spoken to Dr. Sthamer, the German Ambassador in London, on the same lines as Sir A. Chamberlain had spoken to MM. de Fleuriau and Skirmunt, and also to the Italian Ambassador, Signor Bordonaro, as recorded in despatch No. 1323 to Rome of November 2 (not printed). Dr. Sthamer was informed of Sir Austen's hope that M. Briand and Dr. Stresemann would serve on the proposed subcommittee of the League of Nations, but 'expressed the doubt whether it would be possible for the German Minister for Foreign Affairs to take any part in the dispute as his country was on bad terms with both Poland and Lithuania. Sir W. Tyrrell replied that by serving on such a committee, Dr. Stresemann would have a good opportunity of improving this state of affairs.'

No. 34

Mr. Kennard (Belgrade) to Sir A. Chamberlain
(Received November 6, 6.30 p.m.)

No. 174 Telegraphic [*C 8917/4490/92*]

BELGRADE, *November 6, 1927, 5 p.m.*

My telegram No. 171.[1]

French Minister informs me that Pact is to be signed before the end of this month and that Minister for Foreign Affairs is to proceed to Paris in this connection. He states that Monsieur Marinkovic proposes to go to London too.[2]

I have communicated sense of your despatch No. 528[3] to Minister for Foreign Affairs and am to see him tomorrow on the subject but in the meantime would point out that signature of Franco-Yugoslav Pact, however innocent it may be, is not likely to facilitate resumption of Monsieur Rakic's conversation at Rome. French Minister states that French Ambassador there informed Signor Grandi of intention to sign six weeks ago and that neither he nor Signor Mussolini have mentioned matter since. Italian Legation here however expressed the belief that secret clauses of a military nature must be included in Pact.

French Minister tells me that he has not himself received text of Pact as all negotiations have taken place in Paris but while he realizes that signature may make bad impression in Rome he feels that signature may produce salutary effect in Italy.

I had intended to suggest to Minister for Foreign Affairs that as he was to make a declaration on foreign affairs in Skuptchina[4] on November 10th he should make some reference of a friendly nature to Italy and should state that while relations were not as satisfactory as they might be he was prepared to enter into frank discussions with Italian Government. This might have paved the way for Monsieur Rakic to resume conversations.

I fear that announcement of impending signature of French Pact may close the door for the time being at any rate though I presume French Government have fully weighed the possible consequences.

In the meantime it would at any rate be interesting to learn what the main lines of this Pact are and what the real attitude of the Italian Government to it is likely to be.

Addressed to Foreign Office, repeated to Rome.

[1] No. 32.
[2] A similar communication was made to Sir V. Wellesley on November 7 by the French Ambassador in London, who stated that signature of the Franco-Serb-Croat-Slovene treaty would take place during the following week.
[3] No. 31.
[4] *Skupshtina*, the Serb-Croat-Slovene parliament.

No. 35

Mr. Kennard (Belgrade) to Sir A. Chamberlain (Received November 8, 9 a.m.)
No. 175 Telegraphic [C 9001/808/92]

BELGRADE, *November 7, 1927, 9.10 p.m.*

Your despatch No. 528.[1]

Minister for Foreign Affairs in conversation today assured me that he was always prepared to follow advice of His Majesty's Government who were the strongest factor in maintenance of peace in Europe. He drew my attention however to the fact that it was Signor Mussolini himself who had desired to postpone conversations[2] until a more favourable moment that therefore an invitation on the part of the latter had been awaited. His Excellency also pointed out that if Monsieur Rakic began conversations by an undertaking regarding Nettuno conventions he would make concession without perhaps gaining any satisfaction as regards Albania.

Serb-Croat-Slovene Government did not intend to insist on any special interpretation of the pact of Tirana and were ready to sign agreement in any form for maintenance of independence of Albania. Monsieur Marinkovic then stated that he had instructed Serb-Croat-Slovene minister at Rome four days ago to inform Signor Mussolini in accordance with the terms of the pact of Rome of impending signature of treaty with France and to add if he could see him personally, that he was prepared to renew conversation whenever Signor Mussolini thought fit. Monsieur Marinkovic also as I suggested intends to make friendly reference to Italy in his declarations in Skuptchina on his return from Paris.

He was leaving for Paris tomorrow to sign pact but would only remain there two days and proposed to proceed to London if agreeable to you. On my mentioning impression which signature of pact would cause in Rome His Excellency stated that pact which closely followed lines of Franco-Roumanian agreement of 1926 should give no cause for alarm in Italy though Italian press no doubt would react. I urged him to give Italian minister[3] who leaves for Rome today some friendly communication which he could make to Signor Mussolini and he promised to do so. French minister is also to press for renewal of conversations at Rome. I have requested him to impress on Monsieur Marinkovic necessity of preventing as far as possible anti-Italian outburst in the press here on signature of French pact.

Addressed to Foreign Office No. 175, repeated to Rome.

[1] No. 31.
[2] In his telegram No. 261 to Rome of November 10 Sir A. Chamberlain enquired whether Sir R. Graham could confirm the accuracy of this statement.
[3] General Bodrero. For his account of a conversation with Mr. Kennard on November 7 see *I Documenti Diplomatici Italiani*, Settima Serie, vol. v, No. 508.

No. 36

Sir R. Lindsay (Berlin) to Sir A. Chamberlain (Received November 11)
No. 675 [C 9071/857/18]

Confidential
BERLIN, November 8, 1927

Sir,

In continuation of my despatch No. 648[1] of the 27th of October about Mr Parker Gilbert's memorandum to the German Government on German financial conditions, I have the honour to report that I heard a report yesterday to the effect that Mr Gilbert was preparing a further rejoinder to the Finance Minister's reply.[2] I therefore contrived an interview yesterday evening with him and I was relieved to learn that he had no such intention, though in his acknowledgment of Dr Koehler's note he had put in some phrase to the effect that he reserved to himself the right to write further on any points in that note which, on careful reading, might require more elucidation. He told me that he thought the best thing now would be to keep quiet for awhile and watch reactions. Further polemics he thought would be inadvisable. I asked him if he meant to deal with the matter in his next report, which is due to appear at the end of this month. He said he had not yet decided, but he had rather been thinking of confining himself to merely printing the correspondence in the report as an annex with little or no comment, a suggestion which I commended. I think his decision is likely to be taken on the course press discussion of the correspondence may take in the next few days.

2. We had some discussion as to the great advisability of avoiding any acute issues over reparation questions for the present and at any rate until the various elections of 1928 were over. He is quite of this view, both in regard to the French elections, which he believes are likely to go to the Left, and in regard to the American Election of next autumn. In reporting this opinion of Mr Gilbert's I must remind you of his view that his action of the last few days has been designed to prevent the German Government from precipitating a reparation crisis by their ill judged conduct of budget and credit questions.

3. I found him so decidedly sanguine of salutary results from his action that I reminded him of last spring when we had both hoped that his warning letter might have some effect, yet he had had to speak more clearly still in his report of June, and in spite of all, things had gone from bad to worse. He admitted this, but maintained that there was a difference now in that influential circles in Germany had taken alarm. Two days after he had put in his memorandum, while its contents were quite unknown outside a very narrow circle, he had received a visit from a very important German industrialist, a man of almost violently nationalist politics, whom he had never made the

---

[1] No. 28.

[2] This letter of November 5 is printed as annex II to the *Report of the Agent General for Reparation Payments, December 10, 1927*. Mr. Gilbert's acknowledgment of the same date is printed *ibid.* as annex III.

acquaintance of. This gentleman had called uninvited, to say that it was high time the German Government was called to order in finance, and to express the hope that his, Mr Gilbert's, memorandum was couched in the strongest possible language, as nothing else would have any effect. Mr Parker Gilbert told me too that eight or ten of the most powerful industrialists had formed a private committee which was to exert pressure in the sense of financial moderation on the Government, and that they had engaged Dr Luther[3] to conduct proceedings for them as head of the committee. Mr Gilbert was satisfied in general with the way press comment had so far been formulated; and he thought the tone of the provincial papers too was good.

4. We had a good deal of discussion on Mr Gilbert's general relations with the Ministry of Finance and I must say I have much sympathy with his difficulties. Before Dr Koehler's unfailing aimiability [sic], his ceaseless volubility, and his complete disregard of all suggestion, combined with the utter disorganization of the Ministry, Mr Gilbert has been absolutely baffled. Humanly speaking he cannot be blamed for having pitched in this formidable memorandum. Dr Koehler's personality and incompetence is an important and unpleasant feature in the situation.

5. While I was speaking with the Agent General for Reparations, Mr Finlayson was talking to Dr Ritter at the Foreign Office, the chief official charged with the conduct of Reparation matters. I annex a note[4] by Mr Finlayson reporting his conversation and a comparison of Dr Ritter's language with that of Mr Gilbert is interesting.

6. I hardly know what result to anticipate from the excursions and alarms of the last fortnight. Dr Ritter, you will see, expects that the School Bill will fall of its own weight, but it could not in any case have involved any financial commitments for at least two years, so that it did little more than give Mr Gilbert a good debating point for his memorandum, and its sacrifice today will afford no immediate financial relief. The expense of the War Compensations contemplated would I imagine in any case have been spread over many years; and the increase of official salaries is to be prosecuted so far as concerns

---

[3] Dr. Luther had been German Chancellor from January 1925 to May 1926.

[4] This note of November 8 is not printed. Mr. Finlayson stated in particular: 'Dr. Ritter started out by saying that even cumulative stupidity could be productive of real good; the "Dummheiten [follies]" of Dr. Köhler had produced the Gilbert memorandum, for which Ritter was truly thankful, as some such outside objective judgment was necessary to bring the Reich Finance Ministry to a proper sense of its duties. . . . The German view of the immediate outlook on reparations was broadly as under: It would be fatal if, as a result of the present differences of opinion, the reparation problem were again to become immediately acute. The Germans were abundantly alive to the fact that nothing could be got out of Poincaré—he would claim his pound of flesh. But there would be elections in France in May, and, according to their prognostications, the likelihood was the return of a Cabinet of the Left, i.e., a triumph of the Briand or Locarno policy. In Germany there would be elections in the spring and here the probability was, according to Ritter, a considerable swing to the Left with the return of the Socialists to political power. Lastly, towards the end of 1928 there would be a new presidential election in the United States of America. Now, regard being had to the foregoing elements, it was in the general interests of all to keep things smooth and sweet, until we all saw things a bit clearer.'

at least the lower ranks. If, as I imagine, the lower ranks represent something like seven eighths of the whole cost of any civil service, there is not much economy to be realized here. It is not possible to say how detrimental to German credit the prosecution of this, that, or the other item of a programme may be. I suppose that Mr Gilbert has really been attacking a *spirit* of extravagance prevalent in all German governing bodies, and I am sure he is right when he says that important German circles are at his side in this fight. Whether or not he and they are influential enough to change the spirit of a weak Government about to face the electorate should become clear in the course of a very few weeks.

I have, &c.,

R. C. LINDSAY

No. 37

Sir A. Chamberlain to Mr. Kennard (Belgrade)

No. 121 Telegraphic [C 9002/4490/92]

FOREIGN OFFICE, *November 9, 1927, 1 p.m.*

Your telegram No. 176[1] (of November 8th).

I received yesterday communication of intended signature from French Ambassador[2] and almost simultaneously your telegram No. 175[3] (of November 7th). I was not taken by surprise as when I last saw M. Briand in Paris on my way home[4] he told me that signature which had been long postponed could not be much further delayed. He added that he had greatly modified original draft and that present text conformed closely to general policy of League of Nations.

I made no observations then or since on wisdom or opportuneness of this step. I have not seen text of treaty nor have I any other knowledge of its contents.

I have neither approved nor disapproved and if it is suggested that I have expressed any opinion favourable or the reverse you should contradict the report or call upon Serb-Croat-Slovene government to do so as you think best.

The Yugoslav Minister has asked me to receive him this afternoon. I shall speak to him in this sense.[5]

Tell M. Marincovic that I am always glad to see him and should be delighted to receive him here, but that in the interests of Yugoslavia I think he

---

[1] Not printed. This telegram referred to press reports that 'Great Britain regards conclusion of [Franco-Serb-Croat-Slovene] pact with satisfaction' and requested information on any communication made by or views expressed to French or Serb-Croat-Slovene representatives on the subject.

[2] See No. 34, note 2. The communication was made on November 7.

[3] No. 35.   [4] See No. 20.

[5] Sir A. Chamberlain recorded in his despatch No. 546 of November 9 to Belgrade that he had spoken to M. Diouritch as proposed and had asked him to express to M. Marinkovitch, who had already left Belgrade for Paris, the views in the paragraph below. Lord Crewe was also requested to make such a communication to M. Marinkovitch in telegram No. 247 to Paris of November 9.

would be unwise to visit me at this juncture, unless he is prepared to propose simultaneously to visit Signor Mussolini on his way home.

Addressed to Belgrade No. 121. Repeated to Paris No. 245 and Rome No. 259.

No. 38

Sir A. Chamberlain to Sir G. Grahame (Brussels)
No. 680 [C 9042/789/18]

FOREIGN OFFICE, *November 9, 1927*

Sir,

The Belgian Ambassador spoke to me to-day of the position of Belgium, now that she was no longer a member of the Council of the League, in regard to discussions on matters arising out of the Locarno Treaties. He said that this was a matter about which Belgium was particularly concerned since her disappointment at the time of the recent Council elections, and he intimated that it would be most agreeable to Belgium if Great Britain could take the lead in proposing a solution. His Excellency left with me the attached *aide-mémoire*[1] in which the views of the Belgian Government are embodied and where they appear to be expressed rather more clearly and explicitly than the Ambassador stated them.

I told him that I should like time to consider the question. As I listened to his exposition I had understood it to refer only to such conversations as have not infrequently taken place between the representatives of the Locarno Powers at Geneva. From a very hasty perusal of the *aide-mémoire* it would seem that the presence of Belgium at the Council is also envisaged, and the question obviously requires careful consideration and time for reflection.

I am, &c.,
AUSTEN CHAMBERLAIN

[1] Not printed. This *aide-mémoire* is printed in Ch. de Visscher and F. Vanlangenhove, *Documents Diplomatiques Belges 1920–1940* (Brussels, 1964), vol. ii, pp. 456–7.

No. 39

Mr. Kennard (Belgrade) to Sir A. Chamberlain (Received November 11, 9 a.m.)
No. 177 Telegraphic [C 9091/808/92]

BELGRADE, *November 10, 1927, 8.35 p.m.*

(? Rome telegram No. 196).[1]

Serb-Croat-Slovene minister at Rome reports that after expressing his thanks for communication regarding pact with France, Signor Mussolini opened conversation by stating that the moral détente which he had mentioned in their conversation last June[2] had unfortunately not been reached,

[1] Not printed. This telegram of November 9 stated in particular: 'Jugoslav Minister will have personal interview with Signor Mussolini tomorrow evening to inform him of pact with French.'　　　　　　　　　　[2] See Volume III, No. 254.

largely owing to attitude of Yugoslav press. It was not sufficient that he and Monsieur Marinkovic should desire better relations but moment must be awaited when present hatred between the masses of the two nations should have disappeared. Signor Mussolini added that friendship between Great Britain and Italy did not rest on any written agreement but on natural sympathy between the two peoples.

On Monsieur Rakic stating that press, which could not be controlled in Yugoslavia, did not represent the attitude of Serb-Croat-Slovene government, Signor Mussolini stood and conversation ended.[3]

Addressed to Foreign Office, repeated to Rome.

[3] Sir R. Graham reported on this conversation in Rome telegram No. 197 of November 10 in which he stated in particular: 'The conversation ended on a friendly note with which M. Rakic expressed himself well satisfied but he does not think the moment has yet come when general conversations could usefully be resumed or that it would be wise for M. Marinkovic to make a personal visit to Rome as he had thought of doing. I expressed my opinion that the sooner such a visit could take place the better as Signor Mussolini is so susceptible to personal influences.'

On November 11 Sir R. Graham replied, in Rome telegram No. 199, to Foreign Office telegram No. 261 (see No. 35, note 2) referring to his telegram No. 196 as giving a partial explanation, and adding: 'Signor Mussolini holds to his statement that he is always ready to receive M. Rakic but His Excellency does not consider the atmosphere of moral detente between the two countries which is indispensable for a successful prosecution of more general conversations has yet been reached. M. Rakic after his recent interview with His Excellency is inclined to share this view and fears that any mention of Albania might lead to an immediate deadlock.'

No. 40

The Marquess of Crewe (Paris) to Sir A. Chamberlain
(Received November 11, 8.30 a.m.)

No. 228 Telegraphic: by bag [*C 9056/808/92*]

PARIS, *November 10, 1927*

Your telegram No. 247,[1] and your telegram No. 121 to Belgrade.[2]

M. Marinkovic reached Paris this morning, and I sent at once to offer to call on him to-day at his own time, but he preferred to come here this afternoon, and was accompanied by the Serb-Croat-Slovene Minister.[3] He began speaking at once about his conversation with Mr. Kennard described in Belgrade telegram to Foreign Office, No. 175,[4] putting the points to me in much the same terms as those in which he spoke to His Majesty's Minister. He added that M. Rakić was to have an interview with Mussolini yesterday evening or this morning, but he had received no details of this as yet. He hoped to be able to send me some particulars of this in the course of tomorrow. Speaking of the character of the conversations, he repeated that, in his view, they ought to cover the entire history of the last four years, each topic on which there might be a difference of opinion coming under consideration in order of date. In this manner the Treaty of Tirana might be touched on not

[1] See No. 37, note 5.   [2] No. 37.   [3] M. Spalaikovitch.   [4] No. 35.

as a subject of complaint, because Yugoslavia does not complain of it, but in order to get an authentic interpretation of its real bearing as understood at Rome. He remembered that, with regard to your conversations with Mussolini at Leghorn, you had been assured that the independence of Albania is completely respected under the Treaty,[5] but this is exactly the point on which his government would like a first-hand assurance if one may be got.

As to the Convention of Nettuno, M. Marinkovic is prepared to propose its ratification, but he wished to mention two points about this instrument. In the first place, he thought it unreasonable that M. Rakić should open the proceedings by a promise to ratify, because this would be making a preliminary concession to Italian opinion, which might simply be accepted without anything being offered in return. In the second place, he wanted the suggestion for ratification to be simply made in the course of conversation by his Minister as coming direct from his government, and not to appear to have been inspired by the French or British Governments. It would fall naturally into its place as a satisfaction of one of the complaints which the Italian government would probably make. He himself was particularly anxious to deal with this matter, because he was afraid that the Italian government, while recognising the goodwill of the Yugoslav government, believed that the latter were too weak to force an unpopular instrument through the Assembly. He must dissipate this misapprehension, not believing that the Assembly would think of rejecting the Convention, out of which Yugoslavia has as much to gain as Italy.

The Minister proceeded to say something about his hope of visiting London, in order to explain fully the situation. I put to him the consideration mentioned in the last paragraph of your telegram No. 121 to Belgrade, at which he looked a little blank, but I found a rather unexpected ally in M. Spalaikovic, who dreaded that Italy would consider herself slighted if Rome were left out, and that the success of the conversations might be prejudiced. M. Marinkovic began by saying that there were plenty of reasons for going both to Paris and London, where the Yugoslav Ministers had been in continual communication with the respective Foreign Offices, whereas M. Rakic had not been to the Consulta[6] since last June. But after a little more conversation he observed that if he went to Rome now there would really be nothing to talk about, until the detailed conversations were completely under way. So that his wiser plan would be to go direct from Belgrade to Rome, not waiting for the conclusion of the negotiations, but for their being fairly started, when he ought to be able to insure their success. I asked whether, in this case, he proposed announcing at once his visit to Rome, even though it did not take place on his journey homeward, in order to prevent the misapprehension there of which you foresee the probability. The Yugoslav Minister also approved of this, and M. Marinkovic was prepared to inform

---

5 See Volume II, Nos. 235 and 255. A marginal note by Mr. Sargent here read: 'There is a confusion. The Treaty was not signed until after the Leghorn meeting & we had been given no information at that time with regard to it.'

6 The Italian Ministry of Foreign Affairs, located in the Palazzo Chigi.

Signor Mussolini of his intentions as early as possible, though he did not suggest making any public announcement of them.

I said that I would at once inform you of his wishes and views, and I shall be grateful if you can let me know in the course of tomorrow what you feel about the journey to London, in the light of these statements. I fear that M. Marinkovic will be greatly disappointed if you say that you are unable to see him.

In conclusion the Minister spoke of his intended statement on Italian relations in the Chamber at Belgrade. He hoped that by about the 24th of this month he might be able to give a day for the interpellation on Foreign Affairs, though almost all parliamentary days are taken up with the Budget. I asked whether there is a favourable atmosphere in the Chamber for a friendly understanding with Italy, and he said he was sure that a considerable majority of members would support any movement in this direction, so that for this reason he would develop his reply in a form to cover as much ground as possible, employing a friendly tone towards Italy throughout.

The subject of the Franco-Serbian Treaty was not touched on either by the Minister or by myself.

No. 41

Sir A. Chamberlain to the Marquess of Crewe (Paris)
No. 249 Telegraphic: by telephone [C 9056/808/92]

FOREIGN OFFICE, November 11, 1927, 5.50 p.m.

Your Lordship's telegram No. 228[1] (of November 10th. Franco-Serb pact).

Please inform Monsieur Marinkovic of my satisfaction on learning of his intention to proceed with the discussions at Rome, and of the lines on which he proposes to conduct them. I regret that he does not see his way to visiting Rome before returning to Belgrade, but this being so, much as I would like to see him in London, I remain of the opinion that in the circumstances it would be wiser that he should not risk arousing misunderstandings by coming to see me at the present juncture.

I think I am quite 'au courant' with the situation and Serb-Croat-Slovene Minister and Mr. Kennard keep me fully and constantly informed. I appreciate his difficulties but I am convinced that if he comes here now without first announcing publicly that he will visit Rome on his way home, he will prejudice success of the conversations between Monsieur Rakic and Monsieur Mussolini. It would be to my mind insufficient merely to inform the Italian government that he will visit Rome *if* the conversations develop favourably.

I would also deprecate a visit by His Excellency just now for the reason that it might arouse suspicions in Bulgaria and thus weaken the effect of my good offices in the Macedonian question.[2]

[1] No. 40.

[2] In connection with the murder of General Kovachevitch (see No. 26, note 1) Sir A. Chamberlain had instructed H.M. Chargé d'Affaires at Sofia, in Foreign Office telegram

I feel convinced that more harm than good would come out of such a visit owing to the wrong interpretation being placed upon it both in Rome and Sofia.[3]

No. 30 to Sofia of October 8, to urge the Bulgarian Government to co-operate with the Serb-Croat-Slovene Government to put an end to the violence. Further instructions for strong representations were sent to Sir W. Erskine, H.M. Minister at Sofia, in Foreign Office telegram No. 36 of October 23. Foreign Office telegrams Nos. 109 and 113 to Belgrade of October 8 and 23 respectively authorised Mr. Kennard to inform the Serb-Croat-Slovene Government of the instructions to Sofia and to urge them to preserve patience.

[3] Lord Crewe reported in Paris telegram No. 230 of November 12 that he had acted on these instructions, and that M. Marinkovitch would return to Belgrade on November 13 or 14. The treaty of friendly understanding between France and the Serb-Croat-Slovene State signed in Paris on November 11 would be registered with the League of Nations after ratification. This treaty, together with the arbitration convention signed the same day, is printed in *British and Foreign State Papers*, vol. 127, pp. 500–7.

No. 42

Sir A. Chamberlain to Mr. Kennard (Belgrade)
No. 555 [C 9184/808/92]

FOREIGN OFFICE, *November 11, 1927*

Sir,

The Jugoslav Minister reported to me this afternoon M. Marinkovitch's answer to my last communication in the same sense and in much the same terms as I had already learnt it by telegram from Lord Crewe.[1]

I told M. Diouritch that it would have been a great pleasure to receive M. Marinkovitch in London, and that I should still be very pleased to receive him if he felt able to announce publicly before coming here that he would visit Rome on his way home. If, as M. Diouritch had indicated, he thought that for reasons of Jugoslav internal policy it was not wise that he should go to Rome at this moment, I did not desire to contest that view. That depended upon conditions of which M. Marinkovitch must be much better informed than I was myself, but I remained convinced that for him to come here without visiting Rome in the course of this journey would be to increase the difficulties of the Jugoslav-Italian conversations and to lessen my usefulness if indeed my good offices should be required again at any time during those conversations. It was because I so earnestly desired the success of those conversations that I deprecated the visit on any other conditions, and in order that my reasons might be perfectly clear to him and to M. Marinkovitch I handed him an *aide-mémoire* in which they were embodied.

M. Diouritch then asked whether he might speak to me quite personally and as man to man—a formula which always causes me a little anxiety though it is difficult to refuse to admit it. Being permitted to proceed, M. Diouritch said that he had always contended that in the issues pending between Jugoslavia and Italy I had been impartial and that my policy had been what I had declared it to him to be. He might now admit that there

[1] No. 40.

was a time when his Government had not given credence to his statements and suspected that I had undertaken some engagement to Signor Mussolini which I had not disclosed, but my conversation with M. Marinkovitch at Geneva[2] had produced a great effect upon that gentleman and had re-established M. Diouritch's credit with his own Government. M. Marinkovitch now believed that there was little difference between the objects which he was pursuing and my attitude as I had explained it to him, and he was therefore the more anxious to obtain and be guided by my advice. It was for this reason that he had so much desired an opportunity of speaking with me again.

I said that, although M. Diouritch had begun by asking leave to speak to me as man to man, what I was about to say to him I said as Secretary of State to the Minister. If at any time his Government again suspected that I had signed a treaty or undertaken an engagement which I had not disclosed to Parliament, he might deny it on my authority and say that I had offered to him that assurance. I added that in these days no Foreign Minister in this country could venture to make secret engagements or undertake secret obligations. Not only would it be contrary to the pledges I had given to Parliament, but Parliament would not regard itself as bound to implement an engagement which had been concealed from it.

M. Diouritch said that he personally fully appreciated this fact, and it was the knowledge of it that had given him confidence when his Government doubted the accuracy of his information and suspected that he had come too much under English influence.

In the course of the conversation, I took occasion to pay a tribute to the moderation and restraint which M. Marinkovitch had shown in his handling of the situation arising from the recent recrudescence of the Macedonian agitation and murder campaign. I said that I had watched M. Marin-kovitch's conduct with great interest and appreciation, that just as I had urged moderation upon him I had urged the Bulgarian Government to give proper satisfaction, and as I saw M. Marinkovitch persisting in his policy of restraint I had felt authorised to redouble my effort at Sofia to secure that the Bulgarian Government took action appropriate to the circumstances. I was glad to be able to tell him that the latest information which I had received from Sir William Erskine was to the effect that the Bulgarian Government had removed all dangerous komitajis out of the district between the right bank of the Struma and the frontier, that the Bulgarian Government's plan was making satisfactory progress and that further steps would be taken shortly.

I am, &c.,

AUSTEN CHAMBERLAIN

ENCLOSURE IN NO. 42

Aide-mémoire

The great object I have in view in interesting myself in the relations between Yugoslavia and Italy is that I may be able to use my good offices to

[2] See No. 1.

assist both Governments to arrive at a general agreement. Without wishing to discuss in any way the merits of the Treaty recently concluded between Yugoslavia and France, I cannot but observe with regret that its conclusion has produced a most unfortunate effect in Italy and is likely in itself to render more difficult M. Mussolini's task of reaching a general settlement with Yugoslavia. M. Marinković's visit to Paris has given a still wider publicity to this Treaty and has accentuated the irritation in Italy. If in these circumstances M. Marinković came to London to see me without publicly announcing that he is also visiting Rome before his return to Belgrade, I feel convinced that public opinion in Italy would at once draw the most undesirable conclusions, with the result that the success of the forthcoming conversations between M. Rakić and M. Mussolini would be prejudiced, and I would find considerable difficulty in continuing to assist in maintaining contact between the Yugoslav and Italian Governments. Although, therefore, I should much like to see M. Marinković in London, I still am of the opinion that it would be wiser at the present juncture that he should abstain from coming here unless he also visits Rome before returning to Belgrade.

It has been suggested that if M. Marinković does not see his way to visit Rome before his return to Belgrade, he would nevertheless be prepared to go there when the forthcoming discussions between M. Rakić and M. Mussolini have further progressed. I feel, however, that even an announcement to this effect would not be sufficient to counteract the unfortunate impression which a visit to London would produce at the present juncture.

No. 43

Sir W. Max Muller (Warsaw) to Sir A. Chamberlain (Received November 21)
No. 499 [N 5469/23/55]

WARSAW, *November 16, 1927*

Sir,

I have the honour to transmit herewith a short memorandum by Mr Leeper[1] on his first impressions of the changes wrought in Poland during the three years that have elapsed since his former tenure of office here. Though obviously after less than a fortnight spent in Warsaw Mr Leeper has not had sufficient opportunities for forming a final judgment on so intricate a subject, I considered that it might be of interest to you to learn the first impressions of an intelligent and informed observer who had made a close study of Poland in an earlier stage of her post-war development.

2. I do not propose to canvass any of Mr Leeper's remarks, with most of which I am in full agreement, but as one who has lived on the spot during the three years of Mr Leeper's absence I venture to express the opinion that if Mr Leeper had returned to Poland eighteen months ago he would not have found it possible to write as he does about the improved conditions of the

---

[1] Not printed. The gist of this memorandum by Mr. R. A. Leeper, who had recently been appointed First Secretary in H.M. Legation at Warsaw, is indicated below.

country, both external and internal. The improvement, which is patent to every one, not only in material aspects but also in public efficiency and prosperity and in the spirit of the people, dates from shortly after the *coup d'état* of May, 1926, and must be ascribed in large measure, if not entirely, to the driving power of Marshal Pilsudski and to the fear and respect inspired by his name.

3. There is much truth in Mr Leeper's remark that the Poles have recovered confidence in themselves. This tendency, of course, has its good side, but if carried too far, has in it also the germs of future trouble and I fully endorse what Mr Leeper writes as to the necessity for other nations to reckon with this tendency in their relations with the Poles. We have hitherto been wont in our dealings with the Polish Government to adopt a patronizing and superior air, to read lectures on the right course to pursue, and to expect them to follow our advice, such advice being given with the best intentions in the world, but often without due regard to its possible effect on the immediate interests of Poland as they appear to the vast majority of Poles. I fear that if we are to maintain such influence as we still possess here, these methods will have to be modified, and we must learn to pay as much attention to the practical interests and political aspirations of Poland as we do, for instance, to those of Italy.

4. What Mr Leeper writes as to the changed attitude of Poles towards foreigners, and especially I would add towards diplomatists, has much truth in it. When I arrived here seven years ago the three allied Ministers exercised a powerful influence in the councils of the Government. So far as we ourselves were concerned the policy of His Majesty's Government was very unpopular, but the Poles still recognised that they were under a great debt of gratitude to us and that our advice, though frequently unpalatable, was given in their own best interests, and they were keenly desirous of our assistance in overcoming the many difficulties, both political and economic, still confronting them.

5. All this has changed now, foreign representatives, even those of the Great Powers, are seen to be but fallible mortals and, though successive foreign ministers, who invariably belong to what Mr Leeper describes as the cosmopolitan type of Pole, receive our admonitions with proper courtesy and attention, our advice, and even our threats uttered in the name of our Governments, no longer carry such weight with the Polish Government as they did, especially since Marshal Pilsudski became the dominant factor in shaping the policy of this country. Even the French influence, in spite of the frantic efforts of the French Government to maintain it, is not what it was. Certainly the Poles regard their alliance with France as the foundation of their foreign policy, but they look now on the French as their equals, not as their protectors, and they even begin to forget that they owe to French counsels and French work the very instrument with which they mean to defend their independence. Before long the French Military Mission is likely to be a thing of the past, and Marshal Pilsudski and his brother generals will persuade themselves that the Polish army is a child of their own creation.

6. The last few days have provided a fresh illustration of this tendency on the part of the Poles to forget what they owe to the armies of the allied Powers.

During the first years of my residence here Armistice Day, so far as the Poles were concerned, was only observed by a public gathering to which the representatives of the allied Powers were invited in order to listen to speeches of gratitude and devotion. Since last year the programme has been changed, and November 11th has become a day of rejoicing for the liberation of Poland from the German occupation and of glorification of the part played in this achievement by Marshal Pilsudski and the armed forces which he had created. All reference to the share of the allied Powers in bringing about this happy consummation is avoided, and this year the newspapers actually ascribed the principal merit for these historic events to the foresight, courage and organizing power of Marshal Pilsudski.

7. I could quote other instances to prove this growth of exaggerated self-confidence among the Poles and their determination to be treated as equals by other nations, even by the great Powers to whom they owe their very existence as an independent country, but I feel that I have written enough to prove the truth of what Mr Leeper writes as to the effect of the moral influence exercised by Marshal Pilsudski in strengthening the self-reliance of his fellow-countrymen and encouraging them to think and act for themselves in an emergency even at the risk of alienating the sympathies of other nations.

I have, &c.,

W. G. MAX MULLER

No. 44

Letter from Sir W. Tyrrell to Sir R. Lindsay (Berlin)
[*C 9242/857/18*]

Private   FOREIGN OFFICE, *November 17, 1927*

My dear Ronald,

I am so sorry that we are not at present able to send you any official views as regards the situation created by Parker Gilbert's memorandum to the German Government,[1] but the Treasury are not anxious to commit themselves very far for the time being. Meantime, however, I send you for your information copy of a memorandum they have submitted on the subject to the Prime Minister and Chancellor of the Exchequer. If there are any particular points on which you would like further enlightenment let me know and I will try and obtain the information you need.

You will observe our anxiety that you should 'dry nurse' Gilbert.

I am quite sure that nobody can do it more successfully than you and occasionally you may be able to whisper to him the magic word 'watch your step'.

Yrs ever

W. TYRRELL

P.S. If you desire any further information, please let me know & I will 'tap' the Treasury, but perhaps you know more than they do.

W. T.

---

[1] See No. 24, note 5.

Memorandum by Sir R. Hopkins[2] (Treasury)

Copy

A short time ago Mr. Parker Gilbert, Agent General for Reparations, called to see the Prime Minister and discussed with him a draft of a memorandum which he proposed to present to the German Government. He had already shown the draft to Monsieur Poincaré and he presented the document a few days later.

The memorandum comments on the dangers which Mr. Gilbert sees in the present economic situation in Germany and the tendencies of public finance and credit policy. He indicated the need of a halt in public expenditure and public borrowing, and, in regard to credit the need of a properly coordinated policy between the central bank and the finances of the state.

The fact that the memorandum was being presented became known to the Press. It is understood that the German Government did their best to avoid publication and open discussion but were unsuccessful. The memorandum has now been published together with a long reply by the German Government. This reply, the text of which will very shortly be available, appears to be conciliatory in tone; and to that extent, although before the Germans replied the British Ambassador thought a fall of the Government might be possible, the indications for the moment are that the situation will not become acute.

The wide publicity which the matter has had raises the question whether action is called for on the part of the British Government. The Agent General acts in these matters as seems right to him but I think the interests of this country would be best served if his present representations are not pursued too far nor lightly renewed in the immediate future. The in-flow of foreign capital to Germany has rendered possible the transfer of reparations from that country and its abrupt cessation at the present time would be correspondingly unfortunate. Nor would it be in our interest to have any serious issues raised as to the meaning or efficacy of the Dawes Plan prior to the French elections.

I have taken counsel with Sir William Tyrrell and he concurs in the following views.

Although formally the Agent General is appointed by the Reparation Commission, his position following the general understanding of the London Conference[3] is a quite unique and exceptional one, nor would a man of Mr. Gilbert's ability have accepted the post otherwise. There is neither occasion for, nor utility in, seeking to bring compulsion to bear upon him through the Reparation Commission by asking him to report to them prior to further action. Such a request, if pressed, might only lead to Mr. Gilbert's resignation, which in my opinion would be a very grave misfortune. Our touch should be maintained through the Ambassador in Berlin who already sees Mr. Gilbert

[2] Controller of Finance and Supply Services in H.M. Treasury.
[3] Of 1924.

as occasion requires and his influence should, I think, be directed in friendly conversation towards composing the situation.

At the same time we should prepare for eventualities. On the American side we have to consider the possibility of an abrupt cessation of loans and even an insistent call for repayment of loans, if public opinion should get too much alarmed. The presence of an American as Agent General affords security against the occurrence of such a panic, especially given the personality of the present holder of the office and the high regard he enjoys.

There is also the possibility of the French Government getting alarmed at the prospect of a break-down of transfers under the Dawes Plan and proposing to take action in order to secure their continuance. As stated above we need not reasonably expect such a move until after the May elections. We should then be prepared with a scheme or a policy which should enable us to persuade the French to let us take the lead in any negotiations that may be necessary to give effect to the French view then expressed. This seems the best method of preventing the possibility of repetition of the Ruhr experience.

I ought to mention that Lord Blanesburgh, the British Representative on the Reparation Commission, heard indirectly of Mr. Gilbert's consultation with the Prime Minister, and was upset that he had not been called into conference. I suggest that Sir Warren Fisher[4] and I be authorised by the Prime Minister to see Lord Blanesburgh and get the matter into its proper and harmonious perspective.

R. V. N. Hopkins

9/XI

[4] Permanent Secretary of H.M. Treasury.

No. 45

The Marquess of Crewe (Paris) to Sir A. Chamberlain
(Received November 19)

No. 2301 [*W 10719/1182/17*]

PARIS, *November 18, 1927*

Sir,

I have the honour to forward herewith the signed original together with one copy of the Military Attaché's despatch Serial No: 53, No: 6499, addressed to myself on the 16th of November. I have informed the Military Attaché that while in great part the despatch deals with purely military matters, and that a further copy of it is properly sent to the Director of Military Intelligence, there are some passages, such as those dealing with the perusal of papers of all political parties and speeches made by French Ministers, which come near to contravening the instructions contained in his letter of appointment, forbidding the compilation of any political report.[1] Colonel Needham has assured me that it was far from his intention to

[1] In minutes on this despatch in the Western Department of the Foreign Office, views were expressed which were not in entire agreement with Lord Crewe on this point.

infringe this rule in any way, or to forward any expression of opinion on political matters to the military authorities.

2. I observed with no little surprise the statement, understood to be corroborated by the Air Attaché, who is absent on leave at the moment, that while our officers receive every mark of kindness and attention in their private relations with their French comrades, on public occasions they have to submit to treatment which can only be described as slighting. Since in paragraph 4 of his despatch Colonel Needham says that he can cite specific instances of this, I have asked him to give some particulars, and from these it would appear that on at least two occasions French officers of high rank, with whom he is on very friendly terms in private, treated him with marked coldness in comparison with some officers belonging to other nations. It is hardly to be expected that Colonel Needham, although previously well acquainted with many French officers of distinction, can enjoy quite the same relations of personal intimacy with them as did his predecessors Major-General Sir Charles Sackville West, and Major-General Sidney Clive,[2] who happened to have been brought into the closest connection with the French army both during the War and immediately afterwards; but, from Colonel Needham's account, the attitude of French officers went beyond anything that could be explained by this. I confess that I am entirely unable to account for this state of things, which is in singular contrast to that which I myself, and the whole staff of the Embassy, experience on all occasions, public as well as private, when we meet our friends and acquaintances of the French Services.

3. I drew Colonel Needham's attention to the statement in the 4th paragraph of his despatch, that he is led to think that, for some reason, there is a concerted plan to avoid public contact and to minimise our war exploits in France, and asked him if he really meant that the officers in the high command are combined in a wish to depreciate their British comrades, and to do so in public. I added that in my opinion the facts pointed in exactly the opposite direction if any coolness is displayed on public occasions. It can hardly be disputed that general public opinion in France has from time to time been irritated by an excessive assertion, expressed or implied, on the part played by the British Empire in the War. It has been assumed that we took up arms because Belgium's neutrality had been violated, that we came to the rescue of France, and that without us she would have lost the War. This is no doubt true, but it is far from being the whole truth. Some of us recognised at the time, and many more have become aware since, that, if we had stood aside in 1914, and the Germans had become the undoubted masters of Europe, our turn would have come next, even to the point of our probably losing command of the sea. One may be sure that not a few Frenchmen also feel this, and would resent our being represented as simply the saviours of France.

4. In addition to this, there is the feeling here that Britain is the rich country and France the poor one, and that British people have not always been careful in concealing their superiority in this respect, apart from the

[2] Military Attachés in H.M. Embassy at Paris, 1920–4 and 1924–7, respectively.

burden of debt, though here, in comparison with the United States, we may even acquire a slight degree of merit. But, with regard to the ceremonies of which the Military Attaché speaks, at War Memorials etc., I feel that the multiplication of these occasions has an exactly opposite effect to that which we should all desire. They are numerous and in some cases more costly than anything which it is possible for French liberality or charity to provide; and the ceremonials at which they are dedicated are naturally devoted rather to the particular forces which are commemorated than to France and the French. I am glad to know that Sir Fabian Ware, the competent and respected chief of the [Imperial] War Graves Commission, entirely shares my view on this subject, and that he has done his best to limit the number of these Memorials. Personally, I have always regretted that, bearing in mind the fact that the destruction of the manhood and youth of France was considerably greater than that of the whole British Empire, and that a number of her finest Departments were laid waste, England did not erect at some appropriate point in London or at Aldershot a monument after the manner of our Cenotaph in honour of the French Army. No doubt it is far too late now to offer any such suggestion.

5. The foregoing observations explain my meaning in saying that if any coolness is shown on public occasions to British military representatives, it is in no way due to the machinations of leading French Generals or French politicians, but must represent the half-conscious deference to the opinion of Frenchmen generally. The Military Attaché told me that he believed that this is so, and that he did not intend to imply that an example of indifference is being set by those in authority. In conclusion I can only hope that the instances adduced by Colonel Needham are altogether isolated, and even that his appreciation of them may have been in some degree the result of misunderstanding.

I have, &c.,
CREWE

ENCLOSURE IN No. 45

Colonel Needham to the Marquess of Crewe (Paris)

Serial No. 53. No. 6499

Confidential   PARIS, *November 16, 1927*

My Lord,

I beg to bring the following matter to Your Excellency's notice.

Since my arrival here in May last, it has been my custom to endeavour to try to gauge the general atmosphere as regards Franco-British relations, especially the French attitude towards our Army. A good many opportunities have come my way of doing so, e.g. conversations with all sorts of officers and others, official discussions, ceremonies of all natures, perusal of papers of all political parties and of a technical nature, and interviews in connection with my normal office work.

The net result of my observations, which incidentally are corroborated by the Air Attaché, is that where direct contact is concerned, all French officers from Marshal Foch[3] to the junior cadet at St. Cyr are friendly, helpful, and well aware of what they owe us and fully appreciate our work and losses in the war.

On the other hand, a very careful study of the attitude of the senior officers of the Army, even of personal friends like Marshal Foch, Generals Debeney, Gouraud and Weygand[4] on public occasions, leads me to think that for some reason there is a concerted plan to avoid public contact and to minimise our war exploits in France. Whereas in private, in addition to obtaining all the information we require, and being treated with great civility and indeed preferentially to others, in public the reverse is the case to an almost painful degree, occasionally to the point of rudeness. I can cite specific cases of this.

In all the speeches I have heard made by Ministers or Generals, especially in the Nord and Pas de Calais, where our armies exercised a preponderating influence in the war, the speakers have invariably laboriously misrepresented the facts of the case and attributed all allied successes and reliefs to the French and Belgians.

The French press invariably backs up this attitude, and deliberately cuts out or hides any reference to our war action, our losses, or our representation at public functions. The repercussion on the general public is that the un-educated bulk of the population know little or nothing about the assistance rendered to France by Great Britain in the war.

I only forward this memorandum to Your Excellency as I feel convinced that this attitude is not spontaneous, but engineered for some special purpose, e.g. that the population at large should be unaware of France's moral obligations to us and the fact that she owes her very existence to our war efforts. Although the political utility of such an impression is not difficult to gauge, it appears to be a peculiarly foolish attitude to pursue in view of the fact that France must always be largely dependent on us or on our benevolent neutrality in case of European or indeed of any war in which she is implicated.

I have, &c.,
H. NEEDHAM

[3] President of the Allied Military Committee of Versailles (cf. Volume I, No. 1, note 10).
[4] General Debeney was Chief of the General Staff of the French Army; General Gouraud was Military Governor of Paris; General Weygand, a former chief of staff to Marshal Foch, was director of the Centre des hautes études militaires.

No. 46

Sir A. Chamberlain to Mr. Kennard (Belgrade)
No. 127 Telegraphic [C 9277/808/92]

FOREIGN OFFICE, *November 19, 1927, 6.45 p.m.*

Your telegram No. 179[1] (of November 17th).

The Italian Ambassador informed Sir William Tyrrell on November 16th that Signor Mussolini feared the effect in Yugoslavia of the conclusion of the

[1] Not printed.

treaty between France and that country. It might, in his opinion, considerably increase the influence of the military party which surrounded the King and encourage the megalomania of Yugoslavia. Such a state of mind might, M. Mussolini considered, develop into a great danger to peace. In support of this view, Italian Ambassador quoted the recent anti-Italian manifestations in various parts of Yugoslavia and expressed the fear that the Yugoslav government, although they had taken steps to deal with these demonstrations, would not be able to continue to pursue a policy of moderation in view of their public opinion.

In reply the Ambassador was informed that we had looked upon the signature of some such treaty as inevitable since M. Briand had inherited it from his predecessor. On the other hand M. Briand was a guarantee that no improper use would be made of it. In fact since this treaty had been signed, any exaggerated hopes which might have been raised in Yugoslavia would have been turned to disappointment, since this treaty would add considerable weight to the moderating advice which we felt sure the French government would give at Belgrade.

Lastly, Sir William Tyrrell expressed the view that the signature of this treaty had made it more than ever the task of the Foreign Ministers of Great Britain, France and Italy to work for peace in the Balkans and that I had witnessed here with great satisfaction the successful efforts made by M. Mussolini to calm public opinion in his own country and the statesmanlike attitude adopted by him in regard to this treaty.[2]

On November 18th Serb-Croat-Slovene Minister called to express regret of Serb-Croat-Slovene Minister for Foreign Affairs that he could not come to London, and then asked whether I thought Serb-Croat-Slovene Minister at Rome ought at once to start negotiations with Italy for general settlement. I replied that frankly I could not advise an immediate commencement of the negotiations. The signature of the treaty, the advertisement given to it by visit of the Serb-Croat-Slovene Minister for Foreign Affairs to Paris, the emphatic and exaggerated statements of its importance in Yugoslav press, street demonstrations etc. had undoubtedly increased difficulties in way of any negotiations. But I did think Serb-Croat-Slovene Minister for Foreign Affairs would be wise to make friendly statement in Skupshtina as he proposed and emphasize his desire for better relations with Italy. I do *not* deprecate a conversation between M. Rakic and M. Mussolini following on a friendly public declaration by Serb-Croat-Slovene Minister for Foreign Affairs if it is only for the purpose of repeating and emphasizing the declaration, but I cannot advise attempt at resumption of negotiations in view of altered circumstances. I added that at the moment I doubted if I could be of any more use. It would not do for me to address any communication to Rome at the moment. Serb-Croat-Slovene Minister for Foreign Affairs must himself allay irritation at Rome and prepare the way for negotiations and when the time comes for them he must in my view if they are to have any chance of success

[2] For an account of this conversation by Signor Bordonaro see *I Documenti Diplomatici Italiani*, Settima Serie, vol. v, No. 558.

make a real advance such as promising that he is ready to make a solid contribution such as ratification of Nettuno conventions.

Serb-Croat-Slovene Minister appeared to think that because I had criticised policy of Serb-Croat-Slovene government I failed to appreciate their difficulties and causes of complaint given by Italy. To this I replied that if I did criticise Serb-Croat-Slovene government this did not mean that I advocated policy of Italian government. If Italian government had consulted me I might have made similar criticisms to them; but they had not and all I could do was sometimes to use my good offices to explain any misunderstandings and so forth in order to promote settlement of differences. He must clearly understand that I could take no responsibility for Italian policy or attempt to control it in any way.

Serb-Croat-Slovene Minister asked whether I could not now let Rome know that no unfriendly intention should be inferred from fact that Serb-Croat-Slovene Minister for Foreign Affairs had not visited Rome and that his sole reason for not going was fear of a rebuff. I said that I did not think the moment was propitious for any intervention on my part but that I would inform His Majesty's Ambassador at Rome who would decide whether it would be wise to say anything to M. Mussolini.

Please speak to Serb-Croat-Slovene Minister for Foreign Affairs in above sense making it clear that if he wishes my advice I counsel:—

(1) a friendly statement by him in the Skupshtina; this is all the more essential in view of Italian excitement (see Rome telegram No. 203);[3]

(2) no resumption of *negotiations* at Rome at present;

(3) courage to make a real solid offer when negotiations do begin.[4]

Addressed to Belgrade No. 127 and repeated to Rome No. 262.

[3] Not printed. This telegram of November 18 reported on demonstrations in Italy in reaction to Italophobe demonstrations in Belgrade, and on 'a decidedly violent communiqué . . . published in the orders of the day of the Fascist party'; cf. *The Times*, November 19, 1927, p. 14. Sir R. Graham stated that he was endeavouring to meet Signor Grandi 'to see if something cannot be done to damp down this sort of thing; otherwise both sides will get more and more worked up'.

[4] Mr. Kennard reported in Belgrade telegram No. 181 of November 23 (not printed) on the conversation on November 22 with M. Marinkovitch in which he carried out these instructions.

No. 47

Mr. Seeds[1] (Durazzo) to Sir A. Chamberlain
(Received November 20, 7.10 p.m.)
No. 80 Telegraphic [*C 9307/25/90*]

State[2]   DURAZZO, *November 20, 1927, 1.20 p.m.*

My French colleague[3] informed me last night that President of the Republic[4] has admitted to Serb-Croat-Slovene Minister that he is being strongly

[1] H.M. Minister at Durazzo.   [2] A designation of extreme urgency.
[3] Baron de Vaux.   [4] Ahmed Zogu Bey.

urged by Italy to sign immediately a secret Military Convention of which French Minister had apparently heard rumour from Paris. French information is to the effect that Convention covers co-operation in war and contains promises of territorial compensation to Albania in that event. Serb-Croat-Slovene Minister naturally urged President not to sign and French Minister has asked for audience with the same object.

French Minister pressed me earnestly to take similar action at once on the ground that British advice alone would give President sufficient courage to resist Italian demands and so avoid a most serious international complication. I said that Convention of which I knew absolutely nothing might only concern terms of employment of Italian officers here and though I realised the possible dangers, there seemed no need for me to take immediate action for the present as I had recently happened to give the President a personal warning on general grounds to abstain from any startling actions calculated to rouse Serb alarms.[5] French Minister said that much more than Serb alarm was at stake but I stuck to my point of view.

Italian Minister has just returned from a flying visit to Rome and was most reticent when I tried to sound him later without actually mentioning French scare.

I did not tell either French or Italian Ministers that when I saw the President on November 14th His Excellency who was ill and worried asked me whether he should continue, intensify, or radically change his policy. I answered vaguely that the policy had given peace and prosperity to Albania but I added the above mentioned warning.

It is now a year since the Tirana treaty was sprung on us and I earnestly hope that Italians are not preparing a similar stroke now to counteract the effect of the Franco Serbian Treaty.

Addressed to Foreign Office No. 80, November 20th, repeated to Rome and Belgrade.

[5] Mr. Seeds had reported on his interview on November 14 with Ahmed Zogu Bey in Durazzo despatch No. 159 of November 16.

No. 48

Sir R. Graham (Rome) to Sir A. Chamberlain
(Received November 21, 9.20 a.m.)
No. 205 Telegraphic [C 9324/4490/92]

ROME, *November 20, 1927, 7 p.m.*

My telegram No. 203.[1]

I asked Signor Grandi whether Italian government considered the pact[2] of sufficient gravity to warrant intense resentment which it appeared to have aroused here. He replied in the negative saying that pact had been in the air for a long time and although it went perhaps a little beyond the form of recent

[1] See No. 46, note 3.
[2] The treaty between France and the Serb-Croat-Slovene State.

pacts of the same kind yet no serious exception could be taken to its terms. It was unfortunate that French government which had refused to sign when Italo-Yugo-Slav relations were on a good footing, should have chosen this moment to do so when these relations were decidedly more strained. It was of some comfort to note the uneasiness in French press on the subject, further that Monsieur Briand in order to secure ratification had felt obliged to make a false statement to his committee for foreign affairs when he alleged that negotiations for Italian participation were proceeding (? when) there were no such negotiations and Monsieur Briand knew perfectly well that Italy would never enter into a pact which was not only contrary to the spirit of Locarno but would reduce her to role of a French tool in the Balkans. The French would no doubt say that Monsieur Marinkovic had insisted on immediate signature of the pact in order to reinforce position of his government. This reason might pass muster but what had aroused deep suspicion and resentment here had been the way in which the pact was received at Belgrade with a chorus of jubilation and Italophobia. Yet Italian press had maintained its correct and moderate attitude.

I agreed but pointed out that the same could not be said of recent Fascist order of the day[1] which could only be described as insulting to Yugoslavia. I was not aware how far such pronouncements emanated from Italian government but it distressed me to see Italian diplomacy, at moments when Italy enjoyed general European sympathy and had all the cards in her hands, throw those cards deliberately away. It was obvious how much capital the anti-Fascist foreign press could make of such an order, accusing Italy of an aggressive and warlike spirit. Signor Grandi replied that such ideas were ridiculous. Italy had her hands far too full with internal economic problems to dream of war. The order in question did not emanate from the government but was written by Turati[3] and was one needless[4] paragraph in the Fascist order of the day. He was not sure whether Signor Mussolini had seen it but thought it unlikely as His Excellency would never have passed the unfortunate comparison to 'An Austria of the Hapsburgs'. At the same time it must be remembered that Italy also had her internal difficulties to meet. For the past four months she had been exposed to an unexampled campaign of mud-slinging by the whole Yugoslav press unchecked by Belgrade government. She was accused of organising murders, the honour and chivalry of her marine officers were impugned and even the King was insulted. But Italian press had not been allowed to make any reply. This had caused deep dissatisfaction and accusations of cowardice against the government. It was therefore indispensible [sic] to show that there was some force here which could hit back and hit straight. This had been done and further press replies or polemics were thereby rendered unnecessary.

Signor Grandi complained of consistently unfriendly policy of France towards this country. It was not that of Monsieur Briand but of Berthelot and was very short sighted. The Italian nation might not love France but it dis-

[3] Secretary-General of the Italian Fascist Party.
[4] This word was queried in another text of this telegram.

liked Germany more; yet everything was being done to throw Italy into the latters arms. French imagine[d] that question of Upper Adige would keep Germany and Italy still further apart. This was a delusion. The question was Bavarian not German. Dr. Stresemann cared little about it. He might make play with it for the time being and coquet with Monsieur Poincaré. But when the moment came that Germany having rid herself of occupation felt strong again there would be unpleasant surprises; then would come the time when France would regret her present policy towards Italy.

I said that I was more concerned with the present than the future. The policy of His Majesty's Government was to do everything possible to cultivate friendship between France and Italy and to restore Italian and Yugoslav relations to better footing with elimination of all questions which might cause friction. I trusted therefore (having in mind M. Marinkovic's forthcoming speech) that any friendly gesture from Belgrade would be met half way by Rome in the proper spirit. Signor Grandi replied that any such gesture would be duly appreciated.

Insert the following sentence into penultimate paragraph above after the words 'latter's arms'. French were egging on Little Entente[5] to be hostile to Italy. He would say nothing of constant flow of munitions that passed from Marseilles to Spalato.

Addressed to Foreign Office No. 205, repeated to Belgrade.

[5] i.e. Czechoslovakia, Roumania, and the Serb-Croat-Slovene State.

No. 49

Sir A. Chamberlain to Sir R. Graham (Rome)

No. 265 Telegraphic [C 9324/4490/92]

FOREIGN OFFICE, *November 21, 1927, 6 p.m.*

Your No. 205.[1]

I fully approve your language.

See my telegram No. 127 to Belgrade[2] and my telegram No. 84 to Durazzo.[3]

You will see that I have made it plain at Belgrade that I consider that they have done a very foolish thing in a very foolish manner but I earnestly trust that Signor Mussolini is not trying to push Albania into an equally mistaken step. Immediate result of conclusion of an alliance between Albania and Italy would be to afford an apparent justification for French Yugoslav treaty which would appear as merely an intelligent anticipation. It would only increase the tension and add to the dangers of the existing situation.

Above statement of my views is for your guidance if you think it wise to follow up your conversation with Signor Grandi by any further communication.[4]

[1] No. 48. [2] No. 46. [3] See No. 51, note 4.

[4] In an unnumbered telegram of November 21 Sir A. Chamberlain authorized Sir R. Graham to act on a suggestion made in a private letter of November 18 and let Signor Mussolini know why he had discouraged M. Marinkovitch from visiting London as described in Nos. 37 and 41.

No. 50

The Marquess of Crewe (Paris) to Sir A. Chamberlain
(Received November 22, 8.30 a.m.)

No. 231 Telegraphic: by bag [*C 9387/33/18*]

PARIS, *November 21, 1927*

M. Berthelot spoke to Sir Eric Phipps[1] this afternoon in an optimistic manner on the subject of Franco-German relations. He said that he was convinced that Herr Stresemann intended to work in as close collaboration as possible with you and M. Briand at the approaching meeting of the Council of the League at Geneva.

[1] Minister in H.M. Embassy at Paris.

No. 51

Sir A. Chamberlain to the Marquess of Crewe (Paris)
No. 2884 [*C 9443/4490/92*]

FOREIGN OFFICE, *November 22, 1927*

My Lord Marquess,

I asked the French Ambassador to call this morning.

I told him that I was anxious about the consequences of the signature of the treaty between France and Jugoslavia and enquired of him whether he had any information either from Rome or Durazzo. M. de Fleuriau read to me a long telegram from M. Dard at Belgrade, reporting an interview between himself and M. Marinkovic. M. de Fleuriau said that, in consequence of a conversation with Sir William Tyrrell, he had informed M. Briand that I deprecated a visit by M. Marinkovic to London unless he also went to Rome. M. Marinkovic had already left Paris when this message was received, but M. Briand had communicated it to Belgrade and had advised M. Marinkovic that he also thought that an intimation from him that he was prepared to go to Rome for the negotiations would be a good thing. M. Marinkovic had communicated to M. Dard his intention to make a friendly reference to Italy in the Skupshtina and to instruct M. Rakic to resume his conversations with Signor Mussolini as soon as that was done and to indicate that he would himself be prepared to visit Rome if such a visit would be useful. M. Marinkovic had added that he thought Signor Mussolini was mistaken in thinking that a *détente* must first take place between the people before the Governments could usefully negotiate. This seemed to M. Marinkovic to be putting the cart before the horse. It was the Governments which must produce the *détente* and act in advance of public opinion. He appeared to have added once again that I could give useful help in facilitating such a meeting.

As regards Rome, M. de Fleuriau said that the news which he had received from there was reassuring rather than otherwise. There had been some demonstrations in Rome and in one or two other Italian towns, as I had doubtless observed, but he gathered that Signor Mussolini had taken the signature of the treaty as quietly as could be expected.

I thought so much complacency dangerous. I therefore spoke more freely about my anxieties. I said that it appeared to me that the signature of the treaty was in any case a mistake since it involved France unnecessarily in Balkan affairs and was bound to rouse Italian suspicions. No doubt each phrase of the treaty might be examined and shown to be innocent of any warlike or hostile intention, and I had observed that, in the communiqués issued by the French Government and in the larger portion of the French press, there had been an obvious desire not to allow the importance of the treaty to be exaggerated. At first the attitude of the Italian Government seemed to me to have been very much what the Ambassador had described and Signor Mussolini appeared to have spoken with great restraint himself and to have been successful in imposing restraint on others. Then had followed the reaction of Jugoslavia to the news of the signature of the treaty, the demonstrations in Belgrade and other towns, and articles in the press which had given all the importance possible and, as I thought, an exaggerated importance to the treaty and had presented it as a warning addressed by France to Italy. I confessed that all this gave me great anxiety. The Ambassador had not mentioned any news from Durazzo, but Mr. Seeds had reported to me[1] that his French colleague had informed him that Ahmed Zoghou had told the Serb-Croat-Slovene Minister that he was being strongly urged by the Italian Government to sign immediately a secret military convention of which, as it seemed, the French Minister had also received some information from Paris. Mr. Seeds said that the French information was that the convention covered co-operation in war and contained promises of territorial compensation to Albania if war in fact took place. Baron de Vaux had added that the Serb-Croat-Slovene Minister had urged the President not to sign any such convention, that he himself intended to give the same advice and he pressed Mr. Seeds to make like representations. If such a convention were to be signed as a result of the Franco-Jugoslav Treaty, it would be a great misfortune and would singularly increase the dangers of the situation.

M. de Fleuriau for a moment spoke with unwonted warmth. He said that he did not share my view. If such a project existed about which he knew nothing, it had nothing to do with the treaty and would have come about in any case. M. de Fleuriau added that the attitude of Italy towards France was provocative and irritating. In any case he did not believe that the French Minister had any information on the subject from Paris.

I told the Ambassador that I had nothing to confirm the report and indeed that it would seem from a later telegram from Mr. Seeds that the French Minister had perhaps misunderstood to some extent his Jugoslav colleague.[2]

[1] See No. 47.

[2] In Durazzo telegram No. 81 of November 21 Mr. Seeds explained that the Serb-Croat-Slovene Minister had told him that 'he only asked President of the Republic if it was true that a military convention had actually been signed. President answered in the negative but

I could not, however, treat the matter quite so lightly as his Excellency nor indeed if such a project were under discussion could I dissociate it from the signature of the Franco-Jugoslav Treaty.

I must repeat that the treaty itself and still more the manner of its signature seemed to me to increase the difficulties of everyone. I remarked that I was constantly being asked (as indeed M. Dard's message showed) to make representations to Signor Mussolini on behalf of Jugoslavia, but I must insist that I was not the director of Italian policy, that the Italian Government did not seek my advice and that it was only as a friend and with great discretion that I could venture to make any representations in Rome. It was not my business to defend Italian policy, and I certainly assumed no responsibility for it, but I had done my best to bring the two parties together and to remove misunderstandings which stood in the way of friendly intercourse. It was, however, quite unreasonable for M. Marinkovic to follow his own line of policy without consulting me and without regard to my opinion and then look to me to remove the consequences of his action and to avert its dangers. It was all very well to say to me what M. Diouritch had said the other day that I was the only person to whom Signor Mussolini would listen, and up to a point it might be true, but those who desired my good offices must have some regard to my views. It was not reasonable that they should first without consultation with me create a dangerous situation and then turn to me with the expression of an expectation that I should avert the natural consequences of their action. I thought the policy of the treaty was a mistake: it was bound to rouse Italian susceptibilities, it was bound to increase Italian suspicions of Jugoslavia's intention and to render more difficult the relations of France and Italy, and I must be permitted to add to that, to speak of the treaty as a 'Locarno' treaty, was really a complete misnomer. The special feature of the Treaty of Locarno had been that it was a first step in the reconciliation of former enemies, not as in this case a treaty between friends who had never had a quarrel and between whom there was no proximity and no rivalry that was ever likely to provoke a quarrel. In the present case the treaty made France in some sort a Balkan Power and, however innocently it might be explained in France and whatever assurances M. Briand might give, it was inevitable that the Italians should receive the impression that it was directed against them. Moreover Jugoslavia had done everything to fortify this impression. I must confess that the tension in Franco-Italian relations caused me great anxiety. We had every interest in keeping Italy within our orbit and in linking her with the two western Powers. I could not but be anxious lest the course of events should drive Italy more and more into some other combination. It was significant that Signor Mussolini had promised Italy's vote to Hungary in the optants question[3] without regard to the merits of the issues immediately at stake. I did not want to see a new combination growing up between Italy and Germany and whatever remained of the Austro-

was so obviously ill at ease that Serb-Croat-Slovene Minister came to the conclusion that something serious is in preparation.'

[3] Cf. No. 11, note 1.

Hungarian Empire. It was these larger considerations which made me feel that I must lay my anxieties frankly before M. Briand and urge the importance of cultivating good relations with Italy.

By this time the Ambassador had entirely got over the unpleasant impression which my opening had made upon him. He confided to me that personally he had never liked the treaty and thought both the signature itself and the method of the signature mistaken. He went on to say that he understood the reasons which had caused me to speak and the sincere friendship which underlay my observations. M. Briand's policy was in fact the same as my own. He too would have desired that the Great Powers should keep out of the Balkans and henceforth treat Balkan affairs as matters to be settled among the Balkan States. But Italy had made this impossible by her intervention in Albania. He did not attribute this policy to the initiative of Signor Mussolini. He felt that Signor Mussolini inherited it from his predecessors, but he thought it mistaken in the interests of Italy herself, and he hoped that Signor Mussolini was wise enough some day to alter its character. The true policy for Italy was to have only commercial interests on the opposite side of the Adriatic. To base her defence on Dalmatia and Albania was a mistake; her true defence was on Italian soil, but as long as she pursued this mistaken policy the idea of the Balkans for the Balkan peoples was unrealisable. He asked me, however, whether I had any suggestion to make as to how France could improve her relations with Italy.

I replied that I had no specific proposal in my mind, but as he himself had observed the Italians were extremely sensitive. They were the last arrived of the great nations, still not very certain of their position and therefore particularly suspicious and resentful of anything which could be considered as a slight. France, on the other hand, secure in her unquestionable position, could afford to make advances and to show a largeness of mind and liberality of policy which it would be idle to expect from Italy. I repeated that, in my opinion, Signor Mussolini was far too wise to desire to land any troops on Albanian soil. He had said on many occasions—and I believed with perfect truth—that he desired the preservation of peace, that Italy more than most countries needed peace for the completion of the great works of development that he had planned and for the consolidation of the reforms which he was introducing. But there was always a certain danger in a country where the Government consisted of one man, and it was not lessened in his case by his temperament and sensitiveness. Nevertheless my information was that there was no sign anywhere in Italy of any preparations for war. I did not believe that Signor Mussolini had any territorial ambitions in Albania. I thought that his policy there was in fact influenced by fear of Jugoslav policy and that, if he could be reassured on that side, he would offer no menace to Albanian integrity; but he was not prepared to see, for example, another Albanian ruler overthrown merely because he pursued a policy friendly to Italy, and he had had, after all, only too much ground in the past for the suspicions which he entertained.

I repeated that I had felt too much anxiety not to lay my fears frankly

107

before M. Briand. I insisted once again that it was the interest of France no less than of this country to keep Italy in our circle and to prevent her being driven into another and possibly hostile combination, and I added that, after all, the only link which now bound her to us passed through London and it was none too strong.

Finally, just as M. de Fleuriau was leaving I said that I would tell him, for M. Briand's confidential information, that I had in fact instructed Mr. Seeds to enquire whether the Italian Government had proposed such a military convention to Ahmed Zoghou, and if the answer were in the affirmative, to advise Ahmed Zoghou not to enter into any new engagement at the present time, as by so doing he would only involve himself in a controversy in which it was not in the interests of Albania to become engaged.[4] I had also explained my views fully to Sir Ronald Graham and had left him to judge whether he could usefully say anything more to Signor Mussolini.[5] I had just received a telegram from Sir Ronald Graham in which he said that he would await M. Marinkovic's promised statement and would be guided by the effect which that statement produced in Rome.[6]

I am, &c.,

AUSTEN CHAMBERLAIN

[4] Sir A. Chamberlain's telegram No. 84 to Durazzo of November 21 was as here indicated and is not printed.

[5] See No. 46.   [6] Rome telegram No. 206 of November 21 is not printed.

No. 52

Mr. Seeds (Durazzo) to Sir A. Chamberlain (Received November 23, 9.30 a.m.)
No. 82 Telegraphic [C 9444/25/90]

State   DURAZZO, *November 22, 1927, 2.25 p.m.*
Your telegram No. 84[1].

President of the Republic told me that an Italo Albanian Defensive Treaty had been signed today.[2] Duration 20 years. Each party to treat other party's interests as of equal importance to its own. In case of unprovoked difficulties arising between one party and a foreign power, second party would lend the fullest assistance towards an (? economic)[3] solution; should this fail second party—if requested by first—would give all possible military assistance (an annexe to treaty providing that command would be taken by a national of that party in whose territory allied troops operated); neither party to make peace without the consent of the other.

President explained that he had taken this step to protect Albania in face of Franco-Yugo-Slav Treaty. He was able to repeat my advice of a week ago[4]

[1] See No. 51, note 4.

[2] The text of this treaty, with attached exchange of notes, is printed in *British and Foreign State Papers*, vol. 127, pp. 4–6.

[3] It was suggested, probably correctly, on the filed copy of this telegram that this word should read 'pacific': cf. article 3 of the treaty.   [4] See No. 47.

verbatim but would not admit that his treaty was of a nature to rouse Serb resentment. I explained the gravity of the situation and he then declared himself ready to tear up the treaty as it had only been signed by the Minister for Foreign Affairs, or to do anything recommended by His Majesty's Government to remedy matters. I asked whether the treaty could not be kept secret or in abeyance for a while. He said that though he could prevent it being published or laid before Parliament Italian Minister and the Minister for Foreign Affairs were about to draft communiqué to be issued here and in Rome tomorrow. But of course he himself had apparently to sanction the terms of that document.

I was at a loss to know what to do. Finally I took it on myself to beg him to inform Italian Minister that on my suggestion he wished to delay the issue of any communiqué for three days in order to give time for His Majesty's Government to get into contact with Italian Government on the subject of advisability or otherwise of publishing such news at this particular moment. He promised to do so.

Italian Minister called on me later to say that communiqué would be delayed as desired. He stated that treaty constituted an alliance political, financial and military: it was practically copied from certain Anglo-Portuguese treaties and Italian government wished the world now to recognise Albania as an Italian Portugal. He laid stress on the fact that military portion only came into force in the event of unprovoked attack and added that special clause in the annexe provided for withdrawal of Italian troops from Albania after cessation of hostilities. He naturally refused to admit that the moment was not opportune.

Addressed to Foreign Office No. 82, repeated to Rome and Belgrade.

No. 53

Memorandum respecting the Views and Actions of the Agent General for Reparation Payments in regard to the present German Financial Situation[1]

*[C 8907/857/18]**

FOREIGN OFFICE, *November 22, 1927*

The object of the present memorandum is to explain in as clear and as brief a manner as possible, without attempting to estimate the weight of the arguments employed, or to suggest the policy to be adopted by His Majesty's Government, the problems to which public attention has been drawn by the letter from the Agent-General for Reparation Payments to the German Minister of Finance of the 20th October,[2] on the subject of the effect on the continued operation of the Dawes plan of the German Government's financial policy and the inflow into Germany of foreign loans. The problems have two aspects—internal and international.

[1] According to the docket this memorandum was by Mr. Perowne.
[2] See No. 24, note 5.

(1.) *Preliminary*

By the Treaty of Versailles the German Government undertook to make reparation for the loss and damage caused to the Allied Powers as a result of the war. The Reparation Commission was charged with fixing the amount of compensation due in these respects and some payments on account were actually made by Germany. But the German economic and financial situation deteriorated to such an extent throughout the years 1920–23 that a complete default in reparation payments became inevitable. The whole position was, however, materially altered by the adoption by the interested Governments, including the German, of the Dawes plan and its embodiment in the London Agreement of August 1924.

The Dawes plan laid down that an inclusive annual payment should be made by Germany in settlement of her reparation and other treaty obligations. This annuity, for the payment of which special guarantees were provided,[3] was to be paid into the Reichsbank (set up by the plan) to the credit of the Agent-General for Reparation Payments. The number of annuities, however, which Germany would have to pay in liquidation of her total reparation obligation was not fixed.

While the Dawes plan indicated the sources from which payment was to be made to the ex-Allied creditors, it was the Transfer Committee which was charged with the task of ensuring that the money thus collected reached the creditor Powers. The plan provided that this committee should 'regulate the execution of the programmes for deliveries in kind and Reparation Recovery Act payments in such a manner as to prevent difficulties arising with the foreign exchange,' that it should also control the transfer of cash to the creditor Governments by purchase of foreign exchange and that it should 'generally so act as to secure the maximum transfers without bringing about instability of the currency.' The plan laid on the German Government and the Reichsbank the obligation to co-operate with the committee in the discharge of their duties.

There are thus two distinct processes inherent in the Dawes plan, the payment by the German Government into the account of the Agent-General at the Reichsbank of the requisite sums in Reichmarks, and the conversion by the Transfer Committee of those sums into the foreign currencies required in order that the creditor Powers may each receive their allotted share of the annuity. It is conceivable that Germany might produce the requisite sums in Reichmarks, but that the Transfer Committee would be unable to convert them without upsetting the exchange. In fact the committee are empowered at any time to suspend transfer; in that event the sums received on reparation account are to be accumulated in Germany. When the accumulation of funds not transferable has reached a total of 5 milliards of gold marks, the payments by the German Government in German currency are to be reduced and a partial and temporary suspense of Germany's reparation obligations effected. The committee thus have very wide powers and the actual receipts of the

---

[3] *Note on filed copy*: 'Railway and industrial bonds, controlled revenues, &c.'

creditor Governments depend entirely on the committee's decision as to the amounts which from time to time can be transferred without endangering the stability of the exchange. Thus, it does not follow from the fact that transfer may not have been achieved that there has been any failure on the part of Germany to pay what is annually due from her, nor would such a circumstance signify a breakdown of the Dawes plan. It is an eventuality which is actually contemplated in the plan itself.

The plan also fixed the scale of the annuities which Germany was to pay and the proportions in which the various earmarked sources should contribute to each annuity. That is to say, that the plan fixed not only the amount due from Germany each year, but how that amount was to be made up. For 1924–25 the total annuity was fixed at 1,000 million gold marks, for 1925–26 at 1,220 million gold marks; in 1926–27, 1,500 million gold marks have been paid; in 1927–28, 1,750 million gold marks are due; and for 1928–29 (the first 'standard' year), and thereafter, the annuity stands at 2,500 million gold marks. The experts recommended that Germany should make payment from three sources, namely, from railway bonds and transport tax, from industrial debentures, and from the ordinary budget. No budgetary contribution was levied during the first Dawes year, but after smaller beginnings in the second and third years, it reaches 500 million gold marks in 1927–28, and is fixed for 1928–29 and thenceforward at 1,250 million gold marks, or exactly half the total 'normal' annuity. The importance of the budgetary contribution, especially after next year, when the maximum payments become due, is thus evident. Collateral security for the budgetary payments is provided by earmarking the taxes on beer, sugar, tobacco, alcohol and customs, and there is every reason to suppose that the receipts from these sources will be ample to cover the budgetary payments even in a standard year (1928–29, or thereafter).

The Dawes Agreement came into force on the 1st September, 1924, and since that date the sums for which it provided have been duly paid into the reparation account. There have, however, since 1924, been certain developments in the economic and financial spheres in Germany which appear to have aroused a measure of apprehension in regard to the future. This apprehension is shared by Mr. Parker Gilbert, the Agent-General for Reparation Payments, who has felt it necessary to draw attention in writing to certain aspects of the matter on a number of occasions during the last eighteen months— namely, in his private letters to the German Finance Minister of the 20th September,[4] the 11th November,[5] and the 11th December, 1926,[5] the 17th March,[6] the 9th July,[7] and the 20th October, 1927[2] (only the last of which has been published), and in his interim published report of the 10th June last.

[4] Not printed. The gist of this letter which communicated the views of the Transfer Committee is indicated in Volume II, No. 263, paragraph 15.

[5] Not printed. This letter maintained the views expressed in the letter of September 20, 1926.

[6] See No. 24, note 6.

[7] Not printed. This letter maintained the views expressed in the letter of March 17, 1927.

The situation is, of course, further aggravated by the fact that, in September 1928, the first standard Dawes year will begin to run, in which the annuity will, for the first time, reach its full level.

(2.) *Internal Problem, i.e., Governmental Extravagance.*

The German budget has recently revealed an increasing tendency towards extravagance and improvidence, some of the items in respect of which expenditure is incurred being actually objectionable in themselves (e.g. the increased Reichswehr budget and air subsidies), while the conclusion of a reasonable and final settlement of the difficult question of the financial relations between the Reich and the States and communes ('Finanzausgleich', fixing the amount to be handed over by the Reich annually to the States and communes out of the revenue of the Reich), has been again postponed in favour of a fresh provisional arrangement, entailing increased burdens on the Reich, which is to last until April 1929.

According to Mr. Parker Gilbert's view, if the present practice is continued, successive budgetary deficits may be expected, the result of which (unless, of course, they are covered by increased taxation), will be to precipitate a financial crisis at an early date, which, among other things, would jeopardise the future of the Dawes plan, the success of which was by the authors themselves declared to repose on the twin, but inter-dependent, foundations of a stable currency and a balanced budget.

The German Government recognise the position, but do not appear to contemplate the adoption of any counter-measures to avoid this danger. In fact, they are at the moment proposing still further to increase their commitments (School Bill, Salaries Bill, and War Liquidation Measure, now before the Reichstag, all of which have been the subject of adverse comment by Mr. Gilbert).

The causes for this attitude may be ascribed (*a*) to the fact that the spending departments (both of the Central Government and of the local authorities) cannot get rid of their inflation habits, and (*b*) to the weak position of the German Cabinet, which feels unable to insist on stringent measures of economy or even to drop certain new proposed items of expenditure. Were it to do so the interested parties in the Reichstag might withdraw their support and the Government might fall. Moreover, the representatives of those parties have also their own voters to consider. It is, indeed, not impossible that a political crisis, occasioned by this very question, is in sight.

On the other hand, those circles in Germany which realise the danger of national extravagance have welcomed Mr. Gilbert's strictures as a weapon with which to bring influence to bear on the German Government and public opinion in favour of national economy.

(3.) *International Problem, i.e., Foreign Loans.*

The adoption of the Dawes plan certainly resulted in the restoration of the financial stability of Germany, but money for immediate needs was remarkably short; and in order to meet these needs the newly restored German credit was employed to float loans on foreign, principally American, markets. These loans, which are the liability of certain German States, institutions and private concerns, already amount for the three-year period ending the 30th September, 1927, to some £350 million, and the flotation of loans to the further value of £50 million is in prospect.

Mr. Parker Gilbert has raised the question whether the service of these private loans should not have transfer priority over the Dawes annuity in virtue of article 248 of the Treaty of Versailles (which provides that the cost of reparation is to be a first charge, subject to such exceptions as the Reparation Commission may approve, on all the assets of the German Empire and its constituent States). In his letter of the 20th September, 1926, he criticised the statement in the prospectus of a loan which the Prussian Government was at that time preparing to launch on the United States market that neither German law nor any international engagements assumed by the German Government, involved any restrictions upon the acquisition by the Free State of Prussia of the foreign exchange requisite to meet the service of the loan. In the absence of an express exception under article 248 of the Treaty of Versailles, no such statement could properly be made unless qualified by a reference to the priority of reparation payments and transfers. Accordingly, the service of this loan 'must necessarily (in Mr. Gilbert's words) be regarded as secondary to the obligations in respect of the transfer of reparation payments which the German Government has assumed by virtue of the experts plan of [and] the London agreements.' The German Government was not prepared to admit this claim, however, and a controversy ensued which was tranquillised by a letter from the Reparation Commission[8] (which considered that the Agent-General had, in his letter of the 20th September, gone further than was warranted either by the treaty or the Dawes plan) in which the opportunity was taken to restate the case in more moderate terms with a view to preventing a German appeal to arbitration. It is plain, however, from subsequent events, that Mr. Parker Gilbert is not prepared to drop his interpretation of article 248.

In any case, the Dawes plan laid down nothing with regard to any transfer priority for the annuity. As already stated, it is the duty of the Transfer Committee (the organisation which controls the use and withdrawal of the moneys paid into the Reichsbank for reparation account and also the transfer of cash to the Allies) to see that no detriment to the German exchange results from such transfer. No power is, however, given for preventing the transfer of other moneys in the interest of the transfer of the annuity itself, although the committee is empowered by the plan to take such action as may be necessary to defeat any concerted financial manœuvres by the German Government or by any group for the purpose of preventing exchange transactions. The German Government and the Reichsbank are also obliged to facilitate in any reasonable way within their power the work of the committee

[8] For this letter of October 2, 1926, see Volume II, No. 263, paragraphs 16–18.

in making transfers of funds, including such steps as may aid in the control[9] of foreign exchange.

The full German transfer capacity has not yet been tested; but Mr. Parker Gilbert sees reason to fear that, especially if the process of foreign borrowing continues, it will not be great enough to cover both the service of the private foreign loans and such balance of the annuity as may stand to be paid in cash. Unless he can establish the right of reparation payments to a priority in the matter of transfers, it looks to him as if the existence of so great and increasing a volume of foreign loans will militate against, if not completely impossibilitate, the transfer of at any rate the greater part of reparation cash lying in the Reichsbank into the Treasuries of the various Allied Powers entitled to share in German reparation payments. However this may be, the inflow into Germany of the foreign currencies resulting from the flotation abroad of such loans has undoubt[e]dly served to finance such reparation transfers as the Transfer Committee has hitherto found it necessary to effect. It is argued, therefore, that if these loans now cease, it will prove difficult to finance the transfer of any reparation payments at all, especially when the latter suddenly increase, as they are due to do in the next Dawes year beginning September 1928.[10]

On the other hand, it is the view of certain economists that the money that has so far been raised by such loans has, while serving to finance reparation cash transfers to the Allied Powers, not been used to enable German industry to increase its export trade and thus to facilitate the payment of reparation. According to these authorities, it is being employed merely to finance an artificial and dangerous internal trade boom, and is indeed actually undermining Germany's financial situation, inasmuch as it represents in short nothing but an obligation against which there is no real economic set-off.[11] It is further held that until the flow of these loans has been slowed up and money thus rendered dearer, there will be no prospect of stopping the present artificial trade boom in Germany itself and of convincing the German manufacturers of the necessity of increasing exports in order to create that favourable trade balance of which Germany stands so greatly in need. The creation

[9] *Note on filed copy*: 'The relevant passage in the English text of the experts' plan contains the words "in the control"; the corresponding passage in the French text has "maintien de la stabilité". This conflicting wording may lead to trouble in the future.'

[10] *Note on filed copy*: 'A further transfer difficulty may arise from the fact that under the plan the Transfer Committee cannot go into the open market to obtain foreign currencies by means of which to effect the transfer of reparation cash. This operation must be carried out through the president of the R[e]ichsbank, which, in spite of the proviso in the plan to which reference is made above, has shown a tendency to refuse to purchase foreign currencies, thus threatening to impede transfers by producing an artificial dearth in the Reichsbank.'

[11] *Note on filed copy*: 'The German Government also appear to share this fear, for the German Foreign Loans Control Committee ("Beratungsstelle") was "reformed" in virtue of a Cabinet decision of the 8th October last, which also laid down certain new "guiding principles for the better control of the foreign borrowing of public bodies." The committee has only met once, however, since its "reform"—on the 4th November—when no loan schemes were considered, but a discussion took place as to the manner in which the above-mentioned principles were to be applied.'

of such a balance is important not only for the stability of the German currency, but also for enabling the normal transfer of reparation payments to be made.

(4.) *General Observations.*

Mr. Parker Gilbert justifies the action he has taken on the ground that the over-borrowing and over-spending which are at present proceeding in Germany are leading to an early economic and financial disaster, which could not fail to have the most deplorable repercussions in the sphere of international politics, particularly if, as Mr. Parker Gilbert has more than once indicated, there should be any unpleasant suspicion that such a state of affairs had been brought about as a result of Germany not acting with due regard to her reparation obligations. Were such a complete collapse to occur, not merely would the transfer of reparation payments become impossible, but a default in the payment of the annuity itself would probably ensue.

A more personal reason for Mr. Gilbert's action is to be found in the fact that he is convinced of the dangerous inefficiency of the present German Minister of Finance, and wished to expose him in the eyes of his countrymen.

At all events, the publication of his recent letter to Dr. Koehler has, as he intended, at length clearly brought home to public opinion, both in Germany and abroad, those warnings and criticisms which he has been voicing for some time past without producing much effect. The German Government did not wish the existence of this communication to be known, but when this leaked out they pretended that Dr. Koehler had asked Mr. Parker Gilbert to write him such a letter—a statement which the latter has denied. They were finally driven, however, in order to put an end to the circulation of rumours the ultimate effect of which seemed likely to be more harmful than the revelation of the truth, to agree to its publication. The German Government obviously hoped, to begin with, that the whole question would be allowed to drop; they feared that general realisation of the nature of Mr. Parker Gilbert's criticisms and of the fact that, although this was not the first time they had been brought to their notice, no sort of attempt had, however, been made to put the German financial house in order, would react most unfavourably both on their own internal political position and on the position of Germany *vis-à-vis* the rest of the world. The foreign market was already nervous; it might begin unloading its German securities in such a way as to create a panic, and to bring about that very collapse, or at least that shaking of the German economic structure which it is to the interest of everyone, though not for the same reasons, to avoid.

When it became impossible any longer to withhold Mr. Parker Gilbert's letter, the German Government attempted to disarm criticism and minimise any possible adverse effect which might be produced internally or internationally by publication by arranging simultaneously to publish their official reply. This lengthy document, however, is generally agreed to be unconvincing. It has certainly failed of its immediate object; public opinion in Germany is distinctly restive and is already demanding retrenchment, and while it is too soon to estimate the ultimate effect at home and abroad of Mr. Parker Gilbert's remarks, it may be mentioned that messages from America indicate that greater conservatism will henceforward be the order of the day there where German issues are concerned. Meanwhile, Mr. Parker Gilbert has intimated that he does not intend to continue the correspondence and is anxious to prevent any further polemics.

In conclusion, a certain personal problem ought perhaps to be mentioned. Under the Dawes plan the co-ordinating agency between the machinery set up thereunder, the Reparation Commission and the German Government, is to be the Agent-General. Mr. Parker Gilbert was appointed to this post by the Reparation Commission, as laid down in the plan, but he evidently does not consider himself in any sense the subordinate of that body or the subordinate of the Governments whose interests he is representing at Berlin. For example, he did not even inform the Reparation Commission of his intention to address his recent letter to the German Finance Minister, and his attitude towards that body and the Allied Powers in general is somewhat independent.

No. 54
Sir A. Chamberlain to Mr. Seeds (Durazzo)
No. 86 Telegraphic [C 9444/25/90]

State   FOREIGN OFFICE, *November 23, 1927, 4.45 p.m.*
Your 82.[1]

I fully approve your action in asking for delay. Italian Ambassador has asked for interview this afternoon and I may be able to give further instructions after hearing what he has to say.

I regard consequences of new Italo-Albanian treaty in its present form with grave anxiety but since treaty has already been signed without either party giving me any hint of their intention the responsibility for what follows must be theirs alone. I cannot assume the responsibility of advising President to tear up a treaty which he has already signed.

Repeated to Rome No. 271, Belgrade No. 130, Paris No. 251, by bag.

[1] No. 52.

No. 55
Sir A. Chamberlain to Sir R. Graham (Rome)
No. 274 Telegraphic [C 9488/25/90]

State   FOREIGN OFFICE, *November 23, 1927, 11.30 p.m.*
Italian Ambassador sought urgent interview today.

He said he had brought me a little surprise. He then read French translation of long telegram from Mussolini announcing signature of Treaty of Alliance with Albania explaining reasons and purpose of Italian action.[1] He was

[1] For Signor Mussolini's telegram and an account by Signor Bordonaro of the present conversation see *I Documenti Diplomatici Italiani*, Settima Serie, vol. v, Nos. 588 and 590 respectively.

unwilling to leave translation with me but has promised to send me *aide-memoire*[2] as I expressed desire to weigh with due attention exact phraseology of so important a communication.

I told His Excellency that it was less of a surprise than he anticipated as I had already received the same news from Durazzo, but admitted that the news affected me disagreeably. I then told His Excellency that the first rumour had reached me yesterday in a message from Mr. Seeds and of the instructions which I had sent to Mr. Seeds of his action thereon and my further telegram to him this afternoon.[3] I said situation caused me grave anxiety. I had not been consulted in regard to signature or terms of Franco-Yugoslav treaty any more than about present treaty. I thought policy in both cases mistaken and feared it could only increase the difficulties of a situation already sufficiently difficult and delicate. I called Ambassador's attention to opening words of Article 1 of additional protocol to the Pact of Rome—les hautes parties contractantes s'engagent à se communiquer *après une entente préalable* les accords . . .'[4] The Ambassador interrupted me to say that Italy did not consider Albania as part of Central Europe, to which I rejoined that, if the Pact of Rome did not cover Albania, it was difficult to see what purpose it had been meant to serve. I then called Ambassador's attention to the declaration made by the British, French, Italian and Japanese governments on the 9th November 1921 on the subject of Albania[5]—Articles 1, 2, 3, particularly the last-named—and remarked that I scarcely knew what was now the duty of the British Government in view of that engagement. I continued that throughout these differences I had had no other object than as a friend of both countries and one who attached particular importance to a good understanding and collaboration between Italy and Great Britain to smooth away difficulties, to remove suspicions and misunderstanding and to use as far as I was permitted my good offices to promote agreement between the parties. I had indeed gone so far in this direction that, as was admitted by Signor Mussolini in his message, I had actually been accused of being an accomplice in Italian designs. I only recalled these facts to invite the most favourable and friendly consideration for the suggestion which I now made.

This suggestion was that the announcement of the signature of the treaty should be delayed to enable Signor Mussolini to propose to Yugoslavia that, before signing, it should be converted into a tripartite treaty by which Italy and Yugoslavia would alike solemnly bind themselves to Albania and each other to respect and to maintain the integrity and independence of Albania.

I suggested three alternative methods of procedure: first, in my opinion best, that Signor Mussolini should himself make this proposal to the Yugoslav government: second, that if unwilling to do this himself he should authorise

[2] Signor Bordonaro transmitted this *aide-mémoire*, which followed the lines of the first, second, fourth, fifth, and sixth paragraphs of No. 588, *ibid.*, in a letter of November 24 to Sir A. Chamberlain.

[3] See Nos. 47, 51, note 4, 52 and 54 respectively.

[4] Punctuation as in original quotation: cf. *British and Foreign State Papers*, vol. 120, p. 684.

[5] See No. 7, note 4.

me to do it on his authority: third, that if unprepared to make such an advance without being assured that his offer would be accepted, I should make the proposal to Yugoslavia as if it were my own. I could not, however, do this unless I received his assurance that if my proposal were accepted by Yugoslavia it would also be accepted by him, for otherwise assuming Yugoslavia to accept, I should be placed in a humiliating position towards them and in one which would greatly embarrass my relations with the Italian government.

The Ambassador said he would at once transmit my message to Signor Mussolini. He was, however, doubtful whether Mussolini would accept it. I urged its advantages from many points of view. I regarded a treaty of Alliance directed against a third party as a backward step. On the other hand a Treaty of Mutual Guarantee on the real Locarno model would absolutely safeguard Italian interests. It would redound to the credit of Italy and be, I was convinced, an immense relief to all the world, which could not but be anxious about the growing tension in the Balkans.

Please seek immediate interview with Signor Mussolini and press this suggestion on him with all the arguments you can command at the same time urging desirability of further delay in publication.

I am making this suggestion without having seen the text of the treaty and on the assumption that it conforms to the obligations of the Covenant of the League of Nations. You should make this reservation quite clear to Signor Mussolini.[6]

Repeated to Durazzo No. 87,[7] Belgrade No. 131, and Paris by bag No. 252.

[6] With reference to the present telegram Sir A. Chamberlain's telegram No. 277 to Rome of November 24 stated that he relied on Sir R. Graham to make the best use he could of the friendly references to Italy in M. Marinkovitch's statement of November 23 to the Skupshtina. For a report on this statement see *The Times*, November 24, 1927, p. 13. Foreign Office telegram No. 135 to Belgrade of November 24 instructed Mr. Kennard to congratulate M. Marinkovitch on his statesmanlike speech and, if necessary, make it quite clear that Sir A. Chamberlain had no knowledge of the impending Italo-Albanian treaty when he gave the advice in No. 46.

[7] Foreign Office telegram No. 88 to Durazzo of November 23 instructed Mr. Seeds to press the President of Albania further to delay ratification and publication in order to give time for consideration of the above suggestions. The nature of the suggestions was not to be mentioned to him.

No. 56

Record by Sir W. Tyrrell of a conversation with the French Ambassador

[*C 9561/808/92*]

FOREIGN OFFICE, *November 23, 1927*

The French Ambassador told me today, with reference to his conversation with the Secretary of State,[1] in which the latter had pointed out that one of the results of the recent Franco-Yugoslav treaty might be a rapprochement

[1] See No. 51.

between Rome and Berlin, that he had received last night a report from the French Ambassador in Berlin on the subject.

In this report M. de Margerie had informed M. Briand that Dr. Stresemann had enquired of him the other day whether France intended to sign such a treaty and whether it was directed against Germany. Dr. Stresemann explained his request for information by saying that the Italian Ambassador had been to see him and had warned him that the signature of such a treaty was impending and that its objective was Germany. The Italian Ambassador had also added that that was the general trend of French policy in connection with the treaties she was concluding with central European and Balkan states.

M. de Margerie had shown Dr. Stresemann a copy of the treaty and after studying it Dr. Stresemann had declared himself quite satisfied with its contents as far as Germany was concerned.

The French Ambassador in Berlin in conclusion added that several articles had appeared in German newspapers, inspired by the Italian Embassy, warning Germany against the anti-German policy of France.[2]

W. T.

[2] Lord Crewe was informed of this conversation in Sir A. Chamberlain's despatch No. 2954 to Paris of December 1. Sir A. Chamberlain further stated in this despatch: 'The Ambassador saw me again in the evening and repeated this report to me. But I am still uncertain what moral he intended me to draw and what moral he draws himself. It seemed to me to reinforce my plea that France should *cultivate* Italian confidence and friendship.'

No. 57

Record by Sir W. Tyrrell of a conversation with the French Ambassador
[*C 9654/4490/92*]

FOREIGN OFFICE, *November 23, 1927*

I took the opportunity today of calling the attention of the French Ambassador to the effect upon English public opinion of the treaty recently concluded between France and Yugoslavia.

I premised my remarks by saying that I was not speaking under instruction, and that I was addressing him as a personal friend and not as French Ambassador.

I began by telling M. de Fleuriau that, at the time of the signature of the treaty of Locarno, I had only seen one black speck on the horizon, and that was the prospect that French public opinion did not appreciate sufficiently the international character of the policy which had found expression in the Locarno treaty, and I was sorry to say that, in the light of the events of the last two years, my apprehensions had been justified to a certain extent, in spite of the fact that M. Briand's policy had met with universal acceptance in France and, according to my information, the French Government intended to take its stand upon that policy at the forthcoming general election in May of next year.

His Excellency would therefore pardon me if I told him frankly that I was puzzled by this phenomenon. I should have thought that it would have enabled M. Briand to pursue his Locarno policy with greater vigour and to break with the policy of his predecessor, which had aimed at forming alliances with the central European and Balkan powers with a view to increase the security of France against an eventual German aggression. But, far from this being the case, we were now confronted with a Franco-Yugoslav pact which could only be described as a retrograde step. Such a pact must be very welcome to the critics of the Locarno policy, who had approved that policy with a mental reservation that it would only succeed if France played up and consistently discarded the old fashioned policy of reinsurance treaties. If this line of policy were further pursued, it was bound to impair the value of the Rhineland guarantee, which we had given to France unconditionally and which would oblige us to defend, in the case of aggression, French territory in the same way as we should defend British territory. It was bound to puzzle people here, who would ask themselves why does France prefer to such a gilt-edged security the minor advantages of tying herself up with small states whose interests would not always be identical with those of France and might involve her in continental complications that would considerably diminish the advantages she expected from such alliances.

If such an impression took firm root in this country, France could not count upon the whole-hearted support of England in the eventuality of the Rhine guarantee becoming effective, and I asked the French Ambassador whether M. Briand personally realised how much he was impairing the value of the British guarantee by his excursions into the Balkans.

To this M. de Fleuriau replied that he felt quite certain that that aspect of the question was absent from M. Briand's mind in concluding the recent treaty: he had been entirely governed by the idea of backing a government in Yugoslavia which was certainly a great improvement on its predecessor, and that he was thereby contributing to the maintenance of peace in the Balkans. His Excellency, however, regretted that not sufficient attention was paid to the effect of this treaty upon the relations of Italy with France and Yugoslavia, but he assured me that M. Briand never intended the treaty to have a provocative character as far as Italy was concerned, though he admitted that there were several colleagues of M. Briand who did not regret an opportunity of having a slap at Italy.

M. de Fleuriau begged me to consider his observations as made to me in the strictest confidence and I promised to respect his confidence, but I did not conceal from him my grave apprehension that this lack of direction in French policy, probably due to M. Briand's indolence and weakness and also to the disordered condition of the French Ministry for Foreign Affairs, might have a very grave consequence if steps were not taken to make M. Briand realise the seriousness of the situation with a view to his correcting it.

M. de Fleuriau entirely agreed, but he said that it could be remedied if Sir Austen Chamberlain would make an opportunity next month of bringing this aspect of the question to the notice of M. Briand and pointing out to him how necessary it was that there should be more automatic co-operation between the British and French Governments on the lines of Locarno, as his task of explaining French policy to the English public was becoming more and more difficult as the volume of criticism increased. His Excellency added that he felt quite certain that M. Briand would reply to such a suggestion probably by making a speech, in which he would nail his colours to the Locarno mast and unreservedly commit his fellow countrymen to this policy. This speech would be more for foreign than for home consumption, where it was less needed.

W. T.

No. 58

Letter from Sir R. Lindsay (Berlin) to Sir W. Tyrrell
(Received November 25)

[*C 9554/857/18*]

Private   BERLIN, *November 23, 1927*

My dear Willie,

Thank you very much for sending me Sir Richard Hopkins' Minute of November 9th[1] on the recent Memorandum by Parker Gilbert. There are several points in it which have been of the utmost interest to me, but it does not give me any general guidance. I am not at all sure that the situation is one in which any general guidance can be given; but I will try to give my conception of things and where it goes wrong I should welcome correction.

Hitherto there has been an agreeable inflow of American capital into Germany which has facilitated the transfer of reparations without stimulating German exports—a delightful state of things, and would that it could last indefinitely!

But it apparently cannot. The easy flow of American loans and the extravagance of German public bodies brings about a dangerous situation and provokes Gilbert's indictment. He expressed to me his anticipation that these tendencies if unchecked would cause a true crisis in Germany within a few months. This might mean that the whole reparation issue might become very much alive during the American Presidential Election campaign—the last thing we want. Yet I am impressed by the fact that while Gilbert was preparing his memorandum, Finlayson quite independently was reporting in the same sense to you and the Treasury. I rather infer that Gilbert's anticipations of a German crisis in spring or summer were pretty reasonable.

Now there is undoubtedly much perturbation in German Government circles over all this, but I am not sure that they are going of a sudden to become economical. They are weak, incompetent, about to face a general election and anxious to please every one. I do not know what they will decide to do with their War Compensation Bill, but they certainly mean to carry on with the increase of official salaries—a very expensive measure; and Prussia is just budgeting for a deficit of £3¾ million pounds which it blandly expects the Reich to meet.

[1] Enclosure in No. 44.

As for the American loans to States and Municipalities, Gilbert seems to have done his job for the moment at any rate. Half a dozen towns are wailing that they cannot borrow dollars at any price at all. This, I take it, is not a bad thing in itself, but now Schacht comes along and attacks them with baresark fury. He really rather overdoes it and I fear he may frighten America from making any industrial loans, which I take it are unexceptionable. Moreover he allows himself to mix up his finance with politics (he is a strong Democrat) and advocates an Einheitsstaat[2]—a highly controversial issue. I cannot help thinking he would have done better service to the cause of general economy if he had been rather more moderate in his language.

Most of the above is bad, but of course there is still a good side. Industry is carrying on undisturbed, revenue is resilient, the unhealthy stock exchange boom has been fairly knocked down, and who knows but what German investments may again become as attractive as ever to America. Let it be remembered too that if the Americans release the German Confiscated property, this would have the same economic effect as a very large dollar loan.

Now amid all this turmoil it seems to me that my own possible field of usefulness is a narrow one. As to the Germans, they have got to work out their own salvation, and though they may fail to meet the test, yet there are in the country men with influence and heads clear enough to preach the true

[2] Unitary state. The question of a possible Einheitsstaat was discussed at length by Sir R. Lindsay in Berlin despatch No. 742 of December 12 which concluded as follows: 'The possible effect of the "Einheitsstaat," viewed from the standpoint of British interests, is a subject upon which it is possible to express a more decided opinion. It is, I presume, axiomatic that the British Empire owns a fair share of the good things of this world, that its interests will best be served by peace, and that no war against a Great Power could be otherwise than purposeless except as a supreme measure of defence taken with the object of keeping that which it already holds. The case of Germany is far different. The average German, who is convinced that Germany is not responsible for the war and has been shamefully treated by the Treaty of Versailles, in general considers the arguments in favour of peace advanced by his former adversaries as sheer hypocrisy, and that their attitude is due merely to a desire to make him believe that which is clearly absurd. On the whole, he feels that the miseries which he has endured arose not from the war itself but from the fact of losing it, and he would very much like to win the next war in order to be in the enviable position both of retrieving his losses and of revenging himself for his previous misfortune. Apart, therefore, from any particular grievance, such as the Polish corridor or the occupation of the Rhineland, there is a general suppressed tendency to think the exact contrary to that which the British public believes, namely, that a fresh war might do some good and cannot, in any case, do much harm. Now, there are two facts in connexion with the German character upon which the builders of theories can count as a sure foundation for conjecture, and these are, firstly, that the German's meekness decreases in proportion to the increase in his moral prosperity and material well-being, and secondly, that, given the impetus of discipline and organised method, he becomes aggressive. I do not think that it is necessary to expand on a subject which has been so exhaustively analysed in previous despatches, but the matter under discussion in this despatch demands that I should call attention to the plain fact that the "Einheitsstaat" would lead to a Prussianisation of Germany, that a Prussianised Germany, in turn, means an aggressive Germany—since it would constitute a mere return to type—and that, consequently, a situation might arise which would again expose to peril the peaceful policy of the British Empire.'

doctrine. As to Gilbert, I am on good terms with him, but God forbid that I should pretend to be able to influence him. I never knew a man who could take his resolutions in such solitude. He is surrounded at his Office with Commissioners, but not one of them ever knows what he is planning or thinking. I believe he sinks his character of American—and I say this though I know he is in close touch with Mellon,[3] Ben Strong, and other great ones in New York. He regards himself, I believe, as an international person, charged with the duty of administering THE PLAN, and honestly determined to give it a fair chance. He has no illusions as to its being a final solution of anything, and he does not expect that he will have any successor in the post he occupies. I can talk to him about the Plan, but I should only do mischief by urging on him anything that is a purely British point of view. I can represent to him that his remonstrances, if they are justified by German mismanagement, and if they are necessary in the interests of the Plan, still are two edged weapons in so far as they may enable the French to accuse Germany again of a voluntary default; and Gilbert is far too sensible to wish to defend the Plan at the cost of provoking European complications. I might be able to suggest to him that he should be rather more kind to the Reparation Commission in Paris, though this is delicate ground. It was very naughty indeed of him to go to Paris and show his memorandum to Poincaré, and never go near the Reparation Commission at all. He can maintain all his independence and yet humour them more than that. Finally I know that in general what we want is to avert any crisis till after the American elections. I am conscious of numerous subsidiary points arising out of the above; but if there is anything important I have not mentioned or anything else you would wish me to do, please let me know.

Ever yours sincerely
R. C. LINDSAY

[3] Secretary of the U.S. Treasury.

No. 59

Sir R. Graham (Rome) to Sir A. Chamberlain
(Received November 25, 9 a.m.)
No. 210 Telegraphic [*C 9518/25/90*]

ROME, *November 24, 1927, 11.15 p.m.*

Your telegram No. 274.[1]

Text of new treaty[2] was given to press at midday today and full text and notes exchanged are being telegraphed by Reuters.

Signor Mussolini has not been at Palazzo Chigi the last two days and it was impossible to obtain interview with him before tomorrow at 5 p.m.

In the meantime I saw Signor Grandi and read to him assurances[3] under

[1] No. 55.　　　　　　　　　　[2] The Italian-Albanian treaty.
[3] In another text of this telegram 'your telegram' replaced 'assurances'.

reference. He was very reticent saying that I had better await answer of his chief but he made following points fairly clear.

1. Treaty has been in the offing in a more or less vague way for some time past but when the Franco-Yugoslav pact was signed Signor Mussolini decided to rush it through at once.

2. Decision for immediate publication was taken because text had been communicated to French and Yugoslav Ministers at Tirana and newspaper correspondents there had already begun to telegraph correct and incorrect versions.

It was considered dangerous to delay publication of actual text.

3. As regards violation of article 1 of addition to [*sic* ? additional] protocol to pact of Rome Signor Grandi made a lame defence but said that Italian government had never been given any inkling until quite recently that Franco-Yugoslav pact had reached the stage of being initialled 18 months ago.

4. Signor Grandi said that Yugoslavia had always refused to recognise declaration of November 9th, 1921. Had they done so present situation would not have arisen.

5. Signor Bordonaro who appears to have recorded your language accurately had omitted reference to your having been 'accused of being an accomplice in Italian designs'. Signor Grandi said that one of Signor Mussolini's reasons for not giving you any previous information regarding treaty was to obviate recurrence of anything of the kind.

6. My personal impression, although it must await confirmation by Signor Mussolini, is that His Excellency will never agree to convert the treaty into a tripartite one and to bring Yugoslavia into it. You will remember that he always utterly declined to admit Serbs to pact of Tirana. It would be a complete reversal of policy for him to do so. I shall of course do everything possible in the matter but Signor Grandi held out no hopes and was indeed emphatic to the contrary. Should I fail as I expect to, I propose to concentrate on urging that when Italian Minister at Belgrade communicates text of treaty to Yugoslav government he should accompany it with some friendly declaration and an assurance regarding integrity and independence of Albania. M. Marinkovic's statement should be helpful in this.

7. Signor Grandi assured me that text of treaty conformed entirely to obligations of covenant of League of Nations. Article 7 lays down that it is to be communicated to League after ratification.

I spoke very seriously to Signor Grandi as to effect treaty was bound to produce. It was evident that he expected a disagreeable reaction. But he said that there would be no serious consequences unless France wished them. All depended on her attitude. As to Yugoslavia, her head had been completely turned by her pact and it was necessary to administer a cold douche which would bring her back to realities.

We ended a long and unsatisfactory conversation by my saying that the only light I could see was that when things are at their worst they may get better and a point had now been reached when it was absolutely necessary to start an improvement.

Only press comment so far is one in 'Giornale d'Italia' dictated by Signor Grandi to the effect that the new treaty is essentially defensive in character; it is in fact a new and important peace document only serving to consolidate the independence of Albania which Italy has so much at heart.

Addressed to Foreign Office, repeated to Durazzo and Belgrade.

No. 60

Sir A. Chamberlain to Mr. Seeds (Durazzo)
No. 90 Telegraphic [C 9516/25/90]

State   FOREIGN OFFICE, *November 25, 1927, 4.30 p.m.*

Your telegram No. 84[1] (of the 24th November: Italo-Albanian Treaty).

You should ask Ahmed to delay presentation to Parliament and ratification of Treaty for a few days longer so as to give time for my discussions with Signor Mussolini. You should add that I am telling Signor Mussolini that I have made this request.[2]

Repeated to Rome No. 279, Belgrade No. 137 and Paris (by bag) No. 255.

[1] Not printed. In reply to Foreign Office telegram No. 88 (see No. 55, note 7) Mr. Seeds reported that in view of the impending publication of the Italo-Albanian treaty in Rome on November 24 he had felt impelled to withdraw the objection he had made to the President of Albania about publication of the treaty in Durazzo.

[2] Sir R. Graham was instructed accordingly in Foreign Office telegram No. 280 to Rome of November 25.

No. 61

Sir R. Graham (Rome) to Sir A. Chamberlain
(Received November 26, 9 a.m.)
No. 212 Telegraphic [C 9544/25/90]

ROME, *November 25, 1927, 12 midnight*

My telegram No. 210.[1]

I spoke strongly to Signor Mussolini in sense of instructions in your telegram No. 274.[2]

His Excellency replied that he was sending a full and detailed answer to you through Italian Ambassador in London. If he had had no previous consultation with you regarding treaty[3] and had given you no information on the subject it was in order to spare you inconveniences which had been attached to his having mentioned pact of Tirana to you some time before signature.

It was necessary that Italian attitude should be clearly understood.

Albania was to Italy what Egypt was to Great Britain, namely a vital point. Albania was the door of the Adriatic. Like ourselves in Egypt the last thing that Italy desired was to destroy independence of Albania, but it was essential that no other powers should be in a position to threaten Italian interests there. His Excellency had therefore some months ago sought the best means

[1] No. 59.   [2] No. 55.   [3] The Italian-Albanian treaty.

of clarifying and consolidating the pact of Tirana and he had looked up old Anglo-Portuguese treaty of alliance. Indeed the new treaty followed the lines of this instrument in so far as was possible in present conditions.

You would therefore understand that it was impossible to admit Yugoslavia to such a treaty nor had he been able, for reasons already explained to me to delay immediate publication of its terms. But he was instructing Italian Ambassador to assure you that at some future date when Italian-Yugoslav relations had been cleared up he would be quite ready to frame agreement with the latter country on all subjects at issue.

As the Pact of Rome expired in little more than a year such a clearing up was bound to take place at no distant date. Important point in present situation was not Belgrade but Paris.

Everything depended upon French attitude and if that remained friendly and reasonable there would be no trouble with Yugoslavia. He noted that 'Pertinax'[4] had already prompted the Belgrade government to oppose registration of the new treaty with the League. This was not a good symptom. Indeed, Franco-Italian relations caused him anxiety, as they had for some time past been steadily drifting in an unfavourable sense. Personally, he deplored the departure from French Embassy of M. Besnard whose intentions and actions had always been for the best, but who carried no weight at the Quai d'Orsay. The same could not be said of his successor, and His Excellency was awaiting M. [de] Beaumarchais' arrival with interested anticipation. It was essential, if any progress was to be made with Yugoslavia, that Franco-Italian relations should first be cleared up and improved and any help of that you found possible to give in this direction would be warmly appreciated here.

It was, however, as Signor Grandi had warned me, clearly useless to press further for a tripartite treaty and so I urged especially in view of M. Marinkovich's friendly speech (though Signor Mussolini did not seem as pleased with it as he ought to have been) that His Excellency should seize the opportunity of the communication of the text of treaty at Belgrade and Paris to make some friendly and re-assuring statement with regard to the independence and integrity of Albania. Signor Mussolini evidently did not like the idea and said that at Belgrade such a statement would be regarded as cynical.[5] He would, however, wait to see how the treaty was received there and he would consider later whether any assurance of the kind I suggested could be given.

Signor Mussolini insisted that treaty made for independence and integrity of Albania. That country was throughout treated as absolutely equal with Italy. There were indeed ridiculous provisions regarding command etc. upon which Ahmed Zogu had insisted and he . . .[6] his best for it. Signor Mussolini not only had no desire to send armed forces to Albania but the sooner he

---

[4] Pseudonym of M. André Géraud, a prominent French political journalist.

[5] A marginal note on the filed copy here read: 'When this conversation took place, the communication of the treaty to the Jugoslav Gov. had already been effected.'

[6] The text is here uncertain.

could withdraw the twenty or so Italian officers training small Albanian army the more pleased he would be. These officers are all suffering from malaria. Several had had to be withdrawn and one had died. Italian action in Albania only purposed to strengthen that country and to enable it to stand upon its own legs in so far as this was possible.

I asked His Excellency whether there was any truth in press report that President of Albania intended to proclaim himself King. From his guarded reply it is clear that this will take place whenever Ahmed Zogu considers himself in a sufficiently strong position to carry it through.[7]

Addressed to Foreign Office No. 212. Repeated to Durazzo and Belgrade.

[7] For an account of this conversation by Signor Mussolini see *I Documenti Diplomatici Italiani*, Settima Serie, vol. v, No. 613.

No. 62

Sir A. Chamberlain to the Marquess of Crewe (Paris)
No. 2918 [C 9538/4490/92]

FOREIGN OFFICE, *November 25, 1927*

My Lord Marquess,

The French Ambassador called this afternoon to give me M. Briand's reply to the observations which I had made to M. de Fleuriau as recorded in my despatch No. 2884[1] of the 22nd November. M. de Fleuriau said that the message which he read to me bore on the face of it evidence that it was in the main from M. Briand's own dictation. It was to the following effect:—

The negotiations of the French Treaty with Jugoslavia have always been parallel with those of Italy at Belgrade. At the end of 1923, after the settlement of the vexed question of Fiume,[2] and with the view to bringing about better relations, M. Mussolini proposed a treaty to Jugoslavia. To facilitate negotiations with the Serbs, he suggested that the treaty should be tripartite, and proposals were made to France on these lines.[3] The French Government

[1] No. 51.
[2] For correspondence relating to the occupation of Fiume by Italian armed bands under Signor d'Annunzio on September 12, 1919, see First Series, Volume IV, Chapter I, and Volume XII, Chapter II. For an account of the negotiations leading to the agreement subsequently signed on January 27, 1924, by Italy and the Serb-Croat-Slovene State regarding the facilities at Fiume (printed in *British and Foreign State Papers*, vol. 120, pp. 685–706), see *Survey of International Affairs 1924*, pp. 408–22.
[3] Sir R. Graham subsequently reported in Rome despatch No. 26 of January 13, 1928, that he had asked Signor Mussolini whether a similar account of events published by Pertinax was true, and that Signor Mussolini had 'replied that there was no foundation for it whatsoever, that he had never heard any suggestion of a tripartite pact until it was proposed to him, much later, by M. Besnard. I asked if he thought it conceivable that any such idea might have been thrown out in conversation by Senator Contarini [Secretary-General of the Italian Ministry of Foreign Affairs, 1919 to 1926], but he replied that he could not think this possible.' Sir R. Graham further reported that Signor Contarini had explained in a press interview in the *Giornale d'Italia* of January 13, 1928, that it was inexact to speak of *proposals* for a tripartite pact before the end of 1925 and that conversations held between August 1923 and January 1924 never had any official or determined character.

welcomed this initiative, and began conversations with Jugoslavia without precipitation and without *arrières-pensées*. Such is the origin of the treaty which M. Briand has just signed with M. Marinkovic. The Italians being more advanced in their conversations, signed as early as January 1924 the treaty with the Jugoslavs with which the French should have been associated.

Since 1926 M. Mussolini has desired to advance a step further in his engagements with Jugoslavia and his hold over her. He proposed to Belgrade to reinforce the treaty by introducing clauses of a military alliance. M. Nincic did not favour such an arrangement between Italy and Jugoslavia alone; he suggested a return to a tripartite agreement between France, Italy and Jugoslavia.

France has supported at Rome this suggestion which marked afresh her friendly loyalty and her desire for relations of confidence with Italy. The Italian Government, going back on its original proposals, refused on various pretexts to agree to a tripartite pact (they pleaded, for example, that a Treaty of Three was not in complete agreement with Locarno). M. Mussolini, who was not ignorant of the French Treaty which was in course of negotiation with Jugoslavia, intimated that he preferred that the two treaties of Italy and France with Jugoslavia should be signed separately. It was under these conditions that in 1926 the terms of the Franco-Jugoslav Treaty were decided upon with M. Nincic, who passed through Paris, after being in Rome; but from an extreme sense of courtesy, M. Briand preferred merely to initial the treaty in order to allow the Italian Government to sign first its treaty with Serbia, it being understood that the treaty with France should be signed immediately afterwards. French policy has been reasonable, moderate, and so friendly with regard to Italy that M. Briand renewed three times this initialling at intervals of six months, to take into account incidents which have occurred between Italy and Jugoslavia, complaints against the Albanian policy of Jugoslavia based on inexact facts, addressed by the Italian Government to all the Powers[4] and the unilateral signature of the Treaty of Tirana, which prepared the way for the progressive control of Italy over Albania in conditions dangerous to peace, by reason of the state of feeling in the Balkan countries.

The French Government has continued to give in Belgrade the most constant counsels of moderation and patience and to advise the resumption of conversations with Rome, while the Italian Government evaded every occasion of explanations and of understanding, without, however, definitely breaking off the conversations which permitted the hope that these latter would be brought to a conclusion. The French Government were, on the other hand, pressed by the Serb-Croat-Slovene Government to sign, and it was not possible for them to avoid the signature of a treaty of friendship (in conformity with all the principles of the League of Nations and corresponding exactly to its recommendations for a separate pact for the strengthening of peace). It had been stipulated in a letter exchanged between the French and Serb-Croat-Slovene Governments that on the first request of one of the

[4] See Volume III, Nos. 49 and 61.

parties, the treaty should be signed. M. Briand made a point of warning the Italian Government a month and a half before the signature, recalling to them the conditions of agreement in which it had been negotiated without provoking any comments on their part.

The signature assumed so little the character of a particularly solemn act that M. Briand had preferred to postpone a journey of King Alexander to France which was to take place this autumn, and to sign with the Minister for Foreign Affairs as is customary. M. Marinkovic made a point of coming to Paris to settle the question of debts and of a treaty of commerce with France. On the very day of the signature declarations entirely friendly to Italy were made to the press on both sides.

The manifold manifestations in Italy, the articles in the press, becoming more and more hostile, tolerated, if not encouraged, by a Government which is entirely master of its public opinion and of order in its streets, have been the answer to the restraint of the French press, to the moderation of the French Government and to the pressing advice given to M. Marinkovic, to which the latter has paid the greatest respect. He was ready to go to Rome to show his desire for a *rapprochement* with the Italian Government, and he expressed himself in the Skupshtina in the most cordial terms with regard to Italy.

Who could reproach French policy or French opinion with not having shown for years past patience and the desire for an understanding with Italy? These feelings, however, did not go as far as sacrificing without some compensation French interests in Morocco and Tunisia assured by treaties. Had I forgotten the manifestations against French consulates in Italy,[5] the activities of police employed with the connivance of the Garibaldians to compromise the French Government in the eyes of the world,[6] the agitations, the repeated menaces of the Italian press, which cannot publish a line without the authorisation of the Government? Did I know that all French undertakings in Italy, financial and economic co-operation, contracts of association like those of Schneider, were methodically boycotted in order to eliminate French nationals under indefensible conditions? Could I consider praiseworthy theatrical hostile manifestations like the visit of the Italian ships to Tangier, when Italy by three successive agreements had renounced Morocco,[7]

[5] See Volume II, No. 282; cf. also *Survey of International Affairs 1927*, pp. 140–2.

[6] The reference was to the trial in France in January 1927, in connection with an attempted raid into Catalonia, of Colonel Ricciotti Garibaldi, grandson of the Italian patriot Guiseppe Garibaldi (1807–82). Colonel Garibaldi was alleged to have been an agent of the Italian police. For an account of this affair *v. ibid.*, pp. 142–52.

[7] In October 1927 an Italian naval squadron under the Duke of Udine visited Tangier in order to participate in the Fascist festival to celebrate the March on Rome of 1922; see *The Times*, October 26, 27, and 29, 1927, pp. 14, 11, and 28 respectively: see also *ibid.*, November 2, p. 11, for a statement of November 1 by Signor Tittoni, President of the Italian Senate. The three Franco-Italian agreements would appear to be: (i) a secret agreement of December 14–16, 1900, concerning Morocco and Tripoli, printed in E. Rouard de Card, *Accords Secrets entre la France et l'Italie concernant le Maroc et la Libie* (Paris, 1921), pp. 45–6; (ii) a secret agreement of November 1, 1902, regarding their respective interests in the Mediterranean, printed *ibid.*, pp. 47–9; (iii) the declaration of October 28, 1912, respecting Morocco and Libya, printed *ibid.*, p. 50, and in *British and Foreign State Papers*, vol. 107, p. 794.

and when she was in agreement with France (as I had recognised only a few days ago) on the procedure which France was following for the revision of the Statute of Tangier, where the French Government had declared themselves ready to give her satisfaction, after an agreement with Spain, of which the French Government are at the moment examining the terms?[8]

Had France ever declined the proposition of negotiations in agreement with Italy? The French Government had said all along that they were ready for any conversation to this effect. M. Mussolini informed M. Briand at the end of 1926 that he would give his new Ambassador, M. Manzoni, instructions to enter on such friendly negotiations. The French Government accepted this postponement, but to M. Briand's great surprise, when the new Ambassador arrived several months later, he had no instructions to this effect, and for months past, although M. Briand kept him in touch with the situation, he had only made communications of a routine nature without entering on the expected negotiations.

Now as then M. Briand was ready to examine with the Italian Government in the most friendly spirit the possibility of dissipating the misunderstandings between the two countries, and to conclude an agreement assuring peace and friendship between them, guaranteeing them both against any surprise. Certain indications and indirect suggestions allowed M. Briand to hope that these sentiments of the French Government were known in Rome, and might be considered there as answering to the sentiments of friendship which M. Mussolini had several times affirmed, and might perhaps determine him to push a little further his suggestion of last year.

Such is a very exact account of the communication made to me by M. de Fleuriau, who called my particular attention to the last paragraph. I thanked the Ambassador, and said that I was always glad to think that M. Briand would speak to me as frankly as I felt that my friendship for him and for France authorised me to speak to him.

I then informed the Ambassador of the steps which I had taken, whether at Tirana or at Rome, since I last saw him. I told him that I had not yet read the actual text of the treaty, and that my suggestion for its conversion into a Tripartite Treaty was, of course, conditional on its being in conformity with the Covenant of the League of Nations. I added, however, that I had just received a telegram from Sir Ronald Graham saying that he had been unable to see M. Mussolini, with whom he could only secure an appointment to-day, but that a conversation with Signor Grandi (though the latter expressly reserved this subject for M. Mussolini's own consideration) left him little hope of my proposal being accepted.[9] That, I remarked, was the present position

---

[8] M. de Fleuriau had left with Sir W. Tyrrell on November 9 a copy of an undated memorandum which had been drawn up in the Quai d'Orsay in reply to Signor Tittoni's statement (see note 7 above) and which discussed the French position at Tangier and Italian renunciations in Morocco. Lord Crewe reported in Paris telegram No. 232 of November 21, not printed, that M. Berthelot was working on a draft agreement with Spain on the Tangier question which would shortly be taken to Madrid by Señor Quiñones de Leon.

[9] See No. 59.

as far as I was concerned. There was nothing more that I could do; I could only await M. Mussolini's reply.

I am, &c.,
Austen Chamberlain

No. 63

Colonel Ryan (Coblenz) to Sir A. Chamberlain (Received November 29)
No. 166 [C 9657/2050/18]

COBLENZ, *November 26, 1927*

Sir,

With reference to Lord Erroll's despatch No. 161,[1] relative to reductions made in the strength of the British Army of the Rhine, I have the honour to inform you that the French High Commissioner[2] informed the High Commission yesterday that, so far as the French Army of the Rhine was concerned, all the reductions provided for in the recent decisions of the Allied Governments have now been completed.

The French Army of the Rhine now consists of two Army Corps of two Divisions each distributed over the four zones of Mainz, Coblenz, Kaiserslautern and Trier, their headquarters being respectively in each of the above-mentioned centres.

2. The reductions made in the effectives of the three Armies of Occupation will result in the total evacuation before the end of the year of the garrisons of Geilenkirchen and Lindern in the Belgian zone, of Idstein in the British zone, and of Dietz and Pfeiffligheim in the French zone, and important reductions in several other garrison towns, notably Königstein and Wiesbaden in the British zone and Düren, Euskirchen, Coblenz and Germersheim in the French zone.

3. In a letter addressed to the High Commission some weeks ago, the German Commissioner, amongst other matters, drew attention to the disadvantages caused to the watering places of the Occupied Territory by the presence of Occupying troops, and requested that, in the reorganisation of garrisons consequent on the reductions then taking place, every effort might be made to reduce the burdens on these places. Baron Langwerth's observations were passed by the High Commission to the General Officer Commanding-in-Chief the Armies of Occupation.[3] Quite apart from the military considerations involved, it is clear that, in a country so full of spas as is the

---

[1] This covering despatch of November 16 is not preserved in Foreign Office archives. The enclosed report dated November 10 from Lieut.-General Thwaites, General Officer Commanding-in-Chief, British Army of the Rhine, stated that the strength of the British Army of the Rhine had been reduced to 6,250 men (6 infantry battalions) from October 18. Idstein was being completely evacuated and the garrison at Königstein reduced by two companies. A copy of this despatch was transmitted to Paris and Brussels in Foreign Office despatches Nos. 2903 and 706 respectively of November 25 in order that the French and Belgian Governments should be informed.

[2] M. Paul Tirard.

[3] General Guillaumat.

Rhineland, it was impossible to comply fully with Baron Langwerth's request, but his observations were given due consideration by the military authorities, and have received reasonable satisfaction, as reference to paragraph 2 above shows.

It is, however, of interest to note that recent articles in the German press in no way bear out the statement of the German Commissioner that the watering-places of the Occupied Territory are the victims of the Occupation. On the contrary, the newspapers have reported that during the past Summer the number of visitors to the spas of the Occupied Territory is greatly in excess of any figure since 1914, and figures have been quoted for a number of places of more or less importance. As far as the better-known towns are concerned, Wiesbaden is stated to have been visited by 80,000 tourists up to July 27th; Neuenahr by 20,000,—a figure that has never before been attained—while the number of visitors to Coblenz showed an increase of 60% over 1926 and of 20%–30% more than in the best pre-war seasons.

I have, &c.,
R. S. RYAN

No. 64

Sir R. Lindsay (Berlin) to Sir A. Chamberlain
(Received November 27, 3.50 p.m.)

No. 105 Telegraphic [C 9546/25/90]

BERLIN, *November 27, 1927, 2.20 p.m.*

The Minister for Foreign Affairs expressed yesterday lively concern over the Albanian Treaty. The Italian Ambassador[1] had tried to represent it as purely defensive and he had answered that it was the most aggressive treaty he had ever read. The Ambassador had then, on the strength of a statement in some English newspaper, accused Herr Stresemann of having a prejudice against Fascism and of leaning therefore unduly towards French, a charge which the latter would not admit.

[1] Count Aldrovandi.

No. 65

Sir R. Lindsay (Berlin) to Sir A. Chamberlain
(Received November 27, 4.30 p.m.)

No. 106 Telegraphic [N 5644/9/38]

BERLIN, *November 27, 1927, 2.30 p.m.*

Speaking yesterday the Minister for Foreign Affairs did not seem to think the situation in Lithuania one of immediate danger though there was a risk of an attempt by exiles at a *coup d'état* against Waldemaras. He said that if invited to serve on League committee he would not decline. He was very gratified at the conclusion with Polish government of preliminary commercial agreement.[1]

Litvinov[2] in passing through Berlin had told him that British offensive against Russia was now taking the form of overwhelming her with credits and he had suggested that in the interest of German trade the German government would do well to furnish some more. Stresemann answered advising him to take all the English money that he could get. With regard to German credits, they had been provided to remedy a condition of industrial unemployment which now obtained no more and they could not be repeated. Litvinov told him that at Geneva Russian delegation would propose complete disarmament all round. He said they had prepared a complete scheme for limiting forces intended to secure internal order which they would submit if principle of complete disarmament was accepted.

[1] Negotiations for a German–Polish commercial treaty had begun in 1925 but had met with difficulties in connection with the German refusal of a Polish request for the continuance after June 15, 1925, of the duty-free importation of products, notably coal, from Polish Upper Silesia into Germany, as provided in the Geneva Convention of May 15, 1922 (see *British and Foreign State Papers*, vol. 118, pp. 365–585). In June 1925 both governments had imposed restrictions on trade between the two countries. Negotiations for a commercial treaty continued intermittently, complicated in 1926 by the problem of liquidation of German property in Poland under article 92 of the Treaty of Versailles. For documentation on these negotiations in 1926 see *Akten zur deutschen auswärtigen Politik 1918–1945* (Göttingen, 1966 f.), vol. ii, parts 1 and 2, *passim*. On February 13, 1927, Sir W. Max Muller had reported in Warsaw telegram No. 21 that M. Zaleski had informed him that the German Government had declared that they would not proceed with the negotiations until the connected question of the German claim to most-favoured-nation treatment in respect of rights of residence in Poland had been settled, more especially in connection with the recent Polish expulsion of four German engineers: see Volume III, Nos. 17, 56, and 68. On July 26 Sir W. Max Muller had reported in Warsaw despatch No. 338 that he had been informed that on July 18 agreement had been reached between the German and Polish Governments on the provisions regarding rights of residence which would be incorporated in the future commercial treaty between the two countries. Recent conversations at Berlin between Dr. Stresemann and Dr. Jackowski, Political Director in the Polish Ministry of Foreign Affairs, had resulted in agreement on the basis on which commercial negotiations should take place: see No. 70. For an account by Dr. Stresemann of a conversation with Dr. Jackowski on November 17, see *Gustav Stresemann, op. cit.*, vol. iii, pp. 248–51. See also *Survey of International Affairs 1932*, pp. 337–8.

[2] Soviet Vice-Commissar for Foreign Affairs. For his statement to Dr. Stresemann, cf. *Gustav Stresemann, op. cit.*, vol. iii, p. 256.

No. 66

Sir W. Max Muller (Warsaw) to Sir A. Chamberlain
(Received November 28, 9 a.m.)
No. 98 Telegraphic [N 5598/61/59]

WARSAW, *November 27, 1927, 9 p.m.*

My telegram No. 96.[1]

Minister for Foreign Affairs again discussed Polish Lithuanian dispute with

[1] Not printed. This telegram of November 25 reported a brief conversation that day with M. Zaleski who informed Sir W. Max Muller in particular that Marshal Pilsudski had decided to attend the forthcoming meeting of the Council of the League of Nations.

me. He referred with annoyance to Soviet note of November 24th[2] drawing attention to menace to peace involved in dispute and urging moderation on Polish government. Minister for Foreign Affairs admitted language was couched in unprecedently courteous terms for a communication from the Soviet government and that similar warning had been addressed to Lithuanian government and expressed the opinion that primary object was to create favourable atmosphere at Geneva for Soviet proposals for disarmament.

Minister for Foreign Affairs showed even stronger resentment at corresponding verbal representation made to Polish Minister at Berlin by Herr [von] Schubert directly after German Minister for Foreign Affairs' two hours interview with Litvinov. Herr Schubert expressed hope that Poland would not attack Lithuania to which Polish Minister replied he might make his mind quite easy on that point. His Excellency deprecated this tactless action of German Minister for Foreign Affairs so soon after satisfactory commercial negotiations but added that visits of Chicherin or Litvinov to Berlin seemed always to result in some act of folly on the part of the German government.

When I entered the room Monsieur Zaleski was engaged in drafting a circular which he kindly read to me. This circular to all governments including the Soviet government should reach London tomorrow. It declares that Polish government have no designs against independence or territorial integrity of Lithuania but only desire cessation of pretended state of war and restoration of neighbourly relations.[3]

Minister for Foreign Affairs begged me to let you know that there was no foundation for newspaper reports of Polish military preparations; in spite of Russian [? and] German interference and in spite of new appeal of Lithuanian government to the League of Nations,[4] intentions of the Polish government remained entirely pacific; there was no idea of mobilization, not a single soldier had been moved though the frontier guard already on the spot had been re-grouped to protect the railway where it ran along the frontier. Polish government felt more hopeful that an understanding could be reached between the two peoples and there was no need to employ violence when the end could be secured by pacific means. Marshal Pilsudski had addressed a stern warning to numerous Lithuanian refugees in Vilna which included many soldiers that no action against Lithuania would be tolerated. In future Lithuanian refugees would be distributed in other parts of Poland and all Lithuanian soldiers were deprived of their uniforms.

Minister for Foreign Affairs then said that Marshal Pilsudski was now hesitating whether he should go to Geneva. In reply to a question from me as to what might happen if Poland did not obtain full satisfaction at Geneva Minister for Foreign Affairs replied that a serious situation would be created

[2] Printed in translation in Jane Degras, *Soviet Documents on Foreign Policy*, vol. ii, pp. 282–3.

[3] Note No. P. 1881 communicated by M. Skirmunt on November 28 is not printed.

[4] Cf. No. 23, note 2. In Riga telegram No. 60 of November 26 (not printed) Sir T. Vaughan, H.M. Minister to Estonia, Latvia, and Lithuania, resident at Riga, reported that Professor Voldemaras had addressed a second letter (dated November 21) to the League of Nations in respect of Article 11 of the Covenant, complaining of further 'Polish propaganda and machinations against Lithuania'.

especially if Marshal Pilsudski had personally presented Polish case but he could not believe Poland's request which was only one for restoration of peace with a neighbouring state could be refused. If Council proved impotent to impose its will on Lithuania a fatal blow would be dealt to the prestige of the League of Nations. At the same time he could not close his eyes to the possibility of German Minister for Foreign Affairs adopting the same position as he had in Westerplatte question against the unanimous opinion of other members of the Council[5] and in this connection he pointed out that in his conversation with Sir R. Lindsay Stresemann had it is true expressed extreme annoyance with Waldemaras personally not with Lithuania as a whole[6] and his own information from Berlin in no way supported the view that the German Minister for Foreign Affairs was likely to take Polish side against Lithuania.

My impression is that Monsieur Zaleski is mistaken here. As Stresemann said to Sir R. Lindsay the existence of Lithuania is a necessity to Germany and it is therefore in her inte[re]st to promote a pacific settlement of the dispute between Poland and Lithuania and not to afford the former an excuse for attacking and extinguishing Lithuania, a consummation which at the present moment neither Germany nor Russia is strong enough to prevent. It is therefore possible that both German and Russian influence may be employed to induce Lithuania to come to a reasonable arrangement with Poland which will anyhow guarantee her independent existence.

Addressed to Foreign Office No. 93: repeated to Riga.

[5] For the discussion and adjournment on September 27 of the question of the use of the Westerplatte depot for Polish munitions and war material in transit through the Free City of Danzig see *League of Nations Official Journal*, October 1927, pp. 1423–38. On December 12, 1927, the Council adopted a resolution inviting the Governments of Danzig and Poland to open direct negotiations: *v. op. cit.*, February 1928, pp. 181–2.

[6] See No. 23.

No. 67

Sir R. Graham (Rome) to Sir A. Chamberlain (Received November 29, 9 a.m.)
No. 215 Telegraphic [C 9652/25/90]

ROME, *November 28, 1927, 8.35 p.m.*

Signor Grandi informed me today that Signor Mussolini was much upset to learn from Durazzo that the ratification of the treaty of Tirana was being withheld owing to British pressure.[1] His Excellency was surprised and hurt and wondered what it meant. I pointed out that you had endeavoured to delay final conclusion of friendship treaty and ratification (? and) publication until Signor Mussolini had had time to consider your proposals. Signor Grandi replied that as it was unfortunately quite impossible to entertain these proposals, he trusted there would be no further opposition on our part to ratification and he requested me to telegraph to you in this sense. Treaty came before the Italian Chamber on Thursday[2] and if Albanian ratification

[1] Cf. No. 60.   [2] December 1, 1927.

had not been secured by then owing to our intervention, the effect would be deplorable. Immediate publication of treaty had become necessary otherwise it would have appeared in Yugoslavia before it came out here.

Signor Grandi showed me a telegram from Italian Minister at Belgrade reporting the conversation with Monsieur Marinkovic when he informed him of the treaty.[3] Monsieur Marinkovic seemed to have accepted the ratification very philosophically and had said that he had made his recent speech in the Belgrade Chamber in full knowledge that treaty was about to be signed. (This announcement had had a very favourable effect on Signor Mussolini.) Monsieur Marinkovic had complained of not having been notified regarding treaty: this he considered contrary to the spirit of the pact of Rome although he admitted that pact in question concerned Central Europe only and not Albania. General Bodrero reported that interview had been very cordial, a fact which he ascribed in great measure to Mr. Kennard having paid a visit to Monsieur Marinkovic just previous to his own.[4]

Addressed to Foreign Office No. 215, repeated to Belgrade and Durazzo.

[3] See *I Documenti Diplomatici Italiani*, Settima Serie, vol. v, No. 617.
[4] The reference was presumably to Mr. Kennard's conversation with M. Marinkovitch, reported in Belgrade telegram No. 188 of November 25, in execution of the instructions in No. 55, note 6.

No. 68

Sir A. Chamberlain to Sir R. Graham (Rome)
No. 1449 [C 9688/25/90]

FOREIGN OFFICE, *November 28, 1927*

Sir,

Signor Bordonaro called this afternoon.

He said that I had doubtless already received from your Excellency a report of Signor Mussolini's conversation with you.[1] He himself had only received his instructions on Saturday[2] and had not wished to trouble me on that day. In the interval he had received further messages from Signor Mussolini.[3] In order to make sure that he correctly carried out his instructions, he had provided himself with some notes which he would read to me, but before doing so he observed that Mr. Seeds had pressed Ahmed Zoghou to postpone the ratification of the treaty. Signor Bordonaro presumed that this had been done only in order to give time for carrying out my suggestion if it were approved in Rome, and that, since Signor Mussolini was unable to accept it, there was no longer any need for Mr. Seeds to persevere in that course.

I replied that I regretted that Signor Mussolini had not seen his way to accept my suggestion. I agreed that there was no longer any object in delaying the ratification of the treaty, and I had already sent instructions to Mr. Seeds this morning to withdraw his objection.[4]

[1] See No. 61.   [2] November 26, 1927.   [3] *V. op. cit.*, Nos. 610 and 613.
[4] In Foreign Office telegram No. 93 to Durazzo, not printed.

Signor Bordonaro then read a rather lengthy exposition of Signor Mussolini's views. In the first place, he justified the Treaty of Alliance with Albania
as being a 'realistic' security for peace. He contrasted this realistic and practical treaty with other more inconclusive models, and suggested that it was
only by the former, which allowed all interested parties to know exactly what
the position was, that the situation could be stabilised and peace secured. He
then went on to say that the problem of peace between Italy and Jugoslavia
and, indeed, of peace in the Balkans generally, was 'essentially a problem of
Franco-Italian policy.' He regretted the unsatisfactory state of Franco-Italian
relations. He attributed this to a series of acts or defaults on the part of the
French Government, and he mentioned in particular and with obviously
deep and bitter feeling the encouragement given in France to 'the worst
elements' among the Italian refugees. In fact, the relations of the two countries
bore the impress and were the counterpart of their different political systems.
It was the harbouring of these extreme elements in France that obliged the
Italian Government to take the frontier measures which inconvenienced trade
and tourists and gave rise to incidents, which in turn were exaggerated and
used as the excuse for renewed attacks upon Italy by the French press. The
signature of the Franco-Jugoslav Treaty had at first been received with great
restraint in Italy, but then had followed anti-Italian manifestations in Jugoslavia to the strains of the Marseillaise. Italy was expected to exercise a control
of her people and her press which France—a free country—felt unable to
impose within her own territory. Jugoslavia would not have created the
difficulties which she had done if she had not felt herself sustained and encouraged by France. There had been talk at different times of a meeting
between Signor Mussolini and M. Briand, and of some accord between the
two countries, but in Signor Mussolini's opinion such a meeting or the conclusion of such an accord would be useless unless the spirit of the two peoples
first changed. Any such meeting or negotiations must be accompanied by a
manifestation of French goodwill and by the settlement of some of the questions which were the cause of trouble between them. Of these he mentioned
two—the refugees and the French encouragement in every possible way of
the denaturalisation of Italians in Tunis.

The Ambassador having thus concluded his exposition of the Italian case, I
told him that he naturally would not expect me to agree with a great deal of
what he had said. I profoundly regretted that Signor Mussolini had not seen
his way to accept my suggestion to convert the Italo-Albanian Treaty into a
tripartite treaty of mutual guarantee. Since I had last seen the Ambassador[5]
he had sent me the text of the treaty.[6] I must confess that I found in it
several phrases which no doubt might be commented on and explained one
way or another, but in its broad outline the treaty did not seem to me well
calculated to forward Signor Mussolini's peaceful intentions or to secure that
appeasement and stability which he desired. There was, however, nothing
more for me to do in this matter at present. I must, however, say a few words
upon the account which Signor Mussolini had given of French policy.

[5] See No. 55.   [6] In a letter of November 25, not printed.

Frankly, I could not recognise the policy of M. Briand or of the French Government in the picture which he had painted. I could say that throughout the recent troubles, whether in regard to incidents which had arisen between Jugoslavia and Bulgaria, Jugoslavia and Albania, or Jugoslavia and Italy itself, the influence of the French Government had been consistently used at Belgrade to counsel moderation and restraint, and I was quite certain that, if Signor Mussolini had entered into a serious discussion with M. Rakic of the problems which confronted the two countries, no obstacle would have been presented by the French Government to the successful conclusion of such negotiations. I profoundly regretted that on one pretext or another Signor Mussolini had deferred these conversations and had now made this new treaty with Albania. But I might say more. M. de Fleuriau had only the other day informed me on M. Briand's authority that to-day as yesterday M. Briand was ready to examine in the most friendly spirit with the Italian Government the possibility of dissipating the misunderstandings between them and of concluding an accord assuring peace and friendship between them and guaranteeing them both against any surprise. Certain indirect indications and suggestions, M. Briand had added, permitted the hope that these friendly sentiments of the French Government were known at Rome and might be there considered as responding to the sentiments of friendship which Signor Mussolini had several times expressed and might perhaps determine him to carry further the suggestion of last year (compare my despatch No. 2918 to Lord Crewe).[7] These, I said, were the actual words of M. Briand. They showed the spirit which animated his policy and the policy of France. I could not agree with Signor Mussolini that, before any conversations could usefully be undertaken, there must be a *détente* between the two peoples. If all attempts to improve relations were to be adjourned until that *détente* should take place, we should have to wait a long time. It was the business of Governments to move in advance of the populace and themselves to produce the *détente* in popular feeling by resolving difficulties and establishing a friendly agreement. I continued earnestly to desire a result so eminently to the advantage of both parties. Was I to be told that no conversations could take place until, so to speak, the need for them had passed or that they could take place only after the acceptance by France as a preliminary condition of an obligation to expel the refugees and to change her nationalisation laws? I supposed that Signor Bordonaro would next be instructed to complain to me of the fact which I learned from the newspapers that Signor Nitti[8] had been speaking at I knew not what meeting here and to call upon His Majesty's Government to take measures against Italian refugees. That would be to ask the impossible —to call for a complete reversal of British policy—and the precedents which would be cited against me if I attempted it would be precisely the aid and comfort we had given to those who founded Italian unity. I was always ready to use my good offices if I could to smooth away difficulties between nations

[7] No. 62.

[8] Signor F. Nitti, who had been Italian Prime Minister and Minister of the Interior June 1919 to June 1920, had left Italy in June 1924 in opposition to the régime of Signor Mussolini.

with whom we were friendly, but I could not make myself the channel for such a communication.

Signor Bordonaro replied that this was very unfortunate, for the only chance of an improvement in Franco-Italian relations lay in my intervention. I repeated that I was always ready to use my good offices where that was possible, but in this case Signor Mussolini had refused my good offices.

The Ambassador interrupted me to ask what I meant by these words.

I replied that I referred to his refusal[1] of my offer[5] to propose to Belgrade as from myself, the conversion of the Italo-Albanian Alliance into a tripartite treaty of mutual guarantee. Signor Mussolini had refused my offer and had deprived me of any possibility of usefulness. I found myself completely powerless.

The Ambassador was obviously unhappy and disturbed. He again expressed his regret and again insisted that it was only I who could bring about a better state of affairs.

Finally, he read to me the concluding passage of each of the telegrams from which he had previously quoted. The one instructed him to assure me in Signor Mussolini's name that Italy was ready for a peaceful policy and would do nothing to trouble the peace of the Balkans or of the world. The other repeated this assurance in very similar language, but prefaced it with the statement that Italy herself had need of peace. I told the Ambassador that I was glad to receive this renewed assurance from Signor Mussolini of his determination to maintain peace and to pursue a peaceful policy. I did not question the sincerity of his declaration; I only regretted that the means which he took to carry out his policy seemed to me ill chosen for the purpose which he had in view.[9]

I am, &c.,

AUSTEN CHAMBERLAIN

[9] Sir A. Chamberlain sent an abbreviated account of this interview to Sir R. Graham in his telegram No. 284 of November 30 to Rome which concluded: 'In case Signor Bordonaro fails to reproduce my remarks accurately and fully in his report to Signor Mussolini, I request that you will find an early opportunity of conveying to him the substance of this telegram.' For Signor Bordonaro's telegraphic report on the conversation v. op. cit., No. 630.

Sir A. Chamberlain had previously, on November 28, sent the following record in his despatch No. 2941 to Paris: 'I took the opportunity of the visit which the French Ambassador paid to me immediately after my interview with Signor Bordonaro to give him the substance of what had passed between Signor Bordonaro and myself. He said that he was sure that Signor Bordonaro, who was disturbed and anxious about the situation, would report my conversation very faithfully to Rome and that M. Briand would be very grateful to me for what I had said of French policy.'

No. 69

Aide-mémoire handed by Sir W. Tyrrell to the Belgian Ambassador on November 28, 1927

[*C 9042/789/18*]

FOREIGN OFFICE, *November 28, 1927*

The *aide-mémoire* left by his Excellency the Belgian Ambassador with Sir Austen Chamberlain on the 9th November, 1927,[1] contained an expression of the Belgian Government's anxiety lest, now that Belgium has relinquished her seat on the Council of the League of Nations, she should be excluded from discussions which may take place at Geneva between the Powers signatory of the Locarno Treaties in regard to the application of these treaties.

His Majesty's Government fully sympathise with the Belgian Government's desires in this respect, and, in so far as they relate to representation on the Council whenever that body is called upon to consider matters arising out of the Locarno Treaties, which may be regarded as specially affecting the interests of Belgium in the sense of paragraph 5 of article 4 of the Covenant of the League, the Belgian Government may rest assured that the British representative at Geneva will certainly act in the spirit of the agreement recorded at Locarno and will always interpret the above-mentioned paragraph in a liberal sense.

As regards any informal conversations concerning the application of the Locarno Treaties, such as may from time to time take place between the Foreign Ministers assembled at Geneva, His Majesty's Government hope that if the Belgian Minister for Foreign Affairs is at Geneva when conversations of this nature are suggested, he will participate in them in future as in the past. His presence may not, however, always be possible, as the occasions for such conversations sometimes arise unexpectedly and almost accidentally; but in all cases it is most certainly the wish of His Majesty's Government that he should be kept as fully informed in future as in the past of all that concerns the application, execution and development of the Treaties of Locarno. Sir Austen Chamberlain will, in case of need, take steps so to keep in touch with his Belgian colleague through the diplomatic channel on all such matters.[2]

[1] See No. 38, note 1.

[2] This *aide-mémoire* is printed in *Documents Diplomatiques Belges 1920–1940*, vol. ii, pp. 458–9.

No. 70

Sir W. Max Muller (Warsaw) to Sir A. Chamberlain
(Received December 5)

No. 516 [*C 9877/91/18*]

WARSAW, *November 28, 1927*

Sir,

I have the honour to inform you that the results of the recent Polish-German conversations in Berlin, as reported in my telegram no. 99[1] of 27th

[1] Not preserved in Foreign Office archives. According to the docket this telegram referred

November, have had an exceedingly good reception here. Although German policy is still disliked and distrusted, the dislike and distrust for everything German are no longer so strong that the average Pole loses sight of his own interests, and there is no doubt that he is able to discuss his relations with Germany in a far calmer spirit than was once the case. I should say that one result of the customs war, which Germany has waged with small profit to herself, has been to teach the Poles a self-reliance which enables them to negotiate more successfully with the Germans, who for their part are beginning to appreciate the fact that the high-handed methods which they formerly adopted with the Poles are likely to defeat their own ends.

2. It will be observed that the preliminary agreement reached between M. Stresemann and M. Jackowski in Berlin fully justified the optimism of my German colleague whose views I reported in my despatch no. 493[2] of 9th November. Certainly from the Polish side the results were as satisfactory as could have been expected, and, though we are still far from the signature of a commercial treaty, a provisional arrangement regulating the exchange of the principal commodities between Germany and Poland may be said to be in sight.

3. The Poles have on the whole accepted the news without excitement but with genuine satisfaction. It is recognised that the timber convention initialled last week in Berlin and due for signature here in a few days' time will materially assist in securing a favourable trade balance.[3] It is equally recognised that Germany, with the exception of the rabid nationalists, is convincing herself that Poland is now a going concern and that it is foolish for her not to seek to benefit as far as she can from the opening of the Polish market. The economic position in Germany is not sufficiently rosy to enable German industrialists to sacrifice their immediate interests for the luxury of weakening a neighbouring country which has shown itself surprisingly able to withstand the economic blockade. Although the German agrarians are still putting up a fight on the question of pigs, the German Government appear to have reached the conclusion that the time has come for as wide an agreement as

to Warsaw despatch No. 493 of November 9 which reported that Herr Rauscher, the German Minister at Warsaw, had discussed with Sir W. Max Muller the forthcoming commercial talks between Dr. Stresemann and Dr. Jackowski (see No. 65, note 1) and had stated that his Government were prepared to negotiate a provisional agreement based on a system of contingents whereby Germany would offer a generous contingent for imports of Polish coal and a restricted contingent for pigs besides giving special facilities for the Polish timber trade while Poland would grant contingents for imports of German manufactured goods. The docket of Warsaw telegram No. 99 stated: 'Foreign Minister is very satisfied with results achieved by preliminary negotiations in Berlin, which afford basis for conclusion of modus vivendi on principle of contingents and therefore of partial opening of frontier. Concurrent negotiations are to commence at once in Warsaw for modus vivendi and commercial treaty. Former will cover points easily settled, whilst other points will be left over for commercial treaty negotiations, which will probably be protracted.'

2 See note 1 above.

3 The provisional regulation for the timber trade, signed on November 30 by Germany and Poland, is printed in G. Fr. de Martens, *op. cit.*, Troisième Série, vol. xxx, pp. 280–3. It would appear that this regulation was not ratified.

possible and are anxious to agree on as many points in dispute as the pressure of the nationalists will permit. The Poles fully recognise the nature of the conflict in Germany and are prepared to facilitate any genuine effort made by the German Government to reach an agreement. It is indeed confidently expected here that the renewed negotiations which are to be opened this week in Warsaw will lead to some positive result.

I have, &c.,
W. G. MAX MULLER

No. 71

Sir A. Chamberlain to Sir R. Lindsay (Berlin)
No. 112 Telegraphic [N 5644/9/38]

FOREIGN OFFICE, November 29, 1927, 3.10 p.m.

Your telegram No. 106[1] (of November 27th).

You may tell Minister for Foreign Affairs that Litvinov's story as regards the granting to Russia of huge credits is pure moonshine.

Though Moscow is no longer officially represented here the public is being flooded with similar tales of unlimited German credit being placed at the disposal of Russia.

[1] No. 65.

No. 72

Sir A. Chamberlain to the Marquess of Crewe (Paris)
No. 2932 [C 9548/25/90]

FOREIGN OFFICE, November 29, 1927

My Lord Marquess,

With reference to my despatch No. 2918[1] of 25th November on the subject of the Franco-Jugoslav Pact and the Italo-Albanian Treaty of Alliance, I transmit herewith copy of a letter which I have since received from the French Ambassador, and of the reply[2] I have returned thereto. I request your Lordship to inform M. Briand that I have read the messages conveyed to me by the French Ambassador with the greatest attention. You should, at the same time, convey to him my warm appreciation of the instructions sent by him to the French Minister at Belgrade, and you should inform him that it is my earnest desire to continue in close touch with French policy of this character. You should add that I regret that the suggestion which I made to Signor Mussolini for the expansion of the Italo-Albanian Treaty into a tripartite one, has, for the present at any rate, proved unacceptable to him.

[1] No. 62.

[2] This letter of November 29, not printed, thanked M. de Fleuriau for his letter and informed him of the instructions to Lord Crewe in the present paragraph.

2. Lastly, I shall be glad if you will express my satisfaction at the success of the measures taken to restrain the comments of the Paris press, as reported in your telegram No. 235[3] of the 25th [24th] instant.

I am, &c.,

(For the Secretary of State),

ORME SARGENT

ENCLOSURE IN NO. 72

M. de Fleuriau to Sir A. Chamberlain

Ambassade de France, Londres, ce 24 novembre 1927

Cher Sir Austen,

Après vous avoir vu cet après midi, j'ai reçu communication d'un télégramme envoyé au Ministre de France à Belgrade pour faire ressortir les graves inconvénients de manifestations gallophiles et italophobes et les avantages d'une attitude calme et réservée en Yougo Slavie. La signature du traité défensif italo-albanais provoque dans le monde une désapprobation dont la Yougo Slavie tirera grand bénéfice si elle montre une parfaite sérénité. Pour renforcer cet argument, M. Briand parle de vous, cher Sir Austen, sans d'ailleurs faire allusion aux suggestions dont vous avez bien voulu m'entretenir aujourd'hui. Il fait remarquer que le traité italo-albanais vise l'hypothèse improbable d'attaques dirigées par une tierce Puissance contre l'indépendance ou l'intégrité territoriale de l'Albanie, et que ce traité ne modifie pas une situation de fait déjà connue, que même il a l'avantage de rendre publics et patents des engagements qui ne faisaient de doute à personne. Tout recommande donc à la Yougo Slavie l'abstention de démonstrations bruyantes et inutiles.

J'ai reçu aussi ce soir un mot de Briand dont je vous fais part brièvement ce soir avant de causer avec vous de cet autre sujet. Vous aviez dit à mon ami Clauzel[4] que vous recommandiez à M. Briand et à M. Stresemann d'accepter d'être co-rapporteurs du litige polono-lithuanien au Conseil de la Société des Nations. M. Briand ne partage pas votre sentiment parceque lui et M. Stresemann ne représentent pas en la circonstance des tendances opposées qu'il s'agirait de concilier. M. Briand estime qu'il faudra une action de tout le Conseil pour régler une question aussi dangereuse que celle des rapports entre la Pologne et la Lithuanie. C'est à la procédure même qu'il fait objection.

Veuillez agréer, &c.,

A. DE FLEURIAU

[3] Not printed.
[4] Head of the League of Nations Service in the French Ministry of Foreign Affairs.

No. 73

The Allied Military Experts (Berlin)[1] *to Marshal Foch (Paris)*[2]

No. 104 [C 10199/11/18]

BERLIN, *le 29 Novembre 1927*

Compte-rendu sur le degré d'avancement des questions dont le règlement n'était pas terminé au 31 Janvier 1927

Nous avons l'honneur de vous rendre compte ci-après, sous la présentation déjà adoptée dans le précédent Compte-Rendu (N⁰ 82,[3] du 23 Août 1927), de l'état d'avancement au 25 Novembre 1927 des questions qui nous ont été confiées;

a) Armement

Sous réserve que les dérogations demandées par le Gouvernement allemand relativement aux cinq établissements partiellement occupés par la police soient accordé[e]s, ainsi que le suggèrent les Experts,[4] les seuls points qui sont encore en suspens sont la livraison, par la Bavière, de 6 sous-stations de T.S.F. et la mise en place des 4 canons de la défense côtière.

b) Effectifs

De nouveaux progrès ont été réalisés dans la réorganisation de la police.

Les redressements concernant le Ministère de la Reichswehr sont exécutés, sauf en ce qui concerne le recrutement et l'instruction des Officiers d'État-Major.

La suppression des aménagements militaires du matériel roulant des Chemins de fer se poursuit normalement, mais aucun projet de nouveau règlement sur les transports militaires n'a été jusqu'à présent communiqué.

Les redressements relatifs à l'instruction de la Reichswehr dans l'emploi d'armes interdites sont encore en suspens. Aucune proposition nouvelle n'est parvenue depuis le dernier Compte-Rendu.

L'aliénation définitive des établissements administratifs militaires en excédent fait encore l'objet de pourparlers. Des renseignements verbaux ont été fournis sur l'exécution du programme d'aliénation de 1927, renseignements desquels il résulte que ce programme n'a été que partiellement exécuté (environ 50%).

Le Gouvernement allemand a fait connaître que les stocks de vivres de réserve avaient été réduits dans les conditions fixées par la Commission Militaire Interalliée de Contrôle. Quelques visites de vérification apparaissent nécessaires.

---

[1] For the appointment and duties of these experts see No. 76.

[2] A copy of this report was received in the Foreign Office on December 17 under cover of Paris despatch No. 2488 (not preserved in Foreign Office archives).

[3] Not printed.

[4] *Note on original*: 'Lettre N⁰. 103, du 28 Novembre 1927 [untraced in Foreign Office archives].'

Enfin, relativement aux Associations et à la dissolution du Grenz[s]chutz[5] de Prusse Orientale, aucun progrès — sauf une nouvelle communication au sujet du 'Stahlhelm'[6] — n'a été réalisé.

c) Fortifications

Les seuls points restant en suspens sont les deux suivants:

— vérifier l'exécution de certains travaux dans la place de Wilhelmshaven, après mise en position des canons de gros calibre de la Batterie Friedrich-August, et clôturer ensuite le dossier de recensement de cette place;

— éclaircissements au sujet des crédits affectés depuis 1923 aux fortifications et au Grenzschutz.

Un exposé plus détaillé de ces diverses questions est ci-joint.[3]

Le lieutenant-Colonel B. E. M. Janssens Expert militaire belge.	Le Colonel Gosset, CMG, DSO Expert militaire britannique.
Le Commandant Durand Expert militaire français.	Le Colonel Rossi Expert militaire italien.

[5] Frontier protection force.   [6] Steelhelmet association.

No. 74

Mr. London[1] (Geneva) to Sir A. Chamberlain
(Received November 30, 10.45 a.m.)
No. 278 L.N. Telegraphic [N 5650/209/38]

GENEVA, *November 30, 1927, 10.30 a.m.*

Following from Cadogan.[2]

I understand that M. Litvinoff is very anxious to see Secretary of State and is trying to find excuses for staying on into next week, e.g. by prolonging session of Security Committee[3] for a few days. If Secretary of State would be unwilling to receive him in any (event?) it might be well to discourage Litvinoff as soon as possible. I understand when asked whether he had any proposals to make Litvinoff said he was not prepared to make any advances and indicated that he expected Secretary of State to take the initiative.

[1] H.M. Consul at Geneva.
[2] An assistant to the British Delegate to the League of Nations.
[3] See No. 230, below.

No. 75

The Marquess of Crewe (Paris) to Sir A. Chamberlain
(Received December 1, 8.30 a.m.)
No. 241 Telegraphic: by bag [C 9713/25/90]

Confidential   PARIS, *November 30, 1927*

Sir Eric Phipps handed to M. Berthelot this afternoon a private letter from me to M. Briand embodying the message contained in your despatch

No. 2932[1] of yesterday, expressing your appreciation of the instructions sent by the French government to their representative at Belgrade.

2. M. Berthelot informed Sir Eric Phipps in confidence that unofficial pressure had been brought to bear on M. Briand during the last few days to make some friendly gesture towards Italy. M. Berthelot had, therefore, proceeded to draft an 'establishment treaty' between France and Italy whereby 'inter alia' the large number of Italians resident in France would be granted certain privileges, such as most-favoured-nation treatment, etc., and French companies in Italy would, as compensation, receive certain advantages. This draft M. Berthelot said he was going to submit this afternoon at 6.30 to the Italian Ambassador. At this point, the office-keeper announced that Count Manzoni was waiting.[2]

3. M. Berthelot nevertheless proceeded to read out rapidly a long telegram received from the French Ambassador at Berlin giving in greater detail than did Sir Ronald Lindsay in his telegram No. 105[3] of November 27th Herr Stresemann's views on the recent Albanian treaty. Herr Stresemann told M. de Margerie that he considered that this treaty smelt of powder ('sentait la guerre'); he had heard moreover that warlike preparations were now on foot in Albania where great activity was being displayed in munitions depots, etc. Herr Stresemann now understood the meaning of the accusations brought last[4] year against Yugoslavia by Signor Mussolini, who wished to make Italy appear like an innocent lamb and to throw all responsibility for any future difficulties on to the Serbs; he felt that if things continued as at present we were heading for another war in which Italy would be the first to founder (sombrer) and we should all emerge more than ever the economic and financial slaves of America.

4. Herr Stresemann informed M. de Margerie that Signor Mussolini had had the effrontery to wish to publish on his own account the text of the Franco-Yugoslav treaty, which had been communicated to him beforehand by the French government, but, as Herr Stresemann had told the Italian Ambassador,[5] it was fortunate that Signor Mussolini had not carried out his intention for the difference between the two treaties was palpable, one being in strict harmony with the League of Nations whereas the Albanian treaty made no mention of the League beyond stating that it would be registered at Geneva.

5. Herr Stresemann complained of the excess of zeal shown by Count Aldrovandi and then proceeded to state how he had urged on the latter the desirability of sending a really responsible Italian representative, such as Signor Grandi to Geneva. Count Aldrovandi replied that Signor Grandi had no time to spare, whereupon Herr Stresemann had retorted that this was strange seeing that you and he and M. Briand were able to find the time.

[1] No. 72.
[2] For an account of this interview by Count Manzoni see *I Documenti Diplomatici Italiani*, Settima Serie, vol. v, No. 638.　　　　　　　　　　　　　　　　　　　　　　[3] No. 64.
[4] A note on the filed copy suggested that this word should read 'this'.
[5] Cf. *op. cit.*, No. 609.

6. M. Berthelot again told Sir Eric Phipps that he was convinced that the bright spot of the approaching Council meeting at Geneva was Herr Stresemann's manifest intention to work in close collaboration with you and M. Briand at Geneva.

7. M. Berthelot said that a communiqué would probably be issued to the Press on December 3rd to the effect that an establishment treaty between Italy and France would shortly be signed.[6] This would constitute a friendly gesture on the part of the French government and should help to clear the air in so far as Franco-Italian relations were concerned.[7]

[6] For the notes to this effect exchanged between M. Briand and Count Manzoni on December 3, 1927, see *British and Foreign State Papers*, vol. 127, pp. 481–2.

[7] With reference to the present telegram, which was repeated to Berlin by the Foreign Office on December 1, and No. 64, Sir A. Chamberlain sent to Sir R. Lindsay, in Foreign Office telegram No. 114 of December 1 to Berlin, a brief summary of No. 68 with instructions to inform Dr. Stresemann immediately and confidentially of his proposal to Signor Mussolini and of his general attitude (see Nos. 55 and 61).

No. 76

Memorandum by Mr. Perowne respecting the withdrawal from Berlin of the Allied Military Control Experts

[*C 9801/11/18*]

FOREIGN OFFICE, *November 30, 1927*

It is conceivable (though, according to our latest information, not probable) that the Germans may attempt to raise the question of the withdrawal of the Allied experts from Berlin at the forthcoming Geneva meeting.[1]

The agreement initialled by the Secretary of State at Geneva on December 12th, 1926, provided that the Military Control Commission should be withdrawn from Germany on January 31st, 1927, but that 'each of the Governments represented on the Ambassadors' Conference might attach to its Embassy in Berlin a technical expert empowered to reach agreement (qui aura qualité de [pour] s'entendre) with the competent German authorities on all the questions of execution in regard to the settlements reached or to be reached'.[2] French, British, Italian and Belgian experts were accordingly appointed and entered into their functions on February 1st last. The British expert is Colonel Gosset.

The experts' duties were laid down in February by instructions issued by the Ambassadors' Conference. Briefly their mission was: (1) 'de poursuivre l'exécution des redressements visés dans la note collective du 4 Juin 1925'[3] etc. . . . .[4] (2) 'd'en constater l'achèvement.'[5]

[1] Of the Council of the League of Nations.
[2] See Volume II, Annex to No. 355.
[3] The note presented to the German Government by the British, French, Italian, Japanese, and Belgian representatives at Berlin on June 4, 1925, is printed in Cmd. 2429 of 1925.
[4] Punctuation as in original.   [5] See Volume III, No. 12.

147

On February 3rd the C[omité] M[ilitaire] A[llié de] V[ersailles] addressed to the experts a list of the outstanding questions left to the experts for settlement.[6] It is evident that the 'constatation' of such settlement can be carried out in some cases by the examination of documents: in other cases visits of inspection may be necessary. A dispute soon arose in connexion with the question of visits by the experts. The German Government announced that the destruction of certain shelters at Königsberg, Küstrin, and Glogau (the demolition of which had formed the subject of an agreement between the German and the Allied Powers) was complete: but they declined to agree to the experts visiting the sites to verify the completeness of the destructions. It was indeed clear in the view of His Majesty's Government that the experts had no *legal* right to make such local investigations: but it seemed on the other hand essential that the experts should be in a position to confirm by personal observation the execution of any points where they considered it desirable, in order to avoid any suspicion of bad faith on the German side and any necessity for an appeal by the Allied Powers to the League. On June 16th, however, a compromise about the eastern fortifications was reached at Geneva[7] whereby it was agreed that one or two of the experts should be invited by General von Pawelsz, the German technical expert, to inspect with him the work of demolition of the shelters in question. It was also agreed that no precedent should be held to have been created by this 'invitation' though the Secretary of State was careful to remind Dr. Stresemann in conversation at the time that there were also the coastal fortifications to be considered, and he suggested that the German Government might be willing to make a similar gesture in a later analogous case.[8]

The visits to the eastern fortifications concluded in the most successful manner on July 8th, a joint report signed by the German and Allied representatives on that date testifying to the complete discharge by the Germans of their obligations in regard to the destruction of the shelters in question.[9]

Meanwhile it had been agreed among the Allies that visits would be required not only in the case of the eastern fortifications but also in those of the coast batteries, the police, the demilitarization of the Rhineland and the alienation of military establishments. About the middle of July difficulties seemed likely to arise between His Majesty's Government and the German Government with regard to the principle of further visits by the experts. Briefly it was decided that since the German military experts tended to be reasonable but the German Foreign Office to obstruct, the best hope of reaching a solution of the practical issue involved was to leave it to the Allied and German experts to settle between themselves both the number and the nature of the visits to be made. A note to the German Ambassador dated August 9th concluded as follows (after explaining that there was no point in dispute between His Majesty's Government and the German Government in regard to the legal aspect of the visits in question): 'In these circumstances, and encouraged by information which has recently reached me, I venture to

[6] Not printed.
[8] *V. ibid.*, No. 241.
[7] *V. ibid.*, No. 245.
[9] *V. ibid.*, No. 269, enclosure 1.

express the hope that it may prove possible for the German and Allied military experts so to arrange matters among themselves with regard to the manner and circumstances of a final settlement of all the points in regard to German disarmament at present under discussion between them that no further need may arise for the direct intervention in this question of any of the Governments concerned.'[10] This phrase was designed to safeguard the experts in view of the fact that further visits were contemplated.

Since that date a number of visits have in fact been carried out successfully. At the invitation of the German military experts visits have been paid to alienated military establishments in the occupied territory and to the dismantled fortifications in the Rhineland (this question is finished with until further evacuations take place) as well as to certain police establishments elsewhere.

On September 9th the War Office proposed that a date should be fixed for the withdrawal of the experts from Berlin and that the German Government should be notified accordingly. Certain correspondence[6] followed, as a result of which it was agreed that no such notification was necessary and that any intervention on the part of the Allied Governments was inadvisable at present, it being for the German Government rather than for the Allied Powers to take the first step as regards withdrawal. For the present then the negotiations should be left in the hands of the experts.

Accordingly it was decided to instruct Colonel Gosset to attempt to reach a settlement on the following lines.

The experts should be withdrawn when:—

(1) The Police Laws have passed the State Parliaments and the necessary administrative measures have been approved for Prussia and Bavaria:

(2) The programmes for the alienation and transformation of military establishments have been agreed upon and visits paid to selected establishments in the 1927 programme:

(3) The coast defence guns have been mounted and visited:

(4) The German Government report to the Ambassadors' Conference the further progressive execution of the outstanding questions and agreed to invite the necessary experts to make, after withdrawal, certain visits of verification, e.g. to military establishments and police as well as to future dismantlements in occupied territory;

it was clearly to be understood however (i) that the further visits contemplated in (2), (3) and (4) should not constitute a series of visits covering every individual case, but should consist merely of certain test visits and be strictly limited in number, and (ii) that if the German negotiators refused to give the assurances referred to in (4) regarding invitations to the experts to make certain visits of verification after their withdrawal from Berlin, this refusal should not justify the further retention of the experts in Germany, but would only mean that the Allied Governments will have to fall back on the alternative of reserving their right to request the League of Nations to send a

[10] *V. ibid.*, No. 294.

commission for the purpose of verification. Moreover it would be necessary in order to avoid misunderstandings that the Allied requirements regarding all the outstanding questions should be notified to the German Government before the experts are withdrawn.

To conclude: the Foreign Office view may be summarized as follows:—

The experts to be withdrawn as soon as possible and as few 'visits' as possible demanded. On the other hand the Foreign Office has agreed that the experts must be judges of what visits are essential, and that the negotiations should so far as possible be left in the experts' hands. Any initiative as regards withdrawal should come from the German, not the Allied side,[11] and the Allied Governments should not themselves intervene unless and until (a) the experts find it impossible to reach agreement with the German military authorities as regards visits which they consider essential, or (b) the experts have done all they can do for the time being and are in a position to draw up their final report, while making reservations as regards those requirements the execution of which cannot for one reason or another be completed for a considerable time. As it is in the nature of things that the early withdrawal it is hoped to achieve must take place before the full programme contained in the C.M.A.V. letter of February 3rd can have been carried out, it is obviously necessary to fix a stage at which withdrawal can be effected: what that stage should be has been indicated in the instructions which the Foreign Office agreed should be sent to Colonel Gosset (see above) as the basis for his negotiations. When that stage has been reached and it becomes possible to withdraw the experts it will be necessary (a) that the Germans should, in order to avoid misunderstanding, be told the Allied requirements regarding all the questions still outstanding, and (b) that an arrangement should be come to for verifying the subsequent final execution of those questions—failing such an arrangement the experts will still be withdrawn but the right to a subsequent League investigation will be reserved.

Such is the policy of His Majesty's Government.

It was pointed out earlier in this memorandum that the points, the settlement of which was entrusted to the experts, fell into two classes: (1) those where documentary evidence sufficed, and (2) those where visits of inspection would be required. It is understood that the experts are presenting to the C.M.A.V. on December 1st a schedule showing the present situation of their work,[12] but the information at present at the disposal of the Foreign Office is insufficient to define the actual position. As regards class (1) of the points requiring settlement, nothing is known; as regards (2) visits were required in 5 instances; eastern fortifications and Rhineland dismantlements both of

---

[11] In a message to the Director of Military Operations and Intelligence at the War Office transmitted in Berlin telegram No. 109 of November 30, Colonel Gosset had stated in particular 'my impression is that Germans are in no hurry to get rid of experts'.

[12] See No. 73.

which are finished with for the present; police and alienated military establishments in which some visits have already been paid but more are declared to be necessary; and the coastal fortifications where no visit has as yet been paid.

The latest information is that the stage foreseen in Colonel Gosset's instructions will not be reached by March 31st next and that certain difficulties, not yet acute, are to be anticipated in connexion with the remaining proposed visits to police and alienated military establishments and to coastal fortifications. It is hoped not too confidently that these difficulties may be smoothed out by means of negotiations between the experts in Berlin. And meanwhile the War Office are most anxious that the question should *not* be discussed at Geneva if it can be avoided.

J. V. PEROWNE

No. 77

Sir A. Chamberlain to Mr. London (Geneva)
No. 206 Telegraphic [N 5650/209/38]

FOREIGN OFFICE, *December 1, 1927, 3.35 p.m.*

Following for Mr. Cadogan.
Your telegram No. 278 L.N.[1]
Litvinoff's suggestion that he expects me to make advances is a silly impertinence and requires no reply.

If he formally asks for an interview you should transmit his request to me. Otherwise you need take no action.

[1] No. 74.

No. 78

Sir A. Chamberlain to the Marquess of Crewe (Paris)
No. 2966 [C 9723/3636/18]

FOREIGN OFFICE, *December 2, 1927*

My Lord Marquess,
I have received Your Lordship's despatch No. 2250 (699/3/1927) of the 10th November last enclosing copy of a note from the French Delegation of the Ambassadors' Conference, relative to the desire of the German Marine-leitung to mount 30.5 cm. guns on their 'replacement battleships' instead of the 28 cm. guns mounted on those at present in commission.[1]

2. His Majesty's Government do not desire to decide at the present juncture what would be the most secure legal ground on which to meet an official German proposal of the nature indicated; and since the German official who

[1] Not preserved in Foreign Office archives. According to the docket this French note of November 7 proposed that the previous Allied decision on the subject should be maintained. The decision in question was presumably that reached by the Conference of Ambassadors on July 18, 1923, that the calibre of 28 cm. should not be exceeded for naval guns.

approached the French Naval Attaché in Berlin is said to have stated that the German naval authorities do not intend to take a decision on the subject without first obtaining an assurance that the ex-Allied Powers see no objection thereto, it may be presumed that, in the absence of any such assurance, an official German proposal will eventually be forthcoming before a decision to mount the larger guns is taken.

3. Meanwhile, nothing has been said to the German Government which could possibly create the impression that an application in this sense would be likely to meet with success: on the contrary, as stated in paragraphs 2 and 3 of the letter to the Admiralty, a copy of which was enclosed in my despatch No. 2640[2] of October 21st last, the views expressed by Commander Nash will have shown the Marineleitung that such an application is likely to meet with a refusal.

4. I request therefore that Your Lordship will intimate to the French Government through the secretariat of the Ambassadors' Conference or in whatever manner you think best, that no object would appear to be served by discussing this question until an official request is received from the German Government.[3]

I am, &c.,
(For the Secretary of State)
C. HOWARD SMITH

[2] This covering despatch is not preserved in Foreign Office archives. The enclosed letter of October 21 to the Admiralty, not printed, referred to the report by Commander Nash printed as enclosure 1 in No. 13.

[3] On January 14, 1928, Lord Crewe transmitted in Paris covering despatch No. 73 (not preserved in Foreign Office archives) a French note of January 11 which stated that information had been received that after conversations with several naval attachés, the German Ministry of Marine had taken account of the difficulties which the proposed mounting of 30.5 cm. guns would raise and had given orders that plans should be made for future battleships to have 28 cm. guns.

No. 79

Note from M. Briand to the Austrian Minister (Paris)[1]
No. 192 [*C 9774/55/3*]

PARIS, *le 2 Décembre 1927*

Monsieur le Ministre,

La Conférence des Ambassadeurs a examiné l'état d'exécution des engagements pris par le représentant du Gouvernement autrichien dans le procès-verbal signé à Paris le 30 Juillet 1926.[2] Tout en constatant que, sur un certain nombre de points, ces engagements avaient été pleinement exécutés, elle a dû, d'autre part, se rendre compte que, pour d'autres questions, des retards importants s'étaient produits.

[1] This note to Dr. Grünberger was received in the Foreign Office on December 2 under cover of Paris despatch No. 2385 (not preserved in Foreign Office archives).
[2] See Volume II, No. 119.

La Conférence est convaincue que, si le Gouvernement autrichien veut faire preuve de bonne volonté, il a la possibilité de prendre, avant le 31 Janvier prochain, les mesures suivantes, conformes aux engagements qu'il avait contractés et qui n'ont pas encore été exécutés, savoir :

a) faire voter et promulguer une loi sur l'importation et l'exportation du matériel de guerre, identique à la loi allemande;

b) mettre en état de fonctionnement les différentes sections de l'Usine Unique d'État à l'exception des sections de Blumau (poudre) et de Simmering-Heide (fabrication d'armes portatives et de canons);

c) achever la destruction et la dispersion des machines restant encore à détruire et à disperser pour assurer la fin du désarmement industriel, le Gouvernement autrichien ayant d'ailleurs la latitude de détruire le matériel qu'il n'aurait pas réussi à disperser;

d) exécuter les travaux de réduction du dépôt de Gross-Mittel;

e) — effectuer la destruction des bonbonnes de gaz asphyxiants existant encore;

— effectuer la destruction des 25 tonnes de douilles découvertes à Benköe;

— livrer le matériel découvert à Wöllersdorf le 2 Août 1927;

f) fournir tous les renseignements relatifs aux effectifs et emplacements de l'armée fédérale, indispensables pour établir nettement la situation actuelle de cette armée;

g) fournir conformément à la note de la Conférence des Ambassadeurs du 25 Juillet 1927,[3] paragraphe 2e, tous les éclaircissements nécessaires concernant la situation des anciens officiers employés dans l'administration militaire, et donner l'assurance que ces officiers seront réellement mis à la retraite et ne pourront sous aucun prétexte être rappelés dans l'armée fédérale.

Par contre, en ce qui concerne :

1°) la mise en service de la section des poudres et explosifs de Blumau et de la section de fabrication des armes portatives et des canons à Simmering-Heide,

2°) les destructions à opérer dans les installations de Wöllersdorf, de Blumau et de l'Arsenal,

3°) l'organisation et le maintien à Vienne d'une garde communale (Gemeindewache), dans des conditions contraires aux dispositions du Traité de Saint-Germain,

la Conférence, se rendant compte des difficultés que pourrait éprouver le Gouvernement autrichien à satisfaire à cet égard, dans un aussi bref délai, aux demandes dont il a été antérieurement saisi par l'Organe de Liquidation, ne veut pas subordonner le retrait de cet Organe à l'exécution intégrale de ces demandes; en revanche, elle compte fermement que, avant le 31

[3] Not printed. Lord Crewe transmitted in Paris covering despatch No. 1640 of July 28 (not preserved in Foreign Office archives) a copy of this note, No. 157 to the Austrian Legation, which granted, subject to certain conditions, an Austrian request for an increase in the numbers of officers and non-commissioned officers stipulated in the treaty of Saint-Germain to allow for 200 medical officers and veterinary surgeons.

Janvier 1928, le Gouvernement autrichien prendra sur ces trois points l'engagement écrit : *a*) d'entreprendre immédiatement les travaux envisagés aux paragraphes 1°) et 2°) ci-dessus et de les avoir terminés au plus tard le 1er Juillet 1928; *b*) de procéder au licenciement de la garde communale de Vienne (Gemeindewache) dès que la situation intérieure de l'Autriche le permettra; *c*) enfin, d'autoriser des experts militaires, qui pourront être les attachés militaires à Vienne des Gouvernements intéressés, à vérifier ultérieurement et à une date qui sera fixée, d'accord avec le Gouvernement autrichien, l'exécution des engagements ci-dessus, relatifs tant à l'achèvement des travaux qu'à la dissolution de la Gemeindewache.[4]

L'attention de la Conférence a également été attirée sur l'inobservation, par diverses Associations appartenant à différents partis politiques, des dispositions édictées par le Gouvernement autrichien, notamment par les décrets du 27 Décembre 1926 et du 29 Mars 1927,[5] afin d'assurer l'exécution des engagements contenus dans l'article 128 du Traité de Saint-Germain. Les Puissances ont confiance que votre Gouvernement ne perdra pas de vue cette situation et qu'il saura prendre les mesures utiles pour y mettre fin.

C'est dans ces conditions que la Conférence, convaincue que le Gouvernement autrichien aura à cœur de répondre à la confiance qui lui est ainsi témoignée, a décidé de mettre fin le 31 Janvier 1928, à la mission de l'Organe de Liquidation qui demeurera cependant à Vienne jusqu'au 29 Février 1928 pour achever la rédaction de son Rapport final. Ce Rapport sera transmis par les soins de la Conférence au Conseil de la Société des Nations auquel sera en même temps notifiée la cessation du contrôle exécuté en vertu des articles 149 et suivants du Traité de Saint-Germain. Dès ce moment, l'article 159 dudit Traité pourra donc trouver son application.

Je vous serais obligé de bien vouloir porter d'urgence la présente communication à la connaissance de votre Gouvernement.

Agréez, &c.,

A. Briand

---

[4] In note No. 332 of January 17, 1928, to the President of the Conference of Ambassadors Dr. Grünberger stated that his Government undertook to fulfil the three requests in this paragraph.

[5] See Volume III, No. 14, note 10, and No. 295, note 5, respectively.

No. 80

Sir R. Graham (Rome) to Sir A. Chamberlain (Received December 5)

No. 913 [C 9840/25/90]

Confidential　　　　　　　　　　　　　　　　　　　　ROME, *December 2, 1927*

Sir,

I have little to add to my telegram No. 212[1] of the 25th ultimo recording my conversation with Signor Mussolini regarding the new Treaty of Tirana.

[1] No. 61.

I used all the arguments I could think of in order to induce His Excellency to agree to your suggestion that the Treaty should be made tripartite and Yugoslavia admitted to it, but he brushed them aside and was scarcely willing even to discuss the proposal. This did not surprise me as Italian policy has been and is directed to secure a preponderant position for Italy in Albania, and to exclude Yugoslav intervention in any form. Your proposal was made without knowledge of the terms of the new Treaty, but it is clear that Yugoslav participation in it would have afforded them a right of intervention in certain given circumstances. Signor Mussolini was emphatic in repeating his previous assertions that Italy's sole object in her Albanian policy was to fortify that country and enable it to stand upon its own legs in so far as this was possible. He asked why the Belgrade Government regarded this policy with such dislike and suspicion unless they harboured ulterior designs which would be frustrated thereby. To imagine that Italy desired to establish a base in Albania, from which to attack Yugoslavia, was sheer nonsense, and could not be entertained for a moment by anybody who was in good faith or had looked at the map. Italy was doing what she could to support Albania and its government, but desired to avoid becoming involved more than was absolutely necessary. The vital interest of Albania to Italy as the door of the Adriatic was universally recognised. There had been the decision of the Conference of Ambassadors of 1921, and even President Wilson had favoured giving Valona to Italy.

2. I said that no one questioned the vital interest of Italy in Albania. If His Excellency had declared a sort of Monroe doctrine[2] regarding that country, which would exclude the possibility of its falling into unfriendly hands, I did not think that this could be seriously criticised. But it was another thing to endeavour to monopolise the country, and this was bound to excite the suspicion of neighbours. Signor Mussolini replied that he had no desire to create a monopoly. There were some 20 Italian Officers instructing the ridiculous little Albanian army of 6000 or 7000 men. These officers were all suffering from discomfort and illness, one indeed had died and the sooner he could withdraw them the better pleased he would be.

3. I turned to the subject of Italo-Yugoslav relations. I drew attention to M. Marinkovich's friendly speech in the Skupchina. His Excellency had told me that the new Treaty had been in course of preparation for some months past, and was based on the old Anglo-Portuguese Treaty of Alliance. In this case it seemed to me that the signature of the Franco-Yugoslav pact became not only justifiable but evidence of a necessary prevision. Italy had no valid cause of complaint. The main interest of His Majesty's Government in the whole affair was to bring about, more in the interest of Italy than anyone else, a general improvement of relations between Italy and Yugoslavia and Italy and France. Could not His Excellency offer some friendly gesture at Belgrade and Paris calculated to ease the situation?

[2] Cf. the citation from President Monroe's Annual Message to Congress on December 2, 1823, printed in S. F. Bemis, *A Diplomatic History of the United States* (5th ed., New York, 1965), pp. 210–11.

4. Signor Mussolini brushed aside relations with Belgrade as comparatively unimportant, for they were merely the echo of relations with Paris. Franco-Italian relations caused him serious preoccupation. They were bad, and inclined to become worse. His Excellency repeated the old grievances, which are now familiar to you. He said that their effect throughout Italy was profound and was felt in all circles from the highest to the lowest. A war between France and Italy was unthinkable. At the same time it was the only war which would be really popular in this country. The questions at issue between France and Italy were difficult but by no means insoluble, and no one would welcome a solution more than himself. But a frank, friendly and early exchange of views was necessary. I had stated the policy of His Majesty's Government and our desire to be of service to Italy where we could. Our assistance in the matter of Franco-Italian relations would be warmly welcomed.

5. In so far as our further advice to Italy is concerned, the situation seems to me as follows:

(1) Advice regarding Albania is not appreciated, and is in fact somewhat resented.

(2) Advice regarding relations with Yugoslavia is accepted but rarely, if ever, followed.

(3) Assistance in Franco-Italian relations would be welcomed.

6. Since writing the above, I have received and read with deep interest your two conversations with the French Ambassador recorded in your despatches Nos. 2884 and 2918[3] of the 22nd and 25th ultimo. I believe that your language to M. de Fleuriau, in the first of these despatches, exactly sums up the situation in regard to Albania, when you said 'I did not believe that Signor Mussolini had any territorial ambitions in Albania. I thought that his policy there was in fact influenced by fear of Yugoslav policy and that, if he could be reassured on that side, he would offer no menace to Albanian integrity but he was not prepared to see, for example, another Albanian Ruler overthrown merely because he pursued a policy friendly to Italy, and he had had, after all, only too much ground in the past for the suspicions which he entertained.'

7. There is, of course, great force in Mr. Briand's reply to your observations as recorded in your second despatch under reference. I am often at a loss to discover why Franco-Italian relations are in their present condition, and why all efforts to improve them appear to be abortive. My impression is that the Italians feel a 'superiority complex' on the part of the French which is a source of perpetual irritation to them, and the French have not always been tactful by any means. The French press thrusts with a rapier and the Italian press hits back with a bludgeon. I note that the statement is frequently made in Paris and Belgrade that while the Governments there are in no wise responsible for the articles which appear in a free press, all the Italian newspapers are under a strict censorship, and therefore the Italian

[3] Nos. 51 and 62 respectively.

Government must assume responsibility for anything they say. This statement may be to some extent true, but the situation thus created is distinctly one-sided. As a matter of fact the Italian press is not subjected to preliminary censorship, but the editors or writers may be called to account afterwards for any articles that have appeared and may be punished by fine, suppression, etc. In a country where the expression of all views, unless laudatory, on internal affairs, is entirely prohibited, it is perhaps natural that a certain safety-valve should be afforded by allowing more licence in writing of foreign affairs. But I know for a fact that during these last weeks the Italian Authorities have been imposing restraint on their press to an unusual degree, and the providers of strong meat, such as Forges Davanzati,[4] have not been allowed to write as they would like. I should say that the Italian press as a whole has latterly been distinctly moderate. M. de Fleuriau alludes to manifold hostile manifestations in Italy. There have undoubtedly been such manifestations but they were, in so far as my information goes, of a mild character. In Rome, for instance, there was a procession of students with flags shouting: 'Down with France and Yugoslavia', but they were carefully shepherded by carabinieri[5] and police and were not allowed to go anywhere near the French Embassy or the Yugoslav Legation. They were indeed almost immediately told to disperse, and complied. Yet, the French Chargé d'Affaires, M. Roger, in the absence of the Ambassador, came to me in a state of great indignation. He complained bitterly of the 'insult' of having the French Embassy surrounded with carabinieri and militia. M. Rakic, who was protected in the same way, treated it as a joke. Senator Grandi informed me that M. Roger had been to the Palazzo Chigi and had demanded an official apology for these student demonstrations. It is not therefore difficult to imagine the reports which M. Roger despatched to Paris. I cite the above as an instance in which small causes result to an unwarrantable degree in embittering international relations. My Consular reports indicate that there were demonstrations in other Italian towns, but it seems that in each case the authorities dealt with them drastically and at once. A Milanese friend who is on the Superior Council of Education here tells me that after the accounts of the manifestations of Belgrade over the Franco-Yugoslav Pact had reached Italy, the students and young fascisti in all university centres became very excited and difficult to control. On the whole therefore the Italian Government appear to have exercised a sufficient measure of repression.

8. I note that M. Marinkovich, in one of his conversations with M. Kennard, declared that he did not believe Signor Mussolini's irritation over certain articles in the Yugoslav press to be genuine.[6] In this M. Marinkovich is wrong. Signor Mussolini, at an earlier stage of his career, was a socialist and a journalist. He has become a statesman and has dropped his socialism, but his journalistic tendencies cling to him with an obstinate tenacity. He reads any quantity of newspapers of every country and reacts to

[4] Director of *Tribuna*.
[5] Gendarmes.
[6] Mr. Kennard reported this statement in Belgrade telegram No. 188: see No. 67, note 4.

a remarkable degree to criticism. He finds it difficult to allow any attack in some obscure foreign paper to go unanswered. One of his principles is, whenever he is hit, to hit back promptly, and he cannot bear the idea of allowing hostile statements to pass unchallenged or uncontradicted. This is an unfortunate fact, but it always has to be taken into account. At least half the difficulties in restoring good relations between Italy and her French and Yugoslav neighbours come from His Excellency's reactions to their press attacks.

9. In a conversation with the French Ambassador, who has just returned from Paris, I supplemented many previous conversations on the subject by expressing a real anxiety with regard to the way in which Franco-Italian relations were being allowed to drift. I had a great many Italian friends and could not help being struck by the extreme bitterness of their language with regard to France and their constant assertion that they were being driven into the arms of Germany. No one admitted more freely than I did that the Italians could be unreasonable and irritating. But Italy was a Power with 40 million inhabitants and was rapidly, in Signor Mussolini's powerful hands, becoming more efficient and important from a military and many other points of view. It seemed to me extremely short-sighted on the part of France to allow matters to drift and not to make a serious effort to arrest their course. I did not believe that this would be difficult, although more than friendly words would be necessary. M. Besnard declared that he agreed with every word I said, and that he had spoken in this sense in political circles in Paris, not, he believed, without due effect. When he resumed political life in France one of the main points of his programme would be to work for the improvement of Franco-Italian relations.

I have, &c.,
R. GRAHAM

No. 81

Sir R. Graham (Rome) to Sir A. Chamberlain
(Received December 3, 5.15 p.m.)
No. 218 Telegraphic [C 9793/25/90]

ROME, *December 3, 1927, 3.35 p.m.*

Your telegram No. 284.[1]

From what Signor Grandi told me last night it is clear that the Italian Ambassador had made a correct and full report of your language. Signor Grandi said that Bordonaro's telegram[1] was imprinted with deep gloom and he had taken your attitude very much to heart; so indeed had Signor Mussolini. I explained how justified that attitude was and did not consider it could be modified unless Italian government took some forward step in promoting more friendly relations with her neighbours.

Signor Grandi said that Signor Mussolini while he had resented the un-

---

[1] See No. 68, note 9.

fortunate Avala communiqué[2] had been greatly and very favourably impressed by the way in which Monsieur Marinkovic had accepted the new treaty of Tirana not only in his public statements but in his interview with the Italian Minister. If the new French move recorded in Paris telegram No. 241[3] comes to anything there may be a rapid and definite improvement of the whole situation.

Addressed to Foreign Office, repeated to Belgrade.

[2] The reference was evidently to the communiqué on the Italian-Albanian treaty issued by the Ministry of Foreign Affairs in Belgrade through the Avala press agency, summarised in *The Times*, November 26, 1927, p. 14, and November 28, p. 14; a copy was transmitted to the Foreign Office in Belgrade despatch No. 455 of November 29, not printed.

[3] No. 75.

No. 82

Sir A. Chamberlain (Geneva)[1] *to Sir W. Tyrrell (Received December 7)*
No. 32 L.N.C. [N 5796/209/38]

GENEVA, *December 5, 1927*

Sir,

Monsieur Litvinov telephoned late last night after I had retired to bed to ask me for an interview. The message was communicated to me first thing this morning and, after having had it confirmed, I fixed 2.30 to-day to receive him.

2. Monsieur Litvinov began the conversation by thanking me for according him an interview. He said that he spoke without instructions from his government and did not desire to enter upon the past. He did, however, desire to know what steps could be taken to place our relations upon a better footing.

3. I replied that Monsieur Litvinov placed me in some difficulty. I knew he was a member of the Soviet Government, but he began by saying he did not represent it. Monsieur Litvinov interrupted to say that he did represent it. This, I said, removed my first difficulty, but the second remained. Monsieur Litvinov desired not to recur to the events of the past, but it was those past events which had brought about the rupture of relations, and without reference to them it was impossible to reply to his question. His Majesty's Government had had to complain of the interference of the Soviet Government in the domestic affairs of Great Britain and of the constant hostility of Russian agencies throughout the world to the British Empire. What His Majesty's Government required for the resumption of relations was proof that these obnoxious activities had ceased.

[1] Sir A. Chamberlain left London on December 3 for Geneva where he arrived next day to attend the forty-eighth session of the Council of the League of Nations. The minutes of this session are printed in *League of Nations Official Journal*, February 1928: for a report on the session by Sir A. Chamberlain see Cmd. 3021 of 1928. Sir A. Chamberlain returned to London on December 13, 1927.

4. Monsieur Litvinov then referred to the recent speech of Monsieur Rikov[2] as the 'response' to the Prime Minister's speech at the Guildhall[3] and as offering the assurance that the Soviet representatives would observe the normal conditions of diplomatic relations.

5. I replied that Monsieur Rikov's speech seemed to me not so much a response as a retort and that I did not find in it the assurances which we required. Monsieur Rikov took up the position that the conduct of the diplomatic representatives of Russia had always been correct and would continue to be correct, and he disclaimed any power to control the Third International or the Red International[4]. As regards his assurance as to the conduct of the Soviet diplomatic representatives, it was valueless so long as he asserted that we had nothing to complain of in the past. We had published to the world proof of the improper activities of the Chargé d'Affaires in London, not to speak of the connection of Borodin's activities in China with the Soviet authorities in Moscow,[5] but more than this, we were entirely unable to accept the contention of the Soviet Government that they had no responsibility for the Third International and its agents. I need only remind him of the note which had been addressed in the name of Mr. Ramsay MacDonald to the Soviet Chargé d'Affaires in London on the occasion of the Zinoviev letter.[6] There might be some question as to whether Mr. Ramsay MacDonald had intended this note to be delivered or not, but there could be none as to its expressing his view of the responsibility of the Soviet Government for the activities of the Third International. I remarked that our views on that point had been stated by Lord Balfour in a debate in the House of Lords when he observed that all these bodies were one for the purposes of an offensive and only became separate when it was necessary to make excuses.[7]

6. Monsieur Litvinov continued to assert the perfect correctness of the instructions issued to the Soviet diplomats abroad. I enquired what was the value of such an assertion when I had published the telegram of the Soviet

[2] For the speech by the President of the Council of People's Commissars at Kharkov on November 20, see *The Times*, November 26, 1927, p. 13.

[3] For Mr. Baldwin's speech at the Lord Mayor of London's banquet on November 9, see *The Times*, November 10, 1927, p. 9.

[4] i.e. the Red International of Trade Unions.

[5] See items Nos. 1–3 in Part II of Cmd. 2874 of 1927. M. Borodin had recently acted as adviser to the Kuomintang Chinese nationalist party.

[6] Mr. MacDonald, Leader of the Opposition, had been Prime Minister and Secretary of State for Foreign Affairs, January to November, 1924. The note in question of October 24, 1924, to M. Rakovski, then Soviet Chargé d'Affaires in London, is printed as item No. 7 in Cmd. 2895 of 1927. It had enclosed a 'copy of a letter which has been received by the Central Committee of the British Communist party from the Presidium of the Executive Committee of the Communist International, over the signature of M. Zinoviev, its president [1920–6], dated the 15th September', 1924: *v. ibid.*, pp. 30–2. M. Zinoviev, who until recently had been a member of the Presidium of the State Planning Department, had been expelled from the Communist Party of the U.S.S.R. on November 12, 1927.

[7] For this remark in the speech by the Lord President of the Council on June 17, 1926, see *Parl. Debs., 5th ser., H. of L.*, vol. lxiv, col. 466.

Chargé d'Affaires in London asking for information about affairs in China for the special purpose of anti-governmental propaganda in England and suggesting the particular nature of the information which he desired to receive.[8] Why had not the Soviet Government, when they received this telegram, recalled or reprimanded their envoy? Monsieur Litvinov asked how I could tell that he had not been reprimanded to which I replied that their proper course would have been at once to recall him, but, if Monsieur Litvinov was prepared to produce a copy of the reprimand which had been addressed to him, it would certainly be of interest to see it. Had such a reprimand in fact been issued?

7. Monsieur Litvinov replied that he could not bear in mind all the communications which had passed and could not say. As regards the Communist International, he maintained that that was an international body comprising the Communist Parties of Great Britain, Germany, France and other countries, and that it was quite beyond the power of the Soviet Government to exercise any control over it.

8. I again said that I was wholly unable to accept this view. I regarded the Communist International as one of the organs of the Russian Government and, as long as they professed that there had been nothing improper in their diplomatic methods in the past and refused to control the Communist International and like bodies in the future, there was no basis for any agreement between us. I considered that the Communist International was as much a creature of the Politbureau[9] as the Government itself and it was really absurd to tell me that in a country where only one party was allowed to exist and where, even within that party, no opposition was tolerated, the government was not responsible for the activities of such a body.

9. Monsieur Litvinov again reverted to the Prime Minister's speech and said that he had used the word 'assurances'. What were the assurances that we required? I replied that they were proof of the cessation of the hostile activities of which we had complained and security (to use a word with which Monsieur Litvinov would be familiar since he had just been taking part in the Disarmament Conference) against their repetition. My colleagues and I had been most reluctant to break off diplomatic relations. I had issued warning after warning to the Soviet representatives in London.[10] His Majesty's Government had displayed a singular patience and tolerance, but when at last a rupture had become inevitable I was not prepared to run the risks of renewing those relations without security that the old abuses would not be repeated.

10. Monsieur Litvinov finally said that, if we required as a condition of renewal that the activities of the Third International should be controlled by the Soviet Government, that was an impossibility. The Communist International had had a closer connection with Germany for many years than

---

[8] This telegram of April 1, 1927, is printed as item No. 4 in Part II of Cmd. 2874.

[9] The Political Bureau of the Central Committee of the Communist Party of the U.S.S.R.

[10] See Volume I, No. 65, Volume II, No. 90, and Volume III, No. 21: see also Cmd. 2895 of 1927.

with Great Britain but it had not interfered with the relations between Germany & Soviet Russia which had remained perfectly correct.

11. I observed that I had nothing to do with the relations between Russia and Germany, but, since he referred to the Soviet Government's relations with other countries, I was under the impression that there had recently been a little friction with the Soviet Embassy in Paris in consequence of the improper activities of the Soviet Ambassador in Paris.[11]

12. Monsieur Litvinov retorted that that was no doubt true, but that the incident had been happily settled and was at an end. However, since I required a control of the Third International, there was nothing more to be done at present, though he thought that our conversation had not been altogether useless.

13. We then agreed upon the communiqué which was issued to the Press, a copy of which I attach to this despatch. Monsieur Litvinov enquired whether he might take it that nothing more would be said in public, and I replied that I was content to leave it there provided that he did the same.

I am, &c.,

AUSTEN CHAMBERLAIN

ENCLOSURE IN NO. 82

GENEVA, *December 5, 1927*

Monsieur Litvinov having asked Sir Austen Chamberlain for an interview, a meeting took place between them at the Hotel Beau Rivage this afternoon.

The meeting gave occasion for a frank exchange of views upon the relations between the Government of the Union of Soviet Socialist Republics and the British Government. It was not, however, found possible to reach any basis of agreement within the course of the interview.

[11] Cf. No. 27, note 2.

No. 83

Sir W. Tyrrell to Sir R. Graham (Rome)

No. 1479 [C 9811/25/90]

FOREIGN OFFICE, *December 5, 1927*

Sir,

With reference to your despatch No. 894[1] of the 25th November, enclosing the text of the recent Italo-Albanian Treaty of Alliance, I have to inform your Excellency that its terms have now been carefully examined in connection with the obligations assumed by Italy under the Covenant of the League.

2. I am advised that the new Treaty of Defensive Alliance is entirely inconsistent with the spirit of the Covenant, for, in the first place, though it is a treaty providing for the maintenance of the territorial integrity of the two

[1] Not printed.

contracting Powers and for the action which is to be taken to maintain that integrity, there is no reference from beginning to end to the League of Nations or the Covenant, except in the provision that it should be registered with the League of Nations, or to the obligations of the parties as members of the League. In this respect it stands in marked contrast to the Treaty of Mutual Guarantee, initialled at Locarno on the 16th October, 1925. Moreover, it is doubtful how far Italy is in a position to perform her duty as a member of the Council of the League impartially in any matter where Albania is concerned (notably, for instance, under article 15 of the Covenant), seeing that she has in this treaty undertaken to uphold the interests of Albania with the same zeal as she will uphold her own.

3. But the more important question is perhaps whether it can be said that this Treaty of Defensive Alliance violates, not the spirit, but the letter of the Covenant. This is a somewhat difficult question for the reason that it depends upon the interpretation of certain articles of the treaty which are (perhaps deliberately) ambiguous.

4. In article 2 it is provided that there shall be 'an unalterable defensive alliance' between Italy and Albania; the meaning of this expression must presumably be determined by the provisions which follow, namely, the second sentence of article 2 and articles 4 and 5. Under the second sentence of article 2, Italy has to employ 'all her attention and most efficacious means to guarantee the safety of Albania and for the defence of Albania against attacks from without.' A most important point which is left ambiguous is the meaning of the term 'attacks from without.' If it means simply any attack upon Albania by any third Power, then I am advised that it is clearly inconsistent with the Covenant for the reason that it would cover *inter alia* operations against Albania conducted under the ægis and authority of the League in pursuance of article 16 of the Covenant, and it is clearly inconsistent with Italy's duty as a member of the League and her obligations under article 16 for her to protect Albania against measures directed against her in pursuance of the Covenant.

5. It is possible, however, to argue that the meaning of this sentence in article 2 is to be found in article 3. Article 3 provides that: 'In consequence of the obligations assumed under the preceding articles Italy will . . . [2] in the case of Albania being menaced by a war not provoked by Albania, employ all most efficacious means not only to forestall hostilities, but also to secure just satisfaction to Albania,' and this is followed in article 4 by a provision that, in the event of 'all measures of conciliation having failed, Italy pledges herself to follow the fortunes of Albania, placing the whole of her military, &c., resources at the disposal of Albania.' It may be argued that articles 3 and 4 (which begin: 'In consequence of the obligations assumed under the preceding articles') define and express all the obligations created by article 2. The case when the obligations under articles 3 and 4 arise is expressed to be in the event of Albania being 'menaced by a war which she has not provoked,' which is a narrower expression than 'menaced by attack from without.'

[2] Punctuation as in original quotation.

163

While the meaning of the expression 'a war which she has not provoked' is not clear, it might well be argued that it would not cover any case where Albania had made war in violation of her obligations under the Covenant, i.e., by resorting to war against a third State which was complying with an arbitral award (article 13) or against a Power which was complying with a unanimous recommendation of the Council (article 15, paragraph 6), or where Albania goes to war in resistance to measures recommended by the Council to give effect to an arbitral award or a unanimous recommendation of the Council which Albania refuses to accept. If this is the case, the articles will only cover those cases where Albania has an arbitral award or a unanimous recommendation of the Council on her side, or those cases in which, under article 15 of the Covenant, the 'members of the League reserve to themselves the right to take such measures as they think fit for the maintenance of right and justice.' But here the real objection to such a treaty comes in, because Italy is a permanent member of the Council and can always prevent a unanimous recommendation being given against Albania, and she has contracted under article 1 to uphold the interests of Albania with the same zeal as she would uphold her own. If such a case came before the Council Italy's vote ought morally not to be counted for the purposes of ascertaining whether there is unanimity, just as the votes of the parties to a dispute are not counted for this purpose. But I am advised that legally it would not be possible to maintain that in the event of an investigation of a dispute between Albania and Jugoslavia, for instance, under article 15 of the Covenant, Italy was by reason of her Treaty of Defensive Alliance with Albania a 'party to the dispute' within the meaning of paragraph 6 of that article. There are probably many cases where, even though there is no objectionable treaty, a third State, though not a 'party to the dispute,' may be vitally interested in it and be in a position where it is difficult for the State to be impartial. If Egypt became a member of the League, a case might well arise where His Majesty's Government might find themselves in that position.[3]

6. Assuming the effect of the treaty to be as stated above, it is not easy to show by a mere logical reasoning that it necessarily conflicts with the letter of the Covenant.

7. Article 10 of the Covenant provides that the members of the League undertake to 'preserve against external aggression the territorial integrity and political independence of all other members, and that in the case of such aggression or danger of aggression the Council shall advise upon the means by which this obligation shall be fulfilled.' Desirable as it may be that members of the League should wait for and accept the advice of the Council in all such cases, it would be difficult to maintain that it is necessarily

[3] The minutes by Mr. W. E. Beckett, an assistant legal adviser to the Foreign Office, on which this portion of the despatch was based, included in this connection the following passage: 'An even more difficult case is a dispute between Canada and a foreign power—i.e. whether the British member of the Council is the representative of a "party to the dispute" or not. This question has often been discussed but I do not think that any definite opinion on it has yet been given.'

contrary to the Covenant for a member to take any measures to protect the integrity of another member of the League which the Council has not advised, any more than that members are legally compelled to take all the measures which the Council does advise.

8. There is one other point. In certain circumstances Italy, as a member of the League, may be under an obligation to take measures against Albania. If the Treaty of Defensive Alliance disenables Italy to do this, it is contrary to the Covenant. If the second sentence of article 2 has the wider meaning, it is contrary to the Covenant on this ground also. If it has the narrower meaning, then Italy has not prevented herself under these articles from taking such action. The only article which can be advanced for alleging that she has is article 1, when it says that she shall uphold the interests and advantages of Albania with the same zeal as she upholds her own, which is a very vague provision.

9. The position would appear to be, therefore, that an Italian representative would be able to make a good case, taking each article in turn and interpreting one by reference to the other, for saying that there is no particular provision in the treaty which is definitely incompatible with the obligations of the parties as members of the League. In this connection there is one argument which he might fairly use. Under article 20 the members of the League 'solemnly undertake that they will not hereafter enter into any engagements inconsistent with the terms' of the Covenant, and, therefore, if a treaty or a provision in a treaty is susceptible of two interpretations, according to one of which it is consistent with the obligations of the Covenant, while, according to the other, it is not, there should be a presumption that the parties did not intend to do anything inconsistent with their obligations under the Covenant, and that, therefore, the treaty should be interpreted in the sense which is not inconsistent therewith. But the general effect of the treaty is to put Italy in a position which would make it difficult for her, if she carries out her agreement with Albania under the treaty, to fulfil loyally her obligations as a member of the League, and especially as a member of the Council.

I am, &c.,

(For the Secretary of State)

C. HOWARD SMITH

No. 84

Letter from Sir W. Tyrrell to Sir R. Lindsay (Berlin)

[C 9554/857/18]

FOREIGN OFFICE, December 5, 1927

My dear Ronald,

Very many thanks for your letter of November 23rd[1] giving your comments on Hopkins' minute of November 9th[2] with regard to Parker Gilbert's

---

[1] No. 58.   [2] Enclosure in No. 44.

recent criticisms about the German financial situation. I enclose a copy of a letter which I have now sent to Hopkins with regard to this matter.

Meanwhile we shall always be grateful for any reports and such further appreciations of the situation as you see it which you may feel from time to time moved to send us. The situation obviously needs the closest watching and you can rely on us for our part to do what we can to keep you well and fully primed with information with regard to the issues involved.

Yours ever,
W.T.

Enclosure in No. 84

Letter from Sir W. Tyrrell to Sir R. Hopkins (Treasury)

Private   FOREIGN OFFICE, *December 5, 1927*

Dear Hopkins,

As you know I sent Lindsay at Berlin a copy of your minute of November 9th on the subject of the attitude we should adopt towards Parker Gilbert's recent criticisms of the German financial situation. I now enclose a copy of Lindsay's reply[1] in which he outlines his views on the various issues involved. You will, I am sure, be interested to read his estimate of Parker Gilbert. I cannot but think that he is perfectly right in feeling that the utmost discretion must mark all his dealings with that quarter. In fact I doubt whether after what he says we can expect him to act as the instrument through which —to quote the words of your minute—the Treasury should 'maintain touch' with Gilbert, if this means that he is to urge on Gilbert what may (since we don't know the views of the other interested Governments) turn out to be the purely British point of view.

As we understand it, your idea is that it will be best, in the general interest, to damp down all discussion or even suggestions regarding reparations until after the American presidential elections. But may I remind you that in your minute of November 9th you recognised the necessity of having some scheme or policy ready in our pockets in case the flow of American loans to Germany dries up as a result of the Agent-General's warning or in case Monsieur Poincaré sees fit to raise the reparation issue after the French elections in May. It may also be raised by Monsieur Poincaré for electoral purposes *before* the elections, though I think it doubtful, unless the Germans oblige him to do so. In fact, circumstances may in our view arise at any moment when it will be important, as you indicate, that we should be in a position to take the lead with some well-defined policy of our own and we shall therefore, I need hardly say, feel relieved when we are equipped with a scheme such as that adumbrated in your minute.

Yours sincerely,
W. Tyrrell

No. 85

Sir W. Tyrrell to Sir R. Lindsay (Berlin)
No. 1499 [C 9793/25/90]

Confidential　　　　　　　　　　　FOREIGN OFFICE, *December 7, 1927*

Sir,

I was gratified to learn from your Excellency's telegram No. 111[1] of the 2nd December that when you informed Herr von Schubert of my views with regard to the recent Italo-Albanian Treaty and general Franco-Italian relations, as instructed in my telegram No. 114[2] of the 1st December, he assured you that the German Government had no intention of taking any initiative in these matters and would prefer to remain outside them and follow the same attitude which they adopted last spring when the Italian Government made certain accusations against the Serb-Croat-Slovene Government.

2. You will observe from Sir R. Graham's telegram No. 218[3] of the 3rd December (of which a copy is enclosed herein) that the observations which I felt bound to make to the Italian Ambassador in London appear to have had some effect upon Signor Mussolini, and I am in hopes that his Excellency will realise that His Majesty's Government cannot view his present activities with favour, and that he will come to understand that it is by close co-operation with France and this country that the interests of Italy will be best served. At the same time I learn from credible Yugoslav sources that recently the Italian Ambassador at Berlin has endeavoured to interest Dr. Stresemann in some negotiations for the conclusion of some agreement (the exact terms of this agreement are not disclosed). It is stated that Dr. Stresemann did not welcome these overtures, but it may well be that if Signor Mussolini feels that Italy is becoming isolated he may redouble his efforts to find companionship and sympathy in Berlin.

3. So long as Franco-German relations remain as satisfactory as they are at present, I do not anticipate that, should Signor Mussolini endeavour to secure the support of Germany, he is likely to succeed, but I should, nevertheless, be glad if your Excellency would watch events carefully during the coming few weeks, and report whether you see any signs of particular Italian activity.

4. Copies of this despatch have been sent to His Majesty's representatives at Paris, Rome and Belgrade.[4]

I am., &c.,
(For the Secretary of State)
ORME SARGENT

---

[1] Not printed. This telegram reported the remarks made by Herr von Schubert in the absence of Dr. Stresemann as recapitulated below. Herr von Schubert had further stated that if an occasion arose in which the German Government could usefully help towards the maintenance of peace they would not let it slip.

[2] See No. 75, note 7.

[3] No. 81.

[4] In Foreign Office despatches Nos. 3036, 1499, and 617 of December 9 respectively.

No. 86

Sir A. Chamberlain (Geneva) to Sir W. Tyrrell (Received December 12)
No. 39 L.N.C. [W 11525/245/4]

GENEVA, *December 9, 1927*

Sir,

I took an opportunity of speaking to Monsieur Beelaerts van Blokland[1] to-day about the Belgian-Dutch Treaty.[2] I said that I had not wished to make any formal démarche at The Hague, but I desired quite informally to draw his attention to our interests in the matter and to our anxiety at the apparent absence of any steps to renew the negotiations with Belgium. I remarked that the question concerned the public law of Europe and particularly affected our interests, since the arrangement come to in regard to them had fallen with the adverse vote of the Dutch Chamber on the Treaty.

2. Monsieur Beelaerts van Blokland told me that he was already busying himself about this matter. Part of the opposition in the Netherlands had arisen from a failure to consult provincial and other authorities which were interested, and he must now take steps to draw them all into an agreement; but he regarded this as essentially his task as Foreign Minister and would make a point of carrying it through before the elections, which must take place in 1929.

3. Monsieur Briand was with us during this brief interchange of views. It appeared that Monsieur Briand had spoken in a similar sense and had received similar assurances yesterday.

4. I should be glad if you would send a copy of this despatch to His Majesty's Minister in Brussels, who might confidentially inform the Minister of Foreign Affairs of my conversations.[3]

I am, &c.,

AUSTEN CHAMBERLAIN

[1] Netherland Minister for Foreign Affairs.
[2] This treaty of April 3, 1925, together with the collective treaty of May 22, 1926, was published by the Belgian Ministry of Foreign Affairs as item No. 11 in *Documents Diplomatiques relatifs à la Revision des Traités de 1839* (Brussels, 1929): cf. Volume I, No. 499. The treaties of 1839 are printed in *British and Foreign State Papers*, vol. 27, pp. 990–1002. Cf. Volume III, No. 98, for the position resulting from Netherland non-ratification of the Treaty of 1925.
[3] A copy of this despatch was transmitted to Brussels in Foreign Office despatch No. 749 of December 14.

No. 87

The Marquess of Crewe (Paris) to Sir A. Chamberlain
(Received December 10)
No. 2438 [C 10018/167/22]

PARIS, *December 9, 1927*

Sir,

I have the honour to transmit to you, herewith, an interesting despatch addressed to me by the Naval Attaché on the subject of Franco-Italian relations from the naval point of view.

2. I am in general agreement with Captain Pipon's observations. During the last few years I have frequently drawn attention to the growing importance to France of her African Empire containing a total population of some 30 millions. For the security of this Empire and the free exploitation of its manpower by France the safety of the Marseilles–Algiers crossing is essential and will become even more important should regular trans-Saharan communication be established. It is indeed a case of a 'new world called into existence to redress the balance of the old'.[1]

I have, &c.,
CREWE

ENCLOSURE IN No. 87

Captain Pipon to the Marquess of Crewe (Paris)

France No. 19/27.

PARIS, *December 8, 1927*

My Lord,

Although it seems that efforts are now being made by responsible statesmen in France and Italy to improve the feeling between the two Countries, the recent treaties between France and Jugo-Slavia and between Italy and Albania have naturally not assisted to bring the two great Mediterranean Powers closer together. Conversation with naval officers, as well as various articles in the press, reflect an uneasiness with regard to Italian aspirations and Italian naval strength.

It would appear that, if trouble should arise in the Mediterranean, it is most likely to commence in the Adriatic, but, when the fire is once lit, it may quickly spread westwards. In view of this I have the honour to forward to Your Excellency the following brief summary of my views on the naval situation in the Mediterranean so far as it concerns France and Italy.

Notes on present situation in the Mediterranean.

There is small doubt that France aims at the control of the western basin of the Mediterranean in time of war, as she practically looks on her North African possessions as an integral part of the Motherland, and safe communications between these two parts can only be assured by a domination of the waters dividing them.

It would seem that the maritime interests of Italy also lie mainly in her communications through the Western Mediterranean. Quite apart from her ordinary commerce, which is especially important between her and South America, Italy is dependent on sea-borne traffic for most of her coal and many other necessities. During the war a very large proportion of the floating tonnage which passed through the Straits of Gibraltar into the Mediterranean was destined for Genoa, Spezzia and Leghorn.

A glance at the map of the western basin of the Mediterranean shows the important position of Sardinia. Italy has a big naval base at Maddalena and

[1] Cf. the speech made on December 12, 1826, by Mr. George Canning, Secretary of State for Foreign Affairs.

a minor one at Cagliari, and the island is favourably situated for carrying out a 'guerre de course' on French communications.

Both Countries must realize what a weight in the scale Spain will be when her naval programme is realized (it is at present only on the horizon and 10 years will probably elapse before she becomes formidable as a naval Power). This programme, in addition to the construction of a considerable force of submarines and other small craft, provides for the conversion of Port Mahon (Minorca) into a first-class naval base, and if a force hostile to France were also based on this port the communications between Provence and North Africa would be far from secure.

A combination between Spain and France would of course be equally strangling to Italy.

In connection with this, it would seem very bad policy for France to irritate the Spaniards over the Tangier question. Naval Attaché gathered in Madrid that Spain realizes she cannot get what she wants and would be content with a reasonable 'save face'.

Great Britain does not really come into the calculations of France in the Mediterranean question. She knows that she cannot go to war with us. In the course of a most friendly and intimate conversation a few days ago, Admiral Robert (1er Sous-Chef de l'Etat-Major at the Ministry of Marine) said to Naval Attaché—'Of course we, like all other Countries, have naval plans; but I assure you, Commandant, that we never consider England as possibly being anything less friendly towards us than an impartial neutral.'

In the opinion of Naval Attaché, France and Italy are building warships against one another and against no-one else. France's opposition to agreed naval parity with Italy on the score of having two coasts to defend separated by over 1,200 miles of coast-line of foreign Countries is rightly countered by Italy's reply that two coasts are twice as difficult to blockade as one. France is on surer ground, however, when she puts forward her large overseas possessions and long communications as an argument; but as long as the political situation remains as at present and Italy is a strong naval power, it is unlikely that the French colonies would see much of her extra ships.

At the moment France predominates over Italy in battleships, cruisers and submarines, but is rather inferior in flotilla leaders, destroyers and naval aircraft. Both Powers have considerable construction programmes as regards small craft, although that of Italy is not known in such detail or so far ahead as that of France. Delays in construction, financial considerations, etc., make it impossible, however, to forecast far ahead what the state of these fleets will be.

To compare the efficiency of the two navies is of course difficult. It is generally believed that there has been a considerable advance in 'esprit de corps' in the Italian fleet since Mussolini's advent to supreme power; on the other hand they have no traditions, and, in spite of their extensive seaboard, are not really a maritime people.

The French Breton sailor is second to none in the world, and it is from the West of France that the backbone of her naval personnel is formed; but there are many short-service conscripts from other parts of the Country, and the weakness of the Government over communist propaganda is not conducive to discipline and efficiency.

There is apparently a distinct aversion amongst the senior officers in both fleets to exercising in bad weather. This is a well-known Latin 'trait', and during the war was not confined to exercises; but it is probable that the French are less prone to this aversion than the Italians. It is understood that the French captains handle their ships with less caution than their Italian 'confrères'. Italy does, however, carry out manoeuvres and exercises on a larger scale than those of the French navy.[2]

I have, &c.,

J. M. Pipon

[2] In Rome despatch No. 972 of December 30 Sir R. Graham transmitted a corresponding report of December 29 by Captain Burke, Naval Attaché in H.M. Embassy at Rome, who summed up the Italian point of view as follows: '(a) The leaders of Italy have set before them a very high ideal of National greatness. (b) They have firmly in mind the importance of sea power and numbers in attaining their object. (c) They devoutly hope to avoid an open clash with France, and expect that the power of France will peacefully decline as Italy's increases. (d) They are not, nor do they intend to enter into any ship for ship competitive building, but will follow out their own ideas and build up to a standard that they consider commensurate with the country's progress in other directions. . . . As regards disarmament, a very generally expressed view is that disarmament Conferences are not inspired by genuine altruistic motives but are the insidious designs of those Nations who possess as much of the world as they want, in order to hold their possessions with the least possible outlay on Naval insurance: and such methods could have no part in the general scheme of a Nation which is bound to inhabit more of the earth than they at present possess. Another view was, that the result of such a Conference might be to tie Italy down to the "status quo" and at present her Navy is considerably less powerful than that of France.'

No. 88

Sir R. Graham (Rome) to Sir A. Chamberlain (Received December 12)

No. 926 [C 10087/25/90]

ROME, *December 9, 1927*

Sir,

I told Signor Grandi yesterday that you had requested me to meet you at Geneva. I said that it would be useful to me, before I saw you, to obtain a clearer idea of the motives which inspired the present Italian policy with regard to Yugoslavia and France, and especially what exactly the Italians wanted in order to bring about an improvement of relations with the latter country, as I was by no means clear on the subject. Signor Grandi replied at considerable length and, although most of the ground over which he travelled is already familiar to you, he made one or two fresh points which seem worth recording.

2. I had just received your despatch No. 1479[1] (C. 9811/25/90) of the 5th instant, and I said that I was advised that the new Treaty of Tirana was inconsistent with the spirit of the Covenant of the League. I quoted from the

[1] No. 83.

second paragraph of your despatch under reference. Signor Grandi replied that the Treaty made no difference whatsoever. Italy was always bound, with all due respect to her obligations to the League, to maintain the interests of Albania. The new Treaty in no wise altered a situation consecrated by the decision of the Ambassador's Conference of 1921. It was important to understand the motives of Italian policy in the Adriatic. Safety in the Adriatic must always be a cardinal point. Italy had ever been threatened by the nightmare of seeing some great Power establish herself on the Adriatic. In the old days of the Russian Empire, animated by Pan-Slavist ambitions, this Power had been Russia. When Italy was to enter the war under the conditions of the Treaty of London,[2] who was it who had at first blocked an agreement? M. Sazonoff.[3] It was only when the position of the Allies rendered Italian cooperation essential that Russian opposition was withdrawn. Could we absolutely exclude the possibility of a great Slav empire in the future, with Yugoslavia as her outpost on the Adriatic? Italy had fought the Great War to secure her position in the Adriatic and she had lost. D'Annunzio could never be forgiven for having diverted national attention from the political and military interests presented by Dalmatia, to the sentimental interests offered by Fiume. The latter were comparatively negligible. One need only look at the map of the Adriatic to see on one side a defenceless Italian coast, with open ports, and on the other a Dalmatian coast, a natural fortress, with impregnable harbours and submarine bases. However, this situation must now be accepted. All that Italy asked for was that she should be safe in so far as Albania was concerned, and that no other Power should be allowed to establish herself in that country. Signor Grandi repeated the assurances regarding Italian respect for the integrity and independence of Albania. Italy had attempted a policy, which might be described as a 'morphia' policy, of understanding and cooperation with Yugoslavia. What had been the result? The Yugoslavs had been ready to honour any obligations which redounded to their own interests, but had ignored the obligations which were of interest to Italy. Could it be honestly said that Yugoslav policy towards Albania could arouse anything but suspicion? Moreover, Yugoslavia had used Italian friendship to further her own aggrandisement in the Balkans. Italy had had her hands tied and had been unable to intervene on behalf of Bulgaria, Hungary or Greece. Italy had no desire to establish an influence, far less a paramount influence, in these countries. But the policy of the Little Entente, under French direction, towards her was one of hostility. She could not afford to see the whole of Central and South Eastern Europe formed into a solid anti-Italian bloc. She wished to have at least some friends there. It was clear from Signor Grandi's language, that while Italy is ready to be on friendly terms with Yugoslavia, she does not desire any close understanding or cooperation with that country.

[2] The treaty of April 26, 1915, between France, Russia, Great Britain, and Italy is printed in Cmd. 671 of 1920.

[3] M. S. D. Sazonoff, who died on December 23, 1927, was Russian Minister for Foreign Affairs, 1910–16.

3. Signor Grandi repeated that the crux of the situation lay at Paris and not at Belgrade. He complained, on lines familiar to you, of the general French attitude towards Italy, which was one of snubbing and thwarting her aspirations in all quarters from Central Europe to Abyssinia. I said that, without accepting these complaints, I should be more interested to know the points on which French and Italian interests might be made to meet. Signor Grandi replied that I was no doubt well aware of the questions at issue. There was Tangier. All that Italy asked for was a recognition in some form or another of her position as a Great Mediterranean Power. How this was to be done was immaterial. But she knew that any concessions on this head would be due to you and not to M. Briand. She could not therefore be expected to feel gratitude towards France in the matter.

4. A second and more important point was that of Italian nationals in French territory. He would not for a moment pretend that he did not understand the perfectly intelligible French attitude in the matter. But it must be remembered that Italy, in encouraging Italian emigration to France, had sent not only workers, but also an excellent class of small farmer, and had, under a scheme originated by Signor de Michelis,[4] supplied them with capital. By a stroke of the pen these men, their families and their capital, lost their Italian nationality and must become French. This was a bitter pill, as was also the idea that these men or their sons might in the improbable, but not impossible, event of a Franco-Italian war, be called upon to fight their own kith and kin. As regards Tunis, Italy entertained no hope whatsoever of ever obtaining that dependency. The idea was ridiculous. All that she asked for was that the inevitable process of Frenchification of the Italians there should be allowed to take its leisurely course and should not be hurried by immediate legislation. He had tried to put the French and Italian points of view as clearly and as moderately as possible. But it was only natural that the question should arouse a deep feeling in Italy and deep resentment unless handled with tact and consideration. In this connection Signor Grandi referred to the rumours of Italian aspirations in Corsica, which he described as absurd. But he added that the French, by exaggerating them and by organising a counter movement, had brought about a party for Corsican autonomy, with a newspaper of its own. He did not pretend that this party was of greater importance than the autonomy party which had long existed in Sardinia.

5. There remained the question of the 'Fuorisciti' [sic][5] in France. I interposed with the remark that, as you had most justly observed to Signor Bordonaro,[6] it was impossible to ask the French Government to infringe the laws of international hospitality by taking action against these people any more

---

[4] Signor G. de Michelis, President of the International Institute of Agriculture, had been Italian Commissioner-General of Emigration from 1919 until the post was abolished in April 1927. He was President of the International Conference of Emigration held at Rome, May–June 1924.

[5] i.e. fuorusciti, exiles.

[6] See No. 68.

than you could act against Nitti or Salvemini[7] in London. Signor Grandi replied that this was perfectly true, but that it did not present the case in its proper light. The Italian Government had never complained, nor would they ever complain, of the presence of such persons as Nitti or Salvemini in London, or as to our attitude towards them. The British accepted their presence, but they received no official encouragement. Switzerland was full of anti-fascist emigrés, but the Italian Government had never had reason to criticise the attitude of M. Motta,[8] for it had always been perfectly correct. As regards Paris, the same could not be said. The Italian refugees there were a dangerous element which had come to the conclusion that the only hope of upsetting the fascist régime in Italy was by the assassination of Signor Mussolini. They were constantly plotting to this effect. But the Italian ground of complaint against the French was that these persons received official encouragement. They were in close touch with members of the Government, such as M. Herriot,[9] and the French made political use of them as a weapon against Italy. So long as such things continued it was difficult to bring about an improvement in Franco-Italian relations.

6. There was, however, already in the last week, a certain détente. The new Etablissement Treaty signed by M. Briand[10] did not amount to much, and was more favourable to French than to Italian interests. At the same time, it was a step forward and M. Briand's language in connection with it had been much appreciated here. The Palazzo Chigi had just received from Signor Scialoja an account of a conversation with M. Briand at Geneva.[11] It had been of an extremely friendly character, but the only point of real importance was that M. Briand appeared to have offered to appoint a mixed commission to study the question of Italians in Tunis. Signor Grandi doubted whether such a proposal would ever be confirmed in Paris, but if it were, a real step forward had been taken. The idea had been mooted of a meeting between M. Briand and Signor Mussolini; the latter was most favourably inclined towards it. At the same time he felt that such a meeting would be a mistake unless it consecrated agreements already arrived at in diplomatic discussion between the two Governments concerned. A meeting which led to nothing would be worse than useless. Signor Grandi expressed some doubt as to whether conversations with M. Briand, whose good intentions and desire for coming to terms on all subjects were not always endorsed by the Quai d'Orsay, would be as useful as a conversation with M. Poincaré.

7. I had been rather at pains to ascertain Signor Grandi's views than to enter into argument with him, and I thanked him for what he had told me, saying that it certainly cleared my ideas on various points.

[7] Signor G. Salvemini, a distinguished historian, was deprived of his Italian citizenship in October 1926 on account of his anti-Fascist writings.

[8] M. G. Motta was President of the Swiss Federal Council and Head of the Political Department.

[9] French Minister of Education. [10] See No. 75, note 6.

[11] See *I Documenti Diplomatici Italiani*, Settima Serie, vol. v, No. 659.

8. It would cause me surprise if what Signor Grandi told me constituted the whole of Italian aspirations in any future agreement with the French. But whatever Italian hopes may be with regard to any territorial increase in Africa, he made no mention of them.

9. I have the honour to enclose a full summary[12] of an article from the 'Popolo d'Italia' by Signor Arnaldo Mussolini, the brother of the Prime Minister, on the subject of Franco-Italian relations.[13]

I have, &c.,
R. GRAHAM

[12] This summary of an article from the *Popolo d'Italia* of December 4, 1927, is not printed.

[13] In a minute of December 13 on this despatch Mr. Sargent stated in particular: 'Signor Grandi's remarks show serious symptoms of encirclement mania, which will require a long and careful course of treatment.'

No. 89

Letter from Sir R. Lindsay (Berlin) to Sir W. Tyrrell
(Received December 14)
[*C 10145/857/18*]

Private   BERLIN, *December 9, 1927*

Dear Willie,

Gilbert is going off to America this week and so I got hold of him yesterday and I enclose a note of my conversation. I send it in this semi-official form because some of it becomes quite personal. I do not much care for personalities but with a queer man like Gilbert they become important and he is an important element in the whole question of reparations.

With regard to a phrase in your letter to Sir R. Hopkins of December 5[1] about 'maintaining touch' with Gilbert, I see now that I expressed myself badly on the point in the passage in my letter of November 23[2] to which you refer. To a considerable extent I can perfectly well represent to Gilbert purely British views, though I could not promise to be able to do so in all cases. Only, I cannot finesse with him; and we must not hope that he will accept a *British* view if it runs contrary to his conception of his duty as an international official. This is a perfectly proper and honourable attitude for him to assume.

Ever yours,
RONALD LINDSAY

P.S. I attach too a second note on a minor activity of mine. It is of small importance, but perhaps you ought to know of what I have been doing.

R. C. L.

ENCLOSURE 1 IN No. 89

Record by Sir R. Lindsay of a conversation with Mr. Parker Gilbert

December 7, 1927

I had a longish conversation yesterday with Mr. Parker Gilbert about the Dawes Plan and German Finance. I had had no real talk with him for three

[1] Enclosure in No. 84.   [2] No. 58.

weeks and I began by saying it seemed to me things were going pretty badly. In spite of all he had said the Germans were going unconcernedly ahead with their liquidation Law, their salary increases, and the outlines of the budget for 28–29 which had just been published, seemed to me full of ominous possibilities. Gilbert said he had advance copies of the full budget and had been analysing it for his report.[3] It was not such a bad document as all that. The expense side of the extraordinary budget had been greatly reduced— there were improvements of form in the direction of simplification—it was good that no further authorisations to borrow would be required, and the revenue side was favourable. He thought the agitations of the last few weeks had had an effect even though it had not induced the Government actually to jettison any of their projects. He agreed with my suggestion that the further increases in the Reich's contributions to the States was very bad, especially, as he said, in view of Koehler's explicit assurances last spring that his Ausgleich arrangements would involve no increases.[4] He also concurred with me in criticizing the general increases of salaries. This would involve almost inevitably increases in railway rates. He also pointed to the reactions it would have on industry. The steel manufacturers were in for big trouble according to all appearances. 'Inflation pure and simple' said I; and he did not demur.

2. I said that we in England were anxious enough that German finance should be sound and if he could ensure this by his admonitions, all the better; but we also feared greatly the effect on the French, who, if they wished, and if the occasion arose, would be able to use his memoranda etc. to prove the voluntary nature of a possible German default and again advocate policies of active intervention. To this his answer was, in the first place, that Poincaré was a very changed man now and was really quite reasonable. He was glad to see the burden of criticizing German reparation policy and of forcing it in this or that direction, removed from French and transferred to international shoulders. Before the present international organization had been set up he had been compelled to press hard on Germany, all the more for the perpetual opposition he had met with in the process from the British Government authorities. Gilbert believed now that it would be possible to carry Poincaré along, without the risk of renewing past dangers.

3. Moreover, how could he, as an International official, stand by and see the Germans dissipate their assets without speaking? It would be a breach of trust. And, you never can tell how things might turn out—if he were now to keep silent, were there not statesmen in England as well as elsewhere who two years hence might bitterly reproach him for not having spoken out in time? Again, here were the Germans maintaining insistently that once they had paid their gold marks in to the Agent General, their obligations were

[3] The *Report of the Agent General for Reparation Payments, December 10, 1927.*

[4] The reference is presumably to Dr. Köhler's letter of May 22 in reply to that of Mr. Gilbert of March 17 (cf. No. 24, note 6). In this letter Dr. Köhler argued that the new financial settlement of April between the Reich and the States was advantageous from the standpoint of the Reich.

completely discharged. This was quite wrong. He knew the real weaknesses of Article 248,[5] and the difficulties involved in the interpretation of the Plan's stipulations about German steps to 'control exchange'. The truth was that the Plan gives the Germans an invaluable protection to their exchange, and as a corollary they could not be allowed to maintain, without protest, a theory that the payment of gold marks and the transfer of them into foreign currencies are problems completely divorced from each other. He was driving this point home in his forthcoming report.

4. I said I had a good deal of fear lest there should be a premature break-down of the Plan and a crisis just when the American Elections were on. It would be awful if American politicians were to be making hasty election pledges about such a matter as Reparations. I thought the best thing would be now to plan policy mainly with a view to breaking the fall when the collapse did come. He agreed about American elections, but did not think any break-down would occur 'just yet awhile'. If it did come of course it was going to be highly unpleasant to everyone and this was a prospect which had been before everyone's eyes ever since the inception of the Plan. At present there was a very modified sort of receivership in Germany. In case of a break-down of this it was conceivable that the next thing would have to be a complete receivership with a strict financial control all round. I screamed a protest against any such suggestion. All our tendencies, I said, were in the very opposite direction—in that of ending receiverships and pulling out controls; and wherever the meaning of any text was doubtful, we would always be found in favour of the more lax interpretations. He said that that was entirely the American view also.

5. I got a good opportunity to speak about Gilbert's relations with the Reparation Commission in Paris. I said it was none of my business, but I understood they did not always see eye to eye with him in what he did. I was afraid that out of this a strain might develop which would imperil the Plan on a purely extraneous issue. I was aware of the anomalies of the situation. The Commission devolved from but was independant [sic] of the Governments; and he devolved from but was independant of the Commission. Could he not, without sacrificing his independance [sic] in any way, keep in closer touch with Paris, tell them what was in his mind, and, to use an expression he had just used to me, 'carry' them? Gilbert replied scoffingly. The Commission met every month or six weeks; he had attended some of their meetings and had little profit out of it. Between the meetings the Commissioners were never there. Lord Blanesburgh is a busy man; he arrives late one day, works up his questions in the night, attends the meeting next morning and is off again in the afternoon. Carry them, indeed? Did I know Blanesburgh? 'He is a judge, and a very good judge too, and spends half the time in laying down the law, and he does it very well. And the other half he spends in telling you stories, and good stories too, but he does most of the laughing himself.' I said that after all, when the Plan comes to an end the Reparation Commission would still be in existence and would have to carry on and clear

5 Of the Treaty of Versailles.

up things. This must give them some right to have their say in policy. Gilbert's answer to this was that it might be right, but only from the purely legal point of view.

6. I am afraid I have no reason to suppose that I have influenced Gilbert in any single particular; but I also think I may, in the past, have acquired an exaggerated view as to the imminence of any crisis. The whole conversation went on in the most perfect good temper. As he left the room he told me that if I had anything more to say before he left for America he would gladly come round to see me again.

ENCLOSURE 2 IN No. 89

Note by Sir R. Lindsay (Berlin)

Relations between Gilbert and the German Government

About a month ago I spoke to von Schubert about this. He said he was alive to the importance of improving them, and he was trying to organize an office to act as intermediary with the Agent General in which the Foreign Affairs would have a strong representation; he meant it to be rather neutral— suspended between all the three Ministries concerned in Reparation questions. I knew this was not what Gilbert wanted and argued strongly that the office must be definitely in the Ministry of Finance, while agreeing of course that the Foreign Affairs must be strongly represented. We had quite a wrangle, Schubert was quite mulish and I could make no progress. So I changed my tack and pointed out that as there were two parties equally concerned, the Government and Gilbert, why should not he ask Gilbert what he thought of it all? Schubert was immensely impressed with the genial nature of this simple suggestion; his whole face lighted up and he said he would act on it; and he did so in fact, and some time later thanked me for the idea.

2. Awhile later Stresemann referred to my talk with von Schubert. I said we wanted to see a concordat set up between Gilbert and the German Government. ('It is the only concordat I want' he trumpeted). He gave me a rigmarole about the new 'Stelle'[6] in the Ministry of Finance, and of their difficulties, which he hoped were overcome, in securing the right man to be at the head of it. I gathered he was referring to von Brandt,[7] the man Gilbert wants, and urged that he should be given a good position in the Ministry of Finance. Stresemann said he would be 'something like a Secretary of State', which ought to be all right. From the attached note by Finlayson[8] I infer that it is not yet entirely settled, but I do not think I had better interfere any further. The German bureaucrats must settle the rest among themselves, and anyhow there will be a fairly efficient cushion between Gilbert and Koehler.

3. Talking of the latter, Stresemann said to me 'it is always a mistake to turn a Kleinhändler[9] into a Grosshändler!'[10]

---

[6] Office.   [7] Dr. von Brandt was a Director in the German Ministry of Finance.
[8] No such note is attached to the filed copy.   [9] i.e. a retailer into a wholesaler.
[10] On December 20 Sir W. Tyrrell sent copies of these records, together with a record of a conversation between Mr. Finlayson and Dr. Karlowa of the German Ministry of Finance

(not preserved in Foreign Office archives), to Sir R. Hopkins at the Treasury under cover of a letter in which he stated: 'As far as I am competent to judge, these papers reveal three points where there is danger ahead:

'(1) the 1928–29 budget, by increasing the share of the States in the Reich revenue, may provoke Gilbert into renewing his protest against the German Government's extravagance and mismanagement, and thereby stir up again the whole of the reparations question, which we want to see left alone for the present.

'(2) The law increasing salaries may affect the receipts of the Railway Company so as to make it necessary that the railway rates should be raised in order to enable the Railway Company to meet the reparation charges levied directly on railway receipts. If such an increase were opposed, as it evidently would be, by the German Government, a crisis would inevitably arise.

'(3) Gilbert still maintains that the German Government's obligations do not, as argued by the Treasury, terminate when the reparations annuity has been paid over in Reichsmarks, but that by both Article 248 and by the spirit of the Dawes Plan, the German Government are equally concerned in the subsequent problem of the transfer of these Reichsmarks across the exchange. He has, I am told, rubbed this in in his report just published. If he has done so in a too provocative manner, the German Government may demand arbitration on the point, which is what I understand the Treasury particularly wish to avoid.

'I now hear that in this report Gilbert also asserts that the time has come to fix the total amount of German reparations.

'Both these assertions of Gilbert's appear to raise serious questions of policy. The report itself, I understand, is addressed to the Reparation Commission who I presume will consider it at the forthcoming meeting. I shall be interested to know what attitude Lord Blanesburgh will be instructed to take on that occasion. If the Commission accepted the report without comment, would this be held to imply that the Allied Governments, including His Majesty's Government, by their silence have subscribed to the views set forth by Parker Gilbert on the two points I have mentioned?'

No. 90

Sir E. Phipps (Paris) to Sir A. Chamberlain
(Received December 13, 8.30 a.m.)

No. 247 Telegraphic: by bag [C 10107/167/22]

Confidential   PARIS, *December 12, 1927*

I had some conversation to-day with M. Berthelot about Franco-Italian relations and asked him whether he was pleased with the manner in which things were going. He replied that the French government were quite willing to make certain minor concessions to Italy in order to bring about a better atmosphere. For instance, the French, as they had frequently told the Italians, were ready to grant practically all the demands made by the latter to ensure Italy's adherence to the statute of Tangier. They were also ready to sign a pact of non-aggression and arbitration with her.

2. Last week a play of Signor d'Annunzio was performed at the Théâtre Français, the President of the Republic was present at the dress rehearsal and cordial telegrams, published in the press, were exchanged between Signor d'Annunzio and M. Poincaré. The French government had wished to raise Signor d'Annunzio from the rank of Chevalier to that of Commander

of the Legion of Honour, but Signor Mussolini had refused his consent. However, M. Berthelot did not take this tragically.

3. As for making any major concessions to Italy in Tunis or elsewhere, M. Berthelot declared that this was entirely out of the question. The Italians were everywhere in the posture of petitioners and of petitioners who had nothing to bring in return. If any big concessions were made to them they would only open their mouths still wider. If at some future time all the great Powers agreed that Italy, owing to her rapidly increasing population, should be given some outlet therefor, well and good, but then all the Powers concerned and not France alone would have to make sacrifices for Italy's sake.

4. What M. Berthelot now considers of extreme urgency is that conversations should begin forthwith between Italy and Yugoslavia in order to place the relations between the two countries on a better footing before January 27th next, when the unratified Nettuno conventions automatically expire. Instructions to this effect have been sent to the French Minister at Belgrade.[1]

[1] With reference to the present telegram Sir E. Phipps reported in Paris telegram No. 248 of December 13 that M. Berthelot had informed him that, in order to give yet another proof of the desire of the French Government to meet Italian wishes, he had made a successful personal appeal to M. Dubarry, editor of *La Volonté*, to give up issuing an anti-Fascist supplement in Italian to another organ which he published in the south of France.

No. 91

Record by Sir A. Chamberlain of a conversation with Dr. Stresemann (Geneva)[1]
[*N 6049/6049/55*]

Secret   GENEVA, *December 12, 1927*

I had an interesting conversation with Dr. Stresemann this afternoon. I opened it by a reference to the satisfactory settlement of the Polish-Lithuanian dispute,[2] which afforded yet another illustration of how much could be achieved when Berlin, Paris and London were in agreement. This, I continued, was not however the object of my visit.

When Monsieur Briand lunched with me yesterday I had taken the opportunity to read to him a letter which I had received from my colleague, Lord Cushendun, about the Committees on Disarmament and Security.[3] My colleague was anxious to secure such a measure of agreement between France and Great Britain as would enable real progress to be made, and he had expressed the anxiety which the differences existing between our two countries caused him. Monsieur Briand had replied to me that if the

[1] This memorandum was addressed to Sir W. Tyrrell and was entered on the Foreign Office file on December 19.

[2] See *League of Nations Official Journal*, February 1928, pp. 176–8, for the acceptance by Poland and Lithuania on December 10, 1927, of the resolution adopted that day by the Council of the League of Nations.

[3] For this letter of December 9 from the Chancellor of the Duchy of Lancaster see No. 230, note 4, below.

Disarmament discussion could be postponed till after the French elections, public opinion in France would impose a measure of disarmament upon the French Government. He had added that as regards western Europe the Treaties of Locarno had given them sufficient security, but eastern Europe still remained anxious and unrestful, particularly as long as Russia held aloof from any agreement.

Monsieur Briand had suggested that it might perhaps be possible, now that the Polish-Lithuanian difficulty was settled, to secure a pact of non-aggression to which the Baltic States, Russia, Germany, Poland and Roumania should all be parties. I had replied to Monsieur Briand that the case of Roumania seemed to me to offer the greatest difficulties on account of the Bessarabian question,[4] but I should be glad indeed if something could be done in that direction.[5]

I did not ask Dr. Stresemann for any answer at the moment, but I hoped that he would turn the question over in his mind. I well understood that it was as much out of the question for him as for us to undertake obligations additional to those which were embodied in the Covenant, but Monsieur Briand's suggestion did not involve any fresh obligations. It was strictly confined to a pact of non-aggression *inter se* between these different countries.

It appeared that Monsieur Briand had spoken in the same sense to Dr. Stresemann.[6] Dr. Stresemann, like me, had at once called attention to the difficulty presented by the Bessarabian question, but he had gone on to say that the Danzig corridor also presented an insuperable difficulty for Germany. Germany could never admit that East Prussia should permanently remain 'a colony'. The Customs formalities at the frontiers, the locking of the doors and the drawing down of the blinds of the carriages in all trains when passing through the Corridor were a constant source of irritation.

Monsieur Briand had asked Dr. Stresemann whether he had spoken of this matter to Marshal Pilsudski and seemed to suggest that Marshal Pilsudski might not be unwilling to consider it with an open mind, if Poland were assured of the possession of a free port at Danzig and perhaps Memel and proper arrangements made for transit facilities. Dr. Stresemann had replied that he had only just made Marshal Pilsudski's acquaintance and could not

[4] For the British attitude in respect of Bessarabia and the non-operative treaty of October 28, 1920, between the British Empire, France, Italy, Japan, and Roumania (printed in *British and Foreign State Papers*, vol. 113, pp. 647–51) see Volume III, No. 268.

[5] In a letter of December 12, 1927, in reply to Lord Cushendun's letter of December 9 (see note 3 above), Sir A. Chamberlain recapitulated the preceding account of his conversation with M. Briand, adding in particular that M. Briand had described his proposal as 'a sort of Eastern Locarno' and had 'seemed to think that the Soviet Government might be induced to enter into a non-aggression pact which would include Roumania'. Sir A. Chamberlain commented: 'If all this succeeded it might lead us a long way, but for the moment it does not advance us much. I am inclined to think that it would be well for you to take the matter up in the first instance with Fleuriau in London. Possibly we might have a conversation *à trois* and then arrange for you to stop in Paris on your way to the next meeting of the Committee [the League of Nations Committee on Arbitration and Security].'

[6] Cf. *Gustav Stresemann, op. cit.*, vol. iii, p. 258, and pp. 262–3. Cf. *ibid.*, p. 263, for a note by Dr. Stresemann of remarks by Sir A. Chamberlain.

speak of every difficulty to him at a first interview;[7] but he too had evidently derived the impression that it might be possible to do business directly with Marshal Pilsudski which could not be done with any other representative of the Polish Government. He had spoken to the Marshal about the right of the Polish Government to dispossess the German proprietors of estates in Poland on the death of the present possessors. He had remarked that there were now only some 300,000 Germans in Poland where before the war they had numbered over a million. The balance were in Germany, where there was no room for them on agricultural land, and were a charge to the German Government. Was it really necessary for Poland to expropriate the small balance? To his surprise, the Marshal had at once replied that he felt no interest in their dispossession, and Dr. Stresemann had sketched in broad outline a project of compromise which might be satisfactory to the two parties.

Dr. Stresemann told me that he was confident that a commercial treaty between Poland and Germany would be signed early in the New Year and he thought it would be useful if it could somehow be suggested to Marshal Pilsudski that he should invite Dr. Stresemann to Warsaw to sign that treaty in person. Dr. Stresemann would then be able to discuss other matters with him. Dr. Stresemann added that the Marshal had told him that he felt no interest in having great numbers of other races included in Poland. He would sooner govern a compact and homogeneous country, and Poland would be stronger if she had fewer strangers among her citizens.

Monsieur Briand had previously told me that the Marshal had said to him that for his own part he did not care about the Corridor as it was quite indefensible, and I replied, therefore, to Dr. Stresemann that his account of his conversation with the Marshal was very interesting and that I myself had derived the impression rather from the Marshal's general attitude than from any particular words which he had said to me, that he did not himself as a soldier think the Corridor of great value to Poland.

This drew from Dr. Stresemann the statement that he might now tell me that when Monsieur Litvinov came to Berlin on his way to Geneva his first words in regard to the Polish-Lithuanian dispute were not words of peace. Monsieur Litvinov had said that there was going to be war and that the moment war broke out Germany should occupy the Corridor, which nobody could prevent her from doing. Dr. Stresemann had replied that Germany would not have war at any price. She knew what the consequences would be for her. It might be all very well for Monsieur Litvinov who sat at Moscow, but Germany would not take the risk.

Dr. Stresemann then spoke of the policy of Italy. He observed that in yesterday's 'Popolo Romano', the paper edited by Signor Mussolini's brother, there was an article which declared that Germany was hostile to Italy and that Germany meant war and not peace, and that nobody in Geneva believed that she was peacefully inclined. He had spoken to Signor Scialöja about this article and begged him to ask Signor Mussolini what it meant. Did

[7] V. ibid., p. 265.

182

Signor Mussolini mean that he objected to good relations between Berlin and Paris or Berlin and London? Such utterances were really intolerable. Signor Mussolini did not come to Geneva himself. He did not send Signor Grandi, but merely a kind of jurist-observer in the person of Signor Scialöja.

Dr. Stresemann added that in 1923, at the time of the Corfu incident when he was Chancellor of the Reich, Mussolini had proposed to him a treaty of alliance and that he had then answered that he should report this proposal to the Cabinet, but that without consulting them he could tell Signor Mussolini that Germany would have nothing to do with it. Germany was not going to make war or be a party to any war.

Dr. Stresemann went on to say that if Germany, Great Britain and France remained united, we could oblige Signor Mussolini to keep the peace. I thought it well after such frankness on Dr. Stresemann's part to explain to him exactly what had passed between Signor Bordonaro and me, and the instructions which I had given to Sir Ronald Graham for his guidance in further conversations with Signor Mussolini. I gathered both from Signor Bordonaro and Sir Ronald Graham, and indeed also from the great anxiety shown by Count [sic] Paulucci[8], that what I had said to Signor Bordonaro had produced a considerable effect at Rome, and I thought it was not a bad thing that Signor Mussolini should become aware that his proceedings met with approval neither in London, Berlin nor Paris. As regards Franco-Italian relations, my impression was that there was already a little détente produced by the feeling on both sides that they had allowed their fraternal quarrels to develop to a point which was dangerous. Monsieur Briand had talked with great frankness to Sir Ronald Graham and had authorised Sir Ronald Graham to repeat to Signor Mussolini any part of his conversation which Sir Ronald thought might be useful.[9]

A. C.

[8] Marquess Paulucci de Caboli, an Italian citizen, was an Under Secretary-General of the League of Nations. For his account of conversations on December 10–11 with Sir A. Chamberlain, Sir R. Graham, and Mr. Selby see *I Documenti Diplomatici Italiani*, Settima Serie, vol. v, No. 674. No record of these conversations has been traced in Foreign Office archives.

[9] No complete record of Sir A. Chamberlain's and Sir R. Graham's conversation with M. Briand on December 11 has been traced in Foreign Office archives. In a minute of December 14 in which he gave instructions for No. 95, Sir A. Chamberlain stated that he had given verbal instructions to Sir R. Graham, that he was not sure that the French Government were right in giving the advice reported in the last paragraph of No. 90, and that he did 'not like to take the responsibility of supporting it. Indeed I told Sir Ronald to say how I had been urging ratification of Nettuno & to ask how I could be expected to continue to do so after Mussolini had let me down so badly.' In a subsequent minute of December 20 Mr. Selby stated:

'1. The general lines indicated by the Secretary of State to Sir Ronald Graham were those he had already indicated in official telegrams to Rome in regard to Signor Mussolini's attitude. Signor Mussolini did not seem disposed to listen to British advice, and accordingly, the Secretary of State felt that in future it would be better to refrain from giving it, although he could not but deplore the present trend of Italian policy.

'2. Monsieur Briand stated that a draft *projet* had been submitted to Signor Mussolini, but like everything else submitted to him, nothing more had been heard from him.

'3. The Secretary of State, in the course of conversation with Monsieur Briand, asked whether he might be permitted an indiscretion. He said that the Italian complaint was that, although the policy of Monsieur Briand was perfectly fair and reasonable, it was not so with Monsieur Berthelot, who is very anti-Italian, and who made negotiation with France impossible. Monsieur Briand vigorously refuted the suggestion as regards Monsieur Berthelot. He said that he was a very loyal collaborator, and that he could always rely on him to carry out his policy. The Secretary of State asked Monsieur Briand whether Sir Ronald Graham might repeat what he had said to Signor Mussolini. Monsieur Briand readily assented.

'4. The idea of the meeting *à quatre* is on the conclusion of the Franco-Spanish conversations in regard to Tangier. Monsieur Briand is optimistic that these conversations will shortly be satisfactorily concluded, and that then will be the time for meeting *à quatre*, France, Italy, Great Britain [? and Spain], always contemplated when the Franco-Spanish conversations were embarked upon [cf. No. 8, note 5].

'W. S. *20th December 1927.*'

No. 92

Record by Sir E. Phipps (Paris) of a conversation with M. Berthelot[1]
[*W 12025/11838/98*]

PARIS, *December 12, 1927*

Mr. Selby's letter to me of December 10th.[2]

2. I had occasion to see M. Berthelot this morning and I told him in strict confidence that you were considerably perplexed owing to the discrepancy between (*a*) the attitude at Geneva consistently adopted by M. Paul-Boncour,[3] who continued to press on every occasion for the Protocol[4] and who therefore in effect made the British Empire in general and you in particular appear before the world as the 'villain of the piece', when you declined to consider it, and (*b*) remarks made to you by M. Briand and to me by M. Berthelot himself to the effect that French public opinion would never countenance France going to war on behalf of any of the smaller States.

3. M. Berthelot at first seemed somewhat embarrassed, but afterwards opened out and said, speaking in strict confidence, that although on good terms with him, he had the poorest possible opinion of M. Paul-Boncour and had always so informed M. Briand. M. Briand had several times expressed his annoyance on this account, and had pointed out that M. Paul-Boncour was essential to him for the maintenance of his parliamentary position on the

[1] This record was prepared for Sir A. Chamberlain who passed through Paris on December 13 on his return to London.

[2] Not printed. This letter transmitted the instructions from Sir A. Chamberlain on which Sir E. Phipps was acting.

[3] President of the Foreign Affairs Commission of the French Chamber of Deputies since November 1927 and a French representative at Geneva.

[4] i.e. the Geneva Protocol for the Pacific Settlement of International Disputes, adopted by the Assembly of the League of Nations on October 2, 1924, and printed as item No. 3 in Cmd. 2273 of 1924: Mr. Chamberlain's statement to the Council of the League of Nations on March 12, 1925, explaining why His Majesty's Government felt unable to sign the Protocol, is printed as Cmd. 2368 of 1925: see also Volume II, Nos. 20 and 41, and Nos. 211 and 237 below.

Left of the Chamber. M. Briand, it seems, added that M. Berthelot greatly underrated M. Paul-Boncour's abilities, and that he would in all probability some day be President of the Council. (This agrees with the opinion expressed to me lately by M. Henry de Jouvenel,[5] who thinks that it is quite on the cards that M. Paul-Boncour may be called upon to form a Ministry after the elections if the latter go sufficiently to the Left; this, however, M. Léon Blum[6] himself doubts.)

4. I thanked M. Berthelot for his frank explanation, which he admitted was not of a satisfactory nature, but which I said you would certainly understand. I urged him, however, to do all that was possible with a view to placing a 'sourdine' on M. Paul-Boncour's excess of zeal in persisting to advocate on every possible occasion a Protocol which he now must realise that the British Empire would never accept. I added that this would seem to be in the best interests of France herself, for some day the occasion might well arise when it would be proved to the world that M. Paul-Boncour, as official French representative at Geneva, had been only paying lip-service to commitments which France in effect declined to undertake.

5. M. Berthelot took note of my request and promised to see what could be done. I made it clear that our conversation was of a purely private character, and this M. Berthelot quite understood.

Poland and Lithuania.

M. Berthelot is relieved at the settlement affected at Geneva, but fears it may be only temporary as M. Valdemaras' whole 'raison d'étre' depends on his die-hard attitude. M. Berthelot has urged M. Briand to kill him with honey rather than with vinegar, to flatter him and to invite him to a banquet at the Quai d'Orsay or the Elysée; he hopes by this treatment to cause M. Valdermaras' claws to drop out, if only for a time.

ERIC PHIPPS

[5] Senator for the Corrèze and a former member of the French delegation at Geneva.
[6] Deputy for the Seine and Leader of the Socialist group in the French Chamber of Deputies.

No. 93

Mr. Leeper (Warsaw) to Sir A. Chamberlain (Received December 19)
No. 535 [N 6029/1316/55]

WARSAW, *December 13, 1927*

Sir,

On coming to Poland from the East[1] I have been much impressed by the realism of the Poles about Russia. Though Poland is Russia's most important neighbour, and though from past experience Poland has more reason to fear and distrust Russia than any other country, yet I believe that nowhere

[1] Before serving at Durazzo (cf. No. 7, note 1) Mr. Leeper had been First Secretary in H.M. Embassy at Constantinople.

can one listen to less alarmist and more dispassionate opinions about Russia than in Poland.

2. This state of mind is instructive for two reasons. In the first place it shows to what extent the Poles have regained self-confidence in themselves, although but seven years ago the Russian armies were at the gates of Warsaw. This self-confidence is real. It is not boastful, nor is it paraded to impress the foreigner. It is born of a close acquaintance with Russia in the past and a careful study of present conditions there.

3. This brings me to the second reason why the attitude of the Poles towards Russia deserves attention. They have long since ceased to be alarmed by Russian Bolshevism as a real social danger, and they are equally unimpressed by the skeleton of a united Russia as represented by the Soviet Government. They do not believe in the resurrection of the Great Russia, of one central Russian Government exercising any effective control over the huge extent of territory which is still marked Russia on our maps. They do not believe that the semblance of unity achieved by the Soviet Government at the moment when the Russian Revolution was dissolving the Empire of the Tsars can be transferred safely and smoothly into the hands of a Russian Nationalist Government. The fear that lurks at the back of so many minds in Western Europe that one extreme must breed another, that the violence of Bolshevism may lead to the violence of Nationalism, occupies no place of importance in the minds of those Poles who know Russia well. This fear may exist in Posnania, which knew little of Russia in the past, but as one goes further east the Russian mirage disappears from view and melts into the endless plain, which Moscow may interrupt for a moment, but which she cannot mould according to her will.

4. I recently asked an intelligent Pole, who knew both England and Russia well and who some months ago had been sent on an official mission to Afghanistan, why it was that England was more impressed by the spectre of Russian greatness than Poland. He gave me the following explanation. England had been worried by Russia both in her capacity as a large industrial country and in her capacity as an Empire. The Russians had always been good stage-managers. If the Russian theatre had excited the admiration of Western dramatic critics, so too had the Russian political stage produced effects abroad which actual circumstances in Russia behind the stage could not justify. The Bolsheviks had admirably continued the stage-managing effects of the old Empire. With the help of the executive powers of the Jew they had in fact surpassed them. The dramatic appeal of Bolshevism had been exploited to the utmost and, if the play was now dragging somewhat towards the last act, it had at any rate kept alive the interest of its European audience through ten whole years, a run which would excite the envy of any professional stage-manager.

5. In the East the spectacle had been equally impressive. The actors there played their very different roles with great skill. When the social drama of Bolshevism flagged in the West, the national drama of Imperialism came forward with quite an impressive pageantry. He himself had watched this

closely in Afghanistan and had been much impressed by the aspect of Russia as seen from Warsaw compared with the spectacle that caught the eye at Kabul. It was but natural that England with her great responsibilities in the East should keep a watchful eye on these activities and should at times exaggerate the power behind them.

6. The Poles are less impressed by the danger of Russian Nationalism, for they too at one time formed part of the Russian Empire when the central government of the day was engaged on a nationalist policy. Then as now a nationalist policy in Russia was imposed from above; it did not draw its roots from a purely Russian soil. It is since the war that real nationalism has been spreading from Europe into Russia, and this real nationalism has been dissolving the old Empire into its component national parts. Europe has already had an outward and visible sign of this in the separation of Finland, the Baltic States and Poland from Russia, but the same process, though in a less advanced stage, is at work in the Ukraine and White Russia, and is continuing on the same lines among the manifold Eastern races which now form part of the Soviet Union. An international doctrine such as Bolshevism may find points of contact in each of these different units which are slowly growing to national self-consciousness, but it is more doubtful whether a Russian nationalist government on the disappearance of Bolshevism would be able to take over the powers of its predecessor.

7. It is reasoning on these lines which explains the calmness of the Polish attitude towards Russia. The Poles feel, and rightly too, that they are far in advance of Russia, that, though they have been influenced in many ways by the East, their foundations are European, and that, if the peoples of Russia are now being influenced by European nationalism, it will take them many years to remake their life on its new foundations. If their reading of the future be correct it is worthy of close attention in our country, for it means that for many years to come the most stable factor in East Europe will be Poland and not Russia.[2]

I have, &c.,
R. A. LEEPER

[2] In minutes in the Foreign Office certain doubts were expressed regarding the soundness of the Polish views reported in this despatch

No. 94

Viscount Chilston (Vienna) to Sir A. Chamberlain (Received December 19)
No. 272 [C 10274/55/3]

VIENNA, *December 14, 1927*

Sir,

With reference to my telegram No. 36[1] of the 9th instant, I have the honour to transmit, herewith, a copy of the collective Note, signed by myself and my French, Italian, and Japanese colleagues, which we presented

[1] Not printed. The brief report in this telegram was expanded in the present despatch.

personally to the Austrian Chancellor on the 9th instant, in regard to the disarmament obligations and the coming withdrawal of the Organ of Liquidation.

2. After I had addressed Mgr. Seipel in the sense of the instructions received,[2] insisting in particular upon the passing of the required law on war material and drawing attention to the steps which would be taken in the event of failure, His Excellency informed us that he was glad to have a clear understanding of what was expected and what would be the position, for he might have to give some explanation to Parliament when he introduced the Bill, and he seemed to have been not quite clear on some of the points mentioned in the Note previously received by the Austrian Minister in Paris.[3] As to the law, he hoped to lay the Bill next week and he anticipated no difficulty in getting it voted directly after Christmas. He said he was grateful for the goodwill and confidence shown to Austria, who would be considerably strengthened by becoming free of the control of the Organ of Liquidation and thus being on an equal footing in this respect with Germany and Hungary. As to the yet unfulfilled obligations, he believed the number of special machines still to be destroyed would be destroyed by the end of this year; as to the dispersal of machines, the questions of dismantling and of factories, etc. and of information regarding Army personnel, he would do his best to see that satisfaction was given and he was hopeful on all points save in regard to the gas bombs, the destruction of which was rather a lengthy and dangerous matter. He would instruct the authorities to get into touch immediately with the Liquidation Organ on all these points, and he would also keep us informed of any progress made.

I have, &c.,
CHILSTON

ENCLOSURE IN No. 94
*Collective Note presented to the Austrian Chancellor**

VIENNE, *le 9 décembre, 1927*

Se référant à la lettre[3] que le président de la Conférence des Ambassadeurs a adressée le 2 de ce mois à son Excellence M. Grünberger, Ministre d'Autriche à Paris, les Ministres soussignés de Grande-Bretagne, de France, d'Italie et du Japon, au nom de leurs Gouvernements respectifs, ont l'honneur d'appeler l'attention toute particulière de son Excellence le Chancelier fédéral sur les points suivants qui précisent la portée des décisions de la conférence relatives à la levée du contrôle militaire:

1. Ce n'est pas sans regret que la conférence a dû constater que, malgré toutes les facilités données au Gouvernement autrichien pour s'acquitter

---

[2] In a telegram to Vienna dated December 2 Lord Crewe had informed Lord Chilston that instructions addressed by the Conference of Ambassadors to the representatives of the Conference powers at Vienna had been telegraphed to the French Minister at Vienna by the French Ministry of Foreign Affairs. Copies of this telegram and of the instructions, which requested that paragraphs 1–5 and the penultimate paragraph of the enclosure below be communicated to Dr. Seipel, were transmitted to the Foreign Office in Paris despatch No. 2386 of December 2, not printed.   [3] No. 79.

de ses obligations, plusieurs de celles-ci, dont certaines fort importantes, n'avaient pas encore été remplies.

2. Néanmoins, désireux de donner au Gouvernement autrichien une preuve nouvelle de sympathie et de bienveillance, les Puissances ne veulent pas user du droit, qu'elles tiennent cependant du traité,[4] de maintenir en fonction l'organisme de contrôle jusqu'à l'achèvement intégral des obligations incombant à l'Autriche en matière de désarmement.

3. Les Puissances n'ont pris cette décision que parce qu'elles ont la conviction que le Gouvernement autrichien, s'il en a la volonté, est en mesure d'assurer à très bref délai le règlement de la plupart des points encore en suspens; elles sont, d'autre part, persuadées qu'il tiendra à répondre à l'appel qui lui est adressé et qu'il fera l'effort nécessaire à cet effet. En particulier, elles comptent fermement que la loi sur le matériel de guerre sera votée et promulguée avant le 31 janvier.

4. Si leur espoir était déçu, les Gouvernements représentés à la conférence se verraient dans l'obligation, au moment où ils notifieront au Conseil de la Société des Nations la cessation des opérations du contrôle interallié, de lui signaler les questions qui n'auraient pas été réglées, en indiquant l'importance qu'ils attachent à ce règlement.

5. Dans le cas, notamment, où la loi sur le matériel de guerre ne serait pas votée avant le 31 janvier, les Puissances, observant qu'en cette matière les dispositions du Traité de Saint-Germain sont semblables à celles du Traité de Versailles, n'en considéreraient pas moins le Gouvernement autrichien comme tenu de mettre en vigueur et d'appliquer sur son territoire les dispositions ayant les mêmes effets que la loi allemande.

Si, par conséquent, en l'absence de la promulgation de la loi réclamée, il était signalé en Autriche des faits de fabrication, d'importation ou d'exportation de matériel qui aux termes de la loi auraient un caractère illicite, les Puissances considéreraient de tels faits comme constituant autant de violations des obligations de l'Autriche en cette matière et se verraient ainsi amenées à en saisir le Conseil de la Société des Nations en vue d'une application de l'article 159 du traité.

Les Ministres soussignés, en remettant la présente note, expriment de nouveau leur confiant espoir que le Gouvernement fédéral employera tous ses efforts afin d'arriver à un règlement satisfaisant et définitif de cette question.

[4] The Treaty of Saint-Germain.

No. 95

Sir A. Chamberlain to Sir R. Graham (Rome)

No. 288 Telegraphic [*C 10108/808/92*]

FOREIGN OFFICE, *December 15, 1927, 3.30 p.m.*

Paris telegram No. 247[1] (of December 12th: last paragraph).

I am not aware that Nettuno conventions automatically expire on January 27th and I think reference must be to Pact of Rome which expires

[1] No. 90.

in January 1929 and can be either denounced or renewed on January 27th. 1928.

You will have seen from Belgrade telegram No. 193[2] (of December 13th) that Serb-Croat-Slovene Minister for Foreign Affairs has informed Italian Minister that he does not intend to denounce pact and practically invites conversations on the subject.

I shall await report of your conversation with Signor Mussolini before deciding whether to instruct His Majesty's Minister at Belgrade to give any advice in the matter. At present I am disinclined to assume such a responsibility in view of my complete uncertainty as to Signor Mussolini's real intentions.

You should also if possible ascertain from Signor Mussolini what reply he intends to make to Serb-Croat-Slovene Minister for Foreign Affairs' communication.[3]

Addressed to Rome No. 288. Repeated to Belgrade No. 143.

[2] Not printed. This telegram was in the sense here indicated. For the conversation in question between M. Marinkovitch and General Bodrero see *I Documenti Diplomatici Italiani*, Settima Serie, vol. v, No. 672.

[3] Sir R. Graham replied in Rome telegram No. 222 of December 16 that Signor Mussolini had informed him that M. Marinkovitch wished to renew the Pact of Rome in a modified form. Signor Mussolini wished to make some progress with the French Government before entering into discussions with the Serb-Croat-Slovene Government and would therefore propose to M. Marinkovitch an exchange of notes prolonging the Pact for, say, six months in order to give more time: cf. *ibid.*, No. 686.

No. 96

Letter from Sir A. Chamberlain to Sir H. Rumbold[1] (Madrid)

[F.O. 800/261]

FOREIGN OFFICE, *December 15, 1927*

My dear Sir Horace,

Whilst at Geneva, I proposed to Monsieur Briand that he and I should address a personal letter to Quiñones de León expressing our great regret at Spain's withdrawal from the League and our readiness to move the Council at its March meeting to address an appeal to the Spanish Government to re-consider their decision and withdraw their notice before September when otherwise it would become operative, but adding that we could not ask the Council to take such a step unless we ourselves were assured that if the Council did address such an appeal to the Spanish Government it would meet with a favourable response.[2]

Briand warmly approved the proposal and I accordingly submitted to him a draft of what I thought the Council might say and of a letter to Quiñones

[1] H.M. Ambassador at Madrid.
[2] Señor Quiñones had made a suggestion for broadly similar procedure in an interview with Sir E. Drummond, Secretary-General of the League of Nations, whose record, dated November 19, of this interview was received in the Foreign Office.

covering this draft. Briand approved them both and I asked Quiñones to call upon me at the Embassy in Paris on my way home. I there gave him the letter signed by Briand and myself and the sketch of the communication which we were prepared to propose to the Council of the League.[3]

Quiñones was very pleased and I understood from him that he would personally take this communication to General Primo de Rivera, and that he was hopeful of obtaining a favourable reply.

I begged Quiñones to press the General to give the most favourable consideration possible to the latest proposals of the French Government for the settlement of the Tangier question.[4] Briand is very anxious to get this settled and so, I believe, is now the General himself, so that with a small effort I think a solution can be reached. We should then be able to have our meeting *à quatre*.[5] Briand is ready to make the small concessions to Italy for which Mussolini has indicated a desire, and the meeting would therefore both have a *raison d'être* which could be given to the public and would be practically certain to result in an agreement. It would also afford Briand and me an opportunity (much to be desired) of again meeting Mussolini, who lives far too much in isolation, and would enable Briand and him to discuss with, I hope, good results other outstanding questions between France and Italy.

Finally, I told Quiñones that if this were arranged, I was quite ready to suggest Malaga as the place for such a meeting. I told him that I had said nothing to Briand on the subject so far and that I did not know how the French Government would take the suggestion, but I should urge as a reason that Mussolini could come to Malaga in an Italian ship and would not be exposed to the dangers of a land journey. If we could arrange this, it would be a further satisfaction for Spanish national feeling and might help General Primo de Rivera both to accept the settlement of the Tangier question and to reconsider his attitude to the League. I left Quiñones beaming with pleasure. He told my wife that I had brought him extremely good news.[6]

I have to-day told Merry del Val[7] of this conversation, as I did not wish him to grow jealous of my relations with Quiñones or to take offence because I kept him in ignorance of what was passing, but I begged him particularly not to make any report of it to General Primo de Rivera as the letter from Briand and me had naturally been addressed to Quiñones as the late

---

[3] Not printed. The joint letter of December 10 to Señor Quiñones was as indicated in the first paragraph of the present letter.

[4] See No. 62, note 8. In Madrid despatch No. 660 of December 15, Sir H. Rumbold reported that the French Ambassador had told him that the proposals of the French Government, which dealt mainly with certain modifications in the control of the police in the International Zone, seemed to General Primo de Rivera to 'provide a most favourable basis for settlement'.

[5] Cf. No. 8, note 5.

[6] In a letter of December 15 Sir A. Chamberlain instructed Lord Crewe to inform M. Briand of his interview with Señor Quiñones and of the proposal for the meeting at Malaga.

[7] Spanish Ambassador in London.

representative of Spain upon the Council and was, as I have said, to be placed by him personally in the hands of the General.

My conversation with Quiñones, though brief, was of the usual very intimate and confidential kind. I spoke to him of the very satisfactory character of the Council meeting at Geneva and particularly of the loyal and cordial cooperation of Dr. Stresemann with Monsieur Briand and myself. He asked me about Italy. I told him of what had passed between Signor Bordonaro and me, and I was also able to tell him that when Mussolini had knocked at the door of the Wilhelmstrasse he had got an even sharper rebuff.[8] This also pleased Quiñones, who gave me some curious information about Italian-Spanish relations. This conversation does not call for any action on your part, but I should like you to know exactly what has passed in case General Primo should take the initiative in speaking to you about it.

My impression that Primo de Rivera would not now be unwilling to find an excuse for withdrawing Spain's resignation from the League is rather confirmed by something which Villegas told me. He says that the Spanish Ambassador in Rome, who until recently had been very out-spoken in condemnation of the League, has now changed his note. Villegas added that this was *post* and, he thought, *propter* my meeting with Primo.

Yours sincerely,
AUSTEN CHAMBERLAIN

8 Cf. No. 85.

No. 97

Letter from Sir A. Chamberlain to Sir R. Lindsay (Berlin)
[F.O. 800/261]

Private and Personal FOREIGN OFFICE, *December 16, 1927*
My dear Lindsay,

I send for your own personal information a memorandum[1] recording my parting conversation with Stresemann on the day on which we both left Geneva. The cordiality with which Stresemann co-operated with Briand and myself was a particularly happy feature of this Council meeting, and you will get some idea of the relations prevailing between us from the confidences which Stresemann felt able to make to me and I to return as frankly. I do not propose to circulate this memorandum or to say anything of the conversation to Paris, but I shall show a copy of the memorandum to Erskine[2] before he goes to Warsaw and I shall ask him to take some suitable opportunity of telling Marshal Pilsudski of the sympathetic manner in which Dr. Stresemann spoke of him and of saying that I derived the impression that Dr. Stresemann would welcome an invitation to go to Warsaw to sign the Commercial Treaty in person as this would give him an opportunity of further cultivating the acquaintance of the Marshal.

1 No. 91.

2 Sir W. Erskine succeeded Sir W. Max Muller as H.M. Minister at Warsaw in January 1928.

Stresemann, by the way, ought to be grateful to me for having stopped the reference of the Weste[r]platte case[3] to the Permanent Court of International Justice—a reference to which Stresemann had rather reluctantly agreed as part of a bargain which he drove with the Poles but I should not like to claim his gratitude as I did this on general principles and not out of any special tenderness for Germany.

Yours sincerely,
AUSTEN CHAMBERLAIN

[3] See No. 66, note 5.

No. 98

Sir R. Graham (Rome) to Sir A. Chamberlain
(Received December 18, 9 a.m.)

No. 224 Telegraphic [C 10207/167/22]

ROME, *December 17, 1927, 7.20 p.m.*

Signor Mussolini was unable to see Senator Scialoja or myself until yesterday evening when we both gave him accounts of what had happened at Geneva. I spoke to him on general lines which you have always indicated[1] but in view of His Excellency's satisfactory statement to Council of Ministers[2] and complete modification of attitude on the part of Italian press situation had considerably changed since I saw you. His Excellency expressed warm thanks for your friendly messages and for your kind interest without which he scarcely anticipated success in Franco-Italian negotiations.

I told Signor Mussolini of Monsieur Briand's complaint that Italian proposals for negotiations made through French Ambassador at Rome had never been followed up. His Excellency replied that this showed complete misunderstanding. Monsieur Besnard whose intentions had always been excellent but who was not conspicuously clear-headed had told him some time ago before proceeding on leave that he intended to get hold of Monsieur Fromageot[3] at Quai d'Orsay and draft a treaty between France and Italy which he would then communicate. Signor Mussolini had ever since been awaiting this draft but it had never materialized.

His Excellency said that he desired very earnestly a complete understanding with the French and that given good-will on both sides this ought to be comparatively easy. Tangier presented few difficulties. The question of Italian nationals in France was certainly more difficult but not insuperably so if the French would come to realize that an attempt to swallow over a million foreigners at one gulp was bound to cause indigestion. As regards the

[1] See No. 91, note 9.

[2] For a report on Signor Mussolini's statement on December 15, see *The Times*, December 16, 1927, p. 14.

[3] Legal Adviser to the French Ministry of Foreign Affairs.

Balkans His Excellency recognized French right for cultural and political penetration but must the door be shut in face of Italy whose aims were mainly economic and who was a closer neighbour to, as well as having greater interest in the States concerned? An element likely to facilitate general negotiations was fact that Italy did not desire a square metre of territory. His Excellency then corrected him (? self) saying that surely if she asked for slight rectification on her south Tripoli frontier involving a few square miles of desert French could not grudge this 'equitable compensation' in view of vast areas she had acquired in Africa after the war. He might also perhaps seek some assurance that in the unlikely event of existing mandates being reconsidered French would not veto Italian claims. Italy would not come to negotiations entirely empty-handed. She would be ready to come to an agreement with France as to a guarantee over question of Anschluss[4] and she might also be able to offer economic advantages in exchanges between the two countries.

Turning to question of Italian exiles in France His Excellency said that Italian opinion deeply appreciated Monsieur Briand's action in suppressing 'Corriere Degli Italiani'.[5] The measure came none too soon as this obscure rag had on several occasions incited his own assassination even suggesting place and opportunity for the deed. His Excellency was grateful for this and other indications of Monsieur Briand's good-will but he greatly feared that all his efforts to bring about an agreement would be frustrated by other influences. I told him of our conversation with Monsieur Briand regarding Monsieur Berthelot.[1] Signor Mussolini professed scepticism but said that the influences he meant were cartel and free-masons who would move heaven and earth to prevent any agreement being reached. They were now starting a violent agitation about General Capello (see my despatch No. 327[6] April 26th). His Excellency had shown recently that he was always ready to be clement but those who imagined that foreign agitation would help the General were doing the latter a poor service. The anti-Fascist idea was that within the next few years elections in France, Germany and Great Britain might all show a strong swing to the left in which case some combination against Italy, perhaps in the nature of economic blockade might be possible. This was one reason why His Excellency so strongly desired to reach an agreement with France before French elections took place.

[4] i.e. union between Germany and Austria.

[5] With reference to Paris telegram No. 248 (see No. 90, note 1), Sir E. Phipps transmitted in Paris despatch No. 2473 of December 14 (docket only preserved in Foreign Office archives) an extract from the *Petit Parisien* dated December 14, 1927, intimating that the French Minister of the Interior had suspended the *Corriere degli Italiani* for disobeying the terms of a circular issued by the Ministry of the Interior dated October 5, 1926, regarding news on foreigners living in France.

[6] This despatch, not printed, summarised proceedings at the trial of General L. Capello, an Italian Commander during the First World War and a prominent freemason, who was found guilty of complicity with Signor Zaniboni, a former Unitary Socialist deputy, who had confessed to an attempt to assassinate Signor Mussolini in November 1925: see Volume II, No. 108.

I suggested a press truce between Italy and her neighbours. Signor Mussolini replied that he had already ordered Italian papers to cease all polemics.

He evidently entertained very favourably the idea of eventual meeting 'à quatre'.[7]

[7] In a brief report on this conversation in a private letter of December 16 to Sir A. Chamberlain, Sir R. Graham had further stated: 'As regards Yugoslavia he [Signor Mussolini] said that he was also anxious to come to terms but that the negotiations with France must take first place.'

No. 99

Sir A. Chamberlain to Sir R. Graham (Rome)
No. 1540 [C 10315/167/22]

FOREIGN OFFICE, *December 19, 1927*

Sir,

The Italian Ambassador called this morning to take leave of me before proceeding to spend Christmas in Italy. Signor Bordonaro asked what impressions I had brought back from the Council meeting at Geneva. After some reference to the success of the Council's intervention in the Polish-Lithuanian dispute and the added confidence and influence which such success gave to the Council, I spoke to him of my conversations with your Excellency and of our luncheon with M. Briand. I did not go into any details with him, but I told him that already on arrival at Geneva I had felt there was a certain *détente* in the situation and I had seen with great satisfaction its development since, and in particular the response which Signor Mussolini had made, first in an interview with a journalist and afterwards in his statement to the Council of Ministers, to the friendly overture made by M. Briand in Paris. I added that I believed that the French and Spanish Governments were now very near an agreement on the Tangier question, and when their negotiations were finished I hoped the proposed discussion *à quatre* would afford an opportunity for a meeting at some convenient place between Signor Mussolini, M. Briand, General Primo de Rivera and myself. The Tangier question would afford a reason for the gathering and would make it certain that we should accomplish at any rate one piece of work, but I hoped that the conversations which would take place would help to solve other difficulties.

The Ambassador remarked that he had the impression last time we met[1] that I was *un peu fâché* but that he was reassured by my present attitude. I admitted that I had been perhaps a little angry, and still more disturbed, by the latest developments at that moment, since they left me with the feeling that I did not understand Italian policy and could no longer play the part of friendly interpreter which had been my rôle for so long, but I had been

[1] See No. 68

reassured by Signor Mussolini's latest utterances and was well satisfied with the turn which events had taken.[2]

I am, &c.,
(For the Secretary of State),
ORME SARGENT

[2] For an account of this conversation by Signor Bordonaro see *I Documenti Diplomatici Italiani*, Settima Serie, vol. v, No. 687.

No. 100

Letter from Sir R. Lindsay (Berlin) to Sir A. Chamberlain
[*F.O. 800/261*]

Copy
Private

BERLIN, *December 21, 1927*

Dear Sir Austen,

I am very grateful for your letter of the 16th[1] and for the enclosed note of your final conversation at Geneva with Stresemann.[2] He is of an effervescent nature and I think the atmosphere of Geneva is rather apt to go to his head. He telegraphed thence during the last meeting a glowing account of a cordial conversation he had had with Briand. The latter had said to him 'why do you trouble about Poincaré? he really is a changed man, and is now entirely won over to a policy of reconciliation'. And as soon as Stresemann got here his Deutsch National colleagues addressed to him the question 'may we ask Dr. Stresemann whether you did not immediately seize this favourable opportunity for suggesting to Monsieur Briand that he now withdraw all the army of occupation from the Rhineland?' This is an instance of the way in which Stresemann's returns to Berlin are liable also to be a return to mother earth with a heavy bump.

And now I am wondering whether he really could go to Warsaw to sign a treaty, whatever he may have thought before he returned here, and however obviously desirable it is to keep personal touch with Pilsudski and to foster his reasonable inclinations. But I must say I have the impression that Stresemann is in advance of his own public opinion, though perhaps only by a few months; and I cannot help wondering whether the atmosphere of Geneva did not, within those very few hours, rise also to the head of the redoubtable Marshal. I shall try to sound Stresemann as soon as possible. He has been away from Berlin most of the time since his return from Geneva. I am, moreover, far from confident that any treaty with Poland will be ready for signature for some weeks at any rate.

As to the Albanian complications, I have been interested to hear from a good source here that the Italians have, in fact, lately been courting the German Government. Their attitude is described to me as one of atmosphere and tone rather than as anything definite, and there are no concrete proposals whatever. I am also told that the advances are being received with reserve and that there is no indication of the Germans yielding to blandishments and

[1] No. 97.   [2] No. 91.

196

allowing themselves to be beguiled into any rash commitment. It is worth while remembering that Mussolini has before now tried to exert his charm in this direction. When the German-Italian Arbitration Treaty[3] was signed last winter it was Mussolini who wanted to call it a Treaty of Friendship, tried to exaggerate its importance, urged Stresemann to visit Rome for a ceremonious signature; and it was Stresemann who hung back. So long as Stresemann is in office I think there is little risk of rash and short-sighted engagements between Berlin and Rome.

Yours very sincerely,
R. C. LINDSAY

[3] This treaty of December 29, 1926, is printed in *British and Foreign State Papers*, vol. 125, pp. 716–20.

No. 101

Sir A. Chamberlain to Mr. Kennard (Belgrade)

No. 146 Telegraphic [C 10246/808/92]

FOREIGN OFFICE, *December 22, 1927, 2 p.m.*

Your despatch No. 480[1] (of the 16th December. Italo-Yugoslav relations).

I observe that M. Marinkovitch referred to the advice I gave the Yugoslav Minister here on November 18th (see my telegram No. 127[2]), to the effect that the present moment was not opportune for resuming conversations with Rome. This advice was given on the morrow of the signature of the Franco-Yugoslav Treaty and in the circumstances was obviously the only advice possible. The situation however has since been altogether changed.

Please make it clear to M. Marinkovitch that in present circumstances I offer no advice. It is for the two governments to decide when and how to resume their conversations and I do not wish to express any opinion.[3]

Repeated to Rome No. 290 and Durazzo No. 97.

[1] Not printed. This despatch reported conversations held by Mr. Kennard with General Bodrero and M. Marinkovitch regarding the possible renewal or denunciation of the Italian-Serb-Croat-Slovene Treaty of Rome.   [2] No. 46.
[3] Mr. Kennard replied on December 26 in Belgrade telegram No. 198 that M. Marinkovitch fully appreciated Sir A. Chamberlain's attitude and proposed to agree to an exchange of notes prolonging the Treaty of Rome for six months.

No. 102

Mr. Leeper (Warsaw) to Sir A. Chamberlain (Received January 2, 1928)

No. 551 [N 8/8/55]

WARSAW, *December 24, 1927*

Sir,

Now that Poland is making rapid economic progress, after having pulled herself out of the political and financial dry rot of her first years of independence, the moment seems suitable for making certain observations on the methods hitherto adopted by British business houses in England in their dealings with Poland.

2. Poland had a bad name in British financial circles from the very beginning. It is always difficult to live down a bad name, and nowhere, I suppose, is it more difficult than in the City. Poland got her bad name originally both for political and financial reasons. Very soon after the war she came to be regarded, and not unnaturally, as a disturbing element in Europe. She *was* a disturbing element, but, considering the disturbed state of Eastern Europe, she could hardly be anything else, unless she were prepared to abandon her territorial rights. People in Western Europe knew very little about Polish history or the Poles themselves. They were well acquainted with Germany and Russia and, much of what the Poles claimed from the latter States was regarded as territory wrenched from the vanquished rather than stolen property returned to its rightful owner. The pressing need for Western Europe was to conclude peace as quickly as possible and Polish claims undoubtedly delayed that happy day. In fact the Poles became a nuisance so far as their claims against Germany were concerned, while on the Russian side they nearly involved Europe in a new conflagration. They became thoroughly unpopular and nowhere more so than in England.

3. This is now all past history. The irritation and bitterness felt by the Poles for the hesitation shown by His Majesty's Government to admit their claims both against Germany and Russia have disappeared. England is popular in Poland and individual Englishmen are liked and respected more than any other foreigners. So far as the Poles are concerned the English are welcomed here, whether they come to study the country or to do business. It is in England and not in Poland that the past has not been forgotten, and, if there are to be close relations between the two countries in the future, it is in England that the ground has to be prepared.

4. I am prompted to call attention to this need for two reasons. In the first place the political stability of Poland is of real political importance to us. It not only keeps the balance in Europe, but it keeps Bolshevism at bay. But Poland is also important as a market, both as a market for the present and as a centre from which well-established houses can penetrate further east when conditions become favourable. That these opportunities should be neglected by us is not in our interest. It is time that we made an effort to dissipate the suspicions and to induce our own people to come and study conditions in Poland for themselves instead of accepting the tendencious opinions of foreigners, who are ill-disposed to this country, and of entrusting the interests of British firms here to Russian Jews, Letts or any other foreign elements, whose sole qualification is that they are supposed to know Eastern Europe. This is in fact what has been going on for some years past. This Legation has again and again been called upon to support the claim of some British firm represented here by persons who are not English and who belong to some nationality whom the Poles dislike and distrust. It not only hinders the actual business of the moment, but it injures the general interests of British trade here.

5. To those who have spent some time in Poland and have seen with their own eyes the progress which has been made it is a source of wonder and perplexity why Poland is still to so large an extent disregarded by British business and finance. The French Ambassador recently told me that he had been urging his Government to arouse interest in French business circles in the possibilities of Poland. He had no difficulty in convincing his own Ministry of Foreign Affairs that they were very great; the influence, however, of the Ministry of Foreign Affairs with financial circles was not great and the latter were still much more interested in Russian than in Polish possibilities. It had, therefore, been very gratifying to him a short time ago to see the surprise on the face of a leading French financier during a recent visit to Poland. He had opened his mouth wide at the possibilities here and had told M. Laroche that he and many others in France had no idea that Poland had made so much progress.

6. I have recently had an opportunity of speaking to a number of British business men, both those resident in this country, either in Warsaw or in Lodz, and others who had come on a short business visit. In the case of the former I was impressed by the note of optimism which is rare in a British community living abroad and which was certainly quite unknown when I had met these same people three years ago. In the case of those coming from England without any first-hand knowledge of Poland I was struck by their extraordinary ignorance of the country and the unfavourable views which they had picked up in the City. On cross-questioning one of these people I extracted the following confession of faith or—I should say—confession of lack of faith. Poland, he had heard, was unstable politically and was dishonest in business. One could not overlook the constant danger of her being attacked and overwhelmed by her much more powerful Eastern neighbour, Russia, who sooner or later would revive and take her revenge. The Poles too were notorious for their lack of ability in governing themselves. Apart, however, from politics their business morality was very low. Bribery and corruption were rife in the administration and no people had such a bad reputation as the Poles for failure to pay their debts when they fell due.

7. To take first the accusation against the Poles for corruption both in administration and in business. It would be idle to pretend that they have reached British standards in either respect. From Russia they inherited the worst possible traditions and, in judging signs of grace, one must compare the present day with the period immediately after the war. In the administration there has been a very distinct advance, and, though I still hear of cases of bribery in placing government contracts, energetic action is now being taken to expose and punish any such cases which come to the ears of the authorities. A short time ago a representative of an important American engineering firm informed a member of this Legation that he had been greatly impressed by the complete absence of corruption in the municipality.

8. As regards the payment of debts it is true that many British firms have had unfortunate experiences in the past, though I am now told that there has been a distinct improvement. Some years ago times were bad in Poland, the

exchange was uncertain and the risks were great. Orders were and still are largely placed through Jews. The Jews in Eastern Europe have a mentality of their own. They are not necessarily dishonest. They are in most cases perfectly prepared to share the profits, but they do not see the same necessity for sharing the losses. This may help to explain why losses have often been so large.

9. The political distrust is certainly exaggerated. It is of course ridiculous to say that the Poles are less capable of governing themselves than the majority of the present States of Europe. The fear of what Russia may do in the future is typical of the exaggerated importance attached to Russia in England, largely as a result of the propaganda at home both for and against Bolshevism. As I had the honour to point out in my despatch no. 535[1] of 13th December the Poles, who would be most alive to the Russian danger if it really existed, are not in the least alarmed. Russia seems more alarming and impressive the further one gets away from her; the more one can peep behind the scenes the less imposing is the spectacle. But it is this preoccupation with Russia in England which largely accounts for the lack of faith and the lack of interest in Poland. English public opinion and English finance are well-known for their conservatism, for their hesitation in adapting themselves to an entirely new state of affairs. Eastern Europe has undergone the most profound and far-reaching changes, but the old familiar names have not lost their spell and the new have not yet taken their place. The process of education is bound to be slow at home. How can it be most quickly and effectively advanced?

10. I do not believe that any amount of Polish propaganda in England will achieve much. The Poles are always talking of the failure of their propaganda in England. It is but natural that it should fail, for such propaganda will always be suspect. Nor do I believe that carefully organised visits of leading British industrialists to Poland would produce any lasting effect. I venture to suggest that what is really required is something more permanent. English public opinion will only be really influenced by the personal experience of Englishmen, who have lived in the country and who know what they are talking about. If, for example, British business houses, wishing to establish connections in Poland, would send out well-educated young Englishmen, preferably from the Universities, to represent them here, to learn the language and the ways of the country, business would increase and suspicions, bred largely by ignorance, could be dissipated. I suggest that such representatives should, if possible, have had a University education, for in that case not only will they be less hide-bound and more adaptable, but will be capable of mixing on an equality in a society, which may be full of practical defects, but which is certainly not lacking in intelligence and culture.

11. I would add one thing further to this suggestion. It is not desirable on the whole that men should be sent here with a previous acquaintance with Russia. I could quote many instances where that previous experience has

[1] No. 93.

hampered them in Poland and has prevented them from looking at this country with fresh and unprejudiced eyes. What is really essential is that Englishmen who come here should start with a clean slate and should study Poland with a purely British outlook. I believe that such people would succeed with the Poles, and would transact business with far less difficulty than the present type of Jewish representative, and I trust that their experience and the information they could contribute would have a real influence on opinion in the City, which is unlikely to be changed by any artificial propaganda from above.

I have, &c.,

R. A. Leeper

No. 103

Sir R. Lindsay (Berlin) to Sir A. Chamberlain (Received December 30)

No. 769 [C 10507/833/18]

BERLIN, *December 28, 1927*

Sir,

I transmit to you herewith translation[1] of an article from the 'Vorwärts' of the 19th instant regarding the budget of the Ministry of Communications with especial reference to the lax control of expenditure on Aviation and the predominance in the Aviation Department of the Ministry of purely military influence. The article is, I understand, in part the result of the disclosure of some confidential information given to the Reichsrat. The estimates of the Ministry have not yet been issued. When they become available developments will be carefully watched.[2]

2. Meanwhile, however suspicious these indications may be, it would be undesirable to base on them any observations to the German Government. To do so would merely have the effect of disarming completely such German critics of the present state of affairs as may be inclined to speak out.

I have, &c.,

R. C. Lindsay

[1] Not printed.

[2] Certain preceding correspondence regarding German aviation statistics is not preserved in Foreign Office archives. It would appear that Foreign Office despatch No. 1345 to Berlin of October 31 had referred to an enquiry from the Air Ministry regarding publication of the statistics envisaged in the exchange of letters between M. Briand and the German Chargé d'Affaires in Paris on June 9–10 (see Volume III, No. 236) in respect of the year ending March 31, 1927. Sir R. Lindsay had replied to this despatch on December 5 in Berlin despatch No. 729 (docket only preserved in Foreign Office archives), wherein he transmitted a copy of the 'Heeres-Verordnungsblatt' of December 30, 1926, containing a nominal list of pilots (? army officers) authorised to fly: no similar list of naval officers had been traced. Sir R. Lindsay had further reported that the German Secretary of State had given an assurance that other statistics required would be published shortly. On December 16 the Air Ministry had commented, according to the docket of their letter, that publication of the names of the Army and Navy officers permitted to fly under the Paris agreement of May 1926 (see No. 9, note 5) was quite a different matter from publication of lists of aircraft, civilian pilots, factories, &c., in accordance with the German undertaking of June 10, 1927.

No. 104

Sir E. Howard (Washington) to Sir A. Chamberlain
(Received January 7, 1928)
No. 2356 [C 137/49/18]

WASHINGTON, *December 30, 1927*

Sir,

With reference to my despatch No. 2034[1] of the 17th ultimo reporting upon United States press comment on the note which Mr. Parker Gilbert addressed to the German Government on November 6th last, I have the honour to transmit herewith copies of an article entitled 'Urge Revision of Reparation and War Debt'[1] emanating from the Washington Bureau of the New York Herald Tribune and published in the issue of that journal of December 28th.

2. This article amounts to no more than an intelligent surmise that the possible revision of Germany's reparation liabilities may lead to the reconsideration of the allied war debts to the United States; at the same time I have considered it worthy of special reference as an indication of feeling possibly existent in responsible official circles that the future of the war debt agreements cannot be divorced from the question of Germany's ability to meet her reparation obligations under the Dawes plan. On the other hand, Mr. Mellon himself, according to today's New York Times, has seen fit when questioned on the subject by representatives of the press, to indicate strongly that there is no connection whatsoever between reparations and the wartime debts owed to this country. The position thus taken by the Secretary of the Treasury is generally accepted as shewing that the Administration has no intention of deviating from its already declared view that the two problems are entirely separate.[2]

I have, &c.,
ESME HOWARD

[1] Not printed.

[2] Mr. Sargent minuted on January 11, 1928: 'Notwithstanding Mr. Mellon's repudiation —he could hardly have acted otherwise at the present juncture—the view held pretty generally in the Treasury & by the financial experts is that in raising the question of the fixation of the reparation debt Mr. Gilbert acted with the approval, and even possibly at the suggestion, of the U.S. Govt. who wished without committing themselves to give the problem of inter-allied debts an airing before the Presidential election. O.G.S. Jan. 11.'

CHAPTER II

Correspondence on European Questions
January 3–April 13, 1928

No. 105

Sir A. Chamberlain to the Earl of Erroll (Coblenz)
No. 3 [C 10415/304/18]

FOREIGN OFFICE, *January 3, 1928*

My Lord,

I have received your despatch No. 178[1] of December 21st, 1927, relative to the proposal put forward by your Belgian colleague[2] for the initiation of conversations between the High Commissioners at Coblenz with a view to reach agreement, as a preliminary to discussion of the subject with the Reichskommissar, on a plan for hastening the end of the Occupation.

2. I observe that Monsieur Tirard informed Monsieur Forthomme that he did not think that any useful purpose would be served by the initiation of such discussions. Should the latter however revert, in conversation with you, to his proposal, you should be careful to leave him in no doubt that you are unable to support it. Your Lordship is already aware that it is the desire of His Majesty's Government that the occupation of the Rhineland should be terminated as soon as it conveniently may: but I do not consider that Monsieur Forthomme's suggestion would, if adopted, contribute to the attainment of that object. The proposed discussion might indeed do no more than complicate still further the question of the evacuation of the Rhineland, which depends not on local and technical considerations with which the High Commissioners at Coblenz are familiar, but on matters of high international policy, which the Governments concerned alone are competent to decide.

I am, &c.,
(For the Secretary of State)
ORME SARGENT

---

[1] Not printed. [2] M. Forthomme.

No. 106

Sir A. Chamberlain to the Marquess of Crewe (Paris)
No. 28 [C 51/51/18][1]

FOREIGN OFFICE, *January 5, 1928*

My Lord Marquess:

With reference to Your Lordship's despatch No. 2298[2] (7/156/1927) of November 18th last, I have to inform you that His Majesty's Government have recently been considering their attitude towards the question of German railway construction in the Rhineland in its relation to the interpretation of article 43 of the Treaty of Versailles.

2. The problems inherent in questions which arise in connexion with the Rhineland Railway system are of two different natures:

(1) Permanent—that of preventing the development by Germany of those railways for aggressive purposes. Such prevention can be secured only by the application of article 43 of the Treaty of Versailles, which provides that within the demilitarised zone (an area within which the Rhineland railway system is situated) 'the upkeep of all permanent works of mobilisation is forbidden'.

(2) Temporary—that of securing the proper working, etc., of those railways in the interest of the safety, maintenance and requirements of the troops of occupation. The situation in this respect is governed by article 212 of the treaty and by articles 3 and 10 of the Rhineland Agreement.[3]

3. The effect of article 212 of the Treaty of Versailles and of article 10 of the Rhineland Agreement is to place all the communications in the occupied area under the supreme and absolute authority of the Commander-in-Chief of the Allied Armies who has the right to take any measures he may think necessary to ensure their occupation and use. Article 3 of the Rhineland Agreement empowers the Rhineland High Commission to enact ordinances insofar as may be necessary for securing the safety, maintenance and requirements of the occupying troops. In pursuance of its powers under this article the Rhineland High Commission has enacted an ordinance appointing a Railway Commission to represent it and the High Command in the first instance in railway matters and laying on the German authorities the obligation to submit all plans for railway work other than that of ordinary maintenance to the allied authorities for prior sanction. This Commission, as Y[our] L[ordship] is doubtless aware, is sometimes referred to in corre-

---

[1] The approved draft only of this despatch is preserved in the file.

[2] Not preserved in Foreign Office archives. According to the docket this despatch transmitted a copy of a 'report of 15th November from Versailles Committee to Ambassadors' Conference stating that German railway authorities have requested permission to strengthen bridges by which railway line between Odernheim and Staudernheim crossed the River Nahe, and requesting approval for enclosed "avis" recommending that request be refused.' This report, No. 418/1, is not printed.

[3] This agreement of June 28, 1919, between the United States, Belgium, the British Empire, and France and Germany is printed in *British and Foreign State Papers*, vol. 112, pp. 219–24.

spondence as the C.I.C.F.C. (Commission Interalliée des Chemins de Fer de Campagne).

4. In 1922, as you are aware, the Ambassadors' Conference, basing themselves on the above-mentioned article 43, drew up a programme of demands regarding the modification or demolition of railway works in the demilitarised zone. This programme was divided into two parts: (i) relating to constructions in the course of erection, work on which was to be stopped immediately; (ii) relating to existing works which were to be altered or demolished at the moment of the evacuation by the allies of the zone in which they were situated. The German Government were notified of the terms of this programme and invited to co-operate in its execution, the supervision of which was entrusted insofar as the occupied territory was concerned to the Inter-Allied High Command at Mainz, with the Inter-Allied Railway Commission (C.I.C.F.C.) as agent. As regards that portion of the demilitarised zone which lies outside the bounds of the occupied territory this supervision was entrusted to the Military Control Commission.

5. It is not known how much, if any, of this programme has actually been carried out in the occupied area. The German Government protested to the Ambassadors' Conference on two occasions after receiving the Inter-Allied notification of the programme mentioned above, and the Cologne zone was evacuated in January 1926 without any demand for the destruction or modification of railway works in that area having then been made by the Allied Powers. In August 1925, however, the Inter-Allied Railway Commission addressed to the Inter-Allied High Command a statement embodying their recommendations in respect of those demands in the Conference programme of 1922 which related to demolitions etc., in the ten and fifteen year zones. Between that time and June 1927 nothing further was heard on the subject of railway demolitions in the Rhineland in connexion with article 43. The German Railway company however continued, in accordance with the allied regulations enacted in virtue of article 212 of the Treaty of Versailles and articles 3 and 10 of the Rhineland Agreement, to seek permission from the occupying authorities to effect modifications in the Rhineland railway system. It is understood that in no case hitherto, has the desired permission been refused.

6. There are however at the present moment, three German requests under consideration by the allied authorities in respect of work which, although admittedly un-objectionable from the point of view of danger to the security of the armies of occupation, may, it has been suggested, yet involve infractions of article 43 of the Treaty of Versailles. These requests relate to:

(1) The improvement of the lines at Rothe Erde, Walheim and Inden in the neighbourhood of the Belgian frontier;

(2) The reinforcement of certain bridges on the line connecting Odernheim and Staudernheim near Bingen;

(3) The creation of a siding at Kaisersruhe on the Aachen–Würselen line.

7. As regards (1) the situation is not perfectly clear. On June 8th last the Inter-Allied Railway Commission considered an application by the German Railway authorities to be allowed to proceed with the improvements in question. While informing the High Command at Mainz that there was no objection to be taken to these improvements on the ground of danger to the security of the armies, the railway commission indicated that their being carried out might constitute an infraction of article 43. In September General Guillaumat replied expressing the view that it might be possible to oppose the construction of the works in question in virtue of article 43, and he suggested that the Commission might avail themselves of the opportunity to revise their recommendations of August 1925 to include (presumably, though this was not specifically mentioned) a recommendation that the new Aix-la-Chapelle improvements should either be vetoed forthwith or demolished when the time came for the zone in which they are situated to be evacuated. The Inter-Allied Railway Commission has now acted on General Guillaumat's suggestion but its report, dated November 16th,[4] contains no recommendation with regard to these particular constructions.

8. The German applications in respect of the work described under (2) and (3) above have however been referred through General Guillaumat, to the Allied Military Committee of Versailles, and the latter has recommended that the proposals to carry out the works on the Odernheim and Staudernheim line and at Kaisersruhe should be vetoed as constituting infractions of article 43 (a demand for the demolition of the section of railway line referred to under (2) having been included in the Ambassadors' Conference programme of 1922). The Versailles Committee further advises that the German authorities should be informed accordingly.

9. Meanwhile the German Railway Company awaits a reply from the allied authorities in regard to each of the three above-mentioned cases.

10. It is the considered view of His Majesty's Government that whatever decisions may have been taken by the Ambassadors' Conference in 1922 as to what railway works in the Rhineland should or should not be held to constitute a violation of article 43 of the Treaty of Versailles, the effect then given to that article by the programme in question can no longer, now that the Treaty of Locarno is in force, be imposed on the German Government save through a decision of the Council of the League. That this is the correct and only possible view to take is made evident by the fact that, according to the agreement reached at Geneva by the representatives of the Belgian, British, French, German, Italian and Japanese Governments on December 12th, 1926, article 43 of the Treaty of Versailles must be applied as from January 31st, 1927, in the manner laid down by the Council of the League; while according to the resolution adopted by the latter on December 11th, 1926, 'It is understood that the provisions of article 213 of the Peace Treaty with Germany relating to investigations shall be applicable to the demilitarised Rhine zone as to other parts of Germany. These provisions do not provide in this zone, any more than elsewhere, for any special control by

4 Not preserved in Foreign Office archives.

local standing and permanent groups. In the de-militarised Rhine zone, such special groups, not provided for in article 213, shall not be set up except by convention between the governments concerned'.[5]

11. Altogether apart, however, from any question of the right of the ex-allied governments to decide what should or should not be held to be infringements of article 43 of the Treaty of Versailles, it is manifest that the ex-allied authorities in the Rhineland can only impose their veto on any projected alteration of the Rhineland railway system in virtue of article 3 of the Rhineland Agreement and on the ground that the safety of the armies of occupation would be endangered by the construction of such proposed work. As it is apparently admitted that no objection can on that score be entertained to any of the three proposals referred to above, I consider that the Inter-Allied Railway Commission should, without further delay, so inform the German authorities in reply to their several enquiries relative to the above three proposals. It would be convenient however, if these and all future communications of similar character which the commission may have to address to the German railway authorities should be accompanied by a formula to the effect that authority under article 3 of the Rhineland Agreement to proceed with any particular construction is given in each case entirely without prejudice to any question which may arise as to the permissibility of such work under article 43 of the Treaty of Versailles, and on the understanding that the rights of the powers concerned under article 4 of the Locarno Treaty are fully reserved.

12. The adoption of this procedure would have the advantage of rendering unnecessary any direct reference in correspondence with the German authorities to the programme of the Ambassadors' Conference of 1922 and thus avoiding the danger that the German Government might raise the question of its validity if it were again brought to their notice officially in present circumstances. That they would do so is practically certain seeing that, when the 1922 programme of demolitions was communicated to them, they protested, alleging in their notes to the Ambassadors' Conference of August 16th and November 15th, 1922[6] that the demands it contained far exceeded anything which could be justified by the terms of article 43. There is also the further advantage that the existence of the suggested allied caveat would render it more difficult for the German Government to claim that the cost of carrying out any destructions which may eventually be decreed by the Council of the League of Nations as the result of a request from the Allied Powers should be a charge upon the latter and imputable to the Dawes annuity.

13. As regards the present value of this programme drawn up by the Ambassadors' Conference in 1922, it is well to remember that in 1925 the Inter-Allied Railway Commission presented to the High Command at Mainz certain recommendations with regard to that part of the programme which related to demolitions and modifications of the railways in the ten

[5] See *League of Nations Official Journal*, February 1927, p. 162: cf. Volume II, No. 352, Annex A. [6] Not printed.

and fifteen year zones. These recommendations have never, so far as His Majesty's Government are aware, been approved by the Ambassadors' Conference, but they have, as stated in paragraph 7 above, recently been reviewed by the Inter-Allied Railway Commission at the suggestion of General Guillaumat. The report of the commission and General Guillaumat's recommendations in connexion therewith are understood to be at present under the consideration of the Allied Military Committee of Versailles. The fact however remains that notwithstanding the existence of this programme and of the recommendations put forward by the Inter-Allied Railway Commission in August 1925 and November 1927, there is at present no comprehensive and definitive schedule of allied desiderata regarding the railway destructions to be carried out under article 43 on the evacuation of the occupied territory. The 1922 programme moreover may not, it is believed, be entirely adequate to present conditions and it must also be borne in mind that no steps were taken to carry it out so far as destructions in the Cologne zone were concerned when that area was evacuated in 1926.

14. In these circumstances, far from attempting to maintain in the face of the opposition of the German Government that the 1922 programme is still binding on the latter it would, in my opinion, be more convenient were the Ambassadors' Conference now to take a decision cancelling their earlier decisions on this subject (though without communicating with the German Government to this effect), and to direct the Inter-Allied Military Committee of Versailles to investigate anew the question of railway construction in the Rhineland with a view to the submission of a fresh series of recommendations to the allied powers. It should be clearly understood however that the result of the deliberations of the Allied Military Committee of Versailles is not enforceable on the German Government by a decision of the occupying powers, but is to be regarded merely as the material on which the latter will base any demands which they may wish in due course to put to Germany either direct or through the League of Nations in virtue of article 4 of the Treaty of Locarno. With this object in view the Allied Military Committee of Versailles should be instructed when preparing their recommendations to take into account not only strategic but also economic and commercial considerations, and to be careful to limit their recommendations to constructions which constitute such palpable and at the same time such vitally dangerous violations of article 43 as would make it incumbent on the ex-allied governments to appeal, if necessary, to the Council of the League in order to obtain their demolition.

15. I request that you will inform the Ambassadors' Conference of the views of His Majesty's Government as set forth in the preceding paragraphs of this despatch and that you will endeavour to obtain the agreement of your colleagues to the procedure suggested therein.[7]

I am, &c.,

(For the Secretary of State)

ORME SARGENT

[7] Lord Crewe acted on these instructions in a note, No. 17 A.C., of January 9 to the

Conference of Ambassadors (copy received in the Foreign Office under Paris covering despatch No. 44, not preserved in Foreign Office archives). On January 17 the Central Department of the Foreign Office sent a letter to the Chancery of H.M. Embassy at Paris stating that they had been surprised that this note followed so closely the text of the present despatch which had been drafted for the information of H.M. Embassy and not in a form suitable for communication to the Conference of Ambassadors. Mr. Wigram, First Secretary in H.M. Embassy at Paris, replied in a letter of January 19 to Mr. Sargent in which he stated in particular that neither M. Massigli nor his French military advisers had commented on the tone of the British note.

No. 107

Letter from Mr. Sargent to Sir E. Phipps (Paris)

[*F.O. 800/275: Ge/28/1*]

FOREIGN OFFICE, *January 5, 1928*

Dear Eric,

As you will have seen from the recent Germany print,[1] there is trouble again brewing in regard to German reparations. The immediate cause of the trouble is the independent attitude which Parker Gilbert has recently adopted. He has elected, in his correspondence with the German Government and in his periodic reports, to raise various thorny problems which the Reparation Commission and the Treasury do not wish to see discussed, since they feel that any such discussion is at the present time premature and may endanger the smooth working of the Dawes Plan during the coming year when it is going to be put, for the first time, to the real test of full payments. Parker Gilbert, on the other hand, has in this matter refused to consult or even warn the Reparation Commission beforehand as to the line he ought to take with the German Government, and as it turns out the line which he has taken has been, as explained, diametrically opposed to that desired by the Treasury. The question has therefore arisen as to whether the time has not come for the Reparation Commission to assert their authority and to make it clear that they do not necessarily approve the views which Parker Gilbert has recently been expressing. This involves the question as to how in future the Reparation Commission are to restrain Gilbert from further undesirable incursions into reparation politics. Can some sort of liaison be established which will attain the object desired without infringing Gilbert's susceptibilities, since he is very touchy on the subject of his independence and has, I understand, a strong objection to taking anything like orders from the Reparation Commission.

Now Gilbert is going to attend a meeting of the Reparation Commission in the course of this month. On this occasion the whole question is bound to come up and will require very careful handling if a crisis is to be avoided. The Treasury have accordingly arranged an inter-departmental meeting with Blanesburgh on Monday[2] to discuss the line which the latter ought to

[1] The reference was to copies, as printed for confidential circulation, of Foreign Office correspondence concerning Germany.

[2] January 9, 1928.

follow. Lindsay is coming over from Berlin to attend and Goodchild will also be present. In order that this gathering should be complete both Tyrrell and the Treasury feel that it would be most useful if the Ambassador could spare you in order that you may come over and explain to the meeting the attitude the French Government are likely to adopt in this matter from the political point of view.

Will you ring me up, therefore, to-morrow morning and let me know whether you can get away. The meeting is fixed for 3.30 on Monday afternoon and there is a dinner in the evening given by Lord Blanesburgh which you will probably be expected to attend.

Yours ever,
ORME SARGENT

No. 108

Letter from the Marquess of Crewe (Paris) to Sir A. Chamberlain
[F.O. 800/262]

Private and Personal   PARIS, January 6, 1928

My dear Chamberlain,

Phipps has shown me Sargent's letter of yesterday to him on the subject of reparations,[1] and I am sending a despatch[2] announcing his journey to London on Sunday[3] for the meeting mentioned in the letter. He will try if possible to see Poincaré before he goes, so as to be able to give a general impression of the French point of view from the political rather than the purely financial standpoint. The latter is already clear from Poincaré's own statement; the German debt, in his opinion, remains at 6,500 millions,[4] as its original figure, the Dawes plan simply representing a method of collection, and having no special bearing on the official amount.

After Parker Gilbert's first statement I gathered from Goodchild that the Reparations Commission were not a little offended by having simply received an early copy of the document, and having had no previous discussion of its purport. I did not gather that this first utterance, warning the German Government of the necessity for balancing their budget, and protesting against certain projected heads of expenditure, was in substance particularly objected to by the reparations people; but I take it that it is far otherwise with the Report lately published which, though oddly enough it seems to have attracted less attention in the press, makes all manner of forecasts and presumably of recommendations.

It certainly is, as Sargent says, a very delicate and difficult situation. When I first came here at the end of 1922, Poincaré being President of the

---

[1] No. 107.

[2] Untraced in Foreign Office archives.   [3] January 8, 1928.

[4] On April 27, 1921, the Reparation Commission had fixed Germany's reparation liability at 132 milliard gold marks (£6,600 million): see First Series, Volume XV, No. 74, minute 1. The method of payment of this sum was set out in the schedule of payments adopted by the Fourth Conference of London on May 5, 1921: v. ibid., No. 86, minute 5.

Council and Foreign Secretary, the Reparations Commission was run as a French organ, in spite of all Bradbury's[5] protests and efforts, he, with all his knowledge and his excellent qualities, not possessing the faculty of putting points, necessarily disagreeable in themselves, in the least disagreeable way. Nothing could be worse than the official terms then were, though Kemball Cook[6] was to some extent a soothing influence. Now, of course, the position is entirely different. Lord Blanesburgh made himself extremely liked by Barthou[7] before the latter gave up, and gets on admirably with his successor[8] and with the body generally. So far as they are concerned I should expect the forthcoming meeting here to be entirely harmonious.

But no doubt the transference of the site of Government so to speak, to Berlin, makes situations very awkward. I imagine that Parker Gilbert considers himself in no respect the servant of the Reparations Commission, as in any way answerable to them, or in any way under obligation to do more than keep them courteously informed of what he is doing. I equally conceive that their view of his and their functions is completely different. I cannot help feeling that he holds most of the trumps, as the Americans seem to do now in all matters in which money is concerned. If the Reparations Commission stand up to him, and determine to put him in his place, he might resign. Would not this produce an awkward situation? One can hardly suppose that Parker Gilbert has done this entirely off his own bat, and probably Owen Young,[9] and some of the great American banks, if not actually Morgans, have known what he was going to do. I suppose that, whatever happens, the Agent General is bound to be an American, and it cannot be certain that another man of equal capacity with Parker would not be more arbitrary than he is, his personality being regarded as pleasing enough, even by the Reparations Commission. I wonder if it would be possible for the latter to hold some of their meetings at Berlin? It is no doubt a point of honour with the French that the headquarters of the Commission should be in Paris, but I know of no reason why they need be. But if they could, from time to time, hold a plenary meeting at Berlin, supposing the Germans not to regard this as a threat or outrage, would it not enable them to assert their position rather more strongly as against the Dawes machinery?

It will be interesting to hear, as I suppose I shall when Phipps returns, what it is that the Treasury really want. Quite between ourselves, I have never seen that that august body has shown very brilliantly in the matter of reparations, but it has to be remembered that my baptism of fire here, in

---

[5] Lord Bradbury, Chairman of the National Food Council since 1925, had been British delegate to the Reparation Commission 1919–25.

[6] Sir B. Kemball-Cook, Managing Director of the British Tanker Co., had been Assistant British delegate to the Reparation Commission, 1921–6.

[7] M. Barthou, Deputy President of the French Council of Ministers and Minister of Justice, had been President of the Reparation Commission, 1922–6.

[8] M. Chapsal.

[9] Mr. Owen Young, Deputy Chairman of the Federal Reserve Bank of New York, had been a member of the First Committee of Experts appointed by the Reparation Commission in 1924 and Agent General for Reparation payments *ad interim*.

January 1923, took place amid the smoke produced by the appalling fiasco of the Conference at the Quai d'Orsay,[10] a fiasco for which the Treasury were simply and solely responsible, the Foreign Office being prevented from playing any part in the business.

Yours sincerely,
CREWE

[10] The reference was to the Paris Conference on Reparations, January 2–4, 1923: see Cmd. 1812 of 1923, *Inter-Allied Conferences on Reparations and Inter-Allied Debts. Held in London and Paris, December 1922 and January 1923. Reports and Secretaries' Notes of Conversations.*

No. 109

Record by Sir E. Phipps of a conversation with M. Poincaré (Paris)[1]

[C 232/49/18]

PARIS, *January 6, 1928*

I telephoned this afternoon to the Chef de Cabinet of M. Poincaré to ask whether the latter could receive me some time today or tomorrow 'à titre personnel' for a few minutes' conversation. The reply came back almost at once that M. Poincaré would receive me at 4 o'clock today.

2. On entering the room I prefaced my remarks by saying that I had permitted myself to encroach upon his valuable time merely in view of our old friendship and not under instructions from the Foreign Office. I was going to London on private business on Sunday[2] and when I went to the Foreign Office the next day I felt that I should most likely be asked what were M. Poincaré's views on Mr. Parker Gilbert's recent report and on the somewhat independent attitude which he had adopted lately towards the Reparations Commission. I added that anything that M. Poincaré might say to me would be treated as entirely confidential and would in no manner be considered official. M. Poincaré began by declaring his conviction that Mr. Parker Gilbert was particularly well disposed towards the British and French Governments and their points of view in regard to reparations, etc., and that Mr. Parker Gilbert's references to the desirability of fixing the total German debt and to the abolition of the transfer committee only applied to a somewhat remote future, that is to say some time after the next American elections. A few days before making his Report Mr. Gilbert had discussed some of its points with M. Poincaré, but had not referred to these particular ones. Moreover, M. Poincaré says that he knows for a fact that Mr. Mellon, in spite of numerous Press reports to the contrary, is in entire agreement with the attitude adopted by Mr. Parker Gilbert. Mr. Mellon would indeed have publicly contradicted these reports only he fears to do so in view of the approaching elections in America. M. Poincaré here

[1] Sir E. Phipps enclosed this record in a brief letter of January 10 to Mr. Sargent, not printed.

[2] January 8, 1928.

remarked that it was impossible to do any business whatsoever with the United States government at present as their one thought was the elections and the effect that their attitude might have on them. This applied equally to the question of the pact for outlawing war;[3] the latest American proposals here also were made with a view to home consumption. He had wished, owing to the heavy commercial payments due to the United States next year, to make certain modifications in the provisional instalments now being paid over the unratified Debt Agreement,[4] but the United States Government would not contemplate any modification until after the elections.

3. M. Poincaré made it clear to me that he maintained the attitude which he had adopted on December 23rd in the Chamber of Deputies, to the effect that the German debt had been fixed at 132 milliards of gold marks and that there it must be held to remain until the Powers concerned *unanimously* agreed to modify that sum. M. Poincaré here remarked smilingly that of course he did not for a moment believe that Germany would ever be able to pay the 132 milliards, but he considered that the fixing of that sum was a valuable asset both for the French and British Governments in any subsequent negotiations with either Germany or the United States. Indeed he gave me to understand that any diminution of the present French share of that astronomical total would have to be met by a corresponding diminution of French payments to Great Britain. Similarly, M. Poincaré is unwilling to contemplate at present the possibility of fixing the total number of German annuities, so long as the total number of French annuities to America is uncertain. In other words, he will not agree to payments to America and Great Britain over 60 years, for instance, if it be decided that German annuities should only run for 40.

4. I think it is clear that until after the American elections at all events, M. Poincaré will support us in declining to contemplate any modification of the Dawes plan; nor does he think that such is the intention of either Mr. Parker Gilbert or the United States government.

5. M. Poincaré is inclined to think that the tendency of Mr. Parker Gilbert to show undue independence of the Reparation Commission need not be taken too seriously. Mr. Parker Gilbert certainly likes to consult M. Poincaré himself when he comes to Paris just as he likes to consult Mr. Baldwin when he goes to London, rather than address himself to the French or British members of the Reparation Commission, but M. Poincaré thinks that he is so well-disposed towards both countries that this need not be taken too seriously. However, Mr. Gilbert will be lunching with M. Poincaré and M. Briand before the approaching meeting with the Reparation Commission on the 14th January next and M. Poincaré will take the opportunity of impressing upon Mr. Gilbert the advisability in future of consulting the Reparation Commission before launching any reports upon the world.

[3] See Chapter IV, *passim*.
[4] i.e. the agreement of April 29, 1926, negotiated by Mr. Mellon and M. Henry Berenger, then French Ambassador at Washington, in settlement of the French war debt to the United States. The text is printed in *British and Foreign State Papers*, vol. 127, pp. 511–18.

5 [*sic*]. M. Poincaré said that the French Government would much like to proceed to the marketing of the Dawes annuities, but here again no progress could be made until after the elections in the United States.

No. 110

Sir A. Chamberlain to the Marquess of Crewe (Paris)
No. 59 [W 138/138/17]

FOREIGN OFFICE, *January 9, 1928*

My Lord Marquess,

With reference to my despatch No. 2766[1] of the 9th November last I transmit herewith a copy of a letter from the Board of Trade in regard to the increase in the French customs tariff.

2. I entirely share the views expressed in this letter and I request that Your Lordship will communicate with the French Government in the sense desired by the Board.[2]

I am, &c.,
(For the Secretary of State)
G. H. VILLIERS

ENCLOSURE IN No. 110

Letter from the Board of Trade to the Foreign Office

BOARD OF TRADE, *January 5, 1927* [*sic*]

Sir,

I am directed by the Board of Trade to refer to their letter of the 4th November (C.R.T. 3323), relating to the higher Customs duties in France on British goods resulting from the recent Franco-German Commercial Treaty.[1] The Board in that letter, after calling attention to the numerous complaints they have received, expressed themselves for the reasons there given as against further representations to the French Government except in certain special cases.

2. Since that letter was written the Board have received further evidence of the feeling evoked amongst British traders by the continuous increase of trade barriers by foreign Governments and in particular by the recent increases in the French tariff as applied to goods from this country. Thus the President of the Board of Trade received recently a very influential

---

[1] Not preserved in Foreign Office archives. This despatch presumably transmitted a copy of a letter from the Board of Trade dated November 4 (not preserved in Foreign Office archives). According to the docket this letter requested that Lord Crewe should point out to the French Government that the French tariff on asbestos wares and acetylene burners had increased as a result of the Franco–German commercial agreement of August 17, 1927. This agreement, with annexed documents, and the supplementary exchange of notes of October 29, 1927, are printed in *British and Foreign State Papers*, vol. 126, pp. 689–906 and 910–12 respectively.

[2] Lord Crewe acted on these instructions in a note of January 12 to the French Ministry of Foreign Affairs: cf. No. 184. No copy of this note was transmitted to the Foreign Office.

deputation from the British National Committee of the International Chamber of Commerce, a body representing practically all sections of trade and industry, in support of the Resolutions passed by the World Economic Conference held this [last] year at Geneva.[3] This deputation, whilst at variance as to possible remedies, were insistent upon the harm which the increases in trade barriers throughout the world were inflicting upon British interests. They urged most strongly that His Majesty's Government should take every possible step to represent the British case to foreign Governments and to point out where necessary the discrepancy between actual practice and the contents of the Resolutions in favour of lower tariffs passed unanimously at Geneva by the business interests of the countries there represented.

3. As regards France, the Board received recently a deputation from the Manchester Chamber of Commerce at which the same kind of representations were put forward and in particular attention was drawn to the substantial increase in the French rates of duty upon textile machinery. It is, of course, true that in most cases the rates of duty resulting from the Franco-German Agreement are lower, and in many cases substantially lower, than those in the French Tariff Bill against which traders in this country originally protested. But this naturally affords but little satisfaction to manufacturers and traders who find that the result of the agreement is not merely to increase substantially Germany's power to compete with them in the French market, but to increase at the same time the former obstacles to the trade of this country.

4. In all the circumstances the Board have revised their former opinion and now propose, for Sir Austen Chamberlain's consideration, that a formal Note of protest should be presented to the French Government, even though it may not result in any immediate reduction in the rates of duty.

5. The Board suggest that the Note should be of a general character. It should emphasise the fact that the United Kingdom is France's best customer, taking regularly one-fifth of all her exports. Moreover, two-thirds of the imports of French goods into this country continue to be admitted without the imposition of any customs duties whatever. It is a striking fact that the total value of the imports thus freely admitted is in excess of the entire exports to France of United Kingdom goods, practically all of which are dutiable often at high rates.

6. The Note might also draw special attention to the case of those articles in regard to which the United Kingdom occupies a dominant position in the French import trade and which include many of the items notified to the French authorities in the memorandum supplied to them in May last.[4]

---

[3] The League of Nations Economic Conference met at Geneva from May 4 to 23, 1927: for the final report of the Conference see League of Nations document C.E.I. (44) 1 of 1927.

[4] A copy of this memorandum (not preserved in Foreign Office archives) was transmitted to the Foreign Office in a letter from the Board of Trade dated May 19, 1927. According to the docket the letter suggested that a copy of the memorandum, which summarised protests from British traders against the proposed revision of the French Customs tariff, be

The Note might state in this connection that His Majesty's Government feel entitled to represent to the French Government that in considering the duties which should be applied to articles coming within this category, the peculiar position of the United Kingdom, which offers a free market to the bulk of French manufacturers, ought to be given especial weight.

7. The French Government are aware from the memorandum which was supplied in May last of the matters in regard to which British trade was chiefly affected. It might, however, be well to refer, as outstanding instances, to the case of three descriptions of machinery, viz., textile machinery, agricultural machinery and internal combustion engines, in regard to all of which, but especially in regard to the first, considerable feeling has been aroused in this country at the prospective loss of a large and important market. They represent taken together a trade of about a million sterling per annum. In regard to all these classes of machinery the new rates are greatly in excess of those formerly in force and the ad valorem equivalent of the new duties is very high, and indeed almost of a prohibitive character.

8. The Note might also state that His Majesty's Government are continually receiving evidence of a growing feeling amongst traders that the maintenance by this country of the present fiscal system is becoming increasingly difficult to defend in the face of the prevalence in Europe of a policy of high and ever increasing tariffs. Indeed it appears that some European countries, in particular France, are only ready to reduce duties when other countries use high tariffs for bargaining purposes, a method which the United Kingdom has so far not employed.

9. Finally, the Board consider it most important that the Note should particularly stress the recommendations of the World Economic Conference recently held at Geneva and the contrast between those resolutions and the action of the French Government in raising their duties on British goods. The recommendations of this Conference in favour of a progressive lowering of the existing high level of European Customs Tariffs were agreed to unanimously by representatives of the business community from all countries, including France, which took part. It is, therefore, a subject of especial comment by British business interests in this country that, so soon after the

sent to Lord Crewe for unofficial submission to the French Ministry of Commerce with a view to ascertaining if any concessions were likely and that after perusal it might be convenient for an informal discussion to take place in Paris between representatives of the Board of Trade and of the French Ministry of Commerce. A copy of this memorandum was transmitted to Lord Crewe in Foreign Office despatch No. 1431 of May 20 (not preserved in Foreign Office archives). In Paris despatch No. 1211 of May 27, 1927, not printed, Lord Crewe reported that the Commercial Counsellor to the Embassy had handed the memorandum unofficially to the Director of the Commercial Agreements Department of the French Ministry of Commerce and transmitted in his despatch a summary of the indications made by M. Serruys of possible French action to meet points made in Parts I and II of the memorandum. M. Serruys had, however, requested the abandonment of any discussion of Part III, 'Tariff Headings in which overseas parts of the British Empire are interested'. M. Serruys had further said that he would be glad to see Mr. Fountain, Principal Assistant Secretary to the Board of Trade, on May 31: no record of this conversation has been traced in Foreign Office archives.

conclusion of that Conference, steps should be taken in France to increase customs duties on British goods in a manner and to an extent which would seem to suggest that the French Government do not intend to have regard to the conclusions of the Conference when determining their economic policy.

I have, &c.,
H. FOUNTAIN

No. 111

Letter from Mr. Palairet[1] to Sir T. Vaughan (Riga)

[*N 101/101/59*]

FOREIGN OFFICE, *January 9, 1928*

My dear Vaughan,

I had a letter the other day from Princess Gabrielle Radziwill, who is, as you know, a Lithuanian by nationality and employed in the secretariat of the League of Nations. I quote the following extract from it.

'Voldemaras believes it (i.e. Sir Austen Chamberlain's disapproval) is due to Lithuania refusing to join an anti-Soviet bloc. This is an idea which it would be well to dissipate. Unfortunately the former Latvian Prime [Foreign] Minister, Cielens, told Voldemaras that he had been approached by the British Government in view of obtaining his adherence to an anti-Soviet bloc. I enquired whether he (i.e. Voldemaras) had been approached and he said, "No", but that was probably due to his being known unwilling to join it. I vainly suggested it was most unlikely Cielens had had any communication of that kind from the British Government. He was convinced of the truth of his information, and I failed to convince him of the truth of mine!'

The Secretary of State has been shown this, and his comments are as follows:—

'Monsieur Cielens appears to be. . . .[2] He quotes me as having approved his commercial treaty with Russia[3] and at the same time urging him to create or take part in an anti-Soviet bloc.

'By all means let Sir Tudor know—and the Princess also.

'I have never sought in any quarter to make an anti-Soviet bloc. I have carefully refrained from even suggesting to either Paris or Rome that we should be pleased if, following our example, they broke off diplomatic relations. It would on the contrary cause me some anxiety if they did so— especially if Paris did. I do not want the Russians left with no-one to talk to except the Germans.'

[1] Head of the Northern Department of the Foreign Office.

[2] A personal reference is here omitted.

[3] The Soviet-Latvian treaty of June 2, 1927, is printed together with annex and final protocols in *British and Foreign State Papers*, vol. 127, pp. 816–27.

What he says is of course for your private information only; but if you can find any means of disabusing Voldemaras' mind of this particular lie, I hope you will take an opportunity of enlightening him.[4]

Yours ever,

MICHAEL PALAIRET

[4] In a letter of February 1 to Mr. Palairet in reply Mr. E. H. Carr, Second Secretary in H.M. Legation at Riga, explained that M. Cielens had not met Professor Voldemaras since September 1927 when he had had an interview with Sir A. Chamberlain which had 'made a tremendous impression on him. It completely disabused his mind of the "anti-Soviet bloc" theory.'

No. 112

Sir A. Chamberlain to the Marquess of Crewe (Paris)

No. 3 Telegraphic: by bag [C 313/97/21]

FOREIGN OFFICE, *January 13, 1928*

Sir R. Macleay's telegram No. 1 (of January 7th), Mr. Greg's telegram No. 5 (of January 11th), Mr. Kennard's telegram No. 2 (of January 11th) and Sir C. Barclay's telegrams Nos. 2 and 3 (of January 6th and 12th; clandestine arms traffic in Hungary).[1]

It seems clear that Little Entente governments are contemplating some action with regard to this incident. Czechoslavak Minister stated on January 11th that three governments have decided to bring the matter before League of Nations, although this would he added not necessarily mean that they would request an investigation under Article 143 of Treaty of Trianon. Czechoslovak Minister gave impression that he thought his government were attaching undue importance to the incident, but probably they were forced to do so by public opinion, and he hinted that it might be useful to urge moderation on them.

Please inform French government that in my view it is desirable to prevent this incident from developing into a larger political question which might give great trouble to the League of Nations and further embitter relations between Hungary and her neighbours. His Majesty's Government suggest that French and British representatives at Prague, Bucharest and Belgrade should explain to Little Entente governments that right of investigation

[1] Sir R. Macleay, Mr. Greg, and Sir C. Barclay were H.M. Ministers at Prague, Bucharest, and Budapest respectively. Budapest telegram No. 2 is not preserved in Foreign Office archives; the other telegrams under reference are not printed. These five telegrams related to the incident on January 1 at St. Gotthard on the Austro–Hungarian frontier when Austrian customs officials discovered that a consignment described as machinery contained machine gun parts (the total consignment was subsequently found to contain 591 cases of machine gun parts). The consignment had been despatched by a firm in Verona with the immediate destination of Slovenske Nove Mesto on the Hungarian–Czechoslovak frontier. In Budapest despatch No. 15 of January 11 Sir C. Barclay further reported that the consensus of opinion among his colleagues, with which he agreed, was that the consignment was destined for Hungary. For an account of the incident see *Survey of International Affairs 1928*, pp. 161–7.

given to League of Nations by Article 143 of Treaty of Trianon may at some future date be of great value to one or all ex-allied governments. On the other hand the weapon is extremely brittle and might easily break in our hands if not used with care. It is therefore particularly important that the first time that the weapon is used it should be employed in a really important case, because if it failed in its purpose the whole procedure would inevitably be very discredited and therefore be made more difficult to use in really grave emergency. The present incident appears to be not comparatively trivial in itself, but one regarding which it would be extremely difficult to collect sufficient evidence to convict Hungarian government of a violation of the Treaty. In the circumstances therefore it is urged in general interest that Little Entente governments should study other methods of disposing of this incident before committing themselves to an appeal to the League.

At the same time it is suggested that the French and British Ministers at Budapest should be instructed to impress upon the Hungarian government the importance of their putting themselves in the right with regard to this incident as quickly as possible, and to urge (as indeed is hinted by Count Bethlen[2] in Sir C. Barclay's telegram No. 3) that obvious way of doing so is for Hungarian government either to return guns to consignor in Italy direct or agree with Austrian government for their return to Austrian territory for disposal by Austrian authorities as they may think best.

Please invite the views of the French government upon the above with a view to the two governments co-operating to settle this dispute.

Repeated to Prague No. 2, Bucharest No. 3, Belgrade No. 1 and Budapest No. 1, in cypher.

[2] Prime Minister of Hungary.

No. 113

Sir R. Lindsay (Berlin) to Sir A. Chamberlain (Received January 17)
No. 46 [C 414/49/18]

BERLIN, *January 14, 1928*

Sir,

I transmit herewith a note by Mr. Rowe Dutton,[1] recording a conversation he has had with Dr Schacht, President of the Reichsbank. The note has already been sent to the Treasury; but the memorandum referred to in paragraph 3 is not transmitted to you as it is of technical rather than of political interest.

2. Dr Schacht's rather Nietzschian personality induces him to express strongly views which are shared, though not always quite so strongly, by most Germans. He voices his readiness, even his anxiety, to revise and even

[1] This note of January 11 by Mr. Rowe-Dutton, Financial Adviser to H.M. Embassy at Berlin in succession to Mr. Finlayson, who was present at the interview with Dr. Schacht, is not printed.

to smash the Dawes Plan at the first opportune moment. At that moment any concession to be made by Germany, such as the abandonment of Transfer Protection, will be sold only at the highest possible price; and in the meanwhile Germany will strenuously oppose any measure designed to facilitate the normal operation of the Plan, such as an extension of the Reparation Recovery Act. These are understandable views, and having regard to the vehemence with which Dr Schac[h]t holds them, it will always be worth while to pay attention to his utterances and to the tendencies of his thoughts. There is, however, no reason to apprehend that he contemplates at present any premature developments, and moreover his influence, though undoubtedly great, is subject to controls. Even in purely financial matters during the past twelve months it has not always prevailed.

3. It is interesting to note Dr Schacht's reference to the suggestion in Mr Gilbert's Report concerning the fixation of German Reparation liability. He considers that Mr Gilbert's intention was to educate public opinion abroad, especially in France and America, that his action was taken doubtless with American agreement, and that it would have been impossible for him owing to the approaching American election, to utter his warning later.

I have, &c.,

R. C. LINDSAY

No. 114

Letter from Mr. Goodchild (Paris) to Sir E. Phipps (Paris) [1]

[*C 364/49/18*]

Copy

PARIS, *January 14, 1928*

Dear Sir Eric,

I enclose for your information a copy of an unofficial letter which I have sent to Sir Richard Hopkins in regard to to-day's meeting between the Reparation Commission and the Agent General for Reparation Payments, in connection with the latter's Report for the Third Dawes Year.[2]

Yours sincerely,

W. A. C. GOODCHILD

ENCLOSURE IN No. 114

Letter from Mr. Goodchild (Paris) to Sir R. Hopkins

Copy

PARIS, *January 14, 1928*

Dear Hopkins,

The programme envisaged at the conference about reparation held at the Treasury last Monday[3] has been successfully carried out this week-end.

[1] This letter was received in the Foreign Office on January 16 under cover of Paris despatch No. 80 (not preserved in Foreign Office archives).

[2] See No. 89, note 3.

[3] The record of this meeting on January 9 (cf. No. 107) is not printed. At the beginning of the meeting 'Sir Warren Fisher said that everyone would agree as to the desirability of

220

There was an unofficial meeting of the Delegates and Assistant Delegates yesterday evening at which the Chairman read out a draft declaration which he desired the Reparation Commission to make with regard to Gilbert's last Report. This declaration criticised various passages in the conclusions to the Report and in particular emphasised

(1) the intangibility of the 132 milliards[4] fixed by the old Schedule of Payments so long as the Governments represented on the Reparation Commission did not alter the figure;

(2) the incompetence of the Experts who drew up the Dawes Plan to fix a new figure for Germany's reparation debt;

(3) the undesirability of the reference in the Report to the removal of foreign control and transfer protection from Germany, and of putting on the tapis, save in the manner laid down in Article 234 of the Treaty of Versailles, the question of the reduction of Germany's capital debt.

There were other beauties in the declaration which I need not mention. The extracts which I have given are sufficient to show that it would have been impossible for the British Delegate to associate himself with any such statement. So far as the Agent General is concerned, it would have been highly provocative as an official utterance, and the theoretical assumptions made in various parts of it are not in accordance with what I understand to be our general views.

Lord Blanesburgh accordingly pointed out the difficulties which appeared to him to be involved in the proposed declaration and suggested that it would be much better if the Delegates confined their action in the first instance to a frank and informal exchange of views with the Agent General, in the course of which they would probably find it feasible to arrive at a formula regarding the Report which would command unanimity in the Reparation Commission, and not be distasteful to Gilbert.

Lord Blanesburgh's view prevailed, and it was arranged that Gilbert's Report should not be officially considered by the Commission until the suggested unofficial meeting with Gilbert had taken place.

The Commission occupied itself in the course of Saturday morning with the despatch of all the business on its agenda except Gilbert's Report. It then adjourned for a lunch given by the Delegates and Assistant Delegates to Gilbert and the other Dawes Officials (McFadyean, Leverve,[5] etc.) who

maintaining cordial relations with Mr. Gilbert'. Sir R. Hopkins stated that the controversial questions raised by Mr. Gilbert were: '(1) While disclaiming any power to control the German Budget, the criticisms contained in his October Memorandum contained an implicit claim to control the German Budget. (2) His view that Reparation has a transfer priority over the service of foreign loans. (3) His views as to the danger of excessive foreign borrowing by Germany. (4) His view at the end of the Report that the Dawes Plan should ultimately be superseded by one which would fix the Reparation Debt definitely and contain no transfer protection.' No action by His Majesty's Government was considered necessary, and as regards the Reparation Commission the procedure and resolution recorded below were suggested.   [4] See No. 108, note 4.

[5] Sir Andrew McFadyean was Commissioner of the Controlled Revenues at Berlin; M. Gaston Leverve was Commissioner for German Railways.

were in Paris for the week-end in connection with a meeting of the Co-Ordinating Board.[6] The lunch was a successful affair and did a good deal, in my opinion, to promote the atmosphere of friendliness with Gilbert which is what we desire to achieve.

The unofficial meeting was held thereafter. In reply to question addressed to him by various Delegates, Gilbert explained his general frame of mind with regard to the working of the Dawes Plan. I will report officially and more fully as to this in due course.[7] I will confine myself at the moment to saying that the upshot of his remarks was that he felt that the present system under which Germany enjoys a transfer protection is not one which, in his view, makes for an effective execution of the Dawes Plan over any extended period. He thinks that in the interests of the Powers which receive reparation, the fixation of Germany's reparation liabilities at a definite amount and the imposition of responsibility on her to pay that amount without foreign control or transfer protection, would result in enabling the Powers concerned to obtain more from Germany than will, in his view, be the case within a year or two under the existing system. He therefore felt that he would be wanting in his duty if he shut his eyes to what he thought to be the facts of the case, and refrained from mentioning in his Report the really vital elements of the situation.

These expressions of opinion (which were, of course, much more amplified by Gilbert at the meeting, and which I have put in a compressed and possibly crude form), did not elicit any expressions of disagreement from the Delegates present. The Chairman reiterated, as though it were a cabalistic formula, his creed as to the intangibility of the 132 milliards, but Gilbert remarked that this question did not appear to concern the current execution of the Dawes Plan, and nobody else seemed to pay any attention to it.

Eventually a formula was found, mainly at the instigation of Lord Blanesburgh, which I herewith reproduce:

'The Reparation Commission has proceeded with the Agent General for Reparation Payments to an exchange of views on the report addressed to it by Mr. Gilbert at the end of the third year of the operation of the Experts' Plan. The Commission has noted that the Plan has followed its normal development in the course of the third year. The commission has also noted the suggestions of the Agent General which refer to the current working of the Plan, with a view to pursuing the study thereof in cooperation with Mr. Gilbert.

'The Reparation Commission has taken note of the considerations as to the future mentioned by the Agent General in his Report, which will have to be most carefully weighed at the opportune moment by the interested and competent authorities.'

The meeting was then changed to an official one at which the President, after thanking the Agent General for his Report, proposed the above formula

[6] An advisory board, the members of which were the Agent General for Reparation Payments and the Commissioners, which facilitated the interchange of information regarding reparations.   [7] Mr. Goodchild's further report is not printed.

as a resolution to be taken by the Commission. It was agreed to unanimously, and the meeting terminated with expressions of mutual esteem on the part of Gilbert and the Delegates. It is useful to note that Gilbert remarked that he placed the highest value on meetings with the Reparation Commission and considered that it was particularly useful on the present occasion for him to have an opportunity of exchanging views with it.

There seems every possibility in these circumstances of promoting amicable relations between Gilbert and the Reparation Commission, and I think that, so far as one can foresee at present, a difficult corner has been successfully turned.

I have sent a copy of this letter to Sir Eric Phipps and to Rowe Dutton.

Yours sincerely,
W. A. C. GOODCHILD

No. 115

Sir R. Lindsay (Berlin) to Sir A. Chamberlain (Received January 20)
No. 51 [C 499/227/18]

BERLIN, *January 17, 1928*

Sir,

I have the honour to report that on the 12th of January Herr Gessler, who has been Minister of Defence in consecutive Cabinets for over seven years, handed in his resignation to the President on the ground of ill-health. Great efforts have been made to induce Herr Gessler either to withdraw his resignation or to consent to remain titular head of the Ministry of Defence while proceeding on prolonged sick leave. Herr Gessler has, however, obstinately maintained his refusal any longer to be identified with his Ministry, and the Government are, therefore, faced with a problem of some difficulty and one which may possibly, but not probably, cause a Cabinet crisis. It will be remembered that when this Marx Cabinet was formed in January 1927 the Volkspartei, who had been promised four seats, were obliged to surrender one of these seats in order to satisfy the insistence of the Nationalists on obtaining a further Cabinet post for their own party. The Volkspartei demanded at the time that they should have the reversion of the next Ministry which fell vacant, and although this demand was not agreed to in any very explicit form yet its rejection at this juncture may cause some bitterness and even resentment. On the other hand, it is practically certain that the Centre party will not wish to see so important and delicate an office as that of Minister of Defence fall to the Volkspartei, and it is probable that the directing forces in the Cabinet will insist either on leaving the Ministry of Defence without a civilian head or on placing it under the Chancellor himself. Both these alternatives are unsatisfactory: the first would place the Reichswehr completely in the hands of its military chiefs, and the second would throw upon Dr Marx, who already undertakes the office of Chancellor and Minister of the Occupied Territories, a burden which he can scarcely be expected to stand. It is not merely that the difficulty of replacing Herr Gessler renders his resignation an awkward and unpleasant incident, but public curiosity regarding the underlying causes of this resignation has brought to the surface certain unsavoury matters which the present Cabinet may well have wished to inter. Public opinion fully recognises that Herr Gessler who, after the strain of the last seven years, has recently suffered from a series of tragic domestic bereavements, may well feel unable to stand the continual strain of office; yet it is generally felt that his abrupt determination to resign is not unconnected with his anxiety to escape next week's debates upon the Reichswehr estimates. It is inevitable that during the course of these debates the Minister responsible for the estimates will be severely attacked upon such unpleasant incidents as the subsidy paid to the Phoebus Film Company (see my despatch No. 55[1] of to-day's date), the honours accorded to Prince Henry of Prussia on the occasion of his visit to the cruiser 'Berlin',[2] and possibly also the recent seizure of arms at Kiel (see my despatch No. 33[3] of the 12th of January) which are suspected of having come from Reichswehr reserves. Other questions which will arise are the insistence of the Government, in spite of the Reichsrat's opposition on inserting into the Budget an appropriation of R[eichs] M[arks] 9,300,000 for the construction of a 10,000-ton replacement unit for the Navy, an extravagance to which Herr Gessler, whose sympathies are military rather than naval, is rumoured to have been opposed.

2. The extreme difficulty of defending these incidents and appropriations in the face of next week's inevitable hostile criticism and of coping with the conflict between the two legislatures and within the Cabinet itself which has arisen over the appropriation for naval construction, may dispose Dr Gessler to leave, and may deter others from entering a moribund Cabinet for so ungracious a task. It is probable that the Reichstag, realising that a general election is inevitable in three or four months will not wish to force

[1] Not printed. This despatch reported on the scandal in connection with the use of funds of the Reichswehr Ministry to finance the Phoebus Film Company which had since gone bankrupt, with a loss to the German taxpayer estimated at from 4 to 7 million gold marks; cf. Erich Eyck, *A History of the Weimar Republic* (Eng. trans. by H. P. Hanson and R. G. L. Waite, London, 1962), vol. ii, pp. 144–5. Sir R. Lindsay commented: 'This incident is particularly interesting as illustrating the laxity of control under the German budget and audit system to which reference has been made in previous reports. This laxity is especially noticeable in the Ministry of Defence. Owing to the existence of limitations imposed by Treaty on the activities of this Department, it enjoys a halo of martyrdom which excuses it in some measure from the inquisitiveness of the auditor, with the result that funds are diverted to purposes unauthorised by the Reichstag to an extent which is unknown but which everyone thinks considerable. In the case of the Phoebus, Captain Lohmann's [i.e. the responsible officer in the Reichswehr Ministry] personal integrity is not at present called in question, and the purpose to which the millions have been devoted need excite no concern among foreign Governments. But there may be other manipulations unknown or only suspected in which either or both of these considerations do not obtain.'

[2] For an account of this visit by the brother of the former Emperor William II in December 1927, see *The Times*, December 12, 1927, p. 13.

[3] Not preserved in Foreign Office archives. In January 1928 seventeen truckloads of arms destined for export to China had been seized by police and customs officials at Kiel.

an issue at the present moment. On the other hand, the resignation of Herr Gessler has concentrated attention upon the instability of the Marx Cabinet and upon the many delicate sudsidiary [*sic*] questions which have for some time been accumulating to disturb the apparent assurance and placidity of the present Ministry.[4]

I have, &c.,

R. C. LINDSAY

[4] In Berlin despatch No. 66 of January 20 Sir R. Lindsay reported that, despite opposition from the German National and People's Parties, President Hindenburg had appointed General Groener to be Minister of Defence in succession to Dr. Gessler. Sir R. Lindsay commented that General Groener's authority over the Reichswehr would be greater than that of any civilian but at the same time he was 'known to be loyal to the Republic'. Subsequently, in his despatch No. 148 of February 15 commenting on General Groener's speech of February 10 to the Budget Committee of the Reichstag (see *The Times*, February 11, 1928, p. 9), Sir R. Lindsay stated that General Groener's expression of loyalty to the present regime in Germany was for the good 'but it would be optimistic to interpret General Groener's praise of the Republic as more than the acceptance by an intelligent and patriotic man of a state of affairs which he thinks it would be madness to disturb'.

No. 116

The Marquess of Crewe (Paris) to Sir A. Chamberlain
(Received January 19)

No. 95 [*C 461/97/21*]

Urgent

PARIS, *January 18, 1928*

Sir,

With reference to my telegram No. 8[1] of January 15th I have the honour to transmit to you, herewith, a copy of a memorandum which I have today received from the Ministry for Foreign Affairs in regard to the clandestine arms shipment to Hungary.

2. According to a statement made by a member of the Ministry this morning, it would in any case now be too late to invite the Czechoslovak, Yugoslav and Roumanian governments to defer an appeal to the League of Nations in this matter, since it is understood that a note from the Czechoslovak government on the subject will be communicated to the League today.[2]

3. It may be observed that, far from thinking an enquiry under article 143[3] a procedure of great international importance, some sections of French public opinion consider resort to the article in this matter most inadequate

[1] Not printed. This telegram reported that in the absence of M. Briand a memorandum embodying the substance of No. 112 had been handed to M. Berthelot.

[2] The letters from the Czechoslovak, Roumanian, and Serb-Croat-Slovene Governments requesting the Council of the League of Nations to consider the incident at St. Gotthard are dated February 1 and are printed with connected documents in *League of Nations Official Journal*, April 1928, pp. 545–9. *V. ibid.*, pp. 387–97 and 452–3 respectively, for consideration of this question by the Council on March 7 and 10. See also *op. cit.*, July 1928, pp. 905–18, for further discussion by the Council on June 7.

[3] Of the Treaty of Trianon.

(see M. Paul Boncour's declaration to the 'Paris Midi' on January 14th: paragraph 4 of my despatch No. 94[4] of today).

I have, &c.,
CREWE

ENCLOSURE IN No. 116

Note from the French Ministry of Foreign Affairs

Copie

PARIS, *le 18 janvier, 1928*

A la date du 14 Janvier, Son Excellence Lord Crewe a bien voulu informer le Ministre des Affaires Etrangères d'une démarche, faite le 11 janvier auprès de Sir Austen Chamberlain par le Ministre de Tchécoslovaquie à Londres pour lui faire savoir que les Gouvernements tchécoslovaque, roumain et serbe avaient décidé de signaler à l'attention de la Société des Nations les expéditions clandestines d'armes à destination de la Hongrie qui ont été récemment découvertes, sans d'ailleurs que cette initiative des trois Gouvernements intéressés impliquât nécessairement qu'ils demanderaient l'ouverture d'une procédure d'investigation sur cette affaire, conformément à l'article 143 du Traité de Trianon. Sir Austen Chamberlain avait chargé l'Ambassadeur d'Angleterre de marquer qu'il conviendrait d'empêcher que cet incident ne dégénérât en une question politique; les Gouvernements anglais et français devraient donc, d'une part, agir sur le Gouvernement hongrois pour qu'il s'employât à effacer le plus tôt possible la déplorable impression créée par l'incident, d'autre part, intervenir à Prague, Belgrade et Bucarest pour inviter les trois Gouvernements à renoncer à leur projet en faisant valoir l'intérêt qu'ils ont eux-mêmes à ce que le Conseil de la Société des Nations ne fasse usage du droit d'investigation, surtout pour la première fois, que dans une circonstance de réelle gravité.

M. Briand a assurément le plus vif désir de voir observer dans cette affaire, comme dans toutes les difficultés qui peuvent surgir, le principe, que le Gouvernement français ne perd jamais de vue, d'une étroite collaboration de la Grande Bretagne et de la France et il est fermement convaincu que, dans la question qui se pose, les possibilités de règlement favorable dépendent, dans une large mesure, de l'observation de ce principe. Ce n'est cependant pas sans appréhension que le Ministre des Affaires Etrangères verrait les deux Gouvernements, par une action immédiate et alors que la Conférence des Ambassadeurs vient d'être déchargée de ses responsabilités touchant le désarmement de la Hongrie, assumer dans cet incident une responsabilité nouvelle tant à l'égard de la Hongrie qu'envers les Gouvernements de la Petite Entente. Pour suggérer, en effet, à la Hongrie les mesures qu'elle devrait prendre, la Grande-Bretagne et la France devraient, au

---

[4] Not printed. The paragraph under reference reported M. Paul-Boncour's statement that the supervision provided by article 213 of the Treaty of Versailles was illusory, as could be seen in the St. Gotthard incident. The League of Nations would be unable to take up the matter before the March session when 'mutual politeness and fear to speak out' might prevent a full exploration of the matter while the League's machinery was too complicated for speedy application.

préalable, s'être assurées que ces mesures trouveraient à Prague ou à Belgrade un accueil favorable; quant à essayer de détourner les Gouvernements de la Petite Entente de donner suite aux décisions, conformes à l'esprit des Traités, sur lesquelles ils se sont mis d'accord, il faudrait, pour le faire utilement, être en mesure de les renseigner sur les origines de l'affaire ou leur donner l'assurance formelle que les faits dont ils se sont émus ne viendront pas à se reproduire dans l'avenir; il n'apparaît pas au Gouvernement français que ces diverses conditions se trouvent remplies.

Le Ministre des Affaires Etrangères observe d'ailleurs que Sir Austen Chamberlain ne suggère aucune méthode pour donner à la Petite Entente, par une autre voie, les apaisements qu'elle désire manifestement obtenir. Il constate d'autre part que, d'après les renseignements qui lui sont parvenus et qui s'accordent avec ceux dont Sir Austen Chamberlain a bien voulu lui faire part, les Gouvernements intéressés se proposent simplement, à l'heure actuelle, de saisir le Conseil de la Société des Nations des faits qui sont parvenus à leur connaissance, sans se prononcer encore sur l'utilité d'une investigation. M. Briand redoute, dans ces conditions, que la procédure suggérée ne risque de créer la fausse impression que la Grande Bretagne et la France sont d'accord pour chercher à étouffer l'affaire, dans la crainte qu'un débat à Genève puisse prendre un développement fâcheux; il n'est point besoin de souligner les conséquences regrettables que l'impression ainsi créée aurait soit pour l'autorité des deux Gouvernements à Genève, soit pour le prestige de la Société des Nations elle-même.

Le Gouvernement français incline donc à penser que, pour le moment, la Grande-Bretagne et la France agiraient sagement en s'abstenant de chercher à peser sur les Gouvernements de la Petite Entente pour les détourner de donner suite aux intentions dont on est informé à Londres et à Paris. Lorsque le dossier sera soumis au Conseil, il appartiendra à celui-ci de décider en toute indépendance, soit en procédant lui-même à l'examen des documents, soit après avoir provoqué l'avis de sa Commission Permanente Consultative, si les faits dont il se trouvera saisi sont assez graves pour justifier ou non une investigation. Loin d'être l'origine d'une nouvelle complication, le Gouvernement français est convaincu qu'un tel débat pourra utilement contribuer à calmer l'émotion qui s'est manifestée chez les Etats voisins de la Hongrie, à condition que le Gouvernement hongrois profite de cette circonstance pour faire la lumière sur l'incident en donnant les explications franches et complètes qui ont fait jusqu'à présent défaut.

C'est donc à Genève, après avoir pris connaissance des renseignements apportés par les divers Gouvernements intéressés que Sir Austen Chamberlain et M. Briand pourront le plus utilement se concerter afin que leur action commune s'exerce une fois de plus dans le sens que leur paraîtra commander la nécessité de raffermir la paix en Europe et d'assurer le respect des Traités.

No. 117

The Marquess of Crewe (Paris) to Sir A. Chamberlain
(Received January 20, 8.30 a.m.)
No. 11 Telegraphic: by bag [C 488/51/18]

PARIS, January 19, 1928

Your despatch No. 28[1] (C 51/51/18) of January 5th: Rhineland railways.

2. M. Massigli, in his capacity of Secretary of the French Delegation to the Ambassadors' Conference, asked a member of my staff to call upon him on January 18th to discuss the proposals respecting German railway construction in the Rhineland made in the memorandum addressed to the Conference by His Majesty's Embassy on January 9th.[2]

3. M. Massigli said that the position seemed to the Ministry for Foreign Affairs to be as follows. In 1922 the Ambassadors' Conference had communicated to the German government a list of destructions to be effected in the demilitarised zone. Those outside occupied territory had been effected under the supervision of the Military Control Commission. Those inside occupied territory had to be effected before evacuation. In 1926 the Cologne zone had been evacuated. Through an oversight the destructions, which in that zone were unimportant, had not been executed prior to evacuation. The position had now been further complicated by the various German requests to make new constructions. There were therefore two points at issue:

(a) the destructions in occupied territory scheduled by the Conference in 1922; and

(b) the new constructions for which authority was asked by the German government.

4. The British proposal was (1) to reply to the Germans that there was no objection to the new constructions so far as the Rhineland Agreement was concerned, though all rights under article 43[3] were reserved, and (2) to ask the Versailles Committee to review the whole question of destruction, including both (a) and (b) in paragraph 3 above, with a view to the eventual possibility of action by the League of Nations.

5. The Ministry for Foreign Affairs were inclined to doubt the wisdom of this procedure. There seemed to them to be two objections to the British proposal to make an immediate reply to the Germans in respect of new constructions. Such a reply would amount to saying 'You may proceed for the time being but you may eventually have to destroy what you now construct'; and it would be to deal with what was in fact a part of the question only. Why not defer the reply to the Germans respecting new constructions until the Versailles Committee had had time to review the whole question of destruction including both (a) and (b) in paragraph 3 above?

6. If this proposal were approved, it would, when the Versailles Committee had reported, be possible to discuss the whole question with the Germans.

---

[1] No. 106.   [2] See No. 106, note 7.   [3] Of the Treaty of Versailles.

This could be done in the normal course of procedure because in 1922, after the Germans had complained about the demands of the Conference, a promise was apparently made to them that these demands would be reconsidered. That promise had not yet been fulfilled.

7. In reply to a question M. Massigli said that, so far as he could at present tell, the French government shared your view that a decision of the occupying Powers, taken under article 43, was not enforceable on the German government save through a decision of the League. That did not imply that the occupying Powers could not discuss with the German government the question of destructions under article 43 and that they could not try to reach direct agreement with them before the question of an appeal to the League was considered. As in paragraph 14 of your despatch you say that the result of the deliberations of the Versailles Committee 'is to be regarded merely as the material on which the occupying Powers will base any demands which they may wish in due course to put to Germany, *either direct* or through the League of Nations', I gather that you share this view.

8. At the end of the conversation M. Massigli emphasised the French view that preliminary discussion of this matter between the occupying Powers and Germany was in the interests of Germany herself. From the German standpoint a friendly agreement between the two parties was obviously preferable to a League decision. Further, there could be no doubt that if the German government could see their way to conclude an agreement satisfactory to the occupying Powers in this matter, such action on their part would be an important factor in facilitating and even in expediting the evacuation of the occupied territories.

9. To sum up, the French proposal is:—

(1) reference to Versailles Committee of whole question of destructions including new construction;

(2) friendly conversation with Germans on result of this reference;

(3) reference to League only at need and if 'gentlemen's agreement' cannot be reached with Germans.

10. I should be glad to learn your views on this proposal with the least possible delay. If, as I hope, you agree with it, I could join with M. Cambon[4] in submitting it to the Conference.

4 President of, and French representative on, the Conference of Ambassadors.

No. 118

Sir A. Chamberlain to the Marquess of Crewe (Paris)

No. 4 Telegraphic: by bag [C 461/97/21]

FOREIGN OFFICE, *January 21, 1928, 5.5 p.m.*

Your despatch No. 95[1] (of January 18th. Alleged illegal importation of war material into Hungary).

1 No. 116.

In view of M. Briand's reply I do not propose to take any further action in the matter.

Repeated to Bucharest No. 4, Prague No. 3, Belgrade No. 3 and Budapest No. 3 in cypher.

No. 119

Sir R. Graham (Rome) to Sir A. Chamberlain
(Received January 25, 9 a.m.)
No. 5 Telegraphic [C 645/8/22]

ROME, *January 24, 1928, 9.25 p.m.*

New French Ambassador is being given a most cordial reception in official and social circles and in the press. But his first interview with Signor Mussolini was confined to an exchange of civilities and there will be no serious conversations before the end of this or beginning of next week. I had a long and very friendly talk with him this morning but was not reassured on finding Sir E. Phipps' impression as conveyed to me in Mr. Sargent's private letter of the 5th ultimo[1] strongly confirmed. I fear that if French government mean to be stiff he is the man to accentuate rather than soften down their attitude. He said he was considerably perturbed over exaggerated importance attached here to his forthcoming conversations with Italian government as he had very little to give. I replied that it seemed to be important that these conversations should be successful. I had been a good deal disquieted over state of Italian feeling towards France before recent détente and by prevalence of feeling that Italy was being driven into the arms of Germany. Moreover course of Italo-Yugoslav relations would in my opinion be governed by their success or otherwise. Monsieur Beaumarchais answered that the Italian government had already made overtures to the Germans, proposing that in return for an agreement they would withdraw their opposition to Anschluss. As regards Italo-Yugoslav relations Monsieur Marincovic had let Paris know that he wished to conduct them without any French interference. He added that he would of course do his best to render his conversations successful but Italians must in the first instance formulate their demands clearly. I (? gathered) Monsieur Beaumarchais did not seem optimistic as to being able to satisfy them.

I have no confirmation of suggested Italian overtures in Berlin. It would mean a complete reversal of policy as hitherto expressed.

[1] Not preserved in Foreign Office archives.

No. 120

Sir A. Chamberlain to the Marquess of Crewe (Paris)
No. 5 Telegraphic: by bag [C 488/51/18]

FOREIGN OFFICE, *January 24, 1928*

Your telegram No. 11[1] (of January 19th; railway constructions in the Rhineland).

[1] No. 117.

2. We are, subject to the following observations, in agreement with the French proposal as outlined in paragraph 9 of your telegram and especially welcome indication of French acceptance of our view regarding non-enforceability on German government of purely allied interpretation of Article 43 of Treaty of Versailles.

3. It was of course our intention that the ex-allied governments should try by direct discussion with the German government, to reach a friendly agreement as to the applicability of Article 43 to all the constructions at present existing or projected and that a similar course should be pursued in the case of further constructions or demolitions in the future. Reference to the League was only contemplated in the event of agreement proving unattainable. The assumption in last sentence of your paragraph 7 is therefore correct.

4. Such discussions with the German government must however be held as between the governments and you should leave the French in no doubt that His Majesty's Government hold it to be essential that the Rhineland Railway Commission should both in present and in all future cases refrain in correspondence with the German authorities from interpreting Article 43 or basing any of their decisions upon it.

5. For the sake of greater clarity therefore I would suggest that the French proposal should be expanded as follows:

(a) A fresh point should be added recording the view as to the non-enforceability on the German government of a purely allied interpretation of Article 43;

(b) Instructions should be given to the Rhineland Railway Commission in the sense of paragraph 4 above;

(c) Point 1 should be expanded so as to ensure that the Versailles Committee when preparing their recommendations take into account not only strategic but also economic and commercial considerations, and limit their recommendations to constructions which constitute such palpable and at the same time vitally dangerous violations of Article 43 as would make it incumbent on the ex-allied governments to appeal if opposed by the German government, to the Council of the League in order to obtain their demolition;

(d) Point 2 should be elaborated so as to ensure that the conversations are between the governments either direct or through the Ambassadors' Conference and not between the Rhineland Railway Commission or any other organ of the Rhineland Commission or the Rhineland armies on the one side and the German local authorities on the other.

We see no objection to the French desire that the Railway Commission should defer replying to the Germans in connection with new constructions until after the Versailles Committee have considered whole question. But reply cannot properly in our view be withheld if Germans continue to press for an answer. In these circumstances Railway Committee's reply ought to be either (1) on lines suggested in paragraph 11 of our despatch No. 28.[2]

---

[2] No. 106.

or (2) in interim form that reply is being deferred pending consideration by the ex-allied Powers of the whole question which the latter hope subsequently to discuss à l'amiable with the German government.

No. 121

Sir A. Chamberlain to Sir T. Vaughan (Riga)
No. 2 Telegraphic [N 468/46/59]

FOREIGN OFFICE, *January 26, 1928, 6.30 p.m.*

Have you any reason to suppose that obstructive attitude of Lithuania towards negotiations with Poland is due to pressure from Soviet Government?

No. 122

Mr. Kennard (Belgrade) to Sir A. Chamberlain (Received January 30)
No. 37 [C 748/2/92]

BELGRADE, *January 26, 1928*

Sir,

With reference to my telegram no. 10[1] of the 25th January I have the honour to transmit herewith a translation[1] of the protocol which was signed yesterday by the Minister of Foreign Affairs and the Italian Minister for the prolongation of the period foreseen in article 4 of the pact of Rome until the 28th July next.

2. I gather that the Italian Minister made every effort up to the last moment to utilize the opportunity to secure the settlement of some of his claims before the signature of the protocol, but that the only one which has been actually settled, is that of the Lega Culturale Italiana.[2] I further learn that Signor Mussolini in a recent conversation with the S.C.S. Minister at Rome[3] agreed that no condition should be attached to this signature and that he was generally friendly stating that Italy and Yugoslavia had tried to be enemies for the past two years without much success and that they had therefore better now endeavour to be friends.

3. The Minister of Foreign Affairs has been much impressed by this change in Signor Mussolini's attitude and has sent for M. Rakić with a view, no doubt, to giving him instructions as to the line which any future conversations for the renewal of the pact of Rome should follow.

4. I am sending a copy of this despatch to His Majesty's Ambassador at Rome.

I have, &c.,
H. W. KENNARD

[1] Not printed.
[2] Italian Cultural Association.
[3] See *I Documenti Diplomatici Italiani*, Settima Serie, vol. vi, No. 32.

No. 123

Letter from Sir A. Chamberlain to Sir W. Erskine[1] (London)

[F.O. 800/262]

Private   FOREIGN OFFICE, *January 26, 1928*

Dear Sir William,

Upon reflection I do not feel sure that, in reply to your question about National movements in Russia, I gave you as clear an answer as I should, and it may be useful that I should supplement what I said by a brief note.

All news of what is really happening and of the trend of affairs is obviously of interest to us and such movements, if they develop, do not in any way threaten British interests or conflict with British policy; but it is part of our policy, and an essential part, to abstain from any interference in the internal affairs of Russia. We severed diplomatic relations with that country not only because of the constant hostility of Soviet agents to the British Empire in other parts of the world, but because their agents here interfered in our domestic concerns. We must not expose ourselves to any reasonable suspicion that we practise ourselves the policy which we condemned when practised by the Soviet Government. So much I think I said yesterday, but I believe I omitted another point which is of some consequence. If there be any such fissiparous tendency in Russia, it would I am convinced be killed by any external interference. Nothing is more certain to rally Russians to the Soviet Government and to confirm their power than any idea that foreign nations are seeking to break up Russia. I said something of this kind in a speech in the House of Commons last year, and if I can trace the passage I will enclose a copy of it in this letter.[2] I remember meeting Sforza, at that time Foreign Secretary of Italy, at one of the inter-allied conferences held in London about the year 1921 or 1922.[3] Sforza then remarked that he was perhaps the only member of the Conference who was connected by marriage with the old Russian aristocracy and that he had been amazed to find how the then recent attack by Poland on Russia had rallied his Russian friends to the support even of a Soviet Government. I myself am profoundly sceptical as to the real strength of the Separatist movement and in any case I am firmly opposed to allowing ourselves to be in any way mixed up in it.

Yours sincerely,

AUSTEN CHAMBERLAIN

[1] Sir W. Erskine was about to take up his post as H.M. Minister at Warsaw.

[2] Not attached to the filed copy: for this passage in Sir A. Chamberlain's speech of July 28, 1927, see *Parl. Debs., 5th ser., H. of C.*, vol. 209, cols. 1527–8.

[3] Count Sforza, an opponent of Signor Mussolini who had left Italy in 1927, had been Italian Minister for Foreign Affairs, June 1920–July 1921. For conferences at London which he attended see First Series, Volume VIII, Chapter XIV, and Volume XV, Chapters II and IV.

No. 124

Mr. Carr (Riga) to Sir A. Chamberlain (Received January 27, 9 p.m.)

No. 2 Telegraphic [N 484/46/59]

RIGA, January 27, 1928, 7 p.m.

Your telegram No. 2.[1]

None whatever.

Polish Chargé d'Affaires here attributes it to German influence; but this hypothesis appears to me equally doubtful though Lithuanian Minister for Foreign Affairs will doubtless sound German government during his present visit to Berlin.[2]

I feel sure that Lithuanian attitude is primarily due not to any outside influence but to obstinacy of Lithuanian character and to profound conviction of Polish duplicity which causes the friendliest gestures to be regarded with the most suspicion.

[1] No. 121.   [2] January 25–29.

No. 125

Mr. Kimens (Warsaw) to Sir A. Chamberlain (Received February 16)

OTB No. 108/X. 110 [C 1236/357/18]

Confidential   WARSAW, January 27, 1928

Sir,

I have the honour to report that I had to-day the opportunity of discussing with a leading German business man the question of the trade relations between Germany and Soviet Russia.

2. My informant, who at the time of the conclusion of the commercial treaty between the two countries,[1] was a member of the German delegation, told me that the experiences which Germany had gained from the treaty concluded in October 1925 were far from satisfactory and had not come up to the expectations of the German Government, as the result of which a rather hostile feeling was gaining ground in German Government circles and amongst banks and businessmen, towards Russia, and the desire was being expressed either to amend the commercial treaty or to denounce it. It appears that amongst the many grievances Germany resented very strongly that the Russian Government were prepared to pay in cash for goods purchased in the United Kingdom, and more particularly in the United States of America, while in Germany they demanded long credits. It has also been observed that in most cases the contracts were not carried out to the full, and a particular instance was mentioned in respect of a contract for the purchase of 80,000 tons of engineering goods against which only 10,000 were taken.

[1] This treaty of October 12, 1925, is printed in *British and Foreign State Papers*, vol. 122, pp. 707–49.

3. My informant emphasised that it was more particularly the Ministry for Foreign Affairs at Berlin that was laying great stress on the revision of the treaty; he thought that the German Government would insist on the introduction of a number of clauses which would safeguard German interests to a larger degree than they have been under the provisions of the present treaty, and that if it were not possible to obtain the desired concessions Germany might perhaps go so far as to abrogate the treaty.

4. Although the article in 'The Times' of the 24th January by their Berlin Correspondent, entitled 'German-Soviet Trade', contains full details on this subject, I considered it nevertheless desirable to report on the above conversation.[2]

I have, &c.,
R. E. KIMENS

[2] For the suspension on March 15, 1928, of German-Soviet negotiations for the renewal of the treaty of October 12, 1925, following the arrest of five German technicians in the Donbas on charges of espionage and sabotage see K. Rosenbaum, *Community of Fate* (Syracuse, N.Y., 1965), pp. 253 f.

No. 126

Sir R. Lindsay (Berlin) to Sir A. Chamberlain (Received February 3)
No. 99 [C 870/870/22]

Confidential   BERLIN, *January 31, 1928*

Sir,

I have read with interest Sir R. Graham's telegram to you No. 5[1] of the 24th instant regarding Franco-Italian relations, especially the definite statement by Monsieur de Beaumarchais to the effect that the Italian Government had proposed to the German Government that in return for an agreement they would withdraw their opposition to the Anschluss.

2. I heard last month from an excellent source that the Italian Government had in fact been courting the German Government. Their attitude was described to me rather as one of atmosphere than of anything more definite, and no concrete proposals had been made. The advances, I was told, were being received with reserve and there was no likelihood of Germany being beguiled into any rash commitment.

3. When I was with Herr von Schubert yesterday, the conversation giving a favourable opening, I repeated to him, as a report reaching me from a respectable source which I did not specify, the statement of Monsieur Beaumarchais referred to above, and asked him if he had anything to say about it. Herr von Schubert's reply was 'I know nothing about that. No such proposal has ever been made either at Rome or at Berlin.' I observed to Herr von Schubert that the real answer to my question was to be found in the German Memorandum on Security just forwarded to the League of Nations,[2]

[1] No. 119.
[2] See League of Nations, *Documents of the Preparatory Commission for the Disarmament Conference*, Series VI (Geneva, 1928), pp. 176–8.

where the principle is laid down that the real key of the security problem lies not in the preparation of schemes for stopping war when it was once broken out, but in the avoidance of entanglements which are likely to lead to war.

4. In my despatch No. 750[3] of December 16th, 1927, I have referred to the attitude of the German Government towards any entanglement with Italy. There is no telling what confidential whisperings may have passed from Rome to Berlin or through what channel, but I feel confident that at present they are premature. The Anschluss, I think, will in the course of years become a very live issue indeed, but at present it is regarded by Germany as far too dangerous to be touched; and as a quid pro quo for anything, it possesses no attractions whatever.

I have, &c.,

R. C. Lindsay

[3] Not printed. In this despatch Sir R. Lindsay reported with reference to No. 64 a conversation he had had on November 25, 1927, with Dr. Gaus. Sir Ronald had suggested that attempts would be made by Italy and perhaps France to draw Germany into some commitment and Dr. Gaus had agreed that Germany would be unwise to be committed. In a conversation with Sir R. Lindsay the following day Dr. Stresemann 'threw out a remark to the effect that from the strategical point of view it was quite impossible for Italy to move without the permission of Great Britain, and he may have been suggesting that he looked to His Majesty's Government to keep Signor Mussolini quiet'.

No. 127

Letter from Sir A. Chamberlain to Sir E. Drummond (Geneva)

[*F.O. 800/262*]

Private and Personal   FOREIGN OFFICE, *February 1, 1928*

My dear Eric,

I think it is true, as you say in your private and personal letter of the 30th January,[1] that the Council must make an appeal to Brazil at the same time as to Spain, but the circumstances in which the appeal will be made to the two countries and the probable character of their replies are different. I proceed upon the assumption that, by the time the Council meets, we shall know that such an appeal to Spain will be met by a favourable response. I do not think that there is the least chance of a similar reply from Brazil. Alston[2] reports that Lloyd George[3] made a very discreet and impressive appeal to the

[1] Not printed. This letter related principally to a possible appeal from the Council of the League of Nations to Spain and Brazil not to terminate their membership of the League and argued against views expressed by Sir A. Chamberlain in a letter of January 18 (not printed) that such a joint appeal should not be made because the Council would expose itself to a rebuff from Brazil. Sir E. Drummond stated that he was 'convinced that the Latin-Americans on the Council would endanger their whole position with their other Latin-American colleagues if they did not insist that Brazil must be included. Is there not, in favour of the thesis, that the exclusion of Brazil from the appeal would strengthen the hands of those who do not love the League in Latin-America and who repeatedly declare that it is a purely European instrument?'

[2] Sir B. Alston, H.M. Ambassador at Rio de Janeiro.

[3] Mr. Lloyd George, who had been Prime Minister 1916–22, was leader of the Liberal Party in the House of Commons.

Brazilians during his recent visit and that he did so after consultation not only with Alston but also with the Minister for Foreign Affairs, but that this appeal has evoked no response among the public and that the President is less well disposed towards the idea than he formerly was. I myself am inclined to think that, since her quarrel with the League, Brazil has inclined more to the United States, and though the United States are not unfriendly to the League they have not the slightest intention of joining it and, to put it mildly, they would not encourage Brazil to reconsider her attitude.

Nevertheless as I say I agree that we must make an appeal to Brazil, but I am very anxious that, in so doing, we should not lessen the force of our appeal to Spain. I would therefore venture to suggest that, instead of making a single appeal to the two Governments in which every expression is common to them both, we should address a separate appeal to each of them and make some variation in form, if not in substance. I wish you would think this over and see what you can do. I believe that I showed you the letter which Briand and I sent to Quiñones, but for greater security I send you a copy of that letter and its enclosure.[4] They may perhaps help you to put some touches into the Council appeal to Spain which would, so to speak, make it personal to that country and differentiate it from the simultaneous appeal to Brazil which need not be less cordial even though it be rather differently worded. I beg you not to allow these enclosures out of your own personal possession, and if you want to use any of the phrases, transcribe them in your own handwriting before you send them in to the Secretariat. I am so frightened lest any accident should occur when the ship seems getting into port, and have already been a little frightened by seeing in the telegrams to our newspapers from Geneva a statement that in the Secretariat there is a belief that Spain will withdraw her resignation.[5]

Yours sincerely,
AUSTEN CHAMBERLAIN

[4] See No. 96.

[5] In his reply of February 9 Sir E. Drummond suggested procedure on the lines of that adopted by the Council of the League of Nations at its meetings on March 8 and 9: see *League of Nations Official Journal*, April 1928, pp. 405–7 and 432 respectively. The Council's resolution of March 9, together with the covering letters of the same date to the Brazilian and Spanish Governments from M. Urrutia, President of the Council and Colombian delegate thereto, is printed *ibid.*, pp. 584–5.

No. 128

Letter from Sir R. Graham (Rome) to Sir W. Tyrrell

[*C 978/805/21*]

Private and secret   ROME, *February 3, 1928*

My dear Willie,

Many thanks for your letter of January 30, enclosing copy of the telegram which reached you through a secret but reliable source.[1]

[1] This letter is not printed. The enclosed telegram is not preserved in Foreign Office

The telegram is, as you say, unpleasant, but it does not surprise me at all, nor, unless the 'proof of solidarity and friendship' referred to in the last sentence means that Italy will supply machine guns to Hungary, do I consider that it shows Mussolini as 'unstraight', for he would certainly say this kind of thing quite openly. You must remember that the Palazzo Chigi[2] at the present moment is an amateur show. A telegram of this kind, which is rather journalistic than diplomatic, would never have gone out if Contarini were in control. But I think that all it means is that the Italians want to keep in close touch with Hungary with a view to future eventualities. Mussolini is not so much afraid of Yugoslavia as of the French behind her. The Italian point of view, which I have from time to time explained, is as follows:—

They firmly believe in the existence of a military pact between France and Yugoslavia. They also believe in Yugoslavian war-like intentions. They say that Marinkovic is all very well, but that he only represents the nominal Government at Belgrade, the real Government being in the hands of the military party, the White Hand[3] and the King. All these latter elements are bellicose and hold the Italians in contempt. They certainly say openly, and perhaps believe, that they could walk through the Italian army like butter and reach Rome with ease. Recent publications regarding the Manual of the Yugoslav army etc. have not tended to reassure opinion here. To my mind everything depends on the outcome of the Italo-French conversations which Beaumarchais has now initiated, and I wish that I could believe that the French attached as much importance to them as I do. If these go well, then so will the Italo-Yugoslav negotiations and we shall have a quiet time. If they do not, Mussolini will certainly attempt some counter stroke by drawing nearer to Hungary, Bulgaria, if possible Germany and also Greece. This is, in my opinion, the real significance of the telegram you have sent me. But it does not mean any more than this.

I agree with you that both the Hungarians and Bulgarians are rather frightened than otherwise by such overtures.

In a recent *private* conversation with Titulescu,[4] he told me that he had been impressed by the obviously sincere apprehension of Yugoslav intentions that existed here. His own feeling was that the military party and the King at Belgrade constituted the real power and also a real danger. He intended, during his forthcoming visit to Belgrade, to see how the land lay and whether he could not do something to improve relations by recommending Marin-kovic to take some definite step forward, such as the ratification of the

archives. From a docket on the file it would appear that the telegram in question probably corresponded to *I Documenti Diplomatici Italiani*, Settima Serie, vol. vi, No. 6. Mr. Howard Smith had minuted on January 25 that the telegram was 'quite open to the construction . . . that Sig[nor] Mussolini is in this [i.e. the St. Gotthard incident] up to the hilt and is actually aiding an infraction of the treaty of Trianon'.

[2] The Italian Ministry of Foreign Affairs.
[3] A group of army officers.
[4] The Roumanian Minister for Foreign Affairs was visiting Rome.

Nettuno Conventions. In the meantime I see, however, that Marinkovic has fallen from power.[5]

Yours ever,

R. GRAHAM

[5] On February 1 M. Marinkovitch had resigned from the Serb-Croat-Slovene Government, but returned as Minister for Foreign Affairs in the government formed by M. Vukicevitch on February 23.

No. 129

Sir A. Chamberlain to Sir G. Grahame (Brussels)

No. 75 [C 969/969/18]

Confidential   FOREIGN OFFICE, *February 6, 1928*

Sir,

The Belgian Ambassador enquired this morning what view I took of the recent speeches of Dr. Stresemann and M. Briand.[1] His Government had been taken by surprise by this sudden reopening of the question of the occupation and were evidently a little anxious lest important questions should be decided without consultation with them. The Ambassador remarked that it was very unusual for M. Briand to reply so quickly to any foreign declaration, and he was inclined to suspect that the two speeches were the result of a previous arrangement between their authors.

As to this, I observed that the same thought had occurred to me. It seemed to me not improbable that there had been some unofficial exchange of views before Dr. Stresemann spoke through a channel which I knew the two Ministers sometimes employed for that purpose. I thought, however, that the Ministers were mainly concerned to define their policy in view of the coming elections in their respective countries.

The Ambassador remarked that rumours were current in many quarters that these elections would result in a Socialist majority in both cases, whilst in some quarters it was even suggested that the same result would follow as the result of an early General Election here, and it was suggested that the existence of Socialist Governments in the three countries would lead to a more conciliatory policy and an early agreement. For himself he dismissed at once this rumour as far as it concerned Great Britain, and he was not inclined to think that there would be any marked swing to the Left in France or even in Germany.

I replied that there was no possibility of an election here during the current year and that I was inclined to think that, in the other two countries named, the elections would produce no very great change, though they would probably slightly diminish the strength of the extreme parties in each. Upon the general question, I told his Excellency that we recognised the obligation to

[1] For reports on Dr. Stresemann's speech in the Reichstag on January 30 and M. Briand's speech in the French Senate on February 2, see *The Times*, January 31, 1928, p. 11, and February 3, 1928, p. 11, respectively.

consult the other parties interested before taking any decision as regards the occupation. Signor Mussolini had more than once asserted that right for Italy and both the French Government and ourselves had acknowledged it. Belgium could claim it *à fortiori*, since her troops formed a part of the forces of occupation. Our own position was that, since occupation must in any case terminate in 1935, it would be in the interest of all parties that, if possible, it should be brought to an earlier conclusion. We were bound, however, to recognise the difficulties of the French Government, which I supposed were to some extent shared by the Belgian Government. M. Briand had referred to the Thoiry conversations and indicated a readiness to take up again the proposals which were there suggested. His Majesty's Government would be quite prepared to consider any means appropriate to the end which we had in view, but I could not conceal from myself the great difficulties which surrounded any proposal for mobilising financial resources with a view to a lump sum anticipatory payment of reparations. On this subject I had no proposals to put forward and I did not myself believe that either Dr. Stresemann or M. Briand had worked out any scheme. Another suggestion contained in M. Briand's speech was for some form of control of the demilitarisation of the Rhineland. Here again I could not ignore the difficulties which surrounded any such proposal, though if German opinion could be reconciled to it I thought that it would be in the true interest of Germany as well as of the rest of us, for what I feared was not that Germany would seriously infringe the demilitarisation clauses of the treaty, but that at any moment when public opinion was excited she would be suspected of doing so. To compare small things with great, the situation I feared was one very similar to that which had recently occupied attention on the Polish-Lithuanian frontier. The Poles suspected a Lithuanian concentration and the Lithuanians alleged a Polish concentration. We had sent our representatives to the frontier and it had at once become apparent that these mutual suspicions were entirely without foundation. If we could find a simple method of obtaining such assurance as regards the demilitarised zone, it would, I felt, greatly calm opinion and it would avoid the necessity in given circumstances for the elaborate machinery of a League investigation. I had once or twice mentioned this idea to the Germans, but any concession of this kind by the German Government would be very difficult in view of German public opinion.

The Ambassador recurred to his suspicion that the speeches were, to use his own expression, 'a put up job', and the anxiety of his Government lest some sort of agreement was being made without their knowledge and perhaps even to their detriment. He said that the relations of the Belgian and French Governments were not at the moment quite satisfactory. The French Government had tried to impose upon Belgium a commercial treaty of a character which Belgium had been forced to reject, and he apparently connected the speeches in some way with this episode.

I told him that I was quite certain that M. Briand would make no agreement without consultation with the Allies, but I did not anticipate that the matter would be carried any further till after the elections and that it would be very unlike both M. Briand and Dr. Stresemann to have worked out any detailed plans before they made such general declarations of policy.[2]

I am, &c.,

AUSTEN CHAMBERLAIN

[2] In his despatch No. 131 of March 1 to Brussels Sir A. Chamberlain recorded a further conversation that day with the Belgian Ambassador, Baron de Cartier de Marchienne, who referred to a speech to the Belgian Senate on February 21 by M. Hymans, Belgian Minister for Foreign Affairs in succession to M. Vandervelde, in which he had linked the Belgian claim regarding repayment of the German marks left in Belgium in 1918 (see No. 178 below) with the question of an anticipated evacuation of the Rhineland. Sir A. Chamberlain observed to Baron de Cartier that he 'must not expect me to make evacuation dependent upon the question of German marks in Belgium'.

No. 130

The Marquess of Crewe (Paris) to Sir A. Chamberlain (Received February 7)
No. 214 [C 971/472/18]

PARIS, *February 6, 1928*

Sir,

I have the honour to inform you that, happening to meet yesterday M. Clauzel, the Secretary to the French Delegation to the Council of the League of Nations, a member of my staff took the opportunity to ask him what exactly was the meaning of M. Briand's reference to 'control' in the demilitarised area[1] in his speech of February 2nd (see my despatch No. 199[2] of February 3rd).

2. M. Clauzel said that Herr Stresemann was, in the opinion of the Ministry for Foreign Affairs, deliberately obscuring the issue when he spoke of the continuance of 'control' only until 1935. M. Briand had now no intention of trying to secure a permanent and resident 'control' in the demilitarised area after that date. He knew it was impossible. What he was aiming at was to secure that any enquiry ordered by the League of Nations under Article 213 of the Treaty of Versailles or the corresponding articles of the other Treaties of Paris, should function rapidly and efficiently. The importance of this was shown by the recent St. Gotthard incident.[3] M. Clauzel pointed out that this incident had occurred some weeks ago and that it would not be dealt with by the League until March. He said that in the five trucks detained

[1] Of the Rhineland.   [2] Not printed.

[3] In a letter to Mr. Selby of February 4, Sir E. Drummond had stated that M. Avenol, Deputy Secretary General of the League of Nations, had recently returned from Paris and had reported that the St. Gotthard affair 'is of great importance to Briand and to his policy. Briand has always justified the making of concessions to Germany on the ground that the League will look after French interests, and this was specially the case with regard to the cessation of the Inter-Allied Control. An incident now arises which, although of little importance in itself, is being considered both by Briand's friends and by his enemies as a test-case. Those who are opposed to the League and to Briand will be very glad if no action whatever be taken; and it is because Briand's friends feel this so strongly that they are very earnest in insisting that the League must make an enquiry.'

there were believed to be enough machine guns to equip 56 regiments, twice the number accorded to Hungary by the Treaty of the Trianon. So far as the League was concerned, the guns might by now have been scattered all over Hungary and be irrecoverable. M. Clauzel then proceeded to explain that in the matter of possible enquiries under Article 213, including enquiries within the demilitarised area and also in the matter of enquiries under the corresponding articles of the other Treaties, the scheme at present under consideration at the Ministry for Foreign Affairs was to make use of Articles 4 and 11 of the Covenant of the League which laid down that 'the Council shall meet from time to time as occasion may require' and that 'in case of any emergency (war or threat of war) the Secretary-General shall, at the request of any member of the League, forthwith summon a meeting of the Council'.

3. By means of these articles, it seemed to be possible to convene an immediate meeting of the Council if ever in the future any act such as to cause disquiet occurred as regards the state of disarmament of the ex-enemy powers or in the demilitarised zone defined by the Treaty of Versailles. The Council, on being thus convened, would instruct its permanent military advisers to despatch at once the competent commission of enquiry to the point affected. This, M. Clauzel said, was the direction in which the Ministry for Foreign Affairs were now working and this was all the 'control' which they were trying to provide for the demilitarised area. Such 'control' was covered by the Treaty and could not be refused by the Germans.

4. M. Clauzel added that Articles 42, 43 and 44 of the Treaty of Versailles demilitarised the left bank of the Rhine and the 50 kilometre zone east of the river in perpetuity. It followed that the institution of a League enquiry in this area under Article 213 of the Treaty of Versailles was on an entirely different footing from a proposal made by certain people for a League enquiry on the French side of the frontier. The French were free to fortify their frontier as they liked, and the Germans could fortify as they liked to the east of the demilitarised area. It was, in these circumstances, difficult at the moment to see what exactly a League enquiry, which some people suggested should be applied to France as much as to Germany, was, so far as France was concerned, to enquire about. There were Treaty restrictions on the armament of the demilitarised area and on German armaments generally. There were none on the armament of the French frontier or on French armaments.

5. The above information seems generally to confirm that communicated to Sir Eric Phipps by M. Paul-Boncour and reported in paragraph 4 of Sir Eric Phipps' letter to Sir William Tyrrell on February 3rd.[4]

I have, &c.,
CREWE

[4] Not printed. This paragraph reported a conversation between Sir E. Phipps and M. Paul-Boncour on February 2.

No. 131

Sir R. Graham (Rome) to Sir A. Chamberlain
(Received February 9, 9 a.m.)

No. 14 Telegraphic [C 1040/8/22]

ROME, February 8, 1928, 10 p.m.

From private information I gather that Franco (? Italian) conversations have opened none too auspiciously. Signor Mussolini received French Ambassador most cordially and declared that he desired not only improved relations but a close and cordial understanding between France and Italy. He then outlined some of the points to be negotiated. Monsieur Beaumarchais replied that he was in entire sympathy with His Excellency and thought that a settlement ought not to be difficult. He did not however propose to report to Paris in writing on the subject but would wait until he went to Paris about Easter to talk the matter over at the Quai d'Orsay. Signor Mussolini was considerably disappointed and upset at this answer which seemed to show that either French attached little importance to the conversations or had no desire to come to business. He has since been considering possible motives for this dilatory attitude and thinks that it may be due either to political reasons not to go too far before elections or else a wish to see, in first instance, which course Italo-Yugoslav negotiations will take. If the latter it is a case of putting the cart before the horse. In conversations which I have had with Monsieur Beaumarchais on the matter he gave me the impression of thinking there was no reason to hurry and that (? conversations) could be dragged out indefinitely. I disagree with this idea.

No. 132

The Marquess of Crewe (Paris) to Sir A. Chamberlain
(Received February 9, 8.30 a.m.)

No. 21 Telegraphic: by bag [C 1024/51/18]

PARIS, February 8, 1928

At its meeting this morning the Ambassadors' Conference considered the Versailles Committee's report of November 15th, 1927,[1] respecting certain new railway construction in the occupied territory (see my despatch No. 2298[1] of November 18th), this Embassy's memorandum of January 9th (see my despatch No. 44[2] of January 9th) and a French memorandum of February 3rd (see my despatch No. 231[3] of February 8th). These two latter documents deal with the general question of railway construction and destruction in the occupied territory.

---

[1] See No. 106, note 2.   [2] See No. 106, note 7.

[3] This covering despatch is not preserved in Foreign Office archives. The enclosed memorandum expressed views on the lines indicated by M. Massigli in No. 117, and proposed in substance that the Conference of Ambassadors should take the action recorded in paragraphs 2(a) and 4 below and that the Inter-Allied Railway Commission should be instructed to authorise only works which were not affected by article 43 of the Treaty of Versailles.

243

2. It was, in the first place, decided 'to request the Versailles Committee:—

'(a) to submit to the Ambassadors' Conference with the least possible delay a report and proposals respecting the objections made in the German government's notes of August 10th [16th] and November 13th [15th], 1922,[4] to the programme of destructions to be carried out in the occupied territories with a view to the application to the Rhenish railway system of article 43 of the treaty of Versailles; the Committee to distinguish in its proposals between destructions which can be carried out at once and destructions which are not to be executed until the end of the occupation of the zone concerned;

'(b) should this enquiry lead the Versailles Committee to alter the opinion contained in its report of November 15th, 1927, respecting the requests for authority to construct certain works submitted to the Inter-Allied Railway Commission, the Committee to submit new proposals to the conference on the matter;

'(c) to take account in preparing the proposals mentioned in sub-paragraphs (a) and (b) above not only of strategic but also of economic and commercial considerations.'

3. An attempt was made in preliminary conversations with the French delegation to secure the insertion in sub-paragraph (c) above of a formula designed to meet the point made in paragraph 5 (c) of your telegram No. 5[5] of January 24th respecting the desirability of the limitation of the Versailles Committee's recommendations to constructions constituting such dangerous violations of article 43 as would make it incumbent on the interested governments to appeal, if opposed by the German government, to the Council of the League of Nations. The French delegation argued that such a wording of the terms of reference to the Versailles Committee would render it unlikely that agreement would ever be reached by the latter body. From the military standpoint it was difficult to say what was and was not a vitally dangerous violation of article 43. This, in the French delegation's opinion, was a matter which it was preferable to discuss between the different delegations to the Conference on the receipt of the Versailles Committee's report. In the circumstances I thought it useless to insist on the insertion of the words, but the British representative on the Committee will carefully bear the matter in mind during the forthcoming discussions.

4. The Conference also decided that 'after examination of the Versailles Committee's report referred to above the Conference will decide in what conditions the negotiation is to be resumed with the German government on the basis of the programme proposed by the Committee and approved by the Conference. The Conference will at the same time examine the possibility of eventually extending these negotiations to the programme of new constructions planned by the German railway companies.'

5. I would draw your attention to three points arising out of this section of the resolution. First, the reference to 'new constructions planned by the

4 See No. 106, paragraph 12. 5 No. 120.

German railway companies' is a new point. The French contention with regard thereto is that all railways prepare their construction programmes some years in advance and that therefore the occasion of the approaching negotiations might profitably be taken to consider whatever programme the German companies have in mind at the time. The French say that some such discussion of this programme is in the interests of the German companies themselves, who, otherwise, may eventually be compelled to accept modification by the League. As in any case the resolution only provides that the 'possibility' of extending the negotiations to this programme will be considered on receipt of the Versailles Committee's report, I think the sentence might be left as it stands at any rate for the moment.

6. You will note that this section of the resolution does not definitely provide that the forthcoming negotiations will be between the governments either direct or through the Ambassadors' Conference, and not between the Rhineland Railway Commission and the German local authorities. (See paragraph 5 (d) of your telegram No. 5.) The French object to the insertion of this provision at the moment, saying that they prefer first to see the Versailles Committee's report. They point out that it is possible to conceive circumstances in which it would be more convenient to begin at any rate the preliminary details of the negotiations locally. They have as yet no definite views on the point and quite see the advantages of a discussion in Paris. In the circumstances I think it unnecessary to insist on further definition of this point for the moment.

7. As regards the insertion in this section of the resolution of a reference to the respective rights in this matter of the interested governments and of the League of Nations (see paragraph 5 (a) of your telegram No. 5), the French contend that a resolution of the Conference is not the proper place for such a statement. In practice they agree with your view on the point and I would draw your attention in this connection to paragraph 6 of the French memorandum of February 3rd in which it is stated that 'it is certainly true that in the event of a dispute with Germany regarding the interpretation of article 43 the provisions of the Locarno Treaty would apply; that is to say that in the last resort the dispute would have to be referred to the Council of the League of Nations; but no article of the Locarno Treaty is opposed to an understanding being reached between Germany and the Powers signatory of the Locarno Agreements as to the implications of article 43 in the matter of the Rhineland railway system'. I think that at the present stage of the discussion we might rest content with this assurance.

8. The last section of the Conference Resolution provides

'that the Versailles Committee will ask the Commander-in-Chief of the armies of occupation to inform the Inter-Allied Railway Commission:

'(a) that should the German authorities press for a reply to the requests for authority to undertake new constructions which have been addressed to the Commission, the latter will answer that this reply is being postponed pending the completion of the general enquiry into the whole question which the Powers are undertaking with a view to a negotiation which they intend to open with the German government on the matter in the near future;

'(b) that should the Commission receive fresh requests respecting new construction before the Powers have completed their enquiry, it will submit these requests to the Ambassadors' Conference through the Versailles Committee;

'(c) that in no case in its communications with the German authorities will the Commission refer to article 43 of the Treaty without the express authority of the governments represented on the Conference.'

9. I trust that the wording of the preceding section will meet the points made in paragraphs 4 and 5 (b) of your telegram No. 5. The French were unwilling to instruct the Commission never to refer to article 43 as they contended that there was no guarantee that it might not at some moment become necessary to make such a reference. They were, however, ready to forbid the Commission to refer to the article unless authorised by the governments.

10. The fourth and concluding section of the Resolution was inserted at the request of the Belgian Ambassador. It draws the attention of the Versailles Committee to a statement made by His Excellency at the Conference this morning in which the bearing of the question on Belgian security is emphasised. I will forward a copy of this statement as soon as it is received.[6] It makes a special reference to the Rothe Erde, Walheim and Inden improvements and to the Kaisersruhe siding (see paragraph 6 of your despatch No. 287 (C. 51/51/18) of January 5th). These two questions will thus, as well as that of the Odernheim–Standernheim [Staudernheim] line, fall within the scope of the Versailles Committee's enquiry.

11. I have accepted the whole Resolution under reserve of your final approval. I should be glad to receive this at the earliest possible moment as the present proposal is that the Versailles Committee should begin its enquiry on Monday next February 13th.

12. Please send copy of this telegram to War Office.

[6] In his covering despatch No. 243 of February 11 (not preserved in Foreign Office archives) Lord Crewe transmitted a copy of the Belgian note No. 1872 P.C.A. to the Conference of Ambassadors which was as here indicated except that it also referred to proposed modifications to the station at Juliers.
[7] No. 106.

No. 133

The Marquess of Crewe (Paris) to Sir A. Chamberlain
(Received February 10, 8.30 a.m.)
No. 23 Telegraphic: by bag [*C 1050/41/3*]

Immediate   PARIS, *February 8, 1928*

The Ambassadors' Conference examined to-day the Versailles Committee's report of February 6th[1] (see my despatch No. 230[2] of February 8th) regarding the non-compliance by the Austrian Government with certain of the requests conveyed to them in paragraph 2 of the conference's note to the Austrian Minister in Paris of December 2nd, 1927,[3] (see my despatch No. 2385[4] of December 2nd, 1927).

2. Marshal Foch explained the nature of the measures which the Austrian government should have taken in accordance with the conference's request. He drew attention to the importance, in particular, of the Gross-Mittel munition factory, by far the largest armament organization in Austria and the size of which was greatly in excess of the internal requirements of that country. He thought that if the conference, assisted by the Control Commission and later by the Liquidation Organ, had been unable to obtain satisfaction from the Austrian Government in these matters, there was little probability of the League of Nations, with no such machinery at command, undertaking the task with much likelihood of success. M. Cambon, while stating that this question was now technically outside the competence of the conference and would shortly fall within the sole authority of the League of Nations, was of opinion that the failure of the Austrian government to comply with certain parts of the conference request of December 2nd should be brought to their attention. M. Massigli said that either the conference must do nothing but simply inform the League of Nations of the position, in which case it was difficult to see what action that body could take, or else it must ask the Austrian Government to take further steps before the departure of the Liquidation Organ from Vienna on February 29th. The Italian Ambassador thought that the best way of dealing with the matter would be to draw the attention of the Austrian government to the non-fulfilment of certain of their engagements and to ask them what they proposed to do in respect thereof in order to give the conference satisfaction. I said that I had not as yet had time to obtain instructions on this question. I would, however, agree to submit to you a resolution of the conference which, as proposed by the French delegation, would ask the Austrian government why they had failed to fulfil certain of their obligations and what further measures, more satisfactory than those indicated to the Liquidation Organ, they intended to take.

3. This resolution, as finally drafted, reads as follows:—

'It is decided under reserve of the British Government's approval:—

'(a) to take note of the Versailles Committee's report of February 6th;

'(b) to signify to the Austrian Minister in Paris the surprise with which the Ambassadors' Conference has learned of the Austrian government's

---

[1] Not printed. This report No. 23/2 transmitted a report of January 31 by the Organ of Liquidation in Austria regarding the execution of the measures set out in No. 79. The Allied Military Committee of Versailles drew attention, in particular, to the fact that 129 machines remained for destruction and 1457 for dispersal and to a declaration by the Austrian Government on January 31 that it could not reduce the Grossmittel munitions depôt from 34 buildings to 14 as prescribed by the Organ of Liquidation.

[2] Not preserved in Foreign Office archives. [3] No. 79.

[4] See No. 79, note 1.

attitude in the matter of certain requests made of them, and notably that relating to the reduction of the Gross-Mittel factory; the Austrian Minister will further be asked urgently to inform the Conference of the reasons which his government can advance to justify their attitude and of the measures which his government intend to take to settle this question under conditions more in conformity with their obligations than the programme which was brought to the notice of the Liquidation Organ on the eve of the cessation of its functions; the Austrian Minister will be reminded that the governments represented on the Conference will be obliged in notifying the cessation of the operations of allied control to the Council of the League of Nations to bring to the latter's notice those questions which have not been settled and to emphasise the importance which attaches to their settlement;

'(c) to support this communication by representations at Vienna on the part of the representatives of the interested governments, and

'(d) to suspend, until the observations above referred to have been received, all decision as to what further action is to be taken with regard to this matter.'

4. With regard to the above resolution I may explain that it was at one time proposed to include a sentence to show that the questions dealt with in the Versailles Committee's report were from now on within the competence of the League of Nations alone. It was, however, pointed out that such a statement would not be strictly accurate as no notification has yet been made to the League. Thus from the fact that the task of the Conference is terminated it does not seem to be altogether clear that the League's responsibility has begun. I should also explain that the French originally proposed that the Austrian government should be requested to 'submit proposals' for settling the outstanding questions. I secured instead of this wording a simple request that the Austrian government should 'inform the Conference of the measures' it intended to take. My object was to avoid any possibility of a further discussion between the Conference and the Austrian government.

5. It seems to me clear that the Conference should take its final stand on the note of December 2nd and that, as indicated to the Austrian government by the representatives of the Powers at Vienna (see section 4 of enclosure to my despatch No. 2386 of December 2nd),[5] it should leave the latter under no illusion that if any of the requests contained in the note of December 2nd have not been settled there will be no alternative but to draw the League's attention to them. Subject to these considerations, I do not myself see any particular objection to the present proposal. It is, however, essential that if the proposed action is to be taken it be taken at once, as the League should be notified of the termination of control as soon as possible after the receipt of the Liquidation Organ's report at the end of the month. I am afraid that refusal to comply with this proposal, which is supported both by the French and the Italians, might expose us to some criticism in view of what I under-

5 See No. 94, note 2.

stand to be the undoubted military importance of the remaining organisations at Gross-Mittel.[6]

[6] Lord Crewe was informed in Foreign Office despatch No. 339 to Paris of February 13 that Sir A. Chamberlain approved the above resolution. Lord Crewe reported in Paris despatch No. 270 of February 14 (docket only preserved in Foreign Office archives) that a communication in accordance with paragraph 3(*b*) above had been made to the Austrian Minister at Paris.

No. 134

Sir A. Chamberlain to the Marquess of Crewe (Paris)
No. 318 [W 1181/28/98]

Confidential   FOREIGN OFFICE, *February 9, 1928*

My Lord Marquess,

When the French Ambassador had concluded what he had to say on commercial relations as recorded in my despatch No. 317[1] of to-day, I asked him if he had anything of interest to say to me about the recent speeches of Dr. Stresemann and M. Briand.[2] He replied that he knew nothing more than what had been published in the press, but he thought that M. Briand had been considerably incommoded by Dr. Stresemann's speech. M. Briand was now on excellent terms with M. Poincaré. They 'talked Left,' but they wanted to 'lean Right,' and some passages of Dr. Stresemann's speech were, therefore, embarrassing.

I remarked that I had regretted Dr. Stresemann's use of the word 'hypocrisy' in reference to the French attitude. I was told that this was a covert reply to some utterance by M. Paul-Boncour whom Dr. Stresemann did not wish to mention by name, but I was always sorry if a Minister, and above all a Foreign Minister, used language of unnecessary violence. I was convinced, however, that the great mass of the German people would not lend support to any party which attacked the policy of pacification which was symbolised by the word 'Locarno.' I supposed that both Dr. Stresemann and M. Briand were principally occupied in constructing a platform upon which their friends and supporters could stand in the forthcoming elections and that, until those were over, we must mark time.

M. de Fleuriau agreed and observed that it was generally expected in France that there would be a movement to the Right north of the Loire and to the Left south of it, and though a good many personalities would be changed the final result would be much the same.

M. de Fleuriau then spoke of the Disarmament Commission. He remarked that, on the question of reserves, there was really a difference of principle

[1] Not printed. In this despatch, Sir A. Chamberlain recorded that M. de Fleuriau had put forward a suggestion for the negotiation of a commercial treaty between France and the United Kingdom. With reference to No. 110 the Ambassador had 'said that he was ready to give a general support to our representations, but he went on to speak of the peculiar difficulties of France at this moment and of the effect which they had had upon her tariff policy'.

[2] See No. 129, note 1.

between us. French Socialists regarded the conscript system as a guarantee of peace. English Socialists took the opposite view. Obviously that was a question which must be discussed at some time, but the French Government felt that the early resumption of the Disarmament debates was inopportune and inexpedient. It was, however, difficult for any single nation to propose an adjournment, but in conversation with him M. Briand had thrown out the idea that perhaps several nations might combine and by combination share or avert the odium of the proposal.

Passing to the navy, M. de Fleuriau stated that the navy interested French sentiment, that the present condition of the French navy was extremely unsatisfactory and would rouse great discontent if the attention of the public were attracted to it.[3] He added that the present Minister of Marine, M. Leygues, was a man of great influence to whom M. Briand was bound to pay attention. He thought however that further consideration had led to some approach between the French and British views. I said that was also my impression, though I had no specific facts to go upon. After a reference by me to the Air Force, the Ambassador said he believed it would be found that this question must be discussed between M. Briand and me when we met at Geneva and that, though he himself would be very happy to give any help he could, it was only by personal discussion between M. Briand and me that any progress would be made.

I am, &c.,
AUSTEN CHAMBERLAIN

[3] In Paris despatch No. 286 of February 18 Lord Crewe transmitted a report by Captain Pipon who stated that he did 'not consider the state of the French Navy to be anything like so bad as one would be led to believe by M. Fleuriau's remark', and that he was 'of opinion that the navy is in quite a satisfactory condition'. Mr. Broadmead of the Western, General, and League of Nations Department of the Foreign Office stated in a minute of February 21 that it seemed to him that the Naval Attaché had given 'far too narrow an interpretation' to M. de Fleuriau's remarks which did in fact give a good idea of the uneasiness felt in France.

No. 135

Sir A. Chamberlain to Mr. Seeds (Durazzo)
No. 14 [C 1066/6/90]

FOREIGN OFFICE, *February 9, 1928*

Sir,

I received a call to-day from Ilias Bey Vrioni.[1]

After an exchange of greetings he entered into some explanation of the reasons for which the Albanian Government had concluded the recent Treaty of Alliance with Italy. These explanations amounted pretty much to stating that Yugoslavia had had the first offer, but that M. Ninchitch had replied that he could only make a pact *à quatre*, in other words, that he could only make a treaty with Albania when he was in a position to associate Bulgaria

[1] Albanian Minister for Foreign Affairs.

and Greece in the agreement. He had explained that the time had not come when such an agreement with Bulgaria was possible and that at the moment there were questions outstanding between Yugoslavia and Greece which must first be settled. In reply to a question from Ilias Bey as to when these difficulties would be overcome, he could only reply that it might be in a few days or it might take some years. Albania, the Minister said, could not wait indefinitely and had been forced to make her treaty with Italy.

I replied that he already knew my views on the subject. I could not pretend that the course which events had taken had given me satisfaction. I recognised the difficult situation of Albania between the mutual suspicions and jealousies of Italy and Yugoslavia, but just for that reason I had thought that her integrity and independence would best be secured by a tripartite agreement, which would have embraced both these countries. I had done my best to promote such a solution, unfortunately without success. As it was, I accepted the situation which the treaty had created. I took note of the assurances given both by his Government and by the Government of Italy that the treaty had no aggressive or provocative intention but was directed solely to the maintenance of the integrity and independence of Albania, and I should watch its execution in that spirit. This, I remarked, was all that I had to say at the moment. I should always be glad in the measure that was possible to me to facilitate good relations between neighbours in the interests of general peace, but for the moment I had nothing to propose and no counsel which I wished to give.

Ilias Bey made a suitable reply, once again emphasising the pacific character of Albanian policy and Albania's own need of peace. Upon this I remarked that the maintenance of peace was of as much consequence to Albania as to any State in the world in order that the Albanian Government might stabilise the internal situation and devote itself to the development of the country and in particular to the removal of grievances which gave rise to discontent and unrest, and here I added that, since the conversation had taken this turn, I would permit myself to insert one word of counsel. There were elements of disturbance in the Balkans which had their root in the long past and which threatened at times the peace of Greece, of Yugoslavia or of Bulgaria. I would beg the Minister, and through him the President, to see to it that strangers did not disturb the peace of Albania or make use of Albanian soil to hatch their conspiracies. The operations of the Macedonian Revolutionary Committee were dangerous, their directors and agents had no regard for Albania or Albanian interests, and as a friend I begged that the Albanian Government would take care that these people were not allowed to involve Albania in the trouble which they caused.

I need scarcely add that the Minister gave the most explicit assurances on this subject, but the warning may not have been amiss.

I am, &c.,

Austen Chamberlain

No. 136

Mr. Seeds (Durazzo) to Sir A. Chamberlain (Received February 20)
No. 23 [C 1357/1356/90]

DURAZZO, *February 9, 1928*

Sir,

By his Despatch No. 485[1] of the 19th. ultimo [December] His Majesty's Minister at Belgrade transmitted a report by Mr. Vice-Consul Footman on the attitude of certain Albanian elements in Yugoslavia towards the 'Macedonian Revolutionary Organisation' and towards the existing régime in Albania. Mr. Kennard also mentioned a French report as to encouragement alleged to be given by Italian agents to irredentist tendencies in this country as regards those portions of Yugoslavia which are Albanian in character. These reports touch a question which has been somewhat in my mind ever since the conclusion of the Italo-Albanian treaty of alliance.

2. The Italians are not alone in pointing out to the world that the alliance is but the logical consequence of the Pact of Tirana of 1926. This argument is more than merely defensible; it is indeed reasonable in itself: but it inevitably raises the query as to what may be expected to follow logically from the Treaty of Tirana of 1927. If, as the Italians (honestly enough I think) would have us believe that the Alliance represents their maximum in the direction of a protectorate over this country, it is justifiable to ask whether a logical consequence of the new treaty may not prove to be some realisation of Albanian national hopes. Is the logician to take as his starting point the clause of the alliance under which Italy undertakes to uphold the interests of Albania with the same zeal as she will uphold her own? If so, are there any Albanian hopes which might lend themselves to exploitation by Italian Ministers or officials anxious to distinguish themselves in the eyes of the Duce, not to mention those tiresome individuals, the secret agents, who must be up to some mischief in order to earn their pay? In face of these questions, it is natural to think of the Yugoslav frontier and the adjacent lands.

3. The frontier, as drawn by the wisdom of diplomatic Europe, is emphatically not what a frontier should be, in theory at any rate. It does not separate the historical enemies—Serbs and Montenegrins on the one hand and Albanians on the other: important urban centres and many fat lands which should naturally belong to Albania are lying in Serbian hands: on one side of the frontier, for instance, is the tribe of Dibra while the town of that name is carefully included in Yugoslavia: to give Kossovo to Yugoslavia and to call it 'Old Serbia' rouses, in the Albanian, feelings equivalent to those which would be inspired in a Welshman were his country to be renamed 'Old England'. In the course of their hereditary fightings each of the races has had its ups and downs, and though the Albanians now left in Yugoslavia to the Serbian mercies are for the moment the under-dogs, they do not accept such conditions as necessarily permanent. As was only to be expected, these men

[1] This despatch and the enclosed report by H.M. Vice-Consul at Skopje dated December 16, 1927, not printed, were in the sense indicated below.

252

could not but be antagonistic to Ahmed Bey when he originally attained power in Albania proper thanks notoriously to Serb assistance. The situation has, however, changed since then. Ahmed Bey is no longer the creature of the Serbs and the Alliance with Italy holds out at least the prospect of a possible reunion to a greater Albania. It will be remembered that my Italian colleague claimed that even the political refugees, who have more personal reason than the population living permanently in Yugoslavia to hate Ahmed Bey, are being steadily won over to neutrality, if not to actual friendliness. The ground seems therefore well prepared over the frontier against any moment when it might suit Ahmed Bey or his Italian friends to take up the cause of the Albanians under the Serb yoke. From Hoti and Grude in what used to be Montenegro right along the Yugoslav frontier down to Dibra and Ochrida, no inconsiderable area and population await the crusade of an Albanian or Italian Liberator.

4. On the other hand irredentism has hitherto not been a live issue in Albania so far as practical politics are concerned: it has been seldom mentioned to me at all, and then with no great conviction. The President has never spoken to me on the subject: during an interview, not long ago and since the Alliance, I took occasion to mention a certain rumour in that connection and found His Excellency quite uninterested. When I conveyed the same rumour to the Italian Minister, Monsieur Sola explained to me how he and the President were counting on several years of peace in order to carry out the great work of material development in Albania: Ahmed Bey's eyes were, now that Albania was safe from foreign aggression thanks to the Alliance, turned solely toward the interests of internal progress and economic regeneration: the President's policy was the same for this country as Monsieur Mussolini's was for Italy: neither the political refugees nor any Albanian hotheads in Yugoslavia would be allowed to break the peace. And I must confess myself, for the present at any rate, inclined to believe that Monsieur Sola correctly indicated the intentions of the Ahmed-Italian régime: all the more so as the situation described at the close of the preceding paragraph should, with reasonable care, continue to remain favourable from their point of view for some time.

5. But dormant though it be at present, the irredentist question should be borne in mind as one which may present possibilities of liveliness in the future. Above all because it is highly inflammable, in that it may be set alight by more than one interested party:— zealous Italian agents, Albanian patriots over the border, Ahmed Bey to divert attention from internal maladministration, or the Rome Government to counteract Italian unpopularity in Albania, if not to use this country definitely as a threat or a weapon against Serbia and for expansionist aims in the Balkans. There would seem no necessity for the time being for Italy to do more than consolidate her position in Albania. It is however permissible to look ahead to a moment, seemingly inevitable, when Albanian bankruptcy in some form or other will raise even in Italian minds the question 'What have we to show for the millions we have spent on this tiny and poverty-stricken country?' The reply up to date is 'The protection

of Italian interests in the Adriatic': in a few years' time when even more money will have been sunk, the reply may necessarily have to be of a more aggressive character.

6. I am sending copies of this Despatch direct to His Majesty's Representatives at Rome and Belgrade.[2]

I have, &c.,

WILLIAM SEEDS

[2] Sir W. Tyrrell minuted on this despatch on February 27: 'This is disquieting but also very speculative. W.T. 27/2.'

No. 137

Memorandum by Mr. Perowne

[*C 865/49/18*]

FOREIGN OFFICE, *February 9, 1928*

An analysis by Mr. Rowe Dutton, the new Financial Adviser at the Berlin Embassy, of the German Budget estimates for 1928–29 may be seen in Berlin despatch No. 89 in C. 863.[1] This is a very lengthy document, complete with tables and annexes, and need not be read *in extenso*. Copies have already been sent to the Treasury and the B[ritish] D[elegation to the] R[eparation] C[ommission].

The chief points seem to be as follows:—

The Budget for 1928–29 is balanced at $9\frac{1}{2}$ milliards of gold marks, including an extraordinary budget of 146 millions. The figure of $9\frac{1}{2}$ milliards represents a global increase on the two budgets (ordinary & extraordinary) of nearly 700 million over 1927; the extraordinary budget however shows a decrease of 319 millions (this is a satisfactory feature), so that the net increase in the total ordinary budget is actually over 1,000 million. On the other hand if allowances be made for the budgetary contribution to the Dawes annuity and for the payments made by the Reich to the States under the Finanzausgleich, the total budget shows a decrease in respect of general expenditure of 350 million gold marks.

General administrative expenditure shows very little movement, but heavy liabilities have been undertaken in respect of war and other pensions, the salaries of government officials and the compensation of those whose property was sequestrated in the enemy states during the war. The enormous saving under the heading of 'social services' (i.e. unemployment relief) will partly compensate in 1928 for this increased expenditure.

Considerable saving has been effected in economic services (canals, loans to railways, etc.), though provision for aviation has increased by nearly 11 million gold marks. Expenditure on the army and navy on the other hand has not actually expanded, though the estimates are nominally up by $3\frac{1}{2}$

[1] This despatch of January 30 and the enclosed report by Mr. Rowe-Dutton are not printed.

254

million gold marks, but the total budgeted for includes increases in the rates of pay which will involve additional expenditure to an amount of $28\frac{1}{2}$ million gold marks.

The forecast of receipts, in Mr. Rowe Dutton's estimation, is unduly optimistic; though the yield from the taxes has increased, windfalls contributed largely to the balancing of the 1927 budget. The prosperity of 1927 was largely due to the influx of foreign loans and Dr. Köhler appears for the future to be gambling upon the continued inflow of such loans and also on the repetition of windfalls by which the budget has benefitted hitherto.

As regards reduction in expenditure, Mr. Rowe Dutton is 'Certainly not left with any impression of lavish administration' and in general would hesitate to allege that the Government of the Reich has 'unduly overstepped the minimum level of expenditure proper to a great and highly developed country' but he, very pertinently to my mind, asks the question 'Is Germany yet in a position to afford such a level of expenditure?', and adds that if the liabilities undertaken by the government in the present budget are not in themselves excessive, it nevertheless appears that they may have been undertaken too soon and with insufficient assurances that they can continue to be met from the resources at present available. The new budget, in a word, is premature.

The prospect for 1929 is, according to Mr. Rowe Dutton, depressing; not only will reparation payments increase, but a considerable volume of exceptional receipts which have helped to balance the 1927 budget will no longer be available. It is doubtful whether receipts from taxation on its existing basis will continue to expand to an extent sufficient to provide the additional revenues necessary. In the absence of a revision of the Finanzausgleich the problem of the budget of 1929, so Mr. Rowe Dutton concludes, will be a serious one.

Dr. Köhler's speech on January 19th introducing his budget was not a very illuminating example of official optimism. He declared however that little scope existed for economy in the ordinary budget. His remarks on the chapter of reparations do not appear to be very important. He affirmed Germany's intention to do her best by the Dawes Plan and mentioned Mr. Parker Gilbert's reference in his most recent report to the question [?of] the final fixation of the total German reparations liability. He agreed that this total ought to be fixed, as an unsolved reparation question was a fundamental evil under which were suffering not only Germany, but also all countries included in the economic system of the world, but beyond stating that any payments which Germany might make without receiving an equivalent could only spring from a real and transferable surplus of production, his remarks on this score were not particularly important.

For 1929 Dr. Köhler promised a revision of the Finanzausgleich and announced that administrative economies would be effected by a concentration of local authorities, regarding which he gave certain brief details.

In his reply to the critics on January 23rd, Dr. Köhler blamed the reparation question for most of his budget difficulties and defended himself against the charge of undue optimism, but there was nothing of very outstanding importance in his remarks.

On the whole then the present prospects do not seem too promising and if Mr. Rowe Dutton's view is correct, as there seems no reason to doubt, that the German budget, though balanced, is really top-heavy and that the prosperity of 1927 was due to the influx of foreign loans, there appears to be little chance of Germany being able to provide the necessary financial solatium in return for which, plus some form of control, the French have indicated that they are ready to leave the Rhine.

J. V. PEROWNE

No. 138

Sir A. Chamberlain to the Marquess of Crewe (Paris)
No. 9 Telegraphic: by bag [C 1024/51/18]

FOREIGN OFFICE, *February 10, 1928*

Your telegram No. 21[1] (of February 8th: Constructions on the Rhineland railway system).

You may accept resolution.

You should however leave the Conference in no doubt that what is required from the C[omité] M[ilitaire] A[llié de] V[ersailles] is a clear programme of such railway works in the Rhineland as in their opinion call for demolition or modification as constituting patent violations of Article 43.[2] Thus a mere statement to the effect that certain parts of the 1922 programme should be maintained or abandoned, that certain objections made in the German notes of August and November 1922 may be admitted and others rejected, or that any particular 'avis' of the C.M.A.V. itself should be maintained or abandoned, would be useless for the object in view.

It should also be borne in mind that a violation of Article 43 must be the sole criterion for the inclusion in the abovementioned programme of any demand for the demolition or modification of any particular work. We do not desire to object to the attention of the C.M.A.V. being directed to the statement of the Belgian Ambassador regarding the extent to which Belgian security is affected by the projected works at Rothe Erde, Walheim, Inden and Kaisersruhe, but any objection to the construction of these works must be based on Article 43 or on considerations arising out of the security of the armies of occupation. An attempt to justify such objections by arguments based on considerations of Belgian security would of course be doomed to failure in the event of [it] becoming necessary to refer to the Council of the League any difference of opinion between the Allied Powers and the German government on the subject of the works in question.

[1] No. 132.   [2] Of the Treaty of Versailles.

No. 139

Letter from Sir R. Graham (Rome) to Sir A. Chamberlain
[F.O. 800/262]

Copy   ROME, *February 10, 1928*

My dear Sir Austen,

You will have seen from my telegram No. 14[1] of February 8, that the conversations between Mussolini and Beaumarchais do not seem to have started well. The Italians are very anxious to come to terms, but the impression Beaumarchais gives me is that the French are not the least in a hurry and think that matters can be dragged out indefinitely. Nor is Beaumarchais at all the man to bring pressure to bear upon his own Government.

My personal opinion is that it is most important, and even necessary, that the conversations should go forward and should reach an early conclusion, enabling the meeting à quatre to take place. Mussolini will certainly not go to such a meeting for the Tangier question alone, nor unless something has been settled previously with Briand on the other subjects at issue. It is, however, a delicate matter to go any further than we have in urging the French on. I am sure that Briand wants to come to terms, but am rapidly coming to a conviction that the Quai d'Orsay does not, and that Beaumarchais represents the latter rather than the former.

Yours v. sincerely,
R. GRAHAM

[1] No. 131.

No. 140

Letter from Sir R. Lindsay (Berlin) to Mr. Sargent (Received February 13)
[C 1211/48/62]

BERLIN, *February 10, 1928*

Dear Sargent,

I enclose a note of a conversation with Parker Gilbert. It is just possible he may cross over to London to-night and descend on the Treasury on Monday,[1] and as they, the Treasury, might like to turn over in their minds what he said, I have sent you a telegram[2] summarising it, and I am sending a copy of this letter direct to them.

As I say in the note, I was rather out of my depth in this talk and I feel that Gilbert's views should be elicited by an expert before being seriously considered. I indicate a ripple on the water; and if someone in the Treasury will drop a fly there, he may get a rise.

Yours sincerely,
R. C. LINDSAY

[1] February 13, 1928. Mr. Parker Gilbert did not visit London at this time.
[2] Berlin telegram No. 5 of February 10 is not printed.

BERLIN, *February 10, 1928*

I had a conversation last night with Mr. Parker Gilbert in the course of which I asked him about the reactions in America of his suggestion that the total of German Reparation Liability would have to be definitely fixed soon. So far as this simple question was concerned he said the reaction was perfectly good. The general view had been the mere commonsense one, that it was unfair to leave the Germans with an indefinite liability over them and therefore proper that it should be fixed. He then got on to the question of the connection between Reparation and Inter-allied indebtedness.

(Here I may say I got rather out of my depth. I reproduce to the best of my ability what he said but with a warning that it may be inaccurate, and in the hope that someone more expert than myself may be able to elicit from him his real views.)

He said that America is not prepared to admit any logical or theoretical connection between reparation and inter-allied debt. Both political parties had gone strongly on record against it and neither could now admit of any connection without exposing itself to telling attack from the opposition. From the theoretical point of view therefore neither public opinion nor any conceivable government could make any such admission. As a practical matter however it was possible that a connection might be established. The first thing to do would be to fix reparation without regard to the other question, viz. that of debt. In the past, when the Baldwin settlement of Anglo-American indebtedness had been effected,[3] an opportunity presented itself of 'bringing America and Britain to the same side of the table' in all these matters. The policy of the Balfour note[4] was a disappointment of this hope with its insistence of a connection between the two questions. He thought His Majesty's Government were wrong to harp constantly on this theme. But if a fixation of reparation could first be effected, then the practical side of the question would come to the fore. He mentioned (perhaps as one example among other possible ones) that with a definition of reparation the marketing of bonds for reparation purposes over a number of years would become a practical necessity, and this he thought would again bring America and England 'to the same side of the table' where they ought to be.

Gilbert is planning a visit to London and may be leaving to-night. If he does not go to-night he will have to postpone it till the end of this month. He

[3] In January 1923 Mr. S. Baldwin, Chancellor of the Exchequer, and Mr. M. Norman, Governor of the Bank of England, held negotiations with the American Debt Funding Commission respecting the debt incurred during the war by His Majesty's Government to the Government of the United States. His Majesty's Government agreed to issue to the U.S. Government bonds covering the full amount of $4,600 million to be repaid over sixty-two years. The interest for the first ten years was to be 3 per cent. and thereafter $3\frac{1}{2}$ per cent. The agreement was embodied in an exchange of notes of June 18–19, 1923: see *British and Foreign State Papers*, vol. 126, pp. 307–17.

[4] This note of August 1, 1922, from the Lord President of the Council is printed as Cmd. 1737 of 1922, *Despatch to the Representatives of France, Italy, Serb-Croat-Slovene State, Roumania, Portugal and Greece at London respecting War Debts.*

told me he was going to see the Governor[5] but assured me he had no intention whatever of missing out the Treasury. He was genuinely sorry Leith Ross was ill; would want to see Sir Warren Fisher or Sir R. Hopkins; and I think it quite likely he might ask to see the Chancellor. I think he is anxious to keep in close touch with London and I have reason to believe he means in the future to visit Paris far more frequently than in the past.[6]

[5] Of the Bank of England.

[6] Sir A. Chamberlain minuted on February 13: 'N.B. The Balfour Note preceded the Baldwin settlement. There is some mistake in Lindsay's account or in Parker's statement. A.C. 13.2.'

No. 141

Colonel Ryan (Coblenz) to Sir A. Chamberlain (Received February 13)
No. 21 [C 1086/969/18]

Confidential   COBLENZ, *February 11, 1928*

Sir,

I had a long conversation early this week with the French High Commissioner on the attitude of France to the question of the evacuation of the Rhineland which has been brought forward by Herr Stresemann's recent speech in the Reichstag. At the time of this conversation the report of M. Briand's speech had not reached Coblenz. M. Tirard holds, as you know, moderate views, and is in close touch with the Government and with Governmental circles in Paris, which, indeed, has now become, for all practical purposes, his head-quarters. There is nothing new or startling in his views which have been expressed recently in other forms and places. But they give such a clear summary of what one believes to be the present feeling in France as regards evacuation that I venture to think they may be of interest.

2. M. Tirard said that there was, in general, a desire in France to come to a complete settlement with Germany as it was recognised that French interests would be best served by a return to normal relations. There were, however, three considerations which were exercising the French mind at the present moment.

3. The first of these was that there was a certain feeling of disappointment in France both as regards the Reparations question and the Locarno Treaties.

As regards reparations France had made certain sacrifices to reach an agreement and had accepted the Dawes Plan which she had regarded as a final settlement. Now she was being told that this plan was only an experiment (vide Mr. Parker Gilbert's report of December 10th last). She foresaw the time coming when the Plan would be called in discussion and France probably asked to make further sacrifices.

The Locarno Treaties had been concluded on the basis that the Treaty of Versailles was to be left intact. Those people who did not wholeheartedly agree with Locarno had had the consolation that the Treaty of Versailles remained in full force. But now Germany was attacking the Occupation, the terms of which were definitely laid down by the Treaty, on the grounds that its continuance was inconsistent with Locarno. In other words they were using Locarno to batter in the Treaty.

4. The second consideration was that Frenchmen were suspicious of Germany's aims. They knew that German policy was based on realism and developed with mathematical exactitude. A few examples from recent years would suffice to explain French feeling in this respect.

The liquidation of the Ruhr operation was on the point of completion and the French were proposing to keep the Rhineland railways, run by the Regie,[1] as a guarantee of German good behaviour. The Germans protested saying that it was impossible for good relations to be restored so long as the railways were in French hands. Under the pressure of their Allies and to meet the German wishes, they gave way reluctantly and, as they now believe, unnecessarily. And with what result? Only to discover after a few months that Germany not only showed no gratitude to France for having given back this very tangible guarantee but openly attacked her for having dared to take possession of them.

After Locarno Germany protested that the one thing necessary to the restoration of good relations, was the evacuation of the Cologne zone. Without fixing the northern boundary of the second zone, without settling finally the question of the railways in the area, in great haste and with considerable inconvenience to the Armies the zone was evacuated—and what was the result? Was there any recognition on the part of Germany of the action taken by the Occupying Powers? On the contrary. The evacuation of Cologne was only followed by recriminations and complaints that the occupation of Cologne after 1925 had been illegal and that the ex-allied Powers in evacuating had only made a public avowal of the illegality. Since then many alleviations had been made in the Occupied Territories, of a secondary importance, it was true, but they had been received in the same way. The lesson of the past was that there was likely to be no finality in this matter of concessions to Germany.

Germany had now raised the question of the complete evacuation of the Rhineland, saying that the occupation was the one obstacle that prevented a complete understanding between the two countries—the iron curtain between Germany and France—in the language of the Press. But France found it difficult to believe that even with an immediate evacuation the chapter would be closed. France had seen during the last two years the heavy guns of the Press directed in turn with a skill and a determination to which he, Mr. Tirard, was forced to give credit, on the questions of disarmament, of evacuation, of the Colonies, and of the Polish corridor. It reminded them of the closing years of the war, when the German Army with infinite skill concentrated its attacks on the weak sectors of the Allied front, and then, if the resistance was too strong, switched on to a weaker sector. It was the war tactics applied to the present situation. Supposing that an early evacuation

[1] The Régie des chemins de fer des territoires occupés, the Franco-Belgian railway administration.

was agreed to, could one believe that finality would thereby be reached? A study of the past could only lead one to think, as France thought, that the concession of this claim would be but the prelude to further demands in regard to controversial matters, viz:—the Polish Corridor, disarmament, reparations, the Colonies and the 'Anschluss'. To use a metaphor employed before, the Germans were concentrating on limited objectives and an objective once gained was used as a jumping-off ground for the next.

5. The third consideration was the fact that the French were, at least, as realist as the Germans. If there was to be a premature evacuation they asked for some compensation in return. After all, the Occupation, though a diminishing asset, was something tangible. It was a guarantee for another seven years that the Treaty would be complied with, and it was worth something. Since the Germans were making the demand it was for them to suggest the *quid pro quo*.

6. At the conclusion of our talk, I asked M. Tirard what he thought France required as compensation. His reply was vague and unsatisfactory and one is inclined to doubt if the French really know what they want. He spoke of additional guarantees for the Polish frontier, of security for reparations and of some form of control for the Rhineland beyond 1925.[2] In regard to the last-named point, I objected that no form of supervision which any possible form of control would mean was of any practical value and he was disposed to agree.

7. I have only two observations to make on M. Tirard's remarks. The first is that French opinion has advanced some way during 1927. At the beginning of last year there were few French officials acquainted with French public opinion, who would have admitted that negotiations with Germany in regard to the evacuation of the Rhineland were possible. It appears now to be the view that negotiations cannot be avoided, and this seems to be confirmed by M. Briand's recent speech: in other words it seems to be now realised that whatever the letter of Locarno may be, the maintenance of the Occupation is not consonant with its spirit.

In the second place the question of security as concerning the North Eastern frontier of France seems to have dropped into the background. M. Tirard's sole reference to it was in regard to a Rhineland Control after evacuation. I am unable to say if the views of the French Generals have changed or if they have been over-ruled.

I have, &c.,
R. S. RYAN

[2] It was suggested on the filed copy that this date should read '1935'.

No. 142

Memorandum by Mr. Howard Smith

[*C 1403/1403/62*]

FOREIGN OFFICE, *February 15, 1928*

The adaptability of the Locarno System to Central and Eastern Europe

The idea that the system devised at Locarno might be applied with similarly beneficial results in other quarters of Europe came into being concurrently with the initialling of the Locarno treaties in October 1925. Sir A. Chamberlain then expressed to Signor Mussolini, Dr. Benes and M. Ninčić, the Yugoslav Minister for Foreign Affairs, the hope that the principles embodied in the Locarno treaties might be applied to Central Europe and the Balkan States. These leaders recognised indeed that this was a consummation devoutly to be wished, but foreseeing great difficulties, the two latter suggested that the initiative should come either from Great Britain or France. To this suggestion Sir Austen Chamberlain rejoined by explaining that salvation must come from within. It would be useless for the Great Powers to endeavour to impose peace upon the various States into which Central and South East Europe is divided. Each separate government must will peace and work for its realisation; omit no act which can forward it and avoid any action calculated to hinder it. Above all he recommended a policy of conciliation and good-will towards minorities and the co-operation and good-will of the Italian Government.[1]

2. Since the date of this pronouncement little or no progress has been made, and this for a variety of causes into which it will not be necessary to enter in detail. The main cause will probably be found in the unfortunate and growing jealousy between France and Italy in all matters concerned with Central Europe and the Balkans. This lamentable situation as between two of the Great Powers of Europe, both of which are in treaty relations with various of the smaller Central and South Eastern States of Europe, has tended to keep asunder States which might otherwise have come closer together and to have exacerbated suspicions which might, in the nearly two and a half years which have elapsed, have calmed down. At the moment, however, there is a hope that France and Italy may reach an understanding which will substitute a real friendship for the existing masked hostility between them, and should this occur the chances of understandings between ex-allies and ex-enemies in Central and South-Eastern Europe would immediately improve.

3. As things now are the States of Central and South-Eastern Europe are inclined rather to insist on the difficulties which lie in the way of any agreements on the Locarno model,[2] than to endeavour to prepare the way for

[1] See Volume I, Nos. 39–40.

[2] *Note in original*: 'The above statement must be qualified by pointing to the fact that one of the ex-enemy states has been able to make individual arbitration treaties almost precisely similar to the German-Polish and German-Czech (Locarno) [annex E to Cmd. 2525 of 1925] arbitration treaties. Austria has concluded such treaties with Czechoslovakia, Poland [on March 5 and April 16, 1926: see *British and Foreign State Papers*, vol. 125, pp. 103–6 and

understandings of this pattern. They hold to treaties of the defensive type directed against their former enemies, instead of trying to work out understandings on the Locarno model, which is in two words a treaty between one or more ex-allies *with an ex-enemy*, for the settlement of all disputes by some process of conciliation or arbitration and for a system of mutual guarantees in the event of the Treaty being violated.

4. Moreover they are disposed to argue that in no case could there be an effective Locarno Treaty in Central and South Eastern Europe because it would never be possible for any group of States to find a special guarantee by a disinterested Power such as that undertaken by Great Britain under the Locarno Treaty. In fact they argue that the whole merit and substance of the Locarno Treaty consists in the British guarantee. This is an entirely false argument. The British guarantee of the French frontiers is justified and justified solely because for all practical purposes the eastern frontier of France is the eastern frontier of Great Britain. We cannot afford to see a Franco-German settlement of this frontier upset. In fact the British guarantee is not a special guarantee of a disinterested Power but a guarantee given by reason of the fact that Great Britain in regard to the Franco-German frontier does consider herself co-terminous.

5. The above is surely the explanation of and reason for the British guarantee. It followed logically from the circumstances of the time, but it was not absolutely essential for the negotiation of a treaty between France, Belgium, Poland, Czechoslovakia and Germany on the Locarno model. This is proved by the difference between the settlement between Germany and France and that between Germany and Poland. In the case of Poland there is no British territorial guarantee because Great Britain is not vitally interested in the Poland–Germany frontier. But this does not prevent the Locarno system from being applied to the relations between Germany and Poland and Germany and Czechoslovakia as well as between Germany and France. If Great Britain had never entered the war, and if in despite of that the position of the main belligerents at the conclusion of hostilities had been similar to that existing at the time of the signature of the Treaty of Versailles, it might none the less have been possible for France and Germany, with Belgium, Czechoslovakia and Poland, to conclude a treaty of Locarno whereby each state undertook, subject to the League of Nations' decision, to declare war upon any of the others which violated its provisions. In short a general collective guarantee would have taken the place of what appears in the actual Locarno Treaty to be the special guarantee of Great Britain.

6. But another consideration must be borne in mind. The Treaty of Locarno was made possible because France and Germany were each ready to offer the other some valuable *quid pro quo*. Germany surrendered any hope of recovering Alsace-Lorraine, in which she is in any case little interested,

169–73 respectively] and Yugoslavia [a draft agreement initialled at Geneva on September 15, 1926, had not been signed]. There are moreover similar treaties between Czechoslovakia and Poland and Yugoslavia and Poland [of April 23, 1925, and September 18, 1926: *v. op. cit.*, vol. 122, pp. 333–9, and vol. 125, pp. 985–90 ,respectively], and between Italy and Germany.'

accepted the frontiers between France and Germany and Belgium and Germany, as laid down in the Treaty of Versailles, and the demilitarised zone, and in return France relieved Germany of the danger of extended 'sanctions' in the Rhineland, allowed her to become a member of the League of Nations and thus enabled her to secure credits for the rehabilitation of her industries. On the other hand, Germany has never admitted, as she has in the case of her western frontiers, that she accepts her frontier with Poland; she has only declared that she will not seek to alter it by force. And in this attitude she is perfectly logical. In the west she recognised that she never had a good claim to Alsace-Lorraine and she has no grievance at the frontiers laid down by the Treaty of Versailles; but in the east she feels that the treaty settlement is unjust and in the end must be righted. Therefore she insisted on retaining her full right to work for the alteration of the Polish frontier by peaceful means and only agreed to settle with Poland by arbitration disputes *subsequent to the date of the arbitration treaty*. The other signatories in order to obtain the Treaty agreed to forego their demand that the permanence of the German–Polish frontier should be guaranteed. In so doing they made a further important and valuable concession to Germany.

7. If the above analysis is approximately correct, it would seem to follow that treaties on the Locarno model should be possible in other quarters of Europe provided that the following conditions are present:—

(1) There must be an agreement between one or more states of the ex-allied group and an ex-enemy.

(2) The advantage must not be all on the side of the ex-allied states. There must be some strong inducement for the ex-enemy state to enter into a treaty.

(3) There must be special consideration shown for minorities.

8. Can these conditions be applied to Central Europe? There are two ex-enemy states, Austria and Hungary. Although co-terminous and formerly forming a part of the same Empire, they are antagonistic to each other and each raises an entirely different set of problems. Austria is naturally pacific, easy-going and strongly republican. Hungary is militaristic, ambitious and strongly monarchical. Austria is generally contented with her present frontiers, and realises that it will be quite impossible for her to change them (except that she hopes that eventually there will be no frontier between her and Germany and that she will form part of the German Reich). Her frontier with Germany is the same as that existing before the war; her frontier with Czechoslovakia calls for no comment; her frontiers with Hungary and Yugoslavia were settled in her favour by plebiscites, and in her frontier with Italy she is bound to acquiesce as she cannot hope to alter it. But she has one ambition which seems to her natural but which is debarred to her by the Treaty of Saint Germain, namely the Anschluss with Germany; and she feels acutely the treatment to which her former co-nationals in South Tyrol are subjected by Italy. As explained above, there are arbitration treaties on the Locarno model between Austria and Czechoslovakia and Austria and Yugo-

slavia, and thus a beginning towards a Locarno treaty of mutual guarantee has been made. There seems to be nothing to prevent these three countries from concluding such a treaty, but obviously such a combination would be much stronger if Italy could be included, but whether Italy could be brought into such a combination is more doubtful. Austria would hardly welcome an agreement with her unless she were assured of better treatment for the Austrians in South Tyrol, and this Italy would not in present conditions and under the Fascist régime be likely to grant; while on her side Italy would require some guarantee against the realisation of the Anschluss, although it would appear that she is fully covered by the terms of Article 19 of the Covenant. As things now stand Austria can only realise the Anschluss through the operation of that article, and if at some future date the Assembly of the League should advise the revision of Article 88 of the Treaty of Saint Germain, it would hardly be possible for Italy to raise any valid objection. There does not therefore seem any inherent reason why these difficulties should not be surmounted by negotiation.

9. With Hungary the position is very different. She has no kind of inducement at present to come to any agreement with her neighbours. She feels that the Treaty of Trianon is a monument of injustice in that large sections of her former territory have been thereby transferred from her to the Czechs, Roumanians and Yugoslavs, and that these territories contain considerable numbers of Magyars who have been compelled to become foreign subjects. Moreover the agrarian legislation which has been passed in Czechoslovakia, Roumania and Yugoslavia, has severely hit those Hungarian landlords whose estates were situated in the territories now severed from Hungary. Apart from this, Hungarians look upon Czechs and Roumanians (and Serbs to a lesser extent) as inferior races which makes their present superior position doubly detestable. Finally it is these same Czechs, Roumanians and Serbs who induced the Powers to place a veto, which did not appear in the Treaty of Trianon, upon the restoration of a Hapsburg to the Hungarian Throne. A mutual guarantee pact on the lines of Locarno would be of immense benefit to the Little Entente Powers. They are all inclined to fear Hungary, and a pact would remove this fear. Moreover they all have new territories to develop and consolidate and need a prolonged period of peace and freedom from alarms. In present conditions it has no attraction for Hungary because she cannot acquiesce in the permanence of her present frontiers, and thus condition (2) in paragraph 6 above is not present. Therefore it must be for the Little Entente to make it worth Hungary's while. It is not the object of this memorandum to detail how this can be done; this is the business of the Little Entente if they wish for their Locarno and its attendant benefits; but there are one or two obvious lines of approach, viz. frontier rectifications, or undertakings to rectify the frontiers within a specified time; direct negotiations between Hungary and the states of the Little Entente on minority questions instead of recourse to the cumbrous and unsatisfactory procedure undertaken by the League of Nations under the terms of the various minorities treaties; possibly the establishment of demilitarised zones between

Hungary and her neighbours, though the efficacy of this specific is doubtful; and the withdrawal of the veto on a Hapsburg restoration. Italy, now the friend and virtual ally of Hungary, could not but welcome such an agreement and might serve as the guarantor were a guarantee needed; but it seems abundantly clear that the Little Entente must make concessions if they wish to break down Hungary's ill-will. If they will do this a mutual guarantee pact should be possible.

10. The last ex-enemy country to be considered is Bulgaria, and at first sight it would appear that an understanding on the lines of Locarno should be possible between Yugoslavia, Greece, Roumania and Bulgaria with perhaps the addition of Turkey. But on consideration and having regard to the conditions premised in paragraph 6 above, the realisation of such an agreement becomes exceedingly problematical. Bulgaria is at present practically in the hands of the Macedonian Revolutionary Organisation. The aim of this body, which dates from the early days of resistance to the Turks, is to incorporate in Bulgaria those sections of the territory called Macedonia which are now part of Yugoslavia and Greece. Their power is undoubted as is shown by their murder of M. Stambouliiski,[3] the one Bulgarian Prime Minister since the war who endeavoured to work for an understanding with Yugoslavia; and it is known that their influence with the present government is paramount. They wage perpetual war against Serbian administration in southern Serbia by a campaign of assassination and outrage and the Bulgarian government are powerless to prevent them. Any Locarno agreement in the Balkans could only be based on the maintenance of the present frontiers laid down by the Treaty of Neuilly,[4] and it is difficult to see how any Bulgarian Government could, in face of the power of the Macedonian Revolutionary Organisation, accept such a treaty. Moreover through her own stupidity Bulgaria has never acquired the outlet to the Aegean Sea promised to her by the Treaty of Neuilly, and unless she abates her claims the prospect of her obtaining this port must remain doubtful. With Roumania too she has a quarrel over the Dobrudja which the former filched from her in 1913. Where then is Bulgaria's inducement to enter a Locarno Pact? Certainly as things now are the prospect of the realisation of such an agreement seems slender, and clearly Bulgaria cannot be expected to make the first move. But this does not mean that a Balkan Locarno is impossible for all time. There are Bulgarian minorities in Yugoslavia and Roumania and their treatment could with advantage be ameliorated. This might lead to a situation favourable to the conclusion of an arbitration treaty between Bulgaria and Roumania, though the Macedonian Revolutionary Organisation would presumably prevent any similar agreement with Yugoslavia. Then the clearing up of the present points of difference between Greece and Yugoslavia could not but make for greater stability in the Balkans and demonstrate to the Bulgarians

[3] M. Stamboliiski was Bulgarian Prime Minister from October 1919 until his assassination on June 14, 1923.

[4] The Bulgarian peace treaty of November 27, 1919, is printed in *British and Foreign State Papers*, vol. 112, pp. 781–895.

the improbability that their dreams of an alteration of their frontiers can ever be realised. Moreover a 'Balkan Locarno' is for ever on the lips of Yugoslav and Greek statesmen. If they believe it to be the panacea for all their ills, they should at least labour for its realisation and endeavour to produce a situation which would make it possible for Bulgaria to work with them.

11. Finally mention should be made of the pious resolutions adopted by the Assembly of the League in 1926 and 1927.[5] These extolled the Treaties of Locarno and recommended the extension of the system to other parts of Europe. These resolutions were unanimously adopted, and that of 1926 was indeed proposed by the Yugoslav Delegate. The representatives of the Balkan States agreed to the adoption of the resolution that peace can best be secured by the extension of the Locarno system; they make the Assembly's resolution a farce if they now say they can do nothing to make the system applicable to their own problems.

12. These remarks have been confined to considerations of agreements exactly similar to those concluded at Locarno, viz. between one or more ex-allied States and an ex-enemy State. The system need not be so closely confined and the advantages of its extension to other fields will be immediately apparent. Nothing could more make for peace than a Locarno agreement between Italy, Yugoslavia and Albania, but Italy has apparently frustrated this by establishing a virtual protectorate over Albania and by concluding with her a defensive alliance for twenty years. The difficulties between Italy and Yugoslavia might yet be settled on Locarno principles, and Sir Austen Chamberlain has endeavoured to convince Italy of the desirability of this, but we are here concerned solely with the application of the Locarno system only as between former allies and enemies.

13. The conclusion would seem to be that although admittedly there are difficulties, varying in intensity in different quarters and among different groups of states, the system of Locarno can be applied both in Central and South Eastern Europe provided that the ex-allied states will work to create conditions which will offer some real inducement to their former enemies to forego their hostility. As things now are the ex-enemies cannot move first. The first step must come from the ex-allies and if they will take this step, they will secure very material benefits not only for themselves but for Europe as a whole.[6]

C. HOWARD SMITH

[5] *Note in original*: 'A. 119. 1926. IX. and A. 124. 1927. IX.' These resolutions of September 25, 1926, and September 26, 1927, are printed in *League of Nations Official Journal, Special Supplements, No. 44*, p. 120, and *No. 54*, pp. 177–8, respectively.

[6] On February 18 Sir R. Macleay reported in particular in Prague despatch No. 39 that he had asked M. Benes that morning 'whether his idea was to bring about a Central European Locarno Pact. He said Yes, but he wanted to make it clear that he did not expect Great Britain to undertake any positive guarantees in respect of such an Agreement. All that was wanted from His Majesty's Government was the assurance of their moral support, this would, he was confident, be quite sufficient to ensure the success of such an Agreement.'

No. 143

Letter from Sir A. Chamberlain to the Marquess of Crewe (Paris)
[*C 1040/8/22*]

Private   FOREIGN OFFICE, *February 16, 1928*

My dear Crewe,

I am concerned at the course of the Franco-Italian conversations at Rome as disclosed by Graham's telegram No.14[1] of February 8th and by his private letter to me of the 10th[2] of both of which I enclose copies. The attitude adopted by Beaumarchais has evidently produced a chilling effect on Mussolini and appears to denote a dangerous tendency to procrastinate on the part of the French Government. As you know Mussolini has constantly asserted of late that relations between Italy and Yugoslavia depend on the state of Italy's relations with France, so that Beaumarchais' delays will adversely affect Rakitch's negotiations and no progress will be made in either field.

I hope to find an opportunity at Geneva of expressing my anxiety on the subject to Briand personally, but meanwhile will you consider whether you can usefully say anything to him. It would be a real pity (and Briand himself would certainly think it so) if any friction between Beaumarchais and Mussolini prevented the latter from coming himself to the projected meeting à quatre about Tangier.

Yours sincerely,
AUSTEN CHAMBERLAIN

[1] No. 131.   [2] No. 139.

No. 144

Sir A. Chamberlain to the Marquess of Crewe (Paris)
No. 379 [*C 1155/316/18*]

FOREIGN OFFICE, *February 17, 1928*

My Lord Marquess,

With reference to your despatch No. 73[1] (154/1/1928) of January 14th, I transmit to Your Lordship herewith copies of two despatches[2] from His Majesty's Ambassador at Berlin relative to the contemplated armament with five-inch guns of German men of war of the destroyer class.

2. It will be seen that the British Naval Attaché and his ex-Allied colleagues have been approached by the Marineleitung with a request to ascertain the views of their respective Governments as to whether the armament of five-inch guns on the vessels in question is allowable or not, and that Sir R. Lindsay has informed Herr de Haas of the Ministry for Foreign Affairs, with reference to this request, that such questions should be raised as between the Governments direct and not between the Admiralties concerned. Sir R. Lindsay also expressed the view that the Ambassadors' Conference would

[1] See No. 78, note 3.
[2] Berlin despatches Nos. 65 of January 20 and 73 of January 23, not printed.

decide, if the matter was referred to them, that the German Government were not entitled to arm their destroyers with five-inch guns and that indeed some doubt appeared to exist whether the manufacture in Germany of guns of that calibre was not in itself illegal. It will be observed that as the result of this conversation Herr de Haas promised to take the matter up with the Marine-leitung.

3. In these circumstances it would appear either that the German Government will decide to drop the proposal (as in the cases last year of the cruiser 'D' and the proposed twelve-inch guns for the replacement battleships),[3] or that they will put forward an official request to the Governments concerned, either direct or through the medium of the Ambassadors' Conference, with a view to obtaining permission to mount the guns in question. In this connexion I transmit to you herewith a copy of a further despatch[4] from His Majesty's Ambassador at Berlin from which it may be inferred that in all probability no attempt will in fact be made to arm the vessels at present in question with five-inch guns. His Majesty's Government are accordingly of the opinion that no need at present exists for further action on the part of the ex-Allied Powers or of their representatives at Berlin in connexion with this question unless and until an official communication on the subject should be received from the German Government.

4. In order to forestall any independent action by any of the ex-Allied Governments and generally to prevent misunderstandings I request that you will inform the Ambassadors' Conference of the views of His Majesty's Government as set forth in the preceding paragraphs.[5]

I am, &c.,

(For the Secretary of State)

ORME SARGENT

[3] For the proposed German cruiser 'D' see Volume III, No. 203. Sir R. Lindsay reported in Berlin despatch No. 133 of February 10 (not preserved in Foreign Office archives) that the proposal to arm vessels with 12-inch guns (see No. 13) had been dropped.

[4] Berlin despatch No. 109 of February 3 is not printed. This despatch stated that the German Ministry of Foreign Affairs had intervened in the question with the result recorded below. Sir R. Lindsay further stated that it was definitely confirmed that the guns in question had been manufactured and requested guidance as to the line to adopt on the assumption that their manufacture was illegal.

[5] In Paris covering despatch No. 328 (not preserved in Foreign Office archives) Lord Crewe transmitted to the Foreign Office a note of February 22 from the French Delegation to the Conference of Ambassadors recapitulating the exchanges between the naval attachés at Berlin and the German Admiralty and suggesting that the naval experts of the Conference should examine the question with a view to similar instructions being sent by the interested Governments to the naval attachés at Berlin. The despatch further transmitted Note No. 121 A.C. of February 24 from H.M. Embassy at Paris to the Conference of Ambassadors referring to the French note and setting out the views expressed in the present despatch.

Letter from the Marquess of Crewe (Paris) to Sir A. Chamberlain
[*F.O. 800/262*]

Copy

Private   PARIS, *February 17, 1928*

My dear Chamberlain,

With reference to Selby's letter to me of the 13th February,[1] enclosing a copy of the letter from Rome to you of February 10th,[2] I am very glad to be told of the impression which Beaumarchais has left on Ronald Graham's mind. I asked Briand today if he could tell me anything of what was happening at Rome, and he said that the conversations between Mussolini and Beaumarchais are proceeding in the most friendly way. This I might have been inclined to[3] his habitual determination to keep things pleasant by insisting that they are pleasant, even when other people doubt it, but curiously enough Phipps, who was seeing Berthelot this afternoon, had exactly the same story from him. Briand went on to say something about the different questions on which he hoped to be able to meet Italian wishes to some extent. On Tangier, he did not expect any real difficulty in satisfying Italian claims, short of any actual change in the *régime* under the statute. Nor did he anticipate any real obstacles in dealing with Tunis. He himself entertains no jealousy of the Italian preponderance in numbers there, partly because he foresees a future accretion in the French population, and partly because the Italian colonists are quiet and well-conducted, give no trouble, and seem as contented to be under French administration there as the large Italian population is here in France. As to naturalisation in Tunis, he does not in the least mind if the result of discussions is to add to the Italian army a small number of men who would otherwise become French nationals.

The third question was that of the frontier with Tripoli, and the possibility of French access to the South being barred by an Italian claim; but on this, also, he did not anticipate any difficulty in coming to an agreement.

I asked whether he hoped to come to a conclusion on these matters during the conversations *à quatre* which I understood it was still hoped to hold. He said, certainly, and he is looking forward to talking to you about this meeting when you see each other at Geneva. He thought that very possibly it might be suggested that your meeting of Four should take place in May.

He said nothing to me about any questions connected with Italians resident in France, whose position has sometimes been discussed in the Italian press, so probably the Italian Government have not, so far, raised any questions about them. Nor did he allude to a remarkable circumstance which Berthelot mentioned to Phipps, namely that the Italians had hinted at the possibility of a Treaty of Alliance between the two countries. This he said the French

[1] Untraced in Foreign Office archives.

[2] No. 139.

[3] It was suggested in the Foreign Office that the words 'attribute to' had here been omitted.

Government consider as going too fast, but they would at once be prepared to consider an Arbitration Treaty on the customary pattern.

Yours sincerely,
CREWE

No. 146

Letter from Sir R. Graham (Rome) to Sir A. Chamberlain

[*C 1400/8/22*]

Copy

Private and Personal　　　　　　　　　　　　　　ROME, *February 17, 1928*

My dear Sir Austen,

I had a long talk with the French Ambassador yesterday, and it is clear that the Franco-Italian conversations have more or less come to a standstill. Beaumarchais does not propose to do anything more until he has been to Paris at Easter and talked things over at the Quai d'Orsay. He thinks it would be a mistake to hurry matters and that it is best to let the present détente in Franco-Italian relations continue. This is all very well, but will it continue? At present the Italian press is being sat upon by the authorities, but any incident or disagreeable article in a French paper might lead to a different state of affairs. Moreover, if Mussolini got it into his head that he was being played with, he is, as you well know, very capable of some 'Coup de tête'. However, I have expressed my opinion clearly to Beaumarchais, and do not see how anything more can be done.

We were distressed to hear from Lady Chamberlain that she had been ill, and disappointed that her visit here is to be postponed. She will be very welcome in May, but towards the end of that month most people have left Rome and the heat may become unpleasant, but I fear there is no hope of her being able to come earlier?

Yours v. sincerely,
R. GRAHAM

No. 147

Viscount Chilston (Vienna) to Sir A. Chamberlain
(Received February 19, 7 p.m.)

No. 6 Telegraphic [*C 1301/41/3*]

VIENNA, *February 19, 1928, 2 p.m.*

Paris telegram to me of February 14th.[1]

I made representation to the Chancellor to-day[2] in support of conference's note to Austrian Minister as to the attitude of the Austrian government in regard to some of the requests made for complete disarmament.[3] French Chargé d'Affaires has acted similarly. Italian Minister has not yet received instructions.

[1] Not preserved in Foreign Office archives. According to the docket of Paris covering despatch No. 256 this telegram instructed Lord Chilston in accordance with paragraph 3 (*c*) of No. 133.

[2] This telegram was drafted on February 18.　　　　　[3] See No. 133, note 6.

The Chancellor said he had heard of the note which seemed rather a sharp one. He was evidently perturbed at the idea of notification to the League of any failures on the part of Austria but said if this were done he could justify Austria before the League. He thought conference or military committee had misunderstood Austrian attitude or had not been informed by the liquidator of explanations previously given by the Austrian authorities concerning Gross-Mittel etc., the fact that weather conditions at present made destruction very difficult: but two buildings had already been destroyed and work was now being begun on three more. Destruction of remaining fifteen would cost three million schillinge (about 88,000 pounds) which was extremely hard on the Austrian budget and difficult to explain in Parliament.

The Chancellor said he had instructed the Austrian Minister fully to explain to the conference.

Addressed to Foreign Office No. 6. Repeated to Paris No. 1.

No. 148

Viscount Chilston (Vienna) to Sir A. Chamberlain
(Received February 19, 9 p.m.)
No. 7 Telegraphic [Telegrams 48/27]

VIENNA, *February 19, 1928, 5.30 p.m.*

My immediately preceding telegram.[1]

I venture to think that Austrian Government ought not to be taken to task too much on this matter and that there is not much to be gained.

Buildings in question are not factories but old warehouses.

Second report of organ, dated 31st January ([2]apparently not yet seen by military committee when reporting to conference on 6th February,[2] shows improvement on other points.[3] I understand that no machines now remain to be destroyed and that Steyr works are now proceeding to disperse 600 of the 1,200 in question.

(Repeated to Paris.)

[1] No. 147. [2] Punctuation as in filed copy.
[3] With reference to their report of February 6 (see No. 133, note 1) the Allied Military Committee of Versailles transmitted to the Conference of Ambassadors on February 9 in their report No. 27/2 the information from Vienna that 129 machines had been destroyed and only 1206 remained for dispersal.

No. 149

Letter from Sir E. Drummond (Geneva) to Mr. Selby
[C 1467/1403/62]

GENEVA, *February 21, 1928*

My dear Selby,

I send you a record of a conversation which I had with Benes yesterday, and which I think is of interest.

You reminded me the other day that I had objected to certain information which I had sent being treated officially. I remember now to what you referred.

My objection was not that the Department was informed, but that a telegram had been sent to our Representative in Sofia, in which the information was stated to come from me, and he was asked to enquire whether it was accurate. It was that which put me in a somewhat difficult position, as, as a rule, I think that I ought to be treated as an 'unknown source' but I hope reliable.

Yours very sincerely,
ERIC DRUMMOND

ENCLOSURE IN No. 149

Record of Interview

Monsieur Benes came to see me this evening, and told me that the main reason of Monseigneur Seipel's visit to Prague[1] had been to discuss the possibilities of new arrangements in Central Europe. The Treaty between Czecho-Slovakia and Jugo-Slavia[2] came to an end during the present year, and Monsieur Benes was anxious that, in renewing it, account should be taken of the changed situation, and the dispositions of the Little Entente altered accordingly. He had found Monseigneur Seipel quite ready to entertain the idea of a Central European Locarno, and of course he did not intend to ask Austria to forego any rights which she had under the Treaty of Trianon, or the ultimate possibility of the Anschluss. He did not, however, think that he would have any difficulty in persuading Austria to enter into an arrangement for a Mutual Treaty of Non-Aggression, followed up by treaties of Arbitration. His only object was that the countries which had signed these treaties should definitely declare that they would not go to war as between each other, and would settle all disputes which arose by peaceful means. He hoped that Hungary would also agree to such a Pact. In this connection, he had already given the Hungarians definite assurances that nothing in the Pact could override Article 19 of the Covenant.

I said to him that this was very interesting; but what was the attitude of Italy towards it? I had reason to think that they would be somewhat hostile to anything which approached the reconstitution of the Austrian Empire.

Monsieur Benes replied that he feared that there might be some difficulty; but that he intended to meet it by saying to Italy, as he had already said to Germany,—'We shall be perfectly willing that you should become one of the parties to the arrangement, or, if you think that it is directed in any way against you, my country, or any other which is a party to the Pact, would be prepared to sign separate treaties of Non-Aggression, so that any fears which you may entertain will be dissipated.'

I made my previous remark to Monsieur Benes because I had had a long

---

[1] February 13–15, 1928.
[2] This treaty of friendship and alliance signed on August 14, 1920, is printed in *British and Foreign State Papers*, vol. 114, pp. 696–7.

conversation a short time ago with the Marquis Paulucci who explained that, while Locarno could only be regarded as favourable to peace because the countries concerned were so large that they could never combine into a general unity, the same might not be true of a combination of smaller countries in Central Europe, and he displayed some fear that any such Central-European Locarno might be ultimately aimed at Italy.[3]

Monsieur Benes added that he thought that this concrete proposal of his that any country which thought itself endangered by regional treaties of alliance should be allowed either to join the alliance or to conclude a treaty of Non-Aggression and Conciliation with the country of whom it was suspicious would meet the criticism expressed in the German Note against treaties of alliance.[4] For instance, the Germans took objection to the Franco-Polish alliance. The ground of their objection would, however, be taken away if they were offered the conclusion of a Conciliation and Non-Aggression Treaty as between Germany and Poland.

E. D.

February 20, 1928

[3] The reference was possibly to the conversation of which Marchese Paulucci's report is printed in *I Documenti Diplomatici Italiani*, Settima Serie, vol. vi, as No. 121.

[4] The reference was presumably to the German observations on the programme of the work of the Committee on Arbitration and Security of the Preparatory Commission for the Disarmament Conference: cf. No. 126, note 2.

No. 150

Sir A. Chamberlain to Sir R. Graham (Rome)
No. 229 [C 1481/8/22]

FOREIGN OFFICE, *February 22, 1928*

Sir,

The Italian Ambassador spoke to me to-day of the very discouraging impression made upon Signor Mussolini by his conversation with M. Beaumarchais.

I told his Excellency that I was perplexed by the conflicting accounts of the situation which I received from Paris and Rome respectively. M. Briand appeared to be optimistic and, I was confident, had every desire to place Franco-Italian relations on a better footing and every hope of doing so. All I had felt able to do was to communicate to Lord Crewe the impressions which your Excellency had derived at Rome, leaving Lord Crewe free to mention the matter to M. Briand or not as he might think most advisable. The Ambassador then turned to Tangier and enquired whether he was right in supposing that the French and Spanish Governments had reached agreement. I said that I was not quite certain whether anything had yet been actually concluded, but I understood that the last French proposals had given satisfaction in Madrid and I believed that the two Governments were in any case on the eve of agreement.[1] I understood that M. Briand thought the next step

[1] Cf. the Appendix, p. 647.

should be a meeting of the experts of the four Powers to prepare the way for a meeting of the four Ministers. This, the Ambassador said, appeared a prudent and sensible course.

Signor Bordonaro said that he had been further instructed to mention to me two questions which would be coming before the Council of the League of Nations in March. The Ambassador read to me a telegram which he had received from Signor Mussolini in which it was said that the Italian Government had continued to urge Hungary to show a reasonable and conciliatory disposition on the optants question, and Signor Mussolini had taken advantage of M. Titulesco's presence in Rome to give similar friendly advice to him.[2] He regretted, however, to learn that the conversations between M. Titulesco and M. Egri[3] had led to no agreement, and he wished me to know that, if the Hungarians pressed their demand for the nomination of the supplementary judges, the Italian vote would have to be given in their favour. He enquired what my intentions were. I said that my information unhappily coincided with his own. This being so, I presumed that, as *rapporteur*, I should have to summon the Committee of Three,[4] confirm the fact that no solution was possible between the two parties, and then resubmit the report which the Committee of Three had previously presented and of which the major portion, excluding what were called the sanctions, had already been approved by the Council.

The next question mentioned by the Ambassador was the seizure of the machine guns in Hungary. Here again the Ambassador read to me a telegram received from Signor Mussolini, which indicated that, in Signor Mussolini's view, this was an ordinary question of smuggling to which it would be a mistake to apply the procedure of a League investigation. Such investigations in his opinion should be reserved for really serious matters when peace might depend on the issue. The Ambassador was instructed to enquire my views on the subject also.

I therefore said that, in accordance with my usual practice, I must reserve any expression of opinion and full liberty of action until I knew the exact manner in which the matter would be presented to the Council, had the latest facts before me and was in a position to discuss them with my colleagues on the Council. I remarked that, within the last twenty-four hours, a new feature had been introduced into the situation by the decision of the Hungarian Government to break up these machine-gun parts and sell them as scrap. Much might turn upon what exactly the consignment consisted of. If the parts were capable of forming complete machine guns, the consignment might be an isolated incident. If on the other hand they were found to be spare parts, the affair might be regarded in a graver light since that would seem to imply that machine guns must already have been smuggled into the country in excess of what was permitted by treaty. It was therefore, I thought,

[2] See *I Documenti Diplomatici Italiani*, Settima Serie, vol. vi, No. 52.
[3] For a brief account by M. Titulesco of his conversation with M. Egry, a distinguished Hungarian lawyer, see *League of Nations Official Journal*, April 1928, p. 411.
[4] See No. 11, note 1.

important that I should not commit myself to a particular view before going to Geneva and before being completely informed of the situation.

At this point I begged the Ambassador to express to Signor Mussolini my strong hope that, in this and other matters coming before the Council, he would leave a large discretion to his representative. Signor Scialoja was a man much liked by all the Council and carrying great influence with us. Presumably he possessed Signor Mussolini's confidence and would know the general trend of his policy. Surely it was possible to trust such a man. It was very important for the practical working of the Council that its members should have a certain discretion, since in the nature of things the Council could only be effective if its members were agreed, and agreement could only be reached on the spot and by mutual consideration and accommodation. Signor Mussolini knew that, whilst not insensible to ideals, I took a very practical view of the League. I was conscious of the limitations of its influence and authority. Nevertheless it was in my opinion an immense aid to the solution of international differences and a great instrument of peace; but if we all went out narrowly bound by instructions given before our Governments were in full possession of the facts and before there had been any consultation among the members of the Council, it would be hopeless to expect agreement and the Council would really be prevented from functioning at all. I was quite certain that, if it had been possible for Signor Mussolini to take part in meetings of the Council as I had done, he would recognise the truth of what I said and, having seen the Council at work, he would agree that this discretion for the various members of the Council was necessary, and that it could be safely given to them. No doubt there were some cases in which the different representatives must receive definite instructions from their Governments, but I ventured to urge that this was both unnecessary and harmful in the case of most of the problems which the Council had to solve.

The Ambassador then enquired what view I took of the latest interchange of notes between Lithuania and Poland.[5] I told him that I thought M. Zaleski's introduction of the word '*normal*' relations was unfortunate as the Council had deliberately avoided its use, but that otherwise M. Zaleski's attitude had been moderate and reasonable and he had shown himself to be sincerely desirous of coming to an arrangement with Lithuania. M. Valdemaras's reply was discouraging, and I thought it not improbable that the Council would have to take up the question again.[6]

The Ambassador was then about to leave, but I took the opportunity of speaking to him about the Italian proposal to take coal in discharge of reparations.[7] I said that His Majesty's Government frankly recognised that they had no right or ground to make any protest against this proposal, but

[5] For notes of January 8 and February 9 from M. Zaleski to Professor Voldemaras and for the latter's note of January 16, *v. op. cit.*, pp. 577–80; for Professor Voldemaras' note of February 26, *v. ibid.*, pp. 580–1.

[6] For consideration of this question by the Council of the League of Nations on March 9, *v. ibid.*, pp. 430–1.   [7] See below, No. 151.

the reparation coal would take the place of coal which had previously been bought from this country and the change would be a serious blow to a British industry which, as he knew, was actually in a position of great difficulty. I would venture to express the hope that, if the Italian Government could find any other way to secure their proper share of reparations or could in any way alleviate the blow to British industry, they would do so, and we should be very grateful. In this connexion, I asked the Ambassador whether the Italian Government had ever considered proceeding on the lines of our own Reparation Recovery Act. As the Ambassador was unacquainted with this Act, I briefly explained to him its nature, and I undertook to send him a copy of it as it might in any case be of interest to Signor Mussolini. To[8] provide for the rather unlikely event of my having to recur to the subject, I enclose for your information a copy of Cmd. Paper No. 2384, 1925,[9] being the text of an agreement which is now in force between the British and German Governments for amending the method of administering the Reparation Recovery Act, together with a copy of a Memorandum[10] showing the origin of this agreement.[11]

I am, &c.,

AUSTEN CHAMBERLAIN

[8] This sentence appears in the approved draft of this despatch but not in the Confidential print which is the only other text preserved in the file.

[9] Not printed: see No. 16, note 7.

[10] See No. 16, note 3.

[11] Copies of the German Reparation (Recovery) Act and of the Anglo-German agreement of amendment were sent to Signor Bordonaro on February 23.

No. 151

Sir A. Chamberlain to Sir R. Graham (Rome)

No. 20 Telegraphic [C 1377/1175/18]

Immediate   FOREIGN OFFICE, *February 23, 1928, 5.30 p.m.*

My despatches Nos. 180[1] and 204[2] (of February 16th. Italo-German Coal Convention of December 22nd, 1927).

British coal owning and exporting interests are much alarmed at probable effect of Italo-German Coal Convention of December 22nd, 1927, if it

[1] Not preserved in Foreign Office archives. This despatch presumably transmitted a copy of a letter from the Transfer Committee about the agreement of December 22, 1927, operative from February 21, 1928, between the Italian Government and the Rhineland Westphalian Coal Syndicate for an extra supply of one million tons of coal on reparation account as a rider to a contract of March 5, 1925. On January 28, 1928, the Transfer Committee adopted a resolution raising objections to the agreement.

[2] This despatch of February 20 (not preserved in Foreign Office archives) transmitted copies (not printed) of (i) correspondence of February 1–14 between the Foreign Office and the Board of Trade relating in particular to rumours that Italy would buy an extra 6–7 million tons of coal from Germany; (ii) Berlin despatch No. 144 of February 15, in which Sir R. Lindsay reported that it would be possible for Germany to export an extra 5–6 million tons of coal.

materialises, and have now asked that His Majesty's Government should if possible take some action with a view to preventing capture in this manner of Italian coal market by Germany.

Present position as regards Convention will be clear to you from enclosures to my despatch No. 180.

As the Transfer Committee is now making difficulties about approving convention in its present form it has been thought possible that Italian government might be more ready than previously to consider other methods for developing power of absorbing increased reparation receipts and might indeed be prepared in the circumstances to adopt the alternative procedure provided by a Reparation Recovery Act or rather by an agreement in lieu of such act similar to agreements concluded with German government by the British and French governments (see Germany print, November 7th, 1927, section 2[3] and Cmd. 2384, 1925).

Unofficial suggestions in this sense have already been made by Treasury to Counsellor of Italian Embassy and by British Delegation, Reparation Commission, to the Italian representative on that body.

I also took opportunity to refer to the subject on similar lines at interview with Italian Ambassador on February 22nd,[4] while frankly recognising that we had no legal right to protest against Convention.

In view of these new developments I consider it necessary that you should lose no time in calling urgent attention of Italian government to strong feeling which has been aroused in British coal trade by proposals which, if made effective, would replace British by German coal on the Italian market, and while recognising that we have no *locus standi* for objecting express hope that they may be able to find some method of securing their share of German reparations less harmful to British interests: urging in this connexion favourable consideration of alternative procedure of reparation recovery act as less injurious to British coal exports and at the same time possibly more advantageous from Italian point of view. Amount received by His Majesty's Government under Reparation Recovery Act procedure to January 31st, 1928, over £55,000,000.

Despatch[5] follows: but please act immediately since Transfer Committee meets again February 27th and it would be helpful to know the views of the Italian government on the above suggestions before that date.[6]

---

[3] The reference was to copies of (i) Mr. Huxley's memorandum of September 8, 1927 (see No. 16, note 3); (ii) the letter from the Treasury of November 5, 1927 (see No. 16, note 15); (iii) an undated Treasury memorandum (not printed) on the action taken by other Governments in regard to legislation similar to the Reparation Recovery Act.

[4] See No. 150.

[5] The reference was probably to Foreign Office covering despatch No. 227 of February 24 (not preserved in Foreign Office archives) which transmitted a letter of February 20 from the Board of Trade (not printed) proposing the instructions to Sir R. Graham in the present telegram.

[6] In Rome telegram No. 24 of February 27, Sir R. Graham reported that he had seen Signor Mussolini who was very sympathetic about the difficult position of the British coal industry and intended to discuss the situation with his colleagues. On February 29, as

reported in Rome telegram No. 27, the Commercial Counsellor, Mr. Rawlins, was told by officials of the Ministry of Finance that it was impossible for Italy to adopt a scheme for a reparation recovery act owing to the strained relations between Italy and Germany and Germany's inability to undertake further financial commitments. Italy was however ready to examine any plan which H.M. Government could suggest by which Italy could receive cash payments from Germany.

No. 152

Letter from Sir R. Graham (Rome) to Sir A. Chamberlain

Copy   [C 1652/8/22]

Private and Confidential   ROME, *February 24, 1928*

My dear Sir Austen,

With reference to your private letter of February 20[1] and Lord Crewe's private letter to you of February 17,[2] which you were good enough to send me, on the subject of Franco-Italian conversations, I am at a loss to know on what MM. Briand and Berthelot base their rosy views. But I can assure you that my account of feeling here is the correct one. I have had this confirmed from a variety of sources, but today, to make quite sure, when I was seeing Grandi, I induced him to open the subject without alluding to it myself.

De Beaumarchais paid a formal visit of a few minutes to Signor Mussolini on his first arrival, and subsequently had the interview recorded in my telegram No. 14[3] of February 8. Since then he has not been to the Palazzo Chigi at all; there have been no further conversations, although on one occasion when he saw Guariglia[4] he expressed his hopes of coming to an agreement. Grandi said that, as Bordonaro would probably have already told you, Signor Mussolini was seriously disappointed and disillusioned. He had at one moment been angry, but had now concluded that it would be best to treat the matter as a bad joke. Grandi then added that he would be most indiscreet, and, after ringing for a secretary, produced and gave me to read Mussolini's own dictated minute on his conversation with de Beaumarchais.[5]

The conversation opened on the subject of the press, de Beaumarchais assuring Mussolini that he ought not to take articles in the 'Temps' or other papers, by writers of little repute, too seriously. They were not expressions of Government opinion. The conversation then rather languished, but came round to Franco-Italian relations, and the question of which of the two Governments should take the initiative in trying to improve them. De Beaumarchais said that Manzoni had been expected to make some move. Mussolini replied that if this were the point he was perfectly ready to take the initiative himself. He was most anxious not only for good relations and an understanding with France, but even for something closer, if it did not conflict with the provisions and spirit of the Locarno Agreement. De Beaumarchais said that some Italian pretensions, as advanced by the Italian press,

[1] Not printed.   [2] No. 145.   [3] No. 131.
[4] Director-General of Political, Commercial and Private Affairs of Europe and the Levant in the Italian Ministry of Foreign Affairs.
[5] See *I Documenti Diplomatici Italiani*, Settima Serie, vol. vi, No. 68.

appeared excessive, and he quoted claims on the French mandate in Syria. Mussolini replied that he had never thought of Syria, and would not take it if it were offered to him. The points at issue were Tangier, which he believed to be almost settled, Italian residents in France and Tunis, some slight rectification of the Tripolitan frontier, and Italy's position in the Adriatic and the Balkans. Italian pretensions were by no means excessive and it ought not to be difficult to satisfy them. At this point it became clear that de Beaumarchais had no instructions enabling him to open discussions. He said that he was much interested, but that he could not report all this to Paris, and would wait until he went there on leave at Easter in order to discuss them at the Quai d'Orsay. Mussolini, as recorded in my telegram No. 14, was much dashed and disappointed. He minuted that this meant a delay of three months, although he does not seem to have said so to de Beaumarchais. His Excellency's minute concluded by an expression of the view that the French evidently did not mean business, at any rate until after the elections, and that once again French internal political considerations were preventing an agreement between France and Italy. He ended with the words '*dont acte*'.

The above was the minute to the best of my recollection, but I only had the opportunity of reading it once and hastily. I told Signor Grandi that I had reason to believe that both M. Briand and M. Berthelot were optimistic and in a most friendly mood. Grandi replied that on these occasions the language came from Briand and the deeds from Berthelot.

So *that* anyhow is the feeling here, and it does not seem that Campbell's speed record on the sands of Florida[6] is likely to be threatened by de Beaumarchais as a swift negotiator; but you have evidently done all you could in Paris, and I have done all I can with de Beaumarchais here. Possibly the Geneva meeting in March may give an opportunity for a fresh push?

Yours v. sincerely,
R. GRAHAM

[6] On February 19 Captain Malcolm Campbell had set up a world land speed record of 207 m.p.h. at Daytona Beach, Florida.

No. 153

Sir R. Graham (Rome) to Sir A. Chamberlain
(Received February 26, 9 a.m.)

No. 21 Telegraphic [C 1502/179/22]

ROME, *February 25, 1928, 9.30 p.m.*

Interpellations in Austrian national council regarding Upper Adige and chancellor's reply[1] have caused a strong reaction in Italian press.

A violent parliamentary question has been put down for forthcoming meeting of Italian Chamber.

Signor Grandi told me today that Italian government were dissatisfied

[1] For an account of Mgr. Seipel's statement on February 23, see *The Times*, February 25, 1928, p. 11; see also Mgr. Seipel's speech of February 17, *op. cit.*, February 18, p. 11.

with Monsignor Seipel's attitude in view of help which Italy had throughout accorded to Austria. As a mark of disapproval Italian minister had been instructed to come to Rome and remain on leave. But Italian government recognise Monsignor Seipel's difficult position, also that the trouble came not from Austrians but from Herr Stresemann who kept this question alive in order to further his policy of rapprochement to France by persuading German nationalists that Italians were impossible people to deal with. This was part of his policy and Italian government did not complain.

Signor Mussolini would take an early opportunity in the chamber of stating actual situation with firmness and in its true light.

I urged that this statement even if firm should be as moderate and conciliatory as possible.[2]

Addressed to Foreign Office No. 21, repeated to Vienna.[3]

[2] Sir R. Graham reported in Rome telegram No. 23 of February 27 that he had spoken similarly to Signor Mussolini. On March 9 he reported in Rome despatch No. 203 that his German and Austrian colleagues appeared 'well satisfied' that Signor Mussolini's speech of March 3 to the Italian Chamber [v. op. cit., March 5, p. 14] was not couched in more violent terms.

[3] In connection with this matter Sir A. Chamberlain minuted on February 27 that he attached 'no credence to the idea that Germany is *using* Austria—she may, probably she must support her in a certain measure'. Sir A. Chamberlain also stated with reference to a preceding minute by Mr. Howard Smith: 'The "strong feeling growing up" here about the Tyrol will not help the Tyrolese. Nor will Chancellor Seipel's speech nor Austrian parl[iamen]t[ar]y demonstrations. *If* it is possible to help at all, we must proceed quite differently. The battle is between good sense & political wisdom on the one side & human nature on the other. The onlooker sees most of the game & notes all the faults on both sides. But let us be very careful how & when we speak.'

No. 154

Letter from Mr. Sargent to Sir R. Graham (Rome)[1]

[C 1580/1580/22]

Private and very confidential   FOREIGN OFFICE, *February 25, 1928*

Dear Sir Ronald,

We have for some time been receiving information from secret sources that points to the fact that the Italian Government, or at any rate Italian agents, are encouraging and possibly assisting the Macedonian Revolutionary Organisation in their terrorist campaign, and are facilitating the use of Albania as a new base of operations for the Macedonians. I enclose herein a memorandum[2] which we have had prepared which summarises roughly the secret information which we have received.

It seems fairly clear that the Yugoslavs firmly believe that the Italians are encouraging the Macedonians, because, as you will see from our despatch No. 42[3] of the 30th January to Belgrade, the Yugoslav Minister told me that when the Protocol extending the duration of the Pact of Rome was signed at

[1] The approved draft of this letter is the only text preserved in the Foreign Office file.
[2] Not printed.   [3] Not preserved in Foreign Office archives.

Belgrade towards the end of January M. Marinkovitch had taken the opportunity to remind Bodrero that according to this Pact the Yugoslav Government expect to be able to count upon the assistance and support of the Italian Government both at Sofia and at Tirana in their efforts to prevent the Macedonian Committee from using Bulgarian and Albanian territory for their terrorist campaign in Southern Serbia. We do not know what reply if any was made by the Italian Government to Marinkovitch's remarks, and it may be that Bodrero never reported them to Rome.

Meanwhile you will have seen from our despatch No. 160[4] of February 13th that Sir Austen took the opportunity of the visit paid him by the Albanian M.F.A. to hint very plainly to Ilias Bey that the Albanians ought to be careful to see that the Macedonian Revolutionary Organisation did not compromise Albania by using Albanian territory as a basis for their nefarious machinations in Southern Serbia. It is not unlikely that this warning of the Secretary of State will have been reported to Mussolini. As however we cannot be sure of this, we have been wondering whether the time has not come to consider the possibility of our intimating direct to Mussolini that the S[ecretary of] S[tate] is aware of these intrigues and strongly disapproves of them.

We are of course assuming, as I think we must, that our information is sufficiently circumstantial to prove the existence of such intrigues. But we have nothing to show what the motive power behind them is. Do they emanate directly from the Italian Government and are being carried on with the knowledge and approval of Mussolini, or are they the unauthorised work of over-zealous officials and secret agents? But a hint to Mussolini would it seems to us, come in equally useful in either case.

The Secretary of State suggests that his recent conversation with Ilias Bey might afford you a convenient pretext for raising the question with Mussolini. For instance, you might take an early opportunity of telling him of Ilias Bey's visit to Sir Austen and what the latter had said to him regarding the danger of Albania allowing herself to be used as a base of operations by Macedonian terrorists; and then see how he reacts. He ought to regard a communication of this kind ought [sic] as a further proof of our recognition of Italy's special position in Albania and of our determination to do nothing in that country behind her back. The Secretary of State's justification for giving his warning to Ilias Bey would of course be the interest which we have always claimed to have in the maintenance of Albanian independence. Should Albania be allowed to become the basis for the Macedonian Revolutionary Organisation's operations in Southern Serbia through the supineness or connivance of the Albanian Government, the independence of the country would clearly be placed in serious jeopardy, and that for a cause of which the Italian Government have themselves publicly disapproved in the representations which they made to the Bulgarian Government last November.[5]

[4] Not preserved in Foreign Office archives. This despatch transmitted to Rome a copy of No. 135.

[5] See *I Documenti Diplomatici Italiani*, Settima Serie, vol. v, Nos. 523 and 560.

In these circumstances it seems to us that Mussolini could hardly take umbrage at a communication made to him on these lines. You would of course not suggest that the Italian Government are, or are suspected of being, in any way implicated with the Macedonian Revolutionary Organisation, but if Mussolini knows what is going on he will surely be quick enough to realise what your object is in making the communication, and the warning may give him pause. If, on the other hand, he does not know what his subordinates are doing, a communication on these lines may lead him to look into the matter and pull up his over-zealous officials.

This is of course an exceedingly delicate matter, but we cannot help feeling that we may be laying up a good deal of further trouble for ourselves if we allow the Italians to involve themselves still deeper in this dangerous intrigue, without doing anything to make them realise that we know what they are up to and thoroughly disapprove of the dangerous game they are playing. My first idea when I put forward the suggestion that something should be said to the Italians was that the Secretary of State might possibly do it through Bordonaro, but Sir Austen thinks that it would be better and that a hint such as he has in view would be more effective if conveyed personally by you to Mussolini. At the same time he directs that you should have the fullest discretion to speak or to refrain from speaking to him, as you think best, and this is the reason why I have embodied this rather long story in a private letter.

O. G. S.

No. 155

Letter from Sir R. Lindsay (Berlin) to Mr. Sargent (Received March 2)
[*C 1709/307/18*]

BERLIN, *February 27, 1928*

Dear Sargent,

With the approach of the Standard Reparation Year,[1] a question is becoming acute which has been mentioned in previous correspondence, viz., that of extending the scope of the Reparation Recovery Act so that the 26% shall be calculated on all German imports into the Empire instead of on imports into the United Kingdom alone. The Treasury are anxious to bring about this change because they consider that it will materially help His Majesty's Government to absorb their reparation payments in the months after August next, when those payments increase considerably. The exact importance of the operation is only to be described in somewhat technical language and this is best done by the Treasury, to whom I would leave it therefore to demonstrate the advantages which may result from success. I propose to address myself now to some broader considerations of policy which are involved.

There will be opposition to overcome, possibly some from Parker Gilbert, certainly a great deal from the German Government. Behind the latter will

[1] i.e. the fifth year of operation of the Dawes Plan, 1928–9.

be Schacht fighting the proposal tooth and nail. The importance of his attitude can be adequately estimated by the Treasury.

I think the question should be broached to Gilbert by the Treasury when he visits London in the next few days[2] in any case and without our having necessarily decided whether or not we intend to pursue the matter further. To speak to Gilbert does not commit His Majesty's Government to go on with the negotiation in its further stages, and the opportunity of sounding him out is a favourable one which should not be lost. If he were to veto it out of hand I imagine there would be nothing more to be said; but to judge by his attitude when the matter was mentioned before, I expect he would express considerable distaste but go no further than reserve his full right to take whatever view of the scheme he might think proper if and when the Germans accept it. Such an attitude should not I think debar us from approaching the German Government. Gilbert's reactions, however, would require to be carefully observed, and of course if negotiations with the Germans were prosecuted it would be necessary for this Embassy to keep him in touch with them as might be suitable.

The Germans can be trusted to resist strenuously. It is a cardinal feature of their policy to refuse consent to any concession or to any extension of existing agreements of a nature to facilitate reparation payments, and this is of course natural enough. Furthermore, we should be dealing first with a Government just going out of office before a general election, and afterwards with a new Government, probably of the Left parties, unwilling to open its career by infringing the cardinal principle enunciated above and by exposing itself thus to just the form of criticism which a Nationalist opposition would most delight in. Quite possibly they would be open to a deal, but I can think of no quid pro quo to offer, and they would certainly open their mouths very wide. Failing the possibility of buying their consent, we should have to exert very considerable pressure and our best, if not only, leverage would be to play on their reluctance to alienate our sympathies and lose our assistance in general European politics. Even then it might be impossible to overcome their passive resistance. We should have to show a great deal of determination.

The broad question for decision by the Foreign Office and Treasury together is whether the advantages which would result from the extension of the Reparation Recovery Act are worth the effort which would be required to obtain the German consent to that measure and still more, the international friction which will be caused by that effort. I myself am rather in favour of having a shot at it (a) because so far as I can understand it, we have a very good case for demanding the extension of the Act, (b) because we have helped the Germans a good deal in the past and I think they owe us something, and (c) because I am not convinced that any serious disadvantages would accrue if we tried and failed. The Germans might feel sore but I hardly think they would be inclined to retaliate, even if they could find some field in which to retaliate. They are too much dependent on our goodwill in general European policy.

[2] This projected visit did not take place at this time.

In case it is decided to make the attempt, a suggestion may be made as to procedure. It would probably be best to present the German Government pretty soon, say end of March or early April, with a formal proposal and a fully elaborated scheme. It would be unnecessary and useless to press this strongly on the present Government, but an effort might be made to bring about discussion between experts from the technical point of view. The real negotiations should be pressed as soon as the new Government had got into the saddle. This timetable should enable us to judge by July or August whether we were going to succeed or fail.

Yours sincerely,
R. C. LINDSAY

No. 156

Mr. Leeper (Warsaw) to Sir A. Chamberlain (Received March 5)

No. 76 [N 1262/8/55]

WARSAW, *February 29, 1928*

Sir,

I have the honour to report that yesterday I had a long conversation with Mr Frank Symonds [*sic*],[1] the American publicist, who has been in Warsaw for the last ten days chiefly in order to study Polish-German relations and to judge what role Poland is likely to play in Europe both politically and economically within the next few years.

2. Mr Symonds told me that he had come to Poland from Western Europe and Germany with the impression that the questions of the Corridor and Upper Silesia might within a few years' time be revised. His impression in France was that a Franco-German rapprochement would make rapid strides within the next year or two, and that France might gradually, in return for other concessions, disinterest herself in the question of the Corridor. By the year 1930 when the Germans looked for a settlement of Reparations and Debts questions and to the evacuation of the Rhineland by France they might be ready to raise the question of their eastern frontiers and they counted mainly on the benevolent attitude of Great Britain. In his (Mr Symonds') opinion the latter was the decisive factor. Opinion in England was greatly impressed by the rapid recovery of Germany and the weakness of Poland in comparison with her neighbour. There was the same tendency in England as in America to treat with scant respect or interest anything that lay east of Germany. He had, therefore, come to Poland to judge to what extent she must be taken seriously into the calculations of other countries.

3. What had impressed him most since he came to Poland was the unanimity of Polish opinion on the questions of the Corridor and Upper Silesia. There was literally nobody to be found who would entertain the idea of any revision of frontiers, and, what is more, there was not the slightest doubt that Poland would fight rather than yield to any outside decision on these questions. In such circumstances he was convinced that to play with the idea of a

[1] Mr. Simonds was foreign editor of *The American Review of Reviews*.

revision of frontiers was to play with real fire, sufficiently real to start another European conflagration.

4. Mr Symonds asked me whether he was overrating the strength of Polish opinion on these points. I assured him that he was not. If a stay of a few days in Poland had impressed him in this sense, a stay of a few months would carry his conviction still further. Mr Symonds, thereupon, told me that I was merely confirming what the German Minister in Warsaw had told him, namely that no Pole would compromise on the question of the Corridor. Herr Rauscher had also added that Upper Silesia would settle itself without any political changes, as the Polish coal interests would sooner or later join the same cartel with the Germans.

5. We then turned to the question of Poland's economic and political stability. The American loan to Poland,[2] said Mr Symonds, had produced a remarkable change in Germany. In German eyes Poland was now a going concern and Germans were anxious to secure the maximum advantages from the Polish market. The American loan must not be regarded as a sign of American confidence in Poland. There was a superfluity of money in America and with superfluous money one enjoyed the privilege of a gamble. This Polish loan which had started as a gamble seemed likely to end as very good business. Mr Dewey, the American adviser to the Bank of Poland, was optimistic and from his personal observations he thought this optimism justified. Mr Dewey was, as it were, the link between London and Warsaw. Would he adopt the view of the City or that of the Poles, or could he steer a middle course?

6. In reply to this question I said that on the occasion of a recent visit paid by a representative of the Bank of England to Warsaw I had had some conversation both with him and with Mr Dewey on this very point. The Bank of England had not favoured the present loan which, in their opinion, should have been put through under the aegis of the League of Nations, but it was not the practice of the Bank of England to sulk for long when their advice was not taken, and they were already following with attention and sympathy Mr Dewey's progress. First impressions had been good. The social stability of Poland was reassuring, and, if all went well financially for the next two or three years, international finance would open its coffers to Poland.

7. Mr Dewey for his part, I continued, had assured me that he regarded it as one of his main tasks to build a bridge between London and Warsaw. Unless he had achieved this at the end of his three years in Warsaw he would not feel that he had fully accomplished his mission.

8. Mr Symonds then turned to Polish politics which, he said, was more familiar ground to him than that of finance. Mr Dewey was inclined to brush aside political considerations on the ground that, if the country were economically stable, politics might continue to be changeable, but would not become dangerous. This he could not altogether accept. The political future of Poland was most uncertain. The dictatorship must be brought to an end as soon as

[2] The greater part of a stabilization loan of 70 million dollars secured by the Polish Government in October 1927 had been covered by a group of American bankers.

possible. He admitted that Marshal Pilsudski still controlled the machine, but, the longer the machine functioned, the more would it control its inventor. It was the same under every dictatorship and Poland would prove no exception. He had heard that Marshal Pilsudski was thinking of borrowing for Poland many leaves out of the American Constitution. This would, he felt sure, be most unwise. He doubted whether the working of the American Constitution was understood anywhere abroad, least of all in Poland. What then was the way out of the present impasse?

9. On the eve of the elections, the results of which are most uncertain, this question was not an easy one to answer. One can only consider possibilities in order to show that every exit from the present position is not yet closed. The new Diet, I said, is really being summoned as a kind of Constituent Assembly to change the Constitution. Marshal Pilsudski has the direct support of the Centre and part of the Right for this purpose. If he can come to terms with the Socialists—and the latter seem to be showing themselves more amenable —he may secure a working majority to effect the necessary changes. The common opinion is that the Diet would then have fulfilled its functions and could properly be dissolved in order to permit of new elections towards the end of the year. These further elections might give Marshal Pilsudski an opportunity of freeing himself from his present abnormal position and putting himself as a party leader at the head of a Centre–Left parliamentary government. In any case even if the changes in the Constitution were far from ideal it is better that they should be introduced quickly rather than allow the present dictatorship to continue indefinitely. There are already many signs of unwarranted interference on the part of the dictator's subordinates in different spheres of life in which government should not meddle to make it desirable that a halt should be called as soon as possible to the present system.

10. I have ventured to report this conversation at some length in order to convey the views of an intelligent foreign observer on the position of Poland in the general picture of European politics. Mr Symonds' view that Germany is more impressed by the stability of Poland than England is and that Germany will accept the *status quo* as regards her eastern frontiers provided England shows no signs of yielding to the propaganda in favour of revision appear[s] to me of some importance. It is difficult to appreciate these movements of opinion from Warsaw, and I have, therefore, thought it more useful to record the more objective impressions of an outsider coming to Warsaw than those of people like myself, who, from longer residence here, cannot fail to have their views in some measure coloured by the influence of their surroundings.

11. I am sending a copy of this despatch to His Majesty's Ambassador at Berlin.[3]

I have, &c.,

R. A. LEEPER

[3] In a minute of March 6, Mr. Collier expressed his agreement with the views of Mr. Simonds set out in paragraph 3 above but his disagreement with those in paragraph 10. Mr. Collier commented: 'Both the Poles and the Germans know that, apart from our

obligations under the League Covenant, we will not fight either to change the frontier or to preserve it; and they know, too, that nothing short of a threat to fight would stop the Germans from altering the frontier if they saw their opportunity to do so, or the Poles from fighting to preserve it, if an attempt were made to alter it by anything short of overwhelming force.' Mr. Huxley suggested in a minute of the following day the possibility that the German attitude on the eastern frontier might become less rigid.

No. 157

Memorandum by Mr. Perowne

[C 1735/394/18]

FOREIGN OFFICE, *March 2, 1928*

The withdrawal from Berlin of the Allied Military Control Experts

A. . . .[1]

Subsequently a number of visits were successfully carried out. At the invitation of the German Government visits were paid to alienated military establishments in the occupied territory and to the dismantled fortifications in the Rhineland (this question is finished with until further evacuation takes place), as well as to certain police establishments elsewhere. Since the end of November 1927, however, no visits have taken place and there is little doubt that the Germans intend that no more shall be paid if they can be avoided. The C[omité] M[ilitaire] A[llié de] V[ersailles] have, on the other hand, recently declared in an 'avis' which is at present before the Ambassadors' Conference[2] that visits are still required in connexion with four points (if the experts are to be able to guarantee the execution of those points):

(1) Alienation of excess military establishments; an arrangement for the final settlement of this point now awaits the approval of the Ambassadors' Conference.

(2) Stocks of reserve rations. The Germans declare that these stocks have now been reduced to the scale laid down by the Control Commission.

(3) Coast batteries. These are now said to comply with the Allied requirements.

[1] The first six paragraphs of this memorandum are omitted as they were the same as the second to sixth paragraphs of No. 76, subject to minor verbal variation and to the third paragraph of the present memorandum including, after the passage corresponding to the second sentence of the fourth paragraph of No. 76 (ending 'in other cases visits of inspection may be necessary'), 'It is possible accordingly to divide the points the settlement of which was entrusted to the experts into two classes: (I.) those where visits of inspection are required, and (II.) those where documentary evidence suffices.' The heading '(I.) Points where visits are necessary' followed, introducing the fourth paragraph which began as in the third sentence of the fourth paragraph of No. 76, 'A dispute soon arose', &c.

[2] Report No. 52/1 of February 17, received in the Foreign Office on February 22 under cover of Paris despatch No. 303 of February 21, is not printed. The *avis* explained that in December 1926 about 1100 German military establishments had still to be alienated or transformed and that the 1927 programme of alienation was in arrear. The report suggested that German proposals for a four-year programme could be accepted on certain conditions but stated that it was impossible to guarantee that it had been carried out without examination by the experts of the sales contracts or a visit to the sites: see below.

(4) The allocation of police effectives as soon as agreement shall have been reached regarding this point.

(II). Points where documentary evidence suffices.

As regards the larger class of points where documentary evidence is sufficient, progress has also been made since February 1927. It is impossible briefly to state the present position in respect of these points, which are largely ones of detail but include the training of staff officers, the Stahlhelm manual, etc. The only point of any practical importance relates to the police laws of the various German States and the administrative measures (Ausfuhrung[s]-bestimmungen) devolving therefrom. The texts of seven of these laws have yet to be received; the remaining nine laws are either already in force after approval by the Ambassadors' Conference or are under consideration by the Allied authorities. Only two laws of any importance are still completely outstanding (Thuringia and Hamburg).

Such then is in brief the present position with regard to the work of the Allied control experts; it remains however to consider the question of their withdrawal from Germany.

On September 9th, 1927, the War Office proposed that a date should be fixed for the withdrawal of the experts from Berlin, and that the German Government should be notified accordingly. Certain correspondence followed as a result of which it was agreed that no such notification was necessary and that any intervention on the part of the Allied Governments was inadvisable, it being for the German Government rather than for the Allied Powers to raise in the first instance the question of withdrawal. For the time being, the negotiations should be left in the hands of the experts.

An early withdrawal was however desirable from every point of view. In the nature of things this early withdrawal must take place before the full programme contained in the C.M.A.V. letter of February 3rd, 1927,[3] could have been carried out; it was obviously necessary that a stage should be fixed at which withdrawal could be effected. Colonel Gosset was accordingly instructed to try for a settlement as follows:—

The experts would be withdrawn when:— . . .[4]

These are the lines upon which Colonel Gosset has been working since last Autumn, but while distinct progress has been recorded the precise stage defined in his instructions has not yet been reached. The dates at which it has from time to time been estimated that the experts' work would be concluded have progressively receded (the latest suggestion is January 1st, 1929); difficulties are being made about 'visits' in cases where work has been concluded and inspections have been considered advisable; while progress in other directions has been halting.

However that may be, it is the desire of both the War Office and the Foreign Office, and hence the policy of H.M. Government that the experts should be withdrawn as soon as possible. Their continued presence at Berlin

---

[3] Cf. No. 76.

[4] The remaining part of this paragraph was the same as the corresponding portion ending 'the experts are withdrawn' of the ninth paragraph of No. 76, subject to minor verbal variation.

is expensive and no longer of genuine practical value to the ex-Allies, nor is it conducive to the general prosperity of the relations between the latter and the German Government.

Broadly speaking the majority of points of real importance from the British point of view have already been disposed of or are in a fair way to settlement. On the other hand, the presence of the experts has a distinct 'nuisance value' to the Germans which affords an additional reason for the latter to procrastinate over the negotiations for the settlement of the outstanding points.

The C.M.A.V. in a recent 'avis' declared that it would be impossible for the experts to guarantee that the proposed arrangements with regard to the alienation of military establishments had actually been carried out without a visit or inspection of the sales contracts in each case, and that visits would also be necessary in connexion with the coast batteries, the reserve rations and the distribution of police effectives.

This 'avis' is now before the Ambassadors' Conference. Lord Crewe has been instructed that 'inspections of sales contracts and visits of investigation cannot be demanded of the German Government as of right and it is for the allied experts at Berlin to endeavour privately to negotiate with their German colleagues a satisfactory arrangement regarding these matters. Should the German Government be prepared to offer facilities for the inspection of contracts or the making of visits H.M. Government will needless to say be happy to join in availing themselves of such facilities but it is their view that no request for such facilities should be included in any official communication to the German authorities and that there can finally be no question of the maintenance in Berlin of the experts with the sole object either of inspecting contracts or making visits of investigation, or of bringing pressure to bear on the German Government to facilitate such inspections or investigations.

'This being the situation in which the ex-Allied Governments find themselves the experts in Berlin cannot be expected and should not be required to "guarantee" the execution of any of the military clauses of the Treaty.[5] All that they need do in performance of their mission is to receive from the German authorities such assurances and proofs as they are prepared to offer and to report to the Allied Military Committee of Versailles as to the value which they consider ought to be attached to such assurances and proofs.'[6]

There seems no reason to anticipate that these views will not prevail when the 'avis' is considered by the Ambassadors' Conference though the French military authorities demurred to accepting, during the negotiations which preceded the submission of the 'avis' to the Ambassadors' Conference, a British suggestion that neither inspection of sale contracts nor visits ought to be asked for in connection with the particular matter of the alienated establishments.

[5] Of Versailles.

[6] The foregoing instructions were included in Sir A. Chamberlain's despatch No. 388 to Paris of February 18 which further stated that His Majesty's Government did not consider the question of military establishments to be one of primary importance.

None of the questions mentioned in the 'avis' is considered of primary importance and 'visits' while doubtless desirable, can perfectly well be waived from our point of view in all four instances. In fact, as indicated earlier in this memorandum, the only point to which the War Office attach any real importance *is the police question*. In a private letter to Colonel Gosset dated February 14th, Colonel McGrath wrote: '. . .[7] I am sure that we will not agree to your remaining [in Berlin][7] once the police question has made sufficient progress to be assured of a satisfactory solution. Assuming that such a situation will have been reached as soon as the Prussian, Bavarian, Saxon and Thuringian laws have been passed and the necessary administrative measures approved, when do you estimate that this will be?'

From Colonel Gosset's letter of reply[8] and earlier statements made to him in conversation by Hauptmann Doberg and Herr Fo[r]ster,[9] it seems that this stage will have been reached by July or August next. Colonel McGrath in any case expects to be able to raise the whole question of the withdrawal of the experts by next June, by which time there will presumably be further progress to report in connexion also with the other outstanding disarmament points.

For the present then, there is nothing to be done but to allow the experts to continue their negotiations without interference from the governments on either side. There is no reason to suppose that the matter will be raised at Geneva. If however Herr Stresemann should broach the question of the withdrawal of the experts it is suggested that it might be indicated to him that, while H.M. Government agree that an early withdrawal is eminently desirable, a number of points still remain for settlement, and that while negotiations should continue as before between the experts on both sides, a less dilatory and more helpful attitude on the part of the German authorities would inevitably contribute to hasten forward the day on which the allied experts can be withdrawn.

Should occasion present itself for mentioning the matter in conversation with *M. Briand*, stress might be laid on the desirability in the general interest of an early withdrawal of the experts from Berlin, accompanied by a hint that this object will more readily be achieved if the French refrain from insisting too much on points of detail.

It may be added in conclusion that the Belgians and Italians do not at present play any very outstanding role in connexion with the work of the control experts at Berlin. The Belgian expert, whose speciality was fortifications, has been withdrawn and his place taken by an officer from the Belgian Army of Occupation. The Italian expert has also left and his duties have devolved upon the Italian military attaché at Berlin, Colonel Rossi. Both Colonel Rossi and the Belgian officer attend meetings (the Belgian travelling up from the Rhineland *ad hoc*) but do not otherwise 'function'. The

[7] Punctuation as in original quotation.

[8] This letter of February 18 is not printed.

[9] Captain Doberg, a German expert on fortifications and armaments, was assistant to General von Pawelsz. Dr. Forster was a counsellor in the German Ministry of Foreign Affairs.

negotiations and activities vis-à-vis the German authorities in general are now the sole prerogative of Colonel Gosset and Commandant Durand, the French expert.

J. V. Perowne

No. 158

The Marquess of Crewe (Paris) to Sir A. Chamberlain (Received March 5)

No. 372 [C 1748/394/18]

Paris, *March 3, 1928*

Sir,

With reference to your despatch No. 388[1] (C 1202/394/18) of February 18th, I have the honour to inform you that on February 27th I caused to be communicated to the Ambassadors' Conference a memorandum on the question of the German military establishments. Copies of this memorandum are enclosed herein.[2]

2. On March 2nd a member of my staff had an interview with M. Massigli, Secretary to the French delegation to the Conference, in regard to this matter. M. Massigli said that the French delegation was in complete agreement with all the observations contained in paragraph 3 of this Embassy's memorandum respecting the rights of the interested governments with regard to inspections of documents and on the ground. It should be noted, however, that the German government had asked for a fresh concession in the matter of the military establishments (see paragraph 4 of the Versailles Committee's letter to the Conference of February 17).[3] In admitting that concession, as suggested in paragraph 5 of the Versailles Committee's letter, there seemed no reason why the experts should not let their German colleagues know that they counted on the German authorities to invite them to verify the action taken. Such a procedure seemed, in fact, to the French delegation to be preferable to, though not departing from the principle underlying the proposal contained in paragraph 3 of this Embassy's memorandum merely to give the experts instructions 'to endeavour privately to negotiate with their German colleagues a satisfactory arrangement' as regards verifications.

3. M. Massigli explained that the French delegation had in any case no intention of asking that the experts should remain in Germany until the four years' programme as regards the military establishments had been accomplished. It [If] admitted by the German government the annual verifications of the programmes accomplished in preceding years could be carried out by means of special visits paid by the experts to Germany for this purpose, or at need by the Military Attachés of the interested Powers.

4. As regards the three questions (coastal batteries, reserve stocks and police) mentioned in paragraph 8 of the Versailles Committee's letter of

---

[1] See No. 157, note 6.

[2] The enclosed note No. 130 A.C., paragraph 3 of which followed closely the instructions cited in No. 157, is not printed.

[3] See No. 157, note 2.

February 17, M. Massigli said that the work in respect of the first two questions was complete, and that, as in the case of the military establishments, there seemed to be no harm in the experts being instructed unofficially to endeavour to arrange that the German government should invite them to conduct inspections. The division of the police effectives ought, M. Massigli understood, to be complete within a few weeks, and the experts might, in this matter also, let their German colleagues know that an invitation to them to verify the work done would be much appreciated.

5. The only task then remaining for the experts would be that of the status of the police, which was not a matter requiring verification but arose only out of the necessity for the passage of various laws by the State governments. This work ought to be complete by the autumn when the experts could be withdrawn from Germany.

6. The French delegation will make a proposal on the lines of paragraphs 2 and 4 above at the next meeting of the Conference,[4] which it is hoped to hold about March 16. I propose to accept it unless I hear from you to the contrary.

I have, &c.,
CREWE

[4] A French note of March 3 to this effect (not printed) was transmitted in Paris covering despatch No. 501 of March 21 (not preserved in Foreign Office archives).

No. 159

Mr. Leeper (Warsaw) to Sir A. Chamberlain (Received March 12)
No. 86 [N 1431/1431/55]

WARSAW, *March 6, 1928*

Sir,

In my despatch No. 76[1] of 29th February I had the honour to report a conversation with Mr Symonds [Simonds] on the subject of the German attitude towards Poland. Further light on the same subject is thrown by a visit which I received yesterday from a group of British business men representing certain fishing interests in Aberdeen, who have been some ten days in Poland and hope to conclude a contract of considerable importance with the Polish Government in the course of this week. They explained that they had asked especially to see me not so much to talk about the particular business which had brought them to Poland, but to impart to me as well as to the Commercial Secretary some of the experiences which they had had in Warsaw and to discuss the difficulties which were being put in the way of the development of Anglo-Polish trade both in England and in Poland.

2. The spokesman of the party explained, somewhat unnecessarily, that he was a Lancashire man born and bred, and that as such he was accustomed to call a spade not a spade, but a shovel. He was anxious that His Majesty's Legation should be fully alive to the underground machinations of those who were trying to keep British trade out of the Polish market. Those machinations

[1] No. 156.

were being conducted with the greatest vigour and unscrupulousness by our chief rivals, the Germans. For some time past he had been interesting himself in the possibilities of the Polish market, and had lately joined the group representing the Aberdeen fishing interests who were now with him in Poland. Before he came to Poland he had been approached in England by a German group who had offered him the sum of £20,000 in cash and the promise of a share in the profits of another company with a capital of £250,000 if he would not go to Poland or have any business relations with Poland. Not being the cosmopolitan type (again an unnecessary explanation) and being unused to such oriental methods of business as were practised by the Germans, he had summarily rejected the offers in what he described as the broadest Lancashire and had had his curiosity whetted to visit the forbidden land. Now that he had come and had looked round for himself he began to understand.

3. For the first day or two he had frankly been disappointed in Warsaw. There was an air of slovenliness about the streets and the shops which he had not expected. But the people were wide awake. They were intelligent and friendly to us and extremely anxious to develop trade with England. He had met Poles from different parts of the country and he saw great possibilities for British capital. Why did it not come and why did British business men meet with obstacles when they arrived here to do business? These were the two questions which he had examined and he thought that his own experiences and conclusions might throw some light on the answers.

4. In the first place there was still very little confidence in Poland amongst business men at home. It was an unknown country and the Polish Government had sadly neglected to advertise their country. In the absence of knowledge intrigues found a fertile soil. There were two kinds of intrigues. He had already spoken of his own experience of German activity, but he regretted that some of his compatriots, who had interests in Poland, were selfishly trading on the ignorance about the country at home in order to deter others. Of this he had absolute evidence, though he preferred not to mention names. The only answer to these intrigues was publicity and knowledge, and money spent by the Polish Government on such an undertaking would be the best possible investment. As it was a British as well as a Polish interest he would have thought that His Majesty's Government would have given their assistance, but, if it was not the business of His Majesty's Government to advertise other countries, His Majesty's Legation in Warsaw might for their part pass on to the Polish Government some of his criticisms and arouse them to a sense of reality.

5. The other side of the picture was Warsaw itself. He had met with German intrigues in England before he came, but they were nothing in comparison with what had confronted him here. The Germans here, chiefly working through Jews, were practising bribery and every kind of misrepresentation on the largest scale in order to exclude British business. Polish officials were aware of this and had even spoken of it to him, but it was essential that it should be known in England. The Germans were obviously

prepared to fight tooth and nail to secure the Polish market for themselves. They had the advantage of proximity and greater knowledge; we had the advantage of Polish good will, but that was not enough unless we increased our knowledge. When he went home he would do his best to shed a little light in a few dark corners, but who would believe that he knew what he was talking about? To carry conviction it was necessary that the public should know the opinion of His Majesty's Government. How that could be done he must leave to me, but he could not quit this country without conveying the warning that there was much to be done, and that he as a representative of British business had the right to look to his own Government for active interest and support.

I have, &c.,
R. A. Leeper

No. 160

Letter from M. Briand and Sir A. Chamberlain to Señor Quiñones de Leon[1]
[*W 2388/1373/98*]

Copie

GENEVA, *March 9, 1928*

Monsieur l'Ambassadeur,

En décidant aujourd'hui par une résolution unanimement adoptée d'adresser à Son Excellence le Marquis de Estella[2] la lettre que le Président a signée en leur nom,[3] les Représentants des Puissances qui siègent au Conseil de la Société des Nations viennent de marquer en quelle haute estime ils tiennent la glorieuse nation espagnole. Pleinement conscients du rôle éminent que l'Espagne a joué à Genève, convaincus que son absence pèse sur leurs délibérations, persuadés que si elle reprend dans la Société la place qui lui revient, elle y fera sentir dans l'avenir sa présence aussi utilement que dans le passé, ils demandent au gouvernement espagnol de revenir sur l'intention manifestée par lui en 1926 et de ne pas se retirer de l'organisme de Genève.

C'est avec une satisfaction profonde que nous nous sommes associés à la manifestation de nos collègues.

Déjà, au mois de décembre dernier nous avions demandé à Votre Excellence de faire savoir à Son Gouvernement combien nous serions heureux de le voir répondre à l'appel que pourrait lui adresser un jour le Conseil.[4] Aujourd'hui nous nous adressons à Elle pour La prier d'être notre interprète auprès du Marquis d'Estella, au moment où il est appelé à prendre en considération l'invitation du Conseil.

Le Gouvernement Espagnol sait de quels sentiments d'amitié les Gouvernements britannique et français sont animés à son égard: il vient d'en avoir encore des preuves éclatantes. Il peut être assuré, au cas où, comme nous

---

[1] A copy of this letter was transmitted to the Foreign Office under cover of Geneva despatch No. 7 L.N.C. of March 10 (not preserved in Foreign Office archives).

[2] i.e. General Primo de Rivera.

[3] See No. 127, note 5.

[4] See No. 96.

l'espérons, il se déciderait à répondre favorablement à l'appel qui lui est adressé, la France et la Grande Bretagne s'emploieront de toute leur force à faire donner à l'Espagne au sein de la Société la place à laquelle lui donnent droit son histoire et les services qu'elle a déjà rendus à la cause de la paix.

Veuillez agréer, &c.,
ARI. BRIAND
AUSTEN CHAMBERLAIN

No. 161

Letter from Sir R. Graham (Rome) to Mr. Sargent

[*C 2172/1580/22*]

Private and very confidential   ROME, *March 16, 1928*

My dear Sargent,

Your private letter C.1580/G.[1] of the 25th ultimo, regarding alleged Italian encouragement and assistance to the Macedonian Revolutionary Organisation and the use of Albania as a new base of its operations.

2. The Italians in general, and Signor Mussolini in particular, are so extremely sensitive, not to say touchy, on the subject of Albania, that I had to consider carefully how best to proceed. It was undesirable to raise the matter during my discussion with Signor Mussolini regarding the coal question. I hoped, however, to be able to bring it in in the course of some further conversation on other topics. Unfortunately, nothing has arisen which gave me an excuse for seeing His Excellency, and if I had gone to him with nothing but the Secretary of State's warning to the Albanian Minister, my purpose would have been too obvious and might have produced a reaction. On the other hand, I agreed thoroughly with your view that the matter is too serious to be allowed to rest any longer. I therefore thought it best, in the first instance, to throw a fly over Signor Grandi. I had to see him yesterday morning on a variety of minor questions, and I took the opportunity of informing him of Sir Austen Chamberlain's language to Ilias Bey, reading to him, in translation, the penultimate paragraph of Sir Austen's despatch No. 14[2] of February 9. I emphasized, as you suggested, that my communication gave a further proof of our recognition of Italy's special position in Albania and of our determination to do nothing in that country behind her back.

3. No salmon could have risen more readily to my fly. Signor Grandi's immediate answer was that he knew that the Yugoslavs were alleging that the Italian Government were encouraging and inciting the Macedonian revolutionaries. Nothing could be further from the truth. He would admit at once that the Italian Government regarded the Macedonian movement without reprobation, even indeed with a certain degree of sympathy. It was a factor which kept Bulgaria and Greece apart from Yugoslavia and prevented them from being absorbed in the latter's orbit. But this was a very different matter from encouraging revolutionary activity and the Italians

---

[1] No. 154.   [2] No. 135.

well realised the danger of stirring up such a hornet's nest. *On the contrary the Italian agents who were in touch with the revolutionary leaders,* had instructions to impress forcibly upon them that they must keep as quiet as possible, for this was in the best interests of themselves, their movement, and everybody concerned.

4. In so far as regarded Ahmed Zogu, Signor Grandi considered your warning to Ilias Bey as suitable and timely, and the Italian Government could endorse every word of it. His own impression was that Ahmed Zogu was not favourably inclined towards the Macedonian revolutionaries. There was a conflict of aspirations between the revolutionaries and the partisans of a 'greater Albania' over Kossovo and other districts. It was true that the exiled Albanians, hostile to Ahmed Zogu, in view of this conflict of aspirations attacked him for unduly favouring the Macedonians. Anyhow, Sir Austen's warning was all to the good.

5. Signor Grandi said that he would of course report our conversation to Signor Mussolini. So the hint has been given and swallowed. I may very likely have a favourable opportunity of rubbing it in to Signor Mussolini when next I see him.

6. Signor Grandi spoke with freedom and frankness, and I see no reason to doubt the bona fides of his statement, at any rate in so far as the higher Italian Authorities are concerned. But of course this does not cover their minor agents. *Obviously the Italians are in touch with the Macedonian revolutionaries and desire to remain so with a view to making use of them in certain eventualities,* just as the Yugoslavs keep a hand on Albanian revolutionaries of whom they might make use. Unfortunately this is the foggy atmosphere in which we must remain until the air between Italy and Yugoslavia has been cleared. This again depends on the preliminary clearing up of Franco-Italian relations.

7. Signor Grandi added that conditions in Northern Albania were wholly deplorable, and that there was actual starvation. The Italian Red Cross was doing all it could and sending quantities of tinned meat and other forms of food. He did not know who would pay, as Count Volpi[3] absolutely declined to do so, but no doubt the money would be found somewhere. This was only one of the many sacrifices which Italy was making in order to build up a stable Albanian State. It was for this that she provided money, food, financial advisers and military instructors. For it was only when a relatively strong and stable Albania had been called into existence, that the danger of Yugoslav aggression in that quarter would be eliminated. Finally, he repeated the often quoted analogy that Albania is to Italy what Belgium is to ourselves. The country could not be allowed to fall into potentially hostile hands.

Yrs ever,

R. GRAHAM

[3] Italian Minister of Finance.

No. 162

The Marquess of Crewe (Paris) to Sir A. Chamberlain
(Received March 20, 8.30 a.m.)

No. 45 Telegraphic: by bag [*C 2219/8/22*]

Confidential   PARIS, *March 19, 1928*

M. Berthelot in the course of a conversation this afternoon with Sir Eric Phipps showed him a telegram sent by M. Briand late on the night of March 15th to the French Ambassador in Rome containing instructions for his guidance on resumption of his conversations with Signor Mussolini.

2. The general sense of this telegram was extremely friendly and laid stress on the warm desire of the French government to establish really cordial relations with Italy.

3. M. Briand declared his readiness to make extended, though reasonable, concessions respecting Tangier, Tunis and the Tripoli frontier: (in regard to this last-named question M. Briand stated that he would be guided by the spirit of the Pact of London of 1915, but M. de Beaumarchais must bear in mind that French concessions on this point must on no account give Italy access to Lake Chad).

4. M. Briand then proceeded to point out that whilst France was ready to make concessions of the above nature to Italy, that Power had certain desiderata, such as emigration facilities for her surplus population, etc., which could only be gratified by general concessions to be made by all the great powers concerned and not by France alone.

5. Monsieur Briand further declared that he could not contemplate, as the Italians had wished, the signature of a Treaty of Alliance between the two countries, for that would appear to be in contradiction to the spirit of the Treaty of Locarno, but he would be quite ready to sign a Treaty of friendship and arbitration.

6. The telegram to Monsieur de Beaumarchais concluded by a statement to the effect that French policy was based (1) on a close entente with Great Britain, and (2) on friendship with the smaller Powers (Poland, Czechoslovakia, Roumania and Yugoslavia). There was nothing in this policy in any way directed against Italy and he did not suppose Italy could in any way object thereto.

7. After Sir Eric Phipps had hastily perused this telegram Monsieur Berthelot remarked that it was not clear what concessions Italy would be ready to make to France in return for that Power's attitude as defined above; he hoped, however, that Italy would, as a result of the establishment of more friendly relations with France, display an amicable attitude towards Yugoslavia, and if this were so it would be well worth while for France to make important concessions in the interests of general peace. Monsieur Berthelot added that of course there were certain minor points which the Italian government could concede to the French, for instance, they could treat with reasonable fairness, which they did not now do, French citizens engaged in trade and commerce and also French, or partly French, companies and banks

in Italy which were now being squeezed out in a manifestly unfair and ungenerous manner.

8. In regard to 3 above Monsieur Berthelot assured Sir Eric Phipps that if the frontier rectifications brought Italy up to the Sudan His Majesty's Government would be consulted beforehand.

9. In regard to 5 above Monsieur Berthelot told Sir Eric Phipps in confidence that he had persuaded Monsieur Briand that it was essential that agreement over Tangier, Tunis and Tripoli must precede the signature of the Treaty of friendship and arbitration.

No. 163

Sir A. Chamberlain to Sir R. Graham (Rome)

No. 349 [C 2214/1175/18]

FOREIGN OFFICE, *March 19, 1928*

Sir,

In the last paragraph of my despatch No. 318[1] of March 12th I informed Your Excellency that an early opportunity would be taken to consider whether any useful purpose would be served in instructing you at the present juncture to make further representations and suggestions to the Italian Government in connexion with the proposal that the latter should adopt a Reparation Recovery Act procedure in the place of the rider of December 22nd, 1927, to the Italo-German Coal contract of March 5th, 1925. It has now been decided, after a review of the whole situation that it is, in present circumstances, plainly useless for you to continue to urge the Italian Government to adopt the Reparation Recovery Act procedure forthwith.

2. On the other hand it is important that the Italian authorities should not be allowed to assume that the matter has been dropped, and that His Majesty's Government have acquiesced in an indefinite continuance of the present unsatisfactory situation. Without, therefore, actually seeking for opportunities to revert to the question, it would be well that you and the members of your staff should in general as soon as, but not before, the conversations foreshadowed in the succeeding paragraph have taken place, avail yourselves of such opportunities as may present themselves in order to keep the matter alive and to reiterate the hope of His Majesty's Government that the Italian Government will see their way to adopt the procedure which you have previously advocated. It may be hoped that by this means the education of the Italian authorities will have reached a satisfactory stage before or at latest by the time that it becomes necessary for them to envisage the replacement by some other instrument of the rider of December 22nd, 1927, which as you are aware is due to lapse as from March 5th, 1930.

3. The whole question is however of so technical, detailed and complicated a nature that I am conscious that you and your staff must necessarily be at a certain disadvantage when endeavouring to elucidate it with the Italian

---

[1] Not printed.

Departments concerned. Mr. Leith-Ross of the Treasury, who is fully cognisant with the whole question of the Reparation Recovery Act procedure, proposes to be in Rome during the month of April, and would be ready to explain the Reparation Recovery Act procedure and its operation in conversation with the appropriate Italian authorities. I consider it desirable that such interviews should take place and I shall in due course advise you of the dates between which Mr. Leith-Ross intends to be in Rome so that you may make the necessary arrangements to enable him to meet the competent Italian authorities.[2] Pending Mr. Leith-Ross' visit, any further discussion of the subject should, as indicated in the preceding paragraph, be avoided.

I am, &c.,

(For the Secretary of State)

C. HOWARD SMITH

[2] A copy of Mr. Leith-Ross's report of May 3 on his conversations in Rome was received in the Foreign Office on May 7. Mr. Leith-Ross stated in particular that Count Volpi had 'admitted that he would much prefer to take Reparations in cash than in coal, and from this point of view he would have been glad to put into force the Recovery Act arrangement. But the Italian Government were definitely advised that they could not apply the Recovery Act without the consent of Germany, and they had ascertained that such consent could not be obtained. They had had great commercial difficulties with Germany and it was quite useless to try and negotiate an agreement on this point. In the circumstances they had had no option but to increase their coal deliveries, as otherwise they would not have been able to absorb their share of Reparations. They realised that the increase of Reparation coal deliveries meant breaking an old and valued economic relationship with England. They could only hope that this fact might impel the British Government to support an early settlement of Reparations and Debts generally; it was all part of the same question. We need have no fear that the Italians would prefer German coal to British if there were no special inducements for taking German coal.'

Mr. Leith-Ross concluded that 'the Italian Government do not feel it possible to put into force a Reparation Recovery arrangement on the ground that the imposition of such a measure would involve acute difficulties with the German Government. The Italians are undoubtedly right on this point, the German Government having always been markedly hostile to any extension of the Recovery Act. In the circumstances, we are not likely to secure any result by continuing to press the Italian Government on the subject and I recommend that we should not pursue the proposal any further. It could, of course, be brought up again if and when there is any general discussion of reparations or revision of the Dawes Plan.'

No. 164

Letter from Sir E. Phipps (Paris) to Mr. Sargent

[*C 2231/48/62*]

PARIS, *March 19, 1928*

My dear Sargent,

We lunched with the German Ambassador today and after luncheon I had a few minutes private conversation with him.

2. I asked Herr von Hoesch whether he had seen Sauerwein's[1] article in the 'Neue Freie Presse' of March 16th advocating for next spring a general settlement of reparations, debts and evacuation of the Rhineland, but he had not read it.

[1] M. Jules Sauerwein was a correspondent of *Le Matin*.

3. Herr von Hoesch reminded me that we had heard Briand's speech in the Senate together on February 2nd last,[2] and he added that he had been so much struck by M. Briand's language, which was somewhat similar to that used by Sauerwein in his article, that he had immediately asked for an interview with him and had urged him to explain his meaning more fully. This M. Briand had been unable to do and had confined himself to vague and amiable generalities.

4. Herr von Hoesch told me Berthelot had on several occasions in private conversation with him expressed his conviction (as indeed he often has done to me) that the whole question of reparations, debts and Rhineland evacuation must and would be settled comprehensively and simultaneously some time after the instalment of the new American President in March 1929. The Ambassador, however, has always objected and maintains his objections to the Rhineland evacuation being made dependent on the good-will of an unknown President of the United States in the matter of debts and reparations, and he considers it highly improbable that the new President will take the reasonable and generous view which the French like to think probable. The evacuation of the Rhineland was, Herr von Hoesch declared, a question standing entirely by itself, and must not be made dependent on a satisfactory settlement of debts or reparations. It poisoned Franco-German relations and would continue to do so as long as it lasted.

5. I saw Berthelot for the first time to-day since his return from Geneva. He seemed on the whole quite pleased with his stay there and I feel sure that it has had a healthy influence on him, for hitherto he has always been rather inclined to sniff at Geneva and what he used to describe as its atmosphere of intrigue. He spoke more in sorrow than in anger of Titulesco to whose talent, however, he paid due tribute. He deplored the noxious habit to which Titulesco is more and more giving way, viz. the sniffing up at short intervals of large quantities of cocaine.

6. Berthelot seemed rather disappointed in Stresemann, but was impressed by the intelligence and ability of von Schubert, to both of whom he told me that he had expounded his views with great frankness in regard to debts, reparations and the Rhineland evacuation. He said that he had informed them both with great earnestness that it was quite out of the question to expect M. Briand to consent either in June or September to evacuate before the solution of the debts and reparations questions, which was likely to take place some time in the spring or summer of 1929. I gathered that von Schubert had seemed impressed with Berthelot's arguments, but that he had evidently failed to convert Stresemann.

Yours ever,
ERIC PHIPPS

[2] See No. 129, note 1.

No. 165

Sir H. Rumbold (Madrid) to Sir A. Chamberlain
(Received March 21, 9 a.m.)

No. 27 Telegraphic [W 2788/1373/98]

MADRID, March 20, 1928, 10 p.m.

My telegram No. 26.[1]

President of the Council told me today that he would submit draft reply to League Council to his Cabinet tomorrow. He practically said that Spain would resume active membership of League. He admitted Spaniards were a touchy race but manner in which League Council had appealed to Spain to return to the League as well as form of appeal had afforded peculiar gratification to the King and the Spanish government and could not be disregarded.[2]

[1] Not printed.

[2] On March 23 General Primo de Rivera sent a letter to Señor Quiñones de Leon of which the latter evidently communicated a translation to Sir A. Chamberlain. This letter transmitted a copy of the favourable Spanish reply of March 22 (printed in *League of Nations Official Journal*, May 1928, p. 603) to the appeal of the Council of the League of Nations (see No. 127, note 4) and instructed him to inform Sir A. Chamberlain and M. Briand how much the Spanish decision had been influenced by No. 160. The unfavourable Brazilian reply to the Council is printed, *op. cit.*, June 1928, p. 778.

No. 166

Sir A. Chamberlain to the Marquess of Crewe (Paris)
No. 659 [W 2762/138/17]

FOREIGN OFFICE, March 20, 1928

My Lord Marquess,

At an interview with the French Ambassador to-day, I recurred to the suggestion which he had made (see my despatch No. 317[1] of the 9th February last) for the negotiation of a commercial treaty between us. Following the line suggested to me by the Board of Trade, I said that our duties were so limited as not to afford the basis for negotiating a reciprocal bargain such as was commonly made by countries where the tariffs were of a much more general character and were specifically designed for this purpose. In our own case, our customs duties were either imposed for purely revenue purposes and therefore fixed at the lowest rates which would secure the necessary money, or in a few cases as safeguarding duties, and then, too, fixed at the lowest rate which would meet the exceptional circumstances of the industries concerned. In fact as had been pointed out in the note which you addressed to M. Briand,[2] two-thirds of the imports from France entered this country free of any duty whatever. I feared, therefore, that there was no basis here for such a negotiation as he had foreshadowed.

M. de Fleuriau replied that his suggestion had been a purely personal one, but he had reported it to his Government. They had not taken any steps in

[1] See No. 134, note 1.   [2] See No. 110, note 2.

consequence and probably felt that the moment was not opportune, but he was under the impression that, had my reply been favourable, M. Bokanowski[3] would have been inclined to proceed on those lines. In the circumstances, however, we must leave matters as they were.

I then said that this was not all that I had wished to say to his Excellency. I again referred to the note which your Lordship communicated to the French Government, and I observed that His Majesty's Government felt that they had legitimate subject for complaint in respect of the recent tariff policy of the French Government, having regard both to the favourable treatment which French exports enjoyed in the United Kingdom and to the nature of the resolutions passed at the World Economic Conference at Geneva last year, to which representatives of French business interests were party. We had seen with surprise and regret that the French Government, without offering any formal reply to your Lordship's note, had carried through the French legislature measures further increasing the duties imposed on British goods. Protests against many of these further increases of duty, such as those affecting tissues of wool and mohair, boots and shoes, and hæmatite pig-iron, were constantly being received at the Board of Trade and indicated that the patience of British traders was being exhausted and that much irritation existed among them. I observed that happily the most close and intimate political relations existed between our two Governments. These relations were, in fact, the basis on which my own Government certainly and, as I believed, equally the Government of France were basing their respective policies in Europe, and as far as might be in the world at large, and I would beg M. de Fleuriau to press upon his Government that these close intimate and political relations deserved consideration when France was fixing her tariffs. I earnestly hoped that the French Government would give greater consideration to British interests so that our political relations might not be disturbed or injured by a sense of trade grievance.

M. de Fleuriau said he would report what I had said to his Government. Again speaking for himself, he remarked that he thought the trouble arose from a certain duality in our policies. Certainly there was no lack of goodwill in France, but the Ministries of Foreign Affairs and Commerce were not perhaps in as close touch as they should be.

Finally I referred to M. de Fleuriau's complaints about certain points of our customs administration and said that I thought that these could probably be satisfactorily arranged if he would be good enough to instruct his commercial secretary or some other competent authority to take them up with the Board of Customs. These were technical matters which I thought would be best treated by technical experts on either side.

I enclose a copy of the brief which I received from the Board of Trade[4] and upon which my remarks were founded. I shall be glad if your Lordship will mention the matter again to M. Briand.

I am, &c.,
AUSTEN CHAMBERLAIN

[3] French Minister of Commerce.   [4] This letter of March 15 is not printed.

No. 167

Memorandum by Mr. Sargent[1]

[C 2116/652/18]

FOREIGN OFFICE, *March 20, 1928*

Mr. Seydoux tries to make our flesh creep. But when we come to analyse his argument it appears that all his ominous conclusions and forebodings are built up on two very commonplace facts, namely, that Germany and France have been at last able to conclude a Commercial Treaty, and secondly that the French Government have been able to prevent the total collapse of the franc, and establish some sort of practical stabilisation. No doubt both these facts represent solid and indeed remarkable achievements in the realms of economics and finance, and the former of them is evidently facilitating and hastening in a manner which has astonished M. Seydoux the probably in any case inevitable growth of international horizontal cartels and trusts as between France and Germany. Whether British industries have been unwise not to join in this process is beside the point. There is probably another side to this economic aspect of the question which explains British abstention. But in itself this internationalisation of European industry even if we stand aside is, from the political point of view, bound to constitute a powerful weapon to the cause of European peace, and as such cannot but be welcome to this country which requires peace for purely economic and financial reasons, if for no higher motives.

But M. Seydoux, not content, goes a step further and elaborates developments which are going to ensue from this industrial co-operation. By a somewhat sweeping assertion he reaches the conclusion that it is bound to lead to political co-operation between Germany and France which will result in the isolation of Great Britain unless she 'adapts her political conceptions to the new circumstances'. For so I read the rather guarded language of his last paragraph. But if M. Seydoux is assuming that the French in this combination will be able to insist on political co-operation on equal terms, I think he is ignoring numberles[s] obstacles, psychological, sentimental and historic, as well as those created by the war and the Peace Treaty, which for a long time to come will surely prevent any political co-operation between the two countries reaching such intimacy and unity of purpose as to be harmful to Europe and dangerous to Great Britain. But M. Seydoux's facts and evidence are susceptible of another deduction, and that is that as a result of the present developments Germany may prove so much the stronger industrially and economically that she will be able to compel a political co-operation which will amount in reality to a definite control by Germany of France's policy. Such a conclusion is by no means an impossible outcome of the present developments, and perhaps M. Seydoux is thinking of such danger when he says that 'France desires *now* to be on better terms than ever with Great

[1] This memorandum was written in connection with an article which appeared in *The Times* of March 15, 1928, pp. 15–16, by M. Jacques Seydoux, former Assistant Director of Political and Commercial Affairs in the French Ministry of Foreign Affairs.

Britain'. He tries to frighten us with the bogey of isolation, but it may well be that this isolation, if it materialises, will be more dangerous to France than to Great Britain.

We might put these considerations to Paris and Berlin and ask for their views.[2]

O. G. SARGENT

[2] Sir W. Tyrrell minuted as follows on this paper: 'Hardly worth while. M. Seydoux is chasing a mirage of longstanding viz that economics in the case of France & Germany will overcome race antagonism. W.T. 20/3.'

No. 168

Letter from Sir E. Phipps (Paris) to Mr. Sargent
[C 2256/8/22]

PARIS, *March 20, 1928*

My dear Sargent,

Lord Crewe's telegram No. 45[1] of last night.

The following is a point I failed, in my hurry, to mention:—

M. Briand, in his telegram to M. de Beaumarchais, pointed out that the Italian offer to guarantee France against the Anschluss did not constitute any concession on the part of Italy, for it was to the latter's interest at least as much as to that of France that the Anschluss should not take place.

Yours ever,
ERIC PHIPPS

[1] No. 162.

No. 169

Sir A. Chamberlain to Colonel Ryan[1] (Coblenz)
No. 1 Telegraphic [C 2229/51/18]

FOREIGN OFFICE, *March 21, 1928, 5 p.m.*

Following from Sargent.

Your letter of March 17th:[2] (railway construction in the Rhineland).

I. We think despatch by Railway Commission of communication in sense of paragraph 6 of letter from Inter-Allied High Command dated March 13th[3] is undesirable and unwarranted by terms of conference resolution of February 8th.[3] It is also unnecessary because position therein described is

[1] Colonel Ryan was Acting British High Commissioner on the Inter-Allied Rhineland High Commission following the death of Lord Erroll on February 19.

[2] Not printed. This letter stated in particular that in execution of paragraphs (*a*) and (*b*) of section C of the resolution of the Conference of Ambassadors on February 8 (see paragraph 8 of No. 132) General Guillaumat had in a letter of March 13 instructed the Railway Commission to inform the German Railway Company 'that (i) No reply can be made to requests already submitted for authorisation for new works pending an examination of the general question by the ex-allied powers. (ii) That no new work of improvement can be undertaken on the railways until the Conference of Ambassadors has studied the general question.' Colonel Ryan enclosed a copy of General Guillaumat's letter which is not printed. Colonel Ryan further reported that the High Commission had already received a German protest regarding delay in authorizing certain railway improvements.

[3] See note 2 above.

implicit in letter which will in any case, in pursuance of actual terms of paragraph (a) of section (c) of resolution, have to be addressed to German authorities in reply to German Commissioner's complaint to High Commission regarding delay. It is undesirable because allied Powers' right to enforce even a temporary veto on railway construction may be questioned unless safety of the armies is proved to be at stake. In this case allied government's procrastination amounts in effect to temporary veto in the interests of their own convenience and it is obviously better in these circumstances that the situation devolving from such procrastination should eventuate *sub silentio*.[4] Please arrange therefore that despatch of proposed communication be stopped if possible.

II. We agree that it would be preferable if possible that information that allies are reviewing whole question of railway construction in the Rhineland should not first reach German government through subordinate channel of railway committee. As the German government have now through German High Commissioner approached High Commission in regard to the delay in receiving replies to requests for authority to undertake work on lines you should suggest that the latter should take the opportunity to reply direct in the sense of paragraph (a) of section C of the Ambassadors' Conference resolution of February 8th.

[4] Tacitly.

No. 170

The Marquess of Crewe (Paris) to Sir A. Chamberlain
(Received March 23, 8.30 a.m.)

No. 49 Telegraphic: by bag [C 2274/394/18]

PARIS, *March 22, 1928*

Section 1 of my telegram No. 46[1] of March 19th.

At its meeting on March 19th, the Ambassadors' Conference considered the question of the concessions desired by the German government in the matter of the military establishments and of the embarrackment of police, and the possibility of inspection by the experts of the transformations effected by the German government in these matters as well as those of coastal fortifications, reserve stocks and division of police effectives.

2. The conference had before it:

(a) Versailles Committee's reports of February 17th[2] and 27th[3] (see my despatches Nos. 303[2] and 350[4] of February 21st and 29th);

[1] Not printed. This telegram reported on consideration by the Conference of Ambassadors on March 19 of topics other than that to which the present telegram relates.

[2] See No. 157, note 2.

[3] This report, No. 59/1 not printed, explained the argument of the German Government justifying the embarrackment of more than the 35,000 police permitted by the note of November 16, 1925, from the Conference of Ambassadors (see Cmd. 2527 of 1925, item No. 5) and the Conference's resolution of November 26, 1925 (see Volume I, No. 115 §8) and recommended that the German case should be accepted only on certain conditions.

[4] Not preserved in Foreign Office archives.

(*b*) Memoranda from this Embassy prepared on the instructions contained in your despatches Nos. 388[5] and 591[6] of February 18th and March 14th; copies of these memoranda are enclosed in my despatches Nos. 372[7] and 500[8] of March 3rd and 21st;

(*c*) A French memorandum dated March 3rd[9] (see my despatch No. 501[9] of March 21st).

3. No objection was made to the grant of the concessions asked for by the German government, either as regards establishments or embarrackment. The discussion centred round the conditions on which these concessions might be granted. In addition to the conditions set out in paragraphs 5 and 10 of the Versailles Committee's memoranda of February 17th and 27th, paragraph 4 of the French memorandum of March 3rd proposed that the German government should be asked to invite the experts to inspect the transformations effected in establishments, embarrackment, coastal defences, reserve stocks and distribution of police.

4. I made it clear at once that I could not accept this new condition which seemed to be neither equitable nor feasible. The French delegation did not press the point, but Marshal Foch urged that nevertheless inspection was a vital necessity. He realised that it could not be demanded as of right, but he thought that the German government should be warned that, if they refused to admit inspection, the League of Nations would have to be told that the interested governments had not been able to verify the execution of the various questions involved. Marshal Foch considered that, in these circumstances, it would be more satisfactory in the first place to explain the position verbally to the German Embassy in Paris rather than to leave the experts to initiate the discussion with their German colleagues, as suggested in this Embassy's memorandum of February 27th[10] and in a somewhat different form by Monsieur Massigli in the conversation reported in paragraph 2 of my despatch No. 372 of March 3rd.

5. Monsieur Cambon and the Belgian Ambassador supported Marshal Foch, and I thought it impossible to refuse to submit the proposal to you as it is obvious that a decision by the German Government to invite the experts to conduct inspections would be by far the best way out of the difficulty. That result seems to me to be more likely to be obtained at this stage by direct discussion between the Conference and the German Embassy in Paris than by negotiation between the experts and their German colleagues. As in the

[5] See No. 157, note 6.

[6] Not printed. This despatch instructed Lord Crewe to inform the Conference of Ambassadors that His Majesty's Government considered it 'quite unnecessary' to continue the controversy with the German Government on embarrackment of police, but that in view of the importance attached to the matter by the French military authorities no objection would be made to the report referred to in note 3 above.

[7] No. 158: see note 2 thereto for the enclosed note of February 27.

[8] Not preserved in Foreign Office archives. The enclosed memorandum No. 174 A.C. of March 16 stated that His Majesty's Government had no objections to the report referred to in note 3 above.

[9] See No. 158, note 4.

[10] See note 7 above.

case of the interested Governments' eventual requirements respecting the Rhineland railways system, I have little doubt that the adoption of a conciliatory attitude by the German Government in this matter will ultimately react on the French attitude towards the evacuation of the occupied territories (see paragraph 8 of my telegram No. 11[11] of January 19).

6. The following resolution has accordingly been drafted under my reserve:

'It is decided that the Secretary General, in the light of the views developed at the Conference, shall call the attention of the German Embassy in Paris to the different questions raised by the Versailles Committee's reports of February 17th and 27th, and shall impress upon it the great interest which an agreed solution ("solution amiable") of these questions would present.'

7. Unless you see objection on grounds of principle to the procedure outlined above, I would recommend acceptance of the resolution for the reasons set out in paragraph 5 of this telegram. Everyone realises that the interested Governments have no legal right to inspect, and all that the German Government is to be asked to do is, on grounds of political expediency, to invite the experts to inspect.

[11] No. 117.

No. 171

Letter from Mr. Wigram (Paris) to Mr. Sargent
[C 2314/51/18]

PARIS, *March 22, 1928*

Dear Sargent,

Thank you for your letter No. C. 2229/51/18 of March 21 about railway construction in the Rhineland.[1]

2. I pointed out to Massigli this morning the difference between paragraph 8 of the Versailles Committee's letter to Guillaumat[2] and paragraph C. (a) of the Conference resolution of February 8th.[3] Massigli agreed that the Versailles Committee had exceeded the intention of the Conference in this matter and that they had turned into positive action the negative action decided upon. At Massigli's request, Baratier[4] telephoned to Mainz[5] this afternoon to ask that if action had not yet been taken on paragraph 8 of the letter, it should be definitely and finally suspended.

[1] Not printed. This letter enclosed copies of Colonel Ryan's letter of March 17 (see No. 169, note 2) and No. 169 and requested Mr. Wigram to explain the British view to M. Massigli.
[2] Not printed. This letter of March 5 gave the instructions on which General Guillaumat was acting in his letter of March 13: see No. 169, note 2.
[3] See paragraph 8(*a*) of No. 132.
[4] General Baratier was Chief of Staff to Marshal Foch.
[5] i.e. to General Guillaumat's headquarters.

3. I also spoke to Massigli about the German Commissioner's protest and explained to him the nature of the instructions you had sent to Ryan. He had not yet heard of the protest but he was quite agreeable to doing what you want and the matter will be arranged accordingly with Coblenz.

4. If by chance paragraph 8 of the Versailles Committee's letter has already been acted upon,[6] I hope the Germans will not make too much trouble. It is only a question of two or three months now and I am hopeful that we may get a general agreement on the whole of this tiresome question.

Yours ever,
R. F. WIGRAM

[6] Colonel Ryan reported in a letter of March 23 to Mr. Sargent that he had been unable to prevent the despatch to the German Railway Company on March 19 of the communication by the Railway Commission in execution of these instructions. He was informed in Foreign Office telegram No. 4 to Coblenz of March 27 that the Foreign Office agreed with instructions sent by the French Government on March 23 to M. Tirard that the High Commission should reply to the German protest in the terms of paragraph 8(a) of No. 132, adding verbally that the Powers were actively studying the question and hoped to initiate the contemplated negotiations as soon as possible. Colonel Ryan replied on March 31 that an explanation of the Railway Commission's letter of March 19 had been sent to the German Commissioner.

No. 172

The Marquess of Crewe (Paris) to Sir A. Chamberlain (Received March 24)
No. 530 C [W 2922/138/17]

PARIS, March 23, 1928

Sir,

I have the honour to forward you herewith a memorandum by the Commercial Counsellor respecting the relation of Great Britain:

(1) to the recent commercial conventions of France with several European states, and

(2) to the national trade group agreements made between France and other European states in recent years.

I have, &c.,
CREWE

ENCLOSURE IN No. 172

Great Britain and (I) *Recent Inter-State Economic Agreements of France and* (II) *National Trade Group Agreements in Europe*

March 22, 1928

I. *Recent Economic Agreements of France*

This month of March 1928 marks an important date in the contractual economic relations of France with several European States. After years of negotiations (since October, if not since July 1924 at London) the general commercial agreement with Germany, concluded in August 1927, has been ratified, as have been the Saar and the 26 per cent Reparations levy agreements with that country. With her North-Eastern and South-Eastern neighbours, Belgium, Luxembourg and Switzerland, with both of whom trade relations are extremely important, the former taking annually about 17 per cent and the latter 6 to 7 per cent of the value of all French exports, agreements of considerable scope, partly necessitated by the Franco-German agreement, have also been ratified; and with Italy, which takes 4 to 5 per cent of French exports, not only an agreement respecting silks (which had waited many years), but also one covering a number of other commodities, have likewise been rendered definite.

The key agreement, that with Germany, represents in effect the triumph of the German point of view: for, although France since 1919 had reversed her policy from that of most-favoured-nation treatment to that of reciprocity, she has now conceded the minimum rates (which were, however, generally raised considerably *ad hoc*) for the great bulk of the goods of interest to the German export trade; and, as from December 15, 1928, the principle is to have integral application on both sides. The French, it is true, besides raising minimum rates for Germany, had adroitly managed to secure a large dose of reciprocity from various countries before conceding the operation of the most-favoured-nation treatment principle in the German case. The new agreement proved immediately valuable to France: although in force for only four months in 1927, exports to Germany underwent great expansion, and for that year were higher by 2 and 2¾ milliards than in 1926 and 1925 respectively. Special circumstances in 1926, especially the exceptional coal deliveries consequent on the English coal strike, which led to the artificial swelling of German exports to France, debar comparison of 1927 with that year, but, compared with 1925, German exports were not far short of two milliards higher (4·21 against 2·37 milliards).

Great Britain is, in so far as heavier French duties become operative against her, a considerable sufferer by the Franco-German agreement. The tariff rates on most articles of interest to her, save that on coal, have been increased by the raising of the minimum rates applicable to most German products, and although she benefits by certain reductions subsequently secured by Switzerland, Belgium, and Italy, the level has been generally raised to a considerable extent on many important articles (machinery, textile machinery, cutlery, paper, leather goods, chemicals, certain textiles, hosiery, sports goods, etc.). It affords little, or rather no, satisfaction that the new rates are lower than those proposed in the 1927 Government Bill for the general revision of the tariff, these rates having been put forward merely as fighting rates. We were simply not considered seriously in the course of fixing the new rates with Germany, as we are known to be disarmed and to be without effective bargaining power owing to the absence of a regular customs tariff, or of rapidly operative retaliatory powers. The irony of this situation appears more pointed when one recalls two facts: (1) that Great Britain has from time out of mind been far the greatest French market, taking from 18 to 20 per cent of all French exports, whilst Germany took before the war under 13 per cent (average percentage 1909–13 was 12·7 per cent) and since the war 7·6 per cent; and (2) that Great Britain is far the greater exporter to France, our percentage for 1909–13 having been 13 per cent of total imports and that of Germany 12 per cent, whilst for the five years 1922–26 these percentages were 13·3 and 5·4 respectively.

With reference to the suggestion that really important negotiations are pending between France and Germany, which may be of vital interest to the British Empire, the Director of Commercial Relations and Treaties Department of the French Ministry for Commerce, subsequently [*sic*] to the conclusion of the various German agreements, stated to the present writer that no further inter-State commercial agreements with Germany were in contemplation. There would be certain alterations in details of the main agreement to bring them into line with the tariff modifications arranged with Belgium, Switzerland and Italy. Negotiations with Czecho-Slovakia beginning on the 16th March might also cause slight changes under application of the most-favoured-nation principle.

As regards the recent wholesale recasting of the French customs tariffs, it is little short of extraordinary that almost the entire work was consummated by way of negotiations with foreign Powers instead of being effected by ordinary parliamentary procedure: for quite two-thirds of the articles, and these the more important, Parliament had no alternative, if it did not mean to wreck the outcome of several years negotiations, but to accept whole agreements embodying a vast overhauling of tariffs; and, for tariff articles not comprised within such agreements, there was provided, to fill the lacunae, a so-called *additif*, whose parliamentary fate was definitely attached to the fate of the inter-State agreements. That general revision of the French tariff, which, presented in 1927 after four or five years of elaboration, the Government despaired of carrying through the French Parliament, has accordingly been provisionally accomplished on a large scale by the negotiation of agreements with foreign countries. Great Britain was not in a strong position to exercise direct influence on the course of negotiations in which she did not participate, especially as she did not appear anxious to accept the invitation of the French Government to make a commercial treaty.

II. *National Trade Group Agreements in Europe*

Within the last year the only concrete addition of importance in the national trade group agreements structure has been the conclusion of the chemicals agreement, into which Great Britain entered. The Franco-German potash agreement of 1925 concerned directly only the two producers, the parties to the agreement. In general, this policy has been most prominently concerned with the iron and steel trades. Already before the war, when the markets of the world were more absorbent, steel consumption (exclusive of U.S.A.) having increased from 19 million tons in 1900 to 44 million tons in 1913, there had been established some twenty odd international agreements for separate classes of steel products. In view of the greatly developed steel capacity of Western and Central Europe as a consequence of the war, and of the relatively stationary consumption, Continental makers have been alive to the desirability of re-establishing these agreements, or rather of establishing on a broader basis international agreements for the regulation of production (and incidentally for the limiting of markets and regulation of prices). The *steel rails* agreement operative since the summer of 1926 between Great Britain, France, Belgium, Germany, Luxembourg and other countries, revived a pre-war agreement of the same nature: home markets are reserved to home producers, and up to 20,000 tons beyond her quota Great Britain is accorded priority in British overseas territories. In July, 1926, was made an agreement between French, Belgian, German, Czecho-Slovakian, Polish and Hungarian makers of tubes or pipes. Other agreements related to *nails* and *wire*, but fewer countries adhered thereto.

By far the most important international agreement was the five-year *crude* steel agreement of October, 1926, to which then adhered the French, Belgian, Luxembourg and German manufacturers, and at later dates Czecho-Slovakia, Hungary, and Austria.[1] British manufacturers, who were kept fully informed of the negotiations, have not adhered. The agreement states textually that 'the present understanding is open to all countries that wish to join'. Its technical basis is the allotment to each national group of periodic quotas of output in relation to a total periodic output of all national groups, with liberty to exceed quotas, but under obligation to pay a fixed five [fine] per ton of excess; if output is inferior to quota, compensation is payable out of a common fund fed by a fixed levy on all output. Under the original arrangement, Germany received a quota of 43·50, France, one of 31·19, Belgium, of 11·56, Luxembourg, of 8·55, and the Saar, of 5·20 per cent. This agreement was desired by the chief participants for various reasons over and above that of output regulation: the Germans (the most ardent advocates) for general reasons of renewal of open relations with other countries, and for the particular reason that it diminished the inequalities of competition with Belgium, Luxembourg, and France; and the French, because it enabled them to bring their depreciated currency prices more into harmony with appreciated currency prices. Although this agreement was limited to crude steel, understandings between French and German makers of special steels as to respective home markets were then also made.

It cannot be maintained that the general agreement has worked with perfect smoothness. The Germans have made repeated complaints about the payment of fines due by them for excess production or about the restriction on their exports; the Central Europe group (Czecho-Slovakia, Austria, Hungary) have also complained of the heavy fines for over-production. Compromises have been found; the fines have been reduced by half, or export quotas have been raised.

British manufacturers continue to turn a deaf ear to the invitations to adhere to this cartel, having no doubt full knowledge of all the circumstances, and good reasons for their attitude. They probably desire to see it working under more settled conditions of general business and of foreign exchanges, fail to appreciate any permanent advantages for them, object to surrendering

[1] For the text of this convention signed on September 30, 1926, see *Survey of International Affairs 1926*, pp. 481–3. See also Volume II, No. 244.

their liberty of action, are offered, on the basis of their 1925 production, too low a quota, and perhaps feel that their trade organisation is not sufficiently compact and authoritative to apply or enforce regulation of production and distribution of markets. Possibly reasons similar to those that deter the Poles appeal with especial force to them: the former have not yet entered the 'Pact', as they wish to keep open every possibility of the home market and of exportations to Russia and to Germany. In their desire, however, to receive Poland merely for limitations of production, the leaders of the Pact now propose not to admit her as a member, but to create a special position for her, and to offer considerable advantages (e.g., an exportation quota of 300,000 tons and free internal market). British interests with their unrivalled business sense may be supposed to appraise judiciously the pros and cons of entering into this and into other international organisations of national trade groups. They are fully acquainted with all the moves in the game, and may decide finally to enter upon given conditions.

French official and business policy in close contact for many years in this matter has favoured understandings in the ore, coke, and metallurgical industries of France, Belgium, Luxembourg, and Germany, because reciprocal needs were so intertwined and because that sector in Western Europe, though politically divided, formed a single economic complex for the efficient production of steel. In Lord Hardinge's despatch No. 2734 (C) of 22nd November, 1922, paragraph 4,[2] reference is made to the convictions on this point of M. Serruys (he who has been practically the sole negotiator on the French side of the recent series of State commercial agreements), when he said that a large agreement with the German metal industry was essential, and that other countries in Western Europe might well be included in it. On subsequent occasions he has not failed to harp on that string. The business leaders have frequently expressed to the writer the same conviction. French interest in this matter has of course been of first importance owing to the old and permanent reason of ore and coke. Delay in agreement has already made this reason less vital: for France has doubled her pre-war output of coke (but she is still short by 4 million tons a year), and Germany has found other sources of ore supply or has altered her furnaces to a certain extent.

In more recent years, probably quickened by the influence of the widespread so-called rationalisation movement in American and German industry, but really born of the strong advance in France towards large-scale, standardised, and concentrated industry (e.g., metallurgy, coal, ore and potash mining, dyes, heavy chemicals, cement, electrical, locomotive, automobile and other engineering, certain textiles as artificial silk, jute, shipping and transport generally), there came the larger idea of the national organisation of separate groups of industries, with a view to more efficient production within the national unit, and of the subsequent international regulation of total production by voluntary agreements, so as to adjust total production to

[2] Not printed. Lord Hardinge had been H.M. Ambassador at Paris 1920-2.

total consumption. Monsieur Loucheur,[3] the proposer and president of the 1927 Geneva Economic Conference, stated to the writer in January, 1927, that the great major object of that Conference was to lead up first to the national and then to the international organisation of the principal industries, 'so that it would be possible by subsequent international agreements to adjust total production to total consumption, and thus to bring more order and regularity into production whose capacity throughout the world now exceeded, owing to the Great War and post-war creations, consumption capacity'. To the objection that at the present time relatively few branches of industrial activity were ripe for definite centralised regulation, it was replied that a beginning could be made with several great industries such as the coal, coke, iron and steel, chemical, and various sections of the engineering trades. He had Europe only in his mind for this development, and he urged it the more strongly on the ground that the national organisation of industry was making such rapid progress in Germany that, if steps were not taken to follow suit, some disagreeable surprises were in store, and not least for British industry.

Monsieur Jacques Seydoux ('The Times', March 15, 1928) publishes a seeming panegyric on the recent triumphal march of Franco-German collaboration. But negotiations which required three years and occasioned several deadlocks in their course, which resulted in the general raising of French tariff rates prior to conclusion (the German rates had been previously raised), and which were only concluded in August, 1927, after serious threats of tariff war, cannot be said to have manifested that anxiety on the part of the Germans, to which he alludes, 'to follow the rational and practical part of industrial understanding'. Nor is it quite correct that 'the advantages of the first agreements are such that attempts are being made every day to extend them and to create others'. In the last three years France and Germany have made agreements respecting certain steels (and tubes, wire, machine wire, nails), potash, certain chemicals, dyestuffs (but terms secret apparently), and have also made various special compacts as to deliveries of coke and coal both under the reparation in kind and other deliveries (especially as result of 1926 British coal strike). The French, especially under the Loucheur inspiration (for he has always been extensively interested in the trade), have had conversations with the Germans as to agreements respecting light and heavy electrical material (but in this case it may be noted that the same American interests are very great in the French as in the British electrical industries). They have also (with Great Britain and Belgium) come into the minor commercial arbitration scheme for the woollen trade. They have taken an active part in the business of the International Chamber of Commerce, whose seat is at Paris. But it is clearly an exaggeration to contend that daily attempts are made to extend industrial understandings and to create others.

M. Seydoux does not definitely hint that it were well for Great Britain to become a third party to these economic or trade group understandings. Like

[3] M. Loucheur had been French Minister of Finance in 1925 and Minister of Commerce in 1926.

M. Loucheur, however, and like other official and non-official advocates of British participation in Continental trade combines, he has probably as one 'arrière-pensée' the belief that with British participation they would possess in many circumstances a favourable makeweight in face of the obvious de facto and ever more menacing preponderance of Germany on the bases of superior population, industrial and marketing organisation, and output. To some extent, also, French opinion is influenced by the magnitude of the industrial scale in the United States, and by the marked growth of its foreign trade and financial weight. To men like Serruys and Seydoux (who now is a director of the principal 'international' bank in France, which has specialised in financing industrial enterprises in most countries), this aspect of the question—the solidarity of Europe—is not without importance.

Although the French have long been rather eager that Great Britain should join in these European industrial combinations, it is curious to note that they are not slow in emphasising that the necessary organisation for the proper representation of their national industries on an executive body (i.e., one which had to enforce output policies and marketing delimitations) is apparently far from being yet realised in Great Britain. Thus, as regards the coal industry, which in continental eyes distinctly calls for international regulation, it is remarked that the English industry is split into numberless units, has no efficient channels for framing and enforcing policy for the whole industry, and has lost to merchants all control of selling prices, whereas the French industry was thoroughly organised with central control of general policy, production, and prices. The German coal industry has been similarly organised for a good thirty years. It has been frequently remarked in France that the English metal industries were quite inadequately organised for general purposes. They admit that the English chemical industry is sufficiently centralised and organised for the purpose: the British have come into the chemicals arrangement. But in face of their eagerness to have the British in, and their proclamation of their organisation deficiencies, it is not easy to see what great advantage the French expect to derive from their inclusion even in the few international industrial undertakings of importance that have come into being.

J. R. CAHILL

No. 173

Letter from Sir A. Chamberlain to Sir R. Graham (Rome)

[*F.O. 800/262*]

Private and Personal   *March 23, 1928*

My dear Graham,

After the Ambassador had done the business for which he came, as recorded in my despatch of this date,[1] I spoke to him about my suggestion for a meeting between Mussolini, Briand, Primo de Rivera and myself at Barcelona to put

[1] Foreign Office despatch No. 380 to Rome is not printed. For Signor Bordonaro's account of this conversation on Abyssinia, see *I Documenti Diplomatici Italiani*, Settima Serie, vol. vi, No. 175.

the finishing touch to the Tangier agreement. I said that I had spoken of this proposal to Signor Scialoja and Marquis Paulucci at Geneva, but they had both at once said that Mussolini would not come to Barcelona for such a purpose and indeed it was very doubtful whether he would leave Italy at all. I reminded Bordonaro that, at the meeting of the Council which immediately succeeded the signing of the Treaty of Tirana, Scialoja had come to me on account of instructions which he had received from Mussolini. Mussolini had at that moment got the impression that there was a sort of conspiracy against Italy being concocted among the Ministers at Geneva. Scialoja had told me that he saw no sign of it, but that, as I was a friend of Mussolini's, he could speak to me freely in confidence, and that he would be very glad if I would correct or confirm his impression. I had been able entirely to confirm it and to say of my own knowledge that there had been no trace of any such endeavour in the attitude of Briand or any other of the people who were suspected. I now added that this kind of suspicion was almost inevitable when Mussolini saw the other Ministers meet and never joined himself in the gatherings. After all, in post-war Europe the meetings of Ministers had become a normal and most useful instrument of diplomacy and of peace. I accepted the fact that Mussolini could not himself come regularly to Geneva, but was it not a great pity when a good opportunity offered for a meeting that he should refuse to entertain it? At any rate he must not suspect us of plotting behind his back if, when we sought a meeting, it was refused by himself. Was he not further, I asked, depriving himself of his due influence in Europe if he never met us? So much good work was done in these conversations, so many difficulties could be discussed and removed which would never have found their solution in an exchange of despatches. He had not seen Briand since Locarno. I had had the pleasure of meeting him more recently through the accident of my summer holiday,[2] but we could not always be going to Rome and I could not but feel that it would be a great pity if Mussolini did not take advantage of an opportunity when one offered. We should go to finish the Tangier agreement. This would be a sufficient reason of our meeting and a sufficient result of it if there was nothing more that we cared to say when it was over. But I could not help believing that a friendly conversation between him and Briand in which he could really penetrate Briand's mind and purpose would go a long way towards promoting the *détente* in their relations which both desired. I asked Bordonaro to tell Mussolini of the thoughts which had been passing through my head as I had explained them to him, adding that it was not a matter for a despatch, but perhaps he might do it in a personal letter. Bordonaro replied that he would be the more glad to do so because he entirely shared my view and had often pressed on Mussolini the desirability of his going sometimes to Geneva.[3]

There is nothing that I want you to do on this matter at present, but I like to keep you fully informed of all that passes so that if Mussolini should speak to you on the subject you would know how the matter arose.

[2] See No. 1, note 14.

[3] For an account of this conversation by Signor Bordonaro, *v. op. cit.*, No. 182.

I do not expect any immediate change of attitude on M's part even about Barcelona, but—well, Spain returns to the League and nothing but my drip, drip on that stone has worn it away.

Yrs. sincerely,
AUSTEN CHAMBERLAIN

No. 174

Sir R. Lindsay (Berlin) to Sir A. Chamberlain (Received March 27)
No. 246 [C 2441/316/18]

BERLIN, *March 24, 1928*

Sir,

With reference to my despatch No. 73[1] of the 23rd of January respecting the armament of German destroyers, I have the honour to report that Herr de Haas of the German Foreign Office sent a message to the Embassy to the effect that the subject of my previous discussion with him had been studied and that his department was now ready for a discussion of it with the Embassy experts if I agreed. I was rather disappointed at this, and called on Herr de Haas this morning.

2. He said that he had been in communication with the German Admiralty; they had carefully scrutinized the Treaty of Versailles and could find nothing in it prohibiting the use of 5-inch guns. Would I enlighten him. I then went over the ground I had traversed before; I said that from my own examination of the Treaty and its complementary documents I had indeed personally come to the conclusion that the armament proposed was contrary to Treaty; but I was no expert, I was not authorized to discuss treaty interpretations with him, nor could I authorize my staff to do so. If the German Government wanted an authoritative interpretation of the Treaty from the other side, they could raise the question officially; but it was not one which His Majesty's Government could settle single handed—I imagined that they would refer it to their co-signatories represented at the Conference of Ambassadors, and then would arise what might be a very disagreeable controversy. I did not think that His Majesty's Government wanted to have the present satisfactory relations disturbed by such a dispute, and I hoped the German Government shared this view; I felt convinced that this was a foolish moment to choose for a quarrel. I could imagine that some day the German Government might wish to raise the question of the limitations on their armaments, but not to-day, and not over the armament of a few destroyers. It was absurd to attack the Treaty of Versailles with pop guns, and I hoped they would let the question drop. I could tell him that I had in the meanwhile heard nothing of any contemplated action from Paris.

3. Herr de Haas said that the boats had now been launched, the guns constructed, and it was the intention to mount them.[2] I replied that if this

[1] See No. 144, note 2.
[2] Colonel Gosset referred to this statement in a letter of March 28 to Major Calthrop of the War Office (copy received in the Foreign Office on April 3) in which he also stated: 'Two cases have occurred in the last fortnight of finds of concealed arms and war material

317

intention was carried into effect, then indeed the question would be raised. There could be no secrecy in such a matter, and any sailor with an opera glass would be able to see at once that the ships were carrying 5-inch guns, and the controversy which I was deprecating would become inevitable.

4. Herr de Haas thanked me for my visit. He said he would refer again to the Marineamt,[3] and let me know the result in due course. My impression is that the latter, with the narrow view characteristic of German departments, wants to try 5-inch guns on 800-ton ships and deliberately shuts its eyes to the way in which its plans affect the Government as a whole. The Foreign Office, I think, realizes the danger of such a proceeding and I hope it may be able to induce broader views.[4]

I have, &c.,
R. C. LINDSAY

and the accused have been prosecuted under the "Law for the protection of the Republic", instead of under the War Material Law [an English translation of the final text of this law dated July 27, 1927, is printed in *The Board of Trade Journal*, May 17, 1928, pp. 637–8]. My own impression is that the Germans do not intend to apply seriously any of the Laws they have been forced to pass by the Allies. As the present War Minister, General Groener, has stated—"Eid? Das ist ja nur ein Wort, weiter nichts [Oath? That is only a word, nothing more]".

'I do not know that it matters much as long as they destroy the arms under some Law or other, except that the French notice these little things and draw deductions according to their suspicions.'

[3] i.e. the German Naval Department.

[4] In letters of April 4 transmitting copies of this despatch to the War Office and Admiralty the Foreign Office noted that in letters of February 10 and March 24 and of March 1 respectively, the Admiralty and War Office had stated that the manufacture of five-inch guns by Germany was illegal. The Foreign Office expressed the view that the statement by the German Admiralty reported in paragraph 2 above might indicate that there was 'some ground to fear that the German authorities may be preparing to call in question the right invariably claimed in the past by the ex-allied governments to impose upon Germany their own interpretation of the naval, military and air clauses of the Treaty of Versailles'.

No. 175

Sir R. Lindsay (Berlin) to Sir A. Chamberlain (Received March 27)
No. 247 [C 2442/617/18]

BERLIN, *March 24, 1928*

Sir,

In continuation of my despatch No. 202[1] of the 8th of March relating to

[1] Not printed. In this despatch Mr. Nicolson, First Secretary in H.M. Embassy at Berlin, reported on criticisms made in the Reichstag on March 5 by a member of the German National People's Party, Herr Lejeune-Jung, of British commercial policy as being chiefly directed against Germany in spite of the Anglo-German Commercial Treaty of December 2, 1924 (printed in *British and Foreign State Papers*, vol. 119, pp. 369–89). In his reply Dr. Curtius stated that many of Herr Lejeune-Jung's complaints were justified and that Germany would denounce the treaty at the first possible moment: see *The Times*, March 7, 1928, p. 15. Mr. Nicolson commented that there was nothing new in these statements, which 'merely reflect German complaints which have been made from time to time ever since the safeguarding policy [cf. note 2 below] was put into effect in the United Kingdom'.

the declaration of the German Minister of Commerce that the Anglo-German Treaty would have to be denounced at the first due date, I have the honour to report that I to-day spoke on this subject to Herr de Haas at the Foreign Office. He said that Herr Curtius' statement had been made without consultation with the Ministry for Foreign Affairs. He himself, if he had been asked, would have deprecated any such announcement, and he thought it ill-advised; nevertheless there were decided German grievances, and when the time came, if they did not justify actual denunciation, they would certainly necessitate negotiation. He instanced the re-imposition of the McKenna duties,[2] especially so far as Germany was concerned those on musical instruments and on clocks and watches; then there was the duty on gloves, and that on silk, which in spite of the countervailing excise, had a distinctly protectionist character. Germany he said had signed a most-favoured-nation treaty with a free-trade England and the latter was gradually becoming less free-trade; while Germany had since signed a number of tariff treaties with other countries and the United Kingdom was benefiting by every concession any one of those treaties contained.

2. I replied that while the facts might be as he stated, I failed to see that there was any material grievance. With all its duties England was still a free trade country and presented a lower barrier to German imports than any other market in the world. What was the proportion of Germany's gloves, clocks and musical instruments to her whole industry? It must be infinitesimal. And could he name one single British product which was not liable to German duty, except coal which was subject to the still more onerous regime of licence? Possibly our mouse may have grown into a rat, but say what he would, the German hippopotamus was still a hippopotamus. Herr de Haas replied that the German duties were, at any rate, on a moderate scale, while the British rates were very high when they did occur, in fact practically prohibitive, so that the outcry in Germany was very loud. Moreover, he said, except in the case of motor cars, they always seemed to affect articles of especial interest to German producers. The English mouse, he said, was always nibbling at German bread. I said that the English mouse might sometimes find a German crumb, but the German hippopotamus was devouring whole loaves all the time.

I have, &c.,

R. C. LINDSAY

[2] In September 1915 Mr. R. McKenna as Chancellor of the Exchequer had introduced an import duty of 33⅓% on luxury goods such as motor-cars, watches, clocks, musical instruments and cameras. By the Safeguarding of Industries Act, passed in August 1921 (printed in *The Public General Acts*, 11 & 12 Geo. 5, c. 47), a similar duty was levied on certain non-luxury goods with the object of protecting key industries in Great Britain. Both the McKenna duties and the safeguarding duties were abolished by Mr. Snowden in his budget of April 1924 and reimposed and extended by Mr. Churchill, who succeeded Mr. Snowden as Chancellor of the Exchequer in November 1924, in the Finance Acts of 1925 and 1926, printed *op. cit.*, 15 & 16 Geo. 5, c. 36, and 16 & 17 Geo. 5, c. 22, respectively.

No. 176

Letter from Mr. Sargent to Sir R. Lindsay (Berlin)
[C 2297/49/18]

FOREIGN OFFICE, *March 26, 1928*

Dear Lindsay,

To complete the correspondence which has arisen out of Rowe Dutton's letter to Waley of March 3rd,[1] I now send you copy of Hopkins' letter to Tyrrell in answer to the latter's letter which you have already had (see our 'comps.' of March 20th).[2] For your private ear I might mention that Tyrrell's letter of March 19th was largely written in order to show that we viewed with some disquiet the propensity which Rowe Dutton seemed to be developing of continuing the bad old Treasury attitude of attributing sinister and machiavellian motives to every move which Gilbert makes. I am sure you will do your best to check any tendency that you may detect in this direction.

As to the meeting referred to in Hopkins' letter of the 21st, you may like to know that it took place at the Treasury on March 22nd and that Lord Blanesburgh, Tyrrell, Hopkins, Phillips,[3] Waley and myself attended. It was recognised that H.M. Government in theory were in sympathy with the fixation of the reparation debt and the form of transfer arrangements as advocated by Parker Gilbert. On the other hand, in the opinion of the meeting the acceptance even in principle of Gilbert's proposals was subject to the essential condition that the greatest care should be exercised in selecting the opportune moment for putting them forward officially. There was no likelihood that such an opportune moment would occur before the installation of the new United States President in March 1929.

It was found difficult to define the motives which had prompted Parker Gilbert to make this definite effort to get the proposals discussed officially at an early date. It was agreed that it was partly due to his wish to prepare in advance against a forthcoming crisis; partly due to general considerations of justice and economic reconstruction, and lastly to an unconscious desire to get back to America and take up other work. The wishes and advice of Mr. Mellon and of New York financial circles have also probably played a part in determining his present line of action. Tyrrell also called attention to the intimate relations existing between Gilbert and M. Poincaré which seemed

---

[1] Not printed. A copy of this letter to Mr. S. D. Waley, an Assistant Secretary in H.M. Treasury, was sent to Mr. Sargent by Mr. Rowe-Dutton. The letter discussed in particular possible reasons why Mr. Parker Gilbert had recently suggested to Dr. Stresemann, Herr von Schubert, and Dr. Köhler that Germany would do well to seize any psychological opportunity that presented itself to come forward and ask for a fixation of the total German reparation liability.

[2] This printed compliments slip is not preserved in Foreign Office archives. The letter of March 19 from Sir W. Tyrrell to Sir R. Hopkins enclosed therein and Sir R. Hopkins' reply of March 21 enclosed in the present letter are not printed. Sir W. Tyrrell's letter commented on Mr. Rowe-Dutton's letter of March 3 and Sir R. Hopkins' reply foreshadowed the meeting described below.

[3] Mr. F. Phillips, a Principal Assistant Secretary in H.M. Treasury.

to indicate that the two had found means of reconciling their apparently divergent points of view.

It was generally agreed that the effort Gilbert has already made to induce the German Government to raise the question will not find any response in Berlin, at any rate not until after the German elections. Against this, however, it was recognised that we must be prepared for Gilbert to continue his efforts to get his proposals discussed in the near future, and the suggestion was thrown out that if we are compelled to face a premature discussion, the best policy for His Majesty's Government to adopt would be to suggest that the question should be considered by a committee constituted on the same lines and with the same members as the original Dawes Committee.

As regards Parker Gilbert's forthcoming visit to the Treasury where he is to see the Chancellor of the Exchequer,[4] it was agreed that the line to take would be that indicated in the second paragraph of this letter.

As to the action to be taken by the Reparation Commission when it is called upon to consider Gilbert's latest memorandum,[5] it was agreed that Lord Blanesburgh should endeavour to prevent any critical discussion and to dispose of the matter by means of a non-committal resolution on the lines of that adopted in January when the Commission took note of Gilbert's official report.

Since writing this I see that Waley has sent his account[6] of the meeting to Rowe Dutton. It is somewhat different from mine but as the two supplement rather than contradict one another I continue to send you mine for what it is worth.

ORME SARGENT

[4] Mr. Parker Gilbert was due to arrive in London on March 25 for a visit of three days.
[5] This memorandum of February 24 from Mr. Gilbert for the Reparation Commission (not printed) was in confirmation of the views he had expressed at the meeting on January 14 (see the enclosure in No. 114) and argued in favour of fixing the total German reparation liability.   [6] Not printed.

No. 177

Sir R. Lindsay (Berlin) to Sir A. Chamberlain (Received March 30)
No. 251 [C 2530/49/18]

BERLIN, *March 27, 1928*

Sir,

I have the honour to transmit to you a note by Mr Rowe Dutton of a conversation he has had with Dr Schacht, President of the Reichsbank. In the concluding paragraph of this note, he gives an interesting estimate of Dr Schacht's mental processes so far as Reparations are concerned; an important question indeed; for in Germany most politicians are weak, hesitant, swayed this way and that by passing currents or by considerations of very secondary importance, while Schacht is clear headed, and competent; a man who will make up his mind as to what he wants and then pursue his path with determination. He will therefore be an immensely important factor at the moment when great Reparation questions come up for decision.

2. In Mr Rowe Dutton's estimate, I generally concur, but with a slight reservation. In every man's mental make-up there is an intellectual and an emotional side, and in Schacht both are of more than ordinary strength. It is the intellectual side which is usually in charge of the man, and the reactions of which so far as they concern us, have been adequately described in the enclosed note. This side of him is great enough to ensure that normally he will take a scientific view of great problems. But his emotions, besides being strong, are also somewhat conditioned by his origin; for he is a frontiersman from northern Holstein, from a district which three times within a life time has been transferred from one sovereignty to another, and there is something in him of the minority race. This may help to induce an intensity of feeling on national questions that may be anything but scientific, and there is thus a possibility that at given moments and under certain impulses the emotional side of Dr Schacht may display itself in outbursts as interesting to the psychologist as they may be of concern to the politician; but I should anticipate that generally the intellectual side would quickly regain the mastery. If therefore Dr Schacht's attitude towards Reparations turns out to be generally an objective one, we must ascribe this not to any prevalence in him of that mild internationalism which characterises so many great financiers, but rather to the victory of a powerful head over a strongly beating heart.

I have, &c.,

R. C. LINDSAY

ENCLOSURE IN No. 177*

Notes of Conversation with Dr. Schacht on the 23rd March, 1928, by Mr. Rowe-Dutton

I called on Dr. Schacht and enjoyed a somewhat discursive conversation with him on various points.

We started by discussing the formation of new savings in Germany, with the general progress of which Dr. Schacht expressed himself as being far from satisfied. Even the visible savings, such as the new investments in securities and mortgage bonds, were, in his opinion, too much made with merely borrowed money. He thought this even extended to the new savings in the Sparkassen,[1] though this he had so far been unable to prove. It was, however, quite clear to him that when, for example, the Deutsche Bank raised a loan abroad wherewith to make loans to small businesses which were not of a standing to raise loans themselves, that the marks received by the small businesses went through one channel or another to the Sparkassen, &c., and appeared there as new savings. Similarly, too, some part of the visible new savings merely represented the currency equivalent of Devisen[2] borrowed abroad and waiting employment. A similar result was produced by Germans who borrowed marks against the security of borrowed Devisen.

Of course the whole question turned on the volume of consumption in Germany, and, in consumption, he would include even those formations of permanent investment which merely go to raise the standard of living. He

---

[1] Savings banks.   [2] Foreign bills of exchange.

took as an example a splendid new building recently erected for a central office of the health insurance organisation. This was all very well; undoubtedly it meant additional amenities, but, in the present state of Germany, it was an extravagance, and an extravagance which would have some day to be paid for. The people who benefited by this extravagance, namely, the working-classes, knew quite well that they, at any rate, would not do the paying; so the whole question comes down in the end to one of socialism against capital-ism. If the labouring classes are allowed to consume excessively, whether directly or indirectly, the fountain of new savings will be dried up, and the new capital required not to improve, but even to maintain, the existing standards will fail.

Therefore Dr. Schacht felt it his duty to preach a doctrine of saving and to advocate thrift in every sphere. Where the Agent-General emphasises the need of this in his reports, Dr. Schacht was entirely in agreement with him. It was true that such savings would be in the interest of the Allied Powers, but, as he saw it, Germany must give her critics no handle for the charge that by personal or administrative extravagance they had not done all, and more than all, that could be asked of them. When a conference came about to make what he trusted would be a final solution of the present difficulties concerning Europe, he hoped that Germany would be invited as an equal partner and would come to that conference with a record of which she might be proud. I, of course, endorsed this view, that a condition precedent to an eventual settle-ment is that Germany comes with clean hands.

I said that I myself had discerned tendencies towards increasing consump-tion which had alarmed me, but, none the less, were not certain factors to be regarded as favourable? For example, had Dr. Schacht been encouraged by the result of the recent issue of railway preference shares? He said that it might indeed have been worse, but the figures of foreign subscriptions sup-plied to him in confidence by the different banks in Germany showed that foreign subscriptions ranged from 60 per cent. to no less than 85 per cent. If the former figure were somewhat encouraging, the latter certainly was not.

Dr. Schacht had seen the report of the Reichskreditgesellschaft (to which reference is made in the memorandum on capital formation in Germany enclosed with Sir Ronald Lindsay's despatch No. 218[3] of the 15th March, 1928). The figure given therein of the total formation of capital of 7 to 8 milliard R.M., might perhaps be arithmetically correct, but to him such a figure was meaningless. If, for example, it represented copper bars or tons of coal, then he could understand it, but it was bound to include also, for example, new pavements in the streets of Berlin. Surely these two things could not be added together and called new capital. He entirely agreed when I said

[3] This despatch and the enclosed memorandum of March 8 by Mr. Rowe-Dutton on the formation of capital in Germany in 1927 are not printed. In this memorandum Mr. Rowe-Dutton cited a report by the German credit company which estimated the formation of capital at some 12 milliard Reichsmarks, of which 7,600 million Reichsmarks were derived from internal sources. Mr. Rowe-Dutton concluded that on the surface the prospects for 1928 were 'distinctly encouraging' and that the general situation did not call for immediate anxiety.

that I had laid emphasis on the fact that not only must Germany save a sufficient amount to meet her external liabilities, but she must also save it in a form which can be transferred abroad.

Internal savings which could not be transferred abroad too easily expressed themselves, sooner or later, in the form of a rise in the standard of living. Once this was attained there was little or no hope of a subsequent reduction, and for all practical purposes in which we were interested that internal saving had disappeared. This was not merely a German problem; it affected all countries in varying degrees. Too much consumption, too much socialisation ran counter to the aims and objects of the present economic system, which must be capitalistic.

What would be the eventual result of this tendency in Germany? It would be bad enough if only German savings were dissipated in this way; but when, also, this increase in the standard of living was brought about by foreign borrowing, then the consequences might be very serious. When all available assets had been sold to meet the service of unproductive loans, then the foreigner would come forward with yet further claims, which would have to be met by the sales of ordinary shares, buildings, land. There would be an 'Überfremdenheit'[4] of Germany, which would mean sacrifices not only for Germans, but also for their creditors, and could not fail to bring about economic and financial crises of disastrous magnitude.

Dr. Schacht was sure that neither America nor Germany wished the time to come when whole streets of houses would be labelled: 'This street belongs to Charley Dawes.' It was to avoid this contingency that he was doing everything in his power not merely to advocate, but to enforce, saving.

I sought to get Dr. Schacht into an equally expansive mood on the subject of foreign Devisen and his policy with regard thereto, but on this he was anything but communicative. I gather, however, that he thinks the present situation favourable for increasing to some extent the gold holdings of the Reichsbank, and it is not improbable that during the next few months some part of his Devisen will be exchanged for gold. He had seen much theoretical criticism of his Devisen policy in various quarters recently, but he complained that it was all far too theoretical, and suggested that it might have been written under the influence of Keynes,[5] who, he felt, was much too much inclined to assume that the theoretical consequences of a practical action will work themselves out without friction. But, as a practical banker, Dr. Schacht knew that the effect of friction in economic life was often all important. For his part, he was going to interfere with the working of natural laws whenever he thought that by doing so he could relieve the risks of undue friction.

I asked him if he were satisfied with the present situation regarding the loans of public authorities and the Beratungsstelle.

He expressed himself as completely satisfied. There had been a stoppage

---

[4] i.e. excessive foreign indebtedness.

[5] Mr. J. M. Keynes, Fellow of Kings College, Cambridge, had been principal representative of H.M. Treasury at the Peace Conference of Paris and was the author, in particular, of *The Economic Consequences of the Peace* (London, 1919).

of foreign loans to public authorities for almost six months. Now he felt it would be possible to relax pressure a little, and presently to allow a certain amount of foreign borrowing. The public authorities had learnt their lesson. They had found out that Dr. Schacht's views were seriously held and seriously supported, and he felt they had come to accept those views. Compared with the shrieks of rage of last October, the murmur of complaint was now very slight. Indeed, were it not for political repercussions, he would not be surprised if the town authorities openly endorsed what he, Dr. Schacht, had said at Bochum.[6]

Once more, the whole conversation gave me the impression that Dr. Schacht is convinced that the measures which Germany must take in her own interests are exactly those measures which are in the interests of the Allies. Throughout, there was little or no hint of opposition to the payment of reparations as such; certainly there was no word which would lead one to suppose Dr. Schacht would be willing that Germany should suffer if the Allies suffered more. On the contrary, I should say he would be willing that the Allies should benefit on condition that Germany benefits more. He is fully convinced of the truth of the doctrine that prosperity for one is impossible without prosperity for all. This does not, of course, mean that Dr. Schacht will not fight to secure the most favourable possible terms for Germany in any final settlement of reparations, but it does, I think, mean that Dr. Schacht will do his best to bring about such conditions in Germany as will make a reasonable settlement possible. There are many many things as to which he will on the short view, take a line definitely opposed to that of the reparation creditors of Germany, but, on the long view, his policy will be devoted towards creating a permanently prosperous Germany, which, in his view, will offer the greatest possibility for a permanent settlement of the reparation question. If, to prevent an impairment of the permanent prosperity of Germany, he has to bring an early and temporary crisis, he will not hesitate to do so. Just as last May he did not hesitate to smash what he considered the undesirable situation on the stock exchange. His actions may be wrong, but they will at least be honest; nor will they be dictated by any mere personal ambition. In a word, he regards himself as trustee for the future of Germany.

[6] For a report on this speech of November 18, 1927, see *The Times*, November 19, 1927, p. 13.

No. 178

Sir G. Grahame (Brussels) to Sir A. Chamberlain (Received March 28)
No. 281 [C 2465/969/18]

Confidential   BRUSSELS, *March 27, 1928*

Sir,
    I have had the honour to receive your despatch No. 179[1] (C 2122/969/18)

[1] This covering despatch is not preserved in Foreign Office archives. It enclosed a letter of February 27 from the Foreign Office to the Treasury referring to M. Hymans'

of the 22nd instant, enclosing correspondence with the Treasury with regard to the question of the German marks left in Belgium at the end of the war and the claim on the part of the Belgian Government for compensation.

2. I observe that the Lords Commissioners of the Treasury consider that even a partial compensation to Belgium would infringe the rights of the other Powers entitled to reparation, and that Their Lordships state that they trust, if the question be raised by the Belgian Government, the impossibility of any sympathy being shown by His Majesty's Government will be made clear.

3. The origin of this question was the discovery by the Belgian Government, when they re-entered their country at the end of the war, that there were some five and a half milliard German paper marks in circulation, the Belgian population having been forced by Germany during the occupation to accept them at the rate of 1·25 Belgian francs to the mark. The political state of Belgium was critical at that time and there was undoubtedly some apprehension on the part of the Government on arriving from Havre lest serious— possibly subversive—movements should take place. It was at once decided to allow the population to exchange their German marks for Belgian francs at the rate of 1·25 francs to the mark. It is usually said that owing to the delay of some weeks in carrying out this operation, a large quantity of marks were introduced into Belgium, chiefly from Holland, the amount being estimated at six hundred million marks (thirty million pounds). I have not, at this moment, the exact figure actually paid out by the Belgian State in execution of the operation of exchange, but the equivalent in sterling of five and a half milliard German paper marks was nominally £375,000,000.

4. Various abortive negotiations have taken place with the German Government, and the position now appears to be that, even if the latter were ready to grant partial compensation, the ex-Allied Governments would consider that such compensation would prejudice their reparation rights.

5. The Belgians never forget that the chief reason for the impoverishment and even the menace of bankruptcy of the national finances was the disbursement by the State of the equivalent of several hundred million pounds in order to take over from the population the German paper marks left in the country. The leaders of all the principal political parties, including the Socialists, have made it clear that they do not intend to abandon the claim for compensation. M. Vandervelde has spoken as categorically on the subject as the leaders of the Catholic and Liberal parties, and, though they are doubtless at a loss at present how to obtain such compensation, they are certainly on the watch for any opportunity for pressing the claim, and in doing so would have the whole nation behind them.

6. It would have an unfortunate effect on Anglo-Belgian relations if His Majesty's Government opposed such a claim without, in so doing, being closely associated with the French Government, who, as it appears from the correspondence with the Treasury, would be equally prejudiced by any German payments to Belgium for her losses in this respect.

speech of February 21 (see No. 129, note 2) and the Treasury's reply of March 16, the conclusion of which is recapitulated in paragraph 2 below.

7. During the first four or five years after the Armistice, feeling against Great Britain in this country was bitter on account of the attitude of His Majesty's Government who were supposed to be hindering Belgium from obtaining proper reparation. French propaganda during those years certainly encouraged this idea with the object of securing Belgian support of French policy which, during those years, usually ran counter to that of His Majesty's Government. The support of public opinion for the co-operation of the Belgian with the French Government in occupying the Ruhr was largely due to the explosion of grievances thus aroused. During the last three years, there has been a most satisfactory improvement in Anglo-Belgian relations and a progressive cessation of press attacks upon British policy. Circumstances might, however, arise when it would suit once more French politicians that there should be a return of ill-feeling in Belgium against Great Britain. Any isolated action on the part of His Majesty's Government in categorically discountenancing Belgian desires for compensation in the matter of the German marks might once more inflame Belgian opinion against Great Britain.

8. I had a somewhat unpleasant experience a few days ago of the continued existence of Belgian grievances. I was invited by 'Le Jeune Barreau' to attend a lecture to be given by the Prime Minister at the Palais de Justice. The subject, as announced, was 'Face à l'Avenir', though, as it turned out, he discoursed mostly about the past. I was the only ex-Allied representative present. M. Jaspar, who spoke without notes, began his lecture by reviewing the post-Armistice situation, and, apparently being carried away by his feelings, entered upon a long and vehement fulmination about the manner in which Belgium had been treated by her ex-Allies and associates, and about the non-fulfilment of solemn promises given to the martyr-nation during the war. This experience brought home to me anew how near the surface are the former Belgian grievances, of which I heard so much—especially from M. Jaspar, then Minister for Foreign Affairs—during the first three or four years of my mission here.[2]

I have, &c.,
GEORGE GRAHAME

[2] Sir G. Grahame was appointed H.M. Ambassador at Brussels in August 1920.

No. 179

Sir A. Chamberlain to the Marquess of Crewe (Paris)

No. 23 Telegraphic: by bag [C 2274/394/18]

FOREIGN OFFICE, <i>March 29, 1928</i>

Your telegram No. 49[1] (of March 22nd: settlement of outstanding disarmament points).

Experience has shown that the German Ministry of Foreign Affairs are prone to adopt obstructive tactics where the experts and visits are concerned,

[1] No. 170.

and that they are inclined to seize opportunities such as that offered by contemplated conversations between German Embassy in Paris and M. Massigli to take the whole matter into their hands for bargaining purposes. It is for this reason that we have always advocated continuance at Berlin of discussions between the experts without the intervention of the governments concerned. Moreover, visits proposed are in no case essential from our standpoint and we are accordingly all the less desirous that they should become the occasion of a diplomatic controversy.

We are unaware what considerations have led the Conference to the conclusion that desired result is more likely to be obtained at this stage by direct discussion between the Conference and the German Embassy, Paris, than between the experts and their German colleagues, but might it not be as well that the allied ambassadors in Berlin should first be consulted as to whether the proposed démarche is likely to produce a favourable result. Apart from this we are in the circumstances ready to authorise you to accept draft resolution provided

(I) that M. Massigli should put nothing in writing relative to the visits it is desired to make;

(II) that it is understood (as between the Allies) that if the Germans consent as a result of the proposed démarche to invite the experts to pay visits in the instances named (military establishments, coast batteries, reserve rations and police accommodation and distribution) in so far as agreed measures may already have been carried out in such cases the experts will be withdrawn from Berlin without further question immediately these visits (which should of course consist only of test visits in each instance) have been carried out.

You should make it clear to the Conference in intimating the acceptance by His Majesty's Government on the conditions named of the draft resolution, that the withdrawal of the experts proposed above is not to be delayed for the purpose of verifying the execution by the German government of any measures that have *still* to be put into effect, such as the alienation or transformation of the remaining military establishments and the alterations to police barracks.

No. 180

Letter from Sir R. Lindsay (Berlin) to Mr. Sargent
[C 2578/969/18]

Private   BERLIN, *March 29, 1928*

Dear Sargent,

Thanks for your letter of the 26th[1] (C.2231/48/62) enclosing one from Eric Phipps about Reparation, Debts, and Rhineland evacuation.

I have before now expressed myself rather forcibly about the Occupation. I still hold that it is a running sore and a perpetual source of friction between the two countries, who, so long as it lasts, cannot attain to cordial relations. Further that the Locarno Treaties have taken the wind out of its sails as

[1] Not printed. This letter forwarded a copy of No. 164 to Sir R. Lindsay.

a means of giving France security; in this respect it has lost virtue. But in another connection, that with Reparation, I have gradually modified my own view.

It has always been a time honoured device for a victor in war to occupy conquered territory until an indemnity has been paid. 1871 is a locus classicus, where evacuation took place almost department by department as the cash was paid over. A vanquished state will make immense financial sacrifices to get foreign troops out of its territory. The connection between Reparation and Occupation has always been axiomatic, and remains so still if we make due allowance for changes brought about by modern conditions.

Now when the Reparation Commission produced the figure of 132 milliards no one in his senses imagined that this piling of a paper Ossa on a paper Pelion solved the Reparation problem; nor can the Dawes Plan be considered as more than a step, though a great step, towards realities; but there remains a third stage to be traversed, at the end of which we may hope that Reparation may be fixed at such a sum and in such a manner that there will be automatic compulsions on the Germans to pay it without suffering the pressure of an armed occupation by enemy troops. But are not the French justified in maintaining the occupation till the Germans are brought safely through this last stage? And is it not natural that von Hoesch protests that of course Occupation and Reparation are completely separate issues?

The fact that the Treaty of Versailles limits the occupation to fifteen years does not invalidate my argument. This is only a recognition of the fact that with the huge indemnities now payable and with the modern financial methods of capitalization and amortization over a long period, it ceases to be practical politics to contemplate an occupation coinciding in duration with the payment of reparation. We no longer make evacuation depend on the receipt of cash; but on the acceptance of a scheme of payment, the punctual fulfilment of which shall be in the interest of victor and vanquished alike—i.e. the commercialization of the reparation debt.

We have had a blessed pause of six months now in the wrangle over evacuation, but I think the Germans will call an end to the truce as soon as they can after the elections. I have little doubt they would wish to resume hostilities at Geneva in June, but if, as seems likely, their elections take place on May 20, they may have found it impossible to form a Government in time; but I think they are sure to be moving by or before September, quite regardless of the prospects of success. If the elections go to the left the Democratic parties will have to display their patriotism on an issue which appeals strongly to every German in the country; if the Right were to win, of course all the more so.

Yours sincerely,
R. C. LINDSAY

No. 181

Letter from Mr. Kennard (Belgrade) to Mr. Sargent
[C 2641/2/92]

BELGRADE, *March 29, 1928*

Dear Sargent,

I feel a little perturbed as to the course of the Italo-Yugoslav conversations for the renewal of the pact of Rome. It is true that Rakić has had a fairly cordial conversation with Mussolini, but they do not seem to be getting down to business.[1] Now they have little over three months, in which to come to terms and it seems to me essential for the peace of Europe that they should. One hears that the success of these conversations depends on the course of Franco-Italian negotiations, but surely this is an extremely unsatisfactory state of affairs. The foolish Franco-Yugoslav pact is no doubt responsible for it, but if peace in the Balkans is to merely depend on the goodwill between France and Italy, Heaven help us.

It is surely time that Italy and Yugoslavia should make up their minds whether they are going to resume decent neighbourly relations or not. The conventions of Nettuno, assurances re Albania, etc. are mere details and could no doubt be settled provided Mussolini and Marinković conclude some instrument, which will relieve these people of the nightmare of Italian aggression. At present they are so jumpy that they see Italian intrigues everywhere, be it in Bulgaria, Hungary or Albania. Hence their decided tendency to flirt with Germany. One wonders whether, if this state of affairs goes on, the 'Drang nach Osten'[2] may not in the future be renewed on a far more favourable basis.

I do not suppose you are inclined to say anything in Rome and during Marinković's absence[3] it is difficult to do much here; but the weeks are passing and we may find ourselves in July with no progress towards any useful solution and indeed with the possibility that the pact of Rome, which offers a unique opportunity for a general settlement, may altogether lapse. If one felt that Mussolini was prepared to reach a comprehensive understanding, one could put more pressure on these people as regards the ratification of the Nettuno conventions and the settlement of the various Italian claims. As it is, incidents and press attacks occur with the same frequency on both sides and we shall go drifting on until we finally get into a serious mess. The Macedonian Revolutionary Organisation and certain elements in Hungary and elsewhere naturally exploit the situation to the full. I do feel, therefore, that something should be done to make both sides see the urgent necessity of converting the pact of Rome into a really binding and useful instrument for the dissipation of the present suspicions and points of friction.

[1] Mr. Kennard had reported in Belgrade despatch No. 106 of March 15 that the Serb-Croat-Slovene Minister for Foreign Affairs seemed 'well satisfied' regarding this conversation which took place on March 12.

[2] Pressure towards the East.

[3] M. Marinkovitch was taking a cure in France.

I was afraid that we were going to have another St. Gotthard affair at Subotica the other day, but it turned out to be a *bona fide* consignment for Roumania.

It is amusing to note that the *mot d'ordre* must have gone round here to make no comment on the Greco-Roumanian treaty,[4] as I can find nothing in the local press.

One hears of the usual parliamentary crisis after Easter and the government is certainly unpopular. There are even rumours of Ninčić coming back, but it is useless making any predictions at present.[5]

Yours ever,

H. W. KENNARD

[4] The pact of non-aggression, conciliation, judicial settlement and arbitration between Greece and Roumania was signed on March 21, 1928, and is printed in *British and Foreign State Papers*, vol. 130, pp. 780–5.

[5] In his reply of April 14 Mr. Sargent referred to Nos. 162 and 187 and stated that he was sure Mr. Kennard would agree that 'things are a little more hopeful now and that it would be safer for us not to butt in at Rome just yet'.

No. 182

Sir A. Chamberlain to the Marquess of Crewe (Paris)

No. 763 [C 2299/855/18]

FOREIGN OFFICE, *March 30, 1928*

My Lord Marquess,

With reference to Foreign Office despatch No. 699[1] of March 11th, 1927 (C 2146/2146/18) I transmit to Your Lordship herewith copies of semi-official correspondence between this department and the War Office in connexion with the recent illegal entry of Reichswehr detachments into the demilitarized zone.[2]

2. I request that you will explain to the French Government the attitude adopted by His Majesty's Government in regard to this matter before the question is brought before the Ambassadors' Conference.[3]

I am, &c.,

(For the Secretary of State)

ORME SARGENT

[1] See Volume III, No. 41.

[2] This correspondence comprised a letter of March 22 from Major Calthrop, together with its enclosures (not printed) and the Foreign Office reply printed as the enclosure below. Enclosed in Major Calthrop's letter was a letter of March 20 from Major H. T. Martin, Assistant Military Attaché to H.M. Embassy at Paris, forwarding a draft letter from the Allied Military Committee of Versailles to the Conference of Ambassadors regarding press reports from Baden that unarmed detachments of the Reichswehr had taken part in military ski championships held at Feldberg in the demilitarized zone of the Rhineland.

[3] Sir E. Phipps acted on these instructions in H.M. Embassy's note No. 232 of April 5 to the French Ministry of Foreign Affairs which was transmitted to the Foreign Office in Paris covering despatch No. 640, not preserved in Foreign Office archives.

Letter from Mr. Perowne to Major Calthrop

FOREIGN OFFICE, *April 2, 1928*[4]

Dear Calthrop,

Many thanks for your letter No. 0154/6833/M.I.3 of March 22nd about the illegal presence of Reichswehr skiing teams in the demilitarised zone. We have taken copies of the enclosures the originals of which I return to you herewith as requested.

We are advised that the presence of these teams in the demilitarised zone constitutes a technical violation of Article 43 of the Treaty of Versailles, on the assumption, which appears probable, that the detachments in question are to be regarded as 'formed bodies' in accordance with the wording of paragraph 3 of our letter to you of September 17th, 1926.[5] The question whether a ski championship of this description constitutes a military manœuvre in the sense of Article 43 may be more doubtful, but if the above-mentioned assumption is correct it does not appear necessary to establish this contention in order to show that a technical violation of Article 43 has been committed.

Major Martin is quite correct in assuming that the case falls within the category referred to in paragraphs 2 (d) and 8 of our despatch to Paris No. 699 of March 11th, 1927 (see enclosures to our letter to you of March 15th, 1927[6]). You will recollect that it was there laid down that the Ambassadors' Conference and its expert advisers were not to be employed for dealing with cases in this category. We wrote 'in the case of acts committed in the neutral zone the ordinary diplomatic channel must be used by the Allied Governments' until such time as the League should set up some preliminary machinery which would render it unnecessary for the Allied Powers in every trivial case to have recourse to their rights under paragraphs 1 and 2 of Article 4 of the Treaty of Locarno.

There is of course at present no such preliminary machinery in existence for considering whether a violation of Article 43 has in any given circumstance taken place or not. The rules adopted by the Council of the League for the exercise of the right of investigation provided for by the Treaty of Versailles, etc.,[7] are not of course relevant to the present case, as they start from the assumption that the Council has been seized of an infraction of Article 43. This has not yet been done where the skiing teams are concerned and it seems desirable to avoid such a reference if possible.

[4] Date of despatch of this letter to the War Office. The copy sent to Paris was presumably sent after approval of the draft on March 28.

[5] See Volume II, enclosure in No. 224.

[6] Not printed.

[7] i.e. the application, notably in respect of article 213 of the Treaty of Versailles, of the scheme for investigation by the League of Nations into the execution of the naval, military, and air clauses of the treaties of peace, which was approved by the Council on September 27, 1924: see *League of Nations Official Journal*, October 1924, pp. 1592–5 (for a text embodying certain amendments see League of Nations document C. 729. 1926. IX): see also Volume II, No. 297.

Plainly then the ordinary diplomatic channel must be used in this case. The simplest procedure would seem to be for the representatives at Berlin of the Powers forming the Ambassadors' Conference jointly to call the attention of the German Government to the reports in the Baden press, which may be assumed to be correct, and to say that prima facie the presence of the skiing patrols in the demilitarised zone constitutes an infraction of Article 43. The despatch indeed of any Reichswehr detachment to the demilitarised zone whether armed or unarmed, and irrespective of the object of the visit is a technical infringement of the Treaty. At the same time the Powers do not wish to avail themselves of their rights under the Treaty of Locarno in a matter of such small importance and it is proposed therefore that the German Government should extend the undertaking given by them in July 1927 in respect of military bands[8] so as to cover also the entry into the demilitarised zone of any detachment of the Reichswehr whatsoever. If however the German Government decline this suggestion the ex-Allied Powers will be left with no alternative except to make use of their Treaty rights.

While we agree that this is prima facie a case of a rather provocative violation of Article 43 which ought not to be passed over, we do not however feel that His Majesty's Government should take the initiative therein, though we should be quite ready of course to back up the French at Berlin if they attach importance to the matter. We would suggest that Colonel Needham should be instructed to argue, on the lines laid down in our despatch No. 699 of March 11th, 1927, and[9] the Allied Military Committee of Versailles are not competent to deal with the matter and that the French Government, if they attach importance to raising it, should do so through the diplomatic channel.

Copies of this letter and of your letter under reply have been sent to Lord Crewe with instructions to explain our point of view to the French Government before the question is brought before the Ambassadors' Conference.

Yours sincerely,
J. V. PEROWNE

[8] See Volume III, No. 251, note 5.   [9] This word should read 'that'.

No. 183

Letter from Mr. Holman[1] (Paris) to Mr. Sargent

[C 2576/394/18]

PARIS, March 31, 1928

Dear Sargent,

I saw Massigli yesterday and spoke to him in the sense of Foreign Office telegram No. 23[2] (C. 2274/394/18) of March 29th regarding the settlement of outstanding disarmament questions. I first pointed out to him the danger of the contemplated conversations between him and the German Embassy in Paris. He replied that he fully realised the force of that argument. I then laid before him your proposal that the Allied Ambassadors in Berlin should be

[1] Second Secretary in H.M. Embassy at Paris.   [2] No. 179.

consulted as to whether the proposed representations in Paris would produce a favourable result. Although raising no strong objection to the suggestion, Massigli thought that such a step would entail considerable delay. As it is, there has already been a fortnight's delay since the resolution of the Conference and it would probably take some weeks before all the delegations had obtained the views of their representatives in Germany and the Conference had decided upon the line of action to be adopted. M. Massigli explained that the French Ambassador in Berlin was at present away. He was therefore in a difficult position as it would be useless for him to consult the Chargé d'Affaires who would not be in a position to give a considered opinion. He would have to consult the military authorities in Paris.

2. I then discussed with Massigli the points raised in the three final paragraphs of your telegram under reference. He assured me that in the case of the proposed representations in Paris nothing would be put in writing. He said that he was as anxious as we were to get the allied experts withdrawn from Germany and that this could be done as soon as visits of inspection or verification had been made as regards the outstanding questions. He could not say off-hand whether the experts might not require to make certain visits in connection with questions other than those of military establishments, coast batteries, reserve rations and police occupation and distribution. He added that much remained to be done as regards the approval of police laws regarding which the German authorities had shown no desire to take the necessary action. He quite agreed that the experts would not be called upon to stay on in Germany to deal with the final execution of such questions as the alienation of military establishments.

3. I feel that much valuable time would be wasted and little advantage gained by submitting to the Conference your proposal for a reference of the question of the advisability of conversations between Massigli and the German Embassy to the Allied representatives in Berlin. If the French, who are the most interested party as regards visits of verification, feel that the best course in order to obtain satisfaction will be to approach the Germans in Paris, I hardly feel that we can intervene. I at the same time quite realise that we do not wish to become involved in any diplomatic controversy. I would suggest, therefore, if you approve that in the circumstances we should simply address a note to the Conference accepting the resolution contained in paragraph 5 of Lord Crewe's telegram No. 49[3] of March 22nd drawing their attention at the same time to the considerations set out in the three final paragraphs of Foreign Office telegram No. 23. I hardly think that it is necessary to place on record any statement on the lines of paragraph 2 of that telegram.

Yrs ever,

A. HOLMAN

[3] No. 170.

No. 184

Sir E. Phipps (Paris) to Sir A. Chamberlain (Received April 3)
No. 605 C [W 3300/138/17]

PARIS, *April 2, 1928*

Sir,

With reference to the Marquess of Crewe's despatch No. 565[1] of the 28th March, in which His Lordship reported his conversation with M. Briand on the subject of the French Customs Tariff, I have the honour to transmit to you, herewith, copy of the reply of the Ministry for Foreign Affairs to the note which Lord Crewe addressed to them on the 12th January in accordance with the instructions contained in your despatch No. 59[2] (W.138/138/17) of the 9th January.

2. After a reference to Mr. Fountain's visit to Paris last year[3] and to his inability to give any undertaking on behalf of His Majesty's Government as regards British customs duties, the note seeks to defend the moderation of French tariff policy. It mentions, in particular, the duties on certain staple British products, such as coal, textiles, textile machinery and agricultural machinery, and declares that without making any return, His Majesty's Government have benefited by the concessions granted as a result of French commercial agreements with other countries.

3. The note then proceeds to complain of the duties imposed in Great Britain on French goods either for the safeguarding of British industries or for revenue purposes. It also refers to the prohibition on the importation of dyestuffs, which is in force throughout the British Empire.

4. In conclusion the note returns apparently to the suggestion made to Mr. Fountain in Paris by M. Serruys in the course of his conversations on the new French tariff revision proposals to the effect that an understanding might be reached if His Majesty's Government would give an undertaking not to increase the British duties on certain goods of special importance to French export trade in return for a similar undertaking on the part of the French Government as regards staple British products.

I have, &c.,
ERIC PHIPPS

ENCLOSURE IN NO. 184

Copy

PARIS, *le 29 mars 1928*

Par note en date du 12 janvier dernier, l'Ambassade de Grande-Bretagne a bien voulu, d'ordre de son Gouvernement, attirer l'attention du Ministère des Affaires Étrangères sur les augmentations de droits de douane subis,

---

[1] Not preserved in Foreign Office archives. According to the docket this despatch transmitted a copy of an *aide-mémoire* which Lord Crewe had left with M. Briand in accordance with the instructions in No. 166.

[2] No. 110.

[3] Cf. No. 110, note 4.

335

depuis le traité franco-allemand du 17 août 1927, par certaines marchandises britanniques importées en France.

A cette occasion, l'Ambassade a rappelé les conversations échangées entre M. Fountain et les représentants autorisés du Ministère du Commerce et du Ministère des Affaires Étrangères français.

Ce Département a l'honneur d'accuser réception de la communication précitée qui a retenu toute l'attention du Gouvernement de la République. Il regrette de ne pas avoir été en mesure de répondre plus tôt à la note de l'Ambassade, ayant dû consulter, sur cette question, les Ministères techniques qui avaient d'ailleurs déjà fourni de vive voix, aux Services commerciaux de l'Ambassade, les renseignements que ceux-ci leur avaient demandés à ce sujet.

Au cours des conversations engagées avec M. Fountain, celui-ci avait effectivement signalé l'émotion que seraient de nature à causer au Gouvernement et aux exportateurs britanniques toutes mesures tendant à aggraver la protection tarifaire en France. Il avait d'ailleurs déclaré que son gouvernement avait conscience d'être uniquement demandeur, la législation britannique interdisant toute entente tarifaire avec un pays étranger quelconque, et il avait même décliné la proposition qui lui avait été faite de compenser certaines réductions de tarif que la France accorderait à la Grande-Bretagne par l'engagement que prendrait le Gouvernement britannique de tenir compte des intérêts français qui lui seraient signalés, au moment où, à l'occasion du vote du budget, certaines élévations de tarif seraient envisagées à l'égard de produits intéressant particulièrement le commerce français.

Malgré le refus de l'administration britannique d'envisager le moindre engagement d'ordre tarifaire, le Gouvernement français s'est toujours préoccupé, dans l'élaboration des mesures douanières et des conventions commerciales intervenues au cours de ces derniers mois, de ne pas porter atteinte aux principaux intérêts britanniques.

Le Gouvernement de la République croit devoir préciser que les relèvements tarifaires dont se plaint le Gouvernement britannique ont été motivés par le seul souci de réajuster, souvent même d'une façon très incomplète, l'incidence d'un tarif douanier fortement diminué par la dépréciation du franc. Ces réajustements ayant été effectués par étapes, il en est résulté, chaque fois, une augmentation dont les importateurs étrangers se seraient peut-être moins aperçus si, comme dans certains pays, les droits de douane avaient été perçus avec un coefficient compensateur suivant chaque mois les fluctuations du change. Mais le gouvernement français a toujours estimé que la procédure de la perception des droits de douane au pair de l'or était anti-économique pour un pays dont la devise était l'objet de dépréciations successives. Les prix n'augmentant, en monnaie papier, sur le marché intérieur, qu'avec un retard souvent de plusieurs mois sur la dépréciation de la devise, la perception de droits de douane en or eût donné à la production nationale une protection en avance sur les besoins, et de ce fait exagérée. Si le Gouvernement britannique veut bien comparer au tarif français, tel qu'il existait avant la guerre, celui qui résulte de la révision tarifaire à laquelle il a été procédé depuis le mois d'août 1927 à l'occasion des traités conclus avec l'Allemagne, la Suisse, la Belgique et l'Italie,[4] le Gouvernement français est persuadé que cette comparaison fera ressortir quel soin a été apporté à ne pas dépasser, pour l'ensemble du nouveau tarif, le coefficient 5 qui correspond à la dévaluation du franc.

Il n'est pas non plus sans intérêt d'examiner les répercussions de cette révision sur les principales branches de l'importation britannique en France:

1. En dépit des demandes fort équitables formulées par les Houillères françaises et même par les ouvriers des mines en vue d'une péréquation du droit sur le charbon qui, de 1 fr. 20 or avant la guerre, se trouve réduit à 2 fr. papier à l'heure actuelle, le Gouvernement français n'a point voulu modifier la situation actuelle d'où résulte pratiquement une diminution de 66% sur le droit d'avant-guerre.

2. Pour la plupart des produits textiles qui intéressent la Grande-Bretagne, pour tous les tissus cotonniers, pour les tissus de lin ainsi que pour les fils et tissus de jute, la France a réduit les tarifs en vigueur depuis 1926 de 20 à 30% en moyenne. L'Angleterre a eu le bénéfice de ces réductions bien qu'elle-même ait soumis tous les produits de l'industrie de la soie à des droits que l'expérience fait apparaître chaque jour comme presque prohibitifs.

3. De même, au cours des conventions conclues en France avec la Suisse et, ce mois-ci, avec la Belgique, la France a réduit considérablement les droits antérieurement établis par l'accord franco-allemand sur les métiers à filer et à tisser et, d'une manière générale, sur tout l'outillage textile, en telle sorte que la protection afférente à ces produits s'est trouvée pratiquement ramenée à celle antérieure à la révision douanière consécutive à l'accord franco-allemand.

4. Pour des produits qui intéressent particulièrement l'exportation anglaise, tels que les machines agricoles et les tracteurs, le Gouvernement français est intervenu, après les démarches de l'Ambassade de Grande Bretagne, pour faire abaisser, par la Commission des Douanes de la Chambre, les droits primitivement envisagés.

Le Gouvernement britannique a bénéficié, sans contrepartie, de toutes ces concessions, alors que lui-même adoptait ou maintenait les nombreuses mesures résultant de la 'loi sur la défense des industries clés' ou de la 'loi de sauvegarde de l'économie nationale', ou même simplement de besoins fiscaux. Le Gouvernement français a d'ailleurs signalé, à diverses reprises, au cours de ces derniers mois, combien avaient été ainsi gravement atteintes des exportations françaises aussi essentielles que les vins et les soieries, ou certaines industries qui, bien qu'ayant seulement une importance locale, centralisent néanmoins toute l'activité de certaines villes françaises, comme c'est le cas, pour la lunetterie de Morez, pour la ganterie de peau de Grenoble et de Millau, etc.

Il n'est pas non plus inutile de rappeler, pour mémoire, l'obstacle considérable que crée à l'industrie chimique française, devenue largement

[4] For these French treaties of January 21, February 23 and March 7, 1928, see respectively *League of Nations Treaty Series*, vol. lxxii, pp. 275–427, and *British and Foreign State Papers*, vol. 129, pp. 188–257 and 549–61.

exportatrice, la prohibition sur les colorants, qui s'étend à tout l'Empire Britannique et les mesures de restrictions qui entravent l'exportation française du bétail sur pied, celle des cerises, etc...[5] etc...[5]

Le Gouvernement français qui, outre les mesures d'ordre tarifaire mentionnées ci-dessus a également supprimé toutes les prohibitions, à l'exception de certaines restrictions concernant l'exportation des ferrailles, a donc conscience d'avoir strictement conformé sa politique économique aux recommandations de la récente Conférence internationale de Genève à laquelle le Gouvernement britannique a bien voulu se référer dans sa note du 12 janvier.

La stabilisation des échanges et des conditions de la production doit être assurée en même temps que celle de la situation financière, mais ne peut la précéder. L'assainissement des finances de la France a permis au Gouvernement de la République de s'orienter délibérément vers des traités donnant à ses courants commerciaux une stabilisation par la consolidation des droits de douane. La législation britannique ne permettant pas la conclusion de traités comportant de part et d'autre des réductions sur les droits et les taxes en vigueur, le Gouvernement français est toujours tout disposé à rechercher une entente sur un autre terrain, tel que celui d'un accord, aux termes duquel, si l'Angleterre consentait à ne point majorer ses tarifs sur certains produits intéressant particulièrement l'exportation française, la France s'engagerait à ne point aggraver le régime tarifaire des produits cardinaux de l'exportation britannique.

Le Gouvernement français se féliciterait de voir ainsi le commerce franco-britannique à l'abri de toutes modifications éventuelles et il serait heureux que son sentiment rencontrât en la matière comme en tant d'autres, les préoccupations du Gouvernement et des milieux économique[s] de la Grande Bretagne.

[5] Punctuation as in filed copy.

No. 185

Letter from Mr. Sargent to Sir R. Lindsay (Berlin)

[*C 2424/49/18*]

FOREIGN OFFICE, *April 2, 1928*

Dear Lindsay,

With reference to your letter No. 260/4/28 of February 27th relative to the extension of the scope of the Reparation Recovery Act[1] I enclose a copy of the relevant extract[2] from the notes prepared in the Treasury to assist the

[1] No. 155.

[2] Not printed. This extract comprised Note III on 'The method of securing payments in sterling of the full Dawes Annuities which commence in September next' and argued in favour of the extension of the 26 per cent levy to German imports into the British Empire: cf. No. 155. Note I on 'The ultimate final settlement of German reparations' suggested that 'a benevolent reserve' should be maintained: Note II on 'The Title of the Agent General to advise the German Government in regard to the Economy of its Administration' suggested that if Mr. Gilbert raised this question he should be given counsels of caution. None of these Treasury Notes is printed.

Chancellor of the Exchequer in his discussions with Gilbert during the latter's present stay in London.

You will gather from the perusal of this enclosure that there is no possibility of taking the matter up with the German Government early in April as you suggested. Do you think that in all the circumstances this delay will matter very greatly?

Yours ever,
ORME SARGENT

No. 186

Letter from Mr. Sargent to Mr. Holman (Paris)

[*C 2576/394/18*]

FOREIGN OFFICE, *April 2, 1928*

Dear Holman,

Your letter of March 31st about the settlement of the outstanding disarmament points.[1]

2. We quite agree that the proposed reference to the Ambassadors at Berlin can be dropped. You can accordingly as you suggest address a memorandum to the Conference in the sense of the last part of our telegram No. 23[2] which begins with the words 'Apart from this we are in the circumstances ready to authorize you, etc., etc.,' down to the end.[3]

3. You may feel inclined to let Massigli know that we are for our part so little keen on the visits that the French need not expect much assistance in the way of diplomatic pressure from H.M. Government if the conversations with the Germans prove acrimonious and futile.

Yours ever,
ORME SARGENT

[1] No. 183.　　　　　　　　　　　　　　　　　　　[2] No. 179.
[3] Sir E. Phipps transmitted a copy of note No. 227 A.C. which was accordingly sent to the Conference of Ambassadors on April 4 in Paris covering despatch No. 633 of the same date (not preserved in Foreign Office archives).

No. 187

Sir E. Phipps (Paris) to Sir A. Chamberlain (Received April 4, 8.30 a.m.)

No. 60 Telegraphic: by bag [*C 2643/8/22*]

Very confidential

PARIS, *April 3, 1928*

Lord Crewe's telegram No. 45 Confidential of March 19th.[1]

2. M. Berthelot told me to-day in strict confidence that conversations were proceeding satisfactorily at Rome between M. de Beaumarchais and Signor Mussolini, who desires, however, that they should remain entirely secret and that nobody should be informed of the course which they are following: so much did he desire to keep the whole negotiation in his own hands that he was much annoyed with Signor Scialoja for having ventured to discuss it at

[1] No. 162.

Geneva with M. Briand: he told M. de Beaumarchais that he had never authorised Signor Scialoja to do this.

3. Signor Mussolini wishes the negotiations to culminate in the signature of a treaty of arbitration and friendship with three annexes attached thereto, dealing with

(a) Tunis (this question M. Berthelot thinks, is capable of a satisfactory final settlement, pending which it might merely be stipulated in this annex that the present *modus vivendi* will be renewed for periods of one year instead of for only three months, as at present);

(b) The Libyan frontier (here France is ready to make considerable concessions as M. Berthelot told me on March 19th—see Lord Crewe's telegram under reference);

(c) Mandates. Italy, as M. de Fleuriau informed Sir William Tyrrell on March 23rd (see your despatch No. 767)[2] seeks an assurance from France that in the event of a re-distribution of Mandates, Italy and Germany would receive one each; if only one fell vacant Italy would receive it. M. Berthelot fears that the whole negotiation may fail if Signor Mussolini remains obdurate over this question, for the French government decline to admit the possibility of a re-distribution of Mandates, which were permanently allotted by the Great Powers, whose unanimous consent would be required for any such re-distribution. M. Berthelot says that the most the French government would agree to would be some vague assurance that in the (unlikely) event of a *new* Mandate coming up the ex-Allies would give preference to one of their number, rather than to an ex-enemy. (M. Berthelot fears that the adoption of the more precise Italian formula would have the additional disadvantage of enabling the Italians to make bad blood between the French and Germans by pointing to the privileged position which they had been given by France vis-à-vis of Germany.)

4. Signor Mussolini has requested the French government to prepare a draft treaty, whilst he will formulate in writing his demands under annex (b) thereto (Libyan frontier). He greatly desires the signature of the treaty before May 15th when he wishes to announce it in an important speech which he is making in the Senate.

5. M. de Beaumarchais is coming to Paris during the second half of April and will take back to Rome a draft treaty now being prepared by M. Berthelot.

6. It seems to be taken for granted both by the French and by the Italians that the Tangier question will have been settled before May 15th.

[2] With reference to No. 162 this despatch of March 30, not printed, recorded that M. de Fleuriau had informed Sir W. Tyrrell of M. de Beaumarchais' conversation with Signor Mussolini: for a record dated March 19 of this conversation by Signor Mussolini see *I Documenti Diplomatici Italiani*, Settima Serie, vol. vi, No. 167.

No. 188

Sir A. Chamberlain to Mr. Leeper (Warsaw)
No. 166 [N 1991/46/59]

FOREIGN OFFICE, *April 3, 1928*

Sir,

The Polish Minister informed me to-day that the Czechoslovak Government had warned M. Zaleski that Russia appeared to be contemplating some aggressive movement against a neighbour—probably Poland—as a means of escape or at least a diversion from the difficulties of the internal situation. M. Skirmunt believed that similar information had reached Warsaw from M. Herbette.[1] M. Zaleski was not inclined to credit it, but M. Skirmunt enquired whether I had any confirmation. I replied that I had none, and that it seemed to me in itself improbable.

M. Skirmunt then referred to the account of the opening of the negotiations between M. Zaleski and M. Voldemaras appearing in to-day's 'Times'.[2] He observed that the attitude of M. Voldemaras was not very helpful, but that I should have seen that M. Zaleski had given proof of a most patient and conciliatory disposition. I said that I had observed and appreciated M. Zaleski's attitude not only at the conference itself but beforehand, and encouraged by it I had not hesitated to warn M. Voldemaras that, if Lithuanian intransigence caused the negotiations to fail, he could look for no sympathy from His Majesty's Government or the British people. M. Skirmunt spoke with pleasure of the more favourable attitude which the British press had recently taken towards Poland, and I replied that that was the result and the reward of the peaceful policy which the Polish Government were pursuing.

I am, &c.,
AUSTEN CHAMBERLAIN

[1] French Ambassador at Moscow.
[2] For documents relating to these Polish-Lithuanian negotiations at Königsberg, March 30–April 2, and for discussion by the Council of the League of Nations on June 6 see *League of Nations Official Journal*, June 1928, pp. 779–91, and July 1928, pp. 883–8 and 893–7, respectively.

No. 189

Sir R. Lindsay (Berlin) to Sir A. Chamberlain (Received April 10)
No. 275 [C 2779/351/18]

Confidential BERLIN, *April 3, 1928*

Sir,

I have the honour to acknowledge your despatch No. 412[1] (C 2354/351/18)

[1] Foreign Office covering despatch No. 412 is not preserved in Foreign Office archives. The enclosed Warsaw despatches, not printed, referred to Polish decrees of December 23, 1927, and March 16, 1928, extending from ten to thirty kilometres the frontier zone in which domiciliary and trading rights of foreigners were regulated. Warsaw despatch No. 113 reported that M. Zaleski had, in particular, informed Mr. Leeper on March 21 that the German Government had objected to the earlier decree, which had therefore been revised and in its new form represented the limit of Polish concessions.

of the 30th of March enclosing two reports from Mr R. A. Leeper (his Nos. 111 and 113 of the 21st of March) on Polish-German relations. I think it must cause you some amusement to find M. Zaleski complaining that he always received fair words from Dr Stresemann at Geneva,[2] but they were seldom implemented when he returned to Berlin, while Herr v. Schubert was almost at the same moment voicing precisely the same complaint to me about M. Zaleski (see paragraph 2 of my despatch No. 236[3] of the 20th of March). Perhaps you will not feel inclined to decide whether the pot or the kettle is the blacker, but if Mr Leeper will allow me, I think I ought to say what I can for my particular vessel.

2. These negotiations between Warsaw and Berlin have been in progress for many many months. The Commercial Treaty proper will present most formidable difficulties of a very genuine character and hitherto the parties have not really attacked it, being engaged on preliminaries, of which 'settlement' is one. On this point, a loose agreement was reached last July. The new Polish Decree of the 16th of March is not regarded by the German Foreign Office as an actual violation of the July provisorium, but it is, I think justifiably, regarded as a new and unfavourable development in a controversy which it had been hoped was for the time being disposed of. The Germans had come earnestly to desire an end of bickerings, and the Poles had discontinued the expulsions which gave so much offence last year; and the new frontier ordinance is regarded here as a set-back, though it is admitted that in minor particulars it does introduce some alleviations. It is no use saying that similar legislation exists in France, in Italy! and in Soviet Russia!! and that it is directed against the espionage and subversive efforts of any foreign agents. Germans on the western frontier of Poland do not think that they are regarded by the local officials in the same way as other foreigners, and it is not Germans alone who look on Polish voivodes as a law unto themselves.

3. I do not know exactly how official the German representations were which were made about the new ordinance, but the German Minister certainly asked in vain to be precisely informed as to what was planned, and to be consulted if possible in a matter of such importance to the general negotiations pending. At last, on a Friday, he was told that he would be given a copy of the ordinance at once. On the Saturday nothing happened; the Sunday was a dies non; on the Monday he received a telephone message to say that the letter to him containing the ordinance had unfortunately been misdirected—the letter itself arrived simultaneously from the Belgian Legation; and the same day the ordinance appeared in the Official Gazette.

4. Personally, and with every desire to be unprejudiced, I do think that the Polish action in this matter of the ordinance, carried out in this manner and at this moment, has been provocative. I have wondered whether Warsaw thinks that the German elections of next month will go strongly to the Left,

[2] See *Gustav Stresemann, op. cit.*, vol. iii, pp. 364–5, for a note of March 17 by Dr. Stresemann on his discussion with M. Zaleski.

[3] Not printed. This despatch reported a conversation with Herr von Schubert who stated that the German Government were determined to reach an agreement with Poland.

and that they would do well to go slow in their negotiations and perhaps find Social Democrats more malleable next Summer than the present German Cabinet. I am confident that this would be a serious miscalculation. I still think it extremely doubtful whether the forthcoming election will show more than a very moderate transfer of votes from Right to Left; and I also anticipate that a Left Coalition Government, if formed next June, will, at first at any rate, be rather more difficult to deal with than a Nationalist Government, as it will fear that a conciliatory attitude will expose it to attack from the German Nationalists, who have always posed as the monopolists of patriotism.

5. To return to the matter of the ordinance, I would say that on the whole it has not caused any excessive agitation here—rather less than I should have expected—far less than it would have caused last year, and though I do think the incident regrettable, I look on its reactions as showing that relations between Poland and Germany, as seen in Berlin, have essentially improved. Nothing shows the improvement better than Herr v. Schubert's own deportment, for in the Winter of 1926–27 I more than once saw him clench his fists, turn red in the face, and talk, not about Polish pigs but about Polish swine. I even once passed a remark to him about it. Only last week I again saw him turn red and clench his fists, but it was to asseverate that bickerings must come to an end, and Germany and Poland must come to terms. It was Herr v. Schubert who in February of last year, when Dr Stresemann was away on the Riviera, took a leading part in breaking off the Polish negotiations, and though he has always protested to me (perhaps too strongly) that his action was most beneficial, I think that really he was one of the first Germans to see that a wrong course was being followed. I do not go so far as to say that the Germans have never been in the wrong since, but I do think that from last Spring onwards they have tried more honestly to meet the Poles. Perhaps, as the Poles always say, it is the Germans who suffer most in all this tariff war; perhaps as the Russian market becomes more disappointing, the Polish becomes more important to German industry; but the chief reason of the improvement is, I think, the visible consolidation of the Polish State, culminating in the contraction of a loan in America and the appointment of an American Financial Adviser. Anyhow Herr Lewald,[4] the rather stiff German principal negotiator, was promoted to look after the Olympic Games and replaced by Dr Hermes,[5] who, if a bit of an Agrarian, is more conciliatory in manner; and, pace an occasional outburst, the tone of the German press and foreign office has improved. German Hubris has diminished, and I think the proper corollary is that Poland should abandon some of that playful irresponsibility which may be so engaging in children, but is hardly seemly in the conduct of affairs by a Power who aspires to be regarded as of the first class.

I have, &c.,

R. C. LINDSAY

[4] Dr. Lewald was a former State Secretary in the German Ministry of the Interior.

[5] Dr. Hermes, a former German Minister of Food and Agriculture and Minister of Finance, was a member of the Prussian Diet.

No. 190

Sir R. Graham (Rome) to Sir A. Chamberlain (Received April 10)
No. 282 [C 2742/2742/22]

ROME, *April 4, 1928*

Sir,

I have read with much interest the record contained in your despatch No. 659 to Paris[1] of the 20th ultimo of your conversation with the French Ambassador regarding Anglo-French commercial relations. An almost exact analogy exists here to the situation therein described. While political relations between Great Britain and Italy could scarcely be more close and cordial, our commercial relations are in an unsatisfactory condition. The Italian Government, in their desire to protect the lira and home industries, appear to do everything to restrict as much as possible, or even to exclude altogether, foreign commodities. In view of the severe industrial and economic crisis through which this country is passing some allowance must be made for them. But the result of their measures is that I am constantly instructed by you to complain of the excessive duties imposed upon British produce such as motor bicycles, fire bricks, tea, etc. etc. The last minute and abortive efforts to persuade the Italian Government to change their reparations recovery policy in the interests of British coal are well known to you. Apart from the protection of home industries, the apprehension of losing or the hope of gaining foreign markets influences Italian policy as regards Russia, Turkey and other countries; and the main factor which makes the Italians unwilling to adopt a Reparations Recovery Act such as we suggested is and will be the fear of indisposing the German Government and of losing the German, their biggest market, for Italian fruit and other exports. The representations which I am so frequently called upon to make are received in a sympathetic spirit by Signor Mussolini and Signor Grandi, and I know that the latter has pleaded our cause in the proper quarters. But, in so far as the Ministries of Finance and Public Economy are concerned, a very different spirit prevails. I have excellent personal relations with Count Volpi and the Under Secretary of Finance, Prince di Piombino, while Mr. Rawlins is in close touch with the other authorities of the Ministries concerned and is indefatigible in his endeavours to induce a change of mind. But it cannot be said that our efforts in this direction have produced any appreciable results. It is somewhat disconcerting to find that in these Departments not only is there little desire to meet us, but that there is a deep sense of grievance as to the way in which British safeguarding measures hit Italian products such as motor cars, gloves and silk. Moreover, recent instances of Dominions preference appear to have caused special annoyance. I had thought of requesting your permission to send Mr. Rawlins to London in order to explain the position at the Foreign Office and the Board of Trade, but I am doubtful whether he could tell you anything which you do not already know.

[1] No. 166.

344

2. I am at a loss what to suggest. I have already spoken privately at the Palazzo Chigi much in the sense of your language to the French Ambassador as regards the ill effect on political relations of a sense of trade grievance in Great Britain. Possibly you might think it desirable to speak to the Italian Ambassador in similar language to that used to M. de Fleuriau, but I doubt whether this will produce much effect at the Ministries responsible for the existing situation. The only hope seems to be a better understanding and closer cooperation between British and Italian commercial and industrial interests. Possibly the forthcoming visit towards the middle of this month of leading members of the Federation of British Industries may produce some result in the sense indicated, but my previous experience of such missions does not make me sanguine on the subject. Possibly, again, a tighter application of our safeguarding measures might induce the Italian Financial and Fiscal Authorities to realise that they cannot have matters all their own way.[2]

I have, &c.,

R. GRAHAM

[2] This despatch was sent to the Board of Trade which stated in a letter of May 11 to the Foreign Office that it was not considered possible to change British policy.

No. 191

Letter from Sir A. Chamberlain to Sir R. Graham (Rome)

[*F.O. 800/262*]

Confidential   FOREIGN OFFICE, *April 4, 1928*

My dear Graham,

The Italian Ambassador brought to me to-day Signor Mussolini's reply[1] to the appeal which I had made to him to meet Monsieur Briand, General Primo de Rivera and myself at Malaga.[2]

Signor Mussolini said that he did not wish to meet Monsieur Briand unless the meeting were likely to result in an improvement in Franco-Italian relations, but if the conversations now in progress reached such a stage by the time the Tangier agreement was ready for signature as to give an assurance that they would be successful, Signor Mussolini would be happy to come to Malaga.

The Ambassador added on his own account that he saw, from papers which had been circulated to him, that when General Primo de Rivera had broached the subject to Mussolini, Mussolini had given a short and negative reply. He thought, therefore, that the change of attitude on the part of Signor Mussolini might be attributed to the appeal which I had made to him.

AUSTEN CHAMBERLAIN

[1] See *I Documenti Diplomatici Italiani*, Settima Serie, vol. vi, No. 211.
[2] See No. 173.

No. 192

Letter from Mr. Holman (Paris) to Mr. Sargent
[*C 2785/394/18*]

PARIS, *April 5, 1928*

Dear Sargent,

Massigli asked me to come and see him this morning regarding the memorandum which we addressed to the Conference on April 4th on the subject of visits of verification (see our despatch No. 633[1] of April 4th).

2. He said that he quite agreed that, when the visits of inspection had taken place regarding military establishments, coast batteries, reserve rations and police accommodation and distribution, provided, of course, that such visits were authorised by the German authorities the experts should be withdrawn. He pointed out, however, that no mention had been made in our memorandum of the examination of the various police laws. These he said were of special importance and ought to be dealt with too before the departure of the experts. After some discussion he suggested that, if the experts had already been withdrawn, it might be possible for the remaining laws to be communicated by the German authorities to the Versailles Committee direct but in that case it would be most difficult for that body to give their approval without being able to consult the German authorities on various points of detail which might need explanation or discussion.

3. After consultation with the Military Attaché, I explained to Massigli that it might be anything up to a year before all the police laws had been submitted and were found in order. We could not in those circumstances be expected to retain the experts in Germany simply to approve the police regulations. I put forward to him, therefore, as a purely personal suggestion that the experts should work on the police laws until the visits of verification, should they be authorised, had been completed when they would be withdrawn. It might then be possible to request the German authorities to communicate the texts of the remaining police laws to the Military Attachés in Berlin. The latter could examine them, but not being experts in the question, they would not be at liberty to call in the services of the allied expert in the matter, who is, I believe, Durand, whenever such action seemed required. The advantage of having the texts of the laws sent to Berlin would be that the competent German authorities would be at hand if any explanations were required.

4. Massigli seemed to have no deep-rooted objection to this personal proposal, but said that he could not give an opinion without consulting the military authorities. Should Massigli be willing to accept some such scheme, I would propose to address a supplementary note to the Conference on the subject of the procedure to be adopted in dealing with the question of police laws. I trust that you will approve action on these lines, as I feel that this question may prove a stumbling block, if we do not thresh it out now once and for all.

Yrs ever,
ADRIAN HOLMAN

[1] See No. 186, note 3.

No. 193

Letter from Mr. Sargent to Sir R. Lindsay (Berlin)
[*F.O. 800/275: Ge/28/8*]

FOREIGN OFFICE, *April 10, 1928*

Dear Lindsay,

It will be interesting to know what you think of the enclosed minute by Waley, especially after you have had an opportunity of sounding Gilbert on his return from his tour of the Capitals of Europe.

We have up till now failed to extract from the Treasury any record of the Chancellor's conversation with Gilbert (although Hopkins was present). All we have had is Hopkins' memorandum for the Chancellor in anticipation of the conversation (copy enclosed).[1] I am afraid from Waley's present memorandum that it looks as though the Treasury when the time came were unable to resist the temptation, (or perhaps the Chancellor took the law into his own hands) of rubbing Gilbert's nose in the Balfour Note, a course which seems to me to have been rather unnecessary—why scream before one is hurt?—especially as it was one which was bound to give offence to Gilbert. Incidentally this line of approach was never mentioned and still less agreed upon at the meeting at the Treasury on the 22nd ultimo (see my letter of March 26th and Waley's record sent to Rowe Dutton).[2]

Owing to the holidays I have been unable to find out exactly what happened and why, but this will no doubt emerge in the course of the week. Meanwhile I thought I had better use to-day's bag in order, without loss of time, to send you Waley's memorandum for what it is worth. By the way Waley asks that it may be destroyed after being read, as he promised . . .[3] not to repeat what he said in 'writing'.[4]

Yrs.

ORME SARGENT

ENCLOSURE IN No. 193
Minute by Mr. Waley (Treasury)

Confidential—Copy

Sir R. Hopkins

A journalist connected with the 'Times' who appears to be on intimate terms with Mr. Gilbert, told me yesterday that Mr. Gilbert's intention is himself to put forward a proposal for revising the Dawes Plan this Autumn in the hope that the matter will be discussed in the Spring of 1929 and settled by that Autumn. He says that Monsieur Poincaré would agree, and will endeavour to persuade us to adopt the same view in the meantime.

[1] The enclosure was Note I of the notes referred to in No. 185, note 2.
[2] See No. 177.   [3] A name is here omitted.
[4] Mr. Waley subsequently wrote to Mr. Howard Smith on April 19 that Sir R. Hopkins had made no record of Mr. Churchill's conversation with Mr. Gilbert but that Mr. Churchill had 'made the points mentioned in the notes furnished to him and also spoke of the part which the Balfour Note Policy plays as regards our attitude towards reparation questions'.

He says that Mr. Gilbert was very disappointed at his reception here, and complained that when France wanted to be severe on Germany, we wanted to be lenient, and now when France wants to be reasonable, we want to be more severe, adding that at both times we were in the wrong. Mr. Gilbert particularly disloked [*sic*] the emphasis laid here on the Balfour Note.

Mr. Gilbert, he said, has been offered a partnership in Morgans, but feels he must finish his present work before taking it up. He also said that Mr. Gilbert spoke in very friendly terms of Mr. Leith Ross, and greatly regretted his absence.[5]

I do not think that my informant is altogether reliable, but most of what he said is confirmed by what we know from other sources.

[5] Mr. Leith-Ross was on sick leave.

No. 194

Sir A. Chamberlain to Sir G. Grahame (Brussels)
No. 221 [C 2848/969/18]

Confidential   FOREIGN OFFICE, *April 12, 1928*
Sir,

The Belgian Ambassador informed me to-day that his Government were rather troubled by the account which M. Berthelot had given to Baron Gaiffier[1] of his conversations with Dr. Stresemann and Herr von Schubert at Geneva, of which M. Berthelot said that he had informed me and I had expressed my complete approval.

I told the Ambassador that I myself had had no conversations with any of the German representatives on the subject of either reparations or evacuation. M. Berthelot had given me some account of his conversation with Herr von Schubert at a dinner party at which we had both been present, but I had not thought it of sufficient consequence to make any note of it. It appeared to me a resumption of the idea mooted at Thoiry for an early mobilisation of the railway and industrial bonds affected to reparations as a *quid pro quo* for the evacuation of the occupied territory. I desired to see that evacuation took place as early as possible, since the occupation was inevitably a constant source of irritation and useless to us, as it must in any case come to an end long before any danger from Germany could materialise. I should certainly, therefore, not have discouraged any attempt on the part of the French Government to find a scheme which would make early evacuation acceptable to French public opinion, but the more I had looked at the ideas broached at Thoiry the less practical they seemed to me. They involved the raising of a huge loan for which the resources of all the principal money markets of the world would be required, whilst even so the stock or bonds could only be issued at a ruinous discount. This objection seemed to me almost insurmountable, quite apart from the fact that any readjustment of reparations

[1] Baron de Gaiffier d'Hestroy was Belgian Ambassador at Paris. For his report on M. Berthelot's account see *Documents Diplomatiques Belges 1920–1940*, vol. ii, pp. 480–2.

inevitably raised the question of our respective indebtedness to the United States, whilst all the indications which reached me showed that America would be unwilling to link a reduction of her claims on Europe with any scheme connected with the reparations due by Germany to the Allies.

Baron Cartier de Marchienne, who apparently does not like either M. Berthelot or the Americans, made several comments on both, which I need not repeat but only mention lest he should subsequently become persuaded that I was the author of them.

I am, &c.,
AUSTEN CHAMBERLAIN

No. 195

Sir R. Lindsay (Berlin) to Sir A. Chamberlain (Received April 16)
No. 294 [C 2943/49/18]

BERLIN, *April 12, 1928*

Sir,

In talking yesterday with Dr Stresemann, our conversation turned to the presence in Rome at the same moment of Herr Koehler, the German Minister of Finance, and of Mr Parker Gilbert, a subject which has caused as much comment in the German press as in that of other countries. Herr Koehler, the Minister told me, had told him that he meant to spend his Easter holiday in Rome and had asked him whether there would be any objection to his meeting Signor Mussolini if an opportunity presented itself, and Dr Stresemann had replied that he saw no objection. That was all he knew about Herr Koehler's visit; what did I know about Mr Gilbert's. I replied that that gentleman had informed me of his plan before he started and that I thought he merely intended to keep in personal touch with all his principals; and in this view Dr Stresemann concurred.

2. He then turned to M. Poincaré's recent speech at Carcassonne[1] and expressed approval of its sensible tone; he was inclined to infer that M. Poincaré was in favour of hastening on a settlement of the Dawes plan and its connected questions, and what did I think of that. I said that in England I thought most people were anxious at the first moment to substitute a permanent settlement for the Dawes plan, but as to hastening things on, a little caution was necessary. In no case could anything serious be done before the American elections; and apart from that the great difficulty now was the American refusal to admit of any connection between Debts and Reparation. I did not think any of the Allies could give away Reparation rights without some assurance that they would get remissions of debts. I had noticed some talk by Mr Parker Gilbert about hastening on a settlement and it had made me feel uneasy. I had therefore urged him rather insistently to visit London in order that he might receive an unambiguous and authoritative statement as to the views held there. Dr Stresemann quite saw the point of view of the

[1] For a report on this speech of April 1 see *The Times*, April 2, 1928, p. 13.

Allied Powers, but suggested that, without any absolute linking up of debts and reparation, a settlement of both virtually at the same time might perhaps be attained. I said that possibly that might be possible, though I did not know; but what was quite certain was that the Allies could not allow America to say to them 'open your mouth and shut your eyes and see what I will give you'.

3. Dr Stresemann said he thought Mr Gilbert had a good deal of influence in Paris and to judge by M. Poincaré's speeches he seemed almost to have won that statesman round to a hastening on of a Reparation settlement, if not to a separation of Reparation and Debt questions. I said I had heard Mr Gilbert speak of M. Poincaré's complete reasonableness; I thought it quite likely that the latter had come to appreciate that it was inadvisable to emphasize in public any theoretical connection between Debts and Reparation, and perhaps, like all of us at times, he found it wise to say things pleasing to American public opinion; but I held it quite impossible that France when it came to real business, could conclude any settlement of the Reparation question without having previously assured a corresponding settlement of debts.

I have, &c.,
R. C. LINDSAY

No. 196

Letter from Sir R. Lindsay (Berlin) to Mr. Sargent (Received April 16)
[C 2968/307/18]

BERLIN, *April 12, 1928*

Dear Sargent,

I wrote to you a week ago[1] and said I did not much mind a little delay in beginning representations to the Germans about the extension of the Reparation Recovery Act. I said too that I wanted however to begin well before the German election on May 20. This latter point I want now to emphasise strongly, and I should have done so in my previous letter if I had thought there was any risk of a *serious* delay. My reason is not merely that I want the extension to come into force at the earliest moment, for I gather that a month or two doesn't matter; I urge the avoidance of serious delay on purely diplomatic grounds. Assuming, as one must, that a Government of the Left will come into power in June, I think it important that the German Nationals shall not be able to say that we delayed our representations until, or that we only made them when a Government of the Left had assumed office.

I gather now that the Treasury are not nearly so forward in preparing the brief for our negotiation here (communications with the Dominion Government, etc.) as I had imagined, so I shall be grateful if you will stir them up and urge them not to allow any delay that they can avoid. I'd like to begin not later than the last week in April.

[1] This letter of April 5 in reply to No. 185 is not preserved in Foreign Office archives.

Of course possibly the Treasury are not keen on the extension at all. Scientifically speaking all transfers of cash have the same effect on the exchange, whether they are done by buying in the market, by deliveries in kind, or by intercepting sterling through the Reparation Recovery Act. Hopkins says in a recent note[2] that it is only the psychological advantage that is being sought in trying for an extension of the Reparation Recovery Act, and I can quite understand that this psychological element has its importance. Gilbert suggests we should be able to get our money for some time by his purchases in the market, though of course he cannot guarantee this, and of course he has to be still more reserved when the point is referred to a second time. Perhaps therefore the Treasury are not so mad keen on the extension; it is a technical matter on which they have to make up their own minds. If they don't much care, for God's sake let them drop it; Gilbert will be glad enough of course, and the Germans too, and you and I don't want to go out in search of diplomatic trouble. But if they do want it, then for God's sake don't allow them to go cramping our diplomatic style by creating unnecessary delay.

Yours sincerely,
R. C. Lindsay

[2] The reference is uncertain.

No. 197

Letter from Mr. Sargent to Mr. Holman (Paris)

[*C 2785/394/18*]

Foreign Office, April 12, 1928

Dear Holman,

Many thanks for your letter No. 259/26/1928 of April 5th about the withdrawal of the experts.[1] I am sorry that the interposition of the Easter holiday should have delayed my reply.

As regards the Police laws, it seems that nine out of the sixteen have already been passed: and of those which still remain only two are interesting and none of vital importance from our standpoint. There can as you said to Massigli be no question of the retention in Berlin of the experts to deal with the outstanding laws. We quite agree that the experts should continue to work on these laws until the hoped for visits of verification have taken place: but we think that after the experts have been withdrawn, the texts of the remaining laws should be communicated to *the Embassies* not to the Military Attachés whom we are and always have been (cf. Austria) anxious to keep out of control questions.

If our present scheme goes through the experts will be withdrawn as soon as everything which is *at present* ready for inspection has been inspected. But there will still be outstanding points of which the police laws are only one. You will see from the correspondence enclosed in our despatch No. 2590 of

[1] No. 192.

October 15th last[2] that we think it necessary that 'in order to avoid misunderstandings the allied requirements regarding all the outstanding questions should be clearly notified to the German Government before the experts are (actually) withdrawn'.

A schedule of such requirements should in due course be drawn up and submitted to the Ambassadors' Conference for approval (this to enable us here to prevent the inclusion by the French in the schedule of all sorts of nugatory items) with a view to its subsequent communication to the German Government who would be invited to keep the Embassies informed of the progressive fulfilment of the various items. We could not, of course, agree to any subsequent demand being made for the allies to verify the execution of these further items. There would always be recourse to the League if there were serious ground to doubt German good faith in this connexion.

Your proposed supplementary note to the Conference might merely point out, then, that there will still be a number of matters including certain of the police laws, awaiting final settlement at the time when the visits at present in contemplation, should they be authorised, have been paid and the experts consequently withdrawn: and that His Majesty's Government think it important in order to avoid all possibility of misunderstanding, that the allied requirements regarding all the questions still outstanding at that moment should be notified simultaneously with the withdrawal of the experts to the German Government who should be invited, at the same time, to keep the allied Embassies in Berlin informed of the progressive fulfilment of the various items (the list rehearsing these items to be approved by the Ambassadors' Conference before being communicated to the German Government).

Massigli might make it clear to the German Embassy in his conversations that the withdrawal of the experts does not release the Germans from the obligation of continuing to carry out such points of disarmament as may then still be outstanding and that a list of such points will be communicated to the German Government at the time when the experts are withdrawn.

Yours ever,

ORME SARGENT

[2] This covering despatch (not preserved in Foreign Office archives) transmitted copies (not printed) of correspondence of October 5 and 14, 1927, between the War Office and the Foreign Office. Following a suggestion from the former the latter set out the formula cited below.

No. 198

Letter from Mr. Holman (Paris) to Mr. Sargent

[*C 2889/394/18*]

PARIS, *April 12, 1928*

Dear Sargent,

Since writing my letter of April 6th [5th][1] regarding visits of verification, I have seen Massigli who has talked over the whole question with the French

[1] No. 192.

military authorities. The view of the latter is that before taking any action at all on the Conference decision referred to in paragraph 5 of our telegram No. 49[2] of March 22nd, the experts should be instructed to furnish the Conference with a full report explaining the exact position of all outstanding questions. Such a report would show us the present state of the police laws, the questions requiring visits of verification and any outstanding points which needed clearing up. The Conference would then have everything in black and white in front of them and be in a far better position to take a final decision. Massigli asked whether I would submit this proposal to you. My personal opinion is that, although a little time may be lost in obtaining the report, we shall be in a far better position in this way to settle the whole question of outstanding points, and possibly at the same time be able to fix some time limit for the withdrawal of the experts. With regard to visits of verification there is one point which occurs to me, namely what action should be taken in the case of a visit of verification proving unsatisfactory. I presume that your view would be that as His Majesty's Government attach little interest to any such visits you would not be disposed to exert any further pressure on the German authorities in the case of an unsatisfactory one.

2. If you agree to the idea of asking the experts to furnish us with a full report I could arrange with Massigli to invite the Versailles Committee to take the necessary steps. In the meantime should I receive a reply to my letter of April 5th on the subject of police laws, etc., I will hold up any action until I hear from you further.[3]

Yours ever,
ADRIAN HOLMAN

[2] No. 170.

[3] Foreign Office telegram No. 30 to Paris of April 18 transmitted the following message from Mr. Sargent to Mr. Holman: 'We agree that experts should be asked to furnish urgently a full report on present situation. In so informing Massigli you should add that His Majesty's Government are meanwhile reserving their attitude towards all the questions arising out of the Conference decision of March 19th [see No. 170].'

Paris despatch No. 712 of April 20 transmitted a note of April 19 from the Secretariat-General of the Conference of Ambassadors submitting a draft resolution suspending execution of the resolution of March 19 and requesting the Allied Military Committee of Versailles to furnish urgently a report on the outstanding questions before the military experts at Berlin. Lord Crewe stated that he had approved the draft resolution.

No. 199

Letter from Sir R. Lindsay (Berlin) to Mr. Sargent
[*F.O. 800/275: Ge/28/11*]

Private   BERLIN, *April 13, 1928*

Dear Sargent,

Your letter of April 10 about Gilbert's visit to London[1] only reached me yesterday. In the meanwhile I had had a talk with Stresemann about reparation and in my record[2] of it, paragraph 2, you will see mentioned

[1] No. 193.   [2] No. 195.

incidentally what I think of giving Gilbert a little dose of Balfour Note. Rowe Dutton before he came away from London heard that the Chancellor put it in pretty hot and strong. I do not think it will do any harm at all. Gilbert is very likely vexed—see what . . .[3] said to Waley: it sounds to me like a very true account; and I shall be amused to hear what I can from Gilbert when he comes back here (which will not be for a fortnight or so yet). But meanwhile I do not see much good in letting Gilbert stay in a fool's paradise, imagining that we, ex-allies, can let Germany off any reparation obligations without having any assurance whatever against a Jew-bargain from America about Debts. It seems to me quite impossible that we should acquiesce in an American attitude of what Sir A. Chamberlain characterises as 'the open-your-mouth-and-shut-your-eyes-and-see-what-I-will-give-you policy'. The sooner he loses any illusions on that point, the better.

Of course the French are no more going to acquiesce in that policy than we are. Poincaré's speech at Carcassonne is extremely conciliatory in tone and I daresay Gilbert is preening himself on having got the stubborn Lorrainer into such sweet reasonableness. Poincaré has skilfully exuded an atmosphere of great reasonableness which has had its effect on Gilbert and may have some in America. Really all Poincaré did was pointedly to refrain from explicitly connecting debts and reparation together in his speech. This does not mean that he has abandoned the intention of connecting them very closely when it comes to business. He simply cannot do otherwise. But he may have thought that we were likely to go strongly just now on the Balfour note tack, and that therefore he could well afford to rest on his oars for a moment and allow us to take up the running. I doubt if that much matters. The truth is bound to come out clearly and no deception is possible.

Meanwhile Gilbert, though we all feel sure he is in very close touch with Mellon etc., is not an avowed agent of the American Government, though he has all the prestige of America behind him; and so he is in a delightfully irresponsible position, able to press here or press there in the interest of an eventual settlement; and I do not for a moment doubt that he is honestly inspired by the single idea of trying to get a settlement as fair to all concerned as is humanly possible; but meanwhile we are all in rather a difficult position. Someday he may have to come into the open, and it will be interesting if ever again he talks about us getting on the same side of the table as America. That will be worth listening to. But I hope he will say it to someone more capable of understanding it than myself.

Yours sincerely,
R. C. LINDSAY

[3] A name is here omitted.

British policy on disarmament following the Tripartite Naval Conference at Geneva

September 6–December 29, 1927

No. 200

Mr. London (Geneva) to Sir W. Tyrrell[1] *(Received September 7, 10 a.m.)*
No. 247 L.N. Telegraphic [W 8422/61/98]

GENEVA, *September 6, 1927, 11.5 p.m.*

Following from Secretary of State:—

Netherlands delegate gave notice to-day of resolution in following terms:—

'L'Assemblée convaincue que sans rouvrir les discussions sur le protocole de Genève de 1924,[2] il est désirable d'examiner si le moment n'est pas venu de reprendre l'étude des principes qui ont formé la base de ce protocole; considérant qu'il est de la plus haute importance que l'assemblée stimule les travaux de la commission préparatoire de la conférence du désarmement décide de renvoyer l'étude les [des] principes fondamentaux du protocole de Genève et les conclusions du rapport de la commission préparatoire aux commissions appropriées.'[3]

I shall convoke heads of Empire Delegations for its discussion if possible to-night.[4] My present inclination is to oppose at the outset reference to any committee of a resolution which must necessarily reopen protocol discussions.[5]

I am repeating to Prime Minister at Aix.

[1] Cf. No. 1, note 1.

[2] See No. 92, note 4.

[3] See *League of Nations Official Journal: Special Supplement No. 54*, pp. 39–41.

[4] Geneva telegram No. 248 L.N. of September 7 transmitted a message for the Dominions Office that at this meeting 'it was clear that none of the delegates had reason to believe that his Government had changed attitude adopted towards protocol of 1924', and it was 'unanimously agreed that strong effort should be made to avoid reopening of protocol discussions, which could only end in disagreement'.

[5] For the submission by the Netherland delegate to the Assembly of the League of Nations on September 10 of a version of his resolution designed to meet Sir A. Chamberlain's objections and its reference on September 12 to the Third Committee of the Assembly (Reduction of Armaments) *v. ibid.*, pp. 104 and 107 respectively. See also Cmd. 3008 of 1928, p. 3.

No. 201

Sir A. Chamberlain (Geneva) to Sir W. Tyrrell (Received September 8)
No. 6 L.N.A. [W 8499/8313/98]

GENEVA, *September 6, 1927*

Sir,

It would seem clear that the Polish Chargé d'Affaires, in speaking to you of the intention of the Polish Government to negotiate a pact of non-aggression with Germany,[1] must have misinterpreted his instructions. You will have seen, by the accounts which I have sent to you of Monsieur Sokal's conversations first with Sir Cecil Hurst and Mr. Cadogan[2] and afterwards with me,[3] that the idea of the Polish Government was much more general, it being nothing less than to propose to the Assembly the signature of a general pact of non-aggression by all the states members of the League. I have already informed you of the attitude which, in view of previous decisions of the British Government, I felt it necessary at once to adopt towards this proposal.[3] It is true that Monsieur Sokal explained that it was not any part of his idea to seek a definition of the term 'aggressor' or to propose any sanctions, but it seemed to me that the discussion of a new pact in the Assembly and in one of its committees must inevitably raise the old difficulties in regard to these matters. Nor does it appear to me that it is in the interest of the League or of any of its members to belittle what has already been accomplished, by the Covenant itself and by the Treaties of Locarno, by the discussion of fresh instruments which would add nothing to the force of the engagements already taken.

Monsieur Briand spoke to me briefly on the same subject at the opening of the Assembly yesterday and he expressed himself very much in this sense. He said that he had told Monsieur Sokal that we must not on any account revive the differences and difficulties to which the discussion of the Protocol[4] had given rise, and must be assured that any step which we took would meet with general agreement. It would be a fatal mistake to propose even a resolution unless it were one the acceptance of which with unanimity was assured.

I told Monsieur Briand that I had offered to be the medium for communicating the text to the Germans and securing their assent, and he very characteristically suggested that the best thing would be that we should arrange a meeting with them for the purpose of framing the resolution. Monsieur Briand further expressed approval of a proposal, which Monsieur Sokal had apparently attributed to me but which, in fact, came from Monsieur Sokal himself, that in order to give rather more solemnity to the declaration the votes should be taken *par appel nominal*. To this also I agreed.

---

[1] Sir W. Tyrrell had reported this statement by the Polish Chargé d'Affaires in London in Foreign Office telegram No. 162 to Geneva of September 5.

[2] Legal Adviser to the Foreign Office and an assistant to the British Delegate at Geneva respectively.

[3] See Volume III, Nos. 327–8.   [4] The Geneva Protocol of 1924.

Dr. Stresemann has just been with me to ask if I could tell him how the matter stood. He was naturally anxious lest a resolution upon such a subject should be suddenly sprung upon the Assembly without his having any previous opportunity of considering it. I told him in some detail of what had passed between Monsieur Sokal, Monsieur Briand and myself, and he appeared well satisfied with the procedure which we proposed to adopt.

[I am, &c.,]
A. C.

No. 202

Memorandum by Sir A. Chamberlain (Geneva)[1]

[W 8519/8313/98]

GENEVA, *September 7, 1927*

Monsieur Sokal, Delegate of Poland, with the approval of Monsieur Briand, has now proposed to make the following resolution by which he would hope to avoid any re-opening of the discussion on the Protocol[2]:—

The Assembly;

Recognising the solidarity which unites the international community;

And animated by the firm determination to assure the maintenance of general peace;

Recognising that war ought never to be employed as a means of settling differences between states and that, consequently, an aggressive war constitutes an international crime;

Considering that a solemn renunciation of wars of aggression would be of a nature to create an atmosphere of general confidence favourable to the progress of the work undertaken in view of disarmament;

Makes the following declaration:—

1. All recourse to war for the settlement of international differences is and remains forbidden;

2. Differences of whatever nature they may be arising between states can only be settled by peaceful means and, in consequence, the Assembly invites the members of the League of Nations to take note of this declaration and to conform to its principles in their mutual relations.

At first sight, I thought that this resolution might prove generally acceptable, but Sir Cecil Hurst is of opinion that it would in fact involve the acceptance of the principle of universal obligatory arbitration. He accordingly suggests that after the word 'war' in the paragraph beginning 'recognising that war' we should insert the words 'of aggression', that the paragraph numbered (1) should read 'all recourse to a war of aggression is and remains forbidden', and that paragraph (2) should be struck out. This would, of

[1] This unsigned memorandum was prepared for the Prime Minister and sent to him at Aix-les-Bains on September 7. A copy was received in the Foreign Office on September 9 under cover of Geneva despatch No. 9 L.N.A. (not preserved in Foreign Office archives).

[2] The Geneva Protocol of 1924.

course, be quite satisfactory to us but would, I am afraid, not satisfy anyone else and Sir Cecil Hurst is, therefore, at this moment considering at my request a substitute for paragraph 2 which, without pledging us to universal arbitration, would recall the obligations of the Covenant to seek a pacific solution of disputes.

Sokal's resolution has been communicated to the Germans, but I have not yet heard their views about it, but Stresemann has informed me that he agreed generally with the views I had previously expressed and is entirely opposed to re-opening the Protocol discussions. I have just arranged with Politis, one of the Greek representatives here, who was a principal author of the Protocol, that he should make a speech in which, whilst re-affirming his faith in the Protocol, he would announce that he considers the moment inopportune for a fresh discussion of its principles.[3]

The situation is very difficult and much of the temper evoked by the rejection of the Protocol has been aroused afresh, but if I can reach agreement with Briand *and* Stresemann there may be some grumbling but I doubt if there would be any opposition.

P.S. Sir Cecil has now suggested the following text for paragraph 2 which I approve:

'Pacific means should be employed for the settlement of all disputes arising between States.'

[3] The speech made on September 8 by M. Politis, Greek Minister at Paris, is printed in *League of Nations Official Journal: Special Supplement No. 54*, pp. 58–63.

No. 203

Mr. London (Geneva) to Sir W. Max Muller (Warsaw)
No. 1 Telegraphic [W 8547/8313/98]

GENEVA, *September 8, 1927, 11.35 p.m.*[1]

Addressed to Warsaw telegram No. 1.

Following from Secretary of State:

Polish delegate informed us on our arrival of his intention to propose resolution in assembly declaring determination of members of the League not to resort to war. He submitted to us privately text of proposed resolution which was objectionable for reason that it would extend obligations beyond those already imposed by covenant. German delegation whom he also consulted declared themselves unable to accept it. Evidently any such declaration would defeat its own purpose unless it received general support and in particular that of the great powers. British, French and German delegations redrafted resolution with Polish delegate (as far as possible?) in a form that would be acceptable. Polish delegate referred new text to his government who however have now replied by proposing an amendment which practically reintroduces principle which made original draft unacceptable.

[1] Time of repetition as No. 251 L.N. to the Foreign Office (received on September 9 at 9 a.m.).

Please at once impress on Polish government anxiety which I feel at prospect of their making a proposal which will divide the assembly. Their avowed object in introducing resolution is to raise prestige of League and to increase general security. They must see that if they persist in placing certain delegates in a position of having to subscribe to what looks plausible but is in practice unacceptable they will fail in both their objects.

Please impress on Polish government desirability in the interests of all of immediately instructing their delegate to accept text submitted to them by him and accepted by other powers.

If Polish delegate persists in his intention I shall have no alternative but to state clearly the attitude of His Majesty's Government in regard to this and similar resolutions which can only revive abortive protocol[2] discussion. The net effect can only be to throw doubt on the very reality of the guarantees secured to Poland in virtue of covenant and Locarno treaties.[3]

Repeated to Foreign Office No. 251.

[2] The Geneva Protocol of 1924.
[3] Sir W. Max Muller reported in his telegrams Nos. 6–7 to Geneva (72–3 to the Foreign Office) of September 9–10 that he had acted on these instructions and had received assurances that the Polish delegation had been instructed as desired. For the text of the resolution submitted by M. Sokal to the Assembly of the League of Nations on September 9 see *League of Nations Official Journal: Special Supplement No. 54*, p. 84. The resolution was adopted by the Assembly on September 24: *v. ibid.*, pp. 155–6. Cf. also Cmd. 3008 of 1928, pp. 3–4 and 26–7.

No. 204

Sir W. Max Muller (Warsaw) to Mr. London (Geneva)

No. 9 Telegraphic [Telegrams 47/4]

WARSAW, *September 12, 1927, 8.50 p.m.*[1]

Following for Secretary of State:—

'My immediately preceding telegram.[2]

'I saw Acting Minister for Foreign Affairs[3] this morning. He assured me that there must have been some misunderstanding at Geneva to create impression in your mind that Polish Government intended to reject advice of British, French, and German delegations. As a matter of fact, Minister for Foreign Affairs, as soon as he heard of resolution recommended by our four jurists, had himself directed that Polish delegate be instructed to accept it.

'Acting Minister for Foreign Affairs said that, though M. Zaleski regretted that apprehension should have been raised in your mind as to attitude of Polish Government, nevertheless he was glad that you had telegraphed as you did,[4] as this afforded him an opportunity of stating clearly that he had never contemplated opposing wishes of M. Briand and yourself in such a matter.

[1] Time of repetition as No. 74 to the Foreign Office (received on September 13 at 9 a.m.).
[2] Warsaw telegram No. 8 to Geneva was evidently not repeated to the Foreign Office: cf., however, No. 203, note 3.
[3] M. Knoll was acting for M. Zaleski who was ill.   [4] See No. 203.

'Acting Minister for Foreign Affairs concluded that Minister for Foreign Affairs was so anxious to have opportunity of a personal conversation with you in order to dispel any lingering doubts from your mind that he intended to hasten his journey to Geneva in order to arrive there before your departure.'[5]

[5] Sir A. Chamberlain replied in Geneva telegram No. 3 to Warsaw (261 L.N. to the Foreign Office) of September 14 that he would be delighted if it were possible for him to meet M. Zaleski at Geneva: see, however, No. 19.

No. 205

Letter from Sir E. Howard (Manchester, Mass.)[1] to Sir W. Tyrrell

[A 6073/133/45]

Private and confidential   MANCHESTER, MASS., *September 15, 1927*

My dear Tyrrell,

In your letter of the 30th August[2] you say that our American friends are clearly determined to secure themselves against interference by us in the event of their being neutrals in a war in which we are engaged and you don't quite see how we are going to prevent them.

Well, as you may imagine, I have pondered much over this problem, which is one that we may at any moment be called on to solve. If we are called on to face it in the middle of a war, our people will not be in a mental condition to face it reasonably because we shall all be afflicted with war mentality. It is better therefore to try and face it in peace time and as soon as possible.

Now there will—next time, if ever, we are at war—be in regard to this matter a choice of three alternatives only as far as this country is concerned.

1st.   To attempt to prosecute a blockade as in 1914–1918 in spite of this country and risk the financial and economic consequences. I cannot believe that we should be quite so mad as to push our blockade so far as to make this country actually join our enemies and so bring about, as it seems to me, the certain disruption of the Empire. All the same I don't feel quite sure even about this remembering what some of our blockade 'fans' during the last war were prepared to take on in order to prevent cotton &c. from reaching Germany.

2nd.   To arrange with this country beforehand the limits to which we could go in the blockade, so as to make sure that we should not have to count with trouble from a hostile United States.

3rd.   To settle the principles of blockade by International Conference in accordance with the rules of International Law as established before 1914, accepting and defining the doctrine of 'Continuous Voyage'.[3]

[1] H.M. Ambassador at Washington was at his summer residence.
[2] Untraced in Foreign Office archives.
[3] In a letter to Sir W. Tyrrell of November 10 Sir E. Howard explained that in this passage he had in mind: (i) the declaration of Paris respecting Maritime Law, signed by Great Britain, Austria, France, Prussia, Russia, Sardinia and Turkey on April 16, 1856, and

In exchange for this, however, we should obtain from the same Treaty universal acceptance of our thesis of the illegality of the sinking by submarines of merchant vessels whether neutral or belligerent or better still of the use of submarines at all for the purpose of dealing in any way with merchant vessels. This would relieve us of a terrible nightmare and make it really almost impossible to starve us out.

I do not pretend to have done more than think this out in a very superficial way. But although many difficulties suggest themselves I believe that the third alternative does offer the best basis for;

1. Naval disarmament and hence economy.
2. Placing relations with this country on a basis which will make it almost impossible to produce any serious matter of conflict between us—hence a better condition for permanent peace in the Pacific and elsewhere.
3. Removal of much of the jealousy which exists against Great Britain throughout the world.
4. Removal of the nightmare of Great Britain being starved by submarine action.

I had come to these conclusions, as I say, after pondering over the Geneva Conference,[4] when the other day Colonel House[5] came to lunch with us.

He at once attacked the Geneva Conference problem and agreed with me that any satisfactory settlement on the basis of 'parity' was out of the question, the needs of the two countries being so different. I showed him Grey's letter in the 'Times' of August 11 with which he entirely agreed. He then went on

printed in *British and Foreign State Papers*, vol. 46, pp. 26–7 (Mr. Craigie, a senior member of the American and African Department of the Foreign Office, here added in a marginal note on Sir Esme's letter: 'The U.S. are not a party to the Declaration of Paris'); (ii) 'the measure of agreement between U.S. & ourselves, such as it was, regarding "continuous voyage" ', i.e., the doctrine that the real and final destination of goods is the decisive consideration in the definition of contraband; (iii) the unratified declaration of London of February 26, 1909, by Great Britain, Austria-Hungary, France, Germany, Italy, Japan, Netherlands, Russia, Spain, and the United States, and printed as item No. 20 in Cd. 4554 of 1909, *Correspondence and Documents respecting the International Naval Conference, Held in London, December 1908–February 1909*. For the proceedings of the conference, cf. Cd. 4555. The Naval Prize Bill based on the Declaration, printed as House of Commons Bill No. 255 of 1911, was rejected by the House of Lords on December 12, 1911: see *Parl. Debs., 5th ser., H. of L.*, vol. x, cols. 809–94.

Sir E. Howard added: 'Lastly may I emphasize this—The present time is in my opinion v. favourable for the initiation of such pourparlers if H.M.G. approve. The dead leaves of pure isolationism are, I think, beginning to be pushed off by the new spring buds of a will to cooperate. The President would be I am sure more than willing and the leading Senators of the Foreign Relations Committee will not make difficulties if the move comes from the President.

'If, however, we leave the question too long in abeyance, we may find them all so occupied with the question of the Presidential election that they may either have no time to think of anything else or no will to do so.'

[4] For the naval conference between the British Empire, the United States and Japan, proposed by President Coolidge and held at Geneva, June 20–August 4, 1927, see Volume III, Chapter III.

[5] Colonel House had been an unofficial adviser to President Wilson, 1912–20, and had been United States Commissioner Plenipotentiary at the Peace Conference at Paris, 1919.

to say that there was only one possible source of war between our two countries and this was British interference with American neutral trade. I knew, of course, from his book[6] that he took this view but was not prepared for his propounding it so vigorously. He made it quite clear to me—and in this I am sure he was not exaggerating—that Republicans and Democrats are at one on this point of never again allowing American neutral shipping to be interfered with as in 1914–17. He asked me if it would not be possible for us to settle this question of the 'freedom of the seas' now once and for all with the United States and thus eliminate a great danger of collision in the future.

He emphasised that this would be really an immense advantage to us because: 1st. It would enable us to ensure our overseas communications and food supply as nothing else would and 2nd. It would not be a great sacrifice because it was unlikely that there would ever be another war like the last with a country like Germany which was blockaded on both sides by land which fact alone rendered the sea blockade effective.

I replied that speaking for myself entirely I agreed with him in principle (you must have realised by now that I am indeed the pink of indiscretion) but that I thought the moment had not yet come to make any move. I particularly deprecated any move being made by America at present and thought that perhaps next year when I went over to London I might take up the question verbally with the Secretary of State and perhaps the Prime Minister.

He asked me if he should mention it to the President. I begged him not to do so now. It would be necessary if the matter ever was discussed at all to hear what men like Senators Borah, Moses and Swanson[7] had to say about it. Personally I thought they would agree; but I insisted that in any case there could be no question of any settlement in the sense he advocated unless the submarine danger was also eliminated.

He entirely agreed and again stated that nothing would do so much to prepare the way for naval disarmament as this. He went so far as to say that he believed that all other countries would reduce their navies to a minimum leaving us to do what we liked, if only there could be an international settlement on these lines. I said I thought this was too optimistic but I felt it was certain that it would remove one of the principal difficulties in the way of naval disarmament.

House of course does not any longer cut any ice politically, but I am confident that he is quite justified in saying that Democrats and Republicans are agreed on this point and in the main I think his arguments are sound and logical.

I should like to know in due course what you think of the above.

Yours ever,

ESME HOWARD

[6] The reference was to *The Intimate Papers of Colonel House*, edited by C. Seymour (London, 1926).

[7] Senator W. E. Borah of Idaho was Chairman of the Foreign Relations Committee of the Senate; Senator G. H. Moses of New Hampshire was President *pro tempore* of the Senate; Senator C. A. Swanson was a Senator for Virginia.

No. 206

Sir A. Chamberlain (Geneva) to Sir W. Tyrrell (Received September 20)
No. 50 L.N.A. [*W 8894/61/98*]*

GENEVA, *September 18, 1927*

Sir,

M. Paul-Boncour called upon me to-day in order to discuss with me the resolution which he had proposed to the Third Committee.[1] I told him that my whole foreign policy was based on friendship with France; that also I was a good European in my views, but that there was a point beyond which it was impossible for me to go or for me to expect public opinion in England to follow.

2. I deprecated the fact that, my feelings being what they were, circumstances should always seem to arise in the discussions with France putting the two nations as holding opposite views, and I represented to M. Boncour that situations of this kind were bad policy for both nations.

3. I mentioned the protocol[2] and explained the situation at some length, and M. Boncour said that he quite understood and appreciated the frankness with which the matter had been explained to him. He, however, said that he had also his own public opinion in France to consider. The League of Nations was bound to proceed to endeavour to solve the disarmament problem, and it was impressed upon him by the military authorities that the solution of the disarmament problem could not be accomplished without arriving at some agreement with regard to security. He was fully aware of the objections to raising a question which led to disagreement, but he had felt that, things being what they were and public opinion being such as it is in France, he had been obliged to take the course which he had in introducing that resolution.

4. He was, however, anxious to meet me in any way possible, and he would be very glad if it could be arranged that an agreed text should be reached.

5. I laid stress on the undesirability of the second paragraph in the text as it stood, and said that discussion as to the precise value of the various articles of the Covenant would lead us on to very dangerous ground and would cause

---

[1] The text of the resolution on the pacific settlement of disputes submitted on September 16 by the French Representative to this committee of the Assembly of the League of Nations is printed in *League of Nations Official Journal: Special Supplement No. 57*, pp. 39–40, and Cmd. 3008 of 1928, pp. 23–4. In a letter of September 24 to the Foreign Office referring to this resolution the Admiralty in particular requested that 'the British Representatives at Geneva will maintain the view as in the past that the British Government is not prepared to consider in advance the definition of military assistance which it would be disposed to give under Article 16 [of the Covenant of the League of Nations]; and, further, that they will maintain in particular that this country (*a*) will not undertake to establish a blockade, and (*b*) will remain the judge of the type and the extent of the military measures it will take.' In connection with a possible blockade the Admiralty letter referred to Volume III, Nos. 498 and 504, and stated that 'the probability of trouble with America is too real to be risked'.

[2] The Geneva Protocol of 1924.

the question to be raised as to the position created in regard to article 16 by the United States not being a member of the League.

6. M. Boncour said he was fully alive to that position and understood the great alteration from the original conception of the League brought about by the non-adhesion of the United States; he said that the psychology of the various nations did not appreciate this fact, and that, if they were certain that England and France stood together to put in force the sanctions to prevent war, it would suffice to produce the necessary effect.

7. As regards paragraph 3 of the draft, I suggested that this should take the form of inviting the various nations to inform the Council of the measures they would be prepared to take to support the decision of the Council in the case of war breaking out in a particular sphere in which they had special interests—in other words, to say that, in such and such a case, their whole strength would be thrown into the struggle in support of the Council's decision. This was in effect what Great Britain had done by the Treaty of Locarno for the eastern frontiers of France and Belgium. I would prefer if reference could be made to the Covenant as base for such action rather than to the protocol, since the former was actually in force, but the latter was not; but, having regard to the weight given by the French to the protocol, I would not object to judicious reference to it being made in the document.

8. The question then arose as to the competence of the Preparatory Committee[3] to discuss League matters owing to the presence of American representatives. M. Boncour said he did not anticipate difficulty on this ground as he had actually mentioned the matter to the American representatives at the end of the meeting of the Preparatory Committee last year.

9. It was agreed that the details as to the method of giving effect to these proposals and as to the settlement of a text should be discussed between M. Boncour and Lord Onslow,[4] and between Sir Cecil Hurst and M. Fromageot.

10. The above is a very short summary of a conversation which was of considerable length and complete frankness.

I am, &c.,

AUSTEN CHAMBERLAIN

[3] The Preparatory Commission for the Disarmament Conference.
[4] Parliamentary Under-Secretary of State for War.

No. 207

Memorandum by Mr. Roberts (Geneva)[1]

[*W 8953/61/98*]

GENEVA, *September 19, 1927*

Count Bernstorff[2] read a statement to the Third Committee this morning[3] in reply to Monsieur Boncour's proposals.[4] He said that his Government

[1] A copy of this memorandum was received in the Foreign Office on September 21 under cover of Geneva despatch No. 57 L.N.A. (not preserved in Foreign Office archives).
[2] A member of the German Delegation at Geneva.
[3] See *League of Nations Official Journal: Special Supplement No. 57*, pp. 47–8.
[4] See No. 206, note 1.

were quite ready to collaborate in any work calculated to forward the general effort to increase arbitration and security and to help on the realisation of the ideas expressed in Monsieur Boncour's resolution. But he insisted on a distinction between (1) the work that the League should undertake in the direction of disarmament which should be based on the degree of security existing at present and (2) the work which the League might undertake in general to extend arbitration and security in the future.

As regards (1) he moved a resolution (copy of which is attached).[5] As regards (2) he reserved the right to present proposals at a later stage.

The effect of his resolution on disarmament is to ensure that the work of the Preparatory Commission should be kept within its present compass and therefore leaves it to the French to show why, after pressing last year for the calling of a conference of limited scope based upon the present degree of security, they should now be insisting that that work cannot advance unless it is accompanied by an immediate increase in security.

As regards his second point, he made it clear in his declaration that his government were in favour of requesting the Council to undertake at discretion the rest of the work foreshadowed in Monsieur Boncour's resolution, either by setting up a special committee to deal with it as a whole or by setting up a special body to deal with specific aspects of it.

The Committee agreed that the German resolution on disarmament should be sent straight to a sub-committee which already has the Boncour resolution and the Netherlands proposal[6] to work on. This sub-committee was thereupon constituted and is to consist of 12 different countries plus Dr. Benes[7] and the Vice-President.[8] It is to hold its first meeting this afternoon at 4.30.

If we are called upon to come out into the open at an early stage and state our general attitude, and assuming that we have not yet reached an agreement with the French on the lines of the suggestion made yesterday to Monsieur Boncour, I submit that we should do well to make it clear that we are at least no less willing than the Germans to take our share in co-operating in any general search by the rest of the League for increasing general security, even though we are unable at present ourselves to enter into any further commitments.

W. ROBERTS

[5] Not printed.
[6] See No. 200, note 5.
[7] Czechoslovak Minister for Foreign Affairs and Chairman of the Third Committee of the Assembly of the League of Nations.
[8] Of the Third Committee, Dr. J. G. Guerrero, Minister for Foreign Affairs of Salvador.

The Earl of Onslow (Geneva) to Sir W. Tyrrell (Received September 26)
No. 59 L.N.A. [W 9063/61/98]*

GENEVA, *September 22, 1927*

Sir,

Now that the Third Committee of the Assembly has finally approved the text of its main resolution on arbitration, security and disarmament,[1] it may be well to give a short account of the various stages in the drafting of that text, with a brief commentary on the various motives and considerations which gave rise to the successive amendments.

2. It will be remembered that towards the end of an extremely discursive general discussion in the Third Committee, the French delegate, M. Paul-Boncour, submitted a draft resolution which he had framed to express the views of the majority of those who had spoken. For convenience of reference I enclose copy of this draft (Annex I).[2]

3. The draft was, in accordance with the usual procedure, referred to a sub-committee which—still in accordance with precedent—passed it on, after a short discussion, to a less unwieldy Drafting Committee consisting of the British, French, Belgian, Czechoslovak and Netherlands delegates.

4. M. Paul-Boncour's main theme was that the work of the Preparatory Committee had reached a deadlock owing to the necessity of developing 'security' a stage further before any progress could be made with disarmament. The French Government evidently feared that if the Preparatory Committee were to meet again, as provisionally arranged, in November, there was little prospect of making any further advance with disarmament. They were anxious to avoid a failure; at the same time, they dared not propose an adjournment. M. Paul-Boncour had therefore hit on the plan of confiding to the Preparatory Committee itself the study of security, thus furnishing it with a new agenda, with which it could appear to busy itself for some weeks, if not months.

5. His resolution, as originally drafted, was bound to meet with opposition on two different points from the German and British delegations.

6. The German delegate was bound to oppose the idea that the Preparatory Committee could advance no further along the road to disarmament in the present circumstances of security. He reminded us that last year, after the Locarno treaties had been signed, the Assembly directed the Preparatory Committee to 'hasten the completion of the technical work and thus be able to draw up, at the beginning of next year, the programme for a conference on the limitation and reduction of armaments corresponding to existing conditions in regard to regional and general security'.[3] If, he argued, Locarno

---

[1] See *League of Nations Official Journal: Special Supplement No. 57*, pp. 52–7. The Assembly adopted this resolution on September 26, 1927: *v. op. cit., Special Supplement No. 54*, pp. 177–8. See also Cmd. 3008 of 1928, pp. 25–6. Part of this resolution is cited in No. 219.

[2] Not printed: see No. 206, note 1.

[3] For this extract from the resolution adopted by the Seventh Assembly of the League of

afforded sufficient security for a beginning to be made with disarmament in 1926, what has happened since to lessen that security? He declared that he could not go back to Germany and tell his people that the security of Locarno had proved to be non-existent, or at least to be wearing thin. He must insist on the Preparatory Committee continuing its work on disarmament on the existing basis of security, and progress must not wait on some problematical increase of security beyond present conditions.

7. The British objection to the French draft, of course, concerned certain of the methods by which M. Paul-Boncour proposed to achieve greater security—in particular, the idea of a 'systematic preparation of the application of the various articles of the Covenant' and the idea of an 'assouplissement' of the protocol[4]—whatever that might mean. The latter would probably involve a discussion of the text of the protocol itself, which could only revive unpleasant memories and accentuate differences which still exist. We feared that the former was merely a repetition of the device—used on a former occasion—of involving us in an 'elaboration' of the Covenant, which must, in fact, lead to an increase in commitments and perhaps to something very like the protocol itself. Fortunately, M. Paul-Boncour himself, when introducing his proposal in the Third Committee, said that 'to take the articles of the Covenant, to examine the exact obligation that they might imply, and to prepare their systematic application, would lead back to texts similar to those of the protocol.'[5] Sir Austen Chamberlain had already made it quite plain to M. Paul-Boncour, in a private discussion, that the British Government would not be drawn again into any discussion of the protocol, and I was able to quote M. Paul-Boncour's own words against him in support of my refusal to accept the proposal on this point in the form in which he had drafted it. (See Sir A. Chamberlain's despatch No. 50[6] of the 18th September.)

8. I must not weary you with a detailed review of the successive stages of the redrafting of the resolution; it will be sufficient if I draw attention to the changes which have been effected to meet the German and British attitudes. (I enclose copy of the text as finally approved—Annex II.)[7]

9. In view of the explanation of the German point of view given above, it will be readily understood that the German delegate took exception to paragraph 2 of the original draft, maintaining that further security was not indispensable to the work of disarmament. He is now satisfied with a pious hope that it may be possible to bring about 'political conditions calculated to assure the success of the work of disarmament'. He has secured a similar change in paragraph 6 of the original draft, where 'mutual confidence' is now required for the 'complete' success of the Disarmament Conference and is no longer declared to be 'indispensable' for the continuance of the work of the

Nations on September 24, 1926, see *League of Nations Official Journal: Special Supplement No. 44*, p. 108.
 [4] The Geneva Protocol of 1924.
 [5] *V. op. cit., Special Supplement No. 57*, p. 39.
 [6] No. 206.   [7] Not printed. See note 1 above.

Preparatory Committee. This same paragraph now advocates the extension of mutual confidence, instead of its creation, which would have implied a disregard of the Locarno treaties.

10. Further, in order to meet Count Bernstorff, a new passage (paragraph 7 in final draft) was inserted to give effect to his insistence on the fact that the last Assembly directed that disarmament work must begin at once on the basis of existing security.

11. Paragraph 7 of the original draft had, of course, caused Count Bernstorff serious misgivings, as it provides that the study of security was to be entrusted to the Preparatory Committee. For reasons explained above, Count Bernstorff was determined to avoid this, and after some discussion M. de Brouckère (the Belgian delegate) proposed a text which was eventually incorporated in the resolution and figures as paragraph 8 of the final text.[8]

12. It was not until the consideration of paragraph 7 (a) of the original text was reached that it became necessary to face the apparent conflict between the British and French views, and to endeavour to secure a modification that would give satisfaction to the British Government.

13. I at once made a statement to the sub-committee in which I indicated that, subject to a satisfactory interpretation of paragraph 7 (a), the British Government did not wish to raise any essential objection to it. In regard to paragraph 7 (b), I explained that the British Government feared that this would inevitably lead to a renewed discussion of the protocol, and in support of this I quoted M. Paul-Boncour himself. Speaking also of 7 (c), I reminded the sub-committee that the British Government had already taken the most serious engagements to insure against what appeared to be the worst risk in Europe; I referred to the statement already made to the Assembly by Sir Austen Chamberlain,[9] and I expressed the hope that it would be readily understood that the British Government, for their part, did not see their way to contemplate equal sacrifices in all parts of the world. I then suggested that the last paragraph should be replaced by something on the lines suggested by Sir Austen Chamberlain (see his despatch No. 50 of the 18th September) to the effect that Governments should be 'invited to state what measures they would be prepared to take to support the decision of the Council in case of war breaking out in a particular sphere in which they had special interests, in other words, to say that in such and such a case their whole strength would be thrown into the struggle in support of the Council's decision'.

14. This suggestion was not ill-received, and the above text, with verbal alterations, figures in paragraph 7 (c) of the final draft. It will be seen that this paragraph begins with a text, based on M. Paul-Boncour's original proposal, which the latter was anxious to insert, in order to emphasise the need for the conclusion of further pacts on the model of the Locarno treaties. I think this is evidently harmless—it may even be desirable.

[8] i.e. the paragraph numbered 3. This paragraph provided that the Preparatory Commission for the Disarmament Conference should set up a committee to consider guarantees of arbitration and security.

[9] See No. 5, note 3.

15. There remained the difficulty of paragraph 7 (*b*) of the original text. I first of all proposed that it should be replaced by 'the examination of methods to be adopted by the organs of the League of Nations to facilitate the execution by members of the League of the obligations imposed on them by the articles of the Covenant dealing with the pacific settlement of disputes'. The French delegate at once objected to the last words, which would have excluded the consideration of article 16. He observed that it was impossible for us to refuse an examination of the Covenant, as articles 11 and 16 were already being studied by the appropriate organs, in accordance with instructions from the Council. I replied that I must only make it clear at once that we could contemplate no examination that might lead to any extension of the obligations already imposed on us by the Covenant. Eventually a text was agreed upon (paragraph 8 (*b*) of the final text) which, together with the declarations made as to its meaning, which the *rapporteur* has promised to repeat in his report, will, I trust, avert the danger which we had feared.

16. I do not think I need call especial attention to any of the other amendments, which are, for the most part, only verbal.

17. It remains only for me to say that in my opinion the final text may be regarded as satisfactory. I hope it marks the final abandonment of the idea of a general security arrangement, which was the worst feature of the protocol, and which to the minds of most other delegates means that everyone's security shall be guaranteed by the British Empire. The resolution gives a formal blessing to the system of Locarno pacts, and encourages the extension of that system. I fear that it may elicit little response in the way of fresh offers, but even if that proves to be so, it may give us the opportunity of emphasising what we have done already, and it will be an implied hint that if more is to be done it is the turn of someone else to do it. I could not but be secretly amused at hearing, for instance, Danish and Norwegian delegates, who in the past have been readiest to devise general arrangements whereby their defence might devolve on us, now hastily rising to dash any excessive hope that anything may be forthcoming on their side. After that, it will be all the more difficult for them to press us to take any engagements beyond the heavy ones that we have already given.

18. I took steps to keep in touch with the representatives of the Dominions on all points during the discussion. Unfortunately (though an endeavour was made to arrange it) it was impossible for a member of one of the Dominions delegations to be represented on the sub-committee. I gather that the Dominions delegations approve the resolution and are so reporting to their respective Governments.

I am, &c.,
ONSLOW

No. 209

Letter from Sir E. Howard (Manchester, Mass.) to Sir W. Tyrrell

[*A 6073/133/45*]

Private and confidential   MANCHESTER, MASS., *September 22, 1927*

My dear Tyrrell,

With reference to my letter of the 15th instant,[1] which I foolishly forgot to send by the last bag and which therefore only goes by this week's messenger, I enclose a memorandum of a conversation between General Preston Brown, commanding at Boston, and our Military Attaché on the subject of blockade. This shows that fear of future blockade is at the back of the minds not only of Senators but also of Generals and no doubt of Admirals. How much wiser it would have been if the United States Government had made this clear to us before launching us into the Geneva Conference. Anyhow now we really know where we stand, and it is time we considered seriously whether we should just let things slide till a crisis arises, when it will be very difficult to come to an agreement, or try quietly and without any fuss to reach some preliminary agreement with the United States prior to getting the rules of blockade settled by International Law. It seems to me that, this, if we think some action advisable, should be our mode of procedure. We must, however, be careful not to propose this directly to the United States Government as the United States authorities will at once be filled with suspicion that we are out to 'pull the wool' over their eyes. The proposal must be made to come from them. This however does not present any serious difficulties. The question is, whether, if Kellogg or the President does make any suggestion to me in this sense, I should express willingness to submit it to the Secretary of State (Sir Austen, I mean). Personally, I think I ought to do so because I believe that by coming to an agreement on this thorny question with the United States, Great Britain's loss—i.e., the right of unlimited blockade involving the hostility of the United States—will be more than compensated by the gain i.e., the removal of all danger of hostile interference by the United States and the certainty of obtaining the supplies and the credits we need from the United States, while, if we can also include eventually an arrangement for the prohibition of the use of the submarine for blockade purposes, we shall be relieved of a tremendous incubus. The blockade even as exercised in the last war is anyhow a weapon which is only effective after a very long war—and can we stand another long war? Will any other war last for four years? Any move in restraint of blockade and of submarine activities is likely to be welcomed by nearly all European Powers and I think even France and Italy, who might raise objections to the second point, i.e. restriction of submarine activities, would have to bow to general public opinion. I don't know what Japan would do but I take it she would agree.

There is also this to be considered. The United States at present is in the mood for restricting the powers of blockade, but when it comes to have a

---

[1] No. 205.

super-fleet as it will in ten or twenty years will it be so keen on this subject? Will it not be like Great Britain for the last two hundred years, anxious for complete liberty of action in time of war? Will not the positions be completely reversed? It may well be that, unless the powers of blockade are determined shortly by International Law, we shall be the ones who press for restrictions which we shall then find it impossible to persuade the United States to agree to. Our people at home may imagine that this is looking too far ahead to be practical politics. I am not, however, at all sure of this seeing the rapidity of the growth of national pride in this country. Anyhow I feel that this question of the Freedom of the Seas cannot be burked much longer. If it is not brought up by the United States, it will be brought up by Germany or one of the smaller Powers in the League of Nations. It is, I think, essential that we should have an understanding with the United States about it before this happens and the present seems to be a not unpropitious time to lead up to conversations which will lead up to such an understanding.

Perhaps you might show these two letters to the Secretary of State. I have not dared to write to him, as I have been writing him such long private letters that I feel if I go on they will deserve to lie unopened in a heap on his table, like Walter Page's to President Wilson (*vide* Colonel House's memoirs, or is it Walter Page's?).[2]

Yours ever,
ESME HOWARD

ENCLOSURE IN NO. 209

MANCHESTER, MASS., *September 20, 1927*

H[is] E[xcellency],

I submit the following memorandum of a conversation with General Preston Brown on the outcome of the Geneva Conference.

1. By invitation of Major-General Preston Brown, commanding 1st Corps Area (Boston), I visited him at Fort Ethan Allen from 24th to 26th August in order to inspect the troops training at that post.

2. General Preston Brown is an experienced and educated soldier. He has read and thought a great deal about war, and has not allowed his mind to lie fallow since he left the University of Yale to enter the American Army some thirty-three years ago. In the late War he saw something of the British Army in France, and has retained happy recollections of his contact with it. He gives me the impression of being a Southern gentleman, very friendly to England, and with genuine appreciation of what the British Empire stands for. He has been most courteous to my predecessor and to me; my relations with him are cordial and almost intimate as we find that we have many interests in common.

3. On the evening of August 25th, when I was sitting alone with him in his room at Fort Ethan Allen discussing some questions of the late war in which we were both interested, I guided the conversation to the subject of the

[2] Mr. Page had been United States Ambassador to London, 1913–18; *The Life and Letters of Walter H. Page*, edited by B. J. Hendrick, was first published in New York in 1922.

Geneva Conference to find out how an American soldier of his type had reacted to the breakdown of the Conference. What he said amounts to this:

4. The Conference failed because neither side would tell the truth; you (British) want numerous cruisers not only to protect your trade routes—which is obvious—but in order to apply in war your historic weapon of blockade. Small cruisers can do that. We (Americans) want a smaller number of big cruisers to ensure that your blockade does not interfere with our commerce as a neutral. The 10,000-ton cruisers are necessary to us to break your blockade. This country is never again going to put up with what it had to put up with in 1914–15 from both sides. It was the mercy of God and the cooperation of Walter Page and Grey that kept America from coming in on the wrong side last time. Next time He may not be so kind and Page and Grey aren't there. You have no idea how remote we were from the war. In 1914 I was in the Philippines, and in 1915 in Texas, and all we knew of the war there was that British cruisers were stopping American trade and German submarines were sinking our people. If the Germans had not made that mistake we would have come in on the wrong side.

5. General Preston Brown made it clear to me that in his opinion war between Great Britain and the United States was 'unthinkable' only as a result of disagreement between those two Powers alone; as an issue arising out of a state of war between Great Britain and a third party, he considered it 'probable', unless Great Britain modifies her practice of blockade so as to conform with the wishes of the United States.

6. To my remark that, if that was the case, it would be a pity to wait until national passions were at white heat before trying to come to an understanding on the question of blockade, he replied that the blockade question could not be taken up between the two countries too soon 'before the anti-British hot air campaign gets going'. He added: 'We know all about blockade in this country. I remember the South after the Civil War. It is a thing we ought to be able to agree about, as we too may not always be neutrals and may want to use the weapon ourselves as we have in the past.'

7. I would like to emphasise the fact that throughout this conversation General Preston Brown spoke about Great Britain and British policy in a most friendly, and indeed sympathetic way. The impression he left on me was that of a friend anxious to open my eyes to the danger of living in a fool's paradise by assuming that war between our two countries is 'unthinkable' when as a matter of fact in the eventuality which he indicated, it is 'probable', unless steps are taken now to clear up the question of blockade.

R. POPE-HENNESSY

No. 210

Letter from Sir W. Tyrrell to Sir E. Howard (Washington)

[F.O. 800/261]

Private and personal   FOREIGN OFFICE, *September 26, 1927*

My dear Howard,

Before his recent departure for Geneva the Secretary of State asked me to reply to your letter of September 1st[1] about 'peace propaganda' in the United States and Great Britain which he only had time to read and minute before leaving London.

I am very glad you agree that it would be inadvisable to embark upon the propaganda outlined in your letter of July 29th.[2] We feel that public discussion of the disastrous consequences of a war between Great Britain and the United States would produce an effect the reverse of the intention. Instead of soothing public opinion, it would almost certainly spread fear and even consternation on both sides of the Atlantic. A cry would arise not so much for preventing war as for preparing the means to avert these disasters should war unhappily come. If it were sought to demonstrate the impossibility of that war, an irresistible temptation would moreover be provided to the jingoes and paper fire-eaters of both nations to rush into print with ingenious and fearful explanations of what either country could and would. As it is, Hoover appears to have seized the opportunity to indulge in what looks to us suspiciously like sabre-rattling.[2] So little, in fact, do we like this 'propaganda' idea, that I should prefer you not to mention it again to Hoover unless he returns to the charge. In that event it will, I think, be necessary to be quite frank with him and to tell him exactly why the proposal does not appeal to us. We cannot attribute our dislike of the 'propaganda' proposal to the fear that it might excite *our* 'big navyites'. If any such of any moment exist at the present time (which I neither admit nor believe) they cannot be compared with their prototypes in the United States either in numbers or influence. So that if Hoover does mention this matter to you again, please answer him in the sense of this letter.

I need scarcely say that we are fully conscious of the consequences of a war between Great Britain and the United States, and particularly in regard to our imperial structure. I agree with you, however, that such a catastrophe is not 'unthinkable', for all the reasons you mention and for many others. There appear to be forces at work at the present time whose aim it is to point to this country as the great enemy and competitor of the United States in every channel, political and commercial. This is all the more serious when one remembers that of the American population the Anglo-Saxon proportion is rapidly decreasing. What the American people will be, in composition and character, a few generations hence, is a complete gamble. It would, of course, be as absurd to stake one's very existence upon the theory that any two countries must be forever friends as to assume that two countries must be

---

[1] See Volume III, No. 506.   [2] *V. ibid.*, No. 480.

forever enemies. During the last few years we have, I think, given many proofs of our desire for really amicable relations with the United States. I wish we received more frequent evidence than we do that there is some appreciation of this in official and political circles in the United States and that some real as well as emotional value is attached to the friendship of Britain.

Yours ever,

W. T.

No. 211

Memorandum by Mr. Campbell[1]

[W 11899/61/98]

FOREIGN OFFICE, October 8, 1927

Arbitration, security and disarmament

Appended below are (i) a minute by Mr. Kirkpatrick[2] answering the points made in an open letter by Mr. Ramsay MacDonald (Flag A)[3] in support of the Protocol for the Pacific Settlement of International Disputes, commonly called the Geneva Protocol; (ii) a note contesting the statement in a letter by Professor Gilbert Murray (Flag B)[4] to the effect that acceptance of the Protocol would impose no fresh obligations on this country; (iii) a brief note reviewing our position in relation to the cause of arbitration, security and disarmament.

ANNEX I. *Mr. Ramsay MacDonald's letter*

Mr. Ramsay MacDonald questions Sir Austen Chamberlain's reference at Geneva to the attitude of the Dominions towards the Protocol.[5] He goes on to say: 'Moreover, in 1924 the delegates from the Dominions to Geneva unanimously accepted the idea of the protocol and agreed that the various governments should consider it with a view to making what modifications in it might be necessary so that the British Empire might take its place as a truly co-operative partner of the League of Nations.'

This statement is strictly true. The protocol was approved by a resolution of the Assembly, adopted unanimously in the following form: 'The Assembly

---

[1] Mr. R. H. Campbell was a senior member of the Western, General, and League of Nations Department of the Foreign Office.

[2] A member of the Western, General, and League of Nations Department of the Foreign Office.

[3] None of the flagged documents is now attached to the filed copy of this memorandum. The reference was to Mr. MacDonald's letter of September 13 printed in *The Manchester Guardian* of September 14, 1927.

[4] Professor Gilbert Murray was President of the League of Nations Union and Vice-President of the League of Nations International Committee for Intellectual Co-operation. His undated letter is printed *ibid.*

[5] Cf. No. 5, note 3.

welcomes warmly the draft protocol . . .[6] and decides to recommend to the earnest attention of all the members of the League the acceptance of the said draft protocol.' The British and the Dominion delegates voted for the resolution but none signed the Protocol. In view of their action they may be said to have accepted the 'idea' of the Protocol; while some of them fully realised its defects and only voted for the resolution so as to preserve the harmony of the Assembly and because they knew that they were in no way committing their governments, others appear to have come under the influence of the fervour generated by the Assembly and actually voiced general approval of the Protocol.

The present government accepts Mr. MacDonald's version of what passed at Geneva. The Lord Chancellor, speaking in the House of Lords in March, 1925 said: 'The Noble Lord (Lord Parmoor)[7] has said—and of course I take it as absolutely true—that the representatives of the Dominions who were present at the Assembly of the League were favourable to the adoption of the Protocol.'[8] Of course Mr. MacDonald's statement is quite irrelevant except in so far as it conveys to the hurried or thoughtless reader that the Dominions really are favourable to the Protocol. The essential fact is that in the spring of 1925 all the Dominion governments categorically rejected the Protocol and there is absolutely nothing to show that they have in any way changed their mind. With the possible exception of New Zealand none were influenced by Great Britain. All of them in separate documents set forth the reasons which had led to their decision. Copies of these documents will be found at Flag C.[9]

So much for the attitude of the Dominions towards the Protocol itself. Mr. MacDonald goes on to suggest that a commission of the League should be appointed to which the draft of 1924 should be 'submitted for close examination so as to remove from it any mistake that may be embodied in it and simplify it by way of amendments or separate notes so that it may become acceptable as a practical pledge of security and safety to the British or any other people'. It will be seen that Mr. MacDonald's proposal is substantially the same as that in the Dutch resolution which caused all the trouble at the recent Assembly. The latter reads: 'Convinced that, without reopening the discussions on the Geneva Protocol of 1924, it is desirable to consider whether the time has not come to resume the study of the principles on which that Protocol was based; And considering it of the highest importance that the Assembly should give an impulse to the work of the Preparatory Commission for the Disarmament Conference. Decides to refer the study of the fundamental principles of the Geneva Protocol and the conclusions of the

[6] Punctuation as in the original quotation from resolution No. 1 adopted by the Fifth Assembly of the League of Nations on October 2, 1924, printed in Cmd. 2273 of 1924, p. 47.

[7] Lord Parmoor had been Lord President of the Council in Mr. MacDonald's administration in 1924. For his speech on March 24, 1925, see *Parl. Debs.*, 5th ser., H. of L., vol. lx, cols. 655–70, especially cols. 666–8.

[8] For this extract from Lord Cave's speech on March 24, 1925, *v. ibid.*, col. 673.

[9] The reference was presumably to correspondence printed in Cmd. 2458 of 1925, *Protocol for the Pacific Settlement of International Disputes. Correspondence relating to the position of the Dominions.*

report of the Preparatory Commission to the appopriate Committees.'[10] The Secretary of State dealt with this point in his speech[5] against the Dutch resolution when he said: 'But what useful purpose could we serve, what evil consequences might we not incur, if we reopen those troubled debates before there has been from any quarter any indication of a change of mind. All the old controversies, all the old differences of opinion are still expressed.' In making his statement Sir Austen had the full support of the Dominion delegates who agreed at a meeting that everything should be done 'in the first place, if possible, by private persuasion, but in the last resort, if necessary, by a public declaration to prevent any such absurd and mischievous proposal being passed on for the delectation of an Assembly committee', (letter from Mr. Cadogan).[11] It is clear from Mr. Cadogan's letter that the Dominions share our view that the Protocol in the 1924 form cannot be moulded so as to meet our requirements, and that further discussion of it must do unqualified harm. In the circumstances it would be difficult, whatever our own inclination, to put into effect Mr. MacDonald's proposal.

Mr. MacDonald loosely quotes Senator Dandurand's speech (Flag D)[12] in support of his case. It will be seen (page 28) that Senator Dandurand states that although Canada was led to reject the Protocol, largely because of the non-participation of the United States, nevertheless the Canadian Government are ready to consider acceptance of the obligatory jurisdiction of the Permanent Court in disputes of a legal character, subject to certain reservations. This statement has no bearing whatever on the question of the Protocol. He made the same statement in 1924;[13] the Canadian Government made it in March 1925 in the very document in which they rejected the Protocol,[14] and Senator Dandurand himself later said the same thing in a debate in the Canadian House of Representatives [sic]. As a matter of fact, whilst the Canadian Government may in principle be willing to sign the optional clause[15] subject to reservations, they are committed by decision of the Imperial Conference not to do so for the present. This decision runs as follows: 'Whilst the members of the committee were unanimous in favouring the widest possible extension of the method of arbitration for the settlement of international disputes, the feeling was that it was at present premature to accept the obligations under the Article in question. A general understanding was reached that none of the governments represented at the Imperial Confer-

[10] See No. 200.

[11] This letter of September 7 from Mr. Cadogan to Mr. Villiers, head of the Western, General, and League of Nations Department of the Foreign Office, is not printed. For the meeting in question see No. 200, note 4.

[12] *Note in original*: 'Not annexed'. The reference was to the speech made by the Canadian delegate to the Assembly of the League of Nations on September 12, 1927: see *League of Nations Official Journal: Special Supplement No. 54*, pp. 112–13.

[13] *V. op. cit., Special Supplement No. 23*, p. 221, for the relevant passage of M. Dandurand's speech on October 2, 1924.

[14] See item No. 11 of Cmd. 2458, p. 18.

[15] See article 36 of the Statute of the Permanent Court of International Justice of December 16, 1920, printed in *British and Foreign State Papers*, vol. 114, pp. 862–72.

ence would take any action in the direction of the acceptance of the compulsory jurisdiction of the Permanent Court without bringing up the matter for further discussion.'[16]

It will be seen from the above that the attitude of the Dominions is perfectly clear and that we are in a position, should we desire to do so, to answer Mr. MacDonald's attack without any further reference to the Dominion governments.

I. KIRKPATRICK

ANNEX II. *Professor Murray's letter*

The main theme of Professor Murray's letter is summarised in the following passage: 'It shows mere confusion of thought, or deliberate misrepresentation, to pretend that the Protocol imposes new burdens on Great Britain.'

This view has of course been upheld from the start by the supporters of the Protocol; it shows a complete disregard of realities. The question was gone into very fully after the Assembly of 1924. In a paper (Flag E) written in November of that year, the late Sir Eyre Crowe surveyed, in its broader aspect, the difference between the Covenant and the Protocol cum Covenant; a more detailed comparison is contained in a paper written by me about the same time (Flag F).[17] In the light of those and other documents it would be a work of supererogation to enter into any detail here: suffice it to say that the over-riding difference is that, whereas according to the generally accepted interpretation of the Covenant each State retains the right to judge whether in any given circumstances its obligation to apply the sanctions prescribed in article 16 has arisen, it would no longer enjoy that discretion under the Protocol. It is only possible to maintain the contrary view by interpreting the Covenant in the strictest literal sense. In point of fact the tendency has been in the opposite direction. That this was recognised to be so and that the Protocol was intended to add to the obligations of the Covenant, is shown nowhere more convincingly than in the words of the authors of the Protocol themselves. The Report of the First and Third Committees of the Fifth Assembly contains the following passage: 'Article 11 is intended to settle this controversy. The signatories of the present Protocol accept the obligation to apply against the aggressor the various sanctions laid down in the Covenant, *as interpreted in article 11 of the Protocol*, when an act of aggression has been established and the Council has called upon the signatory States immediately

---

[16] The citation is from the report of the Inter-Imperial Relations Committee of Prime Ministers and Heads of Delegations attending the Imperial Conference held in London October–November 1926; see Cmd. 2768 of 1926, p. 28. The Committee's report was adopted by the Conference on November 17, 1926: *v. ibid.*, p. 12.

[17] The minute dated November 17, 1924, by Sir E. Crowe, Permanent Under Secretary of State for Foreign Affairs, 1920–5, is not printed. In it Sir E. Crowe discussed provisions in the Protocol for compulsory arbitration and the rules for the application of sanctions against disturbers of the peace. Mr. Campbell's memorandum of November 10, 1924, was intended 'to throw into relief the principal points of divergence' between the Covenant of the League of Nations and the Protocol, and 'to offer, in addition, a commentary on the more important features which are peculiar to the protocol'.

to apply such sanctions (article 10, last paragraph). Should they fail so to do, they will not be fulfilling their obligations.'; and, again later: 'that is why I said that the great omission in the Covenant has been made good'.[18]

Moreover it should be noted that under the Protocol the discretion of the Council itself is considerably curtailed. In certain contingencies it is bound automatically to order the application of sanctions (e.g. the last paragraph of article 10—'The Council *shall* call upon the signatory States etc.'); under the Covenant such a decision can only be taken on a unanimous vote.

These innovations mean that in certain eventualities a signatory of the Protocol incurs the risk of finding itself drawn into war against its own judgment and against its will. For the British Empire of course this risk would be incomparably greater than for any other member of the League. Thanks to its mobility the British navy would be called upon to take the principal part in military measures against an aggressor in almost any part of the world. Against that the supporters of the Protocol argue that it is inconceivable that any State could for long resist the pressure of the economic and financial sanctions and that the need for military measures would never arise. That, again, shows a complete disregard for realities. Economic and financial sanctions cannot be applied without leading to a state of war with the country against which they are enforced, and to the risk of serious complications with neutrals, particularly with any country not a member of the League.

All this, be it noted, without Parliament having any voice in the matter at all. It is almost incredible that anyone today, particularly the Labour Party, should advocate the resuscitation of the Protocol. Mr. Ramsay MacDonald would doubtless retort that he is not urging its acceptance as it stands, but only after the introduction of the modifications necessary to bring it into harmony with the special circumstances of the British Empire, and that it is the idea rather than the letter of the Protocol that he is advocating. It is not clear what he means exactly by the 'idea' of the Protocol. If he means the essential features, these are compulsory arbitration and the automatic application of the sanctions: eliminate them and there is nothing left. If he means the ultimate end, to which the Protocol is only the means, he must be referring to the slogan 'arbitration, security and disarmament' invented at the Assembly of 1924. If that is what he means the answer is that the present government has done more than any of its predecessors to further those principles; that it has done this and will continue to do it by the methods which seem to it the most practical and fruitful rather than by subscribing to a document which would rob Parliament of all control and might at any moment plunge this country into war over a dispute of no concern to it whatever.

Before leaving Professor Murray's letter, I would draw attention to a reply to him by Mr. Philip Snowden (Flag G), who takes the opposite view and

[18] For these extracts from the report, submitted by M. Benes, of the Third Committee, which formed Part II, 2, of the General Report submitted to the Fifth Assembly by the First (constitutional questions) and Third Committees, see Cmd. 2273 of 1924, pp. 30 and 33 respectively. The passage here italicized was underscored by Mr. Campbell.

makes good his case in an admirably argued statement. Professor Murray's retort (Flag G*)[19] is very feeble and burkes the point at issue.

Finally Professor Murray seems to be condemned out of his own mouth. The report of the British delegates to the fifth Assembly (Flag H)[20] contains (page 15) the following passage: 'The British delegate explained that the willingness of Governments to amend the Covenant must be clearly expressed in the Protocol. In no other way could the danger of creating within the League an inner ring of Powers, bound towards each other by ties and obligations more close than those binding the ordinary members of the League, be avoided. The drafting of amendments to the Covenant was, however, a technical matter, and time was short. He therefore suggested that the Council should be asked to set up a committee of experts to draft the amendments to the Covenant contemplated by the Protocol.'

R. H. C.

ANNEX III. *General survey*

In view of the criticism which this country came in for at the Assembly this year on account of its supposed blocking of further progress along the path of arbitration, security and disarmament, it is desirable to take stock of the situation and see whether such criticism is in any degree justified, and whether there is anything more that we could do for the present to advance the good cause.

The answer to the first point, given by the Secretary of State himself at Geneva, is an emphatic negative. We cannot be justly blamed for refusing to countenance a scheme which, apart from its unsuitability to our particular case, would, we are honestly convinced, disserve rather than serve the best interests of the League itself. Instead, therefore, of following that path we have taken the one which we believe to lead more surely, but in the long run more quickly, to the desired goal. By taking the leading part in formulating the policy which culminated in the Locarno settlement we have not only given ample proof of our own sincerity but have set an example, the value of which has been explicitly recognised by the Assembly. The criticism levelled against this country for not having done more is of course in part the cover employed by others to divert attention from their failure to do as much, and in part the expression of the hope of the smaller European States to feel that they have the guarantee of the British Empire behind them.

This guarantee is one which we cannot possibly give. The next point, then, is whether we should reconsider the question of accepting compulsory arbitration independently of the Protocol, and subscribe to the optional clause of the statute of the Permanent Court. The question has been exhaustively

---

[19] The letter dated September 14 from Mr. Snowden, who had been Chancellor of the Exchequer in Mr. MacDonald's administration of 1924, is printed in *The Manchester Guardian* of September 16, 1927. Professor Gilbert Murray's letter, undated, is printed *op. cit.*, September 20, 1927.

[20] Printed as Cmd. 2289 of 1924, *League of Nations, Fifth Assembly. Report of the British Delegates relating to the Protocol for the Peaceful Settlement of International Disputes.*

considered on more than one occasion. The paper at Flag I[21] contains all the more important opinions expressed up to the summer of 1924, including that, which was adverse, given by Lord Haldane when Lord Chancellor in Mr. Ramsay MacDonald's government. It is unnecessary, indeed impossible, to add to the arguments contained in those documents. Since then the matter was further considered in the summer of 1926 in preparation for the Imperial Conference. The Legal Advisers wrote a paper advocating signature of the optional clause subject to wide reservations to exclude disputes arising out of belligerent action at sea and those arising out of past events. The paper was circulated to the Cabinet with a covering note by the Secretary of State (Flag J).[22] The Cabinet Committee, appointed to consider the question, reported adversely, Lord Robert Cecil[23] alone dissenting. The Imperial Conference endorsed the opinion of the Cabinet Committee and reached the general understanding, quoted in Section (i) of this paper, that none of the governments of the Empire would take any action in the direction of accepting compulsory arbitration without bringing the matter up for further discussion. The grounds on which the considered opinion of His Majesty's government was based are resumed in a paper (Flag K)[24] prepared by the attorney General. Annexed thereto is a note on the views previously expressed by the Dominion governments. Though we have no evidence, beyond the recent speech of Senator Dandurand, to show whether these views remain the same today or have undergone some modification, there is no reason to suppose that they have substantially altered.

The position therefore is that if His Majesty's government decided that the time had come when they might safely sign the optional clause, they only could do so after further consultation with the Dominions, and that in that event, while Canada, South Africa and the Irish Free State might be found either willing or open to persuasion to accept the compulsory jurisdiction of the Court, Australia and New Zealand would probably maintain their opposition.

Whether or not there is occasion for His Majesty's government to revise their attitude is another matter. Nothing has occurred to modify the reasons, as set out in the Attorney General's paper, for the attitude which they have taken up hitherto. Another powerful reason not included among those in the

[21] The reference was possibly to a collection of papers sent to the Colonial Office and the India Office by the Foreign Office on August 13, 1924. This collection contained: (i) a Foreign Office review of opinions expressed on the question dated March 17, 1924; (ii) a memorandum dated May 21, 1924, by Mr. Malkin, then Assistant and since 1925 Second Legal Adviser to the Foreign Office; (iii) a memorandum by Sir C. Hurst of June 18, 1924; (iv) a memorandum by Sir E. Crowe of July 13, 1924; (v) Lord Haldane's memorandum of July 21, 1924, extracts from which are printed in *Parl. Debs., 5th ser., H. of C.,* vol. 210, cols. 2107–8, as cited by Sir A. Chamberlain on November 24, 1927.

[22] See Volume II, No. 68.

[23] Viscount Cecil of Chelwood had been Chancellor of the Duchy of Lancaster from November 1924 to August 1927.

[24] The reference was to a memorandum on Compulsory Arbitration in International Disputes prepared for the Imperial Conference of 1926 by Sir Douglas Hogg.

above-mentioned paper is that given by Mr. Malkin in the earlier part of his note in the document at Flag I, namely that the additional number of cases, or classes of case, which would become arbitrable is very limited. If we exclude those which form the subject of the essential reservations recommended in the later, joint memorandum of the legal advisers, (Flag J) they would amount practically only to those which might be held to affect our vital interests, independence or honour. Even cases in that category we are already bound, under article 15 of the Covenant, to refer to the Council if they are of a nature likely to lead to a rupture.

There seems in short every reason to maintain our attitude.

For purposes of reference, if desired, a list of the States which have signed, and of those which have signed and ratified, the optional clause is annexed at Flag L.[25]

If, then, we cannot agree to the resurrection, in any form, of the Protocol, or sign the optional clause independently of the Protocol, is there anything else we can do to further the cause of arbitration, security and disarmament? After giving much thought to the question, I am unable to make any suggestion. There seems no other or better course than to stand fast on the defence of our policy and our actions, as made by the Secretary of State at Geneva last month. That defence was welcomed by the bulk of opinion in this country, and I have heard it more than once described as a signal service to the League. Our contribution is not necessarily at an end. In course of time we shall no doubt be able to go further on the road of disarmament; but it seems quite unnecessary, indeed positively undesirable, that we should take the lead in any further move at present.

There remains only the question of the attitude to be adopted by the British representative on the Preparatory Committee when it meets again in November, and on the sub-committee which it is to set up. The relevant papers, W 9152 and W 9063, marked to be brought up on the Secretary of State's return, are annexed.[26]

The important point is that contained in the final paragraph of Resolution No. 5. Its meaning is explained in the last two paragraphs of M. de Brouckère's report (see page 3 of the print in W 9152). I do not think that we shall be prepared to indicate any cases, beyond the obligations assumed under the Treaty of Locarno, in which we would bind ourselves in advance to take certain measures and to specify what those measures would be. Such engagements savour too much of the Protocol, and like the general undertaking in that instrument, would rob Parliament of all discretion in matters of peace

---

[25] The list under reference is untraced in Foreign Office archives: cf. however *Parl. Debs.*, *5th ser.*, *H. of C.*, vol. 200, col. 2123, for a list down to December 8, 1926; Guatemala and Germany signed on December 17, 1926, and September 23, 1927, respectively.

[26] W 9152/61/98 was the report of the Third Committee to the Assembly of the League of Nations printed in *League of Nations Official Journal: Special Supplement No. 54*, pp. 453–6. This report, for which M. de Brouckère was *rapporteur*, covered five draft resolutions which were adopted by the Assembly on September 26, 1927. The fifth resolution was that referred to in No. 208, note 1. W 9063/61/98 was No. 208.

and war. We have done it in the case of Locarno, but there would surely be an outcry if we extended it to other cases and other parts of the world in which we have no direct interest. The Secretary of State at Geneva indicated that it was the turn of others to do something. Let us stand fast to that. The smaller States have made so far no contribution at all.

The matter must presumably be considered by the Committee of Imperial Defence, or an appropriate sub-committee, where the views of others departments interested can be heard. If their opinions, as I surmise, are found to be adverse to the British representative taking any leading part, I submit that there is no occasion, on international political grounds, to urge any other policy.

R. H. CAMPBELL

No. 212

Memorandum by Mr. Craigie respecting the Effect on Public Opinion in the United States of Lord Cecil's resignation from the Government[1]

[A 6019/93/45]

FOREIGN OFFICE, *October 11, 1927*

In a despatch dated September 12th last[2] Sir Esme Howard, after quoting a number of American press references to Lord Cecil's resignation, concludes that this event 'has not made any serious impression on public opinion here with regard to the conclusion of the Geneva Conference'. As a corrective of the above inference, Sir Esme quotes a statement recently made to him by Sir Arthur Willert[3] when passing through Washington, to the effect that several financial gentlemen of Sir Arthur's acquaintance who, before the statement issued by Lord Cecil on his resignation, had been of opinion that His Majesty's Government had probably had a good deal of right on their side, now believe that the United States Government were justified in the line they had taken. While admitting that this may be the attitude of certain individuals, the Ambassador is nevertheless inclined to think that public opinion generally regarding the Geneva Conference will not be greatly altered by Lord Cecil's statement.

Sir Esme Howard's above conclusion is not altogether shared by the department, judging from the material at its disposal, nor, I understand, by Sir Arthur Willert, who has just returned from the United States. As examples

---

[1] This memorandum was circulated to the Cabinet. See Viscount Cecil, *A Great Experiment* (London, 1941), pp. 358–63, for his letter of August 9, 1927, to the Prime Minister resigning as Chancellor of the Duchy of Lancaster and consequently as British Representative on the Preparatory Commission for the Disarmament Conference on the grounds of disagreement with the Cabinet on the broad policy of disarmament and on the policy adopted at the Three Power naval conference at Geneva in particular.

[2] Washington despatch No. 1665 here summarised is not printed.

[3] Head of the News Department of the Foreign Office.

of the revival of American self-righteousness to which Lord Cecil's resignation has given rise, I quote the following American press references at random:

1. The Philadelphia Public Ledger (an influential newspaper) published an article on August 31st containing the following paragraph:

'Lord Cecil's letter of resignation was a stinging rebuke to the majority in the Baldwin Cabinet. It seems definitely to prove that the British entered the Geneva Conference only to wreck it. This naturally suggests a little further consideration of the British Navy, of what it has meant in the past and what it may mean in the future.'

Summarising press opinion on September 9th, the British Library of Information in New York declared that large sections of Middle Western opinion interpreted Lord Cecil's resignation as a confession of Great Britain's fault at the Naval Conference, and a clear vindication of the American position. It also served as an occasion for much venting of the obvious dislike in which His Majesty's present Government is held.

2. The St. Louis Globe Democrat stated on August 31st:

'He (Lord Cecil) will dispel the prevalent notion in England that the failure of the Conference was largely due to American stubbornness.'

3. The Pittsburgh Post Gazette, writing on the same date, stated:—

'Lord Cecil has done a service to the Kellogg administration of our State Department'

while such phrases as 'a rebuke to British Toryism' are typical of American editorial comment.

4. The Liberal Scripps Howard Alliance newspapers are so confident that the resignation of Lord Cecil will prove a deadly blow to the Government that they are already counting the seats in the next general election.

5. Southern opinion may be summed up in the words of the Memphis Commercial Appeal of August 31st:—

'Another jolt like that of the resignation of Lord Robert Cecil from the Baldwin Cabinet may open the eyes of the British people as to where the blame must be placed for the failure of the Arms Limitation Conference at Geneva.'

The above quotations appear to me to be representative of most of the American press comment on this question.

Finally, Mr. Coolidge's own view is worthy of note. It is summarised as follows by the correspondent of the 'New York Times' at Rapid City in a message dated Sept. 6th: 'Unless Lord Cecil's retirement from the British Cabinet as a protest against Great Britain's attitude on limitation of auxiliary cruisers . . .[4] causes a decisive reaction against the British Government's position, there appears to be little hope that the movement for reduction of naval armament will succeed in the near future, perhaps not during President Coolidge's term of office.' In other words, the President, who had originally

[4] Punctuation as in original quotation.

383

been reported as still hoping that an agreement might eventually be reached, now considers it a waste of time for him to talk of another Disarmament Conference since Lord Cecil is no longer in the Cabinet.

R. L. Craigie

No. 213

Letter from Sir E. Drummond[1] *(Geneva) to Mr. Cadogan*

[*W 9712/61/98*]

Confidential   Geneva, *October 12, 1927*

My dear Alec,

A very nice question has arisen on which, although I must ultimately settle on my own responsibility, I shall be very glad of your advice.

As you know, the Soviets were invited originally to take part in the work of the Preparatory Disarmament Committee.[2] At that time the Russian-Swiss dispute[3] was still active and the Soviets therefore as usual refused to come to Geneva. After the settlement of that dispute indications reached me from various sources, particularly German, that the Soviets would be willing to send representatives to the Committee if they were re-invited or if they were officially informed that the original invitation still held good. I had no authority to send them any such invitation or information, and I refused to take any action which did not lie strictly within my competence. Further, I had nothing definite from the Soviet Government and it would not have been dignified for the League to re-issue an invitation at the risk of a further refusal.

But the situation is now somewhat changed in view of the Assembly resolutions setting up the Special Committee on Arbitration and Security. I think it is clear that the Soviet Government could not participate in the Arbitration and Security Committee without attending the Preparatory Committee, but from what I have been told previously, and you know it is extremely difficult to understand Russian psychology, the Soviets only require some little encouragement to decide to send members to the Preparatory Committee.

It would be, I think, proper and indeed, right, from the administrative point of view, that I should send to the Soviet Government for information, copies of the Assembly resolutions about the establishment of the Special Committee on Arbitration and Security under reference to the original invitation sent to them to attend the Preparatory Committee. Such action would allow the Soviets to send representatives to the next meeting of the

---

[1] Secretary-General of the League of Nations.

[2] See Volume I, No. 138.

[3] On January 16, 1926, the Soviet Government had stated that it could not be represented on the Preparatory Commission for the Disarmament Conference in Switzerland owing to its dispute with the Swiss Government following the murder in May 1923 of M. Vorovsky, the Soviet delegate to the Lausanne Conference; cf. Volume I, No. 234. For the settlement of the dispute in April 1927, see Jane Degras, *op. cit.*, vol. ii, pp. 180–1.

Preparatory Committee should they wish to do so, while if they do not so desire they need pay no attention to my letter.

But as the result may well be that the Soviet representatives come to both the Committees I should like to know what view would be taken in London on the subject.

As the matter is obviously one which falls within the competence of the Secretariat, we discussed the matter here at one of our meetings of Directors and I found that Sugimura[4] and the Germans were strongly in favour of the action I suggested, indeed, everyone believed that it was the right thing to do. I have delayed final decision until next week because of the importance of the question and therefore I shall be very grateful if you could let me know privately what your opinion is. If, however, you feel, and you may well do so, that you would rather leave the responsibility entirely to me, I shall quite understand, but as far as I can see it is likely, as things are at present, that I shall take the action I have suggested in this letter.

Yours sincerely,
ERIC DRUMMOND

The matter is of considerable urgency as I think I shall have to take a final decision on Wednesday next Oct. 19th.　　　　　　　　　　　　　E. D.[5]

[4] Under Secretary-General in charge of the Political Section of the League of Nations.

[5] Mr. Cadogan sent the following message in reply to Sir E. Drummond in Foreign Office telegram No. 186 to Geneva of October 18: 'Department are disposed to agree that you should act as proposed'. M. Chicherin accepted the invitation on behalf of the Union of Soviet Socialist Republics in a telegram dated October 29, 1927, circulated as League of Nations document No. C.P.D./95 (received in the Foreign Office on November 24).

No. 214

Letter from Sir E. Howard (Washington) to Sir W. Tyrrell

[A 6213/133/45]

WASHINGTON, October 12, 1927

My dear Tyrrell,

Your letter of the 26th ultimo.[1] As you know I agree that any peace propaganda of the kind suggested in my letter of the 29th July[2] would be, as you say, most probably only oil on the flames of the fire-eating jingoes and others who make the public insist on more and more armaments. Therefore it is certainly better dropped. But when you say that Hoover was sabre-rattling, I think you are wrong. He was just thinking aloud and, as his thoughts were those of a possible future President and moreover were in my opinion at least founded on much logic and common sense it certainly seemed to me worth reporting them. Hoover is not at all the sort of man to indulge in sabre-rattling and in manner is the least sabre-rattling that I have ever come across. I am beginning to think he is perhaps one of the half-dozen really big

[1] No. 210.　　　　[2] See Volume III, No. 480.

men I have ever met. When he blurted out during my conversation with Kellogg and himself while the Geneva Conference was in progress—'I don't see why the English shouldn't have all the small five thousand ton cruisers they need. They will never be used against us.'[3]—he was not talking like a sabre-rattler and he clearly annoyed Kellogg by doing so. That unexpected observation of his was the *fons et origo*[4] of the whole of our subsequent conversation re peace propaganda as reported in my letter of 29th July. For it was then that I said 'I wish the people of both countries could be brought to see what the disastrous financial and economic effects of a declaration of war between them would be even if no shot were ever fired.' Kellogg on that waved his hands towards Hoover and said 'There's the man who could get that made clear to the public if you want it.' Hoover agreed that it might be useful and said he would think it over. Then came the further conversation in which he mentioned political implications and blockade which would have to be discussed if the thing were to be done at all. Even if they were not discussed in the original pamphlets, or whatever the documents might be called, they would certainly be discussed after by the Press and Public.

I will certainly be perfectly frank in speaking to Hoover if I do so again about the matter. There are only two things that count with a man like him —complete frankness and absence of funk. If he thinks you are funking an issue he has no further use for you—and that is I think generally the case with Americans. Therefore if you don't mind I prefer rather than leaving it to him to bring up the question again to tell him straight what Sir Austen and you fear and what I also fear i.e. that any discussion on these lines could not but arouse alarm on both sides of the Atlantic which would result in a cry for bigger armaments. That is quite logical and he will fully understand. Therefore I beg you to let me give the whole subject its quietus in this way.

As to the second part of your letter I am sure that most Englishmen *in a responsible position* are fully conscious of the consequences of a war between the two countries particularly in regard to the Empire. This being so, it is obvious that we should do everything in our power to avoid really dangerous causes of friction that might lead to war. Unquestionably the most dangerous of such possible causes is the 'freedom of the seas'. You will by now have got my two letters on this subject.[5] I now enclose a memorandum on it from Colonel Pope-Hennessy, our Military Attaché, which he has sent to the Director of Military Operations at the War Office. I frankly agree with all he says as to the dangers that insistence on the right of complete freedom of blockade may lead us into, and I feel that we should endeavour to settle with our potential enemy in this question while we can do so without loss of face and even perhaps with considerable acquisition of merit.

If you at the Foreign Office decide to pursue this question further, I should like once more to insist on these two points. First, that the first definite overt invitation to discuss the question must come from America. This I could, I feel sure, easily arrange at this end, by letting the President know through a

[3] *V. op. cit.*, No. 418.   [4] Fount and origin.
[5] Nos. 205 and 209.

mutual friend that we would not be averse to such a discussion. Second, that Great Britain and the United States must arrange between them how far they will go before any attempt is made to call an international Conference. If a Conference is called first and there is no previous arrangement between the two greatest naval Powers we shall just have Geneva over again; only the results will be infinitely worse as regards Anglo-American relations. The ground will therefore require most careful preparation and the Press must not be allowed the opportunity to queer the pitch again as at Geneva. I also enclose an article from the Chicago Tribune[6] which is interesting in this connection and shows to what an extent the Press is beginning to dot the i,s as regards the freedom of the seas. We shall certainly hear a good deal about it in the naval debates next session.

Finally you end your letter by saying that while we have shown many evidences of our friendship to the States you wish there was more appreciation of this shown in official and political circles in the United States and that some real as well as emotional value was attached to the friendship of Britain.

I quite agree. I too wish I could see more evidence of this real value. Nevertheless I feel that this is no reason for not continuing our policy of trying to eliminate all causes of friction. We have been successful now as regards liquor smuggling[7]—all complaints against us on this score have ceased—and as regards the settlement of blockade claims,[8] which was a really terrible snag in the path. Why should we not try to get rid of this freedom of the seas bogey especially as I believe with Pope-Hennessy there is little chance of an unrestricted blockade being anything else than a boomerang in the next war? Well, you will no doubt let me know all in good time. But if you at the Foreign Office do think that we might make a move in this direction, let me sound the President first before taking any definite steps. I would only choose someone for this purpose whom I could entirely trust. The moment for such a move is singularly propitious for the President's hands are free as regards the election of 1928.[9]

Lastly, once more I hope that you and the Secretary of State will allow me to speak to Hoover at once in the sense of your letter under reply.

Yours ever,

Esme Howard

[6] The attached copy of an extract from an editorial from the *Chicago Tribune* of July 29, 1927, is not printed. The article stated in particular that the American people 'want a navy able to enforce our rights and interests in the freedom of the seas'.

[7] For correspondence between the United States Government and H.M. Government in pursuance of the convention signed in January 1924 (printed in *British and Foreign State Papers*, vol. 119, pp. 467–9) relative to the prevention of the smuggling of liquor into the United States, in particular from the Bahamas, see *Papers relating to the Foreign Relations of the United States 1926*, vol. ii, pp. 336–58, and Cmd. 2647 of 1926. See also E. Howard, *Theatre of Life* (London, 1935), vol. ii, pp. 501–11, and *Survey of International Affairs 1925*, vol. ii, pp. 436–8.

[8] The notes exchanged at Washington on May 19, 1927, between the United States Government and H.M. Government regarding the disposal of certain pecuniary claims arising out of the War, are printed in *British and Foreign State Papers*, vol. 126, pp. 317–22; see Volume II, Chapter V, *passim*, for the preceding negotiations.

[9] Mr. Coolidge had announced his intention not to run for President in 1928.

Colonel Pope-Hennessy (Washington) to General Charles (War Office)[10]

No. 198

WASHINGTON, *October 10, 1927*

1. The failure of Great Britain and the United States to reach agreement on naval disarmament at the recent Three Power Conference at Geneva gave rise in this country to considerable comment in the Press, to one aspect of which, as exemplified in the attached extract from the 'Chicago Tribune' of July 23rd,[11] I desire to draw attention, as its importance has been borne in upon me in a conversation with a person whom I believe to be well informed and friendly to Great Britain. The substance of that conversation was communicated to you under cover of my No. 188 dated September 22nd, 1927.[12]

2. The proposition to which I desire to draw attention amounts to this:—it is not correct to say that war between Great Britain and the United States is 'unthinkable' since, in certain circumstances, such a conflict is not only possible but even probable; those circumstances being the application by Great Britain of her historic policy of blockade when at war with a third party, while the United States is a neutral as regards the original quarrel, since the United States is determined to maintain 'the freedom of the seas'. However jurists may define, or fail to define, that expression 'the freedom of the seas', to the people of the United States it means the right to trade with Great Britain's enemies as with herself, employing the American Fleet (in the late President Wilson's words) 'to wage neutrality'. I am confident that the people of this country do not intend to submit their overseas trade again to the interference it suffered from both sides during the late war. British interference with American trade during the Napoleonic Wars was the ostensible cause of the War of 1812, and in 1917 it was not American idealism but the interference with American trade by German submarines which ultimately brought the United States into the war against Germany, after all the idealist and other more material arguments in favour of American intervention had been used ineffectively for some two and a half years.

3. Following from the assumption that war between Great Britain and the United States is, at all times and in all circumstances, unthinkable neither plans nor preparations for such a war are made by Great Britain (so we were informed authoritatively at the Senior Officers' War Course at Greenwich which I attended last winter). I believe that the assumption upon which this deduction is based is false and that the deduction is dangerous.

4. The situation, as I see it, is as follows:—

(A). War between the United States and the entire British Empire, united in that war, as original parties to a quarrel is so improbable that it may be ruled out of consideration. I believe that if such a war were ever fought the

[10] Director of Military Operations and Intelligence in the War Office.

[11] Not attached to filed copy: cf., however, note 6 above.

[12] Untraced in Foreign Office archives. The conversation under reference was probably that reported by Colonel Pope-Hennessy to Sir E. Howard in the enclosure in No. 209.

British Empire would in all probability overcome the resistance of the United States, though at a price which would make such a conflict undesirable. In any war between the British Empire and the United States, which does not arise directly out of a Canadian issue, I think that for her own safety, Canada would be driven to proclaim her neutrality. Whether either of the belligerents would admit the validity of such a proclamation is questionable and is beside my present point, as the point I am immediately concerned with is the fact that an Anglo-American war, whatever its outcome, would probably entail the disruption of the British Empire through Canadian action and is therefore to be avoided at almost any cost.

(B). Should the British Empire be at war with another Power and the United States a neutral in that quarrel the present policies of Great Britain and the United States in relation to blockade (using that word in its widest sense of applying the pressure of sea-power to an enemy) will lead to the use of the American Fleet to break the British blockade. The American 10,000-ton cruisers are being built for such a purpose, for which they are well adapted. Should war result, it is to be assumed that the British Empire will only be able to employ against its new antagonist, the United States, whatever margin of sea, land and air power may be available after the demands of the original theatre of war have been met. That margin will be greatly inferior to the power available to the United States, so military or naval success, in such circumstances, is not to be expected. We should be confronted with the alternatives of either going into a war with the United States with the probability of defeat or coming to an agreement with that country which would amount to accepting United States dictation.

5. I submit that the probable course of a war between the British Empire (less Canada) and the United States, arising out of another conflict with a Great Power in which an important portion of the naval and military resources of the British Empire are already committed, leaving only the resulting margin of surplus available for the purposes of the American war, should be examined dispassionately now by the competent authorities.

6. I submit further that if the result of such dispassionate examination shows that in such a war the British Empire is likely to be defeated and disrupted it is incumbent upon H.M. Government to take in advance such steps as may be necessary to eliminate the alternatives either of being drawn into a conflict with the United States arising out of our historic policy of blockade or of being compelled to accept the national humiliation of having to abandon that policy in the face of the world under public pressure from the United States.

7. Should the appreciation by competent authority of the naval, military, air and economic problems involved lead to conclusions approximating to those I have indicated above, the political action to be taken will have to be considered. As this will involve examination of the advisability or otherwise of courses of action which are purely political, I would be drawn out of my province in submitting for your consideration any views I have formed on the subject.

8. An examination of the value in modern war of the policy of blockade, however, comes under a different category, since blockade is directed to the attainment of a military end, the overthrow of the enemy, at the risk of political complications with neutrals which may involve war with the most powerful neutral: an eventuality of decisive military import.

9. The advantages of blockade to a successful blockading power are too patent to need enumeration, and have been set forth fully in standard works on war at sea. Its drawbacks, however, have not been so fully presented, and yet are worthy of some consideration. The danger of drawing into the war a neutral so powerful as the United States has already been referred to and is the most obvious drawback to the use of the weapon of blockade. Another is the fact that it takes time, usually a very long time, for the pressure of blockade to produce an effect upon the civil population so powerful as to induce an enemy government to make peace. Even to hamper the munitions output of a modern industrialised nation so materially as to affect the course of operations takes a long time, though perhaps, in most cases, not so long as to attain results by pressure on the enemy population. I write this in full cognisance of the immense importance of the Allied blockade of Germany in the late war, some of the immediate social consequences of which I observed at first hand in that country when serving with the Military Inter-Allied Commission of Control. One consequence of blockade which struck many observers of post-war conditions in Germany is that the more successful a blockade is in the infliction of suffering upon the population the greater is the risk of the consequent spread of bolshevism in the country blockaded. In view of the present unstable social equilibrium of many European countries, and the fundamental British interest in avoiding the extension of Communism in the world, this possible effect of blockade is not to be discounted lightheartedly in drawing up plans for a future war although in the case of former wars there has been no need to consider it.

10. Another possible consequence of trusting to naval blockade as a principal weapon in the armoury of a nation is the effect of such teaching on the conception of war in the navy itself. If a navy is taught that its primary purpose is anything other than the destruction of the enemy fleet in battle; if it learns that a war can be won by avoiding defeat so long as the economic pressure of blockade is maintained upon the enemy people; then the quality of the command may suffer and opportunities of shortening a war by hard fighting may be neglected. This is a consequence of blockade naturally so antipathetic to the naval mind that in discussions on the subject it may well be overlooked unless brought into consideration by soldiers or others.

11. My object in laying so much stress on some of the drawbacks inherent in the policy of blockade is to emphasise what I believe to be a fact, that, useful as blockade has been as a weapon of war in the past, its utility in the future wars is apt to be overrated, with the consequence that grave danger to the nation may be incurred through unwillingness to modify, in accordance with the conditions of the modern world, a policy which is no longer suited to the needs of the British Empire.

12. So far in this memorandum I have been defending a modification of the policy of blockade in order to avoid the possible evil consequences of such a policy. A drastic modification of that policy can be advocated, however, as a direct benefit to the Empire in time of war whether we are a belligerent or a neutral.

13. If we are a belligerent, such a modification of the practice of blockade as would be agreeable to the United States when a neutral would have the effect of relieving the Navy of a heavy defensive task, of assuring our food supplies and of enabling our trade to proceed unhampered. These last two factors, had they been operative during the late war, would have preserved us from a great measure of the post-war economic evils which still afflict Great Britain and the Empire. From the late war emerges the lesson that it is not enough to win a war, it is also important to win it in such a way as to reduce to a minimum the economic disturbance which war inevitably entails and which affects in a peculiarly vital way the post-war recovery of a nation of shopkeepers.

14. If we are a neutral in some future war, such as one between the United States and Mexico or Japan, 'the freedom of the seas' becomes an important British interest: the freer the seas the greater will be our national profit and the faster our recovery from our present unsatisfactory economic position.

15. To sum up. The conclusions I have come to are:—

The American doctrine of 'freedom of the seas' and the British practice of blockade are irreconcilable. It is therefore misleading to speak of war between Great Britain and the United States as 'unthinkable'. If we adhere to our historic policy of blockade, when we are a belligerent and the United States is a neutral, we will be confronted with the choice of one of two evils, either a war with the United States in which, as we cannot develop our full strength, we will be beaten, or the maintenance of peace with the United States at the price of national humiliation. This dilemma can be avoided only by discarding in advance, when we are still at peace, such portions of our blockade policy (and this may mean the whole of it) as may be necessary to conform to the American doctrine of 'freedom of the seas'. The fact that the British blockade of Germany was one of the main factors in obtaining victory for the Allies in the late war is irrelevant if in a future war (and it is the future, not the past, we now have to consider) it is going to lead to our defeat at the hands of America. Blockade is a weapon of war itself unsatisfactory in modern conditions, so we will not lose much if we abandon it. If we are not willing to do this to ensure peace with the United States, it is fatuous not to prepare seriously for the eventuality of war with that Power.[13]

R. POPE-HENNESSY

[13] In minutes on this memorandum in the Foreign Office, general agreement was expressed with Colonel Pope-Hennessy's views.

No. 215

Memorandum by Sir A. Chamberlain
[*A 6073/133/45*]

FOREIGN OFFICE, *October 16, 1927*

Sir W. Tyrrell,

I am much interested by Sir Esme's letters of Sept. 15th & 20th [22nd].[1]

As you know from our first conversation on my return, my mind had been occupied by the same problem & had reached very similar conclusions. I had indeed already spoken to the Prime Minister about it at our meeting at Talloires[2] & he recurred to it on my return home in consequence of a conversation which he had had with Mr. Vansittart.[3]

It may be useful that I should summarise my own line of thought. It was as follows:—

   i. The U.S. entered the recent conference with a plan of naval limitation rather hastily put together, proceeding from no principle (unless 'parity' be dignified with that name) & based on no clear strategic view of America's policy or needs.

   ii. Only late in the discussions did they become aware of their real case viz:—that whilst 'parity', when interpreted to mean equality of numbers or tonnage, might be necessary to satisfy national pride, but had no basis in strategic necessity, our small cruisers were the instruments of our blockade policy & not as we claimed a purely defensive force. It would seem to me that our representatives were so preoccupied about our food supplies that they had really failed to take the offensive tasks of the small cruisers into consideration at all.

   iii. Blockade is therefore at the root of our difference with the U.S. over naval limitation & is the one question which might lead to war between us. Unless they are belligerents, the U.S. will never again submit to such a blockade as we enforced in the Great War.

   iv. After every considerable war, military & naval authorities are prone to think in terms of that war—till another has been fought, teaching new lessons. Now it is extremely unlikely that, if & when we are again engaged in a serious war, the conditions governing the application of blockade will be at all comparable to those of the last great struggle in which all the great land frontiers of our enemies were closed to trade. The present tendency is to exaggerate the potency of the blockade weapon even when the attitude of the United States is left out of account.

   v. But it cannot be thus excluded from consideration, for

     a. The U.S. have the means & the will to create a navy equal to our own. Their one existing difficulty is men. If there is no agreement between us, they will in time get the men by developing at no matter

---

[1] Nos. 205 and 209 respectively.   [2] Cf. No. 11, note 5.
[3] Head of the American and African Department of the Foreign Office.

what cost their mercantile marine. We shall therefore stimulate a double rivalry—naval & mercantile.

b. If we are engaged in a life & death struggle such as the last, it would be suicidal to add the U.S. to our enemies. Whatever we contend are our rights, we cannot in fact afford to exercise them if it involves war with the U.S. when the U.S. possesses a navy equal in combative force to our own & we are at war with a first-class power.

c. But it is not even necessary for the U.S. to declare war to bring us to destruction. They have only to refuse us supplies & credits in order to deal us a fatal blow.

vi. Not all these arguments apply with equal force to minor conflicts, but the blockade weapon is itself of less consequence to us in such lesser wars & we can in such cases more readily abandon our extremer claims.

vii. Whilst hitherto we, whether as neutrals or belligerents have consistently supported the highest doctrine of belligerent rights, the attitude of the U.S. has been inconstant. They have put those rights high when they were belligerents; they have sought to minimise them when they were neutrals. But now that they have with us the equal-largest navy in the world & like us a very small army; now that with the growth of their international interests they are less certain of being always neutrals, their interests approach our own & this approach should render agreement between us more easy. Our great weapon is their great weapon. They must ask themselves the same question as we have put to ourselves & answered:—Sea-power being our great strength & decisive weapon, shall we bear with the sacrifices which its assertion by others entails when we are neutrals, i.e. the majority of cases, in order to keep it effective for the rare occasions upon which it is our only means of salvation, or shall we take the risk of not being able to use it when its use is vital sooner than suffer the inconvenience of its use by others in circumstances in which that use may cause us some loss & annoyance but can do us no vital injury?

Differing here from Sir Esme, I should say that the higher the U.S. will put belligerent rights, the better for us, but their doctrines must be the same in peace & in war.

I am strongly in favour of an endeavour to reach agreement with them & that as early as possible. The first step is to get our own ideas clear in the F.O.; next to approach the Cabinet &/or the C[ommittee of] I[mperial] D[efence]. Only then can we open discussions with the U.S.A. in whatever manner may seem best.

It will be seen that

1st. I reject the first of the alternatives stated by Sir Esme in his letter of the 15th i.e. to pursue a blockade policy regardless of the U.S.A.

2nd. that I approve his second i.e. to endeavour to come to an agreement with them.

3rd. I would reserve consideration of the suggestion for an international conference until we see the result of our pourparlers with the U.S. Incidentally is not Sir Esme making a rather bold assumption when he speaks in this connection of 'the rules of International Law as established before 1914 . . .'?[4] Was there in fact any general agreement as to these rules? Perhaps he is thinking only of the measure of agreement then reached between the U.S. & ourselves. This in any case would be the starting-point for any reconsideration of our position.

Sir Esme should be supplied with a copy of Mr. Malkin's valuable article on the Declaration of Paris.[5]

If you think well you might send a copy of this memo. to Sir Esme by letter. I doubt whether Colonel House can be of any use to us, but what about Mr. Elihu Root?[6] Ask Howard whether he would think it wise if he happened to meet Root to try another 'indiscretion' with him, more particularly to try the effect on him of my No. vii. I should like to know his *personal* reaction to that argument, but I don't want to get into *any* discussion with the U.S. Govt. till I know what line our own Govt. is prepared to take.

A. C.

[4] Punctuation as in original quotation from No. 205.
[5] This article entitled 'The Inner History of the Declaration of Paris' is printed in *The British Year Book of International Law 1927*, pp. 1–44.
[6] Mr. Elihu Root had been Secretary of State in President Roosevelt's administration, 1905–9, and a United States delegate to the Washington Conference for the Limitation of Naval Armament: for the records of this conference see *Conference on the Limitation of Armament, Washington, November 12, 1921–February 6, 1922* (Washington, 1922); see also First Series, Volume XIV.

No. 216

Memorandum by Mr. Vansittart

[A 6057/133/45]

FOREIGN OFFICE, October 19, 1927

In the negotiation of the Blockade Claims Agreement last December both sides reserved their position on Blockade. That was satisfactory in retrospect, but in prospect too good to be true. The very reservation had a slightly ominous ring: Big Business, Big Navy and the Spirit of Magnitude were hardly likely to leave it at that in the archives of a more or less conciliatory State Department. Within a few weeks of the signature of the Claims Agreement they had showed their hand at Geneva.

It was early suspected in this Department that the blockade question was what really underlay the American attitude, and in August a short memorandum was prepared suggesting the possibility of timely agreement with the United States on this point.[1] That memorandum had already been expanded by Mr. Craigie into the fuller examination herewith submitted when Sir E. Howard's letters of September 15 and 22[2] were received. His mind has been

[1] This memorandum of August 24 by Mr. Craigie is not printed.
[2] Nos. 205 and 209 respectively.

moving on lines similar to ours. America has in fact served notice on us that she will never again admit restrictions such as existed between 1914 and 1917 except perforce—or possibly by prearrangement.

Mr. Craigie's memorandum speaks for itself: so does the naval policy of the United States. But there are further reasons why we should make early effort toward an understanding with America, and this I think is the place to deal with them quite frankly.

The United States as we see or foresee, have growing capacity of objection to our past practice: they have also growing inducement. Some half-dozen years ago the foreign trade of the United States was about 8% of her total. The figures are now advancing by leaps and bounds; and there is a steady American goldfall alike on the New and Old World, especially on Germany. 'Now lies the Earth all Danaë to the stars'[3] and Stripes. The fecund and jovial dollar is in for a lasting entanglement, and behind his shining countenance is the desire to see more of himself. A noticeable tendency to commercial imperialism is likely to grow with his successes.

Further, the most efficient element—at least ultimately—in the United States is the German-American: the others have drive but are often off the fairway, and at greater expenditure of self accomplish no more than their corresponding numbers here. The race is of course a biological gamble, a people *im werden* not *im Sein*;[4] but the Anglo-Saxon element is already down to 25% and the German is increasing in the land.

It is obvious then that on at least three clear and separate grounds our difficulties will increase and not diminish with time. And in justice we must not omit a fourth from this computation, the alarming and deplorable growth of anti-American feeling in this country. It is beside the point that it is worse elsewhere in Europe.

When therefore a sincere and thinking Anglophile like General Preston Brown says that war with this country is not only not 'unthinkable' but 'probable',[5] he speaks with understanding. War between the two countries would now be the most criminal in history; but a set of circumstances is not 'unthinkable' in which such a war might be something more than 'probable'. It is time to effect a revaluation of the assertions to which we have grown accustomed and to see things as they will be; the main trouble is now so clear that it should be easy to meet it half way; but we shall always have to lead in dealing with America. We are within measurable distance of an entirely new America (minor signs of the times are the tendency to broaden the Monroe doctrine, and the whole Central America Policy) that is perhaps the weightiest outcome of the war and that disquiets its own thinkers, especially the Anglo-Saxon remnant. So rapid is this development that the United States have surpassed in a decade the odium we took centuries to accumulate. We are and shall remain a heavyweight, but it seems improbable that we shall eventually be able to take on a cruiserweight plus the United States.

[3] See Alfred, Lord Tennyson, *The Princess.*
[4] In process of development not in being.
[5] See the enclosure in No. 209.

There is no reason why we should ever get into that position. We have much in our favour. We do not of course count watery idealism of the 'unthinkable' which might evaporate at the first heat, idealism being really a local term for sentimentality. There are more substantial considerations of which we should take advantage while the going is good. It is pretty good just now. The odds are that the Republicans will win the next election and that the next president will be Mr. Hoover. He will be better than we think, but not so good as Mr. Coolidge. Moreover would Mr. Olds[6] remain at the Head of the State Department if his law-partner Mr. Kellogg loses his place in the next administration? And Mr. Olds is the best man we are ever likely to get there. We should therefore if possible try to come to an understanding with the present régime by next spring, after which everyone will be absorbed in the November election.

This would be preferable to Sir E. Howard's alternative suggestion of an International Conference. The French failure to ratify the relevant Washington agreement[7] shows that they at least have no intention of restricting the cheap arm of the submarine. At an International Conference we should be squeezed and get little for it. Previous agreement with the United States will make it harder for the others to stand out; and the United States themselves will be easier to deal with *à deux*. (Incidentally it may be questioned whether, until they have got over the impending phase, they are not anyhow better without the League than within.)

A concluding note of caution seems necessary. Sir E. Howard apparently contemplates discussing this question fairly freely with people in the United States who, while not holding any official position, are likely to carry weight with the Administration when the time comes to make an official move. I cannot help feeling that this is a rather dangerous course, for the following reasons:

Any advance by the Ambassador, unless very cautiously made, to Mr. House or a Senator on this subject, will suffice to set rumours circulating that His Majesty's Government are about to move in the matter.

This in turn has the disadvantage that the opposition to any agreement with us will have time to organise and mobilise their forces.

Nothing, moreover, could be more calculated to annoy and antagonise the Administration than that rumours of this kind should reach them indirectly.

Once any rumour of our intention appears in the press the difficulties of reaching a basis of agreement will be quadrupled. Once a *basis* of agreement has been reached, there is of course less danger in publicity.

Finally we must count with the possibility that the present United States Government may not want to negotiate an agreement with us on this subject

[6] U.S. Under-Secretary of State.

[7] The reference was to the treaty signed on February 6, 1922, between the United States, the British Empire, France, Italy, and Japan for the protection of the lives of neutrals and non-combatants at sea in time of war, and to prevent the use in war of noxious gases and chemicals: see Cmd. 1627 of 1922, pp. 19–22. This treaty prohibited the use of submarines as commerce-destroyers.

on any terms which we could accept. If there had been previous publicity respecting our intentions—or even private discussion of them with persons of influence—a refusal by the United States to negotiate would assume the dimensions of a rebuff. It would make it more difficult to reopen the question with the future United States Government—another Republican one— and would tend still further to weaken our whole position in this matter.

It may be confidently anticipated that Mr. Elihu Root would share the views expressed in the Secretary of State's memorandum.[8] But to discuss them with him at this stage would, for the above reasons, lay us open to the risks expressed above. Even Mr. Root cannot be relied upon not to talk.

I venture to think that Mr. Olds should be the medium selected. It might perhaps also be best that the initial soundings on our side should be taken by someone less conspicuous than the Ambassador, anyhow till we are well advanced in regard to our own desiderata for which the earliest possible consideration of the Committee of Imperial Defence would seem required.

Mr. Craigie's very full and careful examination might form the basis of that consideration.

R. VANSITTART

ANNEX TO No. 216

Memorandum by Mr. Craigie respecting the possibilities of an Anglo-American Agreement regulating the exercise by either Power of its belligerent right to intercept private property at sea

Secret   FOREIGN OFFICE, *October 17, 1927*

Contents

I. Premises

II. Grounds for thinking United States [Government] may not prove uncompromising

III. Possible necessity for modification of traditional British attitude

IV. Practices emerging from the war

V. Analysis of (1) probable future British practice; (2) United States objections to British practice during the war; (3) possibilities of agreement with the United States

VI. General conclusions from above analysis

VII. Objections likely to be urged against proposed agreement

VIII. Action suggested

N.B. The purpose of this memorandum is to show that, on the basis of our *existing* practice, agreement with the United States Government, though difficult, would not be impossible. If the Committee of Imperial Defence enquiry which is suggested should demonstrate the desirability in our own interests of some relaxation of the existing rules, agreement with the United States Government would be *pro tanto* facilitated.

[8] No. 215.

397

I. Premises

In approaching this problem it is perhaps permissible to take the following premises for granted:—

(1) It will not be possible for this country as a belligerent to enforce against the United States as a neutral any strong measures in furtherance of a blockade or the seizure of contraband without first arriving at an understanding with the United States Government unless those measures fall incontestably within the recognised rights of a belligerent.

(2) Any such understanding would be more easily reached in a period of peace, when the United States must necessarily consider its position as a potential belligerent, than in a period of war during which the United States, if a neutral, is inclined to view the matter exclusively from the standpoint of a defender of neutral rights.

(3) On the outbreak of a war in which we but not the United States are involved the first acts of detention and capture affecting American vessels and cargoes would, in the absence of any previous understanding, create an atmosphere of resentment and hostility in the United States ill-suited to the conclusion of any satisfactory agreement with this country.

(4) The existence of an Anglo-American agreement on this subject would have an arresting influence on the further development of the American navy, for the wind would to some extent be taken out of the sails of the 'big navalists' in the United States.

II. Grounds for thinking United States Government may not prove uncompromising

As evidence that the United States may be disposed in the future to take a less doctrinnaire [sic] view of the whole question than that exhibited during the war in the Lansing notes,[9] I would mention (a) the final decision of President Wilson not to raise the 'freedom of the seas' issue at the Peace Conference[10] although he was influenced also by the idea that the League would cause neutrality to disappear and (b) the conclusion of the recent Anglo-American War Claims Agreement which removed one of the best

[9] American notes protesting against British measures to prevent commodities of any kind from reaching or leaving Germany are printed in *Papers relating to the Foreign Relations of the United States 1915: Supplement* and *op. cit., 1916: Supplement, passim*; see in particular *op. cit., 1915: Supplement*, pp. 152–6 and 578–601 respectively, for the notes dated March 30 and October 21, 1915, drafted by Mr. Robert Lansing, Counsellor in the U.S. State Department 1914–June 1915 and Secretary of State June 1915–1920 protesting against the British Order-in-Council of March 11, 1915 (printed in *British and Foreign State Papers*, vol. 109, pp. 217–19).

[10] The second point in the peace programme (the Fourteen Points) put forward on January 8, 1918, by President Wilson (printed in *British and Foreign State Papers*, vol. 111, pp. 950–5) had referred to the Freedom of the Seas. It would appear that in the light of a disagreement which arose in October 1918 between the United States and the Allies over the implementation of this point, this question was not discussed at the Peace Conference of 1919: see D. Lloyd George, *The Truth about the Peace Treaties* (London, 1938), vol. i, pp. 74–86, and Lord Hankey, *The Supreme Command 1914–1918* (London, 1961), vol. ii, pp. 853–63. See also *Papers relating to the Foreign Relations of the United States 1918: Supplement I. The World War*, vol. i, *passim*.

means open to the United States of keeping the issue alive for future use against this country.

While it is probable that the American attitude at the recent Geneva Conference was consciously or unconsciously determined—anyhow in its middle and later stages—by the possibility of friction with this country over some future 'blockade' issue, and the determination to have a more decisive say next time, it does not necessarily follow that the United States Government would prove intractable in any negotiations designed to remove this possible cause of future trouble.

In illustration of the tendency of American naval opinion to depart from the strictly orthodox United States attitude on these questions, the following opinion expressed by Rear-Admiral W. L. Rodgers, U.S.N., in the American Journal of International Law is of interest: 'The United States should reconsider its old stand for a rule favouring neutral commerce and lean rather towards one favouring the allied practices in the late war . . .'[11]

A further point to be remembered is that the American blockade notes were despatched in the heat of a contest during which the State Department was indulging in a species of legalistic orgy. Many of the points made are never likely to be heard of again. Indeed the majority of their representations were directed against alleged abuses under our 'blockade' measures rather than against the measures themselves.

III. *Possible necessity for modification of traditional British attitude*

Turning to our own interests in this matter, it is undeniable that the whole situation in regard to the exercise of our belligerent rights at sea has been profoundly modified by the claim and probable determination of the United States to reach an equality of sea power with the Empire. This claim has been admitted in so far as battleships and battle-cruisers are concerned. It has been virtually admitted also for cruisers and auxiliary craft, for there is apparently no intention to engage upon a race with the United States in the construction of subsidiary naval armaments. Even if (as is probable) the United States Government do not immediately build up to our cruiser strength, they will endeavour gradually to approach it and probably to surpass it in the heavier type of cruiser. To maintain the traditional position of British naval dominance or to think from such a premise in the future, is, in already existing circumstances, no longer possible.

Whenever this problem of the exercise of our belligerent rights at sea has been under review by any British Government it may safely be assumed the discussions have always proceeded upon the basis that this country will be able to establish at once and to maintain an unquestioned command of the sea, untrammelled by any serious menace from neutrals. If for this reason alone, it seems worth examining whether the traditional British attitude on the question of interference with belligerent and neutral commerce does not, or must not, need some revision. Moreover the development of the submarine menace and other important changes in the methods of

[11] Punctuation as in original quotation.

conducting naval warfare render it doubtful whether a 'blockade' in the proper sense of the word can ever be made effective in future wars. The balance between a legal right to enforce a stringent blockade and a legal right to guarantee our food supplies in time of war lends itself anyhow to varying appreciations, and the relative advantages seem to call for constant revision to keep pace with the changing conditions of naval warfare and of the economic situation of this country.

The C[ommittee of] I[mperial] D[efence] 'Advisory Committee on Trading and Blockade in time of War' has not yet examined the above questions from the more purely naval point of view, and, before we can get much further in the matter, it is important that such an investigation should be made. What we really want to get at is a clear and exhaustive statement as to the measures which the Admiralty are able and would want (within the limits of international law and altered circumstances) to enforce in any future war in order to exert 'sea pressure'. For the purpose of such an enquiry it would be necessary to examine the differing situations arising in any war in which this country might conceivably be engaged. Broadly speaking such possible future wars are divisible into four main categories: (a) a duel between ourselves and one other nation without the intervention of the League; (b) a war in which several nations are engaged without the intervention of the League; (c) a League war in which we are engaged as one of the coercing Powers; (d) a League war in which we are the Covenant-breaking Power. It is clear that in case (a) the exercise of our right to stop goods from passing to our enemy through a host of neutral States would be relatively more difficult than in cases (b) and (c), and an indication as to how the Admiralty would propose to exert sea pressure in case (a) is especially important. It would also be necessary to know whether, in all these situations, the Admiralty consider that we could or should exercise to the full the rights at present recognised by international law or whether it might now be to our advantage to endeavour, by international agreement, to restrict the full exercise of those rights by others.

IV. *Practices emerging from the war*

In the absence of further data on these points it is only possible in this paper to estimate the chances of an agreement with the United States Government on the basis of the practices which emerged from the enforcement of the 'blockade' during the late war. These practices probably represent the maximum which a Prize Court could be expected to uphold, so that the result of the proposed investigation could scarcely be in favour of increasing (though it might be in favour of decreasing) their severity. Regarded, therefore, as a maximum, they form an interesting basis of comparison with American precept and practice. If an agreement with the United States appears not impossible with our claims placed at the highest level, its conclusion would be *pro tanto* simplified by any recession from these maximum demands. It is proposed briefly to outline each of the principal measures which His Majesty's Government would probably take for the interception of private property at sea; to summarise under each heading the objections raised by the United States Government during the war; and to estimate the chances of future agreement with the United States Government with or without modification of our existing attitude.

V. *Analysis (1) Probable future British practice; (2) United States objections to British practice during the war; (3) Possibilities of agreement with the United States*

Contraband

1. *Visit, Search, Detention and Capture*

(a) *British practice*

The generally accepted precepts of international law (in particular the provisions of the Declaration of Paris, 1856 and the principles underlying the Washington Convention of 1923 [1922] respecting the Protection of the Lives of Neutrals and Non-Combatants at sea) to apply so long as they are observed by other belligerents. (For the position in the event of a flagrant breach of these provisions see under 'Reprisals' below.) An enemy vessel to be captured. A neutral vessel to be diverted to a convenient port for an investigation into the nature and destination of her cargo. The period of detention to last until it has been decided whether proceedings should be instituted against her or her cargo. Vessels carrying cargo covered by 'navicert' permit (see under 'Navicert' below) to receive special facilities. Period of detention for all innocent vessels and cargoes to be the shortest possible.

(b) *United States objections during the war*

The United States Government during the early stages of the war insisted on search at sea instead of at a British port, maintaining that the policy of diversion without examination at sea and merely on suspicion of the existence of contraband was contrary to international law. The United States Government further considered that the detention of innocent vessels and cargoes was in many cases unreasonably long.

(c) *Possibilities of agreement*

As regards diversion, His Majesty's Government urged during the war with much force that under modern conditions the right of search could only be exercised in port, especially in view of the elaborate arrangements in force for concealing the identity of cargoes. Moreover the growth of the size of steamships necessitated their being taken into calm water to be searched. A similar course was pursued in the American Civil War and the necessity of giving the belligerent captor full liberty to establish enemy destination by all the evidence at his disposal was recognised by the American Prize Courts during that war.

To the above arguments may be added the ever increasing danger of submarine attack on a vessel conducting or undergoing search on the high seas; also the fact that the legality of deviation was recognised in various Prize Court decisions during the war.

Unless the policy of the United States Government is to do away altogether with the right to search neutral vessels, there should be no serious difficulty in reaching an agreement with them on this point.

2. *Seizure—doctrine of continuous voyage*

(a) *British practice*

If contraband is found on board, either the vessel herself or the offending cargo may be placed in the Prize Court. The doctrine of continuous voyage or ultimate destination to be applied to 'contraband'. Shipment of contraband goods 'to order' to be regarded as corroborative evidence that the cargo is really destined for the enemy.

(b) *United States objections*

The United States, having applied the doctrine of continuous voyage in their own Prize Courts, do not appear to have protested during the war against the principle underlying the doctrine but rather against the character and sufficiency of the evidence adduced to prove the ultimate destination of contraband goods.

(c) *Possibilities of agreement*

The United States Government are likely to agree, or would find it difficult to disagree, that (except possibly in the case of an island) a refusal to apply the doctrine of continuous voyage would, in modern conditions, divest a belligerent of all power to intercept contraband of war.

3. *Lists of Contraband*

(a) *Existing British practice*

The distinction between absolute and conditional contraband, though difficult to define in practice, to be retained. The 1917 list (with certain additions proposed by the Advisory Committee on Trading and Blockade) to be adopted as the foundation for any future list. It will require modification in detail according to the country against which a war is being waged.

(b) *United States objections*

There were occasional representations against the rapid extension of the contraband list during the war and in particular every effort was made to prevent the inclusion of cotton in the list.

(c) *Possibilities of agreement*

The United States themselves had a long list of contraband during the civil war. To quote Mr. Bryan, speaking as Secretary of State in 1915:—

'The record of the United States in the past is not free from criticism. When neutral, this Government has stood for a restricted list of absolute and conditional contraband. As a belligerent, we have contended for a liberal list, according to our conception of the necessities of the case.'

It is probable therefore that in peace time and when contemplating their position as a potential belligerent the United States would agree to a much longer 'basic' list of contraband than they appeared to think reasonable during the late war. A further element tending automatically to increase the size of the absolute contraband list is the modern practice of Governments taking over in war time the complete control of certain commodities, thus disposing of any possibility of distinguishing between absolute and conditional contraband in respect of those commodities. The United States would probably agree that commodities so controlled must automatically be declared absolute contraband.

It may not be impossible to agree with the United States Government on a reasonably adequate and flexible list of contraband to form the foundation of any list to be issued on the declaration of a war and to be subject to mutual revision from time to time.

4. *Blockade*

(a) *British practice*

According to the Declaration of Paris 'blockades, in order to be binding, must be effective, that is to say maintained by a force sufficient really to prevent access to the coast of the enemy'.

Continental jurists have maintained that access to the coast must be barred by a chain of warships anchored so near to one another than [*sic*] the line could not be passed without obvious danger. Such a blockade is clearly impossible in these days of submarine-infested seas. The Anglo-American practice has been that, if the blockade is maintained by a force sufficient *to render ingress or egress hazardous, and the capture of blockade-runners most probable*, the number or station of the ships is immaterial. But even a blockade on these lines will be increasingly difficult to maintain as time goes on, and it seems not unlikely that a blockade of the future will be a long-distance affair and be applicable to the blockaded country as a whole. The doctrine of continuous voyage would be applied to the commerce of neutral countries bordering the blockaded State, the effect of the whole operation being similar to that achieved under our 'Reprisals' measures of 1915. Whether any Prize Court would uphold such measures if taken in enforcing a formally declared blockade is another matter. Whether moreover such an extension of 'blockade' would not be detrimental to the interests of an island Power no longer safely predominant at sea is a question which the Admiralty will no doubt be prepared to face. But for the purposes of this memorandum it will be assumed that in a future war we might wish to impose something in the nature of a 'long distance' blockade.

(b) *United States objections*

As no formal blockade of the German coast was declared during the last war, the American protests under this head are not strictly relevant. The measures taken under the Reprisals Order-in-Council of March 11th, 1915, were justified by the British Prize Court on the ground of retaliation, not of blockade. Nevertheless the probable attitude of the United States to any future 'long-distance' blockade may to some extent be discerned from the nature of their protests during the war, which are summarised in the Library memorandum of November 2nd, 1925,[12] as follows:—

1. The blockade was ineffective.
2. It did not apply impartially to the ships of all nations.
3. It included *neutral* ports.
4. The measures were retaliatory and therefore illegal.

(c) Possibilities of agreement

If the measures taken in virtue of the Order-in-Council of March 1915 had been the result of a formal declaration of blockade, then *objection 1* above (that the blockade was ineffective) might conceivably have had some force. It should not however be impossible to agree with the United States Government, after a dispassionate examination of all the circumstances, what are the measures of interception which may be expected to satisfy a Prize Court that a blockade is 'effective', regard being had to the present changed conditions of naval warfare. We should, however, have to be careful to do nothing in this respect which might give a third Power a reasonable pretext for declaring our measures to be a breach of the relevant provision of the Declaration of Paris, thus justifying the jettisoning of that Declaration by a potential enemy. *Objection 2* (that the blockade did not apply impartially to the ships of all nations) was based on the fact that we did not touch trade across the Baltic. In any future long-distance blockade it will be difficult to ensure that there is not some arm of the sea unpatrolled, but agreement on this will depend on what is and what is not to be regarded as an effective blockade in future. *Objection 3* (that the blockade included neutral ports) falls to the ground if it is admitted that the doctrine of continuous voyage is to be applicable to a blockade—and the United States cannot consistently resist the applicability of this doctrine to blockade in view of their own practice during the Civil War. Moreover in modern times it is difficult to imagine any blockade which could produce useful results without the application of the doctrine. *Objection 4* (that the measures taken were retaliatory) is examined under the heading 'Reprisals' below.

5. Jurisdiction of Prize Courts

(a) British practice

All breaches of the law of contraband and blockade to be brought before the Prize Court, which will try the case in accordance with the accepted canons of international law, uninfluenced by any domestic enactments which may be held to be contrary to these canons.

(b) United States objections

(1) The United States Government claimed at one time that, as the British Prize Courts were fettered by municipal enactments binding upon

[12] This memorandum (not printed) by Mr. Orchard, a senior member of the Foreign Office Library, was entitled 'Memorandum on the Attitude of the United States Government towards British War Measures'.

them, they were not competent to deal with the complaints of neutral individuals who questioned the validity of those enactments under international law.

(2) The United States Government contended that, when a ship had been illegally brought within the jurisdiction of a belligerent power, it could not be compelled to submit to the domestic laws and regulations of that nation.

(c) Possibilities of agreement

Objection 1 above is simply a misstatement of fact, since the British Prize Courts administer international and not domestic law. They have always asserted their freedom from executive control and their complete independence as a judicial body. Moreover the whole purpose of the proposed agreement would be to decide what *is* the accepted international practice on these points and to bring it into harmony with modern conditions.

Objection 2 is also unlikely to be raised in view of the purpose of the proposed agreement as stated above. Moreover such a principle, if urged now by the United States, might have an embarrassing repercussion on American efforts to suppress liquor-smuggling from the sea. Many arrests which might be characterised by foreign Powers as 'illegal' have nevertheless led to the ship and crew being compelled to submit to the domestic laws and regulations of the United States.

This question of the jurisdiction of the Prize Courts is unlikely to present much difficulty in practice (except possibly in respect of postal correspondence).

6. Seizure and Censorship of Mails

(a) British practice

Under the XIth Hague Convention (1907)[13] the postal correspondence of neutrals or belligerents found on the high seas, whether on board a neutral or an enemy ship, was declared to be inviolable, except when proceeding to or from a blockaded port.

The United States Government agreed during the war that the Convention applied only to correspondence and not to parcel post, securities or negotiable instruments. Moreover it cannot be held to apply to ships voluntarily entering a belligerent port. During the war the mails were removed from all neutral ships touching at or compulsorily diverted to British ports and censored in this country. Intelligence invaluable to the Prize Court and to the naval, military and political authorities was thus obtained, while contraband articles were found in large quantities in postal packets. The Hague Convention was held not to be applicable because all the belligerents were not a party to it and because its stipulations were in any case flagrantly violated every time any German submarine sank a belligerent or neutral ship.

[13] This international convention relative to certain restrictions on the exercise of the right of capture in maritime war, signed on October 18, 1907, is printed with *procès-verbal* in *British and Foreign State Papers*, vol. 100, pp. 422–34.

Our practice in a future war would presumably be the same as in the late war unless all the belligerents are a party to and duly respect the relevant provisions of the XIth Hague Convention. In any event there are cogent arguments in favour of the view that the censorship of mails should be regarded as part of the exercise of the right of visit and search of a vessel in time of war. If this view prevails, possibly Hague Convention No. XI may have to be denounced. All seditious matter to be submitted to prize court proceedings.

(b) United States objections

During the war the United States did not admit that there was any right in international law to censor neutral postal correspondence whether the mail bags had been removed from neutral vessels compulsorily diverted to British waters or from those voluntarily touching at a British port. They further contended that correspondence, including shipping documents, money order lists, etc., even though relating to enemy supplies or exports, were, unless carried in the same ship as the relevant property, entitled to unmolested passage.

(c) Possibilities of agreement

It is doubtful whether we should ever secure any agreement with the United States which does not recognise the full application of the XIth Hague Convention so far as concerns the inviolability of postal correspondence. In the light of our war experience and the invaluable aid received from the censorship of neutral mail it is unfortunate, perhaps, that we should ever have signed that Convention. But the Convention is there and, unless it is denounced, we shall in any future war presumably abide by its provisions so long as these are observed by the enemy (even though not technically party to the Convention). If the Convention is to be retained and observed, there should not be much difficulty in reaching an agreement with the United States Government in this matter. If not, I should not despair of the possibility of our being able to persuade the United States Government of the importance for both countries of keeping their hands free to search the mails wherever found for seditious matter—a course which would probably be upheld by the Prize Court if the Convention were to be denounced.

As regards the removal and censorship of other types of mail from vessels forcibly diverted to a belligerent port, we are not likely to have any serious difficulty with the United States provided that they can be brought to recognise the necessity in modern times of diversion for purposes of search. Neither, as shown in Section 5 above, shall we necessarily have difficulty over the question of 'jurisdiction' which figured so prominently in the war controversies over the mail question.

It may here be remarked that, after the United States entered the war, she imposed a most stringent censorship on all types of correspondence found on neutral vessels voluntarily calling at United States ports. We have, however, no record of the American censorship having examined mails taken from a ship either boarded on the high seas or compulsorily diverted because the United States were not co-operating in the interception or diversion of neutral traffic.

7. 'Rationing' of a neutral bordering upon a belligerent State

(a) British practice

This system, for which there is no precedent in international law, was applied most efficaciously as a result of the conclusion of a series of agreements with Associations of Importers such as the N.O.T. in Holland and the S.S.S. in Switzerland. The seizure of a commodity on the ground that an altogether excessive quantity had already been imported by the particular neutral country of destination which happens to border upon an enemy State was upheld during the war by the British Prize Court to the extent of dismissing a claim for damages. While I understand that we cannot rely on this decision in justifying stoppage merely on the ground of excess, it may be assumed that we shall use such means as are at our disposal to introduce a similar system of 'rationing', where applicable, in any future war.

(b) United States objections

The United States Government protested during the war against interference with goods intended to become incorporated in the 'common stock' of a neutral country. However they appear to have raised no serious objection on this score once the 'Navicert' scheme (see below) and the Agreements with Importing Associations in European countries were in operation. After their entry into the war, the United States co-operated cordially in the application of the 'rationing' machinery, though they were careful not to approve the actual seizure of a neutral cargo in order to render the policy effective.

(c) Possibilities of agreement

Possibly the U.S. Govt. may now take the line that 'rationing' is permissible and reasonable provided it is done by agreement with the neutral States concerned (including the exporting State). But this does not get over the difficulty that there must be a preliminary period of 'rationing pressure' in order to induce importing neutrals to make the necessary rationing agreements. Perhaps, by means of some device similar to the Navicert scheme the United States may be induced to assume a benevolent attitude, but this is undoubtedly one of the points on which it will be difficult to find any basis of agreement with the Americans.

8. Navicert scheme

In March 1916 it was arranged, with the tacit assent of the United States Government, that 'letters of assurance' should be issued by His Majesty's Embassy at Washington to applicant firms in the United States in respect of goods the passage of which through the naval patrols His Majesty's Government were prepared to facilitate. The system, of which very free use was made, was worked by telegraphic consultation between the Embassy and

London, although the Embassy had authority to grant letters without consultation in cases where similar exports from the United Kingdom would not require licences. Details of the scheme are given in the annexed print.[14]

The scheme soon became so popular with shipping companies that many refused to carry any goods not covered by a 'navicert' letter and vessels carrying only cargo thus guaranteed were relieved from practically all disabilities resulting from the 'blockade'. The friction with the United States was greatly reduced through the introduction of this system.

In any agreement with the United States it should be possible to arrange for the setting up, immediately on the outbreak of war, of some such organisation in the country remaining neutral. The arrangements would of course be relatively easy and expeditious so long as no formal blockade is declared and it is merely a question of dealing with a restricted list of contraband. No conceivable breach of sovereignty is involved, since the employment of the facilities offered would be entirely optional for the exporting firm. But even in the early days of a war most reputable firms either in this country or in the United States would probably be glad to make use of the facilities thus made available with the consent of their own government. The absence of knowledge in the early stages of a war in regard to enemy agents, etc. in neutral countries need not prevent the immediate inception of the scheme: its effectiveness for purposes of stopping contraband, small in the initial stages, would increase as experience of enemy methods was obtained. If such an arrangement were to come automatically into operation on the outbreak of a war in which either Great Britain or the United States were involved, the maintenance of smooth relations between the two countries would be enormously facilitated.

9. *Black List, Statutory List, Bunker coal, Insurance, Banking Facilities*

After United States action as a belligerent in the war, no difficulty is anticipated in coming to a reasonable understanding with the United States on the above points.

10. *Reprisals*

The United States held that the measures taken under the Order-in-Council of March 1915 were retaliatory and therefore illegal. On the other hand the British Prize Courts upheld the validity of measures which had been taken as a reprisal for a previous breach of international law.

It is clearly in the general interest that retaliatory measures not specifically sanctioned by international law should not be undertaken either lightly or on the first pretext. It is equally clear that, in the event of a consistent violation of the recognised precepts of international law by one belligerent, the other must, in self-defence and to avoid extermination, adopt either the same or some other measure of reprisal. Moreover some sanction must clearly

[14] Not printed. This document, dated 'Foreign Office, April 7, 1916', was entitled *'Arrangement for the Issue of Letters of Assurance in the Case of Particular Consignments for Scandinavian Destinations'*.

be applied to a State avowedly and consistently violating international law. In the absence of combined action by the neutral Powers, the only possible sanction is retaliation by the opponent. Action by the League of Nations could not be invoked in an agreement with the United States.

A clause providing for 'reprisals', particularly for any breach of the Declaration of Paris or of the principles underlying the unratified Washington Convention respecting submarine warfare, would clearly be an essential part of any agreement with the United States such as is proposed in this memorandum. Its acceptance by the United States Government, within specified and reasonable limitations, is not beyond the bounds of possibility. It would of course be provided that any such measures of reprisal would only be taken with the utmost regard for the commerce of the country remaining neutral and free discussion to this end would be invited.

11. *Article 16 of the Covenant of the League of Nations*

Under this article Member States undertake, *inter alia*, to subject a Covenant-breaking State to the 'prevention of all financial, commercial or personal intercourse between the nationals of the Covenant-breaking State and the nationals of any other State, whether a Member of the League or not'.

This article was drafted at a time when it was thought that, the League being practically all embracing, there would be no neutrals worth considering. As things stand, however, we have to deal with a very powerful neutral and it would be a gross breach of international law to interfere on the high seas with that neutral's commerce without a previous declaration of war on the Covenant-breaking State. If the proposed agreement with the United States dealt with measures to be taken *after a declaration of war* and if war were to be declared by us on a Covenant-breaking State, the provisions of the agreement would, so far as we are concerned, automatically apply to action taken under Article 16. A 'blockade' of the Covenant-breaking State would be declared and full effect would thus be given to the provisions of Article 16. If, however, war were *not* declared by the coercing Powers, our agreement with the United States would not apply and we should be in the same situation as if it did not exist. In either event the conclusion of such an agreement could hardly be held to conflict with our obligations under Article 16.

On the contrary if, in pursuance of Article 16, this country were to declare a blockade against the coast of a Covenant-breaking State or to take other steps to stop its trade on the high seas, it would be of the utmost value that we should at that time have an agreement with the United States defining limits within which such action could be taken without bringing in the United States on the side of the Covenant-breaker.

VI. *General conclusions from above analysis*

The above examination of our probable future procedure, based largely on the practices emerging from the war, does not purport to be exhaustive, but it is I think sufficient to demonstrate that the probable divergences of view between ourselves and the United States are not necessarily insurmountable, even if the British practice be estimated on the basis of the maximum of severity permissible under international law. Any relaxation of our traditional attitude, due to changing conditions, would of course make agreement with the United States correspondingly simpler.

Everything would really depend on whether the United States Government would be prepared to talk at all on this subject. Although there is nothing to prove it at present, they *may* be found to be definitely wedded to their conception of 'freedom of the seas', i.e., abolition of all blockade or contraband measures in time of war. Again they may consider the whole question too 'entangling',[15] though it is hardly more so than the disarmament discussions on which they enter freely. A further possible, though on the whole unlikely, attitude is that the United States Government would prefer to keep this question open because they know that, in any future war in which we are a belligerent, the United States as a neutral would have the 'whiphand' so far as the exertion of naval pressure is concerned.

But, provided that the United States Government are prepared to discuss the subject at all, they may well be found to be amenable to a proposed arrangement which could be pointed to as mitigating the effects of the Geneva failure and as even in the long run facilitating the conclusion of an agreement for the limitation of cruiser construction. For this reason and because we should have to wait a good two years before we could begin discussions with the government which will come into power in March 1929, it would, if possible, be preferable not to defer any discussions on this subject until after the American elections (as had been suggested in my earlier memorandum).[1] The most favourable time for sounding the Americans would be some time between now and the spring. After that the electoral campaign will begin in earnest. The party 'conventions' will be held in the summer and thereafter negotiations with the United States Government on any subject will be difficult.

Should it be decided that such a discussion with the United States Government is feasible and desirable from our point of view, it would have to be undertaken in the first instance with the utmost caution. With the example of the Geneva Conference before us, it seems desirable that the preliminary soundings should be of an entirely informal and unofficial character, responsibility for which could if necessary be repudiated should the soil be found to be unsuitable or the season unpropitious. In this way we should not have prejudiced our position in any way if the present United States Government are found to be unfavourably disposed: we should not have shown our hand and nothing would have occurred to prevent the repetition of the experiment at some later date. In this connection it is important that any preliminary enquiry here as to the desirability and possibility of an agreement on these questions should be regarded as secret.

[15] A reference to Thomas Jefferson's first inaugural address as President of the United States on March 4, 1801, when he advocated 'Peace, commerce and honest friendship with all nations—entangling alliances with none'.

VII. *Objections likely to be urged against proposed agreement*

I foresee two objections which may well be urged against this scheme even if it were held to be otherwise feasible.

The first is the objection of the naval authorities, and in a lesser degree of the legal authorities, to any further attempt at the codification of the law and procedure of prize. The report of the International Law Committee, dated December 1918, on the historical and legal side of the question of the 'Freedom of the Seas'[16] recommends that, as the strongest naval Power, this country should resolutely oppose any further attempt at codification as being both futile and prejudicial to our interests as a potential belligerent.

The arguments in favour of keeping our hands free are of course very weighty: but they require revision if only because during the nine years which have elapsed since that report was written the situation has been profoundly modified by the admission to a virtual equality of naval strength of the power which in the past has shown the greatest energy and determination in the defence of neutral rights. Moreover to leave these problems of prize law in a fluid and indeterminate state is like leaving dynamite lying about loose in a ship which may at any moment encounter a terrific storm. So far as Anglo-American relations are concerned, it is tantamount to keeping in being the one question which might conceivably lead to an eventual explosion. By insisting on keeping our hands free now the Admiralty would run the risk of seeing our activities unnecessarily circumscribed later by a United States determined to 'go the limit' in protecting neutral rights.

The other objection likely to be encountered is that this is a matter which properly comes within the sphere of the League of Nations and should not form the subject of separate negotiation between the two principal naval Powers. But to achieve an agreement on this subject with the League Powers would be a Herculean task of many years' duration which might leave this country shackled as no Anglo-American agreement need leave it. Moreover at the end it would not necessarily bring us nearer to an agreement with the United States.

There are three other very cogent reasons for *beginning* with the United States: (1) She is the Power which, as a neutral, could most seriously threaten to interfere with our naval measures as a belligerent; (2) She is one of the few Powers which need be considered in time of war solely as an *exporter* of neutral goods, for she is only co-terminous with Canada and Mexico, and we would in any case never undertake a blockade of Mexico without previous agreement with the United States. Most other countries are potential *importers* of neutral goods, that is, they adjoin other States with which we might conceivably have to go to war. A definition of the limits, within which naval economic pressure may be applied must if negotiated with a group of potentially *importing* neutral States, be a far more difficult task than one negotiated with a potentially *exporting* neutral State; (3) France has steadily refused to sign the Washington treaty abolishing the use of the submarine for blockade

[16] Not printed.

purposes. She must therefore be assumed to favour this form of warfare. No agreement on this subject appears to me possible which does not proceed on the assumption that the terms of that treaty are to be observed and which does not reserve the right to take reprisals in the event of their non-observance by any belligerent. No such reservation seems possible in any agreement which might be negotiated within the League of Nations so long as France maintains her present attitude.

Once an agreement had been reached with the United States, the task of negotiating with other countries, if still held to be desirable, would be immensely facilitated.

VIII. *Action suggested*

To sum up, *the following action is suggested*:—

(*a*) The Committee of Imperial Defence should conduct an enquiry into this question at the earliest possible moment, particularly as regards the points mentioned under Section headed 'Possible necessity for modification of traditional British practice'. If we are to approach the present United States Government, this should be done within the next two or three months, i.e., before the electoral campaign is in full swing.

(*b*) As soon as agreement is reached as to what we *can* and what we probably will *want* to do in any future war, an early opportunity might be taken to sound the United States Government, discreetly and informally, as to whether they are prepared to discuss these questions; if their disposition is found to be favourable it could then be ascertained whether their views are within a measurable distance of ours.

(*c*) Should the preliminary soundings produce favourable results, the question of opening formal negotiations might be considered after consultation with the Dominions.

R. L. CRAIGIE

No. 217

Letter from Sir E. Howard (Washington) to Sir W. Tyrrell
[*W 10845/61/98*]

Private & confidential   WASHINGTON, *October 25, 1927*

My dear Tyrrell,

I had a curious conversation with Kellogg yesterday. Some days ago I had a letter from Philip Kerr[1] at Chicago (or Big Billville,[2] as it is to be called in future) to say he had met a man called Winston—not Garrett [*sic* ? Garrard] Winston[3]—who said he had recently seen Kellogg. He declared the S. of S.

---

[1] Mr. Kerr, who had been Private Secretary to Mr. Lloyd George as Prime Minister, 1916–21, was Secretary of the Rhodes Trust.

[2] The reference was to the Mayor of Chicago, Mr. William Hale Thompson, who in his youth as a prominent athlete had been known as 'Big Bill'.

[3] Mr. Garrard B. Winston had formerly been Under-Secretary to the U.S. Treasury.

was still much annoyed and irritated over the Geneva Conference & had said that he meant to make a speech shortly showing up the alleged need of the British for all the cruisers they declared they required.

I therefore tackled Kellogg about this & said I had heard to my surprise and sorrow that he intended to reopen the Geneva controversy by attacking our declared need for cruisers. I said I could not believe he really meant to do this as everything had quieted down so satisfactorily without any recrimination or bad blood & that it would be really a misfortune if the whole controversy were to be restarted as it might get out of hand. The situation was still a delicate one, I said, and any move of this sort on his side could not but provoke reactions in G.B. It was as well to let the whole matter rest as much as possible so that we should all be in a better mood to discuss the Washington Treaty[4] when it came up again for discussion in 1931.

He told me he had no intention whatever of making a speech about it but that my informant no doubt referred to the possibility of his (Mr. Kellogg) being summoned to give evidence about the proceedings of the Geneva Conference before the Senate Committee on Naval Affairs. In that case he would have to prepare a statement and would have of course to say what he thought about H.M.G.'s demand for cruisers. I said I thought it would be most unfortunate if now either of us, American or British, were to begin anew doubting or criticising what the others considered necessary for their own security. In my opinion the last Geneva Conference—all things considered— had ended remarkably well—both parties had now stated that they were not going to build against each other—(I referred to the Peace Bridge speeches[5] & to recent speeches in England) both were free to build as much or as little as they thought they required for security and economy & there was plenty of time till 1931 to think the matter out & see if there wasn't some better formula than the three incompatibles, security; economy; parity.

The S. of S. then said that he had noticed that Mr. Baldwin speaking recently had said that H.M.G. intended to carry out the already accepted building programme and nothing more.[6] This he believed amounted built & building to a total, for cruisers, of 378,000 tons. Had the British negotiators given that figure for their requirements matters could easily have been arranged. Why had they insisted on no less than 425,000?

I said I did not know what the total tonnage of the building programme was but I proposed to note the figures he had mentioned as they were interesting. He at once protested, as usual, against my noting anything. He was not saying this to reopen any discussion etc. I nevertheless took the note

[4] The treaty for the limitation of naval armament between the United States, the British Empire, France, Italy and Japan, signed at Washington on February 6, 1922, is printed in Cmd. 1627 of 1922, pp. 3–19.

[5] For the speeches by H.R.H. the Prince of Wales, Mr. Baldwin and General C. Dawes, Vice-President of the United States, at the dedication of the Peace Bridge over the Niagara River between Fort Erie in Canada and Buffalo in the United States on August 7, see *The Times*, August 8, 1927, p. 10, and August 9, p. 10.

[6] *V. op. cit.*, October 8, 1927, p. 12, for a speech by Mr. Baldwin on October 7 at a dinner given by H.M. Government in honour of visiting American Legionaries.

and should be glad to know as a matter of curiosity whether this figure of 378,000 is correct & if so how it is arrived at.[7]

Mr. Kellogg, as happens not infrequently at times, was rather snappy and irritated during part of this conversation. But at the end he said 'Well, we at any rate shall not quarrel over this question'. I said I didn't think we would but that what concerned me more was whether our peoples would quarrel. If all the old accusations etc. were going to be trotted out again when Congress met, I thought the result would be really disastrous and make any arrangement in the future impossible—I have no idea whether I made any impression at all on Mr. K.

One thing I have forgotten to mention. At one time in the conversation he said:—'But if we are to discuss this matter again (meaning by "we" G.B. & the U.S.A.) it is better that *we* i.e. U.S.A. take the initiative.' With this I agreed.

Now lastly may I give a hint for the time when the Navy question comes up in Congress—there will no doubt be the usual wild men who will make every sort of accusation against G.B. etc—I am confident that the best way for our Press to treat them is to take no notice of them at all, hardly to record what they say & to make no comments whatever. 'Non ragionam di lor' ma guarda e passa'.[8] This will greatly annoy them because they always hope by starting an angry controversy to produce what you may call the 'Big Navy' reaction in the crowd here—and their psychoanalysis is quite reasonable.

If we meet their diatribes with absolute silence, I believe they will be nonplussed & have great difficulty in putting any extreme Navy Programme through Congress.

Yrs. ever,

ESME HOWARD

[7] On December 8 Sir W. Tyrrell sent to Sir E. Howard a letter of December 2 from Captain Egerton of the Admiralty who explained in particular that the figures of 378,000 tons and 425,000 tons related to different things, and that: 'The figure 378,000 tons has apparently been evolved by deducting from our forecast of cruiser tonnage in 1931 all vessels over 16 years of age. Such a tonnage, plus a percentage of over-age vessels would, of course, have been acceptable to us for cruisers provided the U.S.A. would have agreed to (a) Restriction in numbers of 10,000 ton cruisers on the 12–12–8 basis; (b) A smaller displacement and armament for other cruisers in the future . . . the 425,000 was a combination of cruiser and destroyer tonnage, and was only acceptable subject to conditions (a) and (b) above, and in addition:—(c) The right to maintain 25% of this tonnage in over-age vessels; (d) Special legislation in regard to such vessels as the "Omahas", "Effinghams" and "Furutakas" &c.' Captain Egerton added that the last proposal was a modification of his proposal at the meeting of junior delegates at Geneva (see Volume III, Nos. 429–30) and expressed some criticism of the recall to London of the British delegates (v. *ibid.*, No. 439).

[8] Do not take any account of them but look and pass on: Dante, *Inferno*, Canto 3, verse 51.

No. 218

Memorandum by Sir A. Chamberlain[1]
C.P. 258 (27) [A 6057/133/45]

Secret   FOREIGN OFFICE, *October 26, 1927*

Belligerent Rights at Sea and the Relations Between the United States and Great Britain

As one result of the failure of the Three-Power Naval Conference, I was led to consider what was the real ground for the apparently unreasonable attitude of the United States towards the British proposals for limitation of armaments. This consideration quickly brought me to the conclusion that the difference between us centred in the use which we make of our naval forces to enforce our view of the rights of a belligerent at sea. This at once raised the question whether it was desirable, and, if desirable, possible, to attempt to reach an agreement with the United States upon the disputed points of international law. On my return home I found that the same problem had been raised independently alike in private letters from the Ambassador at Washington and within the Foreign Office itself.

Sir Esme Howard had set out his views in two private and confidential letters to Sir William Tyrrell, which I print for the information of the Cabinet (Appendix I).[2]

I set out my own line of thought in the memorandum which is printed as Appendix II,[3] and in Appendix III will be found a memorandum by Mr. Craigie[4] which gives a much more detailed examination of the points of difference between ourselves and the Americans, and the possibility of reconciling them.

I know the immense difficulties which surround this question, and I realise that there must be a most careful examination of all that is involved before any such negotiations could be undertaken, but I hold strongly that the examination ought to be made and that the new factors introduced by the rise of United States naval and financial power and by the cost and extent of modern warfare must be taken into account. It cannot be denied that the present difference on this subject between the United States and ourselves is the only matter which makes war between our two nations conceivable. But I go further; I believe that General Preston Brown does not exaggerate when he says that any attempt by us to enforce our rights in a future war where the United States were neutral, as we enforced them in the late war, would make war between us 'probable'. The world position has been altered to our disadvantage, and what was possible in the past may have become impossible for the future; I would, therefore, urge that the question should be referred for consideration by a special Committee of the Cabinet or the C[ommittee

[1] This memorandum and that printed as No. 219 were circulated to the Cabinet.
[2] Appendix I comprised Nos. 205 and 209.
[3] Appendix II comprised No. 215, with the omission of the last paragraph.
[4] Appendix III was the annex to No. 216.

of] I[mperial] D[efence]. I am advised that, if it should appear that there is any possibility of entering upon pourparlers or negotiations with the United States, the sooner we can take action the better would be our chances of success.

A. C.

No. 219

Memorandum by Sir A. Chamberlain

C.P. 256 (27) [*W 10423/61/98*]

Confidential   FOREIGN OFFICE, *October 27, 1927*

The Present Situation in Regard to Disarmament

Sir M. Hankey[1] requested Mr. Cadogan to prepare for the information of the Cabinet Committee on Disarmament a paper that would give in outline the recent history of the question. I believe that Mr. Cadogan's memorandum will be most useful to the Committee in approaching the consideration of the problems referred to them; but as in some respects it does not quite represent my own views, I have thought that my office minute on it might also be of use to the Committee.

A. C.

Annex i to No. 219*

Memorandum by Mr. Cadogan

October 26, 1927

The Geneva Protocol having been formally rejected at the meeting of the Council in March 1925, the Assembly in September of that year was rather at a loss what to do about security and disarmament. Locarno was in the air, but had not yet materialised, so that, as far as security was concerned, the Assembly could only give expression to a pious hope for the success of the policy of partial or regional agreements which had been suggested in the speech in which Sir A. Chamberlain had rejected the Protocol in March. With that it ought to have been content, but certain delegations wished it to go further and, before the first step had actually been taken towards security, insisted on making some provision for 'preparing' the work of Disarmament which might perhaps be expected to follow the establishment of a degree of security not yet realised. We were assured—which was, and remains, quite true—that it would be folly to go into a Disarmament Conference unless the ground had been fully prepared beforehand, and—what was more open to doubt—that it was not too early to begin. So the Assembly asked the Council to constitute the 'Preparatory Committee for the Disarmament Conference', and the Council, as in duty bound, proceeded to do so in December 1925.[2] It was formed of representatives of the States Members of the Council and, by special invitation, of the United States of America, Germany, Russia,

---

[1] Secretary to the Cabinet.   [2] See Volume I, Nos. 42 and 138–9.

Bulgaria, Finland, the Netherlands, Poland, Roumania, and the S.H.S. [Serb-Croat-Slovene] State. To these were added in March 1926 the Argentine and Chile. Subsequently, by their election to the Council in September, Colombia, Salvador and China were also admitted, and by the last elections we have now gained in addition the co-operation of Canada and Cuba. Finally, the inclusion of Greece was specially authorised by the last Council. The Council, moreover, set the Preparatory Committee a *questionnaire*,[3] being a number of theoretical questions on the principles of disarmament, probably unanswerable by any ordinary body of men. Assuming that it was necessary to appoint prematurely a body to 'prepare' a conference for which the world was not yet ready, there could probably have been devised no better means of keeping it occupied for an almost indefinite period. The Preparatory Committee met for the first time in May 1926, and tackled this *questionnaire*.[4] The method which it adopted—not unwisely, in the circumstances—was to recast these questions in a rather more detailed form, and hand them on to sub-committees for study. Most for the questions—certainly the most contentious of them—were referred to Sub-Committee 'A'—a body closely resembling the Permanent Advisory Committee, in that it was formed of military, naval and air advisers of the Governments represented on the Preparatory Committee itself. So-called 'economic' questions were referred to Sub-Committee 'B'. It would be only confusing to enumerate the other off-shoots —Joint Committees, Committees of Experts, &c.

Sub-Committee 'A' dragged on throughout the summer. Seeing that it was composed of experts without power to negotiate, the positive results could not be expected to be great. On certain points there was agreement, and this fact was duly recorded. On others there was complete divergence, and no attempt was made to conceal the fact. So that on many points one found one group of States putting up Answer I. This would be followed in the report[5] by Answer II, devised by another group of States. (In order to avoid complication, I leave out of account cases where three or more answers were submitted.) Then would follow a chapter on the 'advantages' of I, written by its adherents, who, if in combative mood, would also contribute some paragraphs headed 'disadvantages' of II. The adherents of II would certainly reply with 'disadvantages' of I, and might, if they could think of them, add 'advantages' of II. This, of course, had one good result, in that it elicited clear statements of the experts' ideas of their own Government's views. But it had the drawback that it rather shocked the feelings of those Governments who thought that it was time that some dignified progress should be made with disarmament. So that when the Assembly met in 1926 —the Locarno Treaties had been initialled in October 1925 and signed in December—there was a demand that the work should be got on with. We had made a stride towards security, and we must make a plunge in the direction of disarmament. So the Assembly asked the Council to hurry up

[3] *V. op. cit.*, Nos. 135 and 139.   [4] See Volume II, Chapter I, *passim*.
[5] The report of December 1926 of Subcommission A of the Preparatory Commission is printed as League of Nations document No. C. 739. M. 278. 1926. IX: C.P.D. 28.

the Preparatory Committee so that the Disarmament Conference might be summoned before the next Assembly, provided this were not materially impossible. This had all followed fairly logically, but, in effect, it was a breach with the policy to which the League had pledged itself in 1922, when it practically laid down the principle 'Disarmament through Security.' We had got some measure of security in the Locarno Treaties—not the *general* security of the Protocol—and if the theory was correct, some measure of disarmament should follow automatically. The Locarno Treaties were signed in December 1925, but owing to the delay in Germany's entry into the League they were not yet in force. The League should have waited to see what would be the result. But, instead of that, it decreed a Disarmament Conference during 1927, if possible. This really amounted, in the circumstances, to an attempt to get 'Security through Disarmament.'

Thus, when the Preparatory Committee met again in March 1927, everyone went there feeling that this time something really must be done.

Lord Cecil felt that the technical questions had been sufficiently aired in the long discussions in Sub-Committee 'A'. No advantage would be gained by further reiteration of conflicting views, and the time had come to try and combine these views into one acceptable scheme. He therefore proposed to submit to the Committee a draft convention designed, as far as possible, to unite the views of the various Governments. His draft convention was revised by the C[ommittee of] I[mperial] D[efence], and he went out to Geneva in March last with a version of it which His Majesty's Government would be prepared to accept.[6]

Briefly, this draft convention attempted to lay down the *principles* of reduction or limitation of armaments; it did not attempt to allot quotas to each country. For instance, as regards land effectives, it provided that each High Contracting Party should undertake that the number of these 'should not exceed that prescribed in Table I of Annex I.' These 'tables' were left blank, the idea being that it would be for the Disarmament Conference itself to fill in the figures. Similarly, as regards aircraft, 'the number of such aircraft maintained by each of the High Contracting Parties shall not exceed the figure set out in Table III of Annex I.'

There were several points on which we knew (from the discussions in Sub-Committee 'A') that other Governments—notably the French and their adherents—would not be disposed to accept our proposals.

1. We proposed that the limitation of land effectives should apply in some measure to *reserves* as well as to the effectives actually serving with the colours.
2. We insisted on the limitation of *numbers* as well as tonnage of warships in each of a number of distinct classes, whereas the French would consider only a limitation of the *total* tonnage irrespective of class.

[6] See Cmd. 2888 of 1927, pp. 10–12 and 13–25 respectively, for British and French draft disarmament conventions. For documentation regarding discussion of them by the Preparatory Commission see Volume III, Chapter I, *passim*.

3. His Majesty's Government were unable to accept the idea of a *limitation* of expenditure on armaments, though they were prepared to agree to a system of publicity.
4. We were opposed to any idea of strict control or supervision to ensure the carrying out of the Treaty, whereas the French Government, at least, evidently contemplated a special organisation for this purpose.

At the outset of the meeting of the Preparatory Committee, Lord Cecil tabled his draft convention. This at once elicited a counter-draft from the French, and a comparison of the two showed that the above were the main points of difference.

The Committee decided to proceed to a discussion of the various headings *seriatim*, and under each heading to take the provisions of the two drafts and try to evolve a single text. It agreed to open the proceedings with a discussion of effectives. Lord Cecil put the case for a limitation of reserves as well as of effectives with the Colours, and received support from some delegations— notably the Swedes and the Americans. But after long discussion, it became evident that a large majority of the Committee, headed by the French, who received the support of their usual followers, would have nothing to do with any limitation of the numbers of reserves. Lord Cecil, not wishing to reach a deadlock at this stage of the proceedings, and hoping, I think, that if we eventually gave way to the continental nations on land effectives they might let us have our way in naval matters, proposed to pass on to other questions, leaving this one open for the moment. His actual words were these: 'I have done my best and I have been a complete failure. I have not shaken even M. de Brouckère, whose open-mindedness we all know; I have not shaken M. Paul Boncour, who has treated me with such courtesy and consideration all through; and I have not shaken even my friend M. Sato,[7] who has expressed, with his usual courtesy, his great regret for differing from me. There it is; that is the end of it. As we cannot get a unanimous view in favour of the opinion I put forward, it is no good persisting, as these things must be done by unanimous views in all matters. I regret the position my friends take, but I shall not persist, having regard to their attitude.'[8]

The Committee accordingly passed on to the discussion of air armaments. But it may be observed here that the French misunderstood, or misrepresented, Lord Cecil to the extent that they are now inclined to emphasise that the Preparatory Committee broke down on the naval question alone, i.e., on our obstinate attitude in regard to that question, and that there was general agreement on land effectives. Lord Onslow challenged this view at a meeting of the Third Committee of the last Assembly, and I think the challenge ought to be maintained and that, when the Preparatory Committee meets again, we should, in the 'Second Reading,' take the points again in the same order, i.e., effectives first, and fight the battle over again, to show that there are other

[7] Japanese representative on the Preparatory Commission.
[8] See League of Nations, *Documents of the Preparatory Commission for the Disarmament Conference*, Series IV, p. 56; see also Volume III, Nos. 89 and 91.

Governments whose unreasonable attitude is an obstacle in the way of a satisfactory scheme of general disarmament.

In regard to air armaments, something was achieved, there being unanimity in favour of limiting aircraft by number and horse-power.

The Committee then tackled the naval question, and were unfortunately unable to arrive at an agreement except on minor points of detail, and it was agreed to pass on from this question, leaving the conflicting proposals to stand in parallel columns. It is true that the French Government produced a modification of their original proposals which appeared to go some way to meet the British view. On examination, however, it proved that this advance was more apparent than real. Anyhow, it was decided to leave the question alone for the moment, more especially as the Tripartite Naval Conference at Geneva was impending, and it was felt that if agreement could there be reached between the principal naval Powers, the rest might be ready to follow with a good grace. There for the moment we may leave the naval question, observing only that on this point there was a fundamental divergence of view on the very *principle* of limitation, in the same way that there had been a definite absence of agreement on the principles of the limitation of land armaments, though the difference on the naval question has been emphasised—and exploited—by the French, whereas we have not given prominence to what we might rightly regard as an unreasonable attitude on their part in regard to land effectives.

After the rather spectacular failure of the Preparatory Committee to produce any agreement on the naval question, interest in the Committee's proceedings waned. Somewhat perfunctorily it continued to discuss limitation of expenditure and such subjects as 'Organisation,' 'Exchange of Information,' 'Derogations,' and 'Procedure with regard to Complaints and Revision.' Practically no agreement was reached on these points, but delegates were tired of arguing, and the Committee had acquired the habit of setting down its results in two (or more) columns. I do not believe that these last-named points would present any insuperable difficulty. The two difficulties are army reserves and the naval question.

We are in a minority on both questions. In regard to military reserves, we certainly have a good case for demanding their reduction, but we are, of course, bad advocates of that case in that we have no reserves, in the continental conscriptionalist sense, so that all our opponents can insinuate that it is easy for us to ask them to dispense with what we haven't got. In regard to the naval question, we are, of course, in a minority, because we are in an unique position as regards sea-power. That might give us the right to lay down the law to others on this question, but if this principle is admitted we must maintain silence in regard to reservists. It is, of course, unfortunate that the few big naval Powers cannot agree amongst themselves on the naval question. And this brings us to the Geneva Naval Conference, which, instead of facilitating the work of the Preparatory Committee, has made it infinitely more difficult. For, whereas at the Preparatory Committee in April it was not very evident that agreement between the United States and

British Governments would be impossible or even difficult, and the dispute raged between the British and the French, the latter have since witnessed the Americans fighting their battle at the Geneva Conference and cannot but be encouraged in their opposition to our proposals. It is true that the American and French opposition is based on different policies and founded on different considerations, but it is equally determined in either case.

When the Preparatory Committee adjourned at the end of April it was decided in principle that it should meet again in November—in any case, in the course of the present year. It was hoped that direct discussions between Governments might afford hope of agreement on the points in dispute. Unfortunately, as has been seen, the outcome of the Geneva Conference rather dashed this hope, and at the moment no progress can be recorded.

It was to be anticipated that the Assembly in September would take a lively interest in the question, and this proved to be the case. Everyone agreed that the Preparatory Committee must meet as arranged—at least, no one was prepared to suggest its postponement. The French were fully alive to the danger of embarking on another discussion unless some preliminary agreement had been reached beforehand on the difficult points, and they saw in this deadlock an opportunity again of preaching 'Security.' They maintained that the present difficult situation arose out of the mistake made in divorcing disarmament from security, on the interdependence of which they had always insisted, and they proposed that the Preparatory Committee should be instructed to examine the question of 'security', so as to give it something to do even though it might be able to effect nothing in the matter of disarmament. This at once brought them up against the German delegation, and, before examining the development and ultimate fate of this French proposal, it may be well for a moment to consider the position of Germany in the matter of disarmament.

It was certain that once Germany had joined the League the question of disarmament would come prominently to the fore. The Preamble to the military clauses of the Treaty of Versailles runs: 'In order to render possible the initiation of a *general limitation of the armaments of all nations*, Germany undertakes strictly to observe the military, naval and air clauses which follow.' In reply to the German observations on these clauses, the Allied Governments in Paris wrote to the German delegation: 'The Allied and Associated Powers wish to make it clear that their requirements in regard to German armaments were not made solely with the object of rendering it impossible for Germany to resume her policy of military aggression. They are also the first steps towards that general reduction and limitation of armaments which they seek to bring about as one of the most fruitful preventives of war, and which it will be one of the first duties of the League of Nations to promote.'[9] Finally, in the

---

[9] See *British and Foreign State Papers*, vol. 112, p. 274, for this quotation from the allied and associated reply of June 16, 1919, to the German observations of May 29 on the conditions of peace (printed in *Papers relating to the Foreign Relations of the United States: The Paris Peace Conference 1919*, vol. vi, pp. 795–901).

Final Protocol of the Locarno Conference, the signatories gave expression to 'their firm conviction that the entry into force of these treaties and conventions will contribute largely to bringing about a moral *détente* amongst the nations, that it will greatly facilitate the solution of many political and economic problems in conformity with the interests and sentiments of the peoples, and that, in consolidating peace and security in Europe, it will have the effect of hastening appreciably the disarmament contemplated in article 8 of the Covenant of the League of Nations.'

The attitude of Germany on the Preparatory Committee has therefore been that, apart from the general obligation on all Members of the League arising out of Article 8 of the Covenant, Germany has a special interest in seeing others disarm. She has herself been disarmed on the promise that this was the prelude to general disarmament; now that her own disarmament is complete, she wonders when others are going to begin. From 1922 till 1925 the League had upheld the theory that disarmament must wait on security, and that disarmament would follow as a natural result of any real advance towards security. If the League had held to that theory, German clamour for progress with general disarmament might perhaps have been allayed temporarily by representing that a direct approach to disarmament had been found impracticable, and by urging them to hope for results from what had already been achieved in the way of security and from what might be expected of an extension of the Locarno system. But by appointing the Preparatory Committee in 1925, and by instructing it in 1926 to hasten the elaboration of a programme for a Conference, to be convened in 1927, based on the 'existing conditions in regard to regional and general security,'[10] the Assembly intimated that the time was ripe for a definite step towards disarmament, which was justified by existing political conditions. So that when the French delegation, at the last Assembly, proposed to divert the attention of the Preparatory Committee from disarmament to security, the Germans were bound to object. What they said, in effect, was: 'You told us last year that Locarno afforded sufficient security to enable a start to be made with disarmament, and you instructed the Preparatory Committee to prepare a Conference on that basis. Now you say that progress with disarmament is impossible without further progress in the matter of security. What has become of Locarno, and in what way is the situation less favourable now than it was last year? We cannot go back to our people and tell them that Locarno turns out to be of no value for this purpose, and we must insist that the work should proceed on the existing basis. The Preparatory Committee must go on as it is, and finish its work.'[11]

This was rather unanswerable, and these objections on the part of the German delegation were only overcome by a compromise whereby the Preparatory Committee shall meet again in November (or at the beginning of December) and constitute a new offshoot Committee to deal *pari passu* with security.

[10] See No. 208, note 3.
[11] See No. 207.

It was generally understood, when the delegation left Geneva at the end of September last, that this meeting would be purely formal, that the new Committee would be constituted, and that both would then adjourn probably till early next year.

Very little has been laid down in regard either to the composition of the new Committee or in regard to the relations between the two Committees. The Germans, for reasons explained above, objected to the Preparatory Committee mixing itself up with 'security' questions: the French and Belgians wished to emphasise the interdependence of disarmament and security, and pretended to see disadvantages in the multiplication of Committees. Finally the general idea seemed to be that the Security Committee would be a sort of second self of the Preparatory Committee—would be, in fact, the same Committee sitting in a different capacity, with, possibly, some changes in personnel. For instance, whereas a Serb general sat for some time on the Preparatory Committee, the S.C.S. Government might wish to replace him by a more 'learned' member on the Security Committee. The majority of Governments would probably have representatives who could double the parts—unless the two Committees were required to sit concurrently.

As to the prospects of either Committee, it is difficult at the moment to see how they are likely to shape. In the absence of any direct negotiations between the Governments on the points which brought the Preparatory Committee to a standstill in April, we remain where we were, and from the experience then acquired it is not clear that another meeting will bring the parties closer together. If the present situation justifies the continental nations in saying that they dare not depart from the principle of giving military training to every able-bodied citizen, and if the same situation renders it necessary for us to adhere to the line which we took at Geneva in June and July as regards naval matters, no progress is possible, and there would appear to be justification for the French view that 'security' is at fault. But that raises an awkward question with the Germans, and it completes the vicious circle—disarmament proves impossible without security: the attempt at *general* security (Treaty of Mutual Assistance and Protocol) proves impracticable: 'regional' security (Locarno) is attempted, but does not produce disarmament quickly enough, and in the attempt to hasten disarmament we find we are driven back to search for greater security. It is unfortunate that Locarno, which really does 'secure' the situation in the most dangerous part of Europe, does not set an example in disarmament, for the reason that we had already disarmed ourselves, the Germans had had disarmament thrust upon them, and the French—for reasons with which it is possible to sympathise—are in no hurry to achieve disarmament. They have, it is true, introduced a scheme which they maintain involves a reduction of armaments, but for reasons which it is impossible to examine here in detail, it does not amount to a very honest or very useful contribution to the problem. Perhaps one cannot blame them for taking every precaution for defence against so powerful and resourceful a nation as Germany. If a Locarno could have been devised in Central Europe, there might have been less excuse for the Little *Entente*[12], for instance, encircling a practically impotent Hungary with an altogether disproportionate ring of armed forces. But further one travels east the more the Russian menace hangs over Europe, and so long as it is admitted—as we should have to admit in any convention signed without a certainty of the honest participation of Russia—that countries in Eastern and Central Europe must be allowed to reckon with this menace, the value of any agreement that we should be likely to get diminishes. The contagion would spread westward, and if any one country is allowed to keep excessive forces to guard its eastern frontier, its westerly neighbour has no guarantee that these might not eventually be used against it.

All the foregoing seems to lead to no conclusion at all, except the negative one that disarmament cannot be imposed arbitrarily: it must follow automatically—as it certainly would follow—from a real sense of security. No single Government can wish to expend a penny more on armaments than what it judges absolutely necessary for its own safety: every Government would seize any opportunity to reduce military expenditure, and so relieve the voting taxpayer.

Can the new Security Committee achieve anything useful? This seems very problematical. We do not know exactly how it will work, but these are the terms of reference given it by the last Assembly resolution[13]:—

They are to seek security—

'1. In action by the League of Nations, with a view to promoting, generalising and co-ordinating special or collective agreements on arbitration and security.' But it is questionable whether the League can do much to 'promote' in this sphere. If nations are prepared for arbitration and security agreements, they may be able to achieve them, but it is doubtful whether public exhortations from the League will assist them very greatly in their delicate task.

'2. In the systematic preparation of the machinery to be employed by the organs of the League of Nations with a view to enabling members of the League to perform their obligations under the various articles of the Covenant.' This was the most innocuous form to which we were able to reduce the Netherlands–French proposal for a fresh study of the Protocol. We were unable to resist it, as its authors pointed out that the Council had already ordered a study of certain articles of the Covenant, and a Committee had already produced a comparatively innocuous work on article 11.[14] Moreover, the Council is even now prosecuting enquiries into possible means of facilitating the meeting of the Council in emergencies,

[12] i.e. Czechoslovakia, Roumania and the Serb-Croat-Slovene States: cf. the Czechoslovak-Roumanian, Czechoslovak-Yugoslav and Roumanian-Yugoslav treaties of April 23, 1921, August 14, 1920, and June 7, 1921, respectively, printed in *British and Foreign State Papers*, vol. 114, pp. 695–6 and 696–7, and vol. 123, pp. 1046–7.

[13] i.e. the fifth resolution referred to in No. 208, note 1.

[14] The report of the Committee of the Council of the League of Nations, approved by the Council on March 15, 1927, is printed in Cmd. 2889 of 1927: cf. Volume III, Nos. 15 and 47.

means of communication in times of crisis between the various Governments and the seat of the League, &c. But it will almost inevitably involve an examination of article 16 and an attempt at a definition of the obligations arising therefrom, which leads us on to dangerous ground.

'3. In agreements which the States Members of the League may conclude among themselves, irrespective of their obligations under the Covenant, with a view to making their commitments proportionate to the degree of solidarity of a geographical or other nature existing between them and other States.' This, so far as it can be understood, refers to agreements on the lines of the Locarno Treaties, and it is not easy to see exactly what rôle the League is expected to play.

'4. And, further, in an invitation from the Council to the several States to inform it of the measures which they would be prepared to take, irrespective of their obligations under the Covenant, to support the Council's decisions or recommendations in the event of a conflict breaking out in a given region, each State indicating that, in a particular case, either all its forces, or a certain part of its military, naval or air forces, could forthwith intervene in the conflict to support the Council's decisions or recommendations.' By this is meant, presumably, that the Council should collect and register the precise undertakings which any States might be prepared to give it as to the action which they might be ready to take against a Covenant-breaking State. If the question were put to us, we could reply by pointing to our obligations under the Locarno Treaties. It seems to be contemplated that other Governments, even though bound by no 'regional' agreements such as Locarno, might be prepared to offer definite co-operation in support of the Covenant in certain definite circumstances.

In addition to the above, two definite questions have been referred by the Assembly for study by the Security Committee: the proposal of the Finnish Government for assistance to States victims of aggression, and Dr. Nansen's proposal for an optional convention for compulsory arbitration of disputes.[15]

If then, disarmament can only be expected to follow from increased security, what are the prospects of the Security Committee achieving anything tangible on the above lines?

The terms of reference clearly indicate two lines of advance—one by means of increasing 'regional' agreements, and the other by means of an elaboration of the Covenant with a view to making the sanctions provided therein more real and more effective.

The former method depends mainly on the initiative of individual States. It may be adopted and followed by a number of them, but we cannot reckon

<hr/>

[15] For the proposal submitted by the Finnish delegate, Mr. Erich, to the Preparatory Commission for the Disarmament Conference on May 26, 1926, see *Documents of the Preparatory Commission for the Disarmament Conference*, Series II, p. 72. For the proposal submitted to the Third Committee of the Eighth Assembly of the League of Nations on September 14, 1927, by Dr. F. Nansen, Norwegian delegate to the Assembly, see *League of Nations Official Journal: Special Supplement No. 57*, pp. 27–8.

on it, we cannot hurry them, and, in the light of experience, it must be confessed that the direct effect on disarmament is problematical.

The second method is unlikely to produce any real result unless it is pushed to its logical conclusion—which would not be far removed from the Protocol of 1924. And however logical that may be on paper, it is not a matter of practical politics now.

The conclusion, therefore, seems to be as inevitable as it is depressing: States maintain their present armaments because they consider them indispensable to secure them against the dangers with which they are or might be threatened, and the size of these armaments is a measure of the feeling of insecurity that must still exist, for nearly all the armies of Europe are rather a symptom of fear than a gratuitous challenge to others. To dissipate this feeling of insecurity something more drastic and effective is required than isolated 'regional' agreements, and if such a feeling exists, implying distrust and suspicion in all quarters, is it possible to believe that even a Protocol, which must depend for its efficacy on absolute good faith and confidence in the inevitability of its working, would effect such a radical improvement as to change the whole mood of Europe?

A. Cadogan

Annex 2 to No. 219

Minute by Sir A. Chamberlain

October 27, 1927

This is a very able memorandum but I am not altogether happy about it. Mr. Cadogan has not confined himself to a mere exposition of the past but has added or rather interwoven an appreciation of the present & a forecast of the future.

Now this part of his paper is purely & consistently negative & concludes on a note of despair. I think that H.M.G. ought to be far more positive. I suggest that H.M.G. can & should accept without reserve (1) & (3) & (4) of the Reference to the Security Committee. These I should interpret as a call to others to do what we have done by our Treaty of Locarno.

On (2) I should adopt a waiting policy, leaving others to formulate proposals, but I should watch the proceedings carefully to see whether at a given moment it might not be necessary for us to raise definitely the effect of the withdrawal of the United States on the efficacy & practicability of using the methods of Art[icle] 16 & again I would press strongly the acceptance by other Powers (already given by us in principle) of the Finnish financial guarantee fund proposal.

We can also support Dr. Nansen's proposal within carefully defined limits. On this point Sir Cecil Hurst could give the Cabinet Com[mit]tee useful help.

Finally, as regards disarmament, I would urge that the Com[mit]tee should most carefully review the differences recorded in the Report of the Preparatory Committee in the light of the subsequent proceedings at the Three-Power Naval Conference & see how our position is affected by them. It should, I submit, be our object to reach an agreement for such a measure, small & imperfect as it may be, of restriction or reduction of armaments as is actually possible. In this connection we ought particularly to consider what measure of support we may expect & from what quarters on the various points on which we are at present definitely in a minority.

A. C.

No. 220

Letter from Sir W. Tyrrell to Sir E. Howard (Washington)

[*A 6213/133/45*]

Private and secret   FOREIGN OFFICE, *October 28, 1927*

My dear Howard,

Your private letter of the 12th instant[1] in regard to your conversation with Hoover of last July and also the general question of the exercise of belligerent rights at sea, enclosing a memorandum by Pope Hennessy, has been read with great interest.

In view of what you say, the Secretary of State quite agrees that you should speak to Hoover in the manner you propose in paragraph 2 of your letter and, as you say, give the whole subject its quietus in this way.[2]

As regards the general question of an agreement with the United States on the 'blockade' question, the Secretary of State asks me to say that, if and when the time comes that we are ready to discuss these issues with the United States Government, we will consult you as to the best manner of getting them started. He feels, however, that it would be fatal to start them prematurely, or at all, except in the *most* confidential way, and that meanwhile we should say nothing to Colonel House or anyone else.

W. TYRRELL

[1] No. 214.

[2] Sir E. Howard reported in particular in a letter of November 25 to Sir W. Tyrrell that he had spoken accordingly to Mr. Hoover on November 23, and that Mr. Hoover had said he quite understood Sir A. Chamberlain's point of view.

No. 221

Letter from Sir W. Tyrrell to Sir E. Howard (Washington)

[*A 6073/133/45*]

Private and secret   FOREIGN OFFICE, *October 28, 1927*

My dear Howard—

We have been much interested in your letters of the 15th and 22nd September[1] in regard to the possible conclusion of an agreement with the United States on the subject of the exercise of belligerent rights at sea. We on our side have been considering this question very carefully during the last few months, and I cannot do better than send you the accompanying copy of a memorandum[2] prepared by the Secretary of State on your two letters, as showing the direction in which his thoughts are moving. This memorandum

[1] Nos. 205 and 209 respectively.   [2] No. 215.

should at present be regarded as nothing more than a guide to the working of Sir Austen's mind and an assurance that your views have not fallen on deaf or impenetrable ears and that they are being studied with the attention which the subject demands. Above all the Secretary of State asks me to say that the problem is not nearly so simple as his memorandum might encourage you to think: you have indeed only to look at the minutes and discussions on the abortive Declaration of London to see how others have argued on the same lines before and how the Great War, if it did not disprove, at least did not confirm their arguments.

Sir Austen therefore hopes you will most carefully avoid any conversation with anyone—officially or otherwise—which might engage us in discussions on these delicate matters until they have been fully considered here.

We are trying to get you a copy of Malkin's article in the 'British Year Book of International Law', the volume for the year 1927, to which the Secretary of State refers. If we are unable to obtain one in time for the bag, I would suggest that the Embassy might borrow a copy from the Congressional Library.

Yours ever,
W. TYRRELL

No. 222

Memorandum by Sir C. Hurst

[*W 10409/61/98*]

FOREIGN OFFICE, *November 2, 1927*

Mr. Fass of the Treasury came over to see me on October 31st under instructions from Sir Warren Fisher. He wanted to talk about the possibilities of using the meeting of the Preparatory Commission on Disarmament at Geneva at the end of this month as an opportunity for sounding Japan as to whether she would be prepared to enter into a bilateral agreement for the restriction of cruiser programmes, and of seeing whether a corresponding bilateral agreement with France would be possible as to aeroplane construction. When I found that Mr. Fass wanted to talk about disarmament and the prospects of an agreement at Geneva, I got Mr. Cadogan to come and join in our conversation.

The substance of what Mr. Fass had to say was that the prospects of a disarmament agreement emerging from the work of the Preparatory Commission seemed to be remote, that the building programme of the naval authorities in this country was now controlled by what Japan does, that it is the shortage in the number of British aeroplanes as compared with the French which constitutes the basis of the building programme of the Air Ministry, that if things go on as at present Great Britain will before long be obliged to spend £20,000,000 a year on her naval building programme alone, and that the only hope for economy through disarmament seemed to be in bilateral agreements with Japan as to naval matters and France as to aeroplanes. He went on to say that the Treasury idea, which the Chancellor of the Exchequer wishes to have explored, is as to the desirability of sending out some experienced individual, such as Sir George Barstow,[1] with Mr. McNeill[2] when he goes to the meeting of the Preparatory Commission at the end of this month, and as to the opportunity being taken of sounding the Japanese and the French as to their willingness to enter into such bilateral agreements.

We explained to Mr. Fass that the November meeting of the Preparatory Commission was likely to be formal as it was improbable that more would be done than to appoint the new committee and consider what action was necessary in order to approach the study of the new tasks imposed upon the Preparatory Commission.

Mr. Fass said that, so far as concerns naval matters, Japan was likely to begin the building of some new cruisers in February and we should have to begin the construction of some cruisers in March. If anything was to come of the idea of such a bilateral agreement, therefore, time must not be lost.

We assured Mr. Fass that if H.M. Government decided to send out a man like Sir George Barstow to sound the Japanese and French Delegations as to whether anything could be achieved in the way of bilateral agreements, we felt sure the Foreign Secretary would offer no objection. The Foreign Office was out to help, not to make difficulties, in a task of this kind. I also told him that the question of a naval agreement with Japan might open up the way to a demand by Japan for something to increase her security, such as a request for the restoration of the Anglo-Japanese Alliance,[3] and I said I should like to have an opportunity to ask Sir Victor Wellesley whether this possibility rendered the Treasury proposal undesirable. Since then I have mentioned the matter to Sir Victor Wellesley and have sent to Mr. Fass the note of which a copy is annexed.

C. J. B. H.

ANNEX TO No. 222

Letter from Sir C. Hurst to Mr. Fass (Treasury)

FOREIGN OFFICE, *November 3, 1927*

My dear Fass,

I had an opportunity of talking over with Wellesley yesterday the question which emerged from our conversation on Monday and which I said I should like to put to him. This was, you will remember, whether any attempt to come to a bilateral agreement with Japan for the restriction or reduction of

---

[1] Lately Controller of Supply Services in H.M. Treasury and since August 1 a Government director of the Anglo-Persian Oil Company.

[2] Mr. R. McNeill had recently been appointed Chancellor of the Duchy of Lancaster in succession to Lord Cecil and had been raised to the peerage as Baron Cushendun.

[3] The Anglo-Japanese alliance, as embodied in treaties of 1902, 1905, and 1911 (printed respectively in *British and Foreign State Papers*, vol. 95, pp. 83–84, vol. 98, pp. 136–8, and vol. 104, pp. 173–4) had terminated upon the ratification, on August 17, 1923, of the Four-Power treaty signed at Washington on December 13, 1921, between the United States, the British Empire, France, and Japan (printed *op. cit.*, vol. 116, pp. 627–30).

certain types of war vessels might not lead to a desire on Japan's part to secure in return mutual guarantees of security which might have an undesirable political repercussion.

Wellesley thinks that Japan for reasons of economy would welcome proposals for a further reduction of naval armaments and that there is no great risk of her raising the question of the renewal of the Anglo-Japanese Alliance. In any case that risk in itself does not seem sufficient to justify abandoning the idea of sounding the Japanese Government to see whether a bilateral agreement would be possible unless there are other and stronger reasons. He personally would deprecate anything in the nature of a return to the Anglo-Japanese Alliance, but if the Japanese did desire to bring in the security question, it is quite likely that we could find some formula—to the effect that the two parties pledge themselves to co-operate effectively in the efforts of the League of Nations to preserve peace—which would be free from the objections which would attend any return to the idea of an alliance. It is, of course, not certain that the Japanese would desire to bring in the security idea.

Wellesley thinks that Japan may find it very difficult to agree to any naval reductions without American participation. This was the lesson taught by the Geneva Conference of last summer. In his view the key to this problem lies essentially in an approach to America rather than Japan, as without American co-operation nothing is likely to be accomplished.

CECIL J. B. HURST

No. 223

Sir E. Howard (Washington) to Sir A. Chamberlain (Received November 14)
No. 1958 [A 6618/133/45]

WASHINGTON, *November 4, 1927*

Sir:

Mr. Wickham Steed, the well-known British journalist, arrived in America a short time ago with the purpose of attending the Convention of the World Alliance of Churches at St. Louis.

On the 26th October he was entertained at luncheon at Philadelphia by the English Speaking Union, which was attended amongst others by no less a person than Mr. Cyrus Curtis, millionaire owner of the Curtis Press, i.e., 'Philadelphia Public Ledger', 'Saturday Evening Post', etc., which has not generally shown itself particularly favourable to Great Britain.

Mr. Steed in a remarkably interesting speech dealt with the attitude of America to Europe and vice versa.

After saying that America was right to stay out of the League of Nations if she wished, but that he still believed America to be idealistic enough to be solid against any country or countries which she thought were plotting for self aggrandizement and after insisting on the interest of Great Britain to prevent wars, Mr. Steed said—

'However, the leading statesmen of Europe fear hostile neutrality from the United States. I answer them: "You're wrong! The American people never will wish their statesmen to tie the hands of Governments that are trying to prevent aggressive wars."

'I wonder if an Englishman might state frankly here what's in his mind? The United States does not like foreign interference! It wishes to settle things for itself. Is it pardonable to put a simple question to the United States?

'Suppose that we have to take action to prevent a war! Now—if we assume that the United States won't interfere in behalf of the aggressor, are we wrong in that assumption? Is it possible for the United States Government, or a spokesman for America, to let other countries engaged in preventing war know where the United States stand?—through the action of some accredited statesman in laying down a doctrine of peace and enouncing it to the world.

'That enouncement would change the face of the world. War can't be waged successfully today without the participation of the United States. By such an enouncement, those who talk of the "next war" in imbecile ignorance, would be silenced. That peace doctrine enounced by America would be a pillar of safety for the world. And the United States lacks neither the idealism nor the courage to express its convictions.'

This speech was reported verbatim in the 'Philadelphia Public Ledger', in the 'New York Herald-Tribune' which though decidedly friendly to Great Britain is strongly anti-League and isolationist, and I believe in other papers.

Mr. Steed had requested me some time before to arrange for him to see President Coolidge and I accordingly made arrangements for him to pay his respects to the President on November 2nd and, as is usual, to be introduced by me. He called on me the day before and asked me if I thought that there would be any harm in his suggesting to the President, if the occasion should offer, that it would be very helpful in the cause of peace if the United States Government would make a pronouncement declaring that they would not aid financially or otherwise any nation that might be recognised as an aggressor in war. I said I did not think it would do harm except in so far as any suggestion made by Englishmen as to the policy America might pursue was always liable to be misconstrued as a trap for the innocent. Mr. Steed said that the way in which his speech at Philadelphia had been received made him hope that this danger might be more imaginary than real in this case. In any case he assured me that he would tell the President that anything he said was entirely unofficial and that my presence there must not be considered as giving it official sanction.

I had hardly introduced Mr. Steed to the President before Mr. Coolidge opened the conversation by saying that he had read Mr. Steed's Philadelphia speech and began to draw him out as to his ideas on the subject of such a declaration. Mr. Steed then developed his theme much as in the Philadelphia speech urging the necessity of restoring European confidence in American action in time of war, lack of which was, he said, the cause of half the uncertainty now prevailing in Europe as to the future and also of the difficulties in the way of a disarmament policy.

Mr. Coolidge, who seemed much interested and was far less non-committal than I have ever yet seen him, said that of course he might himself make a speech embodying such a declaration but that this would naturally not commit Congress or future Governments in any way.

I ventured then seeing how favourably he regarded the plan, to say, speaking quite personally since I had only heard Mr. Steed's views the day before and had of course had no communication from you on the subject, that I wondered whether it would be possible for a speech by the President to be reinforced by a Senate Resolution. The President said that would certainly carry great weight but he wondered whether Senator Borah as Chairman of the Foreign Relations Committee of the Senate would consent to introduce such a Resolution. Mr. Steed said he was going to see Mr. Borah that morning and the President then said that he would like to hear the result of the conversation with the Senator. He invited Mr. Steed to lunch with him that day.

Mr. Steed immediately afterwards saw Senator Borah and Mr. Hoover. He found the Senator very receptive of the idea and not at all unwilling to consider the plan of a Senate Resolution on the lines suggested provided of course, as I understand, that the United States Government would retain the right of judging who was the aggressor and not be bound by any decision of the League of Nations.

Mr. Hoover, however, was not at first so favourable but Mr. Steed believed that he had convinced him in the end that the United States could really assist the cause of peace very greatly and help to restore the confidence of Europe in the future by taking the action proposed.

Mr. Steed afterwards lunched at the White House alone with Mr. and Mrs. Coolidge. Mr. Coolidge took him to his study and kept him in a tête à tête conversation for over an hour after lunch discussing the condition of European affairs.

The upshot of this is, as I read it, that both Mr. Coolidge whose hands are now free from the shackle of an impending election and Senator Borah believe that the time is coming for some move on the part of leaders of the Republican party in the direction of world idealism, as opposed to mere isolationism. I have for some time felt that public opinion here is moving in that direction. It is not therefore impossible that this suggestion of Mr. Steed may fall on good ground and spring up and bear fruit. If properly cultivated I cannot but think that it might lead to very useful results and materially help the cause of security, disarmament and peace in Europe.

I have, &c.,

ESME HOWARD

No. 224

Memorandum by Sir A. Chamberlain
C.P. 286 (27) [A 6673/133/45]

FOREIGN OFFICE, *November 14, 1927*

Belligerent Rights at Sea

While C.P. 258[1] was being printed for circulation, I mentioned to Sir M. Hankey that I was proposing to bring this subject before the Cabinet. He was good enough to supply me within a few days with a memorandum embodying his strongly-held view that we should enter into no new engagement restrictive of our liberty.

I believe the Cabinet will be glad to have his opinion as well as the observations made upon it and on the whole subject by Sir Cecil Hurst, who is also opposed to negotiation. I therefore circulate them with my own paper.[2]

On one thing we are all agreed—that the question is of immense importance, and that the answer, whether negative or affirmative, is fraught with grave possibilities. I have formed no definite conclusion. I ask the Cabinet for no decision until the question has been thoroughly examined by the most competent committee that we can choose; but I cannot take the responsibility which would be mine if, because I am not prepared at present to give a definite answer to the question which I have raised, I refrained from calling the attention of the Cabinet to it and by my inaction, in fact, decided it in the negative.[3]

A. C.

ANNEX II TO No. 224*

Memorandum by Sir C. Hurst on Sir Maurice Hankey's paper on 'Blockade and the Laws of War'

FOREIGN OFFICE, *November 10, 1927*

The thesis maintained by Sir Maurice Hankey in his paper is that no agreement should be negotiated with the United States on the subject of belligerent rights at sea, because an agreement would hamper this country in applying economic pressure against the enemy, and if the struggle in which Great Britain was engaged was one of vital importance to her, it would be essential to apply such pressure.

[1] No. 218.

[2] Sir M. Hankey's memorandum of October 31, circulated to the Cabinet as annex I to this paper, is not printed. For his subsequent exposition of generally similar arguments, see Lord Hankey, *The Supreme Command 1914–1918*, vol. i, pp. 95–101.

[3] On November 7 Sir A. Chamberlain had expressed similar views in replying to Lord Cushendun, who, in a letter of November 4 had stated that Admiral Lord Jellicoe's book, *The Crisis of the Naval War* (London, 1920) had raised in his mind the question: 'Has the time come when it would be wise for us to abandon, or modify, our traditional doctrine of blockade in time of war? I cannot help thinking—and I have thought a lot about it—that there really is a *lot* to be said for an affirmative answer.'

2. It is no doubt true that throughout the greater part of the XIXth century a belief was widely spread among the public at large that war was a struggle between the contending armed forces and not between the nations concerned. Consequently, there was a movement in favour of excluding so far as possible civilian non-combatants from the effects of the war. The idea dates back to the time of Rousseau. There is, I think, no chance of any similar delusion prevailing in the future. At present all modern States are disposed—some even outwardly—to organise themselves for defence upon the basis that the whole nation is to share in the burden. This point is one which is not without importance, as it affects the vulnerability of this country in time of war owing to the extent to which Great Britain depends upon imported seaborne foodstuffs.

3. Sir Maurice Hankey traces the history of the Declaration of London in a way which suggests that the movement in favour of the Declaration emanated from those who thought principally of the protection of Great Britain's neutral trade when other States were engaged in war, and, secondarily, of protecting Great Britain's seaborne commerce, particularly her imports, from the ravages of her enemy when she herself was engaged in war. This is not correct.

4. The movement which culminated in the Declaration of London originated with the first Secretary of the Imperial Defence Committee (Sir George Sydenham Clarke, now Lord Sydenham). The experiences of the South African War, and perhaps the early experiences of the Russo-Japanese War, had convinced him that the power to seize contraband had ceased to be of prime importance to Great Britain and that the risk of antagonizing neutrals by belligerent seizures effected by British naval forces, coupled by the power which it gave to an enemy to interfere with the commerce of this country in time of war, and also with the injury done to the commerce of this country when a neutral by seizures by foreign belligerents, outweighed the advantages which the right to seize contraband and thereby impose economic pressure upon the enemy conferred upon this country in time of war. In a C.I.D. paper, Secret 41–B, of December 1904, reprinted with additions in April 1906, there is a memorandum by the then Secretary of the Defence Committee on the question of 'The Value to Great Britain as a belligerent of the right of search and capture of neutral vessels,' in which he examines the problem at length and, after a reasoned argument of six pages of print, arrives at the conclusion in paragraph 40 that an international arrangement under which neutral bottoms covered contraband would be to our advantage. There is in the same paper an Admiralty letter dated the 10th June, 1905, expressing doubt upon the problem, and indicating that they were not yet convinced. The value of this letter is that it shows that the proposal raised by the Secretary of the Defence Committee must at least have been considered by the Admiralty.

5. The policy then indicated must have been accepted by His Majesty's Government. It was examined at length by an interdepartmental committee appointed for the purpose of framing the instructions to the British delegates

to the Second Peace Conference at The Hague in 1907, and the recommendations of that body were in favour of international agreement for the purpose
of allowing a neutral's trade to be subject to no other restraint than the
exercise of the right of visit and of effective blockade (see Report, dated the
21st March, 1907, of the 'Interdepartmental committee appointed to consider
the subjects which may arise for discussion at the Second Peace Conference,'
p. 2, paragraph 8 (*b*)). The members of this committee included Sir Charles
Ottley, who was at the time Director of Naval Intelligence at the Admiralty.
It was in pursuance of the policy originated in the Defence Committee paper
referred to above and renewed in the report of the interdepartmental committee of 1907 that the British delegates were sent to The Hague in 1907 to
propose the total abolition of the right to seize contraband of war, leaving
sea power to be exercised solely by means of blockade in the old-fashioned
sense of the term, i.e., the blockade of an enemy coast-line. Great Britain
being thus committed to the principle of restricting the exercise of sea power
in time of war was naturally also in favour of curbing the pretensions of
belligerent prize courts by the creation of an international prize court, which
should be entitled to review the decisions of national prize courts and award
compensation to those whose rights had been ignored by such national prize
courts. It was for the purpose of providing this international prize court with
a code of rules which it was to apply that the Naval Conference was summoned to meet in London in 1908–9 and framed the Declaration of London.
Primarily, it is no doubt true that the Declaration of London was intended
only as a code to be applied by the international prize court, but the whole
situation was controlled by the belief that Great Britain stood to gain by the
total abolition, or, if that were impossible, the restriction, of the right to seize
contraband of war.

6. The policy pursued in 1907 may have been right or may have been
wrong. The events of the war of 1914–18 certainly suggest that the policy
was wrong; but the circumstances of the war of 1914–18 were very peculiar
in that at the time when the application of economic pressure to the enemy
was at its highest every Power of any importance was a belligerent. From the
moment that the United States came in, there was no neutral State of sufficient weight to oppose the Allied operations at sea or to oppose the Allied
measures for the purpose of securing control of enemy imports intended to
reach the enemy country through neutral territory. No man, before the war,
could have foreseen the situation as it emerged during the war, and it would
be a bold man who would prophesy that similar circumstances will arise in
any future war.

7. Sir Maurice Hankey's paper seems to me to underestimate one difficulty
with which British naval operations against neutral commerce must always
contend in time of war, that is, that the legality of the operations will always
be controlled by the prize courts, and that any action which the prize courts
are pleased to determine to be inconsistent with international law will be
invalidated and the Government, in the form of the captors, will be ordered
to pay costs and damages. One has only to remember a case like the 'Zamora'

in 1916 (where the Privy Council held to be invalid a measure which His Majesty's Government had taken for the purpose of requisitioning neutral property and thereby increasing the economic pressure on the enemy) to see that such restrictions as the naval authorities suffered from during the late war were not at all due to international engagements, whether ratified or unratified, by which His Majesty's Government had bound themselves in time of peace. People are apt to forget to-day the extent to which all through the late war the enemy played into our hands by the successive blunders which he committed at sea, thereby enabling His Majesty's Government to introduce all manner of novel measures under the guise of retaliation which no British prize court would have tolerated if the enemy had not made these mistakes. It is true that in time the United States came in on the Allied side, but there, again, we have to thank our enemy for the blunders which brought in the United States against them. British measures at sea for the purpose of harrying American commerce were certainly not the element which made the United States join in the struggle against Germany.

8. I do not for a moment contest the view that it was by means of the Blockade that the war was won, but Sir Maurice Hankey's paper does not seem to me to state fully the case *against* the proposal to sound the United States as to the possibility of an agreement on the subject of belligerent rights at sea. The arguments which he marshals against the Declaration of London are not in my opinion the points of primary importance at the present stage, and the case against attempting to negotiate an arrangement with the United States as proposed in the Craigie memorandum[4] should rest, I think, on other grounds.

9. For one Power to exercise effective economic pressure upon its opponent by means of sea power two conditions must be fulfilled: (*a*) the Power exercising the pressure must have the superiority at sea, and (*b*) the measures which it takes must be measures which are within the admitted principles of international law, or such as for exceptional reasons the prize court will uphold. These two conditions do not operate on a footing of equality; the first is the more essential. Unless the Power which is anxious to effect economic pressure on the enemy has the superiority at sea, it is the enemy which will exert the economic pressure and not the first Power. If Great Britain were engaged in a naval war with a Power which was superior at sea, it is Great Britain which, by reason of her vulnerability on account of her necessary importations of foodstuffs, would feel most the economic pressure which sea power can effect, and the more that the whole nation participates in the struggle and not merely the armed forces, the more precarious becomes the position of foodstuffs which theoretically are intended only for the civilian non-combatant population. Furthermore, without that superiority at sea, the neutrals would not tolerate the interference with their commerce which the exercise of sea power entails.

10. The proposed agreement with the United States would only affect the second of the conditions postulated above. It is useless to make such an agree-

[4] Annex to No. 216.

ment unless it is certain that Great Britain will in the future maintain that superiority at sea which she has exercised in the past. Without that superiority sea power can and will be exercised to Great Britain's economic disadvantage.

11. To what extent does superiority at sea depend on the mere multiplication of ships? I suppose it must now be admitted that, if the United States chose to do so, they could outstrip Great Britain in any shipbuilding race in which they chose to engage. Does the problem of manning the ships built, and does the problem of sailing and fighting the ships when built and manned, so weigh down the scales against the United States and in favour of Great Britain that Great Britain could afford to ignore numerical superiority on the part of the United States and feel that she could maintain her superiority at sea despite American preponderance of ships and guns? These are questions which no layman can answer, but they seem to me to be questions upon which His Majesty's Government must be clear in their own minds before any decision is given on the question of whether an agreement as to belligerent rights at sea would be to our advantage.

12. If the question indicated in paragraph 11 is answered in the affirmative, there must be taken into consideration another question. The type of agreement contemplated in the Craigie memorandum is based wholly on the experience of the past, that is to say, it is proposed to come to an agreement as to the extent to which the belligerent practices of the late war are to be acknowledged to be in accordance with the accepted principles of international law. The problem of past wars in connection with economic pressure at sea was in reality that of the rights of neutrals. To what extent will neutrality prevail in future wars in the way that it has done in the past? To what extent will nations be entitled to appeal to the rights of neutrals? As a contrivance for the maintenance of peace the League of Nations is an attempt to organise general concerted action against a State which goes to war in breach of its undertakings. If the League were universal, there would be no neutrals. That was the hope of its founders, and the intention with which article 16 of the Covenant was drafted. The greater the extent to which the League becomes general, the greater the number of States which will have debarred themselves and their nationals from any attempt to trade with the State against which the concerted action is being taken.

13. The League has not become universal because the United States has not, and so far as one can see at present, is not likely to, become a Member, but from the point of view of naval warfare the United States is the only State now standing outside of the League which is of real importance. Spain and Brazil are likely to come back in time; Turkey, Russia and Mexico are not of first-class importance so far as concerns seaborne commerce. The problem comes back, as before, to that of the United States. At present the League is only seven years old; on the whole it is tending to become stronger rather than weaker, and there is no reason for assuming that within the Membership of the League the covenants of the League will not be enforced. Assume a war, therefore, in which there is an enemy State against which Great Britain,

in collaboration with the rest of the League, is endeavouring to exercise economic pressure, and the United States is standing out and maintaining all the rights of a neutral Power. What is the position?

14. Every State except (*a*) the one against which concerted action is being taken, and (*b*) the United States, will be co-operating to sever all trade and financial relations between the Covenant-breaking State and the outside world. Consequently, it will be bound to prevent the use of its territory for transit purposes for foreign trade with the Covenant-breaking State. No doubt can arise as to the right of a State to control the use of its territory for this purpose. There can be no doubt as to the right in international law of a State to control exports from its own territory, and to impose such conditions as it may choose upon exports from its own territory. There can equally be no doubt as to the right of a State to control imports into and transit through its own territory, and to impose such conditions upon import and transit as it chooses. The only neutral American trade, therefore, with the Covenant-breaking State which, if stopped or controlled by Great Britain, can give rise to dispute is American seaborne trade transported directly to or from the enemy ports.

15. The extensions of belligerent practice which Great Britain was forced to introduce during the late war, and as to the legality of which disputes arose, were wholly concerned with neutral trade on its way to or from the enemy territory via the territory of other neutral States. If one can assume that the League will gradually become stronger and that its Members will fulfil the obligations of the Covenant and stop all transit trade with the enemy across their territory, the difficulty which arose during the late war will not arise in the next war in the same form, if it arises at all, as it arose in the war of 1914–18. The right of a belligerent to control neutral trade on its way to or from the enemy country when in the course of direct transportation to or from enemy ports, is a matter upon which the rules of international law are sufficiently well settled, and are adequate. It is a branch of the law in which it is unlikely that our own prize courts would tolerate unreasonable innovations. It therefore follows that if we can count on the development of the power of the League in the interval before the next Armageddon is likely to break out, this proposed agreement with the United States will be unnecessary. The existing rules of international law give us all we want.

16. If the proposed agreement with the United States is unnecessary, it is obvious that it is undesirable to try and negotiate it, because the attempt to negotiate it would inevitably involve great risk. The effect on the mind of the American people would probably be to make them think that Great Britain was ready to negotiate because she was afraid of the United States and felt that she could not compete. The Big Navy party in America would exploit the situation accordingly. If the attempt to negotiate an agreement failed, the situation would be worse than before.

17. To my mind, therefore, the situation comes to this:—

(1.) Firstly, leaving out of account the anticipated strengthening of the League, an agreement with the United States is undesirable at the present time, because (*a*) if we maintain our naval superiority as against the United States in the future, an agreement would tie our hands and prevent the exercise of economic pressure by the use of sea power, i.e. Sir Maurice Hankey's thesis would hold good; (*b*) if we cannot maintain our naval superiority as against the United States, an agreement of the type proposed would prevent the influence of Great Britain being used to swing the belligerent practice in the direction of what the United States have hitherto meant by the phrase 'the freedom of the seas'. If we lost our superiority at sea, it would be to our own advantage to safeguard our own imports by curtailing belligerent rights as much as possible.

(2.) Secondly, if the League of Nations develops in strength, as one may at present anticipate that it will do, the problem arising from British action under article 16 of the Covenant for the purpose of severing intercourse between the outside world and the Covenant-breaking State, reduces itself to interference with American sea-borne commerce in the course of direct transportation to or from the enemy State. As regards the rights of a belligerent to interfere with this form of neutral sea-borne commerce, the rules of international law are adequate and well established and require no agreement to supplement them.

18. I leave out of account one possible eventuality, namely, that the League will continue to grow in strength, and that in the next war it is Great Britain which will be the Covenant-breaking State with the whole world arrayed against her. In such a war Great Britain would never carry the Dominions with her, and it is an eventuality which need not be considered.

C. J. B. HURST

No. 225

Letter from Sir E. Howard (Washington) to Sir W. Tyrrell

[A 6909/133/45]

Private and confidential   WASHINGTON, *November 14, 1927*

My dear Tyrrell:

With reference to previous correspondence on the question of Maritime Law, I had an interesting little talk with Kellogg after dinner at the Canadian Legation on the 11th instant. The papers that morning had published long telegrams from London reporting Wester-Wemyss' speech in the House of Lords in favour of scrapping the Declaration of Paris.[1] I don't exactly know how it happened but our conversation drifted to this and Kellogg said that he was glad to see that Lord Balfour had sat upon Wemyss' suggestion.[2] I

---

[1] For this speech on November 10 by Admiral Lord Wester-Wemyss, First Sea Lord 1917–19, see *Parl. Debs., 5th ser., H. of L.*, vol. lxix, cols. 19–30.

[2] *V. ibid.*, cols. 40–3.

said, not only Lord Balfour but also Lord Chatham, who is a Civil Lord of the Admiralty,[3] had taken the same line.

I then asked Kellogg whether the old American objections to the first clause of the Declaration of Paris with regard to privateering still held good. He said, 'Certainly not. We are no longer interested in the question of privateering.' I then said, 'It's curious how in these latter days the submarine has, to a great extent, taken the place of the privateer of old days.' He said, 'Yes, that's so, but we certainly do not wish to support the submarine in any way and we should be only too glad to see them altogether abolished. I cannot help thinking that if America and Great Britain were to join hands for the abolition of the submarine we could carry it through.' I said that considering the opposition that France and other countries had made at the time of the Washington Conference[4] I hardly believed that this would be possible. But it might perhaps not be impossible to find some means of restricting the use of submarines in warfare, especially as regards blockade. Mr. Kellogg said he entirely agreed and that any proposal to restrict the use of submarines would certainly have the support of the United States.

This was of course merely an after-dinner conversation, but it shows, I think, the line along which the minds of the Secretary of State and probably also the President are working at the present moment.

I hope you don't think that I exceeded the limits of discretion in saying what I did.

Yours ever,
ESME HOWARD

[3] It was correctly suggested on the filed copy that the reference was to Lord Stanhope, Civil Lord of the Admiralty: *v. ibid.*, cols. 30–6.

[4] See First Series, Volume XIV, Nos. 513, 516 and 527.

No. 226

Memorandum by Mr. Vansittart

[*A 6811/133/45*]

FOREIGN OFFICE, November 16, 1927

I submit a further memorandum by Mr. Craigie, commenting on the memoranda put forward by Sir M. Hankey and Sir C. Hurst[1] which were occasioned by the proposals of this Dept.

Sir M. Hankey's memorandum is very interesting, but I do not feel it to be strictly relevant to the situation with which we have to deal, particularly for the reasons contained in the annexed memorandum. I w[oul]d add that (*a*) we are dealing with an entirely changed situation—changed not in prospect or hypothesis, but in fact, (*b*) that it will change still more and to our disadvantage, and not only from the naval point of view, (*c*) that we don't contemplate giving anything away that the C[ommittee of] I[mperial]

[1] See No. 224, note 2 and Annex II respectively.

D[efence] or Ad[miral]ty definitely wish to retain, (*d*) that all we wish to do is to see how much—and we think it will be much—we can retain of our desiderata by agreement now, rather than by wrangling or fighting later.

Sir C. Hurst's memo. seems to me to have much validity—though perhaps we sh[oul]d not *entirely* concur—if, or may I say IF, we have only to consider the contingency of a League War. But have we? Is it even an even money chance? Opinions on this may differ, but I submit that we cannot leave out of consideration—or provision—the other contingencies.

R. Vansittart

Annex to No. 226

Memorandum by Mr. Craigie[2]

Secret   foreign office, *November 16, 1927*

Some observations on Sir C. Hurst's memorandum of November 10th on the suggestion for an agreement with the United States in regard to the exercise of belligerent rights at sea.

Leaving on one side the more purely legal aspects of the case, there are in this memorandum certain points of a political or semi-political character with which, I think, it is difficult for this Department fully to agree. After discussing the matter with Mr. Vansittart I venture to put forward the following considerations which might perhaps be discussed verbally with Sir Cecil Hurst:

(1) Sir Cecil Hurst's memorandum is in the main based on the assumption that, in order to secure an agreement with the United States on this subject, we must necessarily be called upon to abandon some important right which we have hitherto exercised. Sir Maurice Hankey also looks upon the conclusion of such an agreement as merely a repetition of the errors committed in signing the Declaration of London. But can either assumption be taken for granted at this time?

Taking the Declaration of London first, it is only necessary to mention that one of the most powerful criticisms directed against the Declaration by opponents in this country was that it abandoned the application to conditional contraband of the doctrine of continuous voyage. This abandonment was however at the time more distasteful to the United States Government than to His Majesty's Government and I see no reason to think that the United States views on this point have changed. This and other criticised points in the Declaration represented concessions to the 'continental' Powers—departures from our hitherto accepted doctrine which need not, and indeed should not, be repeated in any Anglo-American Convention.

In my memorandum of October 17th (appendix 3 in C.P. 258/27)[3] I endeavoured to show that, on the basis of our experience during the war, it would be wrong to assume that no agreement with the United States was possible unless it departed from the principles of law which have hitherto

---

² This memorandum was circulated to the Cabinet.   ³ See No. 218, note 4.

441

been observed by either country when a belligerent and which have received the sanction of the British and American Prize Courts. Since then an examination of the United States Naval Prize Code of 1900 (as modified in 1903) has reinforced the above conclusion. Only in the matter of immunity of convoys from search and the immunity of coast fishing vessels from capture does there appear to be any fundamental divergence in so far as the rules of contraband blockade and the capture of enemy vessels are concerned. Writing in the 'Times' of April 10th, 1901, Professor Holland, referring to the Naval War Code stated that 'on most debatable points the rules are in accordance with the views of this country'. This naval code was, on the eve of the London Naval Conference of 1908–1909, submitted to His Majesty's Government by the United States Government as representing their view on these questions at that time. In communicating this document, the State Department quoted a passage from the instructions sent to the United States delegate at the second Peace Conference, from which I extract the following:[4] 'The Order putting this Code into force was revoked by the Navy Department in 1904, not because of any change of views as to the rules which it contained, but because many of those rules, being imposed upon the forces of the United States by the Order, would have put our naval forces at a disadvantage as against the forces of other Powers, upon whom the rules were not binding.' The State Department's note to our Embassy added that the attitude of the United States had not changed since the second Hague Peace Conference and that the relevant portions of the above instructions (including the Code) were as applicable to the London Naval Conference as they were to the Hague Conference. There is nothing to show that the United States Government have since gone back on the views expressed in 1908. Indeed, their relative naval strength having enormously increased since that date, it is reasonable to suppose that the old American thesis of 'free ships, free goods'[5] is also sinking into the background: an America drawing rapidly up to an equality of naval strength with this country is on the whole unlikely in the future to show much enthusiasm for securing the immunity from capture of private enemy ships. If this proves to be the case, I cannot see what important belligerent right we are likely to be asked by the Americans to abandon.

As stated in the earlier memorandum, the principal difficulties to be anticipated relate to the diversion of ships to a home port for visit and search, the substitution of a 'long-distance' blockade for the earlier type of close blockade and the censorship of mails, as exercised during the war. These are all extensions of our earlier practice necessitated by the changing conditions under which both modern trade and modern warfare are carried on. If we play our cards carefully, we may well succeed in bringing the United States

[4] For the State Department's note of September 5, 1908, see *Papers relating to the Foreign Relations of the United States 1909*, p. 297; the instructions to the United States Delegate to the second Peace Conference at The Hague, June 15–October 18, 1907, are printed *op. cit., 1907*, part 2, pp. 1128–44.

[5] Mr. Craigie amended the words in inverted commas to read 'freedom of the seas' in the text of this memorandum printed for circulation.

along with us as a partner in a logical adaptation to present-day necessities of old-fashioned rules no longer capable of giving full effect to the principles on which they were based. But such a result would only be possible at a time when both countries are at peace, not when we are already engaged in a life and death struggle.

(2) The example of a full League war quoted by Sir Cecil Hurst in §§ 14 and 15 of his memorandum is certainly one in which an agreement with the United States would prove less useful than in the case of other types of war. Even in this case, however, it is difficult to agree that such an understanding would be entirely useless from a political point of view. United States dislike of the League and all its works is a factor with which we—who will have to apply the naval pressure in a League war—must count.

But can we afford to neglect the possibility of our being engaged in a war in which the League takes no part?

Under the Covenant as it stands there are several possible ways in which a war could be waged without the League States taking an active part. Thus Article 15 of the Covenant, dealing with disputes between members of the League, contains the following paragraphs:

'If the Council fails to reach a report which is unanimously agreed to by the members thereof, other than the Representatives of one or more of the parties to the dispute, the Members of the League reserve to themselves the right to take such action as they shall consider necessary for the maintenance of right and justice.

'If the dispute between the parties is claimed by one of them, and is found by the Council, to arise out of a matter which by international law is solely within the domestic jurisdiction of that party, the Council shall so report, and shall make no recommendation as to its settlement.'

Again Article 17, dealing with disputes between a member of the League and a State which is not a member of the League, contains the following paragraph:

'If both parties to the dispute when so invited refuse to accept the obligations of membership in the League for the purposes of such dispute, the Council may take such measures and make such recommendations as will prevent hostilities and will result in the settlement of the dispute.'

In none of the cases mentioned in the above paragraph does Article 16 (which imposes what for want of a better term one may call a 'League war') come automatically into operation, and it seems more than probable that in such cases the war may be confined to the parties immediately interested in the dispute. Apart from the above it seems necessary to reckon with the possibly remote contingency that, when League opinion in regard to any particular dispute is fairly evenly divided, the machinery for League intervention may break down at an early stage, thus paralysing any corporate action by the League of Nations.

443

Types of war other than that cited by Sir C. Hurst seem therefore to merit consideration before we can conclude that an Anglo-American agreement is unnecessary.

(3) In paragraph 16 of his memorandum Sir C. Hurst states:

'The effect on the mind of the American people would probably be to make them think that Great Britain was ready to negotiate because she was afraid of the United States and felt that she could not compete. The big navy party in America would exploit the situation accordingly.'

I do not believe that this would be the predominating effect on the mind of the American people, but, even if it were, this circumstance would hardly assist the big navy party in America as suggested. The success of that party's propaganda depends not on a realisation that Great Britain may be afraid of the United States, but on the opposite consideration, namely that the United States have something to fear from the British navy. There is ample evidence to show that it is precisely this danger of a dispute with the British Empire in regard to the treatment of private property at sea which is being used by the big navy party to exert pressure on the Administration and Congress to increase the United States navy to 'parity' of strength with the British navy.

(4) At the end of paragraph 16 Sir C. Hurst states: 'If the attempt to negotiate an agreement failed, the situation would be worse than before'. This of course is true of almost any attempt to negotiate an agreement on any controversial subject, but the danger might be reduced to a minimum if the cautious method of approach which has been proposed were to be adopted and no formal British proposals were to be put forward until we were certain that the United States Government were ready to talk—and to talk reasonably.

(5) Paragraph 17 (1) (b) of the memorandum states:

'If we cannot maintain our naval superiority as against the United States, an agreement of the type proposed would prevent the influence of Great Britain being used to swing the belligerent practice in the direction of what the United States have hitherto meant by the phrase "the freedom of the seas".'

With the conditions in which naval warfare and commercial enterprise are conducted constantly shifting, it would be reasonable to suggest to the United States Government that any agreement come to should be subject to denunciation or revision every five years. If at the present moment the Committee of Imperial Defence should recommend that our claims in the matter of contraband and blockade should be put at the maximum, it seems unlikely that before the expiration of five years the position could have so changed as to necessitate His Majesty's Government urging a revision of the rules of war in the direction of 'the freedom of the seas'. In other words, if the experts are content now with the rules and practices which emerged from the Great War, it seems hardly likely that they would have completely reversed themselves by the year 1932 or thereabouts.

The above points are submitted with all due deference in case they may be considered worthy of further consideration or discussion.

R. L. CRAIGIE

No. 227

Memorandum by Mr. Thompson[1]

[A 6768/133/45]

FOREIGN OFFICE, *November 17, 1927*

The future of Anglo-American relations

While both His Majesty's Embassy at Washington and the British Library of Information in New York have furnished very full reports upon the opinions entertained by the United States press and public upon the Geneva Conference and its failure, little material is available showing the views held in the United States upon the future relations between that country and Great Britain. Nevertheless, it is clear that the abortive disarmament Conference of last summer is likely to have important repercussions upon American feeling towards this country, if not upon British opinion vis-à-vis the United States. The failure at Geneva has certainly done nothing to improve Anglo-American relations; on the contrary, it has strengthened enormously those elements in the United States who are unfriendly to Great Britain and whose object it is to 'show the world' conclusively that while the 19th Century may have belonged to Britain, the 20th Century undoubtedly belongs to the United States.

During the Conference an anti-British campaign of considerable violence raged in the United States press. This was the logical result of some two years of well-organised and persistent big-navy propaganda reiterating emphatically again and again (1) that the United States were tricked into throwing away the naval supremacy within their grasp at the time of the Washington Conference, (2) that scarcely had the Washington treaties been signed than Great Britain set about violating the principle of naval parity by quietly developing an extensive programme of modern cruiser construction, (3) that Britain still clung tenaciously to her sea-power which only a few years ago had been used to the detriment of American commerce, (4) that British and American interests, political and commercial, clashed in every quarter of the globe. While Mr. Charles E. Hughes was Secretary of State[2] this propaganda made but little headway, for he never hesitated to combat it by public speeches and explanations of the Washington treaties and so on. But the advent of Mr. Kellogg meant a change for the worse; instead of a firm and dominating personality at the head of the State Department, there appeared a weak, irritable and not too friendly politician lacking the courage required in the United States to espouse firmly the cause of Anglo-American

[1] A member of the American and African Department of the Foreign Office. This memorandum was circulated to the Cabinet.

[2] 1921–5.

445

friendship. Moreover, the awakening of the United States to their world-wide unpopularity, the attacks of the British press etc., upon the United States war debt repayment policy, and the growing realisation of the average American that the power and resources of his country are well-nigh incalculable, combined together to create the present aggressive and jingo spirit prevalent in the country and particularly in the Government departments at Washington. The attention of the latter is always concentrated upon this country—the leading competitor of the United States politically and commercially.

But what of the future? The shouting of the big-navyites, the rubber controversy,[3] the debt wrangles and so on have all left scars upon the feelings of America towards Britain. At the present time, if it is possible to judge from the press, there is scarcely an American who does not believe that the failure at Geneva must be laid at our door. Many who may have entertained doubts on the subject hardened their hearts when Lord Robert Cecil resigned. It is almost certain that a substantial increase in the naval building programme will be sanctioned by Congress during the next session, during which the coming presidential campaign will give an added incentive to the legislators to strike patriotic and anti-British attitudes. But it is doubtful whether all this will have a permanently bad effect upon the American public unless more fuel, in the shape of further naval disagreements, or anti-American outbursts by the British press on the debt question etc., is heaped upon the fire, now only smouldering. The vast majority of the population are neither militaristic nor imperialistic. They desire firmly to live at peace with the world and to go about their business unhampered by foreign 'entanglements' or disputes. But it is easy to play upon their ignorance, their vociferous patriotism and their latent prejudice against this country. Should we at any time find ourselves involved in serious trouble with some other Power, particularly if the circumstances are such as to call for naval activity, a danger point will have been reached. With the increasing importance attached to their export trade, the United States will not readily suffer the interference which we might consider the situation warranted. This question of the rights of neutrals is being increasingly debated in the United States—and it is perhaps not without significance that the United States Government are not inclined to attach undue importance to the strength of our imperial structure should this be subjected to the sudden strain of a serious Anglo-American quarrel. This we know from Mr. Hoover's admission to Sir Esme Howard that in the event of war between the two countries, he confidently anticipated Canada would declare her neutrality.[4]

G. H. Thompson[5]

[3] For correspondence in 1925–6 regarding requests made on behalf of American manufacturers for relief from British restrictions on the export of raw rubber see *Papers relating to the Foreign Relations of the United States 1925*, vol. ii, pp. 245–67, and *1926*, vol. ii, pp. 358–61.

[4] See Volume III, No. 480.

[5] Sir V. Wellesley minuted on November 17: 'All this points clearly to the need for an early agreement on the subject of blockade which in turn will lead to agreement in regard to naval disarmament. The key to this lies in concessions as regards the right of search. If,

as I strongly suspect, after examination by the competent Auth^ries, the latter turns out to be a wasting asset it will be wise to use it for bargaining purposes before it loses all its value. V.W. 17/11/27.'

No. 228

Memorandum by Mr. Locker Lampson[1]

[*A 6820/133/45*]

Secret   FOREIGN OFFICE, *November 21, 1927*

An agreement with the United States of America in regard to the treatment of private property at sea

There are two major considerations which should be taken into account in dealing with this question.

The first is the change of temper of our people. The influence of the Great War may possibly prove only to have a temporary, although prolonged, effect. It is, however, much more probable that that cataclysm has given birth to quite a new set of ideals, and obliterated another set of ideals which will never be reproduced. Some of the mental decisions in regard to peace and war which have been come to in secret in the recesses of the individual, but which are now being taught and handed down, and which are therefore becoming corporate and national decisions, are probably irreversible, at any rate for a period beyond which it is hardly worth while to look. As a result of this change it is certain that any action which can be construed as jeopardising international peace will henceforth be received with hostility and any obvious lack of endeavour in still further securing that peace will incur the reproach of the vast majority of our population. The delinquency of commission or abstention will be visited upon any British government guilty of it, and the general sympathy of the public, especially of the women, will be for many years, if not for good, on the side of those who discard the very idea of war or even the possibility of war.

This country—and I am only speaking of our own people, is determined to have no more war. It has abandoned the old creed that to avoid war we should prepare for war. It now believes in agreement, in arbitration, in non-provocative give and take, and the feeling is becoming ever more deeply rooted that war is evil, even with the compensating advantages that spoils and glory spelt in the past.

This, I believe, is the temper of our people as a whole, and of course the machinery set up by the League of Nations has, apart from anything psychological, made war more difficult and thrust it into a remoter background.

If all this be true, the condition of mind in which one should approach this question is one in which the notion of actual war by us on a large scale is improbable in the extreme. Unless directly and wantonly attacked, which seems a most unlikely contingency, or unless the League of Nations were

[1] Parliamentary Under Secretary of State for Foreign Affairs.

unanimously committed to some great act of force against a powerful adversary—an almost equally unlikely eventuality—a serious war, so far as we are concerned, would meet with resistance by the great bulk of the nation.

If this on the whole is a faithful presentment of the feelings of the British people, a psychological change that has arisen owing to the Great War, then the case for standing by our rights to deal with private property at sea, as we have done in the past, largely falls to the ground. It falls because public opinion, if there were grave attendant risks of war with the United States, would not allow the right to be exercised. An agreement, on the other hand, such as has been suggested, would eliminate any risk of war with the United States if our Navy were still supreme, a risk which without such an agreement is, in the opinion of those best able to judge, not only probable but almost certain.

The second major consideration relates to the naval power of the United States. If that country should decide to increase its naval strength as against ours, we should within a short space of time lose the command of the seas. It has been argued that the manning of warships, the problem of an inferior discipline and the lack of tradition would present insuperable difficulties for them. It must be remembered, however, that the determination of the United States Government to increase the size of the mercantile marine will give them a reserve of trained man-power on which to draw, and there is little doubt that, if they are determined to get the men and train them properly, they will be able to do so. Nothing is more dangerous than to under-rate a possible opponent. Then what object can there be in trying to preserve the illusion of indestructible sea supremacy, when that supremacy may well be a thing of the past within a few years? There are already signs that the United States may bid for this supremacy and she can easily out-distance us. These are outstanding facts and cannot be gainsaid and they seem to be a sufficient reply to those who take it for granted that in the next great war we should be able to treat private property at sea in the same way as we did in the last.

The reason why an agreement with the United States of America is important is therefore, not only because we do not wish to risk a war with them, nor so much because we desire to preserve a free hand in dealing with private property at sea in the future, as that we want to prevent the United States from themselves having a free hand as soon as their naval power becomes greater than ours. Looking to the future and taking it for granted, as we must do, that within a measurable time they will be the paramount naval Power, it is much more important that American claims should be limited by agreement than that we should nominally maintain our claims and yet in practice be unable to assert them, whilst the United States by that time would be able to assert any they chose to make.

The stronger the navy of the United States becomes the less ready will they be to make any agreement, and *pari passu* the less effective in practice will our own claims become. The rights, belligerent or neutral, claimed by the United States would, in the absence of an agreement, be in fact proportionate to their naval power and this, I think, is the answer to Sir Cecil Hurst's argument.[2]

[2] See Annex II to No. 224.

The past practice of the United States has shown that as a belligerent they are prepared to put forward extreme claims in the matter of interference with neutral commerce, while, when themselves neutral, they appear as the foremost champions of the rights of neutrals. Such inconsistencies have been observable in the past history of other naval Powers, but more especially in that of the United States.

The advantage, therefore, of early negotiations for an agreement is that they are more likely to be successful if early. There are also two subsidiary advantages; one is that such negotiations would take place in a comparatively calm atmosphere before the American election campaign was fully launched. The other is that, if the negotiations were successful, an agreement would materialise and be made public before our own General Election. Such an agreement would make a strong impression upon the mind of the electorate. It would be further evidence of our determination to promote peace in the world, an important factor now that the female vote is being increased,[3] and it would obviously be the forerunner of reduced naval programmes in the future.

It may be urged that the United States are so unpopular at present over here that any attempt to come to an agreement with them that had too much the appearance of a concession would give rise to criticism. But as against this the profound desire for peace already referred to would, in the mind of the average elector, far outweigh any disinclination towards such an agreement arising from a feeling of personal dislike of Americans or their Government, for, while the unpopularity persists, it is always a menace and possible source of serious friction.

The failure of the Geneva Naval Conference was undoubtedly due to the formidable questions of contraband and blockade which lurked in the background all the time, although they were never mentioned. Once got rid of, and [sic] the difficulty of easing the burden of naval taxation on both sides of the Atlantic would be greatly diminished.

In the absence of an early agreement what is there to hope for or look forward to?—

(a) An alteration to our disadvantage in the relative naval strength of the two countries.

(b) A consequent and growing disinclination on the part of the United States to deprive themselves of any weapon in their naval armoury.

(c) A gradual diminution of our own chances of being able to assert our claims without bringing America into a war against us.

(d) The maintenance of a comparatively weaker, but still illogically expensive navy, and the consequent unnecessary burden upon the taxpayer.

[3] Mr. Baldwin had announced in the House of Commons on April 13, 1927, the intention of H.M. Government to introduce a bill to reduce the voting age for women from 30 to 21 years: see *Parl. Debs.*, *5th ser.*, *H. of C.*, vol. 205, cols. 358–60. The bill was introduced on March 12, 1928, and became law on July 2 as Representation of the People (Equal Franchise) Act, 1928 (18 & 19 Geo. 5, c. 12).

(e) The growing sense of disillusionment and disappointment in the country in face of a national policy, at once extravagant, ineffective and dangerous.

For all these reasons and with all due respect to those learned in the law and history of the subject who have compiled the memoranda against an agreement—memoranda which at first sight may seem to be convincing—I believe that it would be throwing away an unique opportunity if, while there is yet time, we did not take steps to see how far the United States may be persuaded to commit themselves with us to some new and friendly arrangement.

Hitherto, so it seems to me, we have been inclined to deal with the United States from a wrong angle. We have treated them too much as blood relations, not sufficiently as a foreign country: and meeting them as blood relations we have been surprised, disappointed and irritated by the differences that exist between us, differences of character and temperament, and this has created antagonisms on their side and on ours.[4] If we had met them and dealt with them more in the ordinary way as foreigners, as indeed they now are, we should have expected dissimilarities and found them, but we should also have observed and felt approximations, and the result would have been that our relations with them would have been better and on a more friendly footing than they are to-day. For jealousies and differences are apt to be all the sharper between members of the same family and sects of the same creed. The Americans are not just Englishmen living in another Continent. They are differently constituted and their habits, feelings, up-bringing, outlook and ideals are not identical. Therefore it is a mistake to treat them as such and to expect identity. So far as this country is concerned, they are largely foreigners, and will not hesitate, should the occasion arise and it suits their purpose, to prove it. The fact that there are some Americans who are sensible of their British origin should not blind us to the fact that the vast majority are not.

G. L. L.

[4] Sir A. Chamberlain minuted in the margin against the two preceding sentences: 'Very true. A.C.'

No. 229

Report of the Cabinet Committee on Policy for Reduction and Limitation of Armaments[1]

*C.P. 293 (27) [W 11069/61/98]**

2 WHITEHALL GARDENS, *November 23, 1927*

The forthcoming proceedings of the Preparatory Commission at Geneva will probably not go far into the discussion of Disarmament. There are only

[1] The filed copy is the revised text of this report as amended and approved by the Cabinet on November 24, 1927. This report was signed by Lord Salisbury, the Lord Privy Seal, Chairman of the Committee, whose other members were Sir L. Worthington-Evans, Secretary of State for War, Sir S. Hoare, Secretary of State for Air, Mr. W. C. Bridgeman, First Lord of the Admiralty, Lord Cushendun and Sir D. Hogg. Mr. Cadogan was joint secretary to the Committee.

four days available at this meeting before the stage is required for the Council itself, and the Preparatory Commission may be expected to be mainly occupied in establishing a Sub-Committee upon Security which was ordered by the last Assembly. But though it is likely that the substantial discussion will be postponed to the early part of next year we cannot be altogether sure that this will be the case. We have some reason to think that our representatives will be confronted with a combination of German and Russian delegates in opposition to France and her friends; we know that the Germans complain of the delay in pushing forward general disarmament; and through the action of the combination to which we have referred this grievance might precipitate a discussion of the merits.[2] Our representatives must therefore not be left without instructions as to the policy of His Majesty's Government.

In the first place, our representatives will realise that we have no reason to regret the introduction of the Security issues into the deliberations of the Committee. Though we are not ourselves able to go very far on these lines, yet they have our warmest sympathy. Moreover, they are likely at the moment to present fewer difficulties than the Disarmament issues themselves. The Committee recommend that if occasion arises our representatives should be guided by the knowledge that, although in the view of the British Government agreement as to the reduction and limitation of armaments does not depend upon a prior settlement as to Security, they have no desire to postpone consideration of matters relating to this vital subject.

As will be seen in the Foreign Office Memorandum, which with the Foreign Secretary's Minute is annexed to this report (Annex 1[3]), the Assembly formulated the reference to the Preparatory Commission upon Security in four propositions. The language of the League of Nations is always obscure, and your Committee therefore have done their best to extract from these propositions in plain English the issues that arise, to divide them into heads, and to submit their recommendations in each case to the Cabinet.

I.—*Promotion of Arbitration and Security Agreements*

The Committee suggest that His Majesty's Government would not be prepared to enlarge the scope of their arbitration agreements beyond the limits which have generally been observed in their existing agreements of this nature. It should be explained that this attitude is dictated to us by the peculiar position of the British Empire. The acceptance, for example, by us of the optional clause by which all justiciable issues are necessarily referred

---

[2] Lord Cushendun had recorded on November 14 that these apprehensions had been expressed to him that day by the French Ambassador who feared a complete breakdown of disarmament negotiations. M. de Fleuriau suspected that this was the desire of the Germans, who would then appeal to the Preamble of Part V of the Treaty of Versailles as giving them a moral right to rearm. The French Ambassador then went on to discuss land armaments and dwelt at length on the difference between the British voluntarily-enlisted army and the French conscripted army which, in his opinion, was a more democratic institution and an inseparable part of republican France.

[3] Annex 1 comprised No. 219.

to the Permanent Court of International Justice, or of a similar clause in bilateral agreements with other Countries, would have to be conditioned by so many reservations as to make the agreement worthless. In the view of the Committee it is clear that disputes arising out of naval belligerent action would have to be reserved. Also, not merely any matter affecting inter-Imperial relations between the Dominions and the Mother Country, or between the Dominions themselves, must be reserved, but until we have received their consent any matter which might react at all upon the internal or external affairs of any of the self-governing Dominions. On this head we are bound by the resolution at the last Imperial Conference.[4] Lastly, there must be a general reservation in regard to those disputes which touch the vital interests, independence and honour, of the State. The truth is that in vital matters we can bind the British Government but we cannot bind the British Parliament in whom, of course, ultimately the power rests. We could not deliver the goods. Such reservations would in our case rob of any real significance any general reference of justiciable issues. These difficulties, however, do not all present themselves to other Countries. It is true that the consideration of vital interests, independence and honour, is of general application, but it may well be that to some Countries the advantages secured by a general arbitration agreement in justiciable issues are so obvious and so important that they may outweigh the risks incurred, especially in the case of those States the defence problems of which are relatively simple. In the general interests of arbitration, therefore, the British representatives should be ready to help forward any Country which is anxious to adopt this method of dealing with international disputes, though obviously care must be taken that they do not use language which may hereafter hamper the Government in resisting political pressure at home to secure the adoption by this Country of the Optional Clause. Broadly speaking, wherever it is feasible our vote should always be cast on the side of arbitration, and where, as in our own case, it is not possible to go very far in that direction, every method of conciliation, as distinguished from arbitration—such, for example, as are contemplated in the Locarno Treaty—should be eagerly embraced.

Political disputes present even greater difficulties than justiciable issues. The Committee are not able to advise any support to the opening of an optional general convention for the arbitration of political disputes on the lines suggested by Dr. Nansen. If this Country were to advocate such a proposal it would be difficult for us to resist the suggestion that we should avail ourselves of it in our own disputes; and I need not say that the objections to such a course on political questions would be far stronger than in respect of the justiciable issues which the Committee have just discussed. There is something to be said, however, for a model draft, on Dr. Nansen's lines, not of a general convention but of a bilateral treaty, which might be useful for all those Countries who wished to make such bilateral treaties, and would prevent them from including undesirable provisions in these instruments, as

[4] See Section Vc of the report of the Inter-Imperial Relations Committee adopted by the Conference on November 19, 1926, printed in Cmd. 2768 of 1926, pp. 25–6.

has often been the case hitherto. Notably the reference of political questions to the International Court is mischievous not merely because that Court is not equipped for the purpose, but what is much more important, the employment of a judicial tribunal for the settlement of disputes incapable of judicial treatment must have a demoralising effect upon the Court.

II.—*Development of the Machinery of the League to enable Members to Perform the Obligations of the Covenant*

The Committee recommend that His Majesty's Government as at present advised should not be prepared to develop any further the policy of sanctions under Article 16 of the Covenant. It follows, of course, *à fortiori* that they would not be prepared to undertake anything beyond our obligations under the Covenant, except in so far as we are committed—very properly committed—under the Locarno Treaty.

III.—*Promotion of Treaties on the Locarno Model in Other Regions*

Here, again, in the view of the Committee, we ought not to enter into any further obligations on Locarno lines. But our representatives should urge other Powers to follow the example which we have set and should help forward as far as possible 'Locarno Treaties' in other regions.

IV.—*Finnish Scheme of Financial Guarantees*

There remains amongst the proposals for the promotion of security the Finnish scheme under which a guarantee of financial assistance is provided for a member of the League who may be the victim of unjust aggression. The guarantee is double. There is a primary guarantee divided amongst the members of the League according to a certain scale, and there is a super-guarantee allocated amongst certain selected wealthy Powers. The Committee recommend that the problem should be treated on the lines indicated to the Council by the Foreign Secretary at the meeting held on the 8th September of this year.[5] But as to the details, the Chancellor of the Duchy of Lancaster has been asked to consult the Treasury and be guided by the decision of that Department.[6]

V.—*Disarmament Proper*

As we have said in this report, in existing circumstances we should be glad if the discussion of the issues involved in Disarmament proper could be postponed. But if they are unavoidable, then we recommend that the representatives of the British Government should be guided by the following

[5] Cf. *League of Nations Official Journal*, October 1927, p. 1127.
[6] In a memorandum of November 18 Lord Cushendun stated that he had discussed the Finnish proposal with a Treasury official. He explained that His Majesty's Government would not have to guarantee more than £12·5 millions and concluded: 'I have satisfied myself that this scheme is not likely to involve H.M. Government in responsibility for further immense war debts of other countries; and that it has more substance than most other edifices of peace.'

instructions. The Committee have been informed by the First Lord of the Admiralty that at the Coolidge Conference although the American representatives did not show themselves very favourable to the British proposals as to capital ships, yet these particular proposals were not included in the total tonnage controversy under which in the event the conference ultimately broke down. Your Committee are of opinion that these British proposals as to capital ships are so important both for the cause of peace and for the cause of economy that they ought to be specially mentioned by our representatives at the Preparatory Commission. The Committee are, however, acutely conscious of the objections to running the risk of reviving the naval controversy with the United States at the present moment. It is evident that anything like renewed friction would be used with most unfortunate results in the course of the Presidential Election which is pending, and they would have been glad if the whole thing could be allowed to sleep for a few months. But as that is impossible they consider that at any rate controversy should be avoided, and they realise that once embarked upon the total tonnage problem of craft other than capital ships and upon the question of 8-inch gun cruisers controversy must necessarily follow. They recommend therefore that our representatives should state the Admiralty proposals as set forth in their Memorandum which is annexed (Annex 2[7]), with special mention of the scheme for the reduction of capital ships, but the controversial questions to which we have just referred should not be pressed against opposition. The recent announcement of the modification in our naval programme[8] should of course be mentioned as evidence of the spirit in which we are pursuing the cause of disarmament, but the fact of this announcement will speak for itself, and in the main perhaps it is better that it should be left to speak for itself rather than that it should be liable to be represented as merely a dexterous move in the diplomatic struggle.

Turning from Naval to Military disarmament, the Committee is confronted with the position assumed by the representatives of France that they will not agree that Reserves should be included in the limitation of effectives. It is difficult to see how any real progress can be made in military disarmament so long as that position is maintained. At any rate, it is likely to be hotly contested, both by the German and the Russian delegation[s], acting, perhaps, as has already been suggested in this report, according to some arrangement of co-operation. It is almost unnecessary to say that, in the view of the Committee the British representatives should avoid being ranged publicly on the side of this coalition against the French. Something, however, they might do by private negotiation with representatives of France, and in any case, although not publicly siding against France, they must not surrender the British view against the French attitude on this question, since if a breakdown

[7] This memorandum of November 18 is not printed.
[8] For the announcement by Mr. Bridgeman on November 16 that in the light of the situation disclosed at the Geneva Conference it had been decided not to proceed with the construction of two cruisers in the 1927–8 programme, see *Parl. Debs.*, *5th ser.*, *H. of C.*, vol. 210, col. 1013.

of the conference should become inevitable, it might be well that the failure should be found to have occurred upon this issue rather than on any point of naval disarmament.

As regards Air disarmament, the Committee find that agreement has already been reached at the Preparatory Commission as to the unit of comparison for Air Forces,[9] and they have every hope that an accord could be come to in respect of this Service. They suggest that future progress should be sought by means of diplomatic conversation, initiated at such times as the Foreign Secretary may think fit, with a view of arriving at a measure of equality as between the Air Forces of Great Britain, France and Italy.

There is one further expedient the discussion of which the Committee has reserved to the last because, at any rate in theory, it is applicable to each of the three Services. This is the proposal by international agreement for a budgetary limitation upon expenditure. The Committee have found the Secretary of State for War and his advisers resolutely opposed to any such limitation upon expenditure upon *matériel*. If the limitation included all expenditure, whether upon personnel or *matériel*, the Secretary of State has gone so far as to consider it less objectionable than any other disarmament device in its application to our already depleted Army. But the other Services would not accord this expedient, even that very moderate form of approval. The objections are, indeed, very formidable:—

(*a.*) Owing to the differences between the rates of pay between conscript and voluntary forces, no medium of comparison can be secured.

(*b.*) It is not possible to forecast developments both within each of the Services themselves, and also as to the assumption of duties by one Service in substitution for another.

(*c.*) The organisation of the three Services is not the same in all countries, e.g. Great Britain and Italy only have separate Air Forces.

(*d.*) Any system of budgetary limitation would be susceptible of misrepresentation to the detriment of Great Britain.

(*e.*) In fixing the limit, so large a margin would be necessary as to render the figure comparatively useless. There would also be an uneconomical tendency to build up to the limit imposed.

The Committee are not able, therefore, to recommend any proposal of budgetary limitation. They would point out, however, that the Cabinet have already assented to a proposal that a formal declaration of intended expenditure in each year should be made at Geneva for each of the fighting Services. Such a declaration would, indeed, not be binding even for the particular year to which it was applicable, but if the form of financial statement were settled and was not varied from year to year, the Council would become aware of any large increase under any head which might be specified, and this

[9] The Preparatory Commission had agreed that the main method of limiting air forces should be the limiting of military aircraft by numbers and total horse-power: see Volume III, Nos. 140 and 160, and Cmd. 2888 of 1927, p. 6.

knowledge might act as a check upon any indefensible excess, or at any rate as a warning to the rest of the world.

To sum up, the attitude of our representatives should, in the Committee's view, be to promote arbitration wherever it is possible and conciliation in every case: to advocate the following of the example of the Western Powers in concluding agreements upon the Locarno model wherever the circumstances make such a course practicable; to support the Finnish scheme of financial guarantee; to state once more, though without controversy, our naval proposals, putting in the forefront the proposed reduction in the size and power of capital ships; to use our influence with the French Government to make military disarmament practicable; and to confirm the international agreement, so far as it has been reached, upon the Air Forces, with a view to establishing a basis of equality between the principal Air Powers of Europe.

Signed on behalf of the Committee,

SALISBURY (*Chairman*)

No. 230

Mr. London (Geneva) to Sir A. Chamberlain (Received December 2, 9 a.m.)
No. 279 L.N. Telegraphic [Telegrams 47/15]

GENEVA, December 1, 1927, 10.50 p.m.

Following from Lord Cushendun:—

'Press have no doubt already given full details of the actual proceedings in the Preparatory Committee and Security Committee.[1]

'It seems generally agreed that at the present session committee cannot do more than occupy themselves with preliminaries.

'Preparatory Committee, after hearing Russian declaration[2] and constituting Security Committee, has done practically all that it can do.

'Security Committee will try to-morrow to draw up more or less detailed programme of subjects. It will probably charge specially appointed *rapporteurs* with study of these subjects in conjunction with the secretary with a view to submitting definite proposals at the next session.

'There remains the question of the date of next session of both committees. German delegate yesterday insisted that some date should be fixed for Preparatory Committee at least one month before March Council. This was at the time accepted in principle. Since then, however, the idea has gradually asserted itself that Security Committee must meet *before* Preparatory Committee. That would mean meeting of Security Committee in January, but preliminary work could not be completed by then.

'Part 2 following.

[1] The minutes of the fourth session of the Preparatory Commission for the Disarmament Conference (November 30–December 3, 1927) and of the first session of its Committee on Arbitration and Security (December 1–2, 1927) are printed in League of Nations, *Documents of the Preparatory Commission for the Disarmament Conference*, Series V (Geneva 1928).

[2] *V. ibid.*, pp. 9–12 and 30–3.

'(Part 2.)

'In conversation with the French delegate this morning we agreed that the Security Committee might be summoned two or three weeks before the March Council, say, 20th February, and that the Preparatory Committee might meet immediately after the Council. M. Boncour explained to me that that was the latest possible date, as, owing to the French elections, he could not be absent from France much after the end of March.

'I impressed upon him the danger of summoning another session for the second reading of the draft convention[3] unless we could see some better prospect of reaching agreement, and I also confessed to him the reluctance I should feel in being perhaps forced into supporting the Germans and Russians against the French on certain points. He quite understood, and, speaking confidentially, said that if, when the time approached, we did not see our way to agree, we must find an excuse—and he was confident that one could be found—for further adjournment. That would mean, owing to the French elections, till July. But he emphasised that this must remain a private understanding between us; it would be impossible now to adjourn till July, and public opinion (by which I suppose he meant his constituents) would demand a date at least as early as March.[4]

'I saw the German delegate this afternoon, and I think that he will agree to the above programme, so that I do not anticipate serious objections from any quarter.'

[3] The text of the draft disarmament convention as drawn up at the first reading in March–April 1927 is printed in Cmd. 2888 of 1927, pp. 27–50.

[4] In a letter of December 9 to Sir A. Chamberlain regarding this conversation Lord Cushendun further reported: 'I represented to Boncour that, relatively speaking, France, owing to her present day military condition and the disarmament of Germany, was in a far more powerful position than she occupied in 1914. She had also considerably added to her security by the conclusion of many treaties, and, above all, by the Locarno pact, which secured for her a powerful guarantee of her Eastern frontier. This condition of France was a powerful and plausible argument which both Germans and Russians would unmercifully use in the forthcoming disarmament conferences in order to place France in a very awkward and invidious position vis-à-vis of world opinion, which was steadily moving in the direction of reduction of armaments. If, therefore, we were to escape from such a position, it seemed to me essential that England and France should agree on a joint programme which could show an appreciable contribution towards a reduction in armed forces. It has occurred to me that my arguments with Boncour would be considerably reinforced if you could see your way to enlist Briand on our side and get him to pour some water into Boncour's wine and urge him to work in the closest co-operation with me when next we meet at Geneva.' For Sir A. Chamberlain's conversation with M. Briand on December 11 see No. 91.

No. 231

Letter from Sir W. Tyrrell to Sir E. Howard (Washington)

[*A 6746/133/45*]

Private and secret   FOREIGN OFFICE, *December 2, 1927*

My dear Howard,

The Secretary of State was most interested in your letter of November 10th[1] and agrees with what you say about the advisability of taking action on the question of belligerent rights at sea without undue delay. At the same time he wishes you to be under no misapprehension as to the formidable character of the arguments that may be advanced against any agreement with the United States on this subject. In this connexion, Sir Austen desires that you should be furnished for your personal and strictly confidential information with the three enclosed memoranda[2] which will give you some indication of the obstacles which lie in the way of any such agreement.

The present position is that a Committee is to be formed to go carefully into the whole question. While the Secretary of State cannot hope for a rapid decision on issues of such gravity and extent, you will be kept informed of all developments.[3]

[1] See No. 205, note 3.
[2] Not attached to filed copy. The reference was possibly to Nos. 218, 224, and the annex to No. 226. In his reply (No. 241) Sir E. Howard commented in particular on the annex to No. 216 (cf. No. 218, note 4) and appendix II to No. 224.
[3] Signature lacking from filed copy.

No. 232

Record by Mr. Cadogan (Geneva) of a conversation with Major Abraham[1]

[*W 11475/61/98*]

GENEVA, *December 5, 1927*

I had a conversation to-day with Major Abraham of the League Secretariat on the subject of the programme of the Security Committee.

It will be remembered that M. Rutgers, the Netherlands representative, was appointed *rapporteur* on the subject of the articles of the Covenant,[2] and he has requested Major Abraham and his Section to assist him in the preparatory work.

Major Abraham seemed rather at a loss to know what form this should take; he had discussed the matter with M. Rutgers, who had apparently only undertaken the work with some reluctance and who was rather apprehensive of the responsibility devolving upon him. The articles which are

[1] This record was received in the Foreign Office on December 10 under cover of Geneva despatch No. 38 L.N.C. (not preserved in Foreign Office archives). Major Abraham was a member of the Political Section of the League of Nations.
[2] See *Documents of the Preparatory Commission for the Disarmament Conference*, Series V, pp. 45–54, for the appointment of the *rapporteurs* by the Committee on Arbitration and Security.

specially mentioned are articles 10, 11 and 16. Article 10 raises, or might raise, the whole question of the definition of an aggressor, and in regard to this Major Abraham is fully informed of our misgivings and objections. I referred him to the Secretary of State's recent speech in the House of Commons and to M. Scialoja's speech at the Assembly to which Sir A. Chamberlain had referred.[3] I suggested that the most that M. Rutgers could do would be to make a historical summary of the question. For instance, he might begin by referring to the Assembly resolutions of 1921 in regard to Article 16 of the Covenant,[4] which require the Council to decide that a Member of the League has broken the Covenant and resorted to war. If this duty devolves on the Council, the latter must evidently have some rule to guide it. It would be necessary to examine the various suggestions that have been made, culminating, of course, in the Geneva Protocol of 1924, with regard to the means of determining an aggressor. At the same time, if these were quoted, it would be necessary in all fairness to refer also the various objections which have been raised to the several proposals. Beyond that, I did not see that any definite suggestion or recommendation could be made as there was evidently a difference of opinion amongst the Members of the League. Major Abraham quite agreed, though he referred to the fact that the Security Committee, or various members of it, had insisted on the necessity of producing concrete and practical proposals which would increase the sense of security in Europe. I agreed that this was certainly the case but I suggested that this was hardly M. Rutgers' business. He had really only been charged with preparing the work and it must be for the Security Committee itself to make definite proposals. Lord Cushendun had been anxious that the *rapporteurs*, in drawing up their reports, should not prejudge the questions or do anything to commit us to any particular view, and in the course of one of his speeches at the Committee he had given expression to this view.

Passing on to Article 11, we agreed that all the useful work that could be done on this topic had already been done by the Committee which met in London in February last and whose report had been approved by the Council.[5]

As regards Article 16, Major Abraham was aware of our difficulties and of the danger to the League itself of forcing us into a position in which we should have to raise them and he assured me that he for his part would do everything possible to avoid an 'elaboration of this article'.

He told me that M. Rutgers had had a conversation with Dr. Benes[6] in which the former had expressed his reluctance to make any definite recommendations. Dr. Benes had, however, said that it was obviously the duty of the *rapporteurs* to make definite proposals and that such would have to be

---

[3] See *Parl. Debs., 5th ser., H. of C.*, vol. 210, cols. 2101–6, for Sir A. Chamberlain's speech on November 24. For M. Scialoja's speech on September 9, cf. No. 5, note 4.

[4] These resolutions in regard to the amendment of article 16 of the Covenant are printed in League of Nations, *Records of the Second Assembly: Plenary Meetings*, vol. i, pp. 806, 807–8, 812, and 814.

[5] See No. 219, note 14.

[6] Dr. Benes was Chairman of the Committee on Arbitration and Security.

submitted to the Security Committee. I doubt whether M. Rutgers will go as far as this, but apparently the intention is that when the *rapporteurs* have made their first draft, there will be a meeting in Prague, probably towards the end of January, under the presidency of Dr. Benes, at which the reports will be collated and put into their final form, and I suspect that if at that time Dr. Benes finds that the reports are colourless he will himself devise all kinds of proposals and recommendations.

It may, therefore, be worth while considering whether in the course of January we should get into touch with Dr. Benes and warn him of the various dangers of raising some of the more acute points of difference.

Major Abraham told me in confidence that the French had made themselves very tiresome in connection with the procedure; and M. Paul Boncour had tried his best to secure that all three *rapporteurs* should be genuine and loyal adherents of the Protocol. He has succeeded in getting one—M. Politis —appointed and it took about an hour to get him to agree to the appointment of M. Rutgers.

I told Major Abraham that he might expect to receive from the British Government by January 1st written statements of their point of view on the various questions involved, and I suggested that these might be of assistance in drawing up the reports.[7]

A. CADOGAN

[7] Attached to Mr. Cadogan's record was the following copy of a minute by Sir A. Chamberlain to Lord Cushendun: 'As regards Article 16, it is to be remembered that it was this Article which at Locarno proved to be Germany's greatest stumbling block. The difficulty was solved by the 'formule du bateau' [i.e. the collective note to Germany printed in Cmd. 2525, annex F, drafted on a boat trip on October 10, 1925] which is worth referring to. Germany will not sign the Protocol or any extension of her engagements. If blockade is required and we are asked to enforce it against a dissenting U.S.A. we shall have to plead "geographical position" and insufficiency of means. A.C. 6.12.'

No. 233

Sir A. Chamberlain (Geneva) to Sir W. Tyrrell (Received December 12)
No. 43 L.N.C. [W 11527/61/98]

GENEVA, *December 10, 1927*

The British Delegate to the League of Nations presents his compliments and has the honour to transmit a copy of a Memorandum which Colonel Temperley[1] has sent to Lord Cushendun recording a conversation with Colonel Réquin, French Military representative at Geneva, on disarmament questions.

[1] Military representative on the British Delegation to the League of Nations.

Record by Colonel Temperley of a conversation with Colonel Réquin

Copy

GENEVA, *December 7, 1927*

Lord Cushendun

Colonel Réquin, French military representative at Geneva, asked me if I would talk over some disarmament questions with him. I replied that I had no fresh instructions and had no authority to speak officially, but should be glad to hear his views. He commenced by saying that his government could never even discuss the limitation of trained reserves, as they were the vital factor in their national defence, and that the French could sign no convention which touched them in any way. I replied that I quite understood their point but that our attitude on the question was much misunderstood. We were not trying to disarm continental countries. We had simply arrived at the conclusion that a limitation of trained reserves was essential to any genuine scheme of disarmament. If any state found itself unable to reduce its armed forces, it could explain its reasons to the Disarmament Conference. This was a political question; we were now only concerned with technical methods of limitation.

Colonel Réquin then said that our two conceptions of disarmament were totally different. The French thought only of peace, while we were concerned with war. The French idea was to reduce the personal burden of service and of expenditure in time of peace but to retain in war the power to use the whole strength of the nation. I said that this was all very well, but we regarded disarmament primarily as a means of reducing the forces available for aggression in war and thereby reducing the chances of war breaking out, which was much more important. If the annual contingent were limited, it would fulfil the French idea of reducing the personal burden as well as our idea of ultimately reducing the numbers available for war, and then we should both be satisfied. We then passed to a discussion of the draft Convention.[2]

I said that the definition in Article A of effectives was very unsatisfactory, as the number of effectives was purely arbitrary as different states had different views as to the period of training necessary to fit the men for immediate employment. I suggested that all that was necessary to say[3] 'who are under the colours' or some such phrase and ignore their degree of training. He agreed that this would be simpler and was what the French delegation really intended. He promised to discuss this with the general staff.

He then brought up the period of service in Article I. He said that if conscript armies were to be pledged not to raise their period of service, voluntary armies should not be allowed to reduce their service in order to create reserves. I reminded him that the German period of service was already fixed by treaty, and I did not suppose he felt anxious about the

---

[2] See No. 230, note 3.
[3] The text appears to be incomplete.

461

British and American armies. I also said that there might be many reasons for reducing the period of service in voluntary armies quite unconnected with the idea of creating reserves.

He then remarked that the French could never accept the German proposal in Article TA for direct limitation of material. It was a question of disclosing the secrets of mobilisation and, however regrettable it might be that there should still be secrets, the time had not yet arrived when we could afford to dispense with them. I said I thought the strongest argument against the German proposal was that used by Monsieur Paul Boncour, who said that it would be perfectly useless unless accompanied by a supervision more rigorous than any state could possibly accept in the full exercise of its sovereignty. I said that we had the gravest doubts as to the possibility of this proposal.

He then said that he was coming to the conclusion that limitation of budgets was really useless and that some striking examples of its uselessness were given at the last discussions of the Preparatory Commission.

He really thought that publicity was the only effective method of dealing with budgets. I said that he was aware that we had long ago come to that conclusion, however attractive budgetary limitation might be in theory.

I then asked him whether the French views on supervision had undergone any change, as it was clear that we could never accept their proposals[4] and that no other Great Power had seen its way to do so. He said that they recognised this and thought that they would be able to accept something less, in the same way that we might do so as regards effectives, since they could not go as far as we wanted in that direction. Monsieur Paul Boncour would not, he thought, abandon his principle, but he could say that for a first step in disarmament and at the first Conference such supervision as we proposed might be sufficient. If, however, at subsequent conferences more detailed methods of disarmament were introduced, then more detailed supervision would be required.

Colonel Réquin then reminded me that Count Bernstorff had said that he would not sign any convention which did not limit trained reserves and material in reserve.[5] He did not see why Germany's failure to sign the Convention should render it null and void. Germany was already disarmed by treaty and it was only a courtesy that she was asked to take part in the discussions. He was doubtless referring to Article 13 of the British draft,[6] which made ratification by all Great Powers (including Germany) necessary to bring the Convention into force. I did not feel called upon to comment on his remarks.

The upshot of it all appears to be that the French are prepared to give way about supervision, to give up limitation of budgets, but to stand firm about

[4] For British views on the proposals on supervision in the French draft disarmament convention of March 22, 1927, see Volume III, Nos. 67 and 85. See also *op. cit.*, No. 43.

[5] For Count Bernstorff's remarks to the Preparatory Commission on March 28, 1927, see *Documents of the Preparatory Commission for the Disarmament Commission*, Series IV, pp. 60–1.

[6] Cf. No. 219, note 6.

trained reserves. He made no suggestions about limiting material and, as our position is so weak in this respect, I left it alone.

I have always been on very friendly terms with Colonel Réquin and the conversation was quite open and frank.

A. C. TEMPERLEY

No. 234

Sir E. Howard (Washington) to Sir A. Chamberlain
(Received December 16, 9 a.m.)

No. 526 Telegraphic [A 7258/93/45]

WASHINGTON, December 15, 1927, 9.5 p.m.

The Washington Post of December 11th publishes an article respecting elevation of guns on United States battleships charging that His Majesty's Government had 'suggested' to State Department that elevation of big guns would be contrary to the spirit of the Washington treaty *after* British Admiralty themselves had increased the range of guns on certain battleships. Article continues that His Majesty's Government relies on the spirit of the treaty in the matter of gun elevation though the spirit of the treaty had no deterrent effect on them in increasing cruisers. It then declares 'Lord Balfour's clear statement that the spirit of the treaty contemplated application of 5–5–3 ratio to all vessels[1] was ignored by British government which began to build 10,000-ton cruisers immediately after the treaty was signed'.

In a further article today the same paper commenting on the new naval programme[2] says in the same vein that United States five years ago scrapped the finest battleships in existence 'relying on expressed assurance of other Powers that they would respect the spirit of the Washington treaty which contemplated substantial equality of naval power in all classes of vessels so far as Great Britain and United States were concerned. Japan was to maintain a fleet 3/5's as strong. But immediately after arms treaty had been signed both Great Britain and Japan began to construct 10,000-ton cruisers which were not included in limitation applied to battleships.'

Further on article says 'the spirit of the Washington treaty has been violated. United States has been put on notice that it cannot depend upon Great Britain to co-operate for naval limitation.'

Article then goes on to say that when His Majesty's Government discovered that they had made a blunder at Geneva an immediate and strenuous

---

[1] Cf., however, Volume III, No. 427. Lord Balfour had been the principal British delegate to the Washington Conference of 1921–2. The Washington Treaty for the Limitation of Naval Armament provided in particular for limitations in respect of capital ships and aircraft carriers. In the case of the United States, the British Empire, and Japan the figures for capital ship replacement tonnage and total tonnage for aircraft carriers were in the ratio 5:5:3, with proportional limitations for France and Italy.

[2] On December 14, the U.S. Secretary of the Navy, Mr. C. D. Wilbur, had presented to Congress a bill (H.R. 7359) for a naval building programme of 71 ships, including five aircraft carriers and twenty-five light cruisers.

463

campaign was begun to dissuade United States from increasing the size of its navy. British spokesmen were sent over to preach Anglo-American love and affection and the First Lord found it convenient to announce that only one cruiser would be laid down this year instead of three.[3]

It quotes that section of President's message to Congress dealing with naval construction (see my telegram No. 511[4]) and says that after this open rebuke there has been a welcome shrinkage in the stream of mingled slush, mush and gush poured over America by British propagandists. I pointed out to Secretary of State and Mr. Castle the unnecessarily irritating effect of this useless and cuckoo-like repetition of the charges repeatedly denied [devised][5] against His Majesty's Government of bad faith and of violation of Washington Treaty. Both agreed that this was much to be deplored but feared that nothing could be done with the owner of the Washington Post. I said I thought that if the Secretary of the Navy were to signify his disapproval it might have some effect.

This afternoon Mr. Castle telephoned to me that Secretary of State had spoken to the Secretary of the Navy and that the latter had consented to speak to the owner of the Washington Post while Secretary of State would himself speak to the editor. I asked him to thank Secretary of State.

[3] See No. 229, note 8.

[4] This telegram of December 6 is not printed. President Coolidge's message to Congress of the same day is printed in *Papers relating to the Foreign Relations of the United States 1927*, vol. i, pp. v–xxv.

[5] Amendment supplied from text in Washington Embassy archives) (F.O. 115/3213).

No. 235

Letter from Mr. Selby to Lord Cushendun

[F.O. 800/261]

FOREIGN OFFICE, *December 15, 1927*

Dear Lord Cushendun,

The Secretary of State thinks it would be useful if I were to record to you briefly two conversations which I had with the Italian naval representative on the Disarmament Conference of last year who was also there for the meeting which you attended—Ruspoli, and the Finnish representative Dr. Holsti, who is to be Rapporteur of the Arbitration and Security Committee.

Count Ruspoli was quite explicit in his view that a larger measure of disarmament would already have been achieved in Europe but for the fact that the Disarmament Conference was impending, of the outcome of which no one had any certainty. The effect of this was to induce individual nations to retain rather larger forces than they would otherwise do in the fear that they might be called upon to make a contribution to disarmament which would jeopardise their national security. Count Ruspoli said he had heard it suggested that, if at the forthcoming conference there was a failure to fix a proportion of armed forces to be maintained by the various nations, a proposal might be made to stabilise the position on the basis of existing armaments.

The Italian Government would be compelled to reject any such proposal for the reason that Italy had already reduced her armaments beyond the limits of national safety. Her army at the present moment did not exceed 136,000 men, while her navy was equally reduced. The question for Italy was rather an increase of her armed forces to enable her to compete with those powers with whom she might come into conflict.

Italy must be at liberty to maintain forces in Europe at least equivalent to other powers, such as France. The French army was, at the moment, very largely in excess of the Italian and a stabilisation of the two armies on the existing basis would place Italy in an impossibly disadvantageous position. So far as the Navy was concerned Italy must maintain the right to at least a one power standard, leaving us, the United States and Japan out of account. The Italian Government were perfectly prepared to agree to a limitation of tonnage on this basis and even to a limitation of the largest size of ship which might be constructed within the tonnage agreed upon, but they could never agree to any limitation by classes, as this would simply involve Italy in building a larger number of small cruisers that [*sic*] she could afford. Count Ruspoli said that four-fifths of the coal, wheat and other necessities for keeping Italy alive came via the Straits of Gibraltar, and Italy could not contemplate any interruption of that trade. Count Ruspoli said that one 10,000-ton cruiser with 8″ guns would probably be able to deal with four 6″ cruisers and keep the Straits open, whereas if there were any limitation as regards small cruisers, Italy would require double the number of smaller cruisers to her opponent. I can see that he had in mind France.

Dr. Holsti, the Finn, came to tell me that he understood from a correspondent in London that the Foreign Office and the War Office had been much displeased with the attitude of the Finnish Delegation at the Disarmament Conference last year, and that the impression prevailed in London that the Finns were tied to the French policy on the subject of land armaments and opposed to us. Nothing, said Dr. Holsti, was further from the truth. The Finnish Government were under no agreement with France and their action at Geneva was entirely independent of French policy. If they happened in this matter to appear to vote with France and against us, it was solely for the reason that the Finnish Government could not at a preliminary Conference where Russia was not represented commit themselves to any reduction of the Finnish forces. They could only agree to a reduction after the Russians had laid their cards on the table, since, for Finland, the danger came from Russia. If, said Dr. Holsti, at the preliminary Conference, the Finnish Government had indicated a willingness to reduce their land armaments when Russia was absent, they could have no guarantee that they would not be called upon to make a further contribution—one which they might not be able to afford—when Russia took part in the Disarmament Conference.

Dr. Holsti emphasised the fact that, so far as naval armaments were concerned, the Finns had given their support to us. He said that the reason for this was that the British fleet was regarded as the most useful instrument in the hands of the Council of the League in the event of an act of aggression by any power, and, accordingly, it was to the interest of Finland as a member of the League to assist Great Britain in maintaining her sea power.

Yours very sincerely,
W. SELBY

No. 236

Sir E. Howard (Washington) to Sir A. Chamberlain
(Received December 31)
No. 2276 [A 7559/3827/45]

WASHINGTON, *December 16, 1927*

Sir:

With reference to my despatch No. 1143[1] of July 7th, I have the honour to report that I asked the Secretary of State yesterday whether he could give me any information as to the negotiations between the United States Government and the French Government relating to the renewal of their Treaty of Arbitration[2] which expires next spring and the Briand proposal for a treaty of wider scope 'outlawing' war between the two Governments.[3]

2. Mr. Kellogg told me that he thought it was impracticable to accept the Briand proposal in its present form. He hoped however that it might be possible to alter the Root Treaty of 1908[2] in such a way as to satisfy to some extent the hopes of all who wished to see the cause of arbitration advanced. With this object in view he thought it might be arranged to omit at the end of Article I of the Jusserand–Root Treaty, which is, I understand, similar in wording to the Bryce–Root Treaty of April 4th, 1908,[4] the words 'provided, nevertheless, that they do not affect the vital interests, the independence, or the honour of the two contracting States'. The sense of the words 'provided they do not concern the interests of third parties' would have in some form or another to remain because obviously in such cases the third parties interested must be consulted. Mr. Kellogg told me frankly that he did not consider this omission would really alter greatly the meaning of the article because already the obligation to submit disputes to arbitration was limited to differences of a legal nature and the interpretation of treaties which in any case would be naturally proper and suitable for arbitration, and the article could not be so construed as to embrace matters of domestic concern

---

[1] See Volume III, No. 396, note 3.

[2] This treaty of February 10, 1908, signed by Mr. Root and M. Jusserand, then French Ambassador at Washington, is printed in *British and Foreign State Papers*, vol. 101, pp. 1019-20.

[3] See *Papers relating to the Foreign Relations of the United States 1927*, vol. ii, p. 616, for a translation of the draft treaty communicated on June 21 to the American Chargé d'Affaires in Paris on behalf of M. Briand. This text is printed in a variant translation in Cmd. 3109 of 1928, *Correspondence with the United States Ambassador respecting the United States Proposal for the Renunciation of War*, pp. 3-4. See Volume III, Nos. 355, 361 and 502.

[4] This Arbitration Convention, signed by Mr. Root and Mr. Bryce, then H.M. Ambassador at Washington, cited in full in No. 262 below, is printed with annex in *British and Foreign State Papers*, vol. 101, pp. 208-10.

such as immigration, taxation etc. I enquired whether he thought that, in case a difference of opinion arose over the terms of the Washington Treaty for the limitation of Naval Armaments the question was one which, under the Root Treaty, should be submitted to arbitration. He said he had no doubt of it since once a Treaty had been ratified, even though it might affect vital interests or national honour, its interpretation under the Root Treaty must, if a dispute arose, be submitted to arbitration.

3. The alteration he had in mind for the new Treaty would, therefore, if agreed to, not really amount to much more than a change of form. He was however doubtful whether the Senate would consent even to this and was determined to consult the Senate leaders before signing any Treaty so as to avoid any dispute later when the Treaty came up for ratification by that body.

4. In this plan of consulting the Senate leaders beforehand, and obtaining their approval and consent before the signature of Treaties, it appears to me that the President and the Secretary of State are certainly acting wisely and will spare themselves and the foreign countries with which they negotiate treaties and conventions much unnecessary labour as well as the unpleasant surprises which have occurred in the past.

5. Finally, Mr. Kellogg again told me that he would only sign a Treaty with France which he would also be prepared to make with Great Britain and Japan, whose Arbitration Treaties,[5] as you are aware, also expire next year though rather later than that of France.

6. Mr. Kellogg added that there was of course no reason to discuss the Bryan Treaties of 1913[6] which continued indefinitely until denounced.[7]

I have, &c.,

ESME HOWARD

[5] For the American–Japanese Convention of May 5, 1908, *v. ibid.*, pp. 1072–3.

[6] For these treaties negotiated by Mr. W. J. Bryan, American Secretary of State 1913–15, see *Treaties for the Advancement of Peace* (Carnegie Endowment, New York, 1920). The treaties with Great Britain and France signed on September 15, 1914, by Mr. Bryan and Sir C. Spring Rice, then H.M. Ambassador at Washington, and M. Jusserand respectively, are also printed in *British and Foreign State Papers*, vol. 108, pp. 384–5 and 470–3 respectively.

[7] For an account of this conversation by Mr. Kellogg see *Papers relating to the Foreign Relations of the United States 1927*, vol. ii, p. 628.

No. 237

Memorandum by Sir C. Hurst

[W 549/28/98]

FOREIGN OFFICE, *December 19, 1927*

A memorandum has now to be prepared for submission to the League of Nations, giving the views of H.M. Government as to the measures which the League might take to promote treaties of arbitration, and to co-ordinate and generalise them.[1]

[1] See the programme and method of work adopted by the Committee on Arbitration and Security on December 2, 1927, printed in *Documents of the Preparatory Commission for the Disarmament Conference*, Series V, pp. 55–6.

For this purpose a study of existing arbitration treaties is recommended by the Security Commission of the League, showing the elements which are universal to them all—as upon these elements a model convention might be based,—and also a study of the scheme which Dr. Nansen put forward at Geneva in 1927 for a draft optional convention for the obligatory arbitration of all disputes.[2]

2. Before these studies can be undertaken there is one point on which the policy of H.M. Government must be indicated. It is one on which, so far as I know, that policy has not yet been declared, and it is useless to prepare the necessary memorandum until it has been so declared.

3. What is the meaning which H.M. Government intend to attribute to the word 'arbitration' in this connection? Is it intended to be synonymous with 'compulsory method of peaceful settlement' irrespective of the nature of the dispute? Or is it intended to apply only to disputes which lend themselves to decision by the application of a rule of law, disputes which are termed 'justiciable' or, in the more accurate language of the Treaty of Locarno, disputes where the parties 'se contest[erai]ent réciproquement un droit'.[3]

4. The above is much more than a question of words, it is one of first-class importance. The reason why it is so necessary to know exactly the sense to be given to the word 'arbitration' is that the Covenant[4] uses the word with the later meaning given above, and the Protocol[5] uses it with the earlier meaning. The Protocol makes elaborate provision for the settlement by arbitration of disputes about which the Council, when handling a dispute under Article 15 of the Covenant, fails to arrive at a unanimous report. The Council only deals with disputes under Article 15 when they are not referred to arbitration (using the word in the Covenant sense). This may be for either of two reasons: (a) that the dispute does not lend itself to decision by the application of a rule of law, i.e. is not justiciable; (b) that the parties refuse to submit the case to arbitration even though the dispute is justiciable, but prefer to have it dealt with as a political issue by the Council. Consequently a dispute can go to arbitration in the Protocol sense of the word which does not and cannot go to arbitration in the Covenant sense of the word.

5. In the industrial and commercial life of every nation the term 'arbitration' is habitually applied to the settlement of disputes which are not justiciable in their nature. A dispute as to the amount of the wages of the guards on the London and North Eastern Railway, or as to the correct price of a piece of land are not matters which can be settled by the application of a rule of law, but they readily lend themselves to the decision of an arbitrator.

Equally in the international world there is no theoretical reason why a state should not agree to allow an arbitration tribunal to settle a ques-

---

[2] Cf. No. 219, note 15.

[3] See article 3 of the Treaty of Mutual Guarantee.

[4] A footnote in the original here cited the amended text of article 13 of the Covenant of the League of Nations adopted by the Assembly in 1921: see League of Nations, *Records of the Second Assembly: Plenary Meetings*, p. 829.

[5] The Geneva Protocol of 1924.

tion rather than go to war, even if the question is purely non-justiciable in character and arises out of the clash of political interests.

6. The importance of the question both from the point of view of security and of disarmament is this. If a dispute occurs between two states, it must be settled somehow. It is only very rarely that a dispute is of such a nature that it can drag on unsettled indefinitely. In general some solution must be found for a dispute; if a solution by peaceful means is not found, it will be solved by war.

7. When a state refuses to pledge itself in advance to agree to submit a dispute to solution by pacific means, other states are entitled to assume that it reserves to itself the right to seek a solution of that dispute by war, and consequently, feeling that they may each be the state with whom solution may be sought by war, are entitled, in determining the extent to which their security would be imperilled by recourse to war in such an eventuality, to determine also the extent to which they can disarm.

8. Under the Covenant resort to war is legitimate whenever the Council, acting under Article 15, fails to arrive at a unanimous decision. In measuring the extent to which disarmament is possible for a Member of the League, that Member is bound to form its estimate of the extent to which its security would be imperilled if war ensued as the result of the Council failing to achieve unanimity in handling a dispute in which it was itself a party.

9. In the eyes of France the possibility of the Council not being unanimous in a dispute in which France was a party is very great. The Council is a political body composed in the main of the representatives of continental states, and the representatives of continental states do not approach their duties in the Council in the spirit in which an Englishman approaches it. France has ever before her eyes the picture of 1914 and considers how the Council machine would have functioned in the crisis preceding the war. She sees that Germany would have backed Austria unhesitatingly in the latter's dispute with Serbia, and therefore the Council would necessarily have been divided; war would then have ensued without any violation of the provisions of the Covenant. If France wants confirmation of her views, she has only to think of Mussolini's instructions to the Italian member of the Council to support Hungary in any event in the Optants dispute[6] at Geneva last September.

10. No French statesman in these circumstances dare regard the Covenant as it stands as a sufficient protection against war. Such interest as there may be in the Protocol of 1924 in France is wholly due to the feeling that to some extent it limited the cases in which war was legitimate under the Covenant; it did so by providing machinery for ensuring a peaceful settlement of a dispute about which the Council could not achieve a unanimous report, and the method was by sending the dispute in such a case to a committee of arbitrators.

11. The attitude of H.M. Government has been made clear as to the compulsory arbitration of justiciable disputes, cases which must come before a court and be settled by the application of a rule of law, but has never been

[6] Cf. No. 150, note 2.

defined on the question of compulsorily referring to some peaceful mode of settlement disputes about which the Council cannot achieve unanimity.

12. Wars do not arise out of justiciable disputes, and consequently a refusal to accept the system of compulsory arbitration for such disputes has no very profound effect on disarmament or security; but with disputes arising out of the clash of political interests it is a different matter. It is out of that class of disputes that wars arise, and if H.M. Government are determined to refuse to accept any compulsory system of solution by peaceful means for political disputes where the Council cannot agree, it will be very difficult for Geneva to make any progress in the direction of security or of disarmament.

13. British opposition to the Protocol has been connected almost entirely with the 'sanctions' provisions of that instrument, and has been occasioned by the fear that we should become involved in war with the United States of America through having to enforce the cessation of American trading with the recalcitrant state. It should be quite possible to separate this part of the Protocol system from the part dealing with the machinery for ensuring a settlement by peaceful means of a dispute about which the Council cannot agree.

14. The suggestion that the continental nations should agree on some such system among themselves and that Great Britain should stand aloof is not attractive to the continental nations. Without doubt the inhabitants of this country rightly regard themselves as the most pacific of peoples. Foreign nations take a somewhat different view. They regard Great Britain as a country which geographically, commercially and even at times politically lies across their path everywhere, and they regard disputes with Great Britain arising from the clash of political interests as by no means unlikely. The possibility of those disputes being solved by war if the Council cannot agree, and if Great Britain refuses to agree in advance to some method of peaceful solution is not one which they can safely ignore.

15. Are H.M. Government prepared to accept some system under which, where the Council cannot agree, a political dispute would necessarily be submitted to some organ for peaceful settlement and war cease to be legitimate under the Covenant?[7]

C. J. B. H.

[7] This paper was referred by Sir A. Chamberlain to the Attorney General who minuted on December 22: 'I think the Memorandum to be prepared should deal with Treaties of Arbitration properly so called, not with all compulsory methods of peaceful settlement. In fact so far as this country is concerned Arbitration Treaties are usually confined to justiciable disputes.

'In my opinion the compulsory settlement [*sic* ? submission] of political disputes to an outside body for decision is the very thing which the Empire could not accept for the reasons embodied in the recent decision of the Cabinet upon the recommendation of the Cabinet Committee [see No. 229], and it is no use recommending to other Nations what we are not willing to do ourselves.

'I think no harm would be done by the Committee of the League of Nations exploring the peaceful settlement of political disputes; but I do not think that we can take a lead in advocating any form of compulsory settlement. D.M.H. 22.12.27.'

No. 238

Letter from Mr. Vansittart to Sir E. Howard (Washington)

[*A 7141/93/45*]

Private and confidential   FOREIGN OFFICE, *December 20, 1927*

Dear Sir Esme,

I enclose a record of a conversation which took place on December 6th between Mr. Frank Simonds[1] and Craigie and in which the former expatiated at length upon the relations existing between Great Britain and the United States and the effect of the breakdown of the Geneva Conference on public opinion in the latter country. In addition to what is reported in the enclosed memorandum, Mr. Simonds on this occasion also expressed anxiety lest the United States should, when the Washington Naval Limitation Treaty came up for revision in 1931, throw over the whole principle of limitation by agreement with Great Britain. Mr. Simonds feared that American opinion was moving in that direction.

I should be very glad to have an expression of your views upon Mr. Simonds' remarks as reported in the enclosed memorandum.

Mr. Simonds is a publicist of such world-wide renown and presumed to have such an accurate knowledge of the trend of American opinion that the views he expresses are a little disturbing.

Yours ever,
ROBERT VANSITTART

ENCLOSURE IN No. 238

Record by Mr. Craigie of a conversation with Mr. Frank Simonds

FOREIGN OFFICE, *December 9, 1927*

I met Mr. Frank Simonds at lunch on the 6th instant. He spoke freely on the naval question, and some of his remarks are perhaps worth recording.

His main thesis was that throughout the United States there was a general feeling that America had been 'let down' by Great Britain, both at Washington and Geneva. As regards Washington, the responsibility probably lay to some extent with the Republican party who, in their anxiety to make a great Republican success of the Washington Naval Conference, allowed the impression to prevail that, while the treaty only specifically referred to battleships, the principle of equality between the British and United States navies applied to cruisers and auxiliary craft. When, therefore, it was found that the British navy continued to be far stronger in cruisers than the American navy, a sense of grievance gradually grew, until President Coolidge issued his invitation to the Geneva Conference. Thereafter public opinion felt convinced that the British Government would not fail to honour at Geneva the principle which they believed to have been accepted at Washington, but never carried into effect. As the Conference proceeded, it dawned on the

---

[1] Foreign Editor of *The American Review of Reviews*.

American people that the British Government had not even then frankly and fully accepted the principle of 'mathematical parity' and the feeling grew that the American Government had once more been 'let down' by His Majesty's Government. This view became general when the conference finally broke down. Mr. Simonds did not wish to defend the accuracy of this American view, but he did wish to emphasise the point that in the United States it was almost universally held, and that nothing could now be done to remove it from the public mind. Since the failure of the Geneva Conference, nothing whatever would prevent the American nation from building rapidly up to what they considered to be full equality with the British navy in respect of tonnage and of offensive and defensive strength. It was true that President Coolidge and the Administration were against competitive building, but so widespread was the feeling in favour of a large navy, that Congress was bound to get the better of the Administration in this matter. He had the best information to the effect that feeling in the West and Middle-West was as strong as on the Atlantic seaboard. We should make a great mistake if we thought that a big navy was any longer merely a matter of 'prestige': there was a definite feeling of 'grievance' behind the movement.

Mr. Simonds laid it down as axiomatic that just as the two countries could, for strategical reasons, never go to war (adding as an aside that the issue would be settled in Canada), so they could never conclude any agreement on any important political subject, owing to the deep and latent distrust with which each side regarded the other. He instanced as the type of agreement which was impossible an agreement in regard to belligerent rights at sea, which had recently been much canvassed in the press of this country.

Mr. Simonds likes to convey the impression that he is acting as the candid friend of this country, and that he merely notes these unpleasant manifestations in his own country, without necessarily approving them. In fact, however, I believe him to be one of the cleverest of the American 'Big Navy' propagandists and, owing to the subtlety of his methods and the wide publicity his articles receive, one of the most dangerous. I have never believed him to be a real friend of this country, and this last conversation has confirmed my suspicions. One incident is worth mentioning. Speaking of Lord Cecil, he said that when in 1917 he had occasion to ask for a second interview with Lord Robert (as he then was) the answer he received was to the effect that Lord Robert would gladly receive him 'provided that he would refrain from treating Lord Robert so much as an equal as he had done on the previous occasion'! I told Mr. Simonds that it was quite inconceivable that Lord Cecil could have sent any such reply, and that it was probably a case of mischief-making on the part of his intermediary. He refused, however, to accept this, and appeared anxious to hug his grievance. He spoke of the incident with so much feeling that for a moment his real sentiments towards this country seemed to me to emerge.

Furthermore, he appeared to me to be not in the least anxious to listen to anything said on behalf of the British case, and to be in fact much less open-minded than he likes to appear in many of his articles. Thus, in the course of the conversation I mentioned that the United States Government had probably entered upon the conference in the belief that, if an agreement could be reached, an immediate economy might be effected in the American programme of cruiser construction: they had probably been disappointed when they realised that this would not be immediately possible. This Mr. Simonds emphatically denied, stating that the American Government had been under no misapprehension on the point. According to yesterday's paper President Coolidge, in his message to Congress, said:—'We know now [i.e. since the Conference][2] that no agreement can be reached which will be inconsistent with a considerable building programme on our part'. This shows that what I had surmised, and what Mr. Simonds had so emphatically denied, proves to have been a fact.

It is a little disturbing to hear from a publicist of Mr. Simonds' experience that feeling on this subject in the United States is so strong and so widespread, but, for the reasons stated above, I doubt whether his opinion on this point should be regarded as accurate, particularly as we have no confirmation from our Embassy in Washington that such anti-British sentiments are noticeable in circles other than those which are normally regarded as 'Big Navy'. An intensive propaganda is undoubtedly being conducted which will culminate about the time when the cruiser construction programme will come up for discussion—namely, by about the middle of February next. While this propaganda must necessarily do some harm, I doubt whether we shall notice any serious ill-effects from it once the supplementary appropriation for new construction has been passed. That, at all events, has been the experience of the past, and I cannot help feeling that is what will happen this time, notwithstanding Mr. Simonds' forebodings.[3]

R. L. CRAIGIE

[2] Square brackets in original quotation.
[3] Sir A. Willert stated in a minute of December 13 that he had been 'much struck while in America last autumn with the effect of Lord Cecil's resignation from the Government. It turned indifference about the failure of the Geneva Conference into suspicion of our motives especially in regard to blockade matters, and that suspicion, I am afraid endures. But it is difficult to believe that a serious Anglophobe, Big-Navy movement is likely to arise in the United States unless our public men and press go out of their way to be provocative and fail to realise that a large part of the present "pother" in Washington over cruisers and so on is due to domestic politics and therefore not to be made too much of abroad.' In a letter to Sir A. Willert of December 13, Mr. Angus Fletcher, Director of the British Library of Information at New York, stated in particular: 'For the first time since I have been in America I have heard the possibility of war referred to or discussed by serious minded people. Only this afternoon Dr. Jesse Jones, of the Phelps-Stokes Foundation, referred to the anxiety expressed by Mr. Taft (brother of the Chief Justice) in conversation on the subject, and asked me if I thought relations were strained.... Of this kind of talk we may expect to hear more as the discussion on the naval appropriations opens out. It is inevitable that the British Navy will be used as a measuring stick, and so the conception of conflict will be presented in an unpleasantly concrete form.... And yet, in spite of these disturbing manifestations, one cannot help feeling that we stand solidly on our feet with the American public.... Of course, Great Britain cannot escape the strain which all relationships with this country impose. And no one is more sensitive to that strain than those who work on the very surfaces of friction. But since those difficulties are inherent in the United States of today, and are not

likely to disappear for a long time, you will not be surprised if we in the Library feel very strongly that the proper method of handling this country cannot be too sedulously sought out and cultivated. If the time has come when we find ourselves confronting the United States it is also true that we are awkwardly circumstanced to confront her. More than ever we shall have to exhibit in our dealings with America the patience of Job, without that old gentleman's tendency to irritation and lamentation.'

No. 239

Sir A. Chamberlain to Sir E. Howard (Washington)
No. 529 Telegraphic [A 7267/93/45]

FOREIGN OFFICE, *December 21, 1927, 7.15 p.m.*

Your No. 527.[1]

His Majesty's Government cannot but feel deeply these reiterated attacks on their good faith which the Administration knows to be utterly unfounded and they would be correspondingly gratified if Mr. Kellogg or other authoritative spokesman could be brought to feel that they ought to be authoritatively repudiated by the United States government but I most strongly deprecate your allowing yourself to be drawn into public discussion where your declarations will only provoke further controversy and where you will certainly not be allowed to have the last word.

I do not know what is the occasion or purpose of the banquet on the 10th but whatever it is I find it impossible to believe that any good can be done by your then entering the lists against the Washington Post or any other newspaper. We are in for a storm and it is not a good moment to spread more canvass [*sic*]. Let us hove to and let the storm blow itself out as far as the public are concerned. But you have already spoken to the Secretary of State in regard to the unfriendly tone of the Washington Post editorials on the naval question. Could you not follow this up by seeing the President and soliciting Mr. Coolidge's co-operation, in the interests of Anglo-American relations, in mentioning at one of the periodical White House press conferences that the United States government do not consider that this country has violated either the letter or the spirit of the Washington treaty? This may be a forlorn hope, but it is worth trying I think, because if it came off it might have very useful results—and even if nothing came of it, it would at least indicate to Mr. Coolidge, privately and without publicity, that His Majesty's Government are concerned over grossly unfair attacks on British policy so unnecessarily made in pursuance of the campaign for increasing the United States navy.

[1] Not printed. This telegram of December 16 referred to No. 234 and outlined a statement which Sir E. Howard proposed to make in a speech at a banquet on January 10, 1928, in repudiation of the allegations made in the *Washington Post*.

Sir E. Howard (Washington) to Sir A. Chamberlain
(Received December 30, 9 a.m.)

No. 535 Telegraphic [A 7523/93/45]

WASHINGTON, *December 29, 1927, 6.45 p.m.*

Your telegram No. 538.[1]

Attacks by 'Washington Post'.

I told Secretary of State this morning that His Majesty's Government felt deeply these attacks on their good faith which they held to be without foundation and believed United States Government also considered unfounded and asked if he or any member of Cabinet would not give them an authoritative denial. I also said that you wished me to convey this to President and that you would be gratified if he could make a statement to that effect at one of the White House press conferences.

Secretary of State said that on my drawing his attention to the articles he had at once called up the Editor of the 'Post' and told him that United States Government had always accepted as completely accurate His Majesty's Government's assurance that they had not elevated guns contrary to treaty and asked him to state this. Editor had merely thanked him but done nothing. He was however quite willing himself to issue statement to press to the effect that United States Government never questioned His Majesty's Government's good faith in the matter.[2] I thanked him for this which I thought would be very useful and added that I hoped he would say something also about repeated statement that His Majesty's Government had violated spirit of treaty by building cruisers. I said that His Majesty's Government's view was that expressed by President in his message to Congress that there was no treaty limitation on cruisers and that all parties to treaty were therefore free in this respect. He replied he would rather not open up this theme at present. He was doing everything possible to prevent wild and bitter statements being made in Senate and in House of Representatives during naval debate and he thought that a statement of this kind might only excite controversy. As he said he would issue statement himself about guns, I did not press for interview with President which is always accompanied by some difficulty if desired for some special political purpose but expressed hope that he would inform President of your feelings in the matter.

[1] Not printed. This telegram of December 26 stated that Sir A. Chamberlain held to the instructions in No. 239, in spite of considerations against them advanced by Sir E. Howard in Washington telegram No. 532 of December 23, not printed.

[2] Sir E. Howard subsequently reported in Washington telegram No. 1 of January 1, 1928, that Mr. Kellogg had issued a statement to the above effect which had been published on December 30–1, and that he had thanked Mr. Kellogg.

No. 241

Letter from Sir E. Howard (Washington) to Sir W. Tyrrell

[A 228/133/45]

Private and secret   WASHINGTON, *December 29, 1927*

My dear Tyrrell,

I have read with great interest and care the enclosures in your letter of the 2nd December marked 'Private and Secret'.[1] Judging by Mr. Craigie's memoranda[2] it would seem that there is no very great distance between our ideas respecting Blockade Law and those of the United States. I agree with him in thinking it probable that the United States, now they are embarked on building a fleet second to none, will not be so eager to champion neutral rights in the future as in the past and that consequently we ought not to find it too difficult to get them to fall in with our general ideas of blockade policy. Taking his points one by one, I begin with *Contraband*.

1. *Visit, Search, Detention and Capture.*—The principal difficulty here would be, I believe, to get the United States Government to agree to diversion of their ships when neutral to a British port, but given the precedents for this established, I understand, during the Civil War, and given the wish to have as much liberty of action as possible in blockade which is certain to result from the possession of greater sea power, I agree with Mr. Craigie that we ought to be able to come to an agreement about this that would suit us both.

2. *Seizure. Doctrine of Continuous Voyage.*—Here too I agree with Mr. Craigie that in the light of previous American practice we ought not to have much difficulty in reaching an agreement.

3. *Lists of Contraband.*—It is possible, indeed probable, that we should have difficulty in reaching an agreement on this subject. It must be obvious that such lists should be flexible. I am inclined however to trust to the new naval spirit in the United States not being over nice in restricting the lists of either absolute or conditional contraband.

4. *Blockade—Rules of Blockade.*—We seem already to be in some sort of agreement on this. Mr. Craigie says 'The Anglo-American practice has been that, if the blockade is maintained by a force sufficient to render ingress or egress hazardous and the capture of blockade runners most probable, the number or station of ships is immaterial.' Now if the United States were at war with a European or Asiatic Power, they would certainly have to impose a long distance blockade because they have no sufficient naval bases near enough to any non-American Power to make a near distance blockade feasible. Presumably we should both of us wish to maintain the provision of the Declaration of Paris as to the effectiveness of blockades but in the long run the measure of such effectiveness can only be established by Prize Courts or in the last resort by an International Court. As however the interests of both countries in this matter are obviously running together, I see no reason to expect any great difficulty in agreeing on this point.

[1] No. 231.   [2] See No. 231, note 2.

5. *Jurisdiction of Prize Courts.*—Until there is a regular recognised international practice as regards right of seizure etc. there is always likely to be controversy over the decisions of the Prize Courts of any country in war time even if they are expected to decide according to principles of international law and not municipal enactments, Orders in Council, etc. If we can come to an agreement with the United States as to what is or is not a legal seizure, the principal difficulty in this respect will have been eliminated.

6. *Seizure and Censorship of Mails.*—There, I must admit, I foresee more considerable objections though even here it is possible that American opinion may now be swayed by the possibility of having some day to declare war on Mexico in which case seizure and censorship of the mails would be almost inevitable. I have no doubt that trouble with Mexico is an eventuality that the United States negotiators will keep always before their eyes in negotiating on the rules of maritime war and blockade.

7. *Rationing of Neutrals.*—The United States fell in strictly with this practice after they entered the war. In this connection it may not be amiss to recall a conversation I had with Mr. Hoover some time ago when discussing the fatal economic effects of a war between the United States and Great Britain.[3] He said he thought such a war from the American side would take this course:

1. Canada compelled to declare her neutrality.
2. All shipments of goods to Great Britain stopped from North America and as far as possible from South America. And all European countries rationed in regard to import of goods from the American Continent so far as this could be done.
3. Certain West Indian Islands occupied by the United States.
4. For the rest, a war of naval, financial and economic attrition.

It interested me very much to get this description of such a war from so clear a thinker as Mr. Hoover and from it I deduce:

That he at least would not oppose in any agreement the long distance blockade or the rationing of neutral countries.

Here again I believe that the Big Navy party would favour our views and that an agreement would not be difficult.

As regards the last three points mentioned by Mr. Craigie, viz. Navicerts, Black List and Reprisals, I cannot see that we need anticipate great difficulty provided we agree on other matters.

As regards Article 16 of the Covenant of the League of Nations, I entirely agree with Mr. Craigie that if we had to take action under that Article it would be of the utmost value that we should have an agreement with the United States defining the limits of such action as could be taken without bringing in the United States on the side of the Covenant-breaking State.

I agree therefore with the general conclusions arrived at by Mr. Craigie which are, given that an agreement of this nature is desirable:—

a. That the difficulties between ourselves and the United States are not necessarily insurmountable.

[3] See Volume III, No. 480.

b. That the best time for sounding the United States Government would be before next spring.

c. Should it be considered desirable that a discussion of these questions between the two Governments take place it is advisable that we proceed with caution, sounding the United States Government first as to whether they care for it. Indeed the invitation for such a preliminary discussion had better proceed from them. If they do desire it and know that we are ready to discuss these questions in a quiet way, I have no doubt that they will propose such a discussion.

As Mr. Craigie says, therefore, soundings of an entirely informal and unofficial character would be necessary.

I have also read Sir Cecil Hurst's and Sir Maurice Hankey's most interesting and, given the premises on which their conclusions are built, most convincing memoranda.[4]

Both, however, if I may say so, seem to lose sight of the one all-important new factor in this question which has altered the whole situation since 1914.

This is that the United States has now become aware of its own strength, that it is determined not to be dictated to in any matter by any country, especially I may say, not by England, and that it can build a navy superior to ours whenever it wants to do so and above all that in Canada it has a hostage on land which we cannot for a moment afford to overlook. By this last I mean that, supposing a war between the United States and Great Britain on account of blockade questions, it is obvious that the first thing the United States would do, would be to send an ultimatum to Canada to declare her neutrality, which would be tantamount to breaking off her connection with the British Empire, or take the consequences. What the consequences would be, I cannot say not being a soldier or a strategician but I can guess that there would be without delay an occupation of the Canadian East–West railway lines somewhere west of the Great Lakes which would cut Canada in two and prevent the revictualling of the Industrial East by the Agricultural West. Could we, especially if we were engaged in a European War, come to the assistance of Canada? I fail to see how we could do so—and having once failed decisively to protect a part of the Empire, would that part ever return to be a part of it again after a war of financial, economic and naval attrition out of which we should come unquestionably so weakened and impoverished that it is doubtful whether Great Britain could ever retain her position as the centre of the Empire?

It therefore seems to me that it is frankly useless for us to argue about Sea Power and quote Mahan[5] to prove that we must keep our hands free in regard to Blockade when there is a country so much more powerful materially, financially, economically and geographically which has just awaked to the

---

[4] See No. 224, annex II and note 2 respectively.

[5] In his memorandum of October 31 Sir M. Hankey had cited from Admiral A. T. Mahan. *The Influence of Sea Power upon the French Revolution and Empire 1793–1812* (3rd ed., London, n d.), vol. ii, p. 289, the passage beginning 'The battle between the sea' and ending 'the other by starvation'.

fact that it can tie our hands for us. There are of course some who argue that the United States will never find the personnel to man a large navy. This is I think a dangerous argument and one which may mislead us considerably. *If public opinion here can be persuaded to believe that England is the enemy and the villain of the piece*, which is the aim of the Big Navalists here, I feel confident the men and everything else will be found.

My opinion therefore for what it is worth is this:

If we come to no agreement now, we shall not be able in war time without incurring risk of either having to eat our own Orders in Council or seeing the United States come into the war against us, be able [*sic*] to enforce a blockade like that of 1914–18, because in war time if the United States are neutral, the Government of the United States will be forced by big business and public opinion to take up strongly 'neutral rights', to convoy American ships in order to break our blockade, and to declare war if the convoys are fired upon or interfered with.

On the other hand, if we get an agreement made in peace time and not in time of national excitement, it is very probable that we shall get with it so much of our conception of the rights of belligerents in blockade that we should be, with the consent of the United States which having agreed to it in peace could hardly repudiate it in war, in a position to enforce our belligerent blockade rights without fear of interference, and therefore much more effectively than if we were constantly hampered by protests and threats of retaliation and reprisals by neutral countries headed by the United States.

The long and short of it is that so far as I can see, we shall never again be able to enforce any blockade whatever unless we have the United States actually on our side or unless the United States Government has previously agreed to the rules we propose to enforce. This seems to me axiomatic.

Yours ever,
ESME HOWARD

CHAPTER IV

The American proposal for the Renunciation of War: discussions at Geneva on Security

December 30, 1927–April 13, 1928

No. 242

Sir E. Howard (Washington) to Sir A. Chamberlain
(Received December 31, 9 a.m.)
No. 538 Telegraphic [A 1/1/45]

WASHINGTON, *December 30, 1927, 1.25 p.m.*

My despatch No. 2276,[1] confidential, respecting renewal of arbitration treaties with America.

Secretary of State yesterday read to me note he is addressing to French government in reply to French Minister for Foreign Affairs' proposed treaty declaring that United States and France would settle all disputes by pacific methods.[2] He therein informs French government that United States government wish to make treaties with all governments looking to peaceful solutions of disputes, and encloses another draft treaty[3] for consideration of French government which is in substance practically the same as the expiring Root treaty[4] except that it lays down that after diplomatic methods and conciliation commission set up by Bryan treaty[5] have failed justiciable disputes are to be submitted to arbitration, the court being either the Hague Court[6] or a special court. New draft does not include any reference to honour, vital interests etc. Mr. Kellogg explained to me that he as a lawyer had never been able to understand the real value of these words. It was clear that whatever Latin countries might do Anglo-Saxon countries would never consent to bind themselves to submit matters belonging to the domestic sphere such as taxes, tariffs, immigration etc. to arbitration unless some treaty right was involved which would make such questions justiciable and therefore arbitrable. It was the same with nations as with individuals. If a man went to law he must prove either violation of law or breach of contract. So nations when having recourse to arbitration must prove breach of international law

---

[1] No. 236.

[2] Mr. Kellogg's note of December 28, 1927, to M. Claudel, French Ambassador at Washington, is printed in Cmd. 3109 of 1928, as enclosure 2 (i) in item No. 1.

[3] This draft Franco-American treaty of arbitration was transmitted by Mr. Kellogg to M. Claudel in a further note of December 28: see *Papers relating to the Foreign Relations of the United States 1928*, vol. ii, pp. 810–12.   [4] See No. 236, note 2.

[5] *V. ibid.*, note 6.   [6] i.e. the Permanent Court of Arbitration at The Hague.

or breach of treaty, which was a contract. Even if France refused proposed new treaty Mr. Kellogg intends to offer it to Great Britain and other Powers having arbitration treaties with the United States in the hope that it may ultimately be universally accepted and prove a real step in advance in the education of public opinion of the world for the promotion of peaceful settlement of disputes. In answer to a question from me whether United States government would include Russia amongst the Powers to be invited to consider this treaty Secretary of State said 'not at present'.

Mr. Kellogg told me that he was telegraphing[7] text of note and draft treaty to United States Chargé d'Affaires in London with instructions to communicate with you as soon as they had been submitted to M. Briand.

Not having been able to study text I cannot venture to offer any opinion on new draft, but I feel that it represents a real effort on the part of United States government, who have no doubt consulted Senate leaders, to give expression to growing desire in this country that this government should make some definite move in the direction of world peace.

[7] Cf. *Papers relating to the Foreign Relations of the United States 1927*, vol. ii, p. 629.

No. 243

Sir E. Howard (Washington) to Sir A. Chamberlain
(Received December 31, 9 a.m.)

No. 539 Telegraphic [A 2/1/45]

WASHINGTON, *December 30, 1927, 4.35 p.m.*

My immediately preceding telegram.[1]

Secretary of State evidently hoped very much that His Majesty's Government would accept his new treaty. He admits it does not really constitute an act that will 'outlaw war' but he believes it goes as far as public opinion here will allow at present. It is not a final measure but an educational one and as complementary to and reinforcing Bryan conciliation treaty seems to me to have merits. In speaking yesterday in a general way of peace and disarmament Secretary of State said to me most emphatically that his government would be ready to sign any treaty tomorrow for total abolition of submarines. I said I believed this would be most valuable forerunner to any Naval Disarmament conference but I doubted whether France and Italy would agree. He also spoke strongly about trying to get Washington convention against poison gas ratified, his own country was, he admitted, one of those which had not ratified but he gave me to understand he wished another effort for ratification to be made. It was of course he said impossible to prevent belligerents from using poison gas but at least any belligerents that did after signing convention would be legitimate subject of reprisals.

[1] No. 242.

No. 244

Sir E. Howard (Washington) to Sir A. Chamberlain
(Received January 9, 1928)
No. 2352 [A 154/154/45]

WASHINGTON, December 30, 1927

Sir,

With reference to my telegram No. 538[1] of today's date, I have the honour to enclose copy of a note[2] addressed to me by the Secretary of State in which he transmits for the consideration of His Majesty's Government and as a basis for negotiation a draft of a proposed Treaty of Arbitration. Mr. Kellogg states that the language of this draft is *mutatis mutandis* identical with that of a draft Treaty which he transmitted yesterday to the French Ambassador for the consideration of his Government, except for a reference to questions involving the Dominions of the British Empire.

2. He concludes by saying that if His Majesty's Government are prepared to negotiate a treaty along these lines he will be glad to enter at once upon such discussions as may be necessary.

3. I have the honour to request that I may receive instructions in due course as to the reply I should return to Mr. Kellogg.

4. I have in my telegram above referred to reported at some length the language used by Mr. Kellogg to me yesterday while reading the Draft Treaty to me and I need not repeat this here.

5. One point I omitted to mention on which Mr. Kellogg laid stress and this was that he had found it necessary after consultation with the Senate to make it clear in the Treaty that any special agreement for setting up a special Arbitral Tribunal, if necessary, defining its powers and settling the terms of reference must be considered as a regular Treaty for which the approval and consent of the Senate would be required. Mr. Kellogg said it was impossible to avoid this.

6. Before concluding this despatch, which I am writing in great haste in order to catch the bag which is closing shortly, I would point out that the present Treaty seems to me to be a distinct advance on the Root Treaty of 1908,[3] inasmuch as it will not be possible for Signatories of such a Treaty to refuse arbitration in any question involving the interpretation of a previous Treaty on the ground that the question in dispute affects vital interests or national honour. Neither, if I read it correctly, will it be possible for Congress in future to maintain the theory that it can at any time by unilateral action terminate a Treaty entered into with another Power.

I have, &c.,
ESME HOWARD

---

[1] No. 242.

[2] This note of December 29 is printed in *Papers relating to the Foreign Relations of the United States 1928*, vol. ii, p. 945. The enclosed draft treaty, comprising a preamble and four articles, is cited in full in No. 262 below.

[3] See No. 236, note 4.

The Marquess of Crewe (Paris) to Sir A. Chamberlain
(Received January 5, 8.30 a.m.)

No. 2 Telegraphic: by bag [A 92/1/45]

PARIS, *January 4, 1928*

M. Léger, who is assistant political director[1] as well as 'Chef de Cabinet' to M. Briand, requested, under instructions from the latter, Sir Eric Phipps to call at the Quai d'Orsay this evening to receive an urgent communication.

2. M. Léger rapidly sketched to Sir Eric Phipps what had passed between the French and United States governments since M. Briand, about a year ago in a public message to the United States, had declared the readiness of the French Government to sign with that country a treaty outlawing war.[2] This rather vague declaration had been received in America by both political parties with a success which had surprised M. Briand himself. In order to meet the earnest wish expressed in the first instance by the American press and public men, and secondly unofficially by the American Ambassador in Paris acting under instructions from his government, M. Briand drafted a short treaty in two articles whereby both countries outlawed war. This draft was taken to America last summer by Mr. Herrick,[3] but in view of the summer holidays was only taken into consideration by the United States government in the autumn.

3. The United States government sometime ago proposed that this draft treaty should be embodied in the preamble of the new arbitration treaty between France and the United States which was to take place of the old Root–Jusserand treaty of February 1908 expiring next month and the Bryan–Jusserand treaty of September 1914. To this course the French government declared that they had no objection whatever. On December 28th last, however, the United States government addressed a note to the French Ambassador in Washington proposing that in addition to the above arbitration treaty between the two countries a multilateral treaty should be signed by all the powers condemning war.

4. This afternoon M. Léger said, the French government had been surprised to learn that the United States government had decided to publish in the press to-day the text of their above-mentioned note. In these circumstances the French government had decided to issue the text to the French press this evening at 7 o'clock. M. Briand hoped that you would understand that he had been unable, through pressure of time, to communicate sooner with you on the subject, but he desired to provide you without delay with a copy of the reply which he was to-night instructing M. Claudel to make to Mr. Kellogg.

[1] Of the French Ministry of Foreign Affairs.
[2] See Volume III, No. 355.
[3] American Ambassador at Paris.

5. The texts of these two notes are enclosed in my despatch No. 23[4] of to-day.

---

[4] This covering despatch is not preserved in Foreign Office archives. The enclosed correspondence of December 28, 1927 (cf. No. 242, note 2) and January 5, 1928, between Mr. Kellogg and M. Claudel is printed as enclosure 2 (i) and (ii) in item No. 1 in Cmd. 3109 of 1928.

No. 246

The Marquess of Crewe (Paris) to Sir A. Chamberlain
(Received January 6, 8.30 a.m.)
No. 3 Telegraphic: by bag [A 106/1/45]

PARIS, *January 5, 1928*

My telegram No. 2[1] of January 4th,—Franco-American Pact.

I saw M. Briand today and told him that I had sent you the substance of Sir Eric Phipps's conversation with M. Léger, recorded in the above telegram. He said that there were two quite distinct matters, the first being that of the renewed pact of friendship and arbitration, which was quite a simple matter; the second being the American proposal for agreements of larger scope and covering most other nations. I said that, as to this latter, I had noticed in some quarters in the press suspicions that the purpose of this suggestion had been to set aside the League of Nations by substituting a series of agreements based on a somewhat different principle from that which had been adopted at Geneva. M. Briand said that of course anything of this kind would be altogether out of the question, and that I would observe that in his reply to the American Government he had been careful to quote the exact words employed in the last resolution adopted by the League of Nations on the subject of an aggressive war.[2] He wished you to know that this reply is to be regarded as simply provisional, because the American suggestion would need close examination from several points of view, and he has no intention of reaching a conclusion about a final reply on this second branch of the subject without full consultation with you regarding its terms. I said that I was sure that you would quite understand how it was that he had felt obliged to make the communication to the press without letting you know beforehand, in view of the haste with which the announcement had been made in America.[3]

---

[1] No. 245.

[2] i.e. the resolution originally proposed by the Polish Delegate: see No. 203, note 3.

[3] In a memorandum of January 7 Sir E. Phipps stated in particular that in a conversation the previous day (cf. No. 109) 'M. Poincaré declared his conviction that the latest American proposals for a general pact to outlaw war were merely made in view of the approaching elections'.

No. 247

Sir A. Chamberlain to the Marquess of Crewe (Paris)
No. 1 Telegraphic [A 106/1/45]

FOREIGN OFFICE, *January 6, 1928, 10.30 p.m.*

Your telegram No. 3.[1]

Please thank Monsieur Briand for his friendly message and the intimation that he intends to keep in touch with me in regard to the American proposals. My intentions are similar, as is also my understanding of the double nature of the proposal (second sentence of your telegram).

I have of course seen text of United States note to French government which is primarily a Franco-American matter, but have received as yet no draft text of arbitration treaty, though I understand from Sir E. Howard that one is on its way to us.

This draft text will, I presume, be in some form a reaffirmation or extension of 1908 treaty. Pending receipt, comment is impossible, but I can of course say at once that on either branch of proposal I agree with Monsieur Briand's observations in fourth sentence of your telegram: as member of the League of Nations we could not accept any text incompatible with our obligations.

There would also seem reason to believe that the draft treaty will contain at least a threefold reservation (1) Monroe doctrine, (2) domestic affairs, (3) matters affecting third parties. I am in some doubt at present as to exact meaning or scope of these reservations, especially the third; at first sight however they would seem to amount to covering in another and more specific way the phrase 'vital interests etc.' in the old treaty. This might be criticised as marking no advance on the 20-year-old text, and being no more on the United States side than a declaration that the United States will not fight for anything—in their view—not worth fighting for.

If on the other hand the draft treaty, when received, proves to be of a more frankly 'all in' nature, shall we not again ultimately be faced with the old difficulty that the rights of war and peace reside in Congress. It is of course probable that the Administration has sounded certain at least of the Senators before launching the present proposals, but the eventual assent of the Senate as a whole to treaties of this nature is a different assumption.

If the treaty is to be of an 'all in' nature it is most important to know whether the Senate are prepared to abandon their previous attitude of insisting on their consent being necessary before any particular dispute is arbitrated. Unless this control by the Senate is eliminated, it enables the United States to avoid arbitration in any case where the Senate object and there can be no equality between the parties, because in other countries the legislature is to a much greater extent led by the Executive government.

The Security Committee will shortly be exploring at Geneva the question of what reservations are necessary in arbitration treaties and the terms in which they should be formulated. It would be embarrassing to ignore these forthcoming discussions in any answer which is sent to the American proposals

[1] No. 246.

and it may be better therefore to delay a final answer until that meeting is concluded.

These are preliminary or cautionary comments, but I offer them as an earnest of my desire to remain in close and constant consultation with Monsieur Briand.

No. 248

Sir E. Howard (Washington) to Sir A. Chamberlain
(Received January 10, 9.30 a.m.)
No. 15 Telegraphic [A 224/1/45]

WASHINGTON, January 9, 1928, 7.50 p.m.

My telegram No. 538[1] and my despatch No. 2352.[2]

Reports in the press regarding Mr. Kellogg's counter proposal to Monsieur Briand and latter's reply received two days ago have been so confusing that I asked Secretary of State today if he would enlighten me.

He then read me Monsieur Briand's reply accepting in substance Kellogg's proposal for a multilateral covenant renouncing war for settlement of disputes but stating that in the opinion of French government such a covenant should be signed first by France and United States and that other countries could then be asked to follow suit. To this Kellogg said he could not agree. Such a covenant must be agreed to by all Great Powers together and signed practically simultaneously. In reply to a question from me he stated that he had not in mind any conference for discussion of such an instrument but thought it could be discussed by himself and representatives of the various Great Powers Great Britain, France, Germany, Italy and Japan to begin with and if agreement were reached could then be extended to other Powers. He admitted instrument of this sort could only have an educative and moral value but that this by promoting world opinion for peace might be very helpful. I said then that I understood this declaration or covenant would be separate and distinct from draft arbitration treaty which is to take place of expiring Root treaty of 1908 copy of which draft treaty was enclosed in my despatch No. 2352 of December 30th. He said this was the case. The first was simply counter proposal to Monsieur Briand's proposal for outlawing war, the second is an arbitration treaty providing definite machinery for settlement of certain kinds of disputes.

He promised me a copy of Monsieur Briand's note which I will forward as soon as possible.

[1] No. 242.   [2] No. 244.

No. 249

The Marquess of Crewe (Paris) to Sir A. Chamberlain
(Received January 10, 8.30 a.m.)
No. 5 Telegraphic: by bag [A 174/1/45]

PARIS, *January 9, 1928*

Your telegram No. 1,[1] of January 6th. Franco-American treaty.

I saw M. Briand to-day and left with him a summary of the observations contained in the above telegram.[2] He is in general agreement with everything you say, and was emphatic on the impossibility of his coming to any agreement conflicting in any respect with the conclusions reached at Geneva. In speaking of the threefold reservation made by America he said that its result is to make the new treaty in effect exactly the same thing as the old. Consequently it seems possible that the Senate may be induced to pass the treaty as a whole, and in so doing, with the use of general terms, abrogate their claim to previous examination of any subject of dispute before consenting to its going to arbitration. The Senate had taken this step in passing some previous treaties, and they might do so again.

M. Briand is awaiting with no little interest the American rejoinder to his reply limiting the general proposal to one of abstention from aggressive war in the terms prescribed at Geneva. He considers that the American move, while not unconnected with the presidential election, is the outcome of an uncomfortable feeling in the country that no sufficiently strong assertion of national feeling against war has lately been made, beyond not very effective participation in the Disarmament Conference.

As to the penultimate paragraph of your telegram, he fully agrees that the final reply to the American proposals should await the opinion of the Security Committee on the subject of reservations to be made in arbitration treaties. He will send here the terms in which ultimately he proposes to reply in order that you may see them before they are definitely settled.[3]

---

[1] No. 247.

[2] A copy of Lord Crewe's memorandum of January 7 for M. Briand was transmitted to the Foreign Office in Paris despatch No. 45 of January 9 (not printed).

[3] In this connection Sir C. Hurst stated in particular in a minute of January 19 that in the light of various conversations with M. Fromageot he surmised that 'the real reason why the French Government were not prepared to enter into a multilateral treaty outlawing war on the same lines as that into which they were prepared to enter in the form of a bilateral agreement with the United States is that they do not feel that they can subject themselves to the same measure of obligation vis-à-vis Italy that they can vis-à-vis certain other countries such as the United States.'

No. 250

Letter from Sir E. Howard (Washington) to Mr. Vansittart

[*A 530/36/45*]

Private

WASHINGTON, *January 10, 1928*

My dear Van,

With regard to the conversation between Mr. Frank Simonds and Craigie, of which you enclosed a record in your private letter of the 20th December,[1] I think I can say the following:

I have a great feeling of appreciation for Mr. Simonds as a journalist. I believe he is always trying to be absolutely objective and that he has probably more knowledge of European conditions than any other living American journalist. What he writes or says is very nearly always worth reading or listening to. From what I know of his writings and conversation, however, I always feel that he is quite unconsciously slightly subject to the old New England anti-British prejudices, which Owen Wister[2] has properly termed 'the ancient grudge'. He would not admit this for a moment but there is hardly an article of his that I can remember to have read which is not slightly tinged with it. He is always willing to give France, and later Germany also the benefit of the doubt; he is not generally willing to do so with regard to Great Britain. This, however, does not prevent my liking him personally and considering that it is well worth while following what he says.

Now, as regards his remarks to Craigie. I agree that there is a general feeling throughout this country which has been assiduously cultivated by the Big Navy people and never sufficiently combated by others that America was let down by Great Britain at Washington and that the British delegation at Geneva was trying to repeat the same performance. It is the Big Navy party, as I said before, which have endeavoured to exploit in every way the view that His Majesty's Government was pledged in principle at Washington to parity not only in battleships but also in cruisers, and for some reason or other—principally because no one here cares to risk unpopularity in Congress by taking up the cudgels in favour of Great Britain—this legend has been allowed to grow until it is very generally believed. During the Geneva Conference and again now with a new Navy Bill before Congress the Big Navyites are exploiting it for all they are worth. Indeed it seems to be almost their principal stock-in-trade. I am rather inclined to think also that it is the best card they have to play.

With regard to the Conference itself I often feel that if we had only quite at the beginning told the American delegation that we were out for parity—ton for ton and ship for ship—and had not endeavoured to prove to them, which I understand we did do, that they did not require what we needed, the whole situation would have been very much changed. It would have then been impossible for the Big Navyites to say that we were endeavouring to evade the principle of parity.

[1] No. 238.   [2] A well-known American novelist.

Now, as regards the feeling throughout the United States on this question, I am convinced from all I hear that there is throughout the greater part of the Middle West, the South and the West very little keen interest in the Big Navy programme. J. A. Spender,[3] who has just come back from a tour all round, has told me that the Press men, whom he mainly saw in the big centres, hardly ever condescended to talk about it. Phillip [Philip] Kerr and Wickham Steed tell me the same thing; and I cannot help feeling that unless we make some mistake by giving the Big Navyites a chance to start another yell about England the interest in Congress will subside in a short time.

The 'New York Times' had a letter from some man the other day, Phillip Kerr tells me, pointing out that under the new naval programme it was proposed to spend more on the American Navy in five years than the whole of the capitulised [sic] value of American Universities throughout the country; also the expensive upkeep is going to be a considerable stumbling block.

As regards Mr. Simonds' final remarks—that the two countries could never conclude any agreement on any important political subject owing to the deep and latent distrust with which each side regarded the other. I frankly think that he was speaking for himself. When he instanced as the type of an agreement one in regard to belligerent rights at sea, it seems to me that he entirely disregarded the fact that the interests of the two countries in this matter are rapidly approaching the point where they will join and continue to run on the same lines. That is really the important factor to be remembered.

What Mr. Simonds said about Robert Cecil, or rather what he told Craigie was Robert Cecil's reply to his request for an interview is, of course, grotesque. But these things we must sometimes expect.

On the whole I have not been too much disturbed by Frank Simonds' articles written during his English visit. The last one that I read on the Navy question was, I think, by no means unfair as representing the British attitude, which he described as John Bull saying to Uncle Sam—'Well, if you must build, build and be damned to you, but for God's sake don't let's quarrel about it.'

One other article I think was, so far as I can judge, not really descriptive of the general feeling in England, as it was extremely pessimistic both as regards the political and industrial future of the country. I think he must have been inspired by some close adherent of Lloyd George's.

Yours ever,

Esme Howard

---

[3] Former editor of the *Westminster Gazette*.

No. 251

Sir E. Howard (Washington) to Sir A. Chamberlain
(Received January 13, 9 a.m.)
No. 17 Telegraphic [A 290/1/45]

WASHINGTON, *January 12, 1928, 2.30 p.m.*

My telegram No. 16.[1]

Secretary of State told me today he could not understand why some French papers seemed to think his proposal for a multilateral treaty would be a blow to League of Nations. That was not at all his intention. He was glad that League should continue to do all the work it could for promotion of peace in Europe. He repeated emphatically that his suggestion was really in the nature of a declaration against war which, though abstract, would have great moral value on public opinion in the countries that signed it and on public opinion generally. He thought that if the countries mentioned in my telegram No. 16[2] would join in such a declaration another article might be added to it allowing other countries that so wished also to sign. But he insisted that he must bar any mention of an aggressive nation as no satisfactory definition of an aggressive nation had yet been found. He said that French ambassador had told him he hoped to be able to hand him French reply on his (Secretary of State's) return from Havana[3] on January 19th.[4]

[1] Not printed. This telegram of January 11 summarised Mr. Kellogg's reply of that date to M. Briand's note of January 5. Mr. Kellogg's note, which had been communicated to Sir E. Howard by the State Department, is printed in Cmd. 3109 of 1928 as enclosure 2 (iii) in item No. 1. Mr. Atherton, U.S. Chargé d'Affaires in London, communicated a copy of the note to Sir A. Chamberlain on January 13.

[2] Great Britain, Germany, Italy and Japan.

[3] The sixth international conference of American States opened at Havana on January 16, 1928: see the Appendix, paragraphs 67–9.

[4] In transmitting to the Foreign Office copies of the Franco-American correspondence of January 5 and 11 Sir E. Howard stated in particular in Washington despatch No. 82 of January 13 that Mr. Kellogg had 'always made it clear that he will not sign any Treaty of the kind proposed by M. Briand with one Power alone since that would lay the United States open to the charge of favouring one country as against others'.

Sir E. Howard commented that 'such a multilateral treaty or declaration as outlined in Mr. Kellogg's latest proposal would have considerable moral force and should not therefore be rejected lightly as wholly unpractical though this criticism is the obvious one to make. I also feel rather strongly that though United States public opinion now rejects the idea of any general arbitration Treaty covering disputes of all kinds there is at the present moment a strong movement towards some more idealistic policy than the isolationist role followed since the war. There is little doubt in my mind that once a Treaty of this sort was signed the people of the United States would begin to ask themselves if it really had any value unless there was some machinery for its enforcement. Once that question began to stir in their minds, it is probably [*sic*] that they would be on the verge of understanding the core of the whole problem which is that, without economic sanction at least for the enforcement of penalties against some Nation which violates the Treaty, there is little real hope of establishing permanent peace.'

Letter from Sir E. Howard (Washington) to Mr. Vansittart

[*A 543/133/45*]

Private and confidential   WASHINGTON, *January 13, 1928*

My dear Van,

Your private letter of the 12th [22nd] December[1] enclosed a memorandum by Craigie recording a conversation with Lord Eustace Percy in which the latter gave his reasons for believing that any conversations with the United States Government regarding the question of belligerent and neutral rights at sea should be put off till after the Presidential Election. You stated that the Secretary of State wished to have my observations on the various points raised by Lord Eustace.

As regards the first point, that it would be a mistake to discuss any question with the United States Government at a time when the primaries for the Presidential Election are on, I should as a general rule entirely agree with Lord Eustace's views. Any President who was again running for office would unquestionably be very chary of embarking on discussions of this kind with a foreign Power, especially England, since the result might well affect his chances of nomination at the Party Convention. This however is not the case with Mr. Coolidge. He is in the most independent position any President can be in and his Cabinet are equally independent. He can afford to snap his fingers at the Primaries and, provided as Colonel House says and as I believe, that this question of belligerent and neutral rights is one that the Senate leaders of both parties want to see settled, there seems to me to be less danger of this particular question being made a party question than any other that might come up for discussion.

As to Mr. Hoover, if he becomes President, being the man with whom to negotiate such an agreement, I am also inclined to agree with Lord Eustace. But we are very far from sure that he will be President and we know that he is a member of the Coolidge Cabinet so that his weight in the present Cabinet will probably be thrown on the side of an agreement. It is quite possible that he may not even be a member of the next Administration.

I do not quite understand what Lord Eustace means by saying that he would prefer to wait five years rather than act now, because in any case this matter must be discussed and settled before the Washington Treaty relating to Capital Ships, etc. comes up for discussion which it must do two years from now.

I am therefore strongly of the opinion that we shall probably never get a more favourable moment than the present for initiating such discussions with the United States Government because:

1. The President is in an independent position.

---

[1] This letter and its enclosure dated December 1, 1927, recording Mr. Craigie's conversation on November 30 with the President of the Board of Trade (not printed) were in the sense indicated below.

2. Mr. Hoover is perhaps the most important member of his Cabinet and while he would not be directly engaged in the discussions his opinion would certainly carry great weight.

3. We have, as Craigie says, in Mr. Olds, the Under Secretary of State an asset of real value as he is probably the man with whom the real discussions would be carried on.

4. Leading Republicans and Democrats in the Senate are, I believe, in favour of such an agreement. Senator Borah speaking of the Geneva Conference to Mr. Philip Kerr two days ago spoke, I understand, strongly in favour of it.

If I may make a suggestion as to the procedure to be adopted in case His Majesty's Government propose to take this matter up seriously I should say that we ought first to enquire of the Secretary of State whether the United States Government would think it worth while, in order to avoid what appears to be now the only possible future cause of serious trouble between the two countries, to discuss quite informally the question of belligerent and neutral rights at sea in order to see whether it is possible for us to arrive at any measure of agreement. If Mr. Kellogg and the President consider that the moment is inexpedient the matter will end there. If on the other hand they are in favour of it, we could suggest that perfectly informal discussions might be initiated between Broderick[2] who has the greatest blockade experience of anyone so far as this country is concerned, myself and the Naval Attaché to the Embassy on the one side and Olds and presumably some representative of the Navy Department here on the other. This should not arouse any attention and we might I think work without the Press ever discovering that anything was going on, just as we did in the Blockade Claims matter. My idea would be to take the points mentioned in Craigie's memorandum[3] one by one, long distance blockade, continuous voyage, absolute and conditional contraband etc. and see how near we could get to each other. I should of course keep the Foreign Office informed of every step taken.

If we find there is no hope of agreement, we should have to give it up, but if we discover that there is practical agreement in most subjects, we could then go on to a negotiation *en règle* in the way the two Governments think best. I really believe this offers the best hope of an agreement. We need not act in a great hurry, no special pressure would compel us to accept solutions without careful study. I daresay the whole period covered by such conversations might be a year or even more. But, if we succeed, we shall have laid the foundation not only for a continuation of the Washington Treaty, which is very important, but also for a naval entente between the two countries which will more than make up for the failure at Geneva.

I do feel, however, that a beginning ought to be made without delay. The present moment despite the coming Presidential Election is far from inauspicious and we ought to avail ourselves of it.

Yours ever,
ESME HOWARD

---

[2] Commercial Counsellor in H.M. Embassy at Washington.   [3] Annex to No. 216.

No. 253

Sir E. Howard (Washington) to Sir A. Chamberlain
(Received January 18, 11.4 a.m.)
No. 26 Telegraphic [A 405/1/45]

WASHINGTON, *January 17, 1928, 5.30 p.m.*

My telegram No. 17.[1]

I should be grateful to know what you think of Mr. Kellogg's last note to the French government regarding treaty to renounce war[2] in order that I may know what line to take in discussing it with him since he is sure to speak about it on his return from Havana. It has struck me on thinking the matter over that perhaps M. Briand's insistence on confining his renunciation to aggressive war if treaty is to be multi-lateral, is because he fears that treaty will be joint and not an identic instrument. It is only natural that if treaty is to be binding on France as regards Germany, which it would be if it is joint treaty and Germany signs it, she could hardly pledge herself not to resort to arms in self-defence if attacked by Germany which is what signature of such a joint treaty would amount to. If on the other hand United States government only contemplates signature of identic treaties of this kind with different Powers, it seems to me that as France would only be binding herself vis-à-vis United States, there is no more reason for French government to wish to restrict treaty to renunciation of aggressive war only than there was when M. Briand first suggested such a treaty in May [April].[3]

I should be glad to know if you agree to this view and if so whether I should mention it to the Secretary of State.

[1] No. 251.   [2] See No. 251, note 1.   [3] See Volume III, No. 355.

No. 254

Sir A. Chamberlain to Sir E. Howard (Washington)
No. 98 [A 2/1/45]

FOREIGN OFFICE, *January 17, 1928*

Sir,

I note from the letter which Your Excellency addressed to Sir W. Tyrrell on November 14th last[1] and from your telegram No. 539[2] of December 30th that Mr. Kellogg has lately assured you emphatically that the United States Government are in favour of the total abolition of submarines.

2. You will be aware that at the Washington Conference the British delegation proposed the abolition of the submarine, and the subsequent course of events is shown in the enclosed extract from a note by Mr. Malkin which appeared in the British Year Book of International Law, 1922–23.[3] The

[1] No. 225.   [2] No. 243.
[3] Mr. Malkin's note entitled 'The Washington Conference' is printed in this yearbook, pp. 179–82; the passage relating to submarines is printed *ibid.*, pp. 181–2.

Washington Treaty of 1922, for the protection of the rights of neutrals etc., which resulted from the discussions mentioned, has been ratified by the British Empire, the United States, Italy and Japan, but not by France.

3. Should you see no objection, I feel that advantage might usefully be taken of the opportunity offered by Mr. Kellogg in the conversations reported in your letter and telegram under reference to suggest to him as a first step, that the United States Government should now urge upon the French Government the advisability of ratifying the treaty above mentioned. Mr. Kellogg will readily appreciate that it is for the United States Government, who convened the Washington Conference, to take such action as may be possible to secure progress in the matter of this treaty.

I am, &c.,

(For the Secretary of State)
ROBERT VANSITTART

No. 255

Sir R. Lindsay (Berlin) to Sir A. Chamberlain (Received January 24)

No. 64 [A 515/1/45]

BERLIN, *January 19, 1928*

Sir,

I asked Herr von Schubert to-day if he had any views to express regarding the exchanges of notes between Paris and Washington about the proposed treaty for preventing wars. He replied that he could only offer purely personal opinions on the subject, which had not yet been before the German Cabinet. Moreover Dr Stresemann having been ill since Christmas, he had only seen him once for twenty minutes and had not discussed this question with him. Hitherto Germany had not been involved in the discussion at all and the only actual event had been that the American Embassy had officially communicated copies of the notes addressed to Paris. He would prefer that Germany should not be drawn in at all, but should remain entirely outside any controversy, and when at the outset thereof, the German press had displayed some 'Schadenfreude'[1] over the French embarrassments, he had disapproved its attitude and exerted himself to modify it. Following the controversy therefore at a distance only and through information derived mainly from the press, he was inclined to sympathise with the American point of view. As to procedure it certainly seemed to him more reasonable from the purely practical point of view that the treaty, if it were to be multilateral, should be discussed at the outset by all prospective parties to it, rather than that other Powers should be invited to adhere to an already signed Franco-American instrument in the terms of which they might wish to introduce amendments. Moreover why should the French Government be allowed to assume the attitude of giving a lead to other Governments? On the substance of the treaty too he was inclined to agree with the American

---

[1] Malicious delight.

point of view and he did not think the French were right in endeavouring to limit the scope of the proposed treaty to wars of aggression. I said that if the French were to express openly what they really felt on this subject, they would probably say 'we consider, rightly or wrongly, but with passionate sincerity, that we were in 1914 the victims of an unprovoked aggression. We believe that we may in a possibly distant future be exposed to the same peril again and we hesitate, in a treaty of indefinite duration, to exclude such a contingency completely from consideration.' Herr von Schubert admitted that the French might argue on these lines but said that their real difficulty in accepting the American proposal arose from their system of alliances with Poland, Czechoslovakia and perhaps other States. Furthermore, for the French to require America to sign a treaty excluding for ever the possibility of a Franco-American war was to bind America never to join in a war on the side opposed to France, and it was just as absurd for France to require this of America as it was for America to require of France that she should for ever leave out of consideration the possibility of an aggressive war being declared on her.

2. Herr von Schubert agreed that the Covenant of the League must be safeguarded from any appearance of impairment, but it was rather a reductio ad absurdum if, in order to safeguard the Covenant, which was directed solely to the maintenance of peace, it became necessary to bring home to the signatories of treaties ('vergegenwärtigen') the possibility of war. He believed that the American proposals would have valuable moral effects in educating Governments in the avoidance of war and he was disposed to welcome this and any similar effort in this direction.

I have, &c.,

R. C. LINDSAY

No. 256

Sir A. Chamberlain to Sir E. Howard (Washington)
No. 30 Telegraphic [A 405/1/45]

FOREIGN OFFICE, *January 20, 1928, 4.35 p.m.*

Your telegram No. 26.[1]

The American proposals are now under my consideration. As soon as I am in a position to do so I shall consult my colleagues and His Majesty's Government will consult the Dominions. Obviously a good deal of time will be required for this consideration and consultation, but if the United States government took six months before replying to the original French proposal, they cannot complain if we also take time to study the draft treaties.

It would be most inexpedient that you should make any suggestion or give any indication of our views until you receive instructions.

[1] No. 253.

No. 257

Record by Lord Cushendun of a conversation with M. de Fleuriau

[*W 645/28/98*]

TREASURY, *January 20, 1928*

I saw the French Ambassador at his request yesterday afternoon and we discussed various aspects of the position at Geneva in regard to Security and Disarmament for an hour and a half.

After referring to the present deadlock on Disarmament, I told M. de Fleuriau how M. Boncour in December had said that if the deadlock continued it might be necessary to adjourn to a later date the resumption of the technical discussions on Disarmament fixed for March 15th.[1] I asked whether the French Government would take the initiative of proposing an adjournment: in view of the imminence of their General Election it seemed to me very reasonable to argue that negotiations of the importance and delicacy contemplated should be handled by a fresh rather than by an expiring Chamber. M. de Fleuriau said positively that the French Government, just for electoral reasons, could not possibly take this initiative. He explained that at the forthcoming Election the country would revert to an old electoral system, on account of this it was extremely difficult to forecast the result, and old party divisions already showed signs of the breaking up: the present Government would therefore on no account take any initiative which might be distorted for electoral purposes.

The discussion then passed to Security and I emphasised how futile it was for M. Boncour at Geneva to harp perpetually on the Protocol of 1924, suggesting always that it was our refusal to accept it which was preventing the solution of the Security problem. I said that if M. Boncour, as I half suspected, harboured the hope that if a Labour Government were returned in this country they would sign the Protocol, I was perfectly convinced that he was wrong, and mentioned that Lord Haldane, Mr. Snowden and Col. Wedgwood,[2] to name only a few, had already declared themselves against it, to say nothing of the fact that Mr. MacDonald himself had abstained from signing it. I added that it had always seemed to me surprising that the French themselves should espouse it so warmly. M. de Fleuriau declared himself personally no admirer of the Protocol, though he thought it had acquired sentimental prestige among rather uneducated people. He proceeded to a digression on Article 16 of the Covenant, charging successive British Governments in particular, and the League of Nations generally of having never had the courage to repudiate the words at the end of the first paragraph obliging Member States in case of war to prevent all intercourse not merely between their own nationals but those of any other State whether a member of the League or not and nationals of the aggressor.

---

[1] See No. 230.

[2] Member of Parliament for Newcastle-under-Lyme. Colonel Wedgwood had been Chancellor of the Duchy of Lancaster from January to November 1924.

I brought the discussion back to the Locarno Treaties and referred to some words used by M. Briand to Sir A. Chamberlain in December, in which he spoke of the possibility of providing security in the East of Europe by an adaptation of Locarno to Russia and her neighbours,[3] and I asked whether we might expect the French Government to produce any concrete proposals in that sense: the recent French-Jugoslav treaty did not seem to meet the case. M. de Fleuriau replied rather warmly that it was not easy to adapt Locarno to the East of Europe; the Locarno agreements were based on a historic and disastrous fact and the determination to overcome it—the blood-stained battlefields of Flanders, the Rhineland and Alsace Lorraine—and he argued that there was no such concrete historic fact in Poland or the Balkans, and that therefore it was no easy matter to find the subject or the formula of guarantee. I replied that though that might be so M. Briand had no doubt considered the differences when he spoke to Sir A. Chamberlain, and it would be very helpful to know more definitely what he had in mind. I went on to say that H.M. Government viewed with dislike a general form of agreement which imposed on them definite obligations to undefined nations; it would be easier for them to make a bilateral treaty after full consideration of their particular relations with the other party to it. I added that for this reason I quite appreciated that M. Briand might wish to sign a Treaty with the United States but would by no means necessarily wish to extend it in the same terms to a number of other Powers.

I then raised the question of the military and naval deadlock in Disarmament, reminding M. de Fleuriau of our former conversation[4] in which he had spoken of universal compulsory service as an essential part of democratic France. I appreciated his point of view, but this did not alter the fact that it was diametrically opposed to our own and that of Germany and Russia, and did in point of fact preclude any real disarmament by land. M. de Fleuriau claimed warmly and rather surprisingly that France to-day had no army— not at least one comparable to our own highly trained force. He again contrasted the merits of compulsory military service, which meant that a Voter who supported war involved thereby either himself or his family directly, with a voluntary Army—a weapon liable to be used irresponsibly by the somewhat irresponsible democracies which characterised post-War Europe. He made it quite clear, as I anticipated, that his Government could not be moved from the position of refusing to limit in any way their military trained reserves.

After saying that this was not more than I had expected, I told M. de Fleuriau that we felt at least as strongly that, as regards naval Armaments, there must be rigid limitation by classes, including two for Cruisers and Submarines. After all, surprise was admittedly an all-important element in war; if we were to eliminate war, let us rule out the factor of surprise by as rigid a limitation as possible. I understood that the main preoccupation of the French in naval matters was with Italy, and I could not see how the British proposals for rigid limitation would in any way affect French security

[3] See No. 91.   [4] See No. 229, note 2.

adversely vis-à-vis Italy. M. de Fleuriau, after the usual remarks about the French being very behindhand in Naval construction, said that he quite appreciated that we intended to maintain our position as regards limitation by classes; he was going to Paris almost immediately, there he would report his conversation and hoped to be able to bring back proposals when he returned next week.

CUSHENDUN

No. 258

Memorandum by Mr. Cadogan

[*W 1335/28/98*]

FOREIGN OFFICE, *January 20, 1928*

M. Sugimura, Under-Secretary-General of the League in charge of arbitration and security questions, called on me yesterday. He brought with him an enormous dossier, of which the less unimportant papers are attached.[1] I must apologise for their volume, and trust that the following notes may render the perusal of some of them unnecessary.

It will be remembered that the Security Committee appointed three Rapporteurs to draw up reports on the three main divisions of the subject of their deliberations. M. Holsti (Finland) is to report on Arbitration, M. Politis (Greece) on Security, and M. Rütgers (Netherlands) on the articles of the Covenant requiring special study. These reports are to be ready almost immediately, and the Rapporteurs are to meet M. Benes (President of the

---

[1] Not printed. None of the documents filed with the present memorandum is now flagged with a letter, but they would appear to be identifiable as follows:

A Note by M. Sugimura, written on December 22, 1927, entitled 'Travaux du Comité d'Arbitrage et de Sécurité'.

B The draft of the introduction to a synoptic analysis of treaties of security other than those of arbitration and conciliation, dated January 7, 1928, by M. Vigier of the Political Section of the League of Nations.

C The draft treaty of mutual assistance proposed by the Assembly of the League of Nations in September 1923, printed as the enclosure in item No. 1 in Cmd. 2200 of 1924.

D An unsigned and undated memorandum addressed to M. Sugimura.

E A minute covering a model treaty of conciliation by M. Giraud of the Legal Section of the League of Nations: part of the minute was incorporated in M. Holsti's report on Arbitration and Conciliation as section 50: see League of Nations, *Documents of the Preparatory Commission for the Disarmament Conference*, Series VI (Geneva, 1928), pp. 131–2.

F A minute by Mr. McKinnon Wood, Acting Director of the Legal Section of the League of Nations, covering a draft prepared in his section for M. Holsti's report.

G The first draft, dated January 12–14, of three chapters for M. Rutgers' report on the Covenant of the League of Nations. These draft chapters corresponded to Chapters I–III and V of the final report, printed *op. cit.*, pp. 142–9 and 154–5.

H An unsigned report dated January 13 regarding a conversation with M. Politis in Paris.

I An unsigned report dated January 13 regarding a conversation with MM. Paul Boncour and Clauzel.

J An unsigned, undated memorandum on 'Les tendances au sujet de l'arbitrage obligatoire à la deuxieme conférence de La Haye'.

Committee) in Prague on January 26. M. Sugimura will attend the meeting, also Major Walters, Sir E. Drummond's private secretary. The latter will subsequently come to London with the reports in their final form (by about the first week in February), and he will be able to give us an account of the proceedings.

M. Sugimura has been visiting Rome, Berlin, Paris and Brussels, and his object in coming here was to inform us of the lines on which the Secretariat, under his direction, were working, and of the result of his interviews in foreign capitals, and to ascertain our views on these questions.

His own attitude seems to be fairly sound and cautious—at least when he describes it in London. Annex I (Flag A) shows his general idea of the way in which the work should be approached. The general gist of his ideas is that the League cannot proceed by the methods adopted in 1924 and frame general comprehensive conventions which, by attempting to provide for every possible eventuality, end in something so cumbrous and top-heavy as to be unworkable. It must proceed rather by the method advocated in 1925, keeping within the limits of what is possible, building only where a firm foundation can be laid. In particular, he emphasises the need of devoting attention rather to making conflicts less likely to arise than to organising means for their determination (and possibly their extension) when once they have arisen.

His practical proposals are:—

I. *for promoting and generalising arbitration and conciliation agreements*:—he would attempt to frame 'model' treaties rather than a general convention. M. Sugimura is quite sound on this point: he quite understands the disadvantage of a general convention, viz. that although one country might be ready to sign an agreement with other specified countries, it might hesitate to sign such an agreement if any other unspecified nation were free later to adhere to it and claim its benefits. He quite sees that this is a powerful argument against signature of the Optional Clause. He suggests that these 'model' treaties might be framed on the lines of (1) the model treaty for the establishment of conciliation commissions, elaborated by the League in 1922,[2] and (2) the Locarno agreements.

He would like, for the present at any rate, to leave aside the question of compulsory arbitration.

II. *for coordinating security agreements*:—in this connection he contemplates a comparative analysis of (*a*) the Treaty of Locarno, the non-aggression pacts signed by the U.S.S.R. with other governments etc., and (*b*) regional agreements such as the Little Entente etc., with a view to the framing of a model treaty of arbitration and non-aggression. This work has already been done by the Secretariat—see Flag B.

(He advocates leaving aside for the present the question of sanctions.)

[2] For the text of the Assembly's resolution of September 22, 1922, on the procedure of conciliation see League of Nations, *Records of the Third Assembly: Plenary Meetings*, vol. i, pp. 199–200.

In his view the important point is to make sure that all these agreements are in conformity with the Covenant, and he suggests that the test would be whether they comply with the terms of articles 6, 7, 8 and 11 of the Draft Treaty of Mutual Assistance (Flag C).

He told me that in Berlin his particular attention was drawn to the Little Entente agreements. He suggested that it might be possible to ask the Parties to those agreements whether they would be able to modify them in such a way as to make them conform to the provisions of the Treaty of Mutual Assistance referred to above, and he was told that that would give satisfaction. (But I rather doubt whether the Little Entente Governments would go even as far as that towards turning their defensive alliance into something more resembling a Treaty of Mutual Guarantee.)

As to the articles of the Covenant, he insists on two principles, both of which are unexceptionable:—(1) Do not bind the hands of the Council; (2) do not attempt to proceed by way of *amending* the Covenant. He would be inclined to leave articles 10 and 16 alone in the hope that the development of arbitration and conciliation may render less likely the necessity for their application.

Flag D is an anonymous minute by someone in the Secretariat, commenting on M. Sugimura's memorandum. It is very verbose and leads nowhere, and can, I think, safely be ignored. The only point in it worth noting is that it draws attention to the fact that the Assembly definitely called for a study of a *general* arbitration convention.[3] Members of the Committee may make use of this argument against M. Sugimura's idea of confining the efforts of the Committee to framing a 'model' treaty.

The studies of M. Sugimura and of this anonymous member of the Secretariat resulted in the drafting of a model treaty of conciliation (Flag E) which is, I think, little more than a combination of the League model treaty of 1922 and the Locarno agreements, with certain modifications. In this connection, M. Sugimura suggested that the machinery of conciliation might be rendered more complete, and the 'gap' in article 15 of the Covenant[4] might be filled, if States would agree by bilateral Treaties to accept as binding a recommendation made by the Council by a two-thirds majority. (The suggestion has been made by M. Politis, see top of page 3 of Flag H.) At first sight it would seem that if any two Governments choose to make such an agreement, that is their affair, but I suggested to M. Sugimura that the matter might require closer examination. If such an agreement were made by two Governments and one of them, in a dispute with the other, in the event refused to accept a recommendation made by two-thirds of the Council, what would be the position? Would the Council be called upon to enforce its recommendation? If so, what would be the situation of those Members of the Council who had voted against it?

After this preliminary work, we have a first tentative draft report prepared by Mr. McKinnon Wood for M. Holsti (Flag F). The first ten pages of this

[3] See the resolution referred to in No. 208, note 1.
[4] i.e. the possibility of legitimate recourse to war if the Council of the League of Nations failed to settle a dispute submitted to it.

are purely historical and require, I think, no comment. They define, in a manner which according to our view is entirely orthodox, the difference between justiciable and non-justiciable disputes, and they recapitulate the measures already taken and the proposals already made for dealing with both kinds. On page 12 the author discusses the possibility and the necessity of coordinating existing arbitration treaties with the Covenant and with each other. As regards the 'promotion and generalisation'[3] of such treaties, the report points out that this is to some extent achieved by constant discussion of the subject at Geneva. Turning to the possibility of positive action, the report suggests that there are two alternative courses, the opening of a general convention or the formulation of a model treaty. The report is quite sound on the difficulties and disadvantages of a general convention, and inclines to the second alternative. The only (possible) advantage of a general convention is that two States, whose relations made it difficult for them to negotiate direct, might be able to adhere to a general convention which would draw both within its orbit.

Lastly there is the draft report of M. Rütgers on the articles of the Covenant (Flag G). Here again, a great deal of the report in its present form is harmless, being mainly in the nature of an historical recital of facts. The rapporteur deals first with Article 10 and recapitulates all the discussions which have taken place at Geneva. He examines the various definitions which have been attempted of the term 'aggression' (the discussions at the time of the Corfu incident,[5] the Treaty of Mutual Assistance, the Protocol[6] etc.). This is all done quite fairly and the conclusion is that there can be no one single simple definition of 'aggression'. It is therefore regrettable that on page 13 he proceeds to suggest certain 'factors' which may contribute to an assumption of aggression, several of these factors being, I should say, more than doubtful.

On Article 11 the report seems to be harmless, and there is a discreet and welcome omission of all reference to Article 16.

At the end of his report M. Rütgers devotes a special chapter to the need for ensuring the maintenance of communications with the League at a time of crisis, and in conversation with me M. Sugimura laid great stress on this as being possibly one of the most practical contributions that can be made to the solution of the problem.

So far, then, I think that this preparatory work need cause us less apprehension than I had anticipated. The Secretariat seem to be on the right lines, and two at least of the Rapporteurs seem to be tractable. M. Sugimura expressed to me personally his doubts about M. Politis, whom he had seen in Paris. We have not seen what M. Politis is drafting, but the Protocol is his particular 'King Charles' head', and M. Sugimura has his apprehensions although the record of his conversation with M. Politis (Flag H) would seem to show that gentleman in most reasonable mood. M. Sugimura told me that he found great distrust of M. Politis both in Rome and Berlin.

[5] See No. 19, note 7.
[6] The Geneva Protocol of 1924.

As regards the impressions he has gathered of the attitude of other Governments, M. Sugimura told me that he found, as he expected, a healthy scepticism in Rome government circles, though amongst certain of the officials he noticed a reasonable disposition to work loyally with the League within the limits of reasonable possibility. In Berlin Herr von Schubert had urged particularly the need of simple and intelligible formulae. Anything so complicated as the Protocol must collapse of its own weight. Germany of course still has misgivings about Article 16. The German attitude in regard to the compatibility with the spirit of the Covenant of certain existing defensive alliances has already been alluded to above. M. Sugimura had seen M. Hymans in Brussels, who was generally in accord with the views expounded by M. Sugimura. A short interview with M. Paul Boncour is recorded at Flag I: M. Sugimura has returned to Paris to continue his discussions there.

As regards our own views, he had found all that he wanted in the communication which we have made to the Secretary-General,[7] with which he professed himself to be in hearty agreement.

The production of M. Politis' report and the meeting at Prague may change the situation, and it is therefore perhaps unnecessary to examine more carefully the documents which have been submitted to us. They are only tentative, and not final texts, but still I think that so far as they go, they are reassuring in that they do not propose much that is mischievous or with which we should have to disagree.

Whether anything that the Security Committee can produce out of such material will have the very slightest effect, for immediate purposes, on the general political situation in Europe or on the state of armaments, is another matter. It is difficult to believe that the most enthusiastic—M. Boncour, Dr. Benes or M. Politis—really think that such a result can be achieved in such a manner, or that any really appreciable advance towards security can be made by the 'promotion and coordination'[3] of treaties which will no doubt be signed when the time is ripe, but which must have a basis in fact. No doubt all these labours keep public opinion focussed on the necessity for devising means for the peaceful settlement of disputes, and in so far contribute to the more rapid evolution of a series of precedents that may one day be strong enough to impose itself as a rule. But that is a long process, and it is fatuous— or dishonest—to suppose that the Security Committee can by a stroke of the pen so change the mood of Governments that on March 15th next they will be prepared to agree to measures of disarmament which they rejected in April last. So I am afraid there will be more 'disillusionment', but the world must be coming to expect that, and to realise that progress in these matters is not one rapid and successful advance but a slow growth nurtured largely on the experience gained from the failure of too ambitious schemes.

A. CADOGAN

[7] The observations of His Majesty's Government on the programme of the work of the Committee on Arbitration and Security are printed in *Documents of the Preparatory Commission for the Disarmament Conference*, Series VI, pp. 166–76.

Flag J is a paper prepared by the Secretariat summarizing the arbitration proposals made at the Second Hague Conference in 1907. It has only academic interest but should perhaps be kept with these papers.

A. C.

No. 259

Memorandum by Mr. Torr[1]

[A 560/133/45]

FOREIGN OFFICE, *January 20, 1928*

The policy, to be adopted with regard to belligerent rights, now under consideration arose from the failure of the Geneva Conference. The conclusions drawn from that failure and from subsequent developments have been that America does conceive of herself as having naval 'needs', that those needs are fundamentally different from our own, that she is likely to build as many ships as her big navy people want and that before many years have passed she may have a bigger fleet than we. The prospect is disquieting. Nevertheless we could afford to be indifferent to America's naval expansion, holding that war between our two countries is unthinkable, were it not for the fact that there is a great bone of contention between the United States and ourselves—viz: the question of belligerent rights at sea. With regard to this question we have received plain intimations that the United States will never again tolerate such interference with their trade as they suffered in the last war and that, in the event of our trying to enforce again a blockade similar to that of 1914–1918, war with the United States is not merely not 'unthinkable' but 'probable'.[2] It is to obviate the danger of friction over this question in some future war time, when tempers will be short, that the policy of agreement in times of peace has been adumbrated. Nevertheless have not our deliberations been overshadowed by another consideration too? Has not there lain at the back of our minds all the while an instinctive dislike of the idea of America owning a navy larger than our own and a hope that if agreement is reached over the blockade rights question, thus eliminating America's need for a big navy, the wind will be taken out of the big navy party's sails and America will cease to build? The policy we advocate attempts in fact to kill two birds with one stone.

2. There is however yet a third factor which has influenced the framing of the policy we now propose. We have had to conciliate the traditional Admiralty view. The Admiralty desire to maintain at the highest level our rights of blockade. We say:—'It is better to give away ten per cent now than to have to give away ninety per cent when the crisis comes. And if we negotiate now we shall only have to give away ten per cent because America herself as a great naval power will want to keep her own hands free.' If our present policy is approved then, we shall be committed to an endeavour to

---

[1] A member of the American and African Department of the Foreign Office.
[2] See the enclosure in No. 209.

maintain belligerent rights at a high level. Thus with our single stone we shall be attempting to bag not two birds but three: viz:—

(a) Removal of the only probable cause of war with the United States;
(b) Reduction of the United States building programme; and
(c) Maintenance at a high level of belligerent rights at sea.

3. Now of these three birds which we hope to bag I submit that the first two are sitting close together, but the third quite a long way off. When we consider the first two we regard America as she regards herself at the moment, i.e. as a champion of neutral rights. It is to defend neutral rights (her own of course) that she requires her big cruisers. That is what we were saying after Geneva. And we felt a half hope that if America's wishes with regard to neutral rights could be met, she would not increase her navy. If we regard the problem thus, we see that to secure the first two of our desired ends—viz: the removal of the only probable cause of war between the United States and ourselves and thereby to remove America's need for a big navy and so retain our own supremacy—we must be prepared to give America, before she builds, the thing that she is building for. We must be prepared in fact to agree to, more or less, 'the freedom of the seas'.

4. The policy of the freedom of the seas is one this country has traditionally opposed, since it would deprive her of her one offensive weapon. Nevertheless there is much to be said for it. It would:—

(a) Remove the one probable cause of war between ourselves and the United States. And the United States is the only country which could break up the British Empire.
(b) Induce (perhaps) America to abandon her big navy schemes. And for an island power like ourselves the existence of a navy bigger than our own is an uncomfortable fact even when that navy belongs to a country with whom war is 'unthinkable'. And is it really unthinkable? Admiral Plunkett[3] thinks not. And certainly United States interests are now as world-wide as our own, with consequent world-wide competition and world-wide possibility of conflict. Indeed, if United States aggressiveness increases, it might well be that war between us would be unthinkable only because in such a war both combatants would be impregnable. We cannot fight the United States; and so long as we maintain our naval superiority they cannot attack us. But without that superiority our position is a very different one. Can we be sure enough of American good-will to risk abandoning our one protection against her possible aggressiveness, if that protection might have been safeguarded at the cost of surrendering our claimed rights of blockade?
(c) Prepare the way for a general disarmament at sea, for without the right of blockade big navies would be nearly as useless as they are expensive. Our special position as an island, dependent on overseas supplies, would of course have to be safeguarded in any scheme of

[3] Commandant of the Third Naval District and of the Navy Yard at New York.

naval disarmament, and to this end something more than a three power agreement would probably be necessary; but if we met the wishes of the United States, and presumably of the continental powers too, with regard to blockade, we should be in a far stronger position than we were at Geneva to urge our claim to a privileged position with regard to the defence of our overseas supply routes.

5. The policy of the freedom of the seas therefore, though novel to this country, is not now, in altered world conditions, one which we can afford lightly to reject. In addition to the points above enumerated, this also has been argued in favour of it:—that the submarine has perhaps so altered the conditions of naval warfare that we might be blockaded ourselves, and that the aeroplane has perhaps so altered the conditions of warfare in general that wars in future will be over long before blockades can become effective.

6. But the policy of the freedom of the seas seems to be one which the Admiralty and the C[ommittee of] I[mperial] D[efence] are not likely to approve. We have therefore gone half way to meet them. Let us endeavour —we say—to keep belligerent rights high; but let us by agreement with the United States lay down rules for them now so that when we come to assert them in time of war, the United States will have no cause of complaint. The United States will agree to this because as a great naval power themselves they will wish to keep their own hands free. They will want to safeguard their own rights of blockade. At once we see how far this bird is sitting from the other two; how fundamentally different is this policy from that we have been considering hitherto. It is a policy of sharing with the United States the mastery of the seas, and it is open to far less obvious objections than the policy of the freedom of the seas. Like that policy it removes the one probable cause of war between this country and the United States—provided of course that when we come to find ourselves at war, the United States sticks to her bond— and unlike that other policy it is calculated to maintain our naval power as regards the Continent undiminished. It does however involve a totally different conception of the United States. For the purpose of this policy we must regard her, and persuade her to regard herself no longer as the champion of neutral rights at sea but as a great and potentially aggressive naval power.

7. Now I submit that we cannot, any more than America, have it both ways. Either we must treat with America as the champion of neutral rights or we must approach her as a confederate in sea power—potentially herself aggressive. We cannot draft an agreement which would satisfy her in both characters at once. If she regards herself as a neutral, she will want belligerent rights kept down. If she regards herself as a great naval power potentially herself aggressive she will want those rights maintained. Our policy towards America must therefore depend on which of these two rôles she decides to adopt.

8. But we have still perhaps a little lapse of time before us in which we may be able to influence her in her choice of rôles. Hitherto, since the war at any rate, she has regarded herself as a neutral. Standing apart, she sees, or

thinks she sees a Europe perpetually menaced by the danger of a new conflagration. She sees the English fleet waiting to interrupt her trade again when that conflagration breaks out. She means to protect her interests against that danger. She will build beyond parity—for that is what even her conception of parity means—and safeguard her European trade. If the clash in Europe comes, we may be faced with the alternatives of war with the United States or complete surrender to her wishes in the matter of blockade. Have we anything to gain by giving way to her in advance, now? To do so means in fact the 'freedom of the seas'. The possible advantages to us of that policy are enumerated in paragraph 4 above.

9. If we should decide that the advantages above enumerated (see paragraph 4) outweigh the disadvantages and that we will endeavour to secure them, then we must approach America as a neutral and without delay. Without delay, because one of the principal advantages we would hope to secure would be an abatement of the American building programme and because the big navyites' argument, which represents the general view in the United States at this moment, is the neutrality argument. There is however yet another reason for not too long delaying. As their fleet grows the United States may, by our own calculation, themselves grow less inclined to an abandonment of naval rights. If it is we then who for the reasons above indicated (see paragraph 4) are to urge the freedom of the seas, we must do it soon.

10. But there is no such need for haste if we are to adopt the policy adumbrated to meet the views of the Admiralty and C.I.D. An agreement maintaining at a high level the naval rights of belligerents is not likely to appeal to America so long as she regards herself as a neutral, at a moment in fact when she is preparing a huge building programme to defend her neutral rights. Before she can conclude such an agreement, she must change her outlook. We shall have to be very subtle if we are to make her do this by mere persuasiveness. But time may work in our favour. When America no longer suffers under a, to her, galling sense of naval inferiority she may well be easier to treat with. At present does not the whole strength of the big navyites' position consist in their compatriots' determination to be in the next war profitably neutral? Would not the big navy men's position indeed be positively strengthened if we were to approach them now with a proposal for maintaining belligerent rights at sea at a high level? We could disguise the proposal, but the 'trap', and such it would be surely called, would not be difficult for the 'victors of Geneva' to expose.

Conclusion

The alternatives therefore which seem open to us would appear to be:—
(a) To move *now*, while America still regards herself as the eternal neutral and is building to defend her neutral rights, for the freedom of the seas and for disarmament; or—if we hold that it is more important for us to maintain our rights of blockade than to try to induce America to refrain from out-building us—

(*b*) To wait. To let the big navyites build, holding ourselves that war between us is unthinkable except over one point, to let America grow sure of her naval strength and grow too, with her growing imperialism, into the realisation that she may herself one day need the offensive weapon of blockade, and *then* to remove one probable cause of war between us by negotiating a definition of belligerent rights.

C. J. W. TORR

No. 260

Letter from Sir E. Howard (Washington) to Mr. Vansittart.

[A 782/133/45]

Private and confidential   WASHINGTON, *January 20, 1928*

My dear Van,

There is one more argument in favour of an arrangement over blockade measures with the United States which I think you might use with advantage. It is this. So long as we have no agreement, the United States are in the happy condition vis-à-vis of us of 'heads I win, tails you lose'—for this reason. If they are belligerents, they will without doubt put the strictest interpretation on to blockade procedure to the detriment of our trade and we shall not be able to do more than protest. If we are belligerents and they are the neutrals on the other hand, they will certainly not hesitate to force us by using convoys either to give up the right of search at sea or else to go to war which, unless I am quite wrong, we simply cannot afford to do. But if we come to an agreement, whatever it amounts to, it will be six to one and half a dozen to the other when war breaks out.

I met Nicholas Murray Butler[1] at dinner at Colonel House's in New York the other night and he was most insistent on getting this matter settled saying it was the only thing that could divide the two countries and was the basis of all real desire over here for a big fleet. I said nothing—fortunately it is not necessary to do so when N. M. B. is present.

Yours ever,
ESME HOWARD

[1] President of Columbia University.

No. 261

Sir A. Chamberlain to Sir E. Howard (Washington)

No. 132 [A 546/406/45]

FOREIGN OFFICE, January 23, 1928

Sir,

The American Ambassador called this afternoon.

It was the first time that I had seen him since his return from the United States. He spent an hour with me chatting pleasantly, but the conversation was not very important or very instructive, for he began it by saying that, though he had hoped to have instructions to speak to me on various matters and had sought for them, he had received none and his visit, therefore, had no object but to resume touch. Naturally, we spoke about the failure of the Three-Power Conference at Geneva and what has followed from it. I found that he shared my regret that, when he first asked me as to the probable attitude of the British Government if they received from the United States an invitation to such a conference, I had not suggested a preliminary and entirely confidential exchange of views as to the proposals which the United States contemplated making. Mr. Houghton said that the President had certainly been greatly disappointed by the failure, but he had not changed his policy. It would have been easy for him to rouse an overmastering feeling in the United States, but he had not done so. The United States had formulated a building programme, and it was a serious one, not to be dismissed as mere pretence, but the Ambassador was convinced that there would be no misunderstanding between the two Governments; his only anxiety arose from the state of public opinion in our respective countries and from the dangers which arise from indiscreet speeches and newspaper controversies. For himself, he said, he had determined that the best service he could render to good relations was to abstain from making any speeches throughout the spring.

I expressed my agreement with the Ambassador's view that in present circumstances the less said the better. I told his Excellency that, even before the conference had broken down, His Majesty's Government had decided to review the programme of naval construction which they had previously approved, and I remarked that he would have observed the reductions which we had made in that programme as it affected the present year and the year 1929.[1] For later years the programme stood subject to such review as it was the normal duty of a Government to make as the time for its execution approached.

The Ambassador observed that it did not seem to him that any useful purpose would be served by attempting fresh negotiations on the subject at the present time. He remarked upon the fact that in the course of the current year, there would be a Presidential election in America and elections in France and Germany, whilst a General Election must take place in this country not later than 1929, and he seemed to find in this series of electional contests an additional reason for deferring any fresh discussions on the subject.

We passed from this subject to the negotiations in regard to arbitration now proceeding between France and the United States. I told the Ambassador that I could not help regretting that there had not been more of that prior consultation in this case, the absence of which had proved so injurious to the success of the Three-Power Conference. He would remember that many months ago he had asked, on Mr. Kellogg's instructions, what would be the attitude of His Majesty's Government towards a proposal for the renewal of the Root Treaty. I had replied that I could take it upon myself to

[1] See No. 229, note 8.

say, without any consultation with my colleagues, that His Majesty's Government would be prepared to renew that treaty, but that if it were desired to enlarge its scope I should have to consult the Cabinet and His Majesty's Government in Great Britain would have to consult the Dominions. He had then told me that there was no question of any change in the treaty, but merely of its renewal,[2] and from that day until I had read in the newspapers the nature of the proposals which the Government of the United States had made to the French Government I had had no inkling of any change in their intentions.

The Ambassador did not accept the justice of my comparison between the two sets of negotiations. He observed that the proposal to outlaw war had come from M. Briand, and he interjected the question, 'Why had M. Briand made it?' I replied that I had had no previous indication of M. Briand's intention and that I had no precise knowledge as to the origin of his proposal. I suspected that it was something in the nature of a brain-wave which had occurred to M. Briand when making a statement intended to improve Franco-American relations and that probably M. Briand himself had no precise ideas when he made his famous declaration.

Mr. Houghton agreed that this was probably so, but he remarked that, in any case, the proposal had originated with M. Briand. Political considerations could no more be neglected in the United States than elsewhere. There were people like Mr. Nicholas Murray Butler and a number of women and Senator Borah who took the matter up and the Administration could not refuse to entertain a proposal which, on the face of it, was an effort to avert the danger of war. Mr. Houghton rather flattered himself that the latest American note placed his Government in a favourable position and was something of a poser for M. Briand. He asked me if I saw any reason why M. Briand should object to make multilateral the terms of a treaty which he had been ready to conclude as between France and the United States. I replied that I thought that M. Briand was right in saying that he could not sign the multilateral agreement without a reservation of France's obligations under the Covenant. I was not clear that the same objection might not have applied to his own bilateral draft.

I asked the Ambassador whether he, who had so long represented his country in Germany,[3] had formed any opinion as to how the proposed multilateral treaty would be regarded by the German Government. It seemed to me to present to them exactly the same difficulty as my original suggestion for the outlawing of war between Germany and Poland at Locarno and as the first draft of the Polish resolution proposed to the last Assembly of the League.[4] I made it clear to Mr. Houghton that I did not press him for a reply on this point, and he did not give me one, though I think he clearly appreciated Germany's difficulty.

I told his Excellency that there had been no consultation between the

---

[2] See Volume III, No. 396.
[3] Mr. Houghton had been American Ambassador at Berlin 1922–5.
[4] See No. 202.

French and British Governments on the subject of the French reply. M. Briand had excused himself for not taking the British Government into his confidence on the ground of the pressure which was exercised upon him by the United States Government to publish it at once. The information which I had had about the treaties had reached me fragmentarily, and it was only last week that I could form a clear view of what was proposed and prepare a memorandum on the subject for my colleagues. I must consult them, and there must, of course, be consultations between His Majesty's Government here and in the Dominions. I hoped, therefore, that the American Government, who had now communicated their draft to me 'for consideration', would not expect me to make an early reply.

The Ambassador said he was unable to speak for his Government, but he thought it would be a very good thing if we could avoid intervening at the present stage between France and the United States in regard to the multilateral treaty. He hoped, however, that no difference would arise in regard to the amendment of the Root Treaty. It appeared to him that the changes therein introduced were more of language than of substance and that the new text amounted to very much the same thing as the old.

As to this, I said that any tribunal which had to interpret a text of a treaty and found that new language had been substituted for that which had appeared in an earlier treaty between the same Powers would naturally say that such a change of language would not have been made unless it were intended to mark a change of substance, and they would seek to establish a difference between the two. I confessed that at present I was not very clear what that difference was. It was one of the points which we should have to examine and upon which it would be absolutely necessary for me to consult the other Governments of the Empire. In regard to a simple renewal of the Root Treaty, the only point which I had had to investigate was the form of treaty proper for signature in the present constitutional position of the States of the Empire, and on this subject I had already been in communication with the Governments of the Dominions.

I am, &c.,

AUSTEN CHAMBERLAIN

No. 262

Memorandum by Sir A. Chamberlain[1]

C.P. 22 (28) [A 154/154/45]

Confidential   FOREIGN OFFICE, *January 24, 1928*

The Franco-American Draft Pact of Perpetual Friendship and the American Draft of an Arbitration Treaty to Replace the Anglo-American Arbitration Treaty of 1908.

I circulate to my colleagues papers bearing on (1) the Franco-American negotiations for the conclusion of a Pact of Perpetual Friendship, and (2) the

[1] This memorandum was circulated to the Cabinet.

American draft of an Arbitration Treaty which has just been communicated to us to replace the existing Root–Bryce Arbitration Treaty on its expiration next June.

The two draft treaties are really quite distinct, and I therefore propose, for the sake of greater clarity, to treat them separately in the following explanatory statement:—

(1.) *Draft Treaty of Perpetual Friendship*

In April 1927 M. Briand, in a public message to the United States, declared the readiness of the French Government to sign with that country a treaty 'outlawing war.' This rather vague declaration was, we are informed by the French Foreign Office, received in America by both political parties with a success which had surprised M. Briand himself. In order to meet the earnest wish expressed in the first instance by the American press and public men, and secondly, by the American Ambassador at Paris, who is stated to have been acting unofficially but under instructions, M. Briand drafted a short treaty of two articles whereby both countries agreed, according to M. Briand's phrase, to 'outlaw war.' The draft treaty, the text of which will be found as Appendix I,[2] was communicated to the United States last summer by the American Ambassador at Paris.

Under the draft treaty it was proposed that France and the United States should agree to 'condemn recourse to war and renounce it respectively as an instrument of their national policy towards each other.' The settlement of disputes of whatever nature was 'never to be sought by either side except by pacific means.'

While it is true that Mr. Borah and other influential personages in the United States, together with a certain section of the United States press, gave a warm welcome to the idea underlying the draft treaty, the reception accorded to it by the Administration was from the first exceedingly cool. Embarrassed by the support given to the proposal by a number of their adherents, yet unwilling to conclude a treaty which, so far as the United States is concerned, might give France a free hand to pursue in Europe policies appearing aggressive in American eyes, the United States Government did nothing at all in the matter until the end of December last. On the 28th of that month Mr. Kellogg suddenly addressed to the French Ambassador at Washington a note in which he stated that his Government were prepared to accept M. Briand's draft, provided that it was turned from a bilateral into a multilateral treaty to be signed by 'the principal Powers of the world' and to be 'open to signature by all nations.' It was suggested that the United States and French Governments should jointly submit such a treaty to 'the other nations of the world.' It is difficult to resist the conclusion that the abrupt launching of this proposal, after the long delay of nine months since the Briand plan was first mooted, has not been timed entirely without an eye on the presidential election which takes place next November. The

---

[2] Not printed: cf. No. 236, note 3.

State Department gave the widest possible publicity to the note almost before there had been time for it to reach the hands of the French Government.

To Mr. Kellogg's note M. Briand replied accepting the idea that the treaty should be multilateral, but suggesting (*a*) that it should first be signed by France and the United States before being submitted to the other nations of the world, and (*b*) that the renunciation of war should apply to a 'war of aggression' only. On the 11th January Mr. Kellogg handed to the French Ambassador in Washington a note in which he expressed satisfaction that M. Briand had agreed to make the treaty a multilateral one, but disagreed with his view that it should first be signed by the United States and France alone. The note went on to express surprise that M. Briand should now desire to limit the scope of the agreement to 'wars of aggression,' as this was not the case with the original French draft. Mr. Kellogg now proposed that the treaty and the subsequent correspondence should be communicated to the Governments of Great Britain, Germany, Italy and France [Japan] for their consideration and comment. It is understood that the French Ambassador at Washington has verbally explained to Mr. Kellogg that, the United States Government having transformed the proposed treaty from a bilateral into a multilateral one, France was obliged to limit its effects to a 'war of aggression' in order to take account of her treaty obligations in Europe.

I may add that Mr. Kellogg, in the course of the conversations on the subject which he has had with our Ambassador at Washington, admitted that the draft treaty did not really constitute an act that would 'outlaw war,' but believed that it went as far as public opinion in the United States would allow at present. Mr. Kellogg did not understand why some French papers seemed to think that the proposal for a multilateral treaty would be a blow to the League of Nations. This was not at all his intention. His suggestion was really in the nature of a declaration against war, which, though abstract, would have great moral value upon public opinion generally. Mr. Kellogg insisted that he must bar any mention of an 'aggressive war,' as no satisfactory definition of an 'aggressive nation' had yet been found.

The above is a brief outline of the history of these negotiations. For convenience of reference the texts of the French and American notes appear as Appendix II.[3]

Turning to the text of the draft treaty,[2] it will be seen that articles 1 and 2 only are of importance.

ARTICLE 1

'The high contracting Powers solemnly declare, in the name of the French people and the people of the United States of America, that they condemn recourse to war and renounce it respectively as an instrument of their national policy towards each other.'

[3] Not printed. These notes were (i) Mr. Kellogg's note of December 28, 1927 (see No. 242, note 2); (ii) the French reply of January 5, 1928 (see No. 245, note 4); (iii) Mr. Kellogg's note of January 11 (see No. 251, note 1); (iv) M. Claudel's note of January 21 in reply (printed as enclosure 2 (iv) in item No. 1 in Cmd. 3109 of 1928).

Everything seems to depend on the precise meaning to be read into the phrase 'renunciation of war as an instrument of national policy.' There ought in theory to be no difference between the sense in which the French Government use the term 'war of aggression' and the sense in which the United States Government use the term 'recourse to war . . .[4] as an instrument of national policy.' In practice, however, there is in the American mind a difference of interpretation, since the United States Government have categorically refused to accept the definition 'war of aggression.'

In attempting to narrow the scope of the treaty to 'wars of aggression,' the French Government no doubt have in mind war in general after the elimination of the three exceptional cases specified in article 2 of the Treaty of Locarno. By that article Germany and France mutually undertook not to resort to war except—

(a.) In exercise of the right to legitimate defence.
(b.) Acting in pursuance of article 16 of the Covenant.
(c.) Acting in pursuance of a decision of the Assembly or Council of the League, or in pursuance of article 15, paragraph 7, of the Covenant, provided that, in this last event, the action is directed against the State which was the first to attack.

The above exceptions appear to cover the cases in which a State has to go to war for reasons other than in pursuit of a deliberate policy of its own, i.e., they cover the cases in which hostilities would not constitute rendering war an 'instrument of the national policy.'

If this is, indeed, the French view, there is really not much difference between the two parties, but hitherto it has passed the wit of man to define 'aggression.' It would not be easy, even if France and the United States agreed that the ideas underlying their respective proposals were the same, to find a formula reconciling France's need to cover her commitments under the Covenant with the American need to exclude any recognition of the League as the body with whom will rest the ultimate decision whether a war is or is not 'aggressive.' To judge from the American press comment, America has not the slightest intention of binding herself in advance to accept a League decision on such a point.

ARTICLE 2

'The settlement or the solution of all disputes or conflicts, of whatever nature or of whatever origin they may be, which may arise between France and the United States of America, shall never be sought by either side except by pacific means.'

The settlement of a dispute is never to be sought except by pacific means. The draft Arbitration Treaty, to which I refer below, cites a number of cases which are to be excluded from the compulsory reference to arbitration. The question therefore arises: if such questions are not susceptible of settlement by arbitration and may yet not be subjected to the arbitrament of war, what

---

[4] Thus in original quotation.

machinery is to be set up for their elimination? It would be interesting to know the views of the authors of the proposed pact on this point.

The French Government have now asked for an expression of our views on the text of this treaty and on the exchange of notes, while the American Government have also communicated the documents to the Foreign Office 'for the consideration of His Majesty's Government.' As the Franco-American negotiations show some signs of breaking down, it seems desirable that His Majesty's Government should avoid, if possible, committing themselves at the present stage to any definite expression of opinion. Moreover, it is not very clear what practical purpose the new treaty would serve, since no machinery is to be set up for dealing with questions which at present are held to be unsuitable for settlement by arbitration. The only arguments in its favour which occur to me are (1) that it may, as Mr. Kellogg suggested in a conversation with Sir Esme Howard, promote the formation of 'world opinion for peace,'[5] and (2) that it may tend to draw the United States away from the policy of complete isolation, and may bring about a better understanding there of European problems, such as the reparations and debt questions. This I am bound to admit is at present a faint hope, but a consideration of the American proposal suggests an enquiry as to what course the United States Government would propose to take if, after they had insisted on making the treaty multilateral, one of the signatory Powers broke its obligations in respect of a third party. A rebuff to the United States Government at this stage may drive the Administration still further into the isolationist camp. On the other hand, there are dangers inherent in the very vagueness and uncertainty of the phrase 'renunciation of war as an instrument of national policy.'

In regard therefore to this instrument, it will be well to refrain from any definite expression of opinion at any rate until the text of the forthcoming French note to the United States Government be known and considered. (Since the above was written the text of the French note has been published in the 'Times,' though it has not yet been communicated to this Office officially. It is stated to have been telegraphed to Washington on the 20th January and the revelant [sic] extract from the 'Times' is printed in Appendix II.)

(2.) *American Draft of an Arbitration Treaty to replace the Anglo-American Arbitration Treaty of 1908*

Mr. Houghton, in the course of an interview with me on the 5th July last, drew attention to the fact that the Anglo-American Arbitration Treaty would expire next June, and enquired informally what was likely to be the attitude of His Majesty's Government in the matter. Would they be prepared to renew this treaty? I replied that I could say confidently, even without consulting my colleagues, that we should be most willing to renew the treaty. In the ensuing conversation he made it clear that he merely wished to know, for the information of his Secretary of State, whether the treaty could be renewed

5 See No. 248.

in its present form. We have therefore been proceeding on the assumption that the United States Government desired to renew the Root–Bryce Treaty in its existing form, and His Majesty's Government in Great Britain have been in touch with the various Dominion Governments with a view to its renewal.

This was the position when, on the 29th December last, Mr. Kellogg addressed to Sir E. Howard a note, in which he transmitted, for the consideration of His Majesty's Government and as a basis for negotiation, the draft of a new Treaty of Arbitration to take the place of the treaty which expires next June (Appendix III).[6] Mr. Kellogg stated that the language of his draft was *mutatis mutandis* identical with that of the draft treaty which he had transmitted on the previous day to the French Ambassador for the consideration of his Government. It may be observed that the French Treaty of Arbitration expires on the 27th February next, so that the necessity for an early conclusion of the negotiations is more pressing in their case than in ours.[7]

The French Government have communicated to us a text (Appendix IV)[8] showing the amendments to the American draft which they propose, and which are shown in italics in the appendix. These amendments are discussed below under the relevant articles of the treaty.

In order to permit a convenient comparison between the new American text and the text of the Root–Bryce Treaty of 1908, the two texts have been placed side by side:—

Draft Treaty of Arbitration submitted by the United States Government
Preamble

The President of the United States of America and His Majesty the King of Great Britain, Ireland and the British Dominions beyond the Seas, Emperor of India, determined to prevent so far as in their power lies any interruption in the peaceful relations that have happily existed between the two nations for more than a century, desirous of re-affirming their adherence to the policy of submitting to impartial decision all justiciable

Arbitration Convention of 1908 between the United Kingdom and the United States of America

His Majesty the King of the United Kingdom of Great Britain and Ireland and of the British Dominions beyond the Seas, Emperor of India, and the President of the United States of America, desiring in pursuance of the principles set forth in articles 15–19 of the Convention for the Pacific Settlement of International Disputes, signed at The Hague, the 29th July, 1899[9] to enter into negotiations for the conclusion

---

[6] Not printed. See No. 244, note 2, and see also below.

[7] In a memorandum of March 3 by Sir A. Chamberlain which comprised a revised version of part (2.) of the present memorandum the preceding sentence and the following paragraph were omitted.

[8] Not printed. The appended French draft treaty sent to Mr. Kellogg on January 7 is printed in *Papers relating to the Foreign Relations of the United States 1928*, vol. ii, pp. 813–14.

[9] This convention is printed with annexes in *British and Foreign State Papers*, vol. 91, pp. 970–88.

controversies that may arise between them, and eager by their example not only to demonstrate their condemnation of war as an instrument of national policy in their mutual relations, but also to hasten the time when the perfection of international arrangements for the specific settlement of international disputes shall have eliminated for ever the possibility of war among any of the Powers of the world, have decided to conclude a new treaty of arbitration enlarging the scope and obligations of the arbitration convention signed at Washington on the 4th April, 1908, which expires by limitation on the 4th June, 1928, and for that purpose they have appointed as their respective plenipotentiaries:

The President of the United States of America: 4

His Majesty the King of Great Britain, Ireland and the British Dominions beyond the Seas, Emperor of India: 4

who, having communicated to one another their full powers found in good and due form, have agreed upon the following articles:

of an arbitration convention, have named as their plenipotentiaries, to wit:

His Majesty the King of the United Kingdom of Great Britain and Ireland and of the British Dominions beyond the Seas, Emperor of India: the Right Honourable James Bryce, O.M., and

The President of the United States of America: Elihu Root, Secretary of State of the United States;

Who, after having communicated to one another their full powers, found in good and due form, have agreed upon the following articles:—

Preamble.—There is nothing in the preamble to which serious objection need be taken. It may perhaps appear a rather sweeping declaration that Great Britain and the United States should state that they are 'desirous of reaffirming their adherence to the policy of submitting to impartial decision all justiciable controversies,' but there can be no great objection to such a statement appearing in a preamble.

French Amendment to the Preamble

Apart from purely verbal amendments, there is only one point to which attention need be drawn; at the end of the preamble the American draft speaks of 'enlarging the scope and obligations of the Arbitration Convention signed at Washington on the 4th April, 1908.' The French substitute a phrase, a literal translation of which is: 'enlarging the scope (of the 1908 Arbitration Treaty) and developing, in conformity with modern international law, its obligatory principles.' The French rendering is probably intended to direct attention to the tendencies towards compulsory arbitration inherent in modern international law.[10]

ARTICLE 1

Any disputes arising between the high contracting parties, of whatever nature they may be, shall, when ordinary diplomatic proceedings have failed and the high contracting parties do not have recourse to adjudication by a competent tribunal, be submitted for investigation and report, as prescribed in the treaty signed at Washington, the 15th September, 1914, to the Permanent International Commission constituted pursuant thereto.

Article 1.—There was no corresponding article in the Root–Bryce Treaty. The article does not appear to have any effect other than that of linking up the new draft treaty with the treaty concluded in 1914 for the establishment of a Peace Commission, commonly known as the Bryan Peace Treaty (see Appendix V).[11] This treaty provides that all disputes between the contracting parties of any nature whatsoever (other than those, the settlement of which is already provided for in existing agreements) shall, when diplomatic methods of adjustment have failed, be referred for investigation and report to a permanent international commission. Hostilities are not to be commenced during such investigation. The commission is composed of five members, one member to be chosen from each country by the Government of that country; one member to be chosen by each Government from some third country; the fifth member to be chosen by common agreement between the two Governments. Since its signature in 1914 no dispute has been referred to this Peace Commission.

Under the new American draft a reference to the Bryan Treaty is definitely to be regarded as the first step to be taken by the contracting parties whenever they have failed to reach agreement through the diplomatic channel or whenever there has been no prior agreement to refer the dispute to some other tribunal.[12]

[10] In the revised version the preceding heading and paragraph were replaced by the following paragraph: 'The wording would, however, require modification to provide for the event of signature by the Dominions and India under separate full powers in the form recommended by the Imperial Conference of 1926. The words "between the two nations" in line 8 of the preamble should perhaps be altered so as to read "between their respective countries." The words "to one another" at the end of the preamble are superfluous.'

[11] Not printed: for the Anglo-American treaty of September 15, 1914, see No. 236, note 6.

[12] The revised version here included: 'This article, if it serves to bring the principle of conciliation into greater prominence, is all to the good.'

517

ARTICLE 2

All differences relating to international matters in which the high contracting parties are concerned by virtue of a claim of right made by one against the other, under treaty or otherwise, which it has not been possible to adjust by diplomacy, which have not been adjusted as a result of reference to the above-mentioned Permanent International Commission, and which are justiciable in their nature by reason of being susceptible of decision by the application of the principles of law or equity, shall be submitted to the Permanent Court of Arbitration established at The Hague by the convention of the 18th October, 1907,[13] or to some other competent tribunal, as shall be decided in each case by special agreement, which special agreement shall provide for the organisation of such tribunal, if necessary, define its powers, state the question or questions at issue, and settle the terms of reference.

ARTICLE 1

Differences which may arise of a legal nature or relating to the interpretation of treaties existing between the two contracting parties and which it may not have been possible to settle by diplomacy, shall be referred to the Permanent Court of Arbitration established at The Hague by the convention of the 29th July, 1899, provided, nevertheless, that they do not affect the vital interests, the independence, or the honour of the two contracting States, and do not concern the interests of third parties.

ARTICLE 2

In each individual case the high contracting parties, before appealing to the Permanent Court of Arbitration, shall conclude a special agreement defining clearly the matter in dispute, the scope of the powers of the arbitrators, and the periods to be fixed for the formation of the arbitral tribunal and the several stages of the procedure.

Article 2, paragraph 1, of the new draft takes the place of article 1 and the first sentence of article 2 of the 1908 treaty.

The drafting of this paragraph is defective by reason of the presence of a double attempt to define the word 'justiciable.' If the dispute relates to a matter in which one party is concerned by virtue of a claim of right against the other, the dispute must necessarily be justiciable. Furthermore, if a justiciable case is in question, it is confusing to define it as 'susceptible of decision by the application of a rule of . . .[4] equity.' 'Equity' is an elusive term, and, in international relations it means something more than strict law. The word 'equity' should preferably be omitted.

Continuation of Article 2

The special agreement in each case shall be made on the part of the United States of America by the

Continuation of Article 2

It is understood that such special agreements on the part of the United States will be made by the President

---

[13] This convention for the Pacific Settlement of International Disputes is printed in *British and Foreign State Papers*, vol. 100, pp. 298–314.

President of the United States of America, by and with the advice and consent of the Senate thereof, and on the part of the British Empire in accordance with the constitutional laws of the British Empire, His Majesty's Government reserving the right before concluding a special agreement in any matter affecting the interests of a self-governing Dominion of the British Empire to obtain the concurrence therein of the Government of that Dominion.

of the United States, by and with the advice and consent of the Senate thereof; His Majesty's Government reserving the right before concluding a special agreement in any matter affecting the interests of a self-governing Dominion of the British Empire to obtain the concurrence therein of the Government of that Dominion.

Such agreements shall be binding only when confirmed by the two Governments by an exchange of notes.

Article 2, paragraph 2.—This paragraph takes the place of the remainder of article 2 of the 1908 treaty. As in the case of the earlier treaty we are faced with the difficulty that the special agreement, the conclusion of which is a necessary preliminary to the reference of any dispute to arbitration, remains subject to ratification by the Senate. This body, therefore, has the power, by refusing to sanction the conclusion of the special agreement, to prevent arbitration upon a matter which admittedly falls within the terms of the draft treaty.[14] In this respect the treaty (like its predecessor) is one-sided, but the

[14] The remainder of this paragraph and the following four paragraphs (ending 'by the Administration') were omitted from the revised version which here included the following passage: 'In this respect the treaty (like its predecessors) is one-sided, because the Senate exercises constitutionally on the treaty-making powers of the Executive a restrictive influence, which, differing in degree from that exercised by the Legislature under British parliamentary institutions, is in practice used remorselessly and with little regard for the wishes of the Administration of the day. This is a difficulty inherent in any treaty with the United States.

'At first sight, the following formula, in which the new wording is in italics, would seem preferable to the present United States draft of article 2, paragraph 2:—

' "The special agreement in each case shall be made on the part of the United States of America by the President of the United States of America, by and with the advice and consent of the Senate thereof, *and on the part of His Majesty's dominions by His Majesty the King in accordance with the constitutional practice.*"

'The expression "His Majesty's dominions," used in this sense means the whole of the British Empire, and not the self-governing Dominions.

'The words "in accordance with constitutional practice" would, I am advised, cover the case where the Government of the day (either in Great Britain or the Dominions) considered the subject matter of any "special agreement" to be of such vital importance that they desired to submit the instrument, before ratification, to the British Parliament or Parliaments concerned. In such a case Parliament would have the same opportunity as the United States Senate to reject the agreement if it thought fit. The proposed wording should enable us to meet a possible objection raised by the United States Government that other important treaties have not been submitted to Parliament with the answer that His Majesty's Government or Governments concerned must be the judges of what is or is not of sufficient importance to merit submission to Parliament, and that the advice they tender to the Crown is based upon such a consideration.

'In a draft treaty which had been prepared originally with a view to the renewal of the

balance might perhaps be redressed by a British reservation of the right similarly to refer any 'special agreement,' before ratification, to the British Parliament—should such reference be deemed necessary. Such a reservation would have the added advantage that, in the event of our finding ourselves called upon under the treaty to submit to arbitration some question involving our vital interests as to which an adverse award could not in fact be honoured, Parliament would have the same right as the Senate to withhold its assent to a recourse to arbitration.

The present position with regard to the renewal of the 1908 Arbitration Treaty with the United States is that, in order to conform with the decisions of the Imperial Conference of 1926, it will be necessary to redraft the treaty so that all the self-governing parts of the Empire can participate directly in and sign it. Mr. Kellogg's draft dealing with the 'constitutional laws of the British Empire' is, therefore, quite out of date and must be considerably modified after consultation with the Dominion Governments.

French Amendments to Article 2

The first sentence of article 2 of the new draft provides that 'all differences . . .[4] in which the high contracting parties are concerned by virtue of a claim of right made by one against the other under treaty or otherwise, which it has not been possible to adjust by diplomacy, which have not been adjusted as the result of reference to the above-mentioned Permanent International Commission, &c.' The French counter-draft proposes the omission of the words 'which it has not been possible to adjust by diplomacy.' The purpose of this French omission is not clear, since the French Government cannot mean to exclude the preliminary attempt to settle a dispute through the diplomatic channel.

At the end of article 2, the French Government propose a new paragraph, as follows:—

'In case it is not possible to conclude the special agreement provided for in the preceding paragraph, action will be taken in accordance with articles 53 and 54 of The Hague Convention of the 18th October, 1907.'

This is probably an ingenious attempt by the French Government to overcome the difficulty raised by the constitutional right of the Senate to consent to (and therefore to reject) a special agreement defining the point to be arbitrated. This Hague Convention embodies machinery for enabling the Arbitration Tribunal to settle the terms of the special agreement or 'compromis' as it is called, if the parties fail to reach an understanding. Under these articles, the 'compromis' is to be settled by a commission of five members, two nominated by each of the parties, and the fifth, who should preside, chosen by agreement, or, failing agreement, by a third Power. Where the two parties are unable to agree on a third Power who is to choose the umpire,

1908 Arbitration treaty with the United States the last part of article 2, from the words "His Majesty's Government reserving," were deleted and replaced by the words: "All special agreements concluded in accordance with the provisions of this article shall not be binding until they have been confirmed by an exchange of notes." '

each of them chooses a foreign Power, and those two foreign Powers between them appoint the umpire. If even this machinery fails to result in the appointment of an umpire, he is to be appointed by lot. The result would be to take the matter out of the hands of the Senate if the Senate declines to approve the special agreement arranged between the executive departments of the two Governments. Judging by a statement made to Lord Crewe, M. Briand is hopeful that the Senate may be induced by this means to pass the treaty as a whole, and, in so doing, abrogate its claim to previous examination of any matter in dispute before consenting to the case going to arbitration.[15] It seems most unlikely, however, that M. Briand's proposal can have any prospect of success, since Mr. Kellogg has informed Sir Esme Howard that it would be 'impossible' for the United States Government to avoid submitting any such special agreement to the Senate before entering upon arbitration.[16] Moreover, the Senate would undoubtedly reject any such proposal, even if it were to be made to it by the Administration.

ARTICLE 3

The provisions of this treaty shall not be invoked in respect of any dispute the subject matter of which—

(*a*.) Is within the domestic jurisdiction of either of the high contracting parties.

(*b*.) Involves the interests of third parties.

(*c*.) Depends upon or involves the maintenance of the traditional attitude of the United States concerning American questions, commonly described as the Monroe doctrine.

This[17] article contains the revised formula for the reservations, to be substituted for the old phrase about vital interests, honour, &c., in article 1 of the old treaty.

[15] See No. 249. [16] See No. 244.

[17] In the revised version this paragraph was preceded by the following paragraph: 'Article 1 of the draft treaty admits of no exception from the category of disputes to be submitted, after the failure of diplomatic methods of settlement, to the conciliation proceedings laid down in the Bryan–Spring-Rice Treaty of 1914. Article 3 of the draft treaty declares, on the other hand, that its provisions shall not be invoked in respect of certain classes of dispute. The two stipulations are clearly in conflict. The intention probably is that article 3 should apply to arbitration proceedings only, and this is confirmed by recent press messages from Washington respecting the recently concluded Franco-American treaty. [For this treaty signed on February 6 see *British and Foreign State Papers*, vol. 128, pp. 817–19.] However, in order to remove any element of doubt, it is proposed that the first sentence of article 3 should be amended so as to read: "The provisions of *article 2* of this treaty shall not be invoked," &c., thus removing any possible restriction on the operation of article 1 of the draft treaty.'

The first heading relates to questions within the domestic jurisdiction of either party.

At the forthcoming meeting of the Security Commission at Geneva the general question of the reservations to be made in arbitration treaties will come up for discussion. If as a result of these discussions it is agreed that some reservation as to matters exclusively within the jurisdiction of one of the parties should be formulated, its text should be studied in detail by a competent committee of lawyers. 'Domestic jurisdiction' is not altogether satisfactory as a phrase to express the underlying idea. By international law the principle is admitted that every sovereign State is supreme over certain questions; that is to say that, except in so far as it may voluntarily limit its freedom of action by treaty, it may act as it thinks best in these matters. Within this field no foreign State has a right to complain of any action which may affect one of its nationals. But the extent of this field is vague and indefinite, and I should feel less uneasiness about using the phrase as a reservation in an arbitration treaty if agreement were a little more general as to what it covered.

It may be mentioned as an example that the United States Government have always held that matters relating to immigration are exclusively of American concern, and there can be no doubt that, under this reservation, they expect to remove from the field of arbitration any dispute with Japan in regard to the immigration question—a matter which has in the past led to much ill-feeling between the two countries.

The second reservation excludes disputes which involve the interests of third parties. It is at this point that some form of words might be added so as to exclude from arbitration any question affecting our belligerent rights at sea. Quite possibly one of the objects of the United States Government is to bring this question within the scope of the treaty; they would claim that the question is 'justiciable' because there is a body of international law which is supposed to govern the exercise of such rights, and they might further maintain that it cannot be held to be excluded under article 3, paragraph (*b*), because it is clearly not an 'interest' of a third party to be blockaded. In the present political situation it would be advisable to find some better means than an explicit reservation of such rights, because the latter course would immediately raise a storm in the United States and be used by the Big Navy party as a useful weapon in their campaign for naval expansion. Perhaps the difficulty could be overcome by some elaboration of paragraph (*b*) which, while not specifically referring to the question of belligerent rights, would nevertheless be sufficiently comprehensive to prevent its compulsory reference to an arbitral tribunal. Whether, however, it is done implicitly or explicitly, I think there can be no doubt that any dispute which might prevent the exercise of naval pressure by the British fleet in time of war must be excluded from the operation of the new treaty.

The third reservation is that of the Monroe doctrine. I confess I do not understand how this reservation is intended to work in practice. The Monroe doctrine is a policy of the United States relating to American countries other than the United States itself. It constitutes a notification to all the world that certain interferences on the part of European States with the republics of the Western Hemisphere will be regarded by the United States as a *casus belli*. If, therefore, a dispute between this country and the United States involves the application of the Monroe doctrine, it will be because some action taken by this country towards a Latin-American republic will be regarded by the United States as such an interference with that republic as to necessitate objection, and, in the last resort, belligerent action by the United States. The United States would not base such intervention on a claim of 'right'; it is merely a policy; consequently the intervention would not constitute a justiciable dispute within the meaning of the treaty, i.e., would not constitute a dispute in which the parties to the treaty would be in conflict as to their respective rights. The United States have no 'right' in the technical sense of that term to intervene; such a right must be based on law or treaty.

If a claim by the United States to intervene is to be elevated into a right, the Monroe doctrine must itself be elevated into something of the nature of a law or a treaty. For that purpose it must be defined. Hitherto it has been of the essence of the Monroe doctrine that, being an American *policy*, it was for the United States to interpret the doctrine and apply it as they pleased. In fact, the Monroe doctrine has grown with the growing strength of the United States and is to-day in the American popular mind a different thing from the doctrine originally proclaimed a century ago.

It seems, on the whole, probable that the United States Government, were they asked to define what is the precise intention of paragraph (*c*) of article 3, would reply, if they were frank, that what they desire to avoid is to arbitrate any dispute which might ultimately call into question the validity of the Monroe doctrine, as expounded by President Monroe, and as further interpreted since that time by various American statesmen. I attach in Appendix VI an extract from President Monroe's Message of December 1823, together with quotations from authoritative American pronouncements in regard to the doctrine.[18]

There are objections to inviting the United States Government to define more precisely the intention of this reservation, chief amongst which is the possibility that it might lead to a dispute between the two countries if some new and wider claim were now to be put forward in response to our invitation. If enquiry is held to be necessary on this point, it could best be made by inviting confirmation by the United States Government, for the sake of clarity and to avoid future misunderstanding, that the doctrine is correctly defined by the various declarations quoted in Appendix V[I].

French Amendment to Article 3

The French suggest the addition of a fourth reservation at the end of article 3, which provides that the treaty shall not be invoked in respect of any

[18] Not printed. The extract from President Monroe's address to Congress was the second and third paragraphs of the citation referred to in No. 80, note 2. For the quotations from authoritative statements on the Monroe Doctrine see Volume I, appendix, paragraphs 145-7.

dispute the subject-matter of which 'depends upon or involves the observance by France of her engagements under the Covenant of the League of Nations.'

At first sight France's engagements under the Covenant of the League of Nations would appear to be covered by the reservation in paragraph (*b*), which excludes questions involving the interests of third parties. But the French have evidently wished to make assurance doubly sure on this point, and it will probably be wise that a similar reservation should be added to the Anglo-American draft.[19]

ARTICLE 4

The present treaty shall be ratified by the President of the United States of America by and with the advice and consent of the Senate thereof and by His Majesty the King of Great Britain, Ireland and the British Dominions beyond the Seas, Emperor of India, in accordance with the constitutional laws of the British Empire. The ratifications shall be exchanged at Washington as soon as possible, and the treaty shall take effect on the date of the exchange of the ratifications. It shall thereafter remain in force continuously unless and until terminated by one year's written notice given by either high contracting party to the other.

In faith whereof the respective plenipotentiaries have signed this treaty in duplicate and hereunto affix their seals.

Done at Washington the ⁴day of   ,⁴ in the year of our Lord one thousand nine hundred and twenty-   ⁴

ARTICLE 3

The present convention shall be ratified by His Britannic Majesty, and by the President of the United States of America by and with the advice and consent of the Senate thereof. The ratifications shall be exchanged at Washington as soon as possible, and the convention shall take effect on the date of the exchange of its ratifications.

ARTICLE 4

The present convention is concluded for a period of five years, dating from the day of the exchange of its ratifications.

Done in duplicate at the City of Washington, this fourth day of April, in the year 1908.

(Signed) JAMES BRYCE.
(Signed) ELIHU ROOT.

---

[19] The preceding heading and paragraphs were replaced in the revised version by the following paragraph:

'It may here be mentioned that all the Powers, including His Majesty, accepted in 1907 a reservation made in almost identical terms by the United States when they signed and ratified the Convention for the Pacific Settlement of International Disputes of that year. A reservation of the Monroe doctrine appears also in article 21 of the League Covenant. Apart, therefore, from the undesirability of becoming involved in a discussion with the United States as to what the doctrine means, the hands of the Powers are tied by their own action in 1907.'

The paragraphs on the French amendment to article 3, amended to take account of the signature of the Franco-American treaty of arbitration, which contained the suggested fourth reservation, were included in the revised version following the comment on article 4.

Article 4 of the new draft corresponds to articles 3 and 4 of the Root–Bryce Treaty. The new draft provides that the treaty shall remain in force continuously unless and until terminated by one year's written notice, given by either high contracting party to the other. The old treaty was concluded for a period of five years only, but has hitherto been renewed without modification at the end of each five-yearly period.[20]

From the British point of view the worst feature of the Draft Arbitration Treaty is that we might find ourselves obliged to submit to arbitration, under its present terms, a question involving the future exercise of our belligerent rights at sea; subject to an amendment being introduced which would exclude this possibility, and subject to the other amendments discussed above, which are mainly designed to prevent possible divergencies of interpretation, the draft treaty does not appear to be open to serious objection. It is, however, impossible to say with certainty that, even if its terms are amended so as to exclude disputes affecting the exercise of belligerent rights, some question of vital importance to this country may not arise which we should be reluctantly compelled to arbitrate. If we are to have complete certainty on this point, it would be necessary once again to make some reservation designed to cover questions involving our vital interests. An explicit reservation of vital interests would, however, defeat one of the main purposes of the new draft (which has even been emphasised by the French), that is, the elimination of the clause relating to the vital interests, the independence or the honour of the contracting parties. We should, moreover, by reverting simply to the old text, lay ourselves open to the criticism that we had made no advance during the last twenty years.

It is in any case premature to express a definite opinion on the draft treaty until we are in possession of the report of the Geneva Security Commission, which is conducting an enquiry into the reservations appropriate to treaties of arbitration. This report may be expected in the course of March.[21] Furthermore, it would be well to await the report of the Cabinet Committee now sitting on the question of our belligerent rights at sea before committing ourselves to a definite opinion as to the manner in which those rights should be reserved in the new draft treaty.

The Dominion Governments have been kept fully informed by telegram of the progress of the Franco-American negotiations, and copies of the two draft treaties were promptly communicated to the Dominions Office. Pending

[20] The revised version here included: 'It would appear preferable to substitute "in accordance with constitutional practice" for "in accordance with the constitutional laws of the British Empire".'

[21] The remaining portion of this memorandum was omitted from the revised version and replaced by the following passage: 'At the time of signature of the Arbitration Convention of 1908 an exchange of notes took place with the United States Government, the terms of which are set forth in Appendix V [not printed: see *British and Foreign State Papers*, vol. 101, pp. 209–10]. It would seem desirable to renew these notes subject to such modifications as are rendered necessary by the altered form of the treaty and by developments which have occurred since 1908.

'A. C.'

the receipt of the reports to which I have referred, it would be well that the Dominion Governments should be informed as soon as possible of the preliminary opinion reached by His Majesty's Government in Great Britain in regard to the two draft treaties and invited to give us the benefit of their observations on these instruments.

A. C.

No. 263

Sir E. Howard (Washington) to Sir A. Chamberlain
(Received February 7)
No. 202 [A 903/1/45]

WASHINGTON, *January 27, 1928*

Sir,

Referring to my telegram No. 26[1] of the 17th instant and to your reply in your telegram No. 30[2] of the 20th instant, I fear that I did not perhaps make my meaning sufficiently clear in my above-mentioned telegram. What I intended to convey was that as the Secretary of State was sure on his return from Havana the following week to wish to talk over the negotiations between himself and M. Briand for an agreement to renounce war, it would be of great assistance to me to know what your views were and whether you wished me to express any opinion on the subject. I felt certain that he would enquire whether I had had any expression of opinion from His Majesty's Government, as indeed he actually did, and I was therefore anxious to be supplied beforehand with some indication of the line I should take.

In suggesting in my telegram that the French Minister for Foreign Affairs possibly feared complications from a joint Treaty of this nature to be signed by all powers that were willing to do so, and that these fears might be allayed if the form of identic Treaties were instead adopted, my only object was, in case His Majesty's Government thought that these negotiations should be saved from the deadlock in which they appear to have entered, to find a formula by which possibly such a deadlock might be avoided.

I hoped I had made it clear in my telegram that I had no intention of making any suggestions to the Secretary of State in this or any other sense on my own account nor of giving any indication of your views without instructions, since I asked in the final paragraph of my telegram for your instructions in the matter. I much regret that I did not make my meaning clear.

In any event I was glad to be able to give Mr. Kellogg a reply in the sense of your telegram No. 30 of the 24th [20th] instant, when he asked me at a dinner given by the Irish Free State Minister in honour of Mr. Cosgrave, President of the Executive Council of the Irish Free State, whether I had heard from you on the subject. I told him that all I knew so far was that the matter was of course receiving your close attention, but that even after proposals were officially submitted by the United States Government it would take some time for His Majesty's Government to reply as you would

---

[1] No. 253. [2] No. 256.

have to consult the Dominion Governments. The Secretary of State said he quite understood this and added that he had not and would not speak to the Canadian and Irish Free State Ministers on the subject as he quite realised that this was a matter of Imperial concern to be dealt with by the British Embassy. I thanked him saying that this attitude was no doubt strictly in accord with the views of His Majesty's Governments in different parts of the Empire.

Mr. Kellogg then informed me that he had recently received a further note from M. Briand which amounted to a refusal, couched in very polite language, to consider the Secretary of State's last suggestion for a multilateral Treaty for the renunciation of all wars on the grounds that this would not be compatible with the obligations of the French Government under the Covenant of the League of Nations. I asked him if he would, as before, let me have a copy of this French note and this he said he would do if I came on his next reception day. I accordingly went to see him this morning and reminded him of his promise. He at once sent for copies of the note and then read it to me. I enclose copies herewith.[3]

Mr. Kellogg in commenting on this said that he could not understand why the arguments now used by M. Briand against a multilateral Treaty of the kind proposed did not apply with equal force to a bilateral Treaty. I said I presumed M. Briand considered that a bilateral Treaty renouncing all wars as between the United States and France would not interfere with French previous Treaty obligations and alliances, because he no doubt thought there was no danger of a war of aggression on the part of the United States against any of the members of the League or of the Nations specially bound to France by defensive alliance such as Poland or Czecho-Slovakia. Mr. Kellogg replied that this might be so but the principle remained the same and to this argument I felt there was no reply.

Mr. Kellogg went on to repeat with great vehemence that he would have none of a bilateral Treaty which would be construed by other friendly Powers as in the nature of a defensive Treaty with France since it would leave it open to her to take what action she liked in Europe and ensure the neutrality towards herself of the United States Government. If France rejected this proposal, he said, he thought he might submit it to the other European Great Powers. He was convinced that if Great Britain, Germany, Italy and Japan agreed to it, the rest of Europe and of the world would eventually come in. He again said that while, being without sanctions, the Treaty could have nothing but moral force, he nevertheless believed that this moral force might be of the greatest value in educating public opinion in the direction of peace and it went as far as public opinion in the United States would go at present. It had at any rate the Foreign Affairs Committee of the Senate in its favour. He would never, he said, have made his proposal without previously consulting the Senate leaders and one reason why his reply to M. Briand's first note of the 27th [sic] June[4] had been so long delayed was because the President was

3 Not printed: for this French note of January 21, cf. No. 262, note 3.
4 The reference was presumably to the draft treaty communicated on June 21, 1927.

by that time away in the West and the Senators were scattered all over the country, so that he had to wait till the autumn to consult them.

From being rather lukewarm over the matter it seems to me that the Secretary of State is now taking it very seriously and is most anxious to get this Treaty through by hook or crook.

I could not but remark to him that it seemed to me that there was much to be said in support of M. Briand's objections since it was impossible to avoid the conclusion that a party to such a Treaty might be called on some day to cho[o]se between its provisions and the commitments under the Covenant of the League and previous Treaties such as those of Locarno mentioned by M. Briand in his note.

Mr. Kellogg said he was not going to hurry over his reply to M. Briand's last note and should not consider it until he returned from his visit to Ottawa after the first week in February.

If I may venture an opinion I should like to submit that, if a formula can be found to reconcile what appear to be the conflicting commitments of the multilateral Treaty proposed by the Secretary of State and the provisions of the League of Nations and the Locarno Treaties, etc., it would be useful and to the general interest of peaceful relations for the future as well as, I think, in the particular interest of Great Britain to have the United States Government bind themselves to such a general renunciation of war, even without sanctions against an aggressor nation. It would have, as Mr. Kellogg says, an educative and moral effect which it may be hoped would gradually lead to some more positive and concrete policy in this country against war, than the United States has up to the present been willing to commit itself to.

I have, &c.,
Esme Howard

No. 264

Memorandum by Sir C. Hurst
[*W 1335/28/98*]

FOREIGN OFFICE, *January 27, 1928*

During the two days which I have spent in Paris I have discussed the arbitration problem at considerable length with M. Fromageot. I have not been able to gather much information as to the line the French will take at Geneva during the meeting of the Security Committee. So far as he is aware M. Fromageot will not be attending that meeting himself and he is not in close touch with M. Paul Boncour.

It is clear that our recent note to Geneva about the promotion of arbitration treaties and about security[1] has been regarded by the Quai d'Orsay as a cold douche on those who wish to make progress, and France numbers herself in this band.[2]

[1] See No. 258, note 7.

[2] Sir R. Graham reported in Rome despatch No. 95 of February 3 that 'Signor Rosso, Head of the League of Nations Department in the Palazzo Chigi, told a member of my staff

The Franco-British arbitration convention[3] comes up for renewal this year and the Quai d'Orsay attitude, as voiced by both M. Fromageot and M. Massigli, is that it is an impossibility to renew this convention in terms which date from 1903.

C. J. B. H.

yesterday that the Italian Government agreed with practically every word of the British memorandum on security. They would have hesitated to have drawn it up themselves, as they would probably have been accused of being obstructive; but they would support the views expressed at Geneva.'

[3] This agreement of October 14, 1903, is printed in *British and Foreign State Papers*, vol. 96, p. 35.

No. 265

Memorandum by Sir C. Hurst[1]
[A 691/1/45]

FOREIGN OFFICE, *January 30, 1928*

While I was in Paris I had prolonged and very intimate talks with M. Fromageot on the negotiations between France and the United States with regard to the treaties for the outlawry of war and the renewal of the arbitration convention, and on the corresponding draft treaty which the Americans have offered to H.M. Government for the renewal of the arbitration convention.

1. The first point we discussed was the difference between the meaning of the terms 'war of aggression' and 'recourse to war as an instrument of national policy'. I wrote a minute[2] on one paper before I went to Paris, saying that, so far as I could see, there was no real difference between the phrases and that I did not quite understand why the French had thought it necessary to introduce the term 'aggression' merely because the treaty was to be multilateral instead of bilateral.

M. Fromageot told me that he agreed with me that there was not in reality any difference between the two phrases, but he said that what had happened was that when the French draft was made public last June, in which France agreed to renounce war, the Belgians and the Czechs had both become excited and had expressed alarm lest the French undertakings to come to their aid would lose their value. It was this which really lay beneath the introduction of the phrase 'war of aggression'. Now that the United States had raised objection to the latter phrase, M. Fromageot was at work to see if he could find some satisfactory substitute. He told me in confidence that he was considering whether the phrase 'guerre engagée malgré l'attitude pacifique de la partie adverse' might not be employed. The idea of this phrase is taken from the treaty between Germany and Russia

[1] This memorandum was circulated to the Cabinet on February 7 under cover of a brief note (C.P. 35 (28)) by Sir A. Chamberlain which referred to No. 262.
[2] Not printed.

concluded about two years ago.[3] It expresses the same idea as 'war of aggression' in different language.

2. The next point that I discussed with M. Fromageot was the reconciliation of the draft outlawry of war treaty with articles 16 and 17 of the Covenant, which oblige France as a Member of the League of Nations to take measures which may have to be belligerent against a non-Member state (which might in her case be the United States) because that non-Member state resorted to war with a Member of the League. M. Fromageot's view was that the words 'nationale et réciproque' in the outlawry of war treaty limited the operation of the treaty to war arising out of relations or disputes between the two parties to the treaty and, therefore, did not run counter to any measures, even of a warlike kind, which France was obliged to take by reason of her commitments in the Covenant of the League.

3. The third point we discussed was the apparent inconsistency between article 2 of the outlawry of war treaty, which requires all disputes to be solved by pacific means, and the presence in the draft arbitration convention of reserves as to the cases to be arbitrated.

M. Fromageot's view is that under the outlawry of war treaty, article 2, if the conciliation proposals had failed to result in recommendations which both parties were willing to accept and which therefore ended the dispute, the dispute would drag on unsettled; neither party could go to war. This is what happens under the Treaty of Locarno where France and Germany reciprocally undertake not to resort to war even though the Council, acting under article 15,[4] may not succeed in framing recommendations which both parties are willing to accept. Want of unanimity in the Council in that case does not entitle France and Germany to go to war with each other, because that war is absolutely prohibited by the wording of the Locarno Treaty. Article 2 of the outlawry of war treaty is not limited to arbitration proceedings; it covers all conciliation proceedings, and in these only recommendations can be made.

4. The fourth point was a small one, namely the omission from article 2 of the French counter draft of the arbitration convention of the words 'which it has not been possible to adjust by diplomacy'.[5]

The reason is that these words are superfluous. The draft arbitration convention provides for the dispute going first to the Bryan Commission, and in the Bryan treaty itself there is a provision excluding disputes which it has been found possible to adjust by diplomacy.

5. The fifth point we discussed was the addition in the French counter draft of the reference to articles 53 and 54 of the Hague Convention of 1907, as to the method of settling the *compromis* or special agreement where the parties are unable to agree upon it.[5] M. Fromageot agreed that the intention had been to avoid the power of the Senate to reject a special agreement. The

---

[3] This treaty of friendship, signed on April 24, 1926, is printed, with attached exchange of notes, *op. cit.*, vol. 125, pp. 738–41; see Volume I, Chapter IV, *passim.*

[4] Of the Covenant of the League of Nations.

[5] See No. 262, part (2).

United States have now made the same objection as they made in 1907. To get over the difficulty the French Government are now submitting to the United States Government a new formula under which the question of the terms of the *compromis* would go to the Court at The Hague for settlement, but the terms of the *compromis* as drawn up by the Court at The Hague would not be binding upon either party unless it were confirmed by the constitutional authorities in each country. This would result in the Senate having the right to reject the terms of the special agreement as settled by the Court at The Hague. It is much less likely that the Senate would reject a special agreement which had been settled in this way than if it had merely been settled by the State Department.

6. The next point which M. Fromageot and I discussed was the French phrase for 'matters solely within the domestic jurisdiction of that Party'. This is one of the reserves proposed in the draft arbitration convention offered by the United States and accepted by the French.

M. Fromageot was disposed to agree with me that the clearer French phrase for this was that used in article 15 of the Covenant, 'question que le droit international laisse à la compétence exclusive de cette Partie' and that this was to be preferred to the French phrase used in the counter draft of the arbitration convention.

7. I also had a long talk with M. Fromageot as to the way in which the reserve as to the Monroe Doctrine would work in practice.

I wrote a minute[2] on this point the other day. M. Fromageot said that technically he agreed with me, but that it was no longer open to the Powers to object to a saving as to the Monroe Doctrine. All the Powers, including Great Britain, had accepted a similar reserve in 1907 made by the United States when they signed and ratified the convention for the pacific settlement of international disputes of that year. Apart, therefore, from the undesirability of becoming involved in a discussion with the United States as to what the Monroe Doctrine means, the hands of the Powers are tied by their own action in 1907. Here I think he is clearly right.

C. J. B. H.

No. 266

Letter from Sir E. Drummond (Geneva) to Sir W. Tyrrell
[A 995/154/45]

LEAGUE OF NATIONS, GENEVA, January 30, 1928

My dear Willy,

1. Newspapers have been carrying all sorts of stories as regards the American–French negotiations. Among others, that the United States Government are sending the correspondence to the Great Powers, asking whether they have any observations, or what their views are.

2. I do not know if such is the case, but if it were, might there not be a possibility of leading America into the primary engagement by which League

Members are already bound—viz., never to engage in war without at least a minimum period for arbitration, conciliation and reflection?

3. Now that this big Naval programme has begun, it would certainly be useful to try to secure a 'cooling off' period for America. In any case, it seems to me that an opportunity is afforded of making progress on the lines which you and I have often discussed, viz., to bring America round to concurrence with any measures taken by the League under Article 16 of the Covenant. Personally, I feel that the French have up to now rather badly mishandled the negotiations. Surely they could have secured from the Americans an acknowledgment that war for the purpose of self-defence was permissable [*sic*]. For instance, if Japan declared war, and attacked America, presumably even Borah would agree that America must fight and must declare war in order to secure belligerent rights. If such an acknowledgment were obtained, it follows that defensive war of such a nature could not be outlawed. Is not the next step, therefore, that, as defensive war is permissible, it is only aggressive war to which American proposals could apply; and, once agreement had been reached that aggressive war was to be outlawed, surely it would be extremely difficult for America to object to any measures taken under Article 16?

4. There is one other point which occurs to me. The American formula spoke of war as an instrument for national policy. If I remember rightly, this phrase is taken from Briand's original note; and it would look as if this wording had been deliberately adopted by Briand in order not to preclude war being undertaken because of international obligations under the League Covenant.

5. The American formula would not, therefore, seem inconsistent with repressive or punitive action under the Covenant, though it would, of course, rule out the 'permitted' war according to Articles 12, 13 and 15—i.e., when there is a division of the Council, and the due period has passed. But would this be a calamity?

6. As I said at the beginning, I do not know if it is true that His Majesty's Government has been asked for an opinion; but if it has, I feel justified in writing this letter, and if not, please forgive me!

Yours ever,
ERIC DRUMMOND

P.S. If all the Great Powers have been asked for their views, might it not be useful to take the opportunity of the next Council Meeting for a personal exchange of opinion between the various Representatives concerned who will be here at the time? Is it not desirable that the most important Members of the Council should take a common line as regards principles, at any rate, in a question which is of vital interest to the League?

No. 267

Memorandum by Mr. Cadogan

[*W 930/28/98*]

FOREIGN OFFICE, *January 31, 1928*

Since the last meeting of the Cabinet Committee on Reduction and Limitation of Armaments, there have been some developments which it may be well to summarise, in order to be able to survey the position in which we find ourselves on the eve of the resumption of serious discussion at Geneva.

In the first place, it will be remembered that the Cabinet Committee held its former sittings in November, before the meetings of the Preparatory and Security Committees at Geneva in December. It was then (in November) hoped that these meetings would be of a purely formal character, and that the actual problems of security and disarmament would not be tackled. This hope proved to be justified and we were not involved in discussion of the Disarmament issues on which we had already found ourselves at variance with other governments. But against the possibility of such discussion, instructions were given to the British Delegate, which were summarised thus: 'To state once more, though without controversy, our naval proposals, putting in the forefront the proposed reduction in the size and power of capital ships; to use our influence with the French Government to make military disarmament practicable; and to confirm the international agreement, so far as it has been reached, upon the Air Forces, with a view to establishing a basis of equality between the principal Air Powers of Europe'.[1] Little difficulty was anticipated in regard to the Air. The two formidable issues were (1) limitation of warships and (2) limitation of trained reserves. In regard to these two points the conclusion really was that on the former we could make no concession and that in regard to the latter we must, partly for tactical reasons, maintain our view that in the absence of any limitation of trained reserves there could be no effective disarmament calculated to affect the general sense of security and so reduce the chance of hostilities.

It was hoped that an adjournment of the discussion for some months—an adjournment which was happily secured—would give time for reflection and for discussion between the governments, and it is time now, on the eve of the resumption of the sessions at Geneva, to review the result of such discussion as has taken place.

On the naval question, there are the discussions which Admiral Kelly[2] had with the French naval authorities in Paris in November last (already circulated to the Committee).[3] These show that, although the French are prepared

---

[1] See No. 229.

[2] Naval representative on the British Delegation at Geneva.

[3] The reference was probably to a despatch of November 29, 1927, from Admiral Kelly to the Admiralty of which a copy was sent to the Foreign Office by Lord Cushendun in Geneva covering despatch No. 75 L.N.C.C. (not preserved in Foreign Office archives). Admiral Kelly's despatch reported on a conversation on November 28 with Admiral

to make a slight advance,[4] this does not, in the view of the Admiralty, alter the situation materially, and the Admiralty memorandum on those discussions concludes:—'It does not appear that there is any reason to modify our attitude on the question of disarmament. The above should show that it is only her present feeling of insecurity that prevents France from agreeing to the British method of limitation, and that as regards sound principles we are on firmer ground than she is.'

Further in regard to the naval question, there is the interview between Lord Cushendun and the French Ambassador on January 19,[5] at which the latter was unable to indicate any further concession on the part of his Government, though he promised to discuss the matter with them during his impending visit to Paris. We have not heard that he has brought anything back with him.

From the above it seems that, on the naval question, the French may make a small advance towards our position, but the Admiralty are clear that this is not sufficient, and are also insistent on maintaining our point of view. The situation therefore is not materially different from what it was in November.

As regards the military question, the situation has undergone, if possible, even less change. Colonel Temperley's conversation with Colonel Réquin

Salaun, Chief of the General Staff of the French Navy. Admiral Kelly stated in particular: 'Admiral Saläun [sic] repeatedly emphasised that the French Navy are very much concerned by the present situation. They consider that for them the question of sea communications is of an importance almost as vital as it is to Great Britain owing to the dependence of France in case of war on her colonial and native troops. On this account, whilst they are not concerned with the Navy of Great Britain, they watch with a jealous eye any development of the Italian Navy, and are particularly interested in the ships to be laid down by Germany to replace their existing fleet when its age-limit is reached. The Germans will then have the right to build 10,000-ton ships, but armed for certain with 11″ guns, and they are trying to obtain permission to mount 12″ guns. These vessels will constitute a serious menace to French communications and France must reserve the right to build vessels when required to counter this menace.' The French proposal for limitation of naval armaments (see Volume III, Nos. 137 and 139) was discussed, and Admiral Kelly stated that: 'The only material concession that could be obtained, but which is one of considerable importance, is that the French are prepared to renounce their claim for the transfer of tonnage except in the last two classes, that is to say that *battleship and aircraft carrier tonnage is not transferable.*' Admiral Kelly commented that 'Throughout the whole conversation there was no sign of any spirit of obstruction, but on the contrary a real desire to work in the closest sympathy with a country with whom their hopes of a peaceful future are so closely united.'

[4] *Note in original*: 'The Admiralty memorandum on these conversations says "As regards transfer of tonnage, the so-called French concession will be seen to amount to nothing, as these classes would not be transferable during the life of the Convention in consequence of the restrictions of the Washington Treaty". I submit that this is not an entirely correct presentation of the situation, as there is a note appended to the replacement table annexed to the Washington Treaty to the effect that "France expressly reserves the right of employing the capital ship tonnage allotment as she may consider advisable, subject solely to the limitation that the displacement of individual ships should not surpass 35,000 tons, and that the total capital tonnage should keep within the limits imposed by the present Treaty". So that Admiral Salaun's proposal *does* in fact amount to a concession.' The Admiralty memorandum in question is untraced in Foreign Office archives.

[5] See No. 257.

(circulated to the Committee)[6] shows that, although the French views on limitation of expenditure, and on control, may be modified, their attitude in regard to the main issue—trained reserves—remains immovable. This is only confirmed by Lord Cushendun's interview with M. de Fleuriau.

If, therefore, our hope was that an adjournment of the Preparatory Committee till March might give time for the governments to reach agreement on the main points at issue, it must be confessed that that hope has been deceived.

It remains, therefore, to consider in these circumstances what will be the probable course of events and what would be our best objective.

There seem to be three immediate alternatives:—

(1) The Preparatory Committee might meet on March 15, and after thorough discussion—which is certain to pass through acrimonious phases— it might be able to agree on the preliminary draft of a convention, for what that might be worth. That is on the assumption that those who have so far opposed our naval proposals become reconciled to them. The rather faint chance of this would be strengthened if we could find some way of making those proposals more palatable to their opponents, but for the moment the Admiralty memorandum must be taken as their last word on the subject, and therefore the prospect of agreement cannot but be regarded as slight. No doubt our opponents may be 'bluffing' to some extent, and only a discussion at the Committee itself would reveal how far they would ultimately be prepared to go. But once embarked on a discussion we run the risk of bringing about the second alternative which, on present information, seems more likely to arise, viz.:—

(2) The Preparatory Committee would meet and after discussion would have to record its failure to produce agreement.

It is quite unnecessary to point out that the results of this would be, at best, regrettable. The failure of a League enterprise entrusted to a special League Committee would produce a very bad effect. For it would be a very definite failure, and a distinct check to the policy of 'Disarmament' and all that is implied thereby. The work would be broken off, and it is difficult to see how it could be re-started in the immediate future. In the second place, the deadlock would arise out of a public difference between ourselves and the French, in which we should have the support, on some points, of only a few undesirable Allies. On principle it is obviously most undesirable to quarrel with the French: on this particular issue it is regrettable that we cannot hope that M. Paul Boncour will do much to smooth the asperities of debate or help us find a way to friendly disagreement.

Apart from this unpleasant aspect of a disagreement at Geneva, there is the probability, or rather the certainty, that it will at once bring up the whole question of German (and other ex-enemy) disarmament. The Germans are never tired of insisting that by the Covenant the Members of the League are bound to disarm, and that by the Preamble to the Military Clauses of the Treaty of Versailles, by the Allied reply to the observations of the German

---

[6] See No. 233.

Delegation to the Peace Conference and by the declaration made at Locarno,[7] German disarmament is only a first step towards general disarmament. They will say that if the latter cannot be achieved—and the breakdown of negotiations would for the moment dash all hope of success—it follows that the former can no longer be insisted on. There is a great deal to be said against this argument, and the point will be dealt with later, but for the moment it is necessary to point out that we shall encounter this difficulty from the German side, and that it may give a good deal of trouble.

Then, from the general European point of view, we must consider that a breakdown of the negotiations may be laid at our door. We have saved the French, on former occasions, from their own folly, and it is difficult to avoid suspecting that they look to us to perform the same service again. It has been instilled into us that the French Government, for home political reasons, are forced to push ahead with disarmament: they quote public opinion in France as demanding that something should be done, and that quickly, and if we suggest caution or throw doubt on the possibility of achieving anything really material in a hurry, they shake their heads and make obscure and nervous allusion to their impending general election. Knowing next to nothing about French politics or the French electorate, it has always surprised me, after all that has happened, that disarmament should be a good election cry in France. Amongst M. Paul Boncour's followers, I can imagine that there are some extremer socialists, who are vaguely pacifist in the same way that kind-hearted people in this country are mildly in favour of being as nice as possible to everyone when they direct their attention to foreign politics. I don't know that he looks for any support to the Communists—I imagine he is very far removed from them. If one were very cynical, therefore, one might be tempted to think that he would be rather embarrassed in May if he had returned from Geneva having agreed to any real scheme of disarmament, but that it might suit his book very well if he were able to return pointing out to his pacifists how he had striven for disarmament and at the same time reassuring the bulk of his electors by pointing out that these schemes had been defeated by the Imperialist and aggressive British Government. After all, it is difficult to believe that a nation which, we are told (*vide* M. de Fleuriau, M. Paul Boncour and French speakers *passim*), will never abandon universal military service, is waiting to throw out a government that does not bring about disarmament. Therefore when we are told that the French elections will turn to a great extent on disarmament, it is impossible not to suspect that, if this is true, there has been suppression of the fact that we are expected to play our rôle, and to be held up to the execration of the French elector for standing in the way of the realisation of an ideal which is excellent to advocate but which might be awkward to put in practice.

It would not be very difficult for the French to represent us as the villain of the piece. If a break is forced on the naval question, it will be easy for them to make much of the fact that we are in a small minority, that that is due to our peculiar position at sea, and that really, as they had suspected all along,

[7] See Annex 1 to No. 219.

what we meant by disarmament was that other nations should disarm on land while we maintained our sea-power unimpaired. They will find many believers in this doctrine.

So the situation is unpleasant. Of course, as has been suggested, we can try to shift some of the blame on to the French by pointing out that any so-called disarmament convention that takes no account of trained reserves is a sham and a delusion. That undoubtedly is the fact, but there again we are in a minority, and there again the fact that we—and the Americans—are the only considerable nation that voluntarily adopts the voluntary system, can be adduced in proof that our arguments are not disinterested. If the Preparatory Committee is really committed to a 'second reading' of the Disarmament Convention in March, probably the best tactics would be to insist on taking the Convention in its present form and going through it Chapter by Chapter. That would involve beginning with land effectives. On that we could make our position quite clear—that a Disarmament Convention that puts no limit on trained reserves will not touch the problem which is the objective of all these activities, and that it is useless to talk of 'security' whilst each succeeding generation is trained to war. We could offer to proceed with the other subjects. If the French refuse, the responsibility for the breakdown is theirs. No doubt they will be able to prove to their own people, and to other conscriptionist countries, that we have been disingenuous in asking for the impossible so as to put them in the wrong. But, on the other hand, our attitude might be defensible at home, and might well receive a good measure of support (including that of Lord Cecil and the League of Nations Union). If the French agree to continue the discussion, they can force a break on the naval question, over which they will try to show us in a still more invidious light. In defending our position at home, we could still make use of the trained reserves argument, for it might be argued that we were disinclined to make sacrifices or to take risks in order to secure an agreement that in any case was foredoomed to futility. And the American building programme might make people here even more suspicious of any attempt to tie our hands in naval matters.

(3) There is the third alternative, of adjourning the Preparatory Committee for some months. This would have the effect of postponing all the inconveniences and dangers of the second alternative. It has twice been resorted to—once in April of last year and once in December. On those occasions it was suggested in all good faith that further time for reflection and discussion between the governments might produce agreement. If this hope was sincere, adjournment was a reasonable policy and not merely procrastination. Our experience of ten months or so, however, must make us realise that with the passage of time the rival policies do not seem to assimilate themselves to each other, and that adjournment does not seem likely to lead anywhere. It is perhaps just possible that if we adjourn over the French election, we might find another government in power in France that might possibly take a different attitude in regard to the military question. But it is difficult to quote this reason. The French themselves might say that the preoccupations of an

election make it difficult for them to take part in a critical debate at Geneva at this particular moment. But M. de Fleuriau gave us no encouragement to think that they would give us this lead. There are therefore difficulties about adjournment even if it were desirable. Who is to decide the adjournment, and what reason are we to give for urging it? Technically, perhaps, the Chairman or the 'Bureau' could notify an adjournment. But in practice all the members will be assembled in Geneva on February 20 for the Security Committee, and the Chairman or the Bureau, in the event of a considerable proportion of the members wishing to meet on March 15, would be subject to a good deal of pressure. Probably it would require a vote of the Committee itself. How are they to be induced to give such a vote? Who is to propose it, and on what grounds? We might say that, as we have been unable to come to an under-standing with other governments on points still in dispute last April, we see no prospect of success and therefore think that no good can come of renewed discussion. Then, in addition to the abuse already suggested, we should incur the reproach that the Big Powers claimed to run the League, that we were afraid of public discussion etc. etc. There would also be the usual outburst from the Germans. Nobody else is likely to propose it, so that if we do not, we must fall back on alternatives (1) or (2). In any case adjournment is no solution, nor, in the light of our experience, does it afford much prospect of a solution. In the not very likely event of some other government proposing adjournment, probably His Majesty's Government would willingly consent to it. If it is no solution, it at least has the advantage of postponing the worst difficulties, and it cannot be said that there is *no* prospect of agreement being found during a further adjournment, though experience does not warrant high hopes.

The above has been written on the assumption that we are committed to work on disarmament on the present lines, whether we really think this the best method or not. It is true that we are pledged several times over to disarm: it is not so clear that we are pledged anywhere to sign a general disarmament convention. It is true that under the Covenant the Council is to 'formulate plans' for reduction, but these are 'for the consideration and action of the *several* Governments'. What we told the Germans in 1919 was that the first step towards general disarmament must be a disarmament of Germany. Germany accepted the military, naval and air clauses of the Treaty of Versailles (and may have carried them out). Without that, evidently no one could disarm. Once that was done, other nations were free to reduce their armaments to 'the lowest point consistent with national safety'. At any rate *we* have done so. After the Armistice we scrapped a large proportion of our fleet—a process which was carried still further by the Washington Treaty. We very soon reduced our army to proportions even more 'contemptible'[8] than those of 1914. Other nations have done something of the same—how much, is a matter between them and their consciences.

[8] The reference was to the allegation that the Emperor William II of Germany had used this word in August 1914 to describe the British Expeditionary Force: cf. *The Times*, October 1, 1914, p. 4.

But it does not seem quite certain that 'plans for the consideration and action of the several governments' necessarily involves a general convention for all-round proportional reduction of armaments. Certainly we are nowhere pledged to reduction to the German level. And if German disarmament, carried to the point to which we believe it has been carried, does not produce sufficient sense of security to enable other nations to spare themselves expense which they must grudge, that is no argument in favour of freeing the Germans from restrictions which do not appear to have been severe enough.

But the League has chosen to act as if it were bound to produce a general disarmament convention. The Germans have seized on this and sought to connect general disarmament with their own disarmament in such a way that they can claim to be freed from their part of the bargain if the Allied Governments do not perform theirs. This course has been adopted with our consent, however reluctant, and we are therefore presumably committed to it, with the result that we are now faced with these three alternatives, one of which is favourable though very remote, and the other two of which present obvious inconveniences, if not dangers.[9]

A. CADOGAN

[9] A copy of this memorandum was sent to the Cabinet Office on February 2, 1928, for circulation to the Cabinet Committee on Policy for Reduction and Limitation of Armaments.

No. 268

Letter from Sir E. Howard (Washington) to Sir A. Chamberlain
[*F.O. 800/262*]

Copy
Private   WASHINGTON, *February 2, 1928*

My dear Chamberlain,

I hope you will forgive me if I jot down in a private letter a few considerations which have come into my mind in connection with the so far abortive proposal made last June by M. Briand to the United States Government for a Franco-American Treaty to renounce war. If I do so it is really more in order that I may have some indication of what His Majesty's Government think about it all than because I set any particular value on my own inferences and conclusions.

In the first place I understand from gossip I have had here that M. Briand was first inspired to make this move by Mr. H. Levinson, a well-known Chicago lawyer, who has evolved a plan for settling allied debts and reparations together and works I believe much in cooperation with Senator Borah. Mr. Levinson has explained to me his debt scheme orally and promised to send me papers respecting it. This then I need not say anything about except to mention the fact that it has Senator Borah's support. Mr. Levinson also spoke to me very enthusiastically about the proposal for a Franco-American anti-war Treaty to be made joint and multilateral which he also assured me had the Senator's hearty support. He hoped it would have the support of Great Britain. I merely stated in reply that it seemed to me personally that such a Treaty worded as at present would not be compatible with our pledges under the Covenant of the League of Nations and the Locarno Treaties but that I did not yet know what views His Majesty's Government would take of such a proposal as it had not been submitted for their consideration. The whole aim of His Majesty's Government, I said, was the maintenance of peace and this had been the object of the pledges and commitments of the Locarno policy. It would obviously not promote that object to take further pledges which might in certain circumstances make it necessary for us to break either the one set or the other.

Mr. Levinson seemed to see this but thought the difficulty might be overcome.

I have reported this conversation not so much because it has any value in itself as because it confirms certain conclusions I had already half arrived at with reference to all this business. These are as follows. Senator Borah is at the back of the whole proposition and Mr. Levinson acted as his agent in Paris last spring if indeed he suggested to M. Briand the idea of taking the initiative. In any case it all fits in so well with Borah's well-known penchant for resolutions outlawing war without incurring any risks or responsibilities to prevent war, that we can well beleive [sic] it has his fullest support. At first the proposal did not meet with great favour with Mr. Kellogg and he put it away from June to October without taking any action on it. His explanation of this that the President was away and the Senate scattered has of course a great deal for it, but I cannot help feeling that if he had been really eager about the plan he would have found ways and means in June or July to consult the Senate leaders and let the President know the result. However this may be, he waited till the autumn. When he did consult Borah he found the latter hot and strong for the proposal as he naturally would be if he had inspired it. Now Borah is one of the leaders of the 'insurgent Republicans' in the Senate who hold the power of balance in that body. It is therefore of the utmost importance to the Executive to conciliate these Senate insurgents and here I think we may find the sudden interest shown by the Secretary of State in the proposal with regard to which he was so lukewarm all the summer. This interest has been awakened by the paternal interest in it of Senator Borah and also by the growing knowledge that the Middle West is beginning to clamour for some definite action by the Government for the promotion of world peace. The Middle West is tired of playing the rôle of 'Der Geist der stets verneint'.[1]

All this, however, does not affect the main question which is: Would it or would it not be a benefit for the peace of the world if this country which is now the most powerful in the world could be brought to subscribe to some general Treaty renouncing war, and would it or would it not be in the interest of Great Britain if this could be brought about without sacrificing any of the pledges His Majesty's Government have given in the interests of peace and

[1] i.e. The spirit which always says no: see J. W. von Goethe, *Faust*.

security in Europe? I cannot but think, as I stated in my despatch No. 202[2] of the 27th ultimo that, provided a formula can be found to reconcile such a Treaty with the provisions of the Covenant of the League of Nations and the Locarno and other defence Treaties registered with the League of Nations, there would be a certain advantage in any arrangement that would bring this country within the ring of those which are openly and of[f]icially working for peace and that any such Treaty, declaration or Covenant as between this country and Great Britain would, always subject to the conditions above-mentioned, be of benefit to us for many reasons I need not go into here, but mainly because I believe that of all wars one with the United States would be the most disastrous to the British Empire and such a Treaty would at least make the United States pause before attacking us.

Having said this I must qualify it by saying this, that in my opinion a declaration renouncing *all war* in the future on the part of any Government is really nothing but sheer hypocrisy and humbug because no Government can obviously consent to renounce the right to defend itself if attacked. This is what makes me wonder how M. Briand could have proposed such a Treaty in the first instance even with the United States which France certainly has no reason to fear.

Mr. Kellogg this morning, in telling me about the new Arbitration Treaty which is to be signed with France as reported in my telegram No. 54[3] of to-day, again reverted to the general Treaty or declaration for the renunciation of all war. He repeated that he was not going to prepare an answer to M. Briand's last note of January 21st (see my despatch No. 202 of January 27th) until his return from Canada which will not be till the 10th instant. He repeated that he could not see what difference there was in principle between the original Briand proposal for a bi-lateral Treaty and his own for a multi-lateral one. He said that if France turned down his next note he thought he should probably make proposals along these lines to all the Great Powers and see what success these would have.

From all this I gather that even if France declines to treat any more we must be prepared to give Mr. Kellogg some answer sooner or later and it would be as well to consider whether it is or is not worth while to try to make this geste on the part of the United States Government of some lasting account to us all and not to cast this country back into the arms of the jingoes, the big navyites and the isolationists who are already rejoicing over the prospective failure of the latest peace move.

Whether the right formula can be found or not I don't know. I can only repeat that it seems to me worth trying for.

In this connection I may say that when Mr. Kellogg was holding forth on the subject this morning I could not help interposing a query as to whether, by a declaration renouncing all war, he meant to include also defensive war. 'Of course not', he replied indignantly, 'no country would give up the right to defend itself if attacked'. I said, 'Then why not insert it?' He said, 'Quite unnecessary', to which I answered that it was impossible to be too clear in the

[2] No. 263.   [3] Not printed.

541

wording of international Treaties and I thought that there might in future be many people who would argue that to renounce all war meant to renounce defensive war also. It would at least be open to that construction. To this he gave no adequate reply and I wonder whether some formula could not be found along these lines excluding defensive wars that might, without prejudicing the Covenant and the Locarno Treaties, indeed while openly and explicitly safeguarding them, meet the objections of the United States Government to the mention of 'aggressive war'.

Some time I should be most grateful if you would let me know what you think about the whole question.

Yours very truly,
Esme Howard

No. 269

Memorandum by Mr. Sargent[1]
[W 930/28/98]

FOREIGN OFFICE, *February 7, 1928*

If the disarmament negotiations definitely break down, I have no doubt that the Germans will seize the opportunity of fishing in troubled waters. But, for the reasons given by Mr. Perowne,[2] I think that it would be unwise to assume that any German Govt. would actually demand the cancellation of the military clauses of the Treaty of Versailles in order that they might reintroduce universal military service & restore to the big armament firms the unrestricted right to manufacture war material of all kinds. A retrogressive policy on such lines would arouse the fiercest opposition among those political parties & classes who dread a return of Prussian militarism. I do not say that they represent necessarily anything like the majority of the German nation but they are certainly sufficiently strong & influential at the present time to prevent any Govt. from embarking on a foreign policy to which they would be opposed.

In the case of a definite breakdown of the disarmament negotiations, the German Govt. would probably adopt a purely opportunist policy, and merely try in every possible discussion to confuse the issue by dragging in the argument that the Allied Govts. had violated the obligations they had assumed in

---

[1] This memorandum was written in connection with No. 267.

[2] In a minute of February 6 Mr. Perowne had stated that he did not 'believe that the Parties of the Left in Germany would ever allow the reconstruction of the pre-war German army (& navy) with its officer caste'. Mr. Perowne further stated: 'The real importance of the removal of the restrictions to which Germany is now subjected lies in the faculty which she would thus obtain to resume the manufacture and export of war material. In the meantime there is no particular occasion to believe in the purity of German intentions where disarmament is concerned: there is serious enough reason to believe that she is not observing her disarmament obligations in various directions (though it is not perhaps feasible or expedient for the Allies just at present to raise this issue) & the knowledge that this is the case may quite possibly keep Germany from making too much noise if the Disarmament discussions were to reach a breakdown or a postponement.'

542

the Treaty of Versailles by not disarming down to the level of Germany. By such methods they certainly make things very unpleasant for us since we would be always finding ourselves on the defensive & called upon to justify ourselves,[3] not only to European but more particularly to American public opinion. Again, it would become more & more difficult for us[3] to insist at the League that Germany should be forced to continue to execute the letter of the military clauses of the Treaty & that the Council should carry out for that purpose the investigations in Germany which the Treaty provides for. In fact we might thus witness a gradual process whereby the military clauses would tacitly become a dead letter & the Germans step by step resume their liberty without having to make any formal demand which would raise in an acute form the internal political question of reintroducing compulsory military service.

O. G. SARGENT

[3] *Note in original*: 'i.e. the ex-Allied Gov[ts]'.

No. 270

Letter from Sir W. Tyrrell to Sir E. Drummond (Geneva)

[A 995/154/45]

Confidential   FOREIGN OFFICE, *February 8, 1928*

My dear Eric,

Many thanks for your interesting letter of the 30th about the Franco-American negotiations for a Pact of Perpetual Friendship and the renewal of their Arbitration Treaty.[1]

The position so far as we are concerned is that the draft Pact of Perpetual Friendship has been communicated to us unofficially but that we have not yet received any official request for our views from either side. The matter is still in the stage of bilateral negotiation between the French and the Americans. The draft Treaty of Arbitration on the other hand has been communicated to us officially by the United States Government with the suggestion that it should be substituted for the existing Root–Bryce Arbitration Treaty expiring next June. An arbitration treaty following the same lines as the draft communicated to us has just been signed between the French and the Americans.

You draw attention very pertinently to the desirability of securing a 'cooling-off period' for America. This had already been to some extent provided for under the Bryan Peace Treaty of 1914, although in practice no dispute has yet been referred to the Permanent International Commission established under that treaty. By article 1 of the new American draft Arbitration Treaty the Bryan Treaty is definitely linked up with the new Arbitration Treaty, so that conciliation proceedings under the Bryan Treaty would, if the Arbitration Treaty is signed, be the first step to be taken by the

[1] No. 266.

contracting parties with respect to any dispute which has baffled diplomatic effort. As no reservation of any kind is made in regard to the type of dispute to be referred to the Bryan Peace Commission, you will see that your 'cooling-off period' will be provided under the new Anglo-American Arbitration Treaty (should it prove acceptable) even if the draft Pact of Perpetual Peace does not come to anything.

You say that surely the French could have secured from the Americans an acknowledgment that war for the purpose of self-defence is permissible. I believe that the French are still trying to find some form of words which, while corresponding to the definition of an 'aggressor nation', will yet be acceptable to the Americans. The difficulty is not so much that America condemns a defensive war but that she maintains that it has so far defied the wit of man to define a 'war of aggression' and furthermore that she objects strongly to acknowledging the right of the League of Nations to decide whether in given circumstances a nation is or is not guilty of aggression. Public opinion in America does not yet seem prepared to go further than to say that, when the moment comes, America herself will decide whether or not one of the warring nations can be classed as an aggressor: if she decides in the affirmative, America will then be prepared to make things as difficult as possible for that aggressor. As things stand there seems little hope of the present United States Government binding itself *in advance* to accept a League decision on such a matter. In other words, they are not prepared to recognise League action against a 'Covenant-breaking state' as necessarily branding that state as an 'aggressor nation'.

There is the further question of a possible conflict of obligations between the draft Pact of Perpetual Friendship on the one hand and the League of Nations Covenant and the Treaty of Locarno on the other hand. In paragraph 4 of your letter you correctly surmise that the original phrase 'renounce war as an instrument of their national policy towards each other' first appeared in Monsieur Briand's draft of a bilateral treaty communicated to the Americans last July [June], and it appears to have been deliberately adopted by Monsieur Briand in order not to preclude war being undertaken because of international obligations under the League Covenant. When they originally proposed a bilateral pact to the Americans, the French considered that the insertion of the words 'national' and 'towards each other' had the effect of limiting the scope of the treaty to disputes exclusively concerning the two countries, thus leaving France's obligations under Article 16 of the Covenant unaffected. The soundness of this view is open to doubt, but in any case the conflict of obligations became quite definite from the moment that America proposed to turn the treaty from a bilateral one between France and the United States into a multilateral one to be signed by all the principal Powers: under the draft Pact the signatory Powers would be precluded from taking warlike measures in any circumstances, while under Article 16 of the Covenant of the League and under the Treaty of Locarno such measures are in certain circumstances recognised to be necessary. It is true that the inclusion in the draft Pact of some formula which would admit the justice of a defensive war might probably bring the text into harmony with the obligations assumed by the signatories of the Treaty of Locarno. It would not, however, necessarily remove the conflict of obligations between the draft Pact and the Covenant of the League unless the United States were definitely to recognise action under Article 16 against a Covenant-breaking state as tantamount to a 'defensive war'. As I have shown above, we are still a long way from such recognition.

You suggest in the postscript to your letter that if all the great Powers had been asked for their views it might be useful to take the opportunity of the next Council meeting for a personal exchange of opinion between the various representatives concerned who will be in Geneva at the time. As I have explained above, we have not yet been asked officially for our views in regard to the Pact of Perpetual Friendship and, so far as we know, the other principal Powers are in the same position. Moreover, so far as we are concerned, it will clearly be impossible for us to express any definite opinion in regard to either of these treaties until we have had time fully to consult the Dominions, who are of course closely and vitally concerned. So far as the Pact of Perpetual Friendship is concerned, any such general discussion would seem in any case to be premature until the French and Americans have been able to find some formula which will eliminate the conflict of obligations to which I have referred above.

I must apologise for such a long letter, but, as the whole subject is rather complicated, I thought it might interest you to have a fairly full statement of the position as it strikes me. You will, I know, regard what I have said as entirely confidential and, for the moment, as representing my personal views only.

Yrs. ever,
W. Tyrrell

No. 271

Letter from Sir A. Chamberlain to the Marquess of Crewe (Paris)
[*F.O. 800/262*]

Confidential   *February 9, 1928*

My dear Crewe,

There is a reference in my second despatch of today reporting my conversation with Monsieur de Fleuriau[1] to the question of the air forces. I think it better to put what passed on this subject in the form of a private letter rather than to include it in a despatch, for Monsieur de Fleuriau preferred himself to deal with the matter in that way in writing to Monsieur Briand.

After Monsieur de Fleuriau had spoken of the army and the navy, I remarked that there was a third arm of our defensive services which we had not yet mentioned. I would preface what I had to say on this subject by telling him that I had advised my colleagues that a war between France and England was at the present time improbable to the extent of being impossible,

---

[1] No. 134.

that the Government had accepted this view as the basis from which they studied problems of defence, and that there was therefore no preparation for the contingency of war with France in any decisions which they took. At the same time I could not but observe that the French had an immense superiority over us in the air arm, and however friendly our relations were with a neighbour, one could not wholly ignore their armament when considering one's own. If France and England had only themselves to think of, I did not suppose that we should have any difficulty in coming to an arrangement upon this question. I imagined that the difficulty, if there were one, arose through the fact that France was thinking also of Germany and Italy. As to Germany, it was prohibited from having a military air force. Would it be possible for us to come to any kind of agreement on the basis that Great Britain, France and Italy should each have an equal air force? Did he think that it would be useful for us to enter into any discussion with the French Government on this basis? I could conceive that, if France stood alone in the face of Italy, she might be unwilling to accept parity with that country, but might not the situation be rather different if the agreement were an agreement *à trois*, so any two of us combined would at any moment have double the force of the third party?

Fleuriau seemed to think this rather an interesting suggestion, but of course he could make no direct answer and could only undertake to pass on my enquiry. I said that I should be glad if he would do so in the most informal manner possible as I was only expressing my personal impressions, and he on his part observed that, with my permission, he would write privately to Monsieur Briand on the subject, as it was possible that a reference to it in a despatch might embarrass him. It was after this that Fleuriau said he was convinced any progress in these matters could only be achieved in conversation between Briand and me in Geneva. It is unlikely, I suppose, that anything will be said to you on this subject, but for your confidential information (and guidance in case of need) I may say that such an agreement is eagerly desired by the Air Ministry. I doubt if anything will come of this, but I have been watching for an opportunity to raise the question informally for some time past.[2]

Yrs. sincerely,
AUSTEN CHAMBERLAIN

[2] Lord Crewe stated in particular in his reply of February 12 that he was afraid that the prospects of Sir A. Chamberlain's suggestion coming to anything definite were not very brilliant, at any rate until the atmosphere between France and Italy had become clearer.

No. 272

Letter from M. de Fleuriau to Sir A. Chamberlain

[*F.O. 800/262*]

Copy
Private

LONDON, *le 9 février, 1928*

Cher Sir Austen,

Je communiquerai à Monsieur Briand votre suggestion touchant les forces aériennes. Mais des renseignements que j'ai pris aujourd'hui m'ont indiqué les difficultés que rencontrera la réalisation de votre projet, du fait de la différence entre les programmes des aviations britannique et française.

L'aviation britannique s'est posé un problème séparé des problèmes que l'armée et la marine veulent résoudre de leurs côtés. Elle prétend défendre par elle-même le territoire de la Grande Bretagne contre les attaques aériennes d'un ennemi et contribuer, toujours par elle-même, à la défense de l'Empire Britannique. Elle s'est donc constitué un Etat-major et prévoit des opérations purement aériennes, dirigées par elle seule comme les opérations navales de l'Amirauté.

L'aviation française, au contraire, n'a pas d'existence et de programme particuliers. Elle est partie de l'armée et de la marine. Elle est organisée, non en vue d'opérations séparées, mais en vue de participer aux opérations de la marine et de l'armée. Son augmentation ou sa diminution dépendent donc de l'augmentation ou de la diminution des forces terrestres ou navales dont les forces aéronautiques sont le complément. Les dispositions et la mobilisation de l'aviation terrestre sont établies en France, non en vue de préparer des opérations uniquement aériennes comme en Angleterre, mais d'après le plan des opérations de l'armée, c'est-à-dire que l'ensemble est dirigé vers les frontières de terre que l'armée a mission de défendre. Le système français de l'aviation explique pourquoi nous avons toujours soutenu à Genève le système du désarmement de l'ensemble des forces terrestres, navales et aériennes. Il sera donc très difficile à Monsieur Briand de rechercher avec vous un équilibre entre des aviations, dont l'une, l'anglaise, est une force indépendante, et l'autre, la française, est une branche de l'armée et de la marine.

Je sais que les promoteurs de l'aviation britannique, arme isolée et indépendante, font grand état de la puissance aéronautique de la France. Il leur est, je l'avoue, difficile de prendre une autre base de comparaison. Mais leur ardeur les entraîne trop loin quand ils font de l'aviation française une menace pour l'Angleterre. Je ne fais pas ici seulement allusion aux relations amicales des deux pays, mais aux dispositions et organisations de l'aviation française qui sont orientées vers le Rhin et non vers la Manche. On ne peut pas dire que les escadrilles françaises ne pourraient pas être dirigées contre l'Angleterre; mais rien n'est prévu pour les lancer de ce côté et il faudrait un travail assez long pour modifier leurs plans et en faire l'épouvantail que montre parfois le 'Daily Express'. J'ajoute qu'aux cours de charger les budgets des aviations française et britannique sont à peu près similaires en totaux.

J'ai pensé bon de vous prévenir immédiatement de ce que j'apprenais et je vous prie, cher Sir Austen, d'agréer l'expression de mes sentiments les plus sincèrement dévoués.

A. DE FLEURIAU

No. 273

Sir E. Howard (Washington) to Sir A. Chamberlain
(Received February 20)
No. 313 [A 1208/36/45]

WASHINGTON, *February 10, 1928*

Sir:

My despatch No. 312[1] of February 9th attempts to set out the probable course in Congress of the Bill (H.R. 7359) for the increase of the Naval Establishment.

2. As the course of the bill will be affected by the attitude of the Administration, of the Congress, and possibly of public opinion, it may be useful if I attempt to set forth some considerations on the attitude of these bodies.

3. The President is said to have been bitterly disappointed by the failure of the Geneva Conference and to have decided that His Majesty's Government were entirely to blame. This is said to have caused Mr. Coolidge to feel some resentment, and, moreover, to have decided to be prepared with a large authorized building programme with which to bargain at a future conference. There is some support for the reported resentment of Mr. Coolidge in the asperity of his reference to Great Britain in the passage dealing with the Navy in his message to Congress of December 6th last.[2] Support for his reported wish for a bargaining counter may perhaps be found in his failure to insert any date for the commencement or completion of the programme in bill H.R. 7359 and in the provision of the bill as presented by the Administration empowering him to suspend construction in the event of a new conference, a provision the inclusion of which he is still said to desire. But whether a time limit for the beginning and completion of the programme be set or not, and whether or not a clause for suspension of construction be included, a competent observer declares that he is determined to sign the bill. It is possible that Mr. Coolidge's reiterated intention to oppose any increase of tax reduction beyond the proposed $225,000,000, his clinging to the Administration's flood control proposals which involve expenditures far below what many persons and districts directly and indirectly interested continue to advocate, his opposition to the more expensive plans put forward for farm relief, can be taken, in part at least, as signs of a wish not to prejudice the undertaking of the naval construction programme, by the necessity at the same time to find vast sums for these internal measures.

4. On the other hand, his notorious passion for economy must not be left out of account in any attempt to appreciate his position. Further, he has now

[1] Not printed: for the Bill H.R. 7359, cf. No. 234, note 2.
[2] See No. 234, note 4.

stated (on January 30th) that his programme contemplates the construction being carried out as conditions dictate and Treasury balances warrant. It contemplates no limitation of time as to its beginning or completion. It is a tentative programme. It does however contemplate the building of the ships as fast as possible. In this attitude Mr. Coolidge is supported by the 'New York World'.

5. Congress undoubtedly contains a sufficient number of persons keen enough in varying degrees to vote, other things being equal, for a great Navy. I am informed by the same observer that the bill will undoubtedly pass both Houses. But degrees of keenness on the subject do indeed naturally vary—and it is possible that the information which has at length been asked for as to the total expenditure on the Navy involved by already authorised construction, by the proposed construction, by the increase of personnel entailed by the latter, and by the maintenance of both, may, when it is forthcoming, so much alarm those less ardent in their pursuit of a place in the Naval Sun, as to cause them to do all in their power to oppose the bill. Mr. Britten,[3] of the Naval Affairs Committee, has already on several recent occasions, shown much nervousness on this head, even seeming to deprecate requests for information on this account! The alarm is likely to be particularly marked among representatives of districts interested in flood control and farm relief. Senators Glass, Nye[4] and Borah are reported to have expressed strong disapproval of the bill, the latter declaring his intention to attack it in the Senate. The 'New York World' states that the House Appropriations Committee and the Senate Finance Committee are determined to fight the new construction bill to a finish. Whether, however, opposition of this sort, even if it takes place, will lead to serious modification of the bill, I cannot prophesy; I mention it to indicate what are the possibilities of delay in debate, and of opposition to the passage, of the bill.

6. The press continues to divide along expected lines. The 'New York World', while endorsing the proposals for construction as redefined by the President on January 30th, attacks them as envisaged by 'the Admirals' at the hearings before the House Committee. It continues to emphasize the enormous sums involved and finds that if these gentlemen have their way 7 billions of dollars would be spent in the next decade. The 'Baltimore Sun' and the 'Springfield Republican' discover the manifest inconsistencies between the denials of competition and assertions of comparisons with Great Britain. The latter deprecates official suggestions that the object of the bill is to give a 'big stick' to be used in future naval conferences and then dropped. It is dangerous to militarize a nation thus. It becomes progressively more militaristic till the catastrophe comes.

7. Even the 'Chicago Tribune' expresses doubts on the advisability of the bill, and whether it merely shows an intention to provide a complete and balanced fleet or something more. Is the programme planned for bargaining purposes? Are the United States trying to tell the world they insist on having

---

[3] Congressman Britten was a representative of Illinois.
[4] Senator C. Glass of Virginia; Senator G. P. Nye of North Dakota.

their own way and will get it by power of their wealth? 'The national wealth has a proper use when applied to national requirements. Such use would be in building an adequate navy with a view to minding our own business. Otherwise it will be regarded as bullying.'

8. A move against the big navy proposals is reported to have been started among members of the Greater New York Federation of Churches. A number of ladies belonging to a patriotic body representing every State of the Union have supported the proposals, after hearing the Secretary of the Navy, Representative Piatt Andrews [Andrew],[5] and Mr. Castle of the State Department. The manifestly competitive complexion of the programme and the great sums involved may be expected to make an impression not entirely favourable on the mass of the people especially in the Middle West.

9. If I might hazard a guess I should say that the bill can probably be passed, either in its present or a slightly modified form.

10. The situation seems however to be sufficiently doubtful to make it highly desirable that no definite position should be taken up in Great Britain either on the United States, or on British, construction plans. The prospect of great expenditure is unlikely to be congenial in all sections of this country. If it is not certain that Great Britain will start a large programme in the future, there may be some hesitation in embarking on a programme that might lead to a race. Nothing however should of course be said on the point in the press. Silence, leaving matters in doubt, seems to be the wisest course. I doubt whether statements that the British programme is being and will continue to be diminished will in the present circumstances necessarily be particularly helpful.

I have, &c.,
(For the Ambassador)
RONALD CAMPBELL[6]

[5] Of Massachusetts.
[6] Mr. R. I. Campbell was First Secretary in H.M. Embassy at Washington.

No. 274

Sir E. Howard (Washington) to Sir A. Chamberlain
(Received February 14, 9 a.m.)

No. 62 Telegraphic [A 1074/154/45]

WASHINGTON, February 13, 1928, 1.45 p.m.

My despatch No. 2352[1] of 1927.

I venture to suggest following considerations on draft of new arbitration treaty though they have no doubt already occurred to you.

(1) Exception by name of Monroe Doctrine.

(a) Might this not be dangerous as giving . . .[2] recognition to any future actions of United States government which they might by an extension call part of the doctrine e.g. forcing a Latin American country to interfere with

[1] No. 244.   [2] The text is here uncertain.

operations of or to refuse concessions to British companies not on the grounds of security of United States but in defence of United States economic policy which is against 'price fixing' or restriction of output? I feel it might be unwise to recognise Monroe Doctrine by name without asking for some kind of definition. This recognition by name seems to me to involve more than a mere consecration of what has in fact been an actual state of affairs. For definitions of doctrine by United States statesmen see enclosures to Mr. Chilton's despatches Nos. 1088 and 1507³ of 1923 also memorandum prepared by Mr. Campbell in connection with survey of relations with foreign countries for C[ommittee of] I[mperial] D[efence] in 1925 or 1926.⁴

(b) Would its effect be irritating to Latin America as apparently ranging us on the side of United States but against the former; and would it seem a renunciation of obligations vis à vis Latin American members of League of Nations?

In view of above especially (a), would it be advisable either to press for omission of reference to Monroe Doctrine or for real definition of it?

(2) Exception of matters involving League of Nations obligations if proposed to His Majesty's Government. Might this not leave force as the only ultimate means of settling disputes arising out of a League blockade in which such clause would in no way bind United States to acquiesce? Would it not be well to omit all reference to our obligations under the covenant?

(3) In any case it seems highly doubtful whether if treaty were signed in present form the peace commission's treaty of 1914 would any longer necessarily cover disputes excepted under Article 3 of draft as Bryan treaty procedure is [sic] embodied in Article 1 and Article 3 could be taken as excepting from such procedure all disputes arising from the subjects mentioned in Article 3 which would notably reduce the value of Bryan treaty. This danger could be avoided by substitution in Article 3 of words 'Article 2' for words 'this treaty'.

³ Mr. Chilton, Minister in H.M. Embassy at Washington, had been acting Chargé d'Affaires June 1923–January 1924. Washington despatches Nos. 1088 and 1507 of 1923 respectively reported speeches made by Mr. Hughes on August 30 and November 30, 1923. Both speeches included Mr. Hughes' summary definition of the Monroe doctrine cited in Volume I, appendix, paragraph 145. For extracts from the earlier speech see *The Times*, August 31, 1923, p. 8. Mr. Hughes' address of November 30, 1923, entitled 'The Centenary of the Monroe Doctrine' is printed in *International Conciliation: Documents for the Year 1924*, pp. 3–22.

⁴ The reference was presumably to the Appendix to Volume I, submitted to Sir A. Chamberlain in April 1926.

No. 275

*Letter from Sir A. Chamberlain to Sir E. Howard (Washington)*¹
[F.O. 800/262]

Private   *February 13, 1928*

My dear Howard,

Any reply which I make to your private letter of February 2nd² must be for

¹ Extracts from this letter are printed in Sir Charles Petrie, *The Life and Letters of the Right Hon. Sir Austen Chamberlain* (London, 1939), vol. ii, pp. 322–3.   ² No. 268.

the present both personal and provisional. The renewal of the Arbitration Treaties with the United States and France offers some difficult problems for this Government and for the Empire and, until we have been able to examine them much more closely, I can do little more than jot down first thoughts as they occur to me.

The first of these thoughts is an echo of the opening pages of your letter. I do not think that there is any reality behind Kellogg's move. His long delay in replying to Briand's proposal, as well as the character of his answer when made, combined to produce upon my mind the impression which I see from your letter you share, that Kellogg's main thought is not of international peace but of the victory of the Republican party. It is one more instance of the common practice of the State Department to use foreign politics as a pawn in the domestic game.

And here I think we have real reason to complain. The Press on both sides of the Atlantic has hardly ceased to echo with criticism of the lack of diplomatic preparation for the Geneva Conference. Yet once again in the face of that experience Kellogg flings a new proposal at our head without one word of preliminary discussion. Nay, it is worse than that; for he instructed Houghton to enquire last summer whether we should be prepared to renew the Treaty in its existing form and to tell me that there was no question of any alteration or extension. If he changed his mind, were we not entitled to some friendly private warning? and would not good manners and good policy alike have indicated that before framing his text he should make some enquiry as to whether the words which suited him were equally suitable to the conditions of the British Empire?

He takes the contrary course. He excepts every question which the United States were ever likely to have covered by the old formula of 'vital interests, honour and integrity'. He does not stop to consider whether his new phrase gives equal protection to the other party. You know our difficulties about going to arbitration on the exercise of our belligerent rights at sea before a tribunal which must necessarily be constituted of Powers who have never accepted the doctrines laid down by our Admiralty Courts and so largely confirmed or extended by the Supreme Court of the United States. Obviously, Kellogg has here raised a question of the greatest difficulty for us and one which is particularly embarrassing in the present state of our relations with the United States. And it is no consolation to me to think that he has done so in good faith as complete as his ignorance!

But that is not all. He refuses the French proposal to make the reference to arbitration automatic and again insists upon the Senate's right to accept or refuse each individual reference. He apparently thinks that he provides an 'equal treaty' by his reference to the constitutional laws of the other country. But our constitution is not written. Its practice and its doctrine are always developing and varying. We shall certainly have to consider very carefully in the light of present day conditions whether we must not reserve the right of Parliament to play the same role as the Senate plays in the American constitution. I very much doubt whether some of the Dominion Governments could sign on any other terms. It is clear that we ourselves could not pay a money indemnity without a vote of Parliament; it is questionable whether we could cede territory, and in any case it would be an unequal treaty which bound us in general terms to arbitrate every question which fell within its four corners but left the other party free to reject arbitration on each individual case as it arose. In this connection I draw your attention to my brief observations in the House of Commons last Wednesday on the immense and often decisive importance which the terms of reference have had in previous arbitrations.[3] The Alabama claims and the Venezuelan boundary dispute[4] are conspicuous examples of this.

How little Kellogg has thought the matter out is shown by his immediate repudiation in his conversation with you of the idea that any country would abandon defensive war. But in that case all he really means to ban is 'aggressive war'. Why must he insist on signing a treaty which says what he does not mean and reject words which say exactly what he does mean and admits to you that he means?

This leads me to the last point raised by your letter. Is it to our advantage to get a platonic declaration (with mental reservations) from the United States, and would it be useful to put such a declaration in the form of a multilateral treaty? On this point it may be worth while to refer to Grey's book.[5] If I remember rightly, when discussing the effect of the war upon the Hague and London Conventions, he concludes with the observation that the lesson to be drawn from our experience is that in future we should sign no similar document which does not bind all the signatory Powers to take action in case of need to uphold it; and it would be a very fair question to put to Mr. Kellogg. If you invite us to sign such a treaty not merely with the United States but, let me say, with Germany or Russia, what action will the United States take if either of them break this provision while we remain loyal to our engagement? It may be one thing to sign such a treaty with a Government and people in whose loyalty you have perfect faith, but it is quite a different

[3] For Sir A. Chamberlain's remarks on February 8, 1928, see *Parl. Debs., 5th ser., H. of C.*, vol. 213, col. 121.

[4] The *Alabama* claims were made by the U.S. Government against H.M. Government in respect of losses inflicted during the American civil war by the *Alabama* and other ships which had been built in Great Britain for the Confederate Government. It was agreed by the Treaty of Washington of May 8, 1871, between Great Britain and the United States for the amicable settlement of all causes of difference between the two countries (printed in *British and Foreign State Papers*, vol. 61, pp. 40–56), that the dispute should be referred to arbitration by an international tribunal: in September 1872 this tribunal awarded the U.S. Government £3¼ m. compensation. For an account of this dispute see *The Cambridge History of British Foreign Policy 1783–1919* (London, 1922 f.), vol. iii, pp. 57–71.

The dispute between Venezuela and Great Britain concerning the boundary of British Guiana was submitted to arbitration by an international tribunal under the Anglo-Venezuelan treaty of February 2, 1897 (printed in *British and Foreign State Papers*, vol. 89, pp. 57–65) and settled by the Paris tribunal of 1899 in favour of Great Britain: see *The Cambridge History of British Foreign Policy*, vol. iii, pp. 222–6.

[5] Cf. Viscount Grey of Fallodon, *Twenty-Five Years, 1892–1916* (London, 1925), vol. ii, pp. 102–3.

thing to involve us in signature of a multilateral treaty with Powers who have not our standard and whose past does not encourage us to place unlimited faith in their loyalty to a 'scrap of paper'. I can see many disadvantages in doing anything which Mr. Kellogg may regard as a rebuff, but I confess that I don't think the world will gain anything by merely helping Mr. Kellogg over his electoral fence. How to deal with his proposals in these circumstances is as knotty a problem as he could have found for us.

14th February, 1928

Since I dictated the above, I have read your despatch No. 202[6] of January 27th. There was certainly a little misunderstanding in my reading of your earlier telegram[7] and I was undoubtedly anxious lest in your anxiety to help us you should make a suggestion which might after all not prove acceptable. If Mr. Kellogg recurs to the matter in conversation with you, you must still say that you are without instructions. But one or two additional thoughts are suggested by your report of what he has said.

He indicated that, if the French decline his multilateral treaty, he might propose it to Japan, Germany, and ourselves. I do not know whether you have seen the Japanese newspapers, but according to Tilley's account[8] they appear to have been so unanimous as to suggest that they were acting on a mot d'ordre. They were certainly very cool in the reception of the proposal and they would appear to feel exactly the same difficulty as regards the League of Nations as was expressed by Monsieur Briand. I suppose that Mr. Kellogg has this information. At any rate, it might be possible for you to suggest that it merits a little consideration.

Then, there is a second reflection which I wonder has not occurred to Mr. Kellogg. He was very strong to you on his determination not to sign a treaty with France to the exclusion of Germany. You can see for yourself that it would be at least as embarrassing to us to be asked to sign a treaty with Germany and without France, and the arguments which Mr. Kellogg uses to defend his own decision would come with at least equal force to our minds in the converse case. The fact that Mr. Kellogg has not thought of this illustrates what seems to me the great weakness in his conduct of foreign affairs. Once he is satisfied that a proposal suits his own particular standpoint, he never seems to ask himself how it may affect others or what is likely to be their point of view, and by making these far-reaching proposals without any previous consultation or soundings he lands both himself and others in positions of difficulty which, I am sure, he never contemplated. If you can inspire him with caution without throwing doubt on our goodwill, you will, I think, do good service to all the world and ourselves in particular. But you alone

[6] No. 263.
[7] No. 253.
[8] In his covering despatch No. 18 of January 2 (not preserved in Foreign Office archives) Sir J. Tilley, H.M. Ambassador at Tokyo, transmitted a memorandum (not printed) summarising Japanese press comments on Mr. Kellogg's proposal for a multilateral pact.

can judge whether it is possible for you to say anything of this kind to him as from yourself alone and not as a message from me.[9]

AUSTEN CHAMBERLAIN

[9] The discretion to speak to Mr. Kellogg granted to Sir E. Howard in this letter was repeated in Foreign Office despatch No. 262 to Washington of February 23 which also recapitulated points made in the first five paragraphs above.

No. 276

Letter from Sir G. Clerk[1] (Angora) to Sir A. Chamberlain
(Received March 5)

[*W 2077/28/98*]

Copy
Private and confidential   ANGORA, *February 21, 1928*

Dear Sir Austen,

Yesterday, at the close of an hour's conversation of the usual sort on current questions and high politics, Tewfik Rushdi[2] suddenly said that he had been rather perplexed (sc[ilicet] 'hurt') at Turkey having received no invitation to the Disarmament Conference. I was not altogether surprised, as he had said the same thing a day or two before to Collins, the local 'Times' correspondent in an interesting interview, of which I am sending an account to Oliphant by this Bag.[3] I replied that I did not know how, or by whom, these invitations were issued, but I hazarded the supposition that the omission of Turkey might be due to delicacy, inasmuch as Turkey was not generally supposed to be enamoured of Geneva and its works. I asked further if the Minister had done anything about it.

Tewfik Rushdi replied that he had instructed the Turkish Representative at Berne to ask the Secretary General of the League of Nations why his country had not been invited, and then embarked upon a discourse, the gist of which was:— (*a*) that Turkey was opposed to 'group' treaties and alliances, which only avoided immediate conflict at the cost of sowing the seed of inevitable future war, and that, consequently (*b*) we should find at Geneva an unexpected, but possibly not the less welcome, supporter of our theory in Turkey, were she included in the conference.

I then enquired if all this meant that he wanted me to do something. Tewfik Rushdi replied that he was speaking in confidence, he had said nothing to any other foreign representative and that he made no sort of official 'démarche', but he would be grateful if I would tell you privately what he had said.

I would venture to observe that, considering the matter entirely from the local angle, there would seem some advantage in the inclusion of Turkey and a certain amount of benefit to us if the invitation is attributed to our good

[1] H.M. Ambassador to Turkey, normally resident at Constantinople.

[2] Turkish Minister for Foreign Affairs.

[3] This letter of February 23 to Mr. Oliphant, Head of the Eastern Department of the Foreign Office, is not printed. It transmitted a detailed resumé, dated February 17, by Mr. J. W. Collins of his interview with Tewfik Rushdi Bey on February 16.

offices. I hasten to qualify the foregoing sentence by adding that it means subordinating personal to political considerations, for Tewfik Rushdi airing 'real politik' at Geneva will be an infliction that will rightly make me, as part cause, profoundly unpopular.

Yours very sincerely,
GEORGE R. CLERK

No. 277

Mr. London (Geneva) to Sir A. Chamberlain
(Received February 22, 6.45 p.m.)
No. 2 L.N. Telegraphic [W 1612/28/98]

GENEVA, *February 22, 1928, 5.46 p.m.*

Following from Lord Cushenden [*sic*].[1]

I discussed with M. Benes this morning[2] prospects of preparatory committee. M. Benes while admitting that in the present circumstances further discussion of draft convention[3] was not likely to be profitable and that most delegations shared this view, thought committee must meet on March 15th. Possibility of postponement had been examined at recent Prague meeting and conclusion was reached that as committee had itself fixed date that date must be adhered to. President could not alter it on his own responsibility though of course on the request of a member or members he might consult all the others as to their wishes. But opposition of single delegation would suffice to negative postponement which could only be decided by committee itself. Committee must therefore meet on March 15th but M. Benes thinks meeting would be of hardly more than formal character. Committee would take note of report of security committee and would have to give some consideration to Russian proposal.[4] After that he thinks it could be adjourned until after pending . . .[5].

[1] Lord Cushendun was attending the second session of the Committee on Arbitration and Security of the Preparatory Commission for the Disarmament Conference, held in Geneva from February 20 to March 7, 1928. The minutes thereof are printed in *Documents of the Preparatory Commission for the Disarmament Conference*, Series VI, pp. 11–225.
[2] This telegram was drafted on February 21.
[3] See No. 230, note 3.   [4] See No. 278, note 2.
[5] The text is here uncertain. Another text of this telegram concluded 'pending elections'.

No. 278

Letter from Mr. Cadogan (Geneva) to Mr. Campbell
(Received February 24)
[W 1714/28/98]

GENEVA, *February 22, 1928*

My dear Ronnie,

After going through the 3 Reports on Security and Arbitration,[1] I wrote a

[1] These three reports are printed with an introduction by Dr. Benes and with annexes in *Documents of the Preparatory Commission for the Disarmament Conference*, Series VI, pp. 123–78, as document C.A.S. 10.

note for L[or]d C[ushendun], of which I annex copy. He wanted it in the form of a memo., which could if necessary be comm[unicate]d to the C[ommit]tee, but he has not yet settled whether he will adopt that procedure. It was to draw attention to all the points in the Reports with which we could not agree.

I have shown it to Hurst, who concurs and has nothing to add, but I thought I had better send it to you in case we have missed anything that matters.

We have been enduring a flow of oratory in a Discussion Générale, which might—most of it—have been omitted.

Yrs.
A. C.

By the way, you sh[oul]d by now have rec[eive]d the ridiculous Russian Disarmament Convention.[2] As we may have to pay it the unmerited compliment of pretending to discuss it, w[oul]d the Service Dep[artmen]ts come out with definite criticisms. It seems a waste of time, but that is a commodity which is not rare with them.

ENCLOSURE IN No. 278

At the opening meeting of the present session of the Committee, the British Delegate indicated the approval with which His Majesty's Government regarded generally the reports submitted by the three rapporteurs and the introductory statement with which they were prefaced. If the following remarks are mainly of a critical nature, it is necessary to remember that they deal only with certain points on which the British Delegate does not find himself in agreement with the authors of the documents under consideration, and that these criticisms must not be taken as implying in any way a modification of the general approval which has already been expressed on behalf of His Majesty's Government. Where the British Delegate cannot accept the views of the rapporteurs it is only fair—and it may be useful—to explain the reasons for divergence.

I

Arbitration and Conciliation

The First report, by M. Holsti, examines the possibilities of developing arbitration and conciliation, and in this connection it weighs the advantages and disadvantages of *general* treaties on the one hand and special treaties between individual States or groups of States on the other hand. The report brings out very well the disadvantages which have been apprehended from general arbitration treaties but it at the same time contemplates the possibility (paragraph 39) of the Committee desiring to draw up such a general treaty on the lines of the draft submitted by the Swedish Government,[3] which combines provisions for arbitration and conciliation. The difficulties which His Majesty's Government would feel in becoming a party to any general treaty

<hr>

[2] *V. op. cit.*, pp. 324–39.   [3] *V. op. cit.*, pp. 162–5.

of arbitration are already explained in paragraph 15 of their memorandum which has been circulated to the Committee.[4] They could not, therefore, accept in their present form Articles 1 and 2 of the Swedish draft treaty.

As regards conciliation, the same difficulties are to be found in the way of a general treaty, though perhaps in this case they may not be so serious.

The last sub-paragraph of paragraph 43 mentions the possibility of strengthening the force and authority of the recommendations and proposals resulting from the procedure of conciliation, and in this connection refers to the observations of the German Government.[5] There is no clear indication of what is in the mind of the author of this report, but various suggestions are made by M. Politis in the second report (paragraph 75), which give rise to certain doubts. These suggestions will be dealt with in examining the second report.

In paragraphs 44–47 the Rapporteur discusses the question of the co-ordination of the work of Conciliation Commissions with the procedure of the Council under Article 15 of the Covenant, and submits various alternatives without pronouncing definitely in favour of any one. In the case of the Locarno Agreements, a dispute is referred in the first instance to the Conciliation Commission, and it is only after failure to agree on the result of the Commission's labours that there is resort in the last instance to the Council. On the whole this seems the better procedure, not only because technically it seems to conform with the report of the Special Committee of Jurists of 1923,[6] quoted in the report, but because for practical reasons full discussion in the Conciliation Commission will have done much to throw light on the case and to facilitate the task of the Council itself, and so long as a time-limit is fixed for the duration of the labours of the Commission, as is suggested in paragraph 43, sub-paragraph No. 3, there would appear to be no serious disadvantage in the delay in bringing the matter before the Council. Direct intervention by the Council before the termination of the hearing by the Conciliation Commission might become necessary in the event of the relations between the parties becoming aggravated to a critical extent during the hearing before the Commission, but in that event the Council's intervention would be invoked under Article 11.

2

Security Questions . . .[7]

[4] See No. 258, note 7.   [5] See No. 126, note 2.

[6] See *League of Nations Official Journal*, April 1924, p. 524, for the report dated January 24, 1924, by the Special Commission of Jurists set up by a resolution of the twenty-sixth Council of the League of Nations on September 28, 1923 (*v. op. cit.*, November 1923, p. 1352).

[7] Part 2 is not printed. This part was the same, subject to minor verbal variation, as the observations of the British Delegation on Security Questions printed in *Documents of the Preparatory Commission for the Disarmament Conference*, Series VI, pp. 183–4, except that: (1) in the third paragraph alternative 1 concluded after 'voted in the minority' with the passage which is printed as the second and third sentences of the fourth paragraph of the final text; (ii) the fifth paragraph included the following passage after the penultimate sentence ending 'consider this inadmissible': 'It may be unfortunate that the gap should exist in the

Covenant, but it must be admitted that the authors showed some wisdom in leaving that gap, and the present proposals' &c; (iii) the penultimate paragraph did not include the last sentence of the final text; (iv) the last paragraph did not include the final passage beginning 'and of which the elucidation' and ending 'the Committee'.

No. 279

Letter from the Marquess of Crewe (Paris) to Sir A. Chamberlain
[*F.O. 800/262*]

Copy
Confidential   PARIS, *February 23, 1928*

My dear Chamberlain,

With reference to your Confidential letter of February 9th on the subject of the Air Forces,[1] and my acknowledgment of it of February 12th,[2] I may draw your attention to a despatch from the Air Attaché here, addressed to myself and dated February 22nd, of which a copy has been sent to the Foreign Office.[3] He notes, on Page 2, that the [French] Government and the Army Commission, which last had called for an increase of the proposed figure of 136 squadrons, have agreed to amend Article 14 which fixed the total number as above, by providing for a 'nombre variable d'escadrilles' with power to create new squadrons by Government decree. This, you see, would give the Government of the day the power of increasing the French Air Service to an unlimited extent, and I do not know how the Air Ministry will regard it, while it can hardly fail to excite Italian opinion. On the other hand, 'a variable number of squadrons' might equally imply a diminution of the total, although the circumstances in which the amendment is proposed seem to preclude this. In any case, since you have been intending to talk to Briand informally about the Air Forces, you will probably think it wiser to hold back any protest about the phraseology of the new measure until you have had an opportunity of seeing him.

Yours sincerely,
CREWE

[1] No. 271.   [2] See No. 271, note 2.
[3] Paris despatch No. 323 of February 23 which transmitted a copy of this report is not preserved in Foreign Office archives. According to the docket the report by the air attaché related to 'amendment of article 14 of projet de loi respecting total number of air squadrons to be maintained'.

No. 280

Sir A. Chamberlain to Sir J. Tilley (Tokyo)
No. 25 Telegraphic [*W 1318/28/98*]

FOREIGN OFFICE, *February 24, 1928, 4.30 p.m.*

Please inform Japanese Government that His Majesty's Government in Great Britain intend to revert to the capital ship question at the next session of the Preparatory Committee on Disarmament. In view of the imminence

559

of the presidential election in America they do not expect any final decision in the sense of an immediate modification of the Washington treaty. It is not their intention in the committee itself to do more than allude to their proposals, in broad terms, as representing an important contribution to the reduction of armaments generally. But they hope to be enabled to take advantage of the presence of the representatives of the Washington treaty powers to discuss and agree upon a fixed date for the advanced meeting, contemplated at Geneva, of the conference prescribed under paragraph 2 of article 21 of the Washington treaty, and to hold possibly some informal exchange of views on the elements of the British proposals. His Majesty's Government think conference should assemble during the autumn of 1928 or at latest in the spring of 1929, i.e. after the American election.

They hope that Japanese government will instruct their representative at Geneva to support his British colleague in endeavouring to secure this object, and they are encouraged in this hope by their belief that the Japanese government fully share their views as to the paramount importance of this question.

No. 281

Sir A. Chamberlain to Sir E. Howard (Washington)[1]
No. 274 [W 1318/28/98][2]

FOREIGN OFFICE, *February 24, 1928*

Sir,

Among the most important of the British proposals at the Geneva naval conference were those which aimed at a reduction of the maximum displacement and armament and an extension of the life of capital ships as fixed by the Washington conference.[3] They were never more than superficially considered owing to the instructions received by the American and Japanese delegations to defer any discussion of them until complete agreement had been reached on the limitation of auxiliary vessels for which the conference had primarily been called. There were indications however that, if such agreement had materialised, these capital ship proposals would have received, at the least, a considerable measure of support. As it was, they were made the subject of the following recommendation incorporated in the joint statement issued on behalf of all delegations at the final session of the conference:—

'Further, the delegates agree to recommend to their respective governments the desirability of arranging between the signatories of the Washington treaty that the conference to be called pursuant to paragraph 2 of article 21 of that treaty should be held earlier than August 1931, the date contemplated under the terms of that instrument, in order that any decisions reached by such a conference may come into force before the

[1] This despatch was also addressed to Paris as No. 437 and Rome as No. 230.
[2] The filed text of this despatch, which bears no signature, is the draft on which the amendments in No. 285 were indicated, as explained in No. 289.
[3] See Cmd. 2964 of 1927, pp. 4–5, and Volume III, No. 364.

capital ship construction program commences, namely, in November of that year.'[4]

2. So great is the value which His Majesty's Government in Great Britain attach to the capital ship question, from the point of view both of limitation and of economy that they propose to revert to it at the next session of the Preparatory Committee on Disarmament. It is not their intention in the committee itself to do more than allude to their proposals, in broad terms, as representing an important contribution to the reduction of armaments generally. But they hope to be enabled to take advantage of the presence of the representatives of the Washington treaty Powers to discuss and agree upon a fixed date for the advanced meeting, contemplated at Geneva, of the conference prescribed under paragraph 2 of article 21 of the Washington treaty. That paragraph runs as follows:—

'In view of possible technical and scientific developments, the United States, after consultation with the other Contracting Powers, shall arrange for a conference of all the Contracting Powers which shall convene as soon as possible after the expiration of eight years from the coming into force of the present treaty to consider what changes, if any, in the treaty may be necessary to meet such developments'.

3. At the time when the above paragraph was drafted, it was the general expectation that the conference thereunder provided for would be held in 1929; it was through delay in ratification that 1931 came to be regarded as the intended year, in consequence of the words 'after the expiration of eight years from the coming into force of the present treaty'. His Majesty's Government are strongly of opinion that the conference should assemble at latest in the spring of 1929, preferably in the autumn of 1928 in order to allow of adequate time for the preparation of the plans of the new vessels to be laid down in 1931 in accordance with the replacement tables incorporated in the Washington treaty. Needless to say, His Majesty's Government have no thought of disturbing the ratios represented by those tables; any alterations agreed upon must of course be so adjusted as to preserve the existing balance intact.

4. If at the same time the representatives of the other Powers concerned were able to give some precursory indications of the views of their governments on the elements of the British proposals, it would be an added advantage in helping to prepare the ground. It would of course be understood that any discussions on that side would be wholly informal and without prejudice to the deliberations of the eventual conference.

5. I shall be glad if Your Excellency will lose no time in notifying the government to which you are accredited of the intention of His Majesty's Government as described above in order that they may have time to consider the matter and to issue appropriate instructions to their representative on the Preparatory Committee.

[4] See *Records of the Conference for the Limitation of Naval Armament Held at Geneva from June 20th to August 4th, 1927* (Geneva, 1927), p. 46.

No. 282

Sir A. Chamberlain to Sir E. Howard (Washington)
No. 275 [W 1318/28/98]

FOREIGN OFFICE, *February 24, 1928*

Sir,

My despatch No. 274[1] of today's date of which a replica was addressed to His Majesty's Representatives in Paris and Rome and an abbreviated version by telegram to His Majesty's Representative in Tokyo,[2] instructs Your Excellency to notify the United States Government of the intention of His Majesty's Government in Great Britain to revert to the capital ship question at the next session of the Preparatory Committee on Disarmament.

2. The following additional remarks, applicable to your case in particular, may be of use to you for your own information and possibly for your guidance in any conversations which you may have with the State Department on the subject.

3. You are aware of the immense importance attached by His Majesty's Government to the proposals which they laid before the Geneva naval conference under this head. So great is the saving which would ensue from the general adoption of these proposals, apart from their value from the point of view of limitation, that His Majesty's Government feel bound to persevere in endeavouring to secure their early acceptance. They are encouraged in this policy by the general attitude adopted towards the capital ship question by the American and Japanese delegations at Geneva, though debarred by their instructions from any formal discussion of our proposals. The American delegates, who at first raised specious objections to them, became less hostile as the conference proceeded, and eventually allowed the British delegates to infer that they personally were by no means unfavourable. The Japanese delegates, who were better disposed from the first but were shy of supporting their British colleagues openly in the face of American opposition, became increasingly outspoken in their approval and finally indicated that they would warmly have supported the British proposals had it been possible to discuss them in conference.

4. It was due no doubt to the personal feelings of the American delegates that they agreed, in company with the Japanese, to the insertion, in the joint declaration made at the final session of the conference of the paragraph quoted in my despatch under reference. That paragraph appears to me amply to justify His Majesty's Government in taking their present course without fear of causing offence or irritation to the United States Government at this juncture. There is, as you will observe, no question of modifying the Washington treaty at this stage—a step which doubtless no American administration would contemplate in present circumstances. All that His Majesty's Government have in view is to fix definitely the earlier date, agreed to in principle at Geneva, for the meeting of the further conference prescribed in

[1] No. 281.   [2] No. 280.

article 21 of the Washington treaty, and to take the opportunity of the presence of the representatives of the Powers concerned to exchange views informally on the elements of the British proposals.

5. I trust that, realising the limited scope of the present aim, and having regard to the importance of the issues involved, the United States Government will see fit to give the matter their careful and favourable consideration.

6. For your own information, I would add that in present circumstances the proposal will not be pressed in the event of it meeting with rigid opposition.

I am, &c.,

(For the Secretary of State)

G. H. VILLIERS

No. 283

The Marquess of Crewe (Paris) to Sir A. Chamberlain
(Received February 28)

No. 336 [W 1819/28/98]

PARIS, *February 27, 1928*

Sir,

I have read Mr. Cadogan's memorandum No. W. 930/28/98 of January 31st (League of Nations Print: January 31st, section 1)[1] on the work of the Preparatory Committee on disarmament.

2. It is not possible for me to comment on the statement contained in paragraph 9 of this memorandum that little progress has been made towards agreement on the main points at issue since the last adjournment of the committee, as I have not seen either of the papers referred to in paragraphs 5 and 8 of the memorandum, apparently recording discussions between the British and French representatives on naval and military disarmament respectively. I should be grateful if copies of these documents could, if no objection is seen, be forwarded to me and if copies of any similar documents might be supplied to me in future.[2]

3. It is particularly on paragraph 14 of Mr. Cadogan's memorandum that I wish to comment in this despatch. Mr. Cadogan is 'surprised after all that has happened that disarmament should be a good election cry in France. Amongst M. Paul-Boncour's followers' he 'can imagine that there are some extremer Socialists who are vaguely pacifist in the same way that kind hearted people in Great Britain are mildly in favour of being as nice as possible to everyone when they direct their attention to foreign politics'. If by the word 'pacifist' Mr. Cadogan means 'pacific' or 'peaceful' I think that he

---

[1] No. 267.

[2] In a letter of March 6 Mr. Campbell sent to Mr. Wigram 'copies of the two documents asked for'. The filed copy of Mr. Campbell's letter bears no reference to these documents. It would appear that he sent to Paris copies of No. 233 and the Admiralty memorandum referred to in note 4 to No. 267. (The paragraphing of the text of No. 267 sent to Paris was not identical to the original printed above.)

under-estimates the strength of this sentiment in France. It is my considered opinion that the great body of the French electorate is profoundly and deeply pacific. The thing above all desired is peace for the very natural reasons that France wants nothing more abroad and that the experience of the last two great European wars has shown that it is French lives and French properties which are usually the first to be exposed to the devastation of war. In the words of M. Poincaré speaking in the Meuse in September last 'we could not take a step in our country lanes or on our hill-sides, we could not walk in our forests or our fields without recognising that if war broke out our poor province must inevitably and at once become the theatre of bloody combats. We must have been mad not to have been lovers of peace.'

4. What in fact the more enlightened sections of French opinion and most French Governments have to struggle against is this very overwhelming desire for peace. Their task is really to ensure that it shall not be indulged to the detriment of French security. It is not merely 'extremer Socialists' who, as Mr. Cadogan, arguing from a British example, states are 'mildly in favour of being as nice as possible to everyone when they direct their attention to foreign politics'. It is the whole Left in the widest sense of the term. 'Déclarer la paix à tout le monde' is a device which, as recently as last summer, committed even M. Briand to a negotiation with somewhat unexpected results.[3]

5. This pacific sentiment was a powerful influence in the defeat of M. Poincaré at the general elections of 1924. Well-informed people consider that it will also, especially in the South, hitherto the stronghold of the Left parties, be mobilised in the forthcoming elections against the supporters of the Government of 'Union Nationale' and the rallying cry of fulfilment of M. Poincaré's financial programme. If the elections do not go as much to the Left as was at one time expected, it will indeed merely imply that fear for the franc is a more immediate issue than fear of war. For these reasons I agree with Mr. Cadogan that the French Government are 'for home political reasons forced to push ahead with disarmament'.

6. Mr. Cadogan observes that 'If one were very cynical, one might be tempted to think that M. Paul-Boncour would be rather embarrassed in May if he had returned from Geneva having agreed to any real scheme of disarmament, but that it might suit his book very well if he were able to return pointing out to his pacifists how he had striven for disarmament, and at the same time re-assuring the bulk of his electors by pointing out that these schemes had been defeated by the imperialist and aggressive British Government.' I wonder whether this is the whole truth. If M. Paul-Boncour returns from Geneva in May having agreed to a real scheme of disarmament, it will only be because he has obtained security first. Subject to obtaining security I find it difficult to believe that any member of the French Government would be sorry to obtain disarmament. I am not sure that it follows, as Mr. Cadogan suggests, that a nation 'which will never abandon universal military service' would disapprove a Government which secured disarmament.

[3] Cf. No. 245.

7. The statement recently made by M. de Fleuriau to Lord Cushendun that 'France to-day had no army—not at least one comparable to our own highly trained force'[4] is, I agree, absurd, but, so far as French opinion is concerned, I think there is force in His Excellency's reference to the 'merits of compulsory military service which meant that a voter who supported war involved thereby either himself or his family directly'.

8. In the matter of 'trained reserves' I am not clear whether it is actually suggested that continental armies should be limited in number, recruited by voluntary enlistment for a long term of service and only allowed to discharge 5 per cent of the total number of their effectives during that term. I am afraid that the dream of the Left in France is precisely the opposite—a scheme of very short service for everybody who is whole in body and mind, a scheme long advocated by Jaurès[5] and actually enacted by the Directory in accordance with the principle of equality taught by the Revolution. This fact no doubt renders 'disarmament' difficult on the interpretation now given to the word, but, as Mr. Cadogan realises, we are liable to be told that, though we may deprecate the existence of 'trained reserves', we maintain for the British navy in the form of the Mercantile and Fishing Fleets, a large body of men who by the nature of their calling are to a great extent 'trained reserves'. French opinion is, not without reason, as nervous of invasion as British opinion is of losing the command of the sea.

I have, &c.,
CREWE

4 See No. 257.
5 M. Jean Jaurès (1859–1914), the leading French socialist politician, had discussed the organization of the armed nation in *L'Armée nouvelle* (Paris, 1911).

No. 284

Letter from Mr. Craigie[1] to Sir E. Howard (Washington)
[A 1074/154/45]

Private and confidential   FOREIGN OFFICE, *February 27, 1928*

Dear Sir Esme,

The Secretary of State asks me to thank you for your telegram No. 62[2] of February 13th last regarding the draft Anglo-American Arbitration Treaty now under consideration, and in doing so to send you copies of two memoranda which have been circulated recently to the Cabinet on the subject of the draft arbitration treaty and the draft Franco-American Pact of Perpetual Friendship.[3] Would you be so good as to regard the enclosed memoranda as most confidential and for your own information only? Sir Austen particularly desires that on no account should any use be made of the information contained therein in any conversations that may take place between Mr. Kellogg and yourself on the subject of these treaties.

1 Mr. Craigie had recently succeeded Mr. Vansittart as head of the American and African Department of the Foreign Office on the latter's appointment as Private Secretary to the Prime Minister on February 2, 1928.
2 No. 274.
3 Nos. 262 and 265.

You will see that your points one and two are dealt with in the two enclosed memoranda. As regards point three, the Secretary of State agrees that this is of importance, and asks me to let you know that it will receive careful consideration. Our information is to the effect that the Americans do not intend that article 3 should be regarded as limiting the scope of article 1, but the point must certainly be elucidated when the time comes.

Yours very sincerely,
R. L. CRAIGIE

No. 285

Sir A. Chamberlain to Sir E. Howard (Washington)
No. 87 Telegraphic [W 1318/28/98]

Immediate   FOREIGN OFFICE, *February 29, 1928, 9 p.m.*

Please cancel my despatches Nos. 274 and 275[1] now on their way to you and substitute for former amended version as follows:

After words 'considerable measure of support' cancel remainder of paragraph 1. Paragraph 2 should read as follows: 'His Majesty's Government in Great Britain attach great importance to this question from the point of view both of limitation and of economy. They therefore propose to revert to it'— etc., etc., down to 'contribution to reduction of armaments generally'. Cancel the whole of remainder of despatch and substitute 'Please inform Secretary of State verbally'.[2]

[1] Nos. 281–2.
[2] Sir R. Graham was similarly instructed in Foreign Office telegram No. 30 to Rome of February 29 with reference to Foreign Office despatch No. 230 to Rome (see No. 281, note 1).

No. 286

Sir A. Chamberlain to Sir J. Tilley (Tokyo)
No. 28 Telegraphic [W 1318/28/98]

Immediate   FOREIGN OFFICE, *February 29, 1928, 10 p.m.*

My telegram No. 25[1] and your telegram No. 38.[2]

Similar instructions were sent to His Majesty's Representatives in capitals of other three Washington Treaty Powers but have just been modified in the sense of limiting notification to announcement of intention of His Majesty's Government to revert to capital ship question at forthcoming meeting of Preparatory Committee.

Please ask Japanese Government to regard your message as having stopped at that point, explaining to them in confidence that in view of present situation in America it was thought better to go no further than that at this juncture.

[1] No. 280.
[2] Not printed. This telegram of February 29 from Mr. Dormer, Counsellor in H.M. Embassy at Tokyo, referred to No. 280 and reported that the Japanese Vice-Minister for Foreign Affairs had enquired whether a similar communication had been made to any other Power.

Lord Cushendun (Geneva) to Sir A. Chamberlain (Received March 2)
No. 6 L.N.C.C. [W 1977/28/98]

GENEVA, *February 29, 1928*

Sir,

With reference to my despatch No. 2 (LNCC)[1] of February 24th, regarding the proposals made by the German Delegation to the Security Committee providing for the prescription by the Council of provisional measures to be taken by parties to a dispute and of an armistice in the event of hostilities having broken out, I have the honour to state that an informal discussion took place yesterday afternoon between the British and German Delegations.

2. Dr. Gaus,[2] who is the author of these proposals, explained briefly what had actuated the German Government in formulating them. He referred to the fact that the German Delegate had taken more than one opportunity, during the course of discussion in the Security Committee, to emphasise that in the view of his Government regional security pacts, though doubtless making a valuable contribution to security, were not the only means of attaining security, must not *necessarily* be adopted by all States wherever situated, and could in no case with any advantage be imposed on States unwilling to conclude them. Speaking quite frankly, Dr. Gaus explained that his Government could never in any circumstances apply to the eastern frontier of Germany the same treatment that they had applied to the western frontier. They could never by any possibility make an Eastern Locarno pact with Poland. In these circumstances, they had cudgelled their brains to find some other formula, and had produced the present proposals. They might not be ideal, but the German Government could go no further, and in point of fact what they were now offering was not to be dismissed too lightly. It really gave an additional guarantee for peace.

3. The British Delegation drew attention to the various difficulties presented by the proposals as they stood. These were not unlike certain provisions of the Geneva Protocol, the objections to which had been stated by His Majesty's Government on various occasions. There is of course the further objection that it appears to be contemplated that the proposals should be embodied in a Protocol open for signature by all States. Assuming that this were done and that His Majesty's Government found themselves unable to sign, they would be constantly open to reproach for their failure to do so and would be subject to attacks similar to—and perhaps even more violent than—those which they have incurred by not signing the Optional Clause of the Statute of the Permanent Court of International Justice.

---

[1] Not printed. This despatch reported a conversation between Lord Cushendun and Dr. von Simson, German Delegate to the Committee on Arbitration and Security, regarding the German suggestions printed in *Documents of the Preparatory Commission for the Disarmament Conference*, Series VI, p. 225. Lord Cushendun then expressed reservations on generally similar lines to those reported below.

[2] Legal Adviser to the German Ministry of Foreign Affairs.

4. The German Delegation agreed that the text of the proposals as they stood might be variously interpreted, and that extreme interpretations would be not only inconvenient but possibly even conducive to results the reverse of what were intended. Either the wording would have to be carefully revised, or reliance must be placed on the Council itself, in the event, giving a liberal and reasonable interpretation. They quite recognised that it was not to be expected that governments could here and now give an opinion on their proposals, and the German Delegate, Herr von Simson, intimated that he would be quite content simply to introduce the proposals in the Security Committee and agree that they should be referred to governments for their opinion.

5. While the Drafting Committee this morning were discussing the text of a model regional security pact, it was suggested that something on the lines of these German proposals should be inserted therein. If this suggestion is adopted, that might afford an acceptable solution. His Majesty's Government do not at present contemplate signing any further security pact. There would seem to be no objection to other States, who may be desirous of entering into such a pact, embodying in them engagements of this nature.

6. The Plenary Committee began a discussion of the German proposals this evening.[3] The German Delegate, in introducing them, admitted that alterations of form might be desired, but urged that the Committee should at least accord them serious consideration. He stated that his Government did not desire that they should be included in any regional or collective pact of security but proposed that they should be embodied in a Protocol to be opened for signature by all States and to come into force when signed by a specified—and not too large—number.

7. I observed that I was doubtful whether these proposals would in fact be a material addition to security. I recalled the objections I had already felt obliged to raise against general treaties open for signature by all States regardless of particular and local circumstances. If the German Delegation desired that the proposals should be carefully examined, I could only consent provided it were clearly understood that the conclusions reached would be submitted to Governments for their opinion and to the Permanent Advisory Commission for a detailed examination. I then proceeded to criticise the several proposals more in detail.

8. The French Delegate (Monsieur Paul-Boncour) accepted the German idea in principle, while indicating that it would have to be elaborated in detail. He was unable to refrain from insisting that the more important problem was to find some means of providing that the Council could enforce its recommendations—a text from which he so constantly preaches.

9. The German Delegate replied to my criticisms that they might apply to some extent both to the report by the Committee of the Council on Article 11 of the Covenant, and to the Treaty of Locarno. But he agreed that his proposals, or rather his suggestions, should be referred to governments.

10. Monsieur Sokal (Poland) gave a general blessing to the spirit under-

---

[3] For the minutes of this meeting, v. op. cit., pp. 100–6.

lying the proposals, and endorsed Monsieur Paul-Boncour's observations on the subject of enforcement by the Council.

11. On the proposal of the President, the Committee agreed to adjourn discussion of the proposals to a later session, thus giving the governments an opportunity in the interval of submitting any observations which they might desire to make. If the Committee should thereafter desire to draw up a definite text, that text would again have to be submitted to the governments.

I have, &c.,
CUSHENDUN

No. 288

Lord Cushendun (Geneva) to Sir A. Chamberlain (Received March 2)
No. 8 L.N.C.C. [W 1979/28/98]

GENEVA, February 29, 1928

Sir,

In continuation of my despatch No. 3 (LNCC)[1] of February 25th, I have the honour to inform you that the Security Committee on Monday, February 27th, resumed its discussion of the conclusions in the report on Security by Monsieur Politis.

2. I am only too conscious of the difficulty of giving any clear impression of the proceedings of League committees. Their methods of work are such that at the end of a sitting it may not be too easy, even for those who have participated, to say exactly what, if anything, has been decided. To anyone reading condensed reports, the difficulty must be enormously increased. In the case of the Security Committee it may be useful to explain that the general idea has been for the full Committee to discuss the reports, so that each Delegate may have an opportunity of stating particular views of his own Government. In the light of these discussions the Drafting Committee, consisting of twelve members, examines draft texts or resolutions framed to meet, so far as possible, the general sense of the plenary Committee. These drafts are constructed in the first instance by the Secretariat or submitted by individual members. They are examined more or less in detail by the Drafting Committee, which decides the general sense of the alterations to be made. The actual final drafting is then left to a Committee of Three, consisting of Sir Cecil Hurst, Baron Rolin-Jaequemyns[2] (Belgium) and Monsieur Politis (Greece).

3. On the resumed discussion in the Plenary Committee of the Security report, the most important points dealt with were those in paragraphs 95 and 96.[3] I had previously circulated to the Committee a written statement of criticisms of Monsieur Politis' report (copy enclosed),[4] and I supplemented

---

[1] Not printed.

[2] Belgian Delegate to the Committee on Arbitration and Security.

[3] For discussion of these paragraphs of M. Politis' report on February 27 see *Documents of the Preparatory Commission for the Disarmament Conference*, Series VI, pp. 83–4.

[4] The British observations referred to in No. 278, note 7, are not printed.

this with a speech in which I expressed doubt as to the wisdom or even the propriety of seeking, as it were, to go behind the Covenant. If it were really desired to 'close the gap' in the Covenant, surely the correct method of procedure would be by formal amendment of that document, and not by resort to devices such as those now suggested.

4. I am bound to say that Monsieur Politis made a handsome acknowledgement of the justice of my observations and of the force of my particular criticisms and accepted wholeheartedly and entirely the British view. He recognised that the 'gap' must for the present continue to exist. He feared that even the multiplication of treaties containing undertakings not to resort to war would not wholly close it. The only remedy which he could see, and to which he dared to look forward as a possibility, was that ultimately all States would agree to submit disputes of all kinds to arbitration.

5. Though various of the other conclusions of the Security report came in for some discussion, I think it unnecessary to report them in any detail.

6. Yesterday the Committee began and ended its discussion of the report by Monsieur Rutgers on the Articles of the Covenant.[5]

7. Monsieur Marcovitch (Serb-Croat-Slovene State) opened the proceedings with a complaint that the rapporteur, while making in his report an accurate and valuable survey of the various discussions which had taken place from time to time on the different Articles, made no definite or concrete proposal. This omission was especially to be regretted in the case of Article 16. The French Delegation had also circulated a written statement of criticisms which to some extent endorsed this complaint (copy enclosed).[6]

8. The Chairman (Dr. Benes) explained that at the recent meeting at Prague there had been a long discussion of this very point, and it had resulted from that discussion that, whereas Article 11 had already been applied in several instances by the Council, so that precedents existed which could be analysed and codified, there had fortunately been no occasion yet for the application of Article 16, and consequently the necessary data were not available. In response to Monsieur Marcovitch's request, however, he suggested that the Drafting Committee might be asked to submit proposals. I at once urged the unwisdom of this proposal, and it was eventually decided to give no instruction to the Drafting Committee during the present session. My protest received valuable support from Monsieur Politis, who represented that for the moment nothing could be done on these lines: he pointed out, for the satisfaction of Monsieur Marcovitch and those who thought with him, that the Security Committee, like the Preparatory Committee for Disarmament, was destined to be a permanent body: it might be that at a later date it would be found possible and convenient to undertake this work.

9. Finally, in regard to the Finnish scheme of financial assistance to States victims of aggression,[7] it was decided to nominate four members—Monsieur

---

[5] V. op. cit., pp. 87–100.

[6] Not printed. The French observations on M. Rutgers' report are printed op. cit., pp. 184 bis–ter.

[7] See No. 219, note 15.

Veverka[8] (Czechoslovakia), Monsieur Valdes-Mendeville (Chile), Monsieur Erich (Finland), and Monsieur Rutgers (Netherlands)—to form, with three members of the Financial Committee, a Joint Committee for the further study of this project. I made the reservation, which was accepted, that the detailed proposals that might result from this examination must be referred in the first instance to governments.

10. This evening the Committee meets to consider the German proposals (which are dealt with in my despatch No. 6 (LNCC)[9] of today's date), and will then have finished the first stage of its work. According to the provisional time-table it will not meet again until the afternoon of March 2nd, to examine the results of the work of the Drafting Committee and to pronounce its final judgment thereon.

11. Of the work of the Drafting Committee, which has held several sittings, it is difficult to write in detail. The general scheme of draft model treaties of arbitration and conciliation and of security, of various types, has been agreed. The Committee of Three sits for the first time this afternoon to try and put the drafts into final shape. It remains for the Drafting Committee to agree the texts of resolutions for giving effect to the instructions of the last Assembly for the promotion and co-ordination of arbitration and security agreements.

I have, &c.,
CUSHENDUN

[8] Czechoslovak Minister at Berne.   [9] No. 287.

No. 289

Letter from Mr. Campbell to Sir E. Phipps (Paris)

[W 1318/28/98]

FOREIGN OFFICE, *February 29, 1928*

My dear Eric,

There has been a muddle in connexion with our despatch No. 437.[1] As the original drafts appeared to have got lost, the department submitted some flimsy copies which had been made at the time and obtained authority to send them. The original drafts have since turned up from Lord Salisbury, to whom the Secretary of State had sent them, with a suggestion that they should be considerably modified. The Secretary of State has accepted Lord Salisbury's suggestion.

I enclose an amended version,[2] which we can only ask you to substitute for the previous one. I am afraid there is nothing for it but for you to ask the

[1] See No. 281, note 1.

[2] The enclosed amended version of despatch No. 437 to Paris comprised two paragraphs. The first paragraph was the same as the first three sentences of the first paragraph of No. 281, ending 'support' (cf. No. 285). The second paragraph read as follows: 'His Majesty's Government in Great Britain attach great importance to this question, from the point of view both of limitation and of economy. They therefore propose to revert to it at the next session of the Preparatory Commission on Disarmament. I shall be glad if you will so inform the French government verbally.'

Quai d'Orsay to return you the copy which you left with them and allow you to substitute a verbal notification on the new lines.

Lord Salisbury's point was that we could not safely go further than the abbreviated notification without risking arousing a press campaign in America. Perhaps you could tell the Quai d'Orsay that on reconsideration His Majesty's Government think it better to go no further at present than you are instructed to do in the amended version. But you will be the best judge yourself of how to put it. We can only apologise for putting you into this position, but it was not our fault.

R. H. CAMPBELL

No. 290

Sir A. Chamberlain to Sir G. Clerk (Constantinople)
Unnumbered Telegraphic [W 1963/28/98]

Private   FOREIGN OFFICE, *March 1, 1928, 8 p.m.*

Your letter of 23rd February to me[1] and your letter of 21st February to Secretary of State.[2]

There is at present no such thing as disarmament conference but only a preparatory committee (and a security committee which is practically the same thing). As regards these short answer would be that they were naturally chosen from among members of the League, only exceptions being United States and Russia with their immense populations and one would naturally ask why Turkey does not apply to join League and so put herself on equality with other States. But as you will be coming on leave shortly Secretary of State thinks it unnecessary to send you further information as matter can be discussed with you on arrival. He will however request Lord Cushendun to support Turkish request to be represented on preparatory committee if made formally by Turkish government.[3]

OLIPHANT

[1] For this letter to Mr. Oliphant see No. 276, note 3.

[2] No. 276.

[3] This telegram was repeated as No. 5 to Geneva. Telegram No. 6 to Geneva of March 3 instructed Lord Cushendun to take action in accordance with the last sentence. Mr. Knox, Acting Counsellor resident at Angora, replied to the present telegram in a letter of March 8 to Mr. Oliphant in which he stated in particular that he had spoken on the lines of this telegram to Tewfik Rushdi Bey who 'expressed his thanks for the trouble that had been taken and for the promise of eventual British support. He had now instructed the Turkish Minister at Berne to sound Eric Drummond on the matter.' For the decision taken by the Council of the League of Nations on March 9 to issue an invitation to Turkey to be represented on the Preparatory Commission, see *League of Nations Official Journal*, April 1928, p. 432.

No. 291

Sir A. Chamberlain to Sir E. Howard (Washington)
No. 89 Telegraphic [W 2009/28/98]

Immediate   FOREIGN OFFICE, *March 2, 1928, 3.30 p.m.*

My telegram No. 87.[1]

There has been unfortunate leakage (vide telegram from Paris published by 'New York Herald Tribune')[2] of proposals in my cancelled despatch.[3] His Majesty's Government do not propose to raise now question of date of next Washington conference but only to revert to capital ship question at forthcoming meeting of Preparatory Committee on disarmament. As there is risk of matter being misrepresented it will be well for you to act immediately without awaiting arrival of despatch[3] to which above quoted telegram refers.

Please inform Secretary of State verbally that His Majesty's Government attach such importance to their capital ship proposals, from the point of view both of limitation and of economy, that they propose to revert to them in the Preparatory Committee. Secretary of State will recall passage bearing on this question contained in the joint declaration made by the three delegations at final session of Geneva naval conference. It is not intention of His Majesty's Government to seek detailed discussion of their proposals in the committee itself but merely to revert to them in general terms as an important contribution to disarmament generally and one which they therefore hope will be pursued at some future date.

[1] No. 285.
[2] In telegram No. 17 of March 2 to Paris regarding this press leakage Sir A. Chamberlain commented that the 'United States government will thus obtain first news of our intention from the press. It is particularly unfortunate that it should have been first version which was disclosed in that instructions which it contained were subsequently amended for the very reason that there was felt to be some risk, in mentioning dates, of arousing press campaign in America.'
[3] No. 281.

No. 292

Mr. London (Geneva) to Sir A. Chamberlain (Received March 3, 9.30 a.m.)
No. 9 L.N. Telegraphic [W 2015/28/98]

Immediate   GENEVA, *March 2, 1928, 11.45 p.m.*

Following from Lord Cushendun:

Report to be presented by Security Sub-Committee to Preparatory Committee will probably be a voluminous and ill-digested document which will include all the various memoranda and observations of the three rapporteurs and the various delegations as well as the documents now being prepared by drafting committee in an attempt to give them some sort of coherence. From private talks with Monsieur Benes and other delegates I gather the idea is that in order to give opportunity for governments to consider this report before finally instructing their representatives on the preparatory committee, it will be necessary when latter meets on March 15th to adjourn it till a later date, after giving consideration to Russian proposals, which everyone, with the probable exception of the Germans, hope to see dismissed as summarily as is decently possible. I cannot, however, discover a delegate who is prepared to move rejection of Russian proposals. Polish delegate came to see me yesterday and expressed the hope that I would undertake this duty; I declined to give any promise to that effect.

Meanwhile I hear from a reliable source that the Russians themselves are desperately anxious for domestic reasons that their disarmament proposals should be taken seriously and have some measure of success, however exiguous, which can be pointed to the[1] justification for Soviet government's departure from rigorous avoidance of League. M. . . . -stein[2] is reported to have said in private that if Russian proposals were turned down *in toto* 'it would mean postponement for many years of any possible collaboration' between the Soviet government and the League. As any such collaboration appears much more likely to be embarrassing than helpful, the threat is not one that I should consider a serious menace.

Another factor that has come to my knowledge may make it difficult to adjourn Preparatory Committee without full discussion of the whole question of disarmament. It is that Americans are coming to the Committee with the intention of 'playing a very active part' and that their chief naval expert will be Admiral Long who is said to be a pronounced anglophobe. American delegation may therefore come prepared to discuss, and we must be prepared to present our case on that date.

[1] In another text of this telegram this word read 'in'.

[2] The text is here uncertain. The reference was to M. Boris Stein, Soviet observer at the Committee on Arbitration and Security. A record (not printed) of a conversation on March 1 in which he spoke as here indicated to M. Colban, Director of the Disarmament Section of the League of Nations, had been communicated to Mr. Cadogan by Sir E. Drummond on March 2. In this conversation M. Stein stated that the Soviet Government were not pursuing some utopian idea and realised that they could not hope for 100% satisfaction, but even 2% or 3% satisfaction would make further collaboration possible.

No. 293

Sir E. Howard (Washington) to Sir A. Chamberlain
(Received March 12)
No. 472 [A 1774/1/45]

WASHINGTON, *March 2, 1928*

Sir,

With reference to my despatch No. 202[1] of January 27th, I have the honour to state that on the 27th ultimo, Mr. Olds, Under-Secretary of State, handed to me, at the request of Mr. Kellogg, the note[2] which the latter that day

[1] No. 263.

[2] This note of February 27 is printed as enclosure 2 (v) in item No. 1 in Cmd. 3109 of 1928.

addressed to M. Paul Claudel, French Ambassador, in reply to M. Briand's last note respecting the proposed Treaty to renounce war. As Mr. Olds told me that a copy of this note would be at once communicated to you by the American Embassy in London, I did not think it necessary to telegraph about it.

After reading it I ventured to express to Mr. Olds my personal opinion that I agreed with the view expressed in the note that there was little, so far as the principle of the matter was concerned, to choose between a bilateral Treaty as originally proposed by Mr. Briand and a multilateral Treaty as proposed by Mr. Kellogg. The difficulties stated by M. Briand to exist in the way of the second seemed to me to be almost as applicable to the first. But, even if this was admitted, it appeared to me that inasmuch as no country would forego the right of self defence, it would not be strictly honest to renounce all wars, while making a mental reservation in favour of defensive war.

Mr. Olds was evidently inclined to agree with this point of view but he said that this note was not by any means intended to shut the door on a further exchange of views on the subject and that it was hoped that it might help to clear the air, with which I am disposed to agree.

Mr. Kellogg spoke to me again on the subject after dinner a night or two ago. He began by stating that he entirely agreed with a memorandum which you had submitted to the Disarmament Commission of the League of Nations and could subscribe to every word of it. I have unfortunately not yet received a copy of this memorandum[3] and was obliged to confess to Mr. Kellogg my ignorance of its contents. Mr. Kellogg told me that it argued in favour of restricting arbitration to justiciable cases and for other disputes in favour of applying the 'conciliation' procedure adopted by the 1914 Bryan Treaties.

I told him that I had for a long time past held that the Bryan Treaties were perhaps the most important ever contracted in the interests of permanent peace and that if the principle they embodied could be made general it would help on the cause of peace more than any other multilateral Pact or Covenant could do. He seemed not disinclined to this view though still maintaining that a general Treaty renouncing war would have a beneficial effect.

If I may venture an opinion, it seems to me that perhaps a solution may be found to the difficulties inherent in the Briand–Kellogg proposal for a renunciation of war, whether bilateral or multilateral, by embodying in a multilateral joint Covenant, which all Nations could sign, such as the United States Government evidently desires, a platonic expression of the renunciation of war as a national policy of the signatories. Next there might be a clause for the arbitration of justiciable disputes to arise in the future. This would eliminate both any claims likely to be made against His Majesty's Government on account of past blockade measures and also claims by British subjects on account of the repudiated loans to Southern States of the United States of

[3] The reference was to the British observations on the programme of work of the Committee on Arbitration and Security (see No. 258, note 7) of which a copy had been sent to Washington on February 21.

America which the United States Senate always fear. Finally there should be a third clause for the reference of all other disputes not settled by diplomatic methods to a conciliation commission like those set up by the Bryan Treaties.

By an arrangement of this sort it appears to me that we should perhaps achieve two objects both of which would, I venture to think, help on the cause of peace which is the great aim of His Majesty's Government.

1st. All nations would presumably become Signatories to such a Covenant. This would thus have the public opinion of the entire world behind it which is unfortunately lacking to the League of Nations.

2nd. We should bring back the United States into the circle of nations striving to establish an era of peace and open the door to them for closer cooperation in this sense which they closed when they refused to join the League of Nations.

If, on the other hand, we entirely reject the present American overtures, we may, I greatly fear, simply set back the tide which is beginning again to flow fairly strongly in this country in favour of greater cooperation with the rest of the world and this set-back would in this year of a Presidential election be a real misfortune.

Although such an arrangement as I have outlined would not quite correspond to Senator Borah's proposal to 'outlaw war'[4] it will go as far in that direction as any reasonable person would believe practicable at present and would in all probability meet with the approval of the Senate.

From the short conversations which I have reported with the Secretary of State and Mr. Olds, I am inclined to think that they might welcome a suggestion in this sense as a way of escape out of what appears to be a blind alley constructed of interminable notes passing between the State Department and the Quai d'Orsay.

I understand of course that no suggestion of this kind can be offered by His Majesty's Government unless and until they are consulted but, as they may be consulted very shortly, I have ventured to submit the above considerations to you for what they are worth.

I have, &c.,
Esme Howard

4 Cf. No. 268.

No. 294

Lord Cushendun (Geneva) to Sir A. Chamberlain (Received March 5)
No. 11 L.N.C.C. [W 2062/28/98]

GENEVA, *March 3, 1928*

Sir,

It will be observed that in his study of the Scheme of Financial Assistance to be given to States threatened with Aggression,[1] the rapporteur of the

1 i.e. Chapter VI of M. Rutgers' memorandum on articles 10, 11 and 16 of the Covenant of the League of Nations (cf. No. 278, note 1).

Security Committee (Monsieur Rutgers) suggests (paragraph 203) that the Council might avail itself of this plan before Article 16[2] comes into play.

2. As previously reported, the Security Committee have nominated four members to form, with representatives of the Financial Committee, a small joint-committee to elaborate this scheme of financial assistance. They have held one sitting but have made little progress, and it is expected that their work cannot be finished during the present session but that they will have to have a special session before the next session of the Security Committee.

3. At present they have only discussed one or two of the broad aspects of the scheme, and one of the points to which they have devoted their attention is the question raised by M. Rutgers in the passage in his report referred to above. No conclusion has been reached and the Committee are at present somewhat divided on the point.

4. I am not aware of the view of His Majesty's Government on this particular point, which was not specifically raised before the appearance of the report in question. But, seeing that one of the motives which actuated His Majesty's Government in accepting the scheme was that it might prove a powerful deterrent to any State contemplating aggression, and might, to that extent, render less likely the necessity of enforcing all the sanctions which might be implied in Article 16 of the Covenant, I assume that His Majesty's Government would have no objection in principle to the idea that the Council might mobilise the scheme even in the course of a dispute and before hostilities have actually broken out. As the report of the joint committee will probably not come before the present session of the Security Committee, it will not be necessary for me now to be instructed on this point, which might be examined in the meanwhile by the competent departments.

I have, &c.,

CUSHENDUN

2 Of the Covenant of the League of Nations.

No. 295

Letter from the British Delegation (Geneva) to Western Department
[*W 2173/28/98*]

GENEVA, *March 4, 1928*

Dear Western Department,

We send you herewith two memoranda by Lord Cushendun, one containing his views as to the procedure to be adopted towards the Russian proposals, and the other a record of a conversation which he has had with Monsieur Paul-Boncour. The Secretary of State[1] has seen these and has written the following minute on them: 'Lord Cushendun's two reports should go home

1 Sir A. Chamberlain spent a few hours in Paris on March 3 before going on to Geneva where he arrived the next day to attend the forty-ninth session of the Council of the League of Nations (March 5–10, 1928): for the report by the Secretary of State on this session, see Cmd. 3098 of 1928. The records of the session are printed in *League of Nations Official Journal*, April 1928. Sir Austen returned to London on March 11.

"for consideration by Lord Salisbury's Committee and for instructions" '.
Will you therefore take the necessary action, please.

Yours ever,

Delegation

Enclosure 1 in No. 295

Geneva, *March 3, 1928*

From conversations which I have had with several Delegates to the Security Committee, it is evident that they are very much exercised in their minds as to the most expedient course to pursue with reference to the Russian proposals which are to be presented to the Preparatory Committee on the 15th March. The desire has been expressed, on the one hand, that these proposals should be rejected as summarily as possible, while, on the other hand, the opinion is held that this course would have the disadvantage of enabling the Russian Delegate to present a full and carefully prepared case in support of their very drastic proposals for disarmament, while no sufficient reply would be forthcoming, with the result that for propaganda purposes the Russian move would achieve a very considerable success. At the same time, it is felt that for the Preparatory Committee to embark upon an extempore discussion of these proposals would probably mean an ineffective reply as regards the scheme as a whole.

In these circumstances, it has occurred to me that possibly the following procedure would be as effective for the purpose we have in view as any other that can be devised, and would also have the effect of bringing about, for a plausible reason, an adjournment until a later date of the work of the Preparatory Committee, which I think is very generally desired, though no one seems prepared with a practical plan for bringing it about. What I would propose is that, when the Russian Delegate has elaborated his scheme, some member of the Committee should declare that the Russian proposals involve too many grave considerations of a far-reaching nature for it to be possible for the Committee to deal with them off-hand in an adequate manner. He would also point out that the Committee has been engaged for more than a year on the discussion of disarmament based on certain draft conventions, and that it is very doubtful whether the Russian proposals could be brought into relation, either by amendment or otherwise, with these drafts, or whether they would not necessarily involve the complete abandonment of the scheme of work hitherto followed and their substitution as a completely new scheme. In these circumstances, would it not be the best course to appoint a small Sub-Committee—say, of five representatives—to consider the Russian proposals with a view to determining whether they can be combined in any way with the draft conventions which have up to the present been the basis of discussion, and also to report on the merits and practicability of the Russian proposals. Such a report should give a complete and detailed answer to the Russian case in a form that could be published in the European Press and which would have the advantage both of proving that the Russian proposals

578

had been carefully and sincerely examined and also of supplying a fully reasoned rejoinder to them. The proposed Sub-Committee should be instructed to make their report to the Preparatory Committee at a future date, to be fixed after a sufficient interval for their report to be considered by the Governments; and, when received, it would be possible for the Preparatory Committee simply to adopt the report, thus obviating the necessity of further discussion on the Russian proposals.[2]

CUSHENDUN

ENCLOSURE 2 IN No. 295

GENEVA, March 4, 1928

Monsieur Paul-Boncour came to pay me a farewell visit yesterday evening. After discussing for a few minutes his personal electoral prospects, I told him how sorry I was that he would not be at Geneva to answer the Russian proposals, which I foresaw would prove tiresome. Monsieur Paul-Boncour contented himself with repeating that it was a very tiresome business.

We then got on to the second reading of the Disarmament synoptic texts,[3] and Monsieur Boncour repeated his view that, as England and France were not in agreement, the discussion should be adjourned. In answer to my question 'Until when?', he said the beginning of July. The reason for this date was not clear at the time, but later in the conversation he said that he anticipated that several of the Delegations here would press for a further meeting of the Security Committee at the end of June to read for a second time the Security Report which is now being drafted, and he also expected that the German proposals, on which I have already reported in my despatches Nos. 2 (LNCC)[4] and 3 (LNCC)[5] of the 24th and 25th February respectively, would then be discussed. So he evidently thought that the second reading of the Disarmament synoptic texts could conveniently be taken immediately after the second reading of the Security Report, granted always that the French and British were by then in agreement: failing that, he thought the adjournment should, if possible, be indefinite.

Monsieur Boncour then said that it was the naval questions which were preventing an agreement between the British and the French. When I asked

[2] In a minute on this memorandum and on the record of Mr. Colban's conversation with M. Stein (see No. 292, note 2) Mr. Palairet stated: 'Whether the Soviet proposals are put forward in good faith or not, it seems to me essential that we should treat them as if they were. To reject them without discussion—however unpractical they may be—would, it seems to me, put us in the wrong, not only in the eyes of Russia, but in those of liberal-minded men and women throughout the world, who are anxious that no avenue towards world-peace should be left unexplored, even if it turns out on examination to be a blind-alley. The summary rejection of these proposals would also furnish the Russian propagandists with fresh material for accusing us, and the other Powers, of insincerity in the cause of disarmament; while it would, as M. Stein pointed out, injure, if not destroy, all prospect of Russian co-operation with the League in the future. I therefore submit that the proposals should be treated as sincere and serious; and the method suggested by Lord Cushendun seems to me excellent. C. M. PALAIRET March 9.'

[3] See No. 230, note 3.

[4] See No. 287, note 1.

[5] Not printed.

him what the French had to offer in this respect, he referred to the French compromise proposals put forward towards the end of the session of the Preparatory Committee last April,[6] and added that he thought that Admiral Kelly's discussions with the French Admiralty last November[7] had brought an understanding rather nearer. I expressed some doubt, and said that our Admiralty were very set in their own views, especially as regards the necessity of sub-dividing cruisers into two classes. To this Monsieur Boncour replied that, speaking personally and as one not fully conversant with the views of his own Admiralty, he did not think that this would prove an insuperable obstacle. He emphasised, however, that not only he, but also Count Clauzel and Captain Deleuze[8] who *were* au courant with the general views of the French Admiralty, had no definite instructions: these had not been given because it seemed clear that the second reading of the synoptic texts would not be taken at the meeting due to begin on March 15th.

I told Monsieur Boncour that I would report what he had told me to Sir Austen Chamberlain: if there seemed any prospect of reaching an understanding, how, in his opinion, should the preliminary negotiations be conducted. Monsieur Boncour suggested that I and Admiral Kelly should discuss things with Count Clauzel and Captain Deleuze; these conversations could, if necessary, be continued between now and the anticipated meeting of the Security Committee at the end of June, when it was desirable that he and I should be able to bring the conversations to a definite agreement—and we left the position at that.

In the course of the discussion, Monsieur Boncour said that he supposed the reason why we had not hitherto sounded them on the naval deadlock was because we wished first to see what the attitude of the Americans was likely to be. I neither contested nor accepted this.

CUSHENDUN

---

[6] See Volume III, Nos. 137 and 139.   [7] See No. 267, note 3.
[8] Naval representative on the French Delegation at Geneva.

No. 296

Lord Cushendun (Geneva) to Sir A. Chamberlain (Received March 12)
No. 14 L.N.C.C. [W 2342/28/98]

GENEVA, March 7, 1928

Sir,

With reference to my despatch No. 10 (LNCC)[1] of March 3rd, I have the honour to report that the plenary Committee met on Monday, yesterday and

---

[1] Not printed. This despatch reported on the work of Sir C. Hurst, M. Politis and Baron Rolin-Jaequemyns in drafting texts and their consideration by the drafting committee of the Committee on Arbitration and Security.

today to continue its examination of the work of its Drafting Committee.[2] The Committee approved the texts of six model treaties, as follows:—

(A) A Model General Convention for the Pacific Settlement of all International Disputes (Annex 1).[3]

(B) A Model General Convention on Judicial Settlement, Arbitration and Conciliation (Annex 2).

(C) A Model General Conciliation Convention (Annex 3).

(D) A Model Collective Treaty of Mutual Assistance (Annex 4).

(E) A Model Collective Treaty of Non-Aggression and the Pacific Settlement of Disputes (Annex 5).

(F) A Model Bi-Lateral Treaty of the same type (Annex 6).

2. These model treaties, as you are aware, have been elaborated by the Drafting Committee working at high pressure, and it is generally agreed that if they are to be models in fact as well as in name, they will probably need revision. The Committee has therefore decided that it should proceed at a later session to revise them at a second reading in the light of observations which the governments may see fit to offer during the interval. Another reason for further reflection and study lies in the need for ensuring that they are in harmony with existing agreements of a similar type. The Committee will also have to decide whether to express a preference for one model over any other.

3. In addition to the above, the Committee has approved the texts of the following introductory notes and resolutions:—

(1) An introductory note to the general conventions on arbitration and conciliation (C.A.S. 34—Annex 7).

(2) An introductory note to the model treaties of non-aggression and mutual assistance (C.A.S. 35—Annex 8).

(3) A resolution on the introduction to the three memoranda prepared at Prague[4] (C.A.S. 31—Annex 9).

(4) A draft resolution for submission to the next Assembly recommending the model conventions on Arbitration and Conciliation to the consideration of all governments (C.A.S. 32—Annex 10).

(5) A similar draft resolution on the model treaties of non-aggression and mutual assistance (C.A.S. 33—Annex 11).

---

2 The minutes of these meetings of the Committee on Arbitration and Security on March 5, 6, and 7 are printed in *Documents of the Preparatory Commission for the Disarmament Conference*, Series VI, pp. 106–22.

3 Annexes 1 to 16 are not preserved with the filed copy of this despatch in their original form. Included in the file is a copy of C.P.D. 108 (C.A.S. 39), the report of the Committee on Arbitration and Security of the Preparatory Commission for the Disarmament Conference on the work of its second session, printed *ibid.*, pp. 185–225. This report includes texts of the documents originally annexed to the present despatch as follows: annexes 1–3 (conventions A–C) are printed as Section III (*b*); annexes 4–6 (treaties D–F) as Section IV (*b*); annex 7 as Section III (*a*); annex 8 as Section IV (*a*); annex 9 as Section II; annex 10 as Section III (*c*); annex 11 as Section IV (*c*); annex 12 as Section III (*d*); annex 13 as Section IV (*d*); annex 14 as Section III (*e*); annexes 15 and 16 as Sections V (*b*) and (*a*) respectively.

4 See No. 278, note 1.

(6) Two draft resolutions for submission to the Assembly recommending action by the Council in regard to these two classes of model treaties (C.A.S. 20 and 21—Annexes 12 and 13).

(7) A resolution on the Optional Clause of the Statute of the Permanent Court (C.A.S. 24—Annex 14).

(8) A resolution on communications with the League in case of emergency (C.A.S. 19—Annex 15).

(9) A resolution on Articles 10, 11 and 16 of the Covenant (C.A.S. 37—Annex 16).

4. The texts of some of these resolutions have already been forwarded in previous despatches, but in order to give a clear idea of the results of the Committee's work during its present session I have thought it well to include a complete list in the present despatch.

5. It will be seen that five out of the six model treaties are of a general type. The Committee has decided to proceed at its next session to draft bilateral treaties. The Drafting Committee has explained that it gave its attention first to multilateral treaties as these presented more difficulties from the drafting point of view, whilst there would be little difficulty in adapting their provisions to serve as model bilateral treaties, and the Committee has been careful in its introductory note to point out that it has no intention of indicating thereby any preference for general conventions.

6. The character of the three model arbitration treaties may be summarised as follows.

Under *Convention A*, justiciable disputes are submitted to the Permanent Court or to a special arbitral tribunal. They may, however, be submitted, in the first instance, by agreement to a conciliation commission. Non-justiciable disputes must be submitted to a conciliation commission, and in the event of a failure to reach a settlement the dispute must be brought before an arbitral tribunal.

Convention B. This convention follows the same lines as the arbitration and conciliation conventions concluded at Locarno.

Convention C. This convention provides only for submission of disputes to a conciliation commission.

7. The composition and duties of the conciliation commissions, as laid down in the above three conventions, are in general reproduced from the provisions of the Locarno treaties. Greater latitude has, however, been granted to the parties; in particular it is stipulated that the conciliation commission may be either permanent or constituted *ad hoc*.

8. In order to preserve as much elasticity as possible the Committee has thought well to make ample allowance in these model conventions for reservations, but it has tried to regulate and classify them in order to avoid uncertainty. The most important reservation refers to 'disputes concerning broad clearly-defined subjects, such as territorial status' (see Convention A, Article 36). Thus any State, when acceding to the convention, may exclude any class of dispute, but must indicate the class of dispute with greater definition than is afforded by the customary reservation as to vital interests.

Reservations shall apply only to disputes submitted to arbitration, unless it is expressly stated that they shall also apply to disputes submitted to a conciliation commission. Finally, all disputes as to the interpretation of the terms of the Conventions, including disputes as to the scope of reservations, are, in each case, to be referred for decision to the Permanent Court.

9. As regards the security treaties, the most comprehensive is Treaty D, which combines provisions for non-aggression, peaceful settlement of disputes and mutual assistance. It differs, however, from the Rhineland Pact in several respects: (*a*) It contains no clause guaranteeing the maintenance of the territorial *status quo*; (*b*) it provides for no guarantee by third States; and (*c*) it contains a number of provisions for the peaceful settlement of disputes which are not to be found in the Rhineland Pact but are included in the arbitration conventions concluded at Locarno.

10. In accordance with its policy of providing as much elasticity as possible, the Committee has included in its introductory note above referred to (C.A.S. 35), indications of the various alternative provisions which have not been included in the text but which might be substituted by those governments who desire to conclude a security pact.

11. You will remember that early in the proceedings I moved a resolution by which the Committee were invited to endorse certain statements of principle which are set out in the introduction[4] to the three memoranda prepared under the chairmanship of Dr. Benes. The German Delegation were unwilling to accept as it stood the third proposition in this resolution. They refused to subscribe to the principle that the conclusion of security pacts presents the only practical or possible form of supplementary guarantee. After considerable difficulty they were induced to agree to a modified form of this resolution, which was approved yesterday by the plenary committee, and which will be found under (3) above (Annex 9).

12. When the draft resolution for submission to the Assembly recommending the model arbitration conventions came before the Committee yesterday, the Netherlands representative reverted to a suggestion which he had previously made in the Drafting Committee. This was that these model conventions should not only be recommended to governments but should be included in protocols which should be opened at once for signature by all Members of the League at the next Assembly. This suggestion received no support in the Committee. The Swedish representative, without opposing the terms of the draft resolution, said he would have preferred a resolution under which the model conventions were merely presented to the Assembly. In this way, the Assembly would have been left free to decide what it would do with them. The remainder of the Committee did not share his view and agreed that as the draft resolution will be introduced at the beginning of the Assembly the latter will be perfectly free to accept, amend or reject it, as it thinks fit.

13. It will be observed that among the draft resolutions which the Committee has approved for submission to the Assembly is one dealing with the Optional Clause. In order to avoid the possibility of any embarrassing misunderstanding, I took occasion when this resolution came up before the

plenary Committee to restate the attitude of His Majesty's Government on this question. I pointed out that in his memorandum the rapporteur had been himself unable to suggest any practical proposal for further action by the organs of the League in this matter beyond recognising that the development of the Permanent Court's jurisdiction constituted an important application of the principle of arbitration. I thought, therefore, that the Committee were prudent in refraining from including in their resolution any practical proposal and in merely reiterating the opinion that as many States as possible should sign the Optional Clause if they found it in their power to do so.

14. I should add that owing to other work on which the Financial Committee is engaged, the Joint Committee set up to examine the scheme of Financial Assistance has not been able to make any progress. This matter has, therefore, been left over to the next session.

15. At its final session this afternoon the Committee listened to an able exposé by Monsieur Politis of the general lines which the Drafting Committee had followed in preparing the model treaties. He concluded by emphasising the conciliatory spirit in which all members of the Committee had co-operated notwithstanding the fact that the most delicate and difficult subjects were under discussion, and he expressed his conviction that this fact was a good omen for the political preparation which must precede the conclusion of agreements on the basis of the models which had now been drawn up.

16. Before separating, the Committee decided to meet again not later than the end of June. In addition to the revision of the model treaties, it will then have to draw up model bi-lateral treaties, to examine the suggestions of the German Delegation and to continue the study of the articles of the Covenant.

17. The reports on its second and third sessions will be placed on the agenda of the next Assembly.

I have, &c.,
CUSHENDUN

No. 297

Letter from Sir E. Drummond to Sir A. Chamberlain (Geneva)
[*F.O. 800/262*]

Copy
Personal

GENEVA, *March 7, 1928*

My dear Foreign Secretary,

Some of us who have been working for the League for a long time past believe that the reply made and treatment given to the recent Note from Kellogg on the possibility of the abolition of war must be of the very greatest importance to the whole future of the League.

That Note raises very definitely certain fundamental problems with regard to the relationship of the League to war, and it seems probable that American opinion towards the League and its decisions will in the future be very largely influenced by what now happens.

This being the case, is it really wise that any Power, however important, should speak on behalf of the League as a whole? So much depends on the answer, that I cannot think that the other Members of the League should disinterest themselves in the matter. It may be that the American proposals have come at an inopportune and inconvenient time, but I hope that they will be considered very seriously.

It seems to me to be extremely probable, if not certain, that the next Assembly cannot but interest itself in these proposals and in any reply which has been returned to them.

Yours very sincerely,
ERIC DRUMMOND

P.S. Since writing the above, rumour is current that you have expressed yourself here as hostile to the Kellogg proposals, and I cannot but fear the results if such a story continues to gain currency.[1]

[1] In a letter of March 1 to Mr. Cadogan regarding consideration of Mr. Kellogg's note of February 27 to M. Claudel Sir E. Drummond had stated in particular that he and M. Avenol, Deputy Secretary-General of the League of Nations, agreed that 'it might be dangerous at this stage to suggest to the Americans anything which might imply that sanctions against Pact-breakers should be discussed'.

No. 298

Letter from Sir A. Chamberlain to Sir E. Drummond (Geneva)

[*F.O. 800/262*]

Personal   GENEVA, *March 7, 1928*

My dear Eric,

Your letter in regard to Kellogg's proposals[1] has just reached my hands. I know no such hot-bed of gossip as Geneva and no place where more baseless rumours are current. I have not expressed any opinion on Kellogg's proposals at present and shall not give expression to any opinion until I have been able to consult the Dominions and reached a conclusion with my own Government.

The position at present is that Kellogg proposed to us to make a Treaty of Arbitration similar to that which he offered to France in place of the renewal of the Root Treaty which he had previously proposed. This is the only proposal officially made to us and upon which we are asked for a reply. As regards the multilateral pact, Kellogg communicated it to us 'for consideration' only and did not and has not invited our comments. There are obvious difficulties about both documents, the first of which is to find out what each of them really means, but both must and will receive very careful consideration by His Majesty's Government, who certainly do not desire any fresh difficulty with the United States.

As to your further suggestion that the Council should in some way intervene in the discussion between Kellogg and Briand, I confess that it does not

[1] No. 297.

585

smile to me. I should have thought that both parties would consider it an impertinence on the part of any Member of the Council who suggested it. Kellogg, as far as I understand, has suggested to the French Government that those two Governments should communicate the correspondence and proposals to certain other Governments named by him, but has never shown any desire for the League to take a hand in the discussion. If Briand thinks it necessary to consult the Council, he will no doubt do so, but surely that is a question for him to decide and it would be inexpedient for the rest of us to interfere unasked.

With reference to the earlier part of this letter, I ought perhaps to add that it was only after my return from your house last night that I saw a copy of Kellogg's latest note.[2]

Yours sincerely,
Austen Chamberlain

[2] Sir E. Drummond replied in a letter of March 8 in which he stated in particular: 'Nothing was further from my mind than a Council discussion. All I wanted was to point out that it seemed to me dangerous that the French Government should act unadvised as the sole spokesman for the League in a matter of the greatest importance to its future.'

No. 299

Letter from Mr. Malkin to Sir C. Hurst (Geneva)

[A 2100/154/45]

FOREIGN OFFICE, *March 7, 1928*

My dear Cecil,

There is going to Geneva by tonight's bag a draft to Washington[1] about the new arbitration treaty. It is based on verbal instructions by the Secretary of State and we were accordingly asked to confine ourselves to criticism of the words and to raise any points of substance in separate minutes. As the draft is certain to be submitted to you at Geneva and I have not been dealing with the question before, I have confined my energies to one small alteration of wording. But I wish you would consider the following point.

I am not at all sure that the problem of finding a formula which will (a) effectively exclude the possibility of having to arbitrate questions arising out of the exercise of our belligerent rights at sea, (b) get through the Senate, is not an insoluble one. I confess that I do not like the suggestion made in this despatch,[1] and I do not like any other suggestions which I have heard. The one made in the despatch is extremely wide and would exclude any question arising in the course or out of a war. But to my mind the main objection to it, and to any other proposals which I have heard, is that it is not based on any principle which it is possible to defend in argument with the Americans. The only principle on which it is based is that the exercise of belligerent rights is so important to us that we cannot agree to arbitrate any question connected therewith, and however satisfactory such a contention may appear in this

[1] The reference is uncertain.

country it is not likely to be received, especially in existing circumstances, with uproarious approval on the other side of the Atlantic. In these circumstances I have been trying to discover any principle on which it might be possible to base a formula which would cover us. The only one I can think of is the following; I admit that I am not particularly enamoured of it, but when things are so difficult any suggestion is perhaps worth considering.

Now it seems to me that one of the most presentable reasons which one can give for declining to arbitrate one's action is uncertainty as to the law by which the legality of that action is to be determined. If international law, by which it was agreed that states had to regulate their actions, were complete, precise and definitely known, there would really be no justification for refusing to arbitrate any juridical question which could be determined by the application of some branch of that law, but so long as this is not so (and it is notoriously not so as regards the rules of war at sea) it is perfectly reasonable for a state to whom the matter is of importance to decline to commit itself in advance to arbitrate questions as to which there is no law universally admitted as binding upon the nations. The administration of criminal justice would break down if there were complete uncertainty as to whether particular acts constituted a criminal offence or not, and so long as it is uncertain whether particular forms of belligerent action are legal or not we cannot be expected to submit any belligerent action of ours to the decision of an arbitral tribunal. And in this connection it is perhaps material to note that under the treaty cases are not going to the Permanent Court of International Justice but to the Permanent Court of Arbitration so that even the composition of the tribunal will be unknown until the case arises.

Might it, therefore, be possible, by basing ourselves on the above considerations, to get out of our difficulty on some such lines as the following? Provide in your treaty that all justiciable cases are to go to arbitration under it which can be decided by reference to some treaty provision which is binding upon both parties, or to a rule of law which they have both accepted. Provide, further, that in other justiciable cases the parties shall endeavour to agree in the 'compromis' as to the rules of law to be applied (compare the three rules of Washington)[2] but if they cannot agree, with the result that it becomes apparent that there is no universally accepted rule of international law which is applicable to the case, either party shall be entitled to decline to conclude the 'compromis', so that the case would be left to be dealt with under the conciliation procedure. The idea would want more working out, and there are doubtless any number of objections to it, but it does seem to me to be based on a defensible principle.

I have written the above really to ease my conscience. Personally I don't believe that any arbitration treaty with the United States is worth having in practice, because no arbitration treaty with that particular country is going to lead to arbitration except in cases where the U.S. are willing to arbitrate, and I regret infinitely that Kellogg was not content to stick to his

[2] The reference was evidently to the rules set out in article VI of the Washington treaty of May 8, 1871: see No. 275, note 4.

original suggestion and merely extend the old treaty, since I am afraid that the negotiations for a new one will have a bad effect on Anglo-American relations; but as things are I suppose we all ought to contribute any suggestions which we can, though if you put this one of mine straight into the wastepaper basket there will be nobody more delighted than myself.

Yours ever,
WILL MALKIN

No. 300

Sir W. Tyrrell to Sir E. Howard (Washington)
No. 106 Telegraphic [Telegrams 48/29]

Confidential. Immediate   FOREIGN OFFICE, *March 8, 1928, 10 p.m.*

We have seen telegram of 2nd March from Lewis to the 'Times',[1] who, after talking to press department here, decided that they would not publish it.

After describing disclosure in 'New York Herald-Tribune',[2] message goes on to state that there had been a good deal of discussion that morning in Washington on assumption that story was correct. It was recalled at State Department that American objection at Geneva was not to principle of British proposal but to its introduction at conference called to discuss limitation of auxiliary craft. Subject always to condition that 5–5–3 ratio were not disturbed, there was no reason to suppose that State Department would be other than favourably inclined to reduction of size and extension of life of capital ships. Professional sailors did not like idea at Geneva and did not like it now, but that had produced no argument for maintenance of *status quo*. It had been possible to arouse feeling on question of Anglo-American parity and to persuade public opinion of necessity for 10,000-ton cruisers, but further limitation of capital ships subject to maintenance of Washington ratio would be welcome to all except sailors and naval lawyers. Generally speaking, therefore, if it was intention of His Majesty's Government to seek in advance of conference in 1931 consent of Washington signatories to reduction of size and extension of age limit it might with reasonable confidence count on support of United States.

If above is anything like a correct estimate it is of great interest to us. It is not necessarily in conflict with remarks made to you by Secretary of State (your telegram No. 81[3]), who, apart from question of date, seems to have

[1] Not preserved in Foreign Office archives. According to the docket of a covering minute by Mr. Norton of the News Department of the Foreign Office this telegram was from the Washington correspondent of *The Times*, Mr. W. H. Lewis, and related to British proposals regarding capital ships. The docket of Mr. Norton's minute stated: 'The facts, except any reference to the first note to the French Government were explained to the "Times" representative who promised not to publish the telegram.'

[2] See No. 291.

[3] This telegram of March 3 is not preserved in Foreign Office archives. According to the docket it reported a conversation with Mr. Kellogg 'who was relieved that His Majesty's Government did not intend to raise now the question of date of next Washington conference. He had been perturbed about the Paris telegrams to New York papers but after

confined himself to observation that British proposals in themselves were not suitable for discussion in Preparatory Committee.

We should be grateful for expression of your personal views as to reliability of Lewis's estimate, which appears to indicate possibility of our being able to make some headway with our proposals, leaving aside contentious question of date of conference. You will of course use your own judgment as to any cautious soundings which you may wish to take before expressing opinion. Above all we wish to avoid anything in nature of controversy with United States Government or risk of press campaign at present juncture. All that will be useful to us for the moment is your impression of the direction in which American official opinion is moving upon the question of the size and extension of life of capital ships.

We should be glad to have a reply by Monday,[4] when the Cabinet Committee meet.'

Sir E. Howard's explanation he said he was not surprised that a leakage had occurred in Paris. He still held the view that there was no special reason to bring this matter before the preparatory committee.'

[4] March 12, 1928.

No. 301

Sir E. Howard (Washington) to Sir A. Chamberlain (Received March 20)
No. 534 [A 1917/36/45]

WASHINGTON, *March 9, 1928*

Sir,

With reference to my despatch No. 480 of 29th February last,[1] I have the honour to transmit to you herewith a copy of the pamphlet No. 205[2] recording the hearings of the House Committee on Naval Affairs on the Naval Construction bill (H.R. 7359) on February 1, 2 and 3.

2. On these dates Admiral Hilary P. Jones gave evidence. His remarks and his answers to questions are of considerable interest as giving his views on the respective positions taken up by His Majesty's Government and the United States Government at the Geneva Naval Disarmament Conference, and on questions arising therefrom. The entire record in fact merits attention. Though there are so many points of interest that it is useless to mention

[1] Not printed. This despatch reported in particular that 'the Naval Committee of the House of Representatives yesterday reported out the Bill for Naval Construction. This measure, as now advocated by the Committee, provides for the construction of fifteen cruisers and one aircraft carrier before July 1st, 1931, at an estimated cost, distributed over three years of $274,000,000. Thus the original proposal backed by the Navy Department amounting to twenty-five cruisers and five airplane carriers at a cost of $740,000,000, spread over five years, has been reduced as regards cruisers more perhaps in appearance than in actual fact, but, nevertheless, greatly reduced as far as airplane carriers are concerned. The total result is of course to produce a reduction of expenditure which will allay the alarm of the taxpayers.'
[2] This pamphlet, which recorded the statement of Admiral Jones, who had been a U.S. Delegate to the Geneva Naval Conference, in the sense indicated below, is not printed.

them individually, I would call attention to Mr. Britten's rather childish concluding remarks, on page 1235, in which he says that Admiral Jones convinced the Committee that His Majesty's Government were entirely to blame for the failure of the Conference, that a great opportunity to lift the burden of costly naval competition had been 'spiked by the heel of British Navalism'.[3]

3. Copies of this pamphlet have been sent direct to the Admiralty by the Naval Attaché of this Embassy.

I have, &c.,

Esme Howard

[3] Mr. Thompson minuted as follows on this despatch: 'I have read through these hearings and Admiral Jones' evidence is well worth studying, not so much in order to understand his attitude at Geneva, but so that we may be able to judge to some extent what the United States desiderata will be when the next Naval Limitation Conference convenes. I think I am right in saying that before the proceedings opened at Geneva last year, no official warning was received from the Washington Embassy of the importance attached by the Americans to the 8″ gun, our oversea naval bases, our preponderance in merchant shipping, the difference between our "bread" and our "wealth" lines or ocean trade routes, etc., etc.

'Admiral Jones, acting to perfection the part of a prosecuting counsel damning an absent and unrepresented accused in the shape of Great Britain, concentrated on all the above points, our demand for seventy cruisers and so on, with telling effect.

'The Admiral also emphasized the rivalry between Great Britain and the United States in foreign markets. In fact, it is clear from his evidence that the United States Navy Department have had under careful study what might be expected to happen in the event of an Anglo-American war, which to them anyway does not appear to be an unthinkable contingency.

'The unexpected and successful reaction of American public opinion against the naval programme as originally drawn up shows that similar views are not held by the population in general, and further that "big-navy" propaganda is not so effective as we feared. But it seems to me that we would do well to bear in mind the aggressive outlook of the Navy Department who have never forgiven or forgotten that the cup of naval superiority was dashed from their lips when the Washington Conference of 1921 led to the scrapping of much of the great naval expansion programme of 1916.

'G. H. Thompson 22/3'

No. 302

Letter from Sir E. Howard (Washington) to Sir A. Chamberlain
[F.O. 800/262]

Copy
Private and confidential   WASHINGTON, *March 9, 1928*
My dear Chamberlain,

I was very greatly obliged by the receipt of your letter of the 13th and 14th February[1] and highly appreciated your kindly taking so much trouble in giving me your thoughts about Kellogg's renunciation of war proposals. As regards the latter's mental attitude towards them, I would not go so far as to say that he does not think they have any value in themselves and that he only made them for electioneering purposes. I think he is quite sincere in

[1] No. 275.

saying he believes they will have a moral and educative value (words which he has repeated to me more than once) but I am equally sure he would never have cared enough about them to propose them if there had not been a serious demand in great sections of the country that the Government should do something towards helping to promote the cause of world peace. As I have already written the tide of isolation in this country is ebbing.

What I want to point out in this matter is that if we can find some means of making Kellogg's proposals harmonize with our previous commitments, we shall be helping on those in this country who wish to co-operate. If on the other hand we turn these proposals down without good reason we shall be playing into the hands of the isolationists, big Navyites and jingoes in this country who will at once cry out, 'We told you so. Europe will never take any real peace measure. She believes only in force so we must arm as much as we can to protect ourselves'. They are beginning this cry already.

It is not therefore a question of helping Kellogg or anyone else over the electoral fence (he will be out of office anyhow after 4th March, 1929) but of trying to change the trend of policy of this Government by allaying the suspicion the people unfortunately entertain of Europe and everything European.

Now there is no doubt that neither Kellogg nor Borah, the putative Father of all this 'Renunciation of War' proposal, have any intention of renouncing defensive War though they are scared at the idea of anyone mentioning aggressive war. I hear, however, that the State Department have already informed the French Government that they will not insist on renunciation of defensive war if a formula can be found to exclude it. But as regards arbitration we should have to go further than that. We should have to protect ourselves as you point out from arbitration on the doctrines laid down by our Admiralty Courts and the Supreme Court of the United States which we adopted in our blockade. The United States would wish also without doubt to protect itself against arbitration of the repudiated Southern Loan Claims. In any case, the Senate would never pass a 'compromis' having these in the terms of reference. We could mutually get over this difficulty by declaring that we will only refer all *future* justiciable disputes to arbitration. If the United States Government objected to that, we have only I think to hint at the Southern Loans to get our way.

I entirely agree with you in thinking that every country that makes an arbitration Treaty with the United States must safeguard itself by saying that every 'compromis' containing terms of reference must be submitted not only to the Senate but also to the Parliament of the other country if it has a Parliament. Only so can there be any equality. Surely such a clause would not necessarily conflict with our constitutional practice which can be modified to meet special cases? The terms of reference are of course of the utmost importance and I cannot help thinking that Parliamentary criticism of them would in any case be useful rather than the reverse.

As regards your suggestion that we might fairly ask the United States Government what action they will take if one of the Signatories of the

Multilateral Treaty breaks its engagements, I can but say that this would be a perfectly fair question but that given the present state of public opinion in this country the answer is a foregone conclusion. It would simply be that they will in no circumstances pledge themselves to take any action. But if they do not, neither would the rest of us, so it would not be 'an unequal treaty'. Only, as Kellogg has often explained to me, it would be self-understood that if any Power broke its faith, the other Signatories would be released from their obligations under the Treaty vis-à-vis that Power and could of course concert as to what measures they would adopt. I don't see any great objection to this because it binds none of us to any definite action. This, of course, will greatly weaken and emasculate the Treaty, if it ever comes into being, but still it will, I am convinced, be a good step forward to get the United States into some general Treaty of the kind.

This is why in my despatch No. 472[2] of the 2nd instant I ventured to submit for your consideration the plan of making the new arbitration Treaties which are to replace the Root–Bryce Treaties of 1908, take the multilateral form desired by the United States Government. I suggested very diffidently that they should consist like the French Treaty of three parts:

1. A declaration of the renunciation of war as a national policy.
2. Arbitration of justiciable matters in future.
3. Submission of all disputes—not settled by diplomatic methods—to the procedure laid down by the Bryan–Sprince [Spring] Rice Conciliation Treaty of 1914 to which like you I attach the highest importance. Had the European Powers had such a Treaty in 1914 and been willing to abide by it, unquestionably war would have been averted.

If Kellogg refers to the question again in speaking to me, I will certainly emphasize the necessity of caution and prudence in dealing with this very complicated and difficult problem. As you say his mentality, like that of most Americans in this respect, leads him to believe that once all American difficulties have been overcome, all difficulties have been overcome. They have not yet learnt to look at the other fellow's point of view and are inclined to treat him at first as a fool or a knave for having one. But with patience and perseverence [sic] one can get them to see that a box has four sides and not one only.

I see from the Geneva correspondent's telegram to the New York Times this morning that the opinion held by the Representatives of the Great Powers there is that the offer of the United States to co-operate for peace must not be brusquely turned down but that the correspondence between the United States and France should continue in the most friendly fashion in the hope of finding some satisfactory formula. I am glad of this, if true.

Yours very truly,
ESME HOWARD

[2] No. 293.

No. 303

Sir E. Howard (Washington) to Sir A. Chamberlain
(Received March 11, 9 a.m.)
No. 92 Telegraphic [W 2329/28/98]

Confidential   WASHINGTON, *March 10, 1928, 11.57 p.m.*

Your telegram No. 106.[1]

Feeling that I could give no reliable reply to question asked, I took opportunity of handing to Secretary of State this morning an *aide-mémoire* based on your despatches Nos. 274 and 275[2] and your telegrams Nos. 87 and 89[3] to enquire confidentially whether he could give me any idea of what his government really felt about reduction of size and extension of age of battleships. After once more emphasizing his view that this was a matter which could only properly be discussed in future conference of all signatories of Washington treaty and that earliest date for this was January 1931, he went on to say that while he could not of course commit himself he did not think United States authorities would oppose proposal in principle. He said even Navy Department during Geneva conference had not opposed it but only considered it should not have been raised then because it was a matter with regard to which France and Italy must be consulted. On my enquiring whether he thought there would be any objection to His Majesty's Government sounding other signatories to Washington treaty to find out their views, he said he would have none.[4]

[1] No. 300.   [2] Nos. 281–2.
[3] Nos. 285 and 291 respectively. Sir E. Howard's *aide-mémoire*, dated March 9, is printed in *Papers relating to the Foreign Relations of the United States 1928*, vol. i, p. 245.
[4] For an account of this conversation by Mr. Kellogg, *v. ibid.*, pp. 245–6.

No. 304

Memorandum by the British Delegation (Geneva)[1]
[W 2475/28/98]*

GENEVA, *March 10, 1928*

At Lord Cushendun's suggestion, Sir Austen Chamberlain discussed yesterday with M. Briand the disarmament position with reference to the forthcoming meeting of the Preparatory Commission on the 15th March.

Sir Austen Chamberlain began by regretting that on the two crucial military and naval questions the French and British were diametrically opposed. British public opinion, with its traditions, believed that voluntary armies were defensive and that conscript armies implied offensive war,

[1] This unsigned memorandum, which was circulated to the Cabinet, was entered on the Foreign Office file on March 13, 1928. The first paragraph of the memorandum together with a slightly variant version of the second paragraph, omitting the last sentence, and the fifth paragraph, omitting the last nine words, is printed in Cmd. 3211 of 1928, *Papers regarding the Limitation of Naval Armaments*, as item No. 10.

whereas he was fully aware that to the French compulsory military service seemed a guarantee of a pacific policy and a voluntary army appeared in the dangerous light of a Praetorian Guard. He went on to say that we had been reconsidering what we thought essential from the naval point of view, and he told M. Briand of the modified proposals which appear in section 2 of the Admiralty memorandum of the 7th February (P.R.A. 27).[2] British public opinion realised that concessions were necessary from all parties for a general settlement to be reached, and if he could point to a concession by the French in naval matters it would probably acquiesce in his giving in on the military side. On the other hand, we could not abandon the British standpoint on the question of army reserves unless we could justify this concession by pointing to a similar concession made to us in the naval sphere. He did not want to be driven in the matter of the limitation of military reserves to vote against France with Germany, and still less with Russia.

M. Briand said that this must on no account happen. Experience at Geneva showed that, if Great Britain and France stood together, what they agreed upon would be accepted by others. He then turned to the Russian proposals for complete disarmament, and said that they ought to be subjected at the outset to some searching questions. There were two forms of war: ordinary war between nations and civil war within nations; the latter was hitherto the avowed object of the Union of the Socialist Soviet Republics, whose present scheme aimed only at preventing the first form. They should be asked point-blank whether they equally abjured the other form.

As regards procedure, M. Briand suggested that when the Preparatory Commission met the Russian scheme should be referred to a committee for these and other technical criticisms, and that this period of examination

[2] This memorandum is filed in Foreign Office archives only in its later form as P.R.A. 27 (23) Revise of February 11. It set out recommendations regarding the action to be taken by Lord Cushendun at the Preparatory Commission for the Disarmament Conference decided on at a meeting on February 6 between Mr. Bridgeman, Lord Cushendun and Vice-Admiral Sir F. Field, Deputy Chief of the Naval Staff. At this meeting 'it was considered that the difference between our principles for the limitation of naval armaments and those advocated by France and other continental nations might, and probably would, threaten to cause a breakdown of the conference, and, with this contingency in view, it was decided to recommend that our Delegate should take the following action—I. He should commence by restating that, in the opinion of Great Britain, the extension of the principles of the Washington Treaty of definitely limiting naval armaments by the strict classification of vessels, with a maximum displacement and calibre of gun for each class, is considered to be by far the most effective means of achieving the results desired and eliminating competitive building. Under this proposal vessels should be divided into the following classes:—(i) Battleships. (ii) Aircraft Carriers. (iii) Coast Defence Vessels. (iv) Cruisers in two classes. (v) Flotilla Leaders and Destroyers. (vi) Submarines in two classes. (vii) Small vessels exempt from limitation, the basis of discussion of this classification being that adopted by the Three Power Conference at Geneva.'

If the opposition to this classification proved insuperable, the delegate was empowered to alter it to the form set out in No. 306 below. If this second alternative failed, the British Delegate was to suggest that limitation should be imposed by each nation publishing a programme which should not be exceeded during the period of the regulating treaty. Finally the memorandum proposed the action in Nos. 280–1.

should be used by the French and British to reach an understanding on their military and naval attitudes.

Turning to the navy, M. Briand asked for a personal copy of the revised Admiralty proposals of which Sir Austen Chamberlain had informed him. He said that he would put them to the French naval authorities and use all his influence to obtain their acceptance.

If, however, he was to be successful, he would need our co-operation. He had often told the French Admiralty that a naval war with the British was out of the question, and he was quite prepared to meet the criticism he had encountered for agreeing at Washington to a very small battleship allotment; the French would, in fact, never vote money for large numbers of battleships. The real naval crux for France was Italy. At the Three-Power Conference the British and the Americans had disagreed over the basis of estimating cruiser requirements; France had *vis-à-vis* Italy much the same case that we had as regards the United States. In each case our oversea responsibilities were much greater and our sea communications much longer. It would be to our mutual advantage, when the proper time came, jointly to press that those factors should form the basis of assessment of the cruiser strength which States could justifiably claim. Sir Austen Chamberlain undertook to have this idea studied by the competent authorities on his return home.

Sir Austen Chamberlain and Lord Cushendun discussed the above exchange of views the same evening; Admiral Kelly and Mr. Cadogan were present.

It was agreed that as regards the Russian proposals M. Briand's idea corresponded almost exactly with our own; at the same time, it was not for us, in view of our special relations—or absence of relations—with Russia, to bell the Russian cat. Mr. Cadogan was therefore instructed to repeat privately to Count Clauzel M. Briand's remarks about the question to be put to the Russians and the procedure to be adopted, and was to suggest that if Count Clauzel would propose this line at the Preparatory Commission, he could count unreservedly upon our prompt and loyal support. If Count Clauzel was reluctant himself to take the lead, it would be equally satisfactory if he persuaded the representative of one of France's allies to do so.

As regards the naval and military questions, it was agreed that M. Briand's proposal was a sufficiently satisfactory basis of negotiation to recommend for the consideration of the Admiralty in the first instance and later of the Cabinet. As far as the near future was concerned, it offered hope of an Anglo-French agreement by the time the two draft disarmament texts came to be read a second time, possibly in July; in the remoter future, viz., the Disarmament Conference and possible negotiations preliminary to it, it would at any rate ensure that we had French support in a matter vital to us, whereas at present we had none, having alienated at the Three-Power Conference the Americans, who had been our ally at the Preparatory Commission.

Admiral Kelly undertook to put in the form of a private letter, for Sir Austen Chamberlain to hand to M. Briand, the Admiralty compromise proposals; the initiative as regards M. Briand's own proposal for the basis of estimating cruiser strength would be left to the French.

Finally, as regards the immediate position, Mr. Cadogan was instructed to make it absolutely clear to Count Clauzel, as from Sir Austen Chamberlain, that we would not tolerate any insinuation from the French that the adjournment, upon which we were now mutually agreed, was due to our intransigence in naval matters; if we learnt that they were putting this about, we should give out categorically that the real obstacle to a second reading was the French refusal to limit in any way their trained reserves—a question on which we could come to an agreement with the Germans, if we so wished, at any moment.[3]

[3] Mr. Cadogan spoke accordingly to Count Clauzel of the French Delegation at Geneva on March 10. He stated in particular in his record of this conversation (copy received in the Foreign Office on March 19) that Count Clauzel took his observations in good part but enquired: 'Would it be considered inconvenient by us if, in the event of there being a vote on the question of the adjournment of the second reading, he, as French representative, were to abstain from voting? I told him at once that I feared it would be extremely inconvenient, for I pointed out that such abstention on the part of the French representative could not fail to heighten the impression which might exist in certain quarters and notably in our own country, that all the delay and all the obstruction came from the side of His Majesty's Government.'

No. 305

Memorandum by the British Delegation (Geneva)[1]
[W 2474/28/98]

GENEVA, *March 10, 1928*

Air Disarmament

In the course of Sir Austen Chamberlain's general discussion with Monsieur Briand on disarmament recorded in a separate memorandum,[2] Sir Austen Chamberlain raised also the question of Air forces. He said that His Majesty's Government did not seriously consider the eventuality of an air warfare between France and Great Britain: there was, however, a degree of disparity between the Air forces of the two countries which, if reached, must disturb public opinion. He was, therefore, troubled by information that the French Chamber had recently voted something like a minimum of 150 Air squadrons, with the possibility of an unlimited increase. He believed that our squadrons were at most one-third of this number.

Sir A. Chamberlain reminded Monsieur Briand that he had recently raised this question with Monsieur de Fleuriau[3] and had suggested a parity agreement as between Great Britain, France and Italy; he now wished to make clear what he had not at the time explained to the Ambassador—that the parity contemplated by His Majesty's Government referred to metropolitan

[1] This unsigned memorandum which was circulated to the Cabinet was entered on the Foreign Office file on March 13, 1928.

[2] No. 304.

[3] See No. 271.

forces only, i.e. forces capable of being used immediately for home defence. In addition to these and outside the proposed arrangement would be the squadrons on which Great Britain relied (in some cases almost exclusively) for the defence of territory in the East.

Monsieur de Fleuriau had replied to his original proposal that the fact that France had no separate Air force would make any parity arrangement impossible on administrative grounds alone:[4] Sir Austen Chamberlain could not really accept this as a sufficient obstacle, seeing that, however organised, French and British Air forces would, in fact, be used for approximately the same purposes and duties.

[4] See No. 272.

No. 306

Letter from Sir A. Chamberlain to M. Briand (Geneva)[1]

[W 2473/28/98]

GENEVA, *le 10 Mars, 1928*

Mon cher ami,

Je vous envoie ci-joint le projet de compromis au sujet de la classification de bâtiments de guerre dont je vous ai parlé hier.[2]

Agréez, mon cher ami, l'assurance de mes sentiments de haute considération.

ENCLOSURE IN No. 306[3]

I. Bâtiments de ligne.
II. Bâtiments porte-aéronefs.
III. Bâtiments d'un tonnage entre 10,000 et 7,000 tonnes.
IV. Bâtiments d'un tonnage inférieur à 7,000 tonnes.
V. Bâtiments sous-marins.
VI. Petits Bâtiments exempts de limitation.

avec les stipulations suivantes:

(a) Tout nation peut transférer du tonnage des catégories supérieures aux catégories inférieures à l'exception du tonnage des Classes Nos. I et II, en tenant compte d'une limite de la proportion du tonnage global qui peut être utilisée pour les sous-marins.

(b) Toute nation ayant un tonnage global dans les six classes inférieur à 80,000 tonnes est libre de toute classification.

[1] An unsigned copy of this letter was received in the Foreign Office on March 13 from the British Delegation at Geneva. The docket on the Foreign Office file stated that this letter was from Sir A. Chamberlain.

[2] See No. 304.

[3] A slightly variant English text of these proposals is printed in Cmd. 3211 of 1928, footnote on p. 17. The French text is printed as item No. 15 in the French official publication, *Limitation des armements navals* (Paris, 1928).

No. 307

Letter from Sir C. Hurst (Geneva) to Mr. Malkin
[W 2964/2964/17]

GENEVA, *March 10, 1928*

My dear Will,

The papers about the renewal of the Anglo-American Arbitration Treaty will not, I fancy, be dealt with by the Secretary of State until he gets back to London. There has been no time for him to go into the question here. I have written a minute on the draft,[1] indicating great doubt as to whether the lines it indicates afford an advantageous basis for the new arbitration treaty with the United States and urging that various aspects of the question should be further explored in London. To this minute I have added your letter[2] suggesting that the difficulty about disputes arising out of the exercise of belligerent rights at sea should be got over by the inclusion of a reserve in respect of all matters about which the rules of international law are at present unsettled.

I do not imagine that you have had time to study the model draft treaties which we have been turning out in great numbers in Geneva. These drafts were all prepared by a little Committee of Three, consisting of Politis, myself and Rolin-Jacquemyns, the Belgian. The main Drafting Committee numbered over a dozen people and was attended by a vast horde of members of the Secretariat and others and was far too big a body to prepare texts. In the little Committee of Three we could discuss things with freedom and when preparing the draft article about reserves which a state accepting the Conventions can make,[3] I told Politis that I felt convinced that there must be some power to make reserves about matters on which the rules of international law were at present unsettled. What I had in mind was disputes arising out of belligerent action at sea. The wording of reserve (d) was worked out with the very intention of enabling this class of cases to be excluded. I thought it better not to specify the class.

You will see from the above that our minds have worked on somewhat parallel lines. Let me now proceed to the other side of the question.

It is not in an arbitration treaty between us and the United States that I think the reserve ought to be made in this way, because Great Britain and the United States are the two countries whose views on questions such as contraband and blockade are in theory similar. The division is supposed to be between the Anglo-American point of view and the continental point of view. I rather shrink myself from formulating a reserve in a treaty with the United States which implies, when you think it out, that the British views on the subject of maritime law are purely individual to our own country.

[1] This minute of March 7 (not printed) related to a British revised draft (reference uncertain) for an Anglo-American treaty of arbitration. The main point made in this minute is recapitulated in the final paragraph of the present letter.

[2] No. 299.

[3] The reference was to article 29 of the draft general convention for judicial settlement, arbitration and conciliation (Convention B): cf. No. 296, note 3.

The unattractive looking paper which I enclose[4] is the result of my own efforts to think out a scheme for the renewal of the Anglo-French Arbitration

[4] The enclosed memorandum of March 9 by Sir C. Hurst for Sir A. Chamberlain on the renewal of the Anglo-French arbitration agreement of 1903 is not printed. Sir C. Hurst stated that he had ascertained from M. Fromageot that its renewal in existing terms would cause 'considerable disappointment' to the French Ministry of Foreign Affairs. Sir C. Hurst expanded the points made in the second paragraph above and stated: 'The present situation, however, is that a draft General Arbitration Treaty is now to be submitted for consideration by Governments in terms which would enable H.M. Government to accept it without risk. If they did so, the necessity of renewing the various existing bilateral arbitration treaties would disappear.

'3. The acceptance, however, of a general arbitration treaty subject to far-reaching reserves is open to objection. It would involve a somewhat violent departure from the previous policy of H.M. Government, who have announced not infrequently that they cannot accept any system of general compulsory arbitration, and in their recent memorandum [see No. 258, note 7] on the subject of compulsory arbitration laid stress upon the argument that obligations of this nature which they might be willing to accept towards one state they might not be willing to accept towards another and that the method of signing a general undertaking, even when coupled with the power to make exceptions as to the categories of disputes to be arbitrated, lacks that flexibility which enables the measure of the obligation to be varied in the case of the particular states towards which the obligation is being accepted.

'4. In these circumstances it would, I submit, be better to try and find some new form of arbitration treaty with France which would safeguard the points to which H.M. Government attach importance and which would satisfy the desires of those elements of the public at home which are tending to become critical of the policy which H.M. Government are following with regard to this question of compulsory arbitration. I am not aware of the extent to which you share that view, but I myself am becoming a little apprehensive that this question may be thrown into the arena of party politics in England, and I think this would be unfortunate. It would be very advantageous if some new text could be found of an arbitration treaty with France which fulfilled the two conditions mentioned above.' The attached draft treaty prepared by Sir C. Hurst is not printed. Sir C. Hurst suggested that the arbitration treaties of February 1 and 27, 1904, with Italy and Spain respectively (printed in *British and Foreign State Papers*, vol. 97, p. 57 and pp. 80–1 respectively) should be renewed at the same time in similar terms; and a similar treaty made with Germany whose attitude as inferred from Dr. Gaus was that 'they would like to have a treaty with Great Britain, that they feel that it would not be wise for them to take the initiative, but that they would accept practically anything which H.M. Government offered. . . . If satisfactory arbitration treaties with the above Powers could be signed simultaneously, it would demonstrate the determination of the Great Powers of Europe to maintain that close co-operation which began at Locarno and might, in the case of Spain, provide you with the means of ensuring Spain's return to the League. The League must necessarily play an appreciable part in the machinery of these treaties and it would be reasonable to stipulate that that with Spain shall not come into force until she has terminated her withdrawal from the League.'

Sir C. Hurst then raised the question whether His Majesty's Government should include in such arbitration treaties a clause binding the parties to the treaty not to make war upon each other and concluded: 'There are strong arguments for and against the inclusion of such a clause, but on the whole I think the arguments against including it should prevail, unless it is thought that the inclusion of such a clause in a treaty with France might be of help in connection with reducing the air armaments which Great Britain is bound to maintain so long as she has to maintain anti-aircraft defence against an attack by France. The reasons against the inclusion are that critics will maintain that there must be some method of settling disputes and, if war is eliminated, it is illogical not to accept compulsory arbitration, at least for justiciable disputes. Apart from this it is conceivable that if Great Britain

Treaty, and you will see in that that I have contemplated a different solution for this question. At present I am disposed to think that if we can get a satisfactory clause through in arbitration treaties with the continental states, rendering prize court decisions final on the same footing as the decisions of national courts in matters within the domestic jurisdiction of a state, we shall be on safer ground. If we are going to proceed upon any such lines as I have suggested, the Anglo-American Treaty is the worst place for the purpose, because it is as between Great Britain and the United States that there have been on occasions claims commissions which have revised prize court decisions. There was the famous commission under the Jay Treaty;[5] there were, I think, some prize decisions under review in the commission of 1853,[6] and there was the commission under the Treaty of Washington of 1871. Relations between Great Britain and France have been disturbed by no such vagaries.

Some little time ago on a paper[7] dealing with an effort made either by Holland or Sweden (I forget which) to make claims arising out of decisions in the prize courts during the war, I wrote a long minute[7]—moved thereto by one[7] of Eric Beckett's—on the subject of the extent to which, by the practice of the last two centuries, nations had acquiesced in the view that in time of war captures and condemnations were subject to prize court determination and that these decisions were final. Eric Beckett will probably remember the paper and can give you sufficient details to enable you to trace it. I wish you would get hold of it and read it, because I believe that the idea running through that minute does give a sufficient ground for maintaining that, by the general law of nations, a state can claim finality for its prize court decisions. If it can claim finality, there is no ground on which a foreign state can ask for an international review of the proceedings. I can only hope that in 1907 when we were sent to The Hague with instructions to propose a scheme for an international prize court, the representatives of H.M. Government said nothing inconsistent with the above line.

I am very disquieted at the line it is proposed to take as regards the renewal of the Anglo-American Arbitration Treaty. I have told the Secretary of State in a minute that, in my view, by admitting a reserve for the Monroe Doctrine and dropping the reserve as to vital interests we are excluding from arbitration the only vital interests of the United States and making no

concluded treaties of this character with her important neighbours in the west of Europe, those Powers might desire to follow the example and contract similar agreements with each other. It is unlikely that France would be willing to conclude a treaty containing this provision with either Italy or Spain. For the present I have omitted from the draft treaty annexed any such provision, but it could easily be inserted if thought desirable.'

[5] This Anglo-American treaty of November 19, 1794, negotiated on behalf of the United States by Chief Justice John Jay, is printed *op. cit.*, vol. 1, pp. 784–801.

[6] The reference was to the Mixed Commission, which sat in London from September 1853 to January 1855, set up by the Convention between Great Britain and the United States for the settlement of outstanding claims, February 8, 1853, printed *op. cit.*, vol. 42, pp. 34–8.

[7] The reference is uncertain.

provision for safeguarding our own, and to do this in a way which would aggravate opinion in Latin America seems to me singularly Quixotic. Far better no arbitration treaty at all than one which gives all the advantages to the United States and none to ourselves. If the Americans refuse to renew the existing treaty in the old terms, it would be better to have no treaty at all. Men like Politis speak with contempt of the new Franco-American treaty.

Ever yrs
CECIL J. B. HURST

No. 308

Sir A. Chamberlain to Sir E. Howard (Washington)
No. 114 Telegraphic [A 1725/154/45]

FOREIGN OFFICE, March 13, 1928, 12.45 p.m.

Please inform the United States Government officially that His Majesty's Government in Great Britain are very carefully considering the draft arbitration treaty enclosed in Mr. Kellogg's notes [note] of December 29th,[1] and are in communication with His Majesty's Governments in the Dominions regarding it, and that Your Excellency will be instructed to reply to Mr. Kellogg's communication as soon as possible.[2]

[1] See No. 244, note 2.
[2] In Washington covering despatch No. 571 of March 16 (not preserved in Foreign Office archives) Sir E. Howard transmitted a copy of the note of the same date (not printed) which he had presented to Mr. Kellogg in pursuance of the above instructions.

No. 309

Sir A. Chamberlain to Mr. London (Geneva)
No. 14 Telegraphic [W 2567/28/98]

Immediate   FOREIGN OFFICE, March 13, 1928, 4.50 p.m.

Following for Lord Cushendun.

Cabinet Committee have considered position in regard to forthcoming discussions of Preparatory Commission and have submitted proposals to Cabinet, also [who] have approved them in the following form.

With regard to Russian proposals M. Briand's suggestion is approved, viz: that proposals should be subject at outset to searching questions such as are they calculated to prevent not only war between nations but also civil war the instigation of which has hitherto been avowed object of Soviet government. In supporting French attitude we leave a great deal to your discretion but in regard to these questions you will of course be careful to avoid using any language which might be construed into implying that His Majesty's Government was obstructing reduction in armaments so as to be able to suppress legitimate labour movement. Russian proposals should then be referred to special committee for examination and report as suggested in your memorandum W/2173/28/98 of March 3rd.[1] Adjournment of Preparatory Commission is desirable, but British responsibility for seeking such adjournment should if possible be avoided. Interval between adjournment and next meeting of Preparatory Commission should be utilised to forward the compromise between France and ourselves in regard to land and sea armaments as outlined in conversation between Sir Austen Chamberlain and M. Briand,[2] i.e. support of France to our naval proposals as stated in Section II of Admiralty memorandum No. P.R.A. (27) 23 Revise,[3] to be secured by withdrawal of open resistance on our part to French views on army reserve. Having regard to events of last year, however, it is very important that open discussions on cruiser questions should if possible be postponed till after American Presidential election. The present occasion should not be lost for publicly putting forward British Admiralty's proposals in regard to capital ships since having regard to public opinion at home and abroad the value of seizing the initiative on this proposal outweighs any risk of displeasing Americans, and ultimately no report on reduction of naval armaments would be complete without it. Once case has been placed before the public as a British proposal actual date of consideration is not of material importance, provided agreement is reached in such time as will enable proposals to become effective before Washington Treaty expires.[4] In view therefore of American objection discussion as to this date should at the present moment be avoided.

If either French or Italians suggest that the ratio allotted to them under the Washington Treaty is too low, Admiralty entertain no objection to their ratio being raised from 1·7 to 2. Any suggestion however of this kind must of course emanate from them and not be put forward by you.

The submission to the League of a model statement of expenditure on armaments is agreed to generally in the form proposed by the committee of experts.[5] But it should be preceded by a sentence as follows 'This form is to be used only for the comparison of one year's expenditure with another of each particular country. It cannot be used for the purpose of comparing the military, naval and air strengths of different countries'. Besides this certain minor technical amendments are being studied and it is possible we may send them to you if there is still time.

[1] Enclosure 1 in No. 295.
[2] See No. 304.
[3] See No. 304, note 2.
[4] In a message to Lord Cushendun in Foreign Office telegram No. 15 to Geneva of March 14 Lord Salisbury suggested that the sense might be clearer if the following passage were substituted for the preceding four words: 'Before the capital ship replacement programme commences under the provisions of the Washington Treaty.'
[5] The Committee of Eleven Experts on Budgetary Questions had recommended a model form of return in Subcommission B of the Preparatory Commission for the Disarmament Conference in their final report of July 1, 1927 (League of Nations document C.P.D. 90).

No. 310

Mr. London (Geneva) to Sir A. Chamberlain
(Received March 14, 4.40 p.m.)
No. 33 L.N. Telegraphic [*W 2536/28/98*]

GENEVA, *March 14, 1928, 3.58 p.m.*

Following for Deputy Chief of Naval Staff from Admiral Kelly No. 2.

Second discussion with Long[1] shows that Americans and French have been discussing in Paris. Americans prepared to accept French proposal[2] as basis for discussion with following modifications. Battleship and aircraft carrier tonnage not transferable to other classes. Other categories to be surface vessels between 10,000–3,000 tons, then 3,000 tons and below, then submarines.

Transfer of tonnage in these categories to be permitted, only limited to a percentage of say 10%. Exempt class to be provided for. French decision not yet known. If French agree they to make new proposal and not to give in as concession to proposal by others.

It is emphasized that Admiralty proposals have not been mentioned or discussed in any way; conversations have been exclusively confined to America's attitude at forthcoming meeting.[3]

[1] No record of Admiral Kelly's first conversation with Admiral Long on March 13 has been traced in Foreign Office archives, but it may have been transmitted in Geneva telegram No. 32 L.N. of March 13 (not preserved in Foreign Office archives). According to a memorandum of May 1 by Mr. Cadogan it appeared from this conversation that, 'if the United States Government would agree to the division of cruisers into two classes, they would put the maximum tonnage of the smaller class as high as 8,300 tons. They would accept a maximum individual tonnage for submarines, but would not agree to their division into two classes.'

[2] See No. 295, note 6.

[3] Mr. Cadogan's memorandum of May 1 further stated that 'on March 15 the French Admiral, who had just returned from Paris, told Admiral Kelly that though the British Admiralty's proposal had not yet been completely studied, it was unlikely to be considered acceptable. The French Admiral thought that there was little separating the French from the Americans and that an agreement with the latter was quite possible. It seemed that the French might be prepared to extend the period of notice of transfer of tonnage from one year to 18 months.'

No. 311

Mr. London (Geneva) to Sir A. Chamberlain
(Received March 14, 4.50 p.m.)
No. 34 L.N. Telegraphic [*W 2569/28/98*]

GENEVA, *March 14, 1928, 3.58 p.m.*

Following from Lord Cushendun:—

My telegrams Nos. 32[1] and 33[2] containing messages from Admiral Kelly to the Admiralty.

[1] See No. 310, note 1.   [2] No. 310.

Discussion was . . .[3] between Admiral Long and Admiral Kelly and was of informal nature. Admiral Kelly of cou[r]se gave no indication of latest Admiralty proposals.

Situation as reported and as I see it is that Americans will not accept scheme which divides cruisers into two classes. Gibson's[4] speech at the close of naval conference[5] gave some reason to hope that they might but it now seems clear that they will not.

If as alleged Americans and Japanese are now prepared to accept French compromise proposal of last year[6] I fear we shall be left in a minority of one on naval tonnage question. Obviously if this is so all hope of agreement is gone but what gives me more immediate concern is question of tactics. If as suggested in London we are to take subjects in order of air, navy, and army and if French find us in situation of being alone against the rest on naval question they will break on that without giving us a chance of tackling them on military principles where we should have some not inconsiderable allies.

I still hope for and will work for an adjournment but I cannot be sure that we shall not slip into a second reading[7] and if this happens might it not in the circumstances be better to begin on chapter one, effectives? When we find that conscription countries will not abandon universal military service we could express regret that in our view this renders convention almost meaningless for purposes of security and probably useless for purposes of disarmament and that further discussion seems to us unprofitable. It will be unfortunate that we shall find ourselves joining with Germans and Russians against French but we shall or ought to have support also of Americans, Swedes and Dutch, and others. Would not that be better than finding ourselves possibly in minority of one on naval question and having to bear the whole responsibility for breakdown? Moreover if it is dangerous at present to raise cruiser controversy in the United States, to take effectives first and break on that point is best method of preventing all discussion of naval question.

[3] The text is here uncertain.
[4] Mr. Hugh Gibson, American Ambassador at Brussels and head of the American Delegation to the Preparatory Commission for the Disarmament Conference, had been head of the American Delegation to the Naval Conference at Geneva in 1927.
[5] See *Records of the Conference for the Limitation of Naval Armament, op. cit.*, pp. 42–6, for this speech of August 4, 1927.
[6] See No. 295, note 6.
[7] Of the draft disarmament convention.

No. 312

Mr. London (Geneva) to Sir A. Chamberlain
(Received March 15, 9 a.m.)
No. 35 L.N. Telegraphic [Telegrams 48/30]

GENEVA, *March 14, 1928, 10.35 p.m.*

Following from Lord Cushendun:—

'Netherlands delegate (chairman of Preparatory Committee) asked me this vening to meet him and French, Czechoslovak and Greek delegates to discuss the procedure to be followed in committee.

'Almost everyone here is agreed on necessity for adjourning second reading,[1] and even the German delegate will not press objection too strongly if a plausible reason for adjournment can be suggested, and I think that he would regard proposal to refer Russian scheme to sub-committee as affording sufficient excuse, seeing that until verdict is pronounced on that scheme it would be useless to proceed with the second reading.

'At the meeting this evening it was decided that the chairman should to-morrow give account of the work done since last session. Friday[2] would be devoted to statements by *rapporteurs* on work of Security Committee. On Saturday discussion of Russian proposals would begin. By Monday or Tuesday, president would be in a position to say that discussion seemed likely to be inconclusive, and would himself make proposal for reference to sub-committee, which would involve adjournment.'

[1] Of the draft disarmament convention.   [2] March 16, 1928.

No. 313

Mr. London (Geneva) to Sir A. Chamberlain
(Received March 16, 9.30 a.m.)

No. 38 L.N. Telegraphic [Telegrams 48/30]

GENEVA, *March 15, 1928, 11.15 p.m.*

Following from Lord Cushendun:—

'Your telegram No. 14.[1]

'Do you still wish me to refer to our battleship proposals, even if the second reading is adjourned? I could, of course, do so, though it might appear to be inconsistent to support adjournment and at the same time make such a declaration. It might provoke a discussion on the disarmament proposals generally, which we are anxious to avoid, and possibly be taken as provocative by American journalists.

'The German representative asked me privately whether the discussion of the Russian scheme by the proposed sub-committee would be public or private, as hitherto in sub-committee proceedings at Geneva. The Russians would strongly oppose a private discussion, but I see no reason for departing from the usual practice.

'Would it be permissible for me, in response to the request made by the chairman today (see my telegram No. 37[2]), to state that certain conversations

[1] No. 309.

[2] Not printed. This telegram from Mr. Cadogan reported on the first meeting of the fifth session of the Preparatory Commission for the Disarmament Conference on March 15. For the minutes of this meeting see *Documents of the Preparatory Commission for the Disarmament Conference*, Series VI, pp. 231–3. *V. op. cit.* for the minutes of ensuing meetings. In Geneva telegram No. 37 L.N. Mr. Cadogan stated that the Chairman would be glad to have information on any endeavours by governments to reach agreement by negotiation in respect of disagreements at the Commission's session in March–April 1927. The relevant extract from Mr. Loudon's speech is also printed in Cmd. 3211 of 1928 as item No. 11.

have in fact lately taken place, which may make agreement in the near future not impossible? If I could say something of the kind that might make adjournment more plausible, and, further, in the event of the French and American representatives referring to prospect of agreement, would not leave me silent and isolated.'

No. 314

Memorandum by Sir C. Hurst

[A 1774/1/45]

FOREIGN OFFICE, *March 15, 1928*

I infer that in due course the American Ambassador will hand to the Secretary of State a copy of this U.S. note to France[1] with the proposed treaty in draft form.

After studying its contents and after having had the advantage of discussing it verbally with Mr. Malkin and Mr. Craigie, I think that H.M. Government would stand to gain more than they would lose by accepting the proposal and agreeing to sign a multilateral treaty with America and the other Great Powers, open to accession by the smaller Powers. It is, however, in my opinion improbable that the United States Government intend that the text of the treaty can be quite so bald and simple as the various notes indicate. Mr. Kellogg's last note to France (February 27,[1] paragraph 4) implies a treaty containing an unequivocal renunciation of war with no exceptions stipulating when nations would be justified in going to war. On the other hand Mr. Olds' statement to the Ambassador (Despatch No. 472[2] of March 2, p. 2) seems to imply willingness to admit an exception in favour of war in self-defence.

Assuming the above is really what the United States mean and that Belgium could be brought in as one of the contracting Powers by reason of her commitments under Locarno, and assuming further that, as Senator Borah seems to suggest, violation of such a treaty by having recourse to war would absolve the remaining parties from its obligations, Great Britain would stand to gain more than she would lose by accepting it. The United States on the other hand stand to lose all round—but that is their business.

Let me give some illustrations to make my meaning clear.

Before doing so, however, let me add that I assume that the treaty would become operative as soon as all the Big Powers parties had ratified, irrespective of whether the smaller states exercised or not their option to accede. Let me also add that in Latin America the smaller states would be unlikely to join because what they fear is not *war* by the United States but intervention—theoretically pacific—but in fact depriving them of control in their own house. Consequently with them the new treaty would operate to prevent their replying by war (if they felt able to do so) to United States coercion. If

[1] See No. 293, note 2.   [2] No. 293.

they made war for the sake of recovering their freedom, it would be they and not the United States who broke the treaty.

As *Illustration I* let me take the following. Venezuela grievously wrongs British subjects in her territory. Diplomacy secures no redress. The machinery of the League secures no redress. Great Britain ultimately, without committing any violation of the Covenant, has to make war on Venezuela, secures by treaty a promise to pay compensation and also the right until payment to occupy a defined portion of Venezuelan territory—a clear infraction of the Monroe Doctrine. The United States will be debarred by the new treaty from making war on Great Britain to uphold the Monroe Doctrine. This is a clear gain to Great Britain; the United States alone stand to lose.

Illustration II. Sweden in violation of the Covenant makes war on Finland. The Members of the League decide to enforce against Sweden article 16 of the Covenant. In pursuance thereof the British navy cuts off all seaborne American trade with Sweden. The United States protest but will have debarred themselves from going to war with Great Britain. Again a clear gain to Great Britain; the United States alone stand to lose.

Illustration III. Yugoslavia accedes to the proposed treaty to secure some assurance against Italian aggression. Bulgaria for some reason stands out. Italy accordingly changes her Balkan policy and by astute manœuvres drives Bulgaria into acts which justify Italian invasion. Italy then makes peace on terms which establish Italian hegemony in the Balkans. France, Germany, Great Britain are all prescribed by the treaty from effective opposition.

Advantage to the cause of peace—Nil—. To what extent will the treaty have effected Mr. Kellogg's purpose? 'From the broad standpoint of humanity and civilisation all war is an assault upon the stability of human society and should be suppressed in the common interest.'[3]

In view of Illustrations I and II, I can scarcely believe that the United States have thought out the situation. At any rate if the United States Ambassador comes to the Foreign Office to talk about the proposed treaty, the Secretary of State may like to put these cases to him.

It may be that the American Administration are merely out to make a vote-catching proposal, but a scheme that entails the non-enforcement of the Monroe Doctrine and which would also render the wonderful new fleet useless for the only purpose so far advanced in favour of its construction seems a curious way to set about winning an election.

Great Britain, on the other hand, seems, as I have pointed out, to gain. Locarno would not be prejudiced; nor would the working of the Covenant; if it were provided that a violation of the new treaty by any party absolved the remainder from the obligation of complying with it any further.

As regards the point made in paragraph 3 of Mr. Kellogg's note of February 27, 1928, i.e. that the multilateral treaty cannot be inconsistent with the obligations of the League if the bilateral draft proposed by France is not so, the answer is that which M. Fromageot gave me in Paris, viz. that France in the bilateral treaty only renounced war as an instrument of her

[3] See Mr. Kellogg's note of February 27: cf. note 1 above.

policy against the United States and in their reciprocal relations; consequently it did not prevent France from implementing her obligations under the Covenant. This argument would not apply equally to a multilateral treaty. If the contention is sound, it is exceedingly subtle; it will never be understood by the man in the street; and I venture to suggest that France should be left to grapple with that point herself.

C. J. B. H.

P.S. Mr. Malkin has suggested that *Illustration III* can be put more effectively if one assumes a mere change of Balkan policy on Italy's part: the adoption of an aggressive policy aiming at hegemony without any recourse to war. Such policy being perfectly safe because France, G[rea]t Britain, Germany & perhaps Yugoslavia would all be debarred from supporting in the last resort their opposition by war.

He would add a fourth illustration, a case where Gt. Britain would certainly lose. Soviet Russia accedes and under cover of the treaty propagands more violently than ever against British rule in India & elsewhere. Gt. Britain debarred by the Treaty from war for the protection of interests her people might think vital.

C. J. B. H.

No. 315

Sir E. Howard (Washington) to Sir A. Chamberlain (Received March 27)
No. 578 [A 2141/2141/51]

WASHINGTON, *March 15, 1928*

Sir,

With reference to my despatch No. 469[1] of 2nd March, I have the honour to enclose herewith copy of the Convention of Maritime Neutrality which was recently signed at Havana by all the twenty-one American States represented at the Pan-American Conference.[2] This Convention is of particular interest at the present time as it gives us the first indication of the lines along which the United States Government would be prepared to go in negotiating any agreement for the 'freedom of the seas'.

2. Article 1 of the Treaty lays down that belligerent warships have the right *to detain and visit on the high seas* or in territorial waters that are not neutral, any merchant vessel for the purpose of ascertaining its character and nationality and whether it carries cargo prohibited by international law or has committed any violation of the blockade. If the merchant-vessel does not heed the hint to stop, the warship may pursue it and detain it by force. Outside of this hypothesis the vessel may not be attacked except when, after being requested to stop, it shall fail to observe the instructions given to it.

---

[1] Not printed.
[2] Not printed. This convention, signed on February 20, 1928, is printed in *British and Foreign State Papers*, vol. 130, pp. 386–92.

3. The vessel shall not be put out of navigable condition before the crew and the passengers have been transferred to a safe place.

4. Belligerent submarines are subject to the preceding rules. Should the submarine be unable to capture the vessel in accordance with those rules, *it shall not have the right to continue the attack nor to destroy the vessel.*

5. Article 2 states that the detention of the vessel, as well as of its crew, due to a violation of neutrality, shall be made *in the manner that best suits the State effecting the same and at the expense of the offending vessel.*

6. These are the two principal articles dealing with the Blockade.

7. Article 1, clearly, I think, admits the principle of the long distance blockade which is considered of such importance by His Majesty's Government. It also does not prohibit a belligerent taking ships into one of his own harbours for examination. It seems to me that had the United States Government been anxious to put on record their objections to this practice they would have seized this opportunity to do so.

8. Section II, Articles 3 to 14, on the 'duties and rights of belligerents,' while important, is not of immediate interest for the purpose of this despatch.

9. Section III, dealing with the 'Rights and duties of Neutrals,' states in Article 15, that among the acts of assistance emanating from neutral States and the acts of commerce effected by individuals, only the former are contrary to neutrality.

10. Article 16 declares that the neutral *State* (but evidently not the citizen of the State), is forbidden—

(*a.*) To deliver to the belligerent directly or indirectly and for any reason whatever, warships, munitions, or any war material.

(*b.*) To make loans or grant credit to a belligerent during a war.
Credits granted by a neutral State to facilitate the sale or exportation of its food products in raw are excepted from this prohibition. The only bearing that this would have on the blockade question is the prohibition on States to supply arms or munitions, etc., and to make loans or grant credits to a belligerent, which becomes a violation of neutrality.

11. On the other hand, Article 22 distinctly affirms that neutral States are not obliged to prevent the exportation or transit, at the expense of any one of the belligerents of arms, munitions, and in general everything that may be useful to its military forces. The meaning of this Article which appears at first sight to conflict with Article 16 is that neutral governments are not obliged to prohibit the transit or export of munitions of war purchased privately. The remainder of the articles are not of importance from the blockade point of view.

12. It may, I think, be safely inferred from the above that in any discussion respecting maritime law in time of war, the United States Government may be expected to raise no objection to—

(*a.*) long distance Blockade.

(*b.*) detention of vessels on account of violation of the blockade (Article 1) in the manner that best suits the belligerent State.

13. Further, as nothing is said against belligerents taking neutral vessels into port for examination, we may presume that no objection will be raised on that score.

14. Finally the doctrine of continuous voyage and ultimate destination being essentially an American doctrine, we may assume that this will not be disputed, and once that is granted, the natural corollary is the right of the belligerent to ration neutrals so that they should not receive goods in excess of their ordinary peace time requirements, since any excess may be presumed to be intended for an enemy destination.

I have, &c.,
ESME HOWARD

No. 316

Sir A. Chamberlain to Mr. London (Geneva)
No. 17 Telegraphic [W 2650/28/98]

FOREIGN OFFICE, *March 16, 1928, 6 p.m.*

Following for Lord Cushendun.

My telegram No. 14.[1]

Although Admiralty view is that there would be no objection to an increase in the ratios of tonnage allotted to France and Italy under the Washington treaty, you will doubtless bear in mind that the Dominions, who are also parties to the treaty, have not yet been consulted. We cannot therefore commit ourselves to the Admiralty view at the present juncture nor are we consulting the Dominions until the situation is clearer.

[1] No. 309.

No. 317

Mr. London (Geneva) to Sir A. Chamberlain
(Received March 17, 9.30 a.m.)
No. 41 L.N. Telegraphic [Telegrams 48/31]

GENEVA, *March 16, 1928, 11.40 p.m.*

Following from Lord Cushendun:—

'If scheme of referring Russian proposals to sub-committee is adopted there may be some difficulty over sub-committee's composition. Idea is that it should consist of five members, including Russian representative. I fear this latter is probably inevitable; it is in accordance with invariable League precedure [*sic*] that originator of proposal should be represented on body that examines it; moreover, it is perhaps only practical to give Russians chance of explaining proposals and, if necessary, answering enquiries. Polish and Serb States would be nominated to sub-committee, and would, I understand, have no objection.

'Unfortunately none of the Great Powers are willing to serve.

610

'I think this is unfortunate and that we could not be confident of smaller Powers dealing with Russian proposals in the way they should be dealt with. Though I should have no desire to serve on sub-committee I must submit that it is desirable for at least two of the Great Powers to be included, and that it would probably be best that we and French should volunteer to serve.

'French representative here (who is only substitute delegate) says that his Government are most unwilling, and, even if I extract promise from him to refer to Paris, I am not sure he would represent the matter strongly.

'If you approve therefore would you put the matter before M. Briand and ask him to consent to French representation on sub-committee?'

No. 318

Sir E. Howard (Washington) to Sir A. Chamberlain
(Received March 27)
No. 593 [A 2127/36/45]

WASHINGTON, *March 16, 1928*

Sir,

I have the honour to enclose an article which appeared in the American Review of Reviews for this month written by the well-known American journalist, Mr. Frank Simonds.[1] He puts his propositions very clearly, and, though what he says is, naturally enough, coloured by patriotic prejudices from which none can altogether escape, his conclusions though often exaggerated in scope are rarely without some solid foundation in fact.

2. He argues on page 287, for instance, that the decision of the United States made plain at Geneva to have a fleet equal in power to that of Great Britain means the ruin of the system of peace created by and through the League of Nations, for that system rests on provisions of the Covenant which bind all members to unite in using various weapons for coercing any country guilty of making war. Chief among all these weapons is the double one of blockade and economic embargo. As for the naval weapon, primary reliance was obviously placed on the British fleet. But what, asks Mr. Simonds, very pertinently, could the British fleet accomplish against Italy, Germany or France (when anyone of these deliberately destroyed the peace of Europe) if the United States refused to recognise the blockade, declined to share in the embargo, determined to use its superior fleet to break the blockade and permit its products to reach the nation under the ban of the League? Britain, he says, was faced by the possibility that the attempt to employ her fleet to carry out a League decision would bring her into collision with the United States. This made it inevitable that Britain would not only refuse to act in advance but would at once begin recasting her policy to escape such entangling possibilities.

3. It is strange that even so clear-sighted a political thinker as Mr. Simonds does not see that it is not so much the American fleet which makes a war

[1] Not printed. This article was entitled '"America Comes of Age"—in Europe'.

between Great Britain and the United States 'unthinkable' and a contingency to be avoided at almost all costs as the geographical distribution of different parts of the Empire and particularly the position of Canada which is and has been for years past practically defenceless against the superior power of the United States. The increased power of the American fleet only increases the impossibility for Canada of actively siding with the rest of the Empire in case of a conflict with the United States. Mr. Simonds goes on to argue in that part of his article entitled 'Outlawing War' that M. Briand's original proposal of June last for a Franco-American Treaty renouncing war was based on the assumption that no war had ever taken place between the United States and France and was now unthinkable. He was therefore but planning a pleasant little Franco-American picnic, the exchange of polite, friendly but meaningless words. This Mr. Kellogg by his multilateral proposal suddenly changed into a prospective international exchange of pledges which would compromise not only the French situation but the whole European system of security pacts as evolved after the war. America, therefore, concludes Mr. Simonds, was not only to the European mind embarking on a naval programme envisaging world supremacy but was also seeking to break down the League of Nations it would not join.

4. I need, of course, hardly say that this was not at all Mr. Kellogg's intention. He has no spite against the League but from the first he declined to be drawn into M. Briand's Franco-American picnic because he foresaw quite rightly that such a treaty entered into between France and the United States alone would have been tantamount to a defensive alliance and would in any case have been so considered by other European countries. In this he was no doubt completely justified. Apart from this however it seems to me that Mr. Simonds is correct in stating that the British Empire could not for the sake of the League or indeed anything else except for its own territorial integrity or a question of real national honour risk a conflict with the United States.

5. Any such conflict appears today at present as remote as the planet Mars, except over one issue and that is the conduct of a blockade by Great Britain either on behalf of the League or for her own national interests. Would it not therefore be advisable in the interests both of the Empire and the League that we should endeavour to come to an agreement with the United States Government, while this is possible, regarding the rules of blockade and thus know exactly how far we can go, when the time comes if it ever does come for us to enforce a blockade, without risking a disastrous conflict with this country?[2]

I have, &c.,

ESME HOWARD

[2] In a private letter of March 23 to Sir A. Chamberlain Sir E. Howard stated, however, that recent developments in the political situation in the United States made a Democratic victory in the forthcoming Presidential election 'far from unlikely', and that he thought it would be 'safer and wiser' to await the outcome of the election before making any move as a Democratic Government would not endorse any arrangement reached with their predecessor.

No. 319

Letter from Mr. Cadogan (Geneva) to Mr. Campbell

[W 2728/28/98]

GENEVA, *March 16, 1928*

My dear Ronnie,

I enclose a document which Count Bernstorff announced yesterday afternoon that he would circulate to the Committee and which reached me this morning.[1]

It is not quite clear what Count Bernstorff's intentions are, whether he wishes an instruction to be given to the Secretariat for their guidance in drawing up the Statistical Year Book, or whether he wishes these proposals of his to be incorporated in some way in a Chapter on publicity of the Draft Convention on Disarmament. However that may be, I am sure that most of his proposals will meet with the warmest objections from all the Service Departments, and it might perhaps therefore be as well to obtain from them, if possible, any particular observations which they wish to make and which may furnish us with the material for opposing anything that may seem to them objectionable.

The Service representatives here are, of course, examining these proposals and furnishing Lord Cushendun with a brief on the subject.

If the Service Departments have any special observations, they ought to reach us by Wednesday[2] morning at the latest. We are having a meeting on Monday afternoon to begin the discussion of the Russian proposals and that might last for a day or two, though I hope not longer. So that it is quite possible that Count Bernstorff may demand a discussion of his proposals about Wednesday.

Yrs.

ALEC

[1] Not printed. This proposal by the German delegate concerning the last paragraph of article 8 of the Covenant of the League of Nations is printed with attached tables as document C.P.D. 111 in *Documents of the Preparatory Commission for the Disarmament Conference, Series VI*, pp. 315–23.   [2] March 21, 1928.

No. 320

Sir A. Chamberlain to Mr. London (Geneva)

No. 18 Telegraphic [Telegrams 48/31]

FOREIGN OFFICE, *March 17, 1928, 6.45 p.m.*

Following for Lord Cushendun from Lord Salisbury:—

'Your telegrams Nos. 34[1] and 38.[2]

'Conversation between admirals seems to show an attitude on the part of the French wholly inconsistent with attitude of M. Briand in his conversation with Sir A. Chamberlain on 9th March. On the other hand, your later telegrams seem strictly in line with that conversation. We assume that you

[1] No. 311.   [2] No. 313.

now anticipate an adjournment after the Russian proposal has been discussed, but if it proves after all impossible to secure this, we authorise you to change the order of subjects and to begin on chapter 1, effectives, and then proceed as you suggest.

'We agree that if adjournment is secured it will be impossible to drag in capital ship proposals. As, however, the naval Powers have been notified that we shall mention them, and as it will be tactically useful to direct public attention to them, we suggest, for your consideration, that before leaving Geneva you should communicate the British battleship proposals to the representatives of the Washington Convention Powers, with a note saying that you were about to put them forward when the commission adjourned, and that you think they would like to have them for consideration before the next meeting of the commission. You might also arrange for publication of the proposals, describing them as a most notable move towards economy and limitation of armaments.

'We leave it entirely to your discretion what line you should take on the question whether Russian discussion should be private or public.

'A further telegram will be sent to you in regard to the last paragraph of your telegram No. 38.'

No. 321

Mr. London (Geneva) to Sir A. Chamberlain
(Received March 18, 10 a.m.)
No. 43 L.N. Telegraphic [W 2657/28/98]

GENEVA, *March 17, 1928, 10.15 p.m.*

Following from Lord Cushenden [*sic*].

My telegram No. 41.[1]

My French colleague now informs me that he had a meeting to-day with the Czechoslovak, Serb, Polish and Roumanian representatives. All of them now dislike (? idea of) referring the Russian proposal to a sub-committee, mainly for the reason that they are all alarmed at the prospect of serving on it. They therefore propose the following scheme. When the Russian proposal comes up for discussion speeches should be made to the effect that, though the first impression created by these proposals was that they were unacceptable, some of the delegations now consider that there may be certain elements that might be incorporated in draft convention. They would then propose that the bureau should be asked to incorporate as much as possible of the Russian scheme in a 'synoptic analysis'. The Russians may say that this ought not to take long, but the reply would be that the governments must have an opportunity of examining the result and this would take some time. Hitherto the Russian proposals had been regarded as an alternative to work already done, and to examine them from the point of view of the possibility of incorporating them in draft convention is to view them from

[1] No. 317.

a different angle. Personally I think this gives just as plausible an excuse for adjournment as the proposal to refer to sub-committee and can be worked more easily. I have therefore told my French colleague that I agree.

I learn that the Swedish delegation intend to propose that no fixed date should be fixed for the next session, but that it should be left to the bureau to determine as soon as an intimation is received that conversations between governments give the hope of a successful issue. My United States colleague in conversation expresses approval of this idea.

No. 322

Sir A. Chamberlain to Mr. London (Geneva)
No. 19 Telegraphic [*Telegrams 48/31*]

FOREIGN OFFICE, *March 18, 1928, 12.30 p.m.*

Following for Lord Cushendun:
'Your telegram No. 38,[1] last paragraph.
'If the French refer to the conversations there can be no objection to your doing the same, but otherwise we should prefer you not to mention them.'

[1] No. 313.

No. 323

Sir A. Chamberlain to Mr. London (Geneva)
No. 20 Telegraphic [*W 2754/28/98*]

FOREIGN OFFICE, *March 19, 1928, 10 a.m.*

My telegram No. 14[1] (of March 13th: Russian Disarmament Proposals). Following for Lord Cushendun.

It may be useful to cite the great part Russia has played in providing arms for Chinese civil war purposes. For example documents seized in the raid on Soviet premises in the Legation quarter at Peking last year include two acknowledgments by the Chinese General Feng Yu-hsiang dated August 1926 for arms to the value of 6,400,000 roubles and 4,500,000 roubles respectively.[2] The arms covered by these receipts include 31,000 rifles, 51,000,000 small arm ammunition, 220 machine guns, 60 field guns, 58,000 rounds gun ammunition etc. Similar assistance was given to Kuomintang armies at Canton[3] but figures are not available.

This provides pertinent illustration of Monsieur Briand's point that Soviet are not averse from war in itself and indeed make its fomentation a principal instrument of their policy, their disarmament proposals being a purely political move.

[1] No. 309.
[2] The Soviet Legation had been searched by Chinese police on April 6, 1927. Relevant documents, including two receipts signed on August 15, 1926, by Marshal Feng Yu-hsiang, Commander-in-Chief of the Kuominchun or People's Army of North China, are printed in *The China Year Book 1928* (Tientsin, n.d.), pp. 792–823.
[3] Cf. the Appendix, paragraph 50.

No. 324

Mr. Cazalet[1] (Geneva) to Sir A. Chamberlain
(Received March 19, 1.5 p.m.)
No. 44 L.N. Telegraphic [W 2711/28/98]

Immediate   GENEVA, *March 19, 1928, 11.40 a.m.*

Following from Lord Cushendun:

Your telegram No. 18.[2]

It is true that conversation between the admirals is inconsistent with the attitude of M. Briand in his conversation with the Secretary of State. M. Briand is probably as yet unaware of conversations between French and American naval experts and they of his with Sir A. Chamberlain. If M. Briand can over-rule the French naval authorities we must give him time to develop his idea. If he cannot, the prospect of agreement on naval question seems more remote. In either event an adjournment seems more than ever necessary. I still hope we may get adjournment by the device indicated in my telegram No. 43[3] and I hope we may get the President to propose it. There is the risk that if this is proposed the Russian delegate may think it will serve his purpose to pretend that the League is trifling with his scheme and playing for time and may withdraw it with reflections on the good faith of capitalist governments represented on the League. We should then be faced with the problem of what to do about the second reading.[4] I should hope to get the President to suggest an adjournment, but if neither he nor anyone else would do so I should in the last resort, but only then, propose it myself. I quite realise that it is undesirable that we should make the proposal (see your telegram No. 14)[5] but it seems to me essential that we should secure an adjournment.

[1] H.M. Vice-Consul at Geneva.   [2] No. 320.   [3] No. 321.
[4] Of the draft disarmament convention.   [5] No. 309.

No. 325

Sir E. Howard (Washington) to Sir A. Chamberlain
(Received March 21, 9 a.m.)
No. 104 Telegraphic [A 1965/154/45]

WASHINGTON, *March 20, 1928, 5.15 p.m.*

My despatch No. 525.[1]

Secretary of State handed me this morning note[2] suggesting the following alterations in draft arbitration treaty forwarded in my despatch No. 2352[3] of December 30th last.

[1] This despatch of March 9, not printed, transmitted copies of the exchange of notes of March 1–5 between Mr. Kellogg and M. Claudel following the signature of the Franco-American arbitration treaty (see No. 262, note 17): these notes are printed in *British and Foreign State Papers*, vol. 128, pp. 819–20.

[2] This note is printed in *Papers relating to the Foreign Relations of the United States 1928*, vol. ii, pp. 946–7.   [3] No. 244.

Article 1 of draft to be suppressed and in Article 2 words 'the permanent international committee [commission] constituted pursuant to treaty signed at Washington September 15th, 1914' to be substituted for words 'the above-mentioned permanent international commission' and Articles 3 and 4 to be re-numbered two and three respectively.

Object of this change is to place United States proposal to His Majesty's Government on the same basis as those made and about to be made to other governments and also to make it absolutely clear that the new arbitration treaty does not in any way affect or modify treaty of September 15th, 1914.

Secretary of State told me that similar draft treaties had been submitted to Italy, Japan, Norway, Germany, Spain and Portugal and would shortly be submitted to Austria-Hungary [sic], Denmark, Holland, Sweden and Switzerland and possibly to other countries except Latin American countries which will be asked to discuss special arbitration conventions according to resolution passed at the recent Pan-American Congress.[4]

4 For this resolution of February 21, 1928, cf. the Appendix, paragraph 69.

No. 326

Sir A. Chamberlain to Mr. Cazalet (Geneva)
No. 23 Telegraphic [W 2728/28/98]

Important FOREIGN OFFICE, *March 20, 1928, 7.30 p.m.*

Following for Cadogan.

Your letter of March 16th.[1]

Admiralty views are as follows:

The German proposals disregard the governing principle in article 8,[2] namely, the recognition of the right of governments to make arrangements in accordance with their own national safety. Revelations of a State's armaments in tables X to XIV would *ipso facto* disclose the insecurity of that State, i.e. revelation is not consistent with the State's national safety as laid down in paragraph 1 of article 8. Further, the German proposals raise issues which can only be dealt with when there has been some agreed limitation of armaments and also when questions connected with the private manufacture of arms have been agreed to.

As regards tables XIII and XIV, statements of outputs would reveal shortages in manufactures of arms. Suggestion that the exact localities of factories should be communicated—objectionable as inviting air bombardment by a prospective enemy. Suggestion that private firms should be obliged to reveal their output—very objectionable and likely, in many cases, to damage a firm's business.

Much information wanted in tables of no practical value as a country could arrange to purchase armaments from abroad, or again chemicals could

1 No. 319.   2 Of the Covenant of the League of Nations.

rapidly be produced by dye firms, even although no arrangements had been made in peace.

Tables X onwards demand disclosure of what must be kept secret in the interests of defence.

No. 327

Mr. Cazalet (Geneva) to Sir A. Chamberlain
(Received March 21, 9 a.m.)
No. 46 L.N. Telegraphic [W 2818/28/98]

GENEVA, *March 21, 1928, 12.5 a.m.*

Following from Mr. Cadogan.

My telegram No. 45.[1]

During the debate yesterday afternoon[2] British delegate intimated to President that he wished to join debate to-day. Learning however last night that no other delegate had asked leave to speak and not wishing to bear whole brunt of attack on Russian proposals, Lord Cushendun let it be known that he withdrew his request and that in any case he would not speak first though he would be ready to join the debate and support any of his colleagues who would criticize Russian proposals or would be prepared to move any of innumerable resolutions which they have not been backward in drafting for dealing with those proposals. This caused considerable consternation amongst the delegates who spent this morning eagerly discussing amongst themselves which of their colleagues should undertake the duty from which they one and all recoiled. This discussion was bound to be inconclusive and when committee met this afternoon[3] no one had any idea of probable course of events except Italian delegate (General de Marinis) who had been left out of the swirl of the discussion and who was found sitting in his place having asked leave to speak and having typewritten speech ready before him. This when delivered proved to be proposal for summary rejection of Russian proposals. Emboldened by this example French delegate (M. Clauzel) made a speech which though rather colourless could not be taken as expressing approval of Russian project. Lord Cushendun considered this afforded him opportunity of stating British view and he made long speech report of which will doubtless appear in tomorrow's press. Speech produced profound and immediate effect. Japanese and Canadian delegates followed in support and there are many applications for leave to speak tomorrow from delegates who are now emboldened to endorse views which have been expressed for them.

You will see Lord Cushendun took occasion to refer to British capital ship proposals[4] and it is interesting to note that none have been more enthusiastic in their congratulations than the American delegation.

---

[1] Not printed. This telegram of March 19 reported on the meeting of the Preparatory Commission that day: see *Documents of the Preparatory Commission for the Disarmament Conference*, Series VI, pp. 237–43.

[2] This telegram was evidently drafted on March 20.   [3] *V. ibid.*, pp. 243–53.

[4] Cf. No. 281, note 3.

No. 328

Sir A. Chamberlain to the Marquess of Crewe (Paris)
No. 19 Telegraphic [W 2831/28/98]

FOREIGN OFFICE, *March 21, 1928, 12.55 p.m.*

Lord Cushendun's speech at Geneva.[1]
Please call M. Briand's attention at once to this speech, saying that he will observe that Lord Cushendun took exactly the line which M. Briand suggested to me at Geneva.[2] Beg M. Briand to send immediate instructions to French representative to give Lord Cushendun his full and outspoken support. Lord Cushendun has belled the cat but he ought not to be left to bear the whole burden when carrying out an agreed policy.
Repeated to Geneva No. 26 in R, for information.

[1] See No. 327.   [2] See No. 304.

No. 329

Sir A. Chamberlain to Mr. Cazalet (Geneva)
No. 27 Telegraphic [W 2831/28/98]

Immediate   FOREIGN OFFICE, *March 21, 1928, 3.15 p.m.*
Following for Lord Cushendun.
Cabinet desire me to express to you their warm appreciation of your powerful speech.

No. 330

Mr. Cazalet (Geneva) to Sir A. Chamberlain (Received March 22, 9.30 a.m.)
No. 47 L.N. Telegraphic [Telegrams 48/31]

Immediate   GENEVA, *March 21, 1928, 9.16 p.m.*
Following from Lord Cushendun:
'Your telegram No. 26.[1]
'Am most grateful for instructions to Paris, but hope that it is clearly understood that French support is now needed less for combating Russian proposals than for securing adjournment of second reading. When M. Briand had his conversation with you it was assumed that one procedure might be followed for dealing with both subjects. I cannot guarantee that this will be so. Some delegates have spoken in favour of the simple rejection of Russian proposals, and might not agree to bring them into connexion with the draft convention that awaits second reading. Russian delegate might himself withdraw them in view of their reception. We may therefore to-morrow even be faced with necessity of discussing what to do about the second reading, apart

[1] See No. 328.

altogether from the Russian proposals. It seems to me, in the absence of any prospect of immediate agreement, to be of the highest importance to adjourn second reading, but we cannot be left alone to bear the brunt of moving the adjournment, and it is essential for the French, who, I believe, are no more desirous of taking the second reading now than we are, to give us their fullest support, even if they will not take the lead.

'If the French will not take the lead I should in the last resort feel compelled to do so myself, though I quite realise how undesirable this might be. I am not without (? hope that) president may yet be induced to formulate proposal for adjournment, basing himself on statements made by certain delegates this afternoon, but I cannot count on this.'

(Repeated to Paris.)

No. 331

Mr. Cazalet (Geneva) to Sir A. Chamberlain (Received March 22, 9 a.m.)
No. 48 L.N. Telegraphic [Telegrams 48/31]

GENEVA, *March 21, 1928, 11.25 p.m.*

Following from Lord Cushendun:
'My telegram No. 46,[1] last paragraph.
'My statement regarding capital ships was, as you see, introduced incidentally in a speech to which it was not very directly pertinent. I do not know what prominence it will have been given in the press. Will you therefore advise me whether you think the matter has sufficient publicity, or whether I am to take any further action on lines indicated in your telegram No. 18?'[2]

[1] No. 327.   [2] No. 320.

No. 332

Sir R. Lindsay (Berlin) to Sir A. Chamberlain (Received March 23)
No. 238 [A 2034/1/45]

BERLIN, *March 21, 1928*

Sir,

In continuation of my despatch No. 64[1] of the 19th of January respecting the correspondence between M. Briand and Mr Kellogg on the renunciation of war as an instrument of national policy, I have the honour to report that the Secretary of State yesterday turned to this question in conversation with me. He again expressed his general sympathy with the American proposal and said he had been following the correspondence with much interest. Mr Kellogg's last note was he thought very forcible and it would be difficult for M. Briand to avoid giving a definite answer. Had I any idea how the

[1] No. 255.

matter was viewed by yourself? I said I had understood that Mr Kellogg's proposal had come up at Geneva at a meeting of the five Representatives[2] and so I imagined that Dr Stresemann must know more about your views than I did. Herr von Schubert replied that at Geneva all you had said had been that you had no further cognizance of the problem than that the correspondence had been communicated to you, and Dr Stresemann had done no more than repeat a similar statement for so far as he was concerned. Herr v. Schubert had greatly regretted that no opportunity had presented itself for close discussion of the issue with you. I said I thought it perhaps possible that you would greatly prefer not to have to take any position at all on the question. Herr v. Schubert thereupon advocated the Kellogg proposal in much the same language as I reported in my above-mentioned despatch; if the French Government could renounce war in a Treaty with America, they ought logically to be able to do so in a multilateral treaty; and it was a reductio ad absurdum to plead the Pact, which was designed to prevent war, as an obstacle to the renunciation of war. He had moreover been looking at the results of the discussions of the Committee on Security and he was appalled at the complications. If agreement were reached any treaty would have to be so involved as to be almost incomprehensible, and he felt strongly that no treaty could be really forceful unless it were short and perfectly clear. Here was such a treaty advocated by the United States Government, and he believed it might be a valuable contribution to the cause of peace. I said that speaking entirely for myself, as I had no knowledge of your views, I agreed with him in his preference for short and unambiguous treaties, but only on condition that they were true. Here was Mr Kellogg advocating a renunciation of war all round, and everyone knew that the United States Government would go to war without hesitation on account of any marked violation of the Monro[e]-Doctrine; and no doubt too the Governments of Europe if they examined their own minds would each one of them find some vital interest rather than imperil which they too would have recourse to war; how then could they honestly declare that they renounced war completely. The difficulty in the present case was a tactical one, namely that it was impossible to proclaim from the housetops some simple truths which it was perfectly easy for any two men to say to each other.

2. I infer from Herr v. Schubert's language that if the German Government is invited to adhere to a multilateral treaty of the kind now under discussion between the French and American Governments, it will immediately accept the invitation.

I have, &c.,

R. C. LINDSAY

---

[2] No record of a meeting of the British, French, German, Japanese and Italian representatives at Geneva has been traced in Foreign Office archives.

No. 333

Sir A. Chamberlain to Mr. Cazalet (Geneva)
No. 31 Telegraphic [Telegrams 48/31]

Important   FOREIGN OFFICE, *March 23, 1928, 2 p.m.*

Following for Lord Cushendun:—

'Your telegram No. 48.[1]

'It seems to us desirable that, having seized the initiative in matter of capital ships, we should make our possession of it indisputable. Unless you see any objection, we think that you might well emphasise British proposals in a note of the type mentioned in my telegram No. 18,[2] which would arise naturally as an explanation in detail of the broad suggestion in your speech. If you agree, we authorise you to act accordingly.'

[1] No. 331.   [2] No. 320.

No. 334

Memorandum by Mr. Cadogan (Geneva)[1]
[W 2990/28/98]

GENEVA, *March 23, 1928*

New Russian Draft Convention[2]

The new Russian Draft Convention for the Partial Limitation of Armaments is open to the same objection as the Russian Draft for the Total Abolition of Armaments,[3] in that the fundamental principle which underlies the whole draft appears to be totally unacceptable. The whole idea of this new Russian Draft is to divide States into three or four categories, according to the size of their existing armaments, and to impose fixed reductions on all armies, fleets and air forces, not according to a uniform percentage but varying in proportion to the size of the existing forces. The working of this system is shown by *Article 1* of the Russian Draft, which divides States into four groups:

(1) those who have more than 200,000 men with the colours,
(2) those who have more than 40,000 men with the colours,
(3) those who have less than 40,000 men with the colours,
(4) the so-called 'disarmed' States, i.e. the ex-enemy States.

[1] This memorandum was received in the Foreign Office on March 26 under cover of Geneva despatch No. 20 L.N.C.C. (not preserved in Foreign Office archives).

[2] A manuscript note by Mr. Cadogan on the filed copy here read: '(This was only distributed on the night of March 23, about 8 p.m., and it must be understood that the following notes are only a short summary and commentary done hastily the same night for L[or]d Cushendun's convenience.)' The annexed Soviet draft convention for the reduction of armaments (document C.P.D. 117) is printed in *Documents of the Preparatory Commission for the Disarmament Conference*, Series VI, pp. 347–55.

[3] Cf. No. 278, note 2.

Article 2 lays down that the armies of the first class shall be reduced by one-half, those of the second class by one-third, those of the third class by one-quarter. The rather difficult problem of what to do with the fourth class is dismissed by the remark that the 'determination of the size of the land forces of States in this group will be fixed according to special conditions which must be established by the Disarmament Conference'.

The Russian proposal seems to assume that the distribution of forces in present circumstances is entirely arbitrary and is not proportioned either to the population or to the length of frontiers or to any other reasonable consideration. After reading through the somewhat offensive preamble and 'dispositions générales' it is clear enough that the Soviet Government imply that the States who at present maintain the larger forces are those who have the more aggressive intentions. If this assumption were correct, there might be some argument in favour of reducing the largest armies in a more drastic manner than the smaller armies. But if we assume, as it is fair to assume, that the distribution of armed forces is more or less proportional to the needs of the various States, it is quite obvious that the Russian proposal would do nothing but upset the whole equilibrium and consequently introduce complete insecurity. For if there were two neighbouring countries, A and B, one of which, A, had 201,000 men, and B had 180,000 men, under the Russian scheme A would be forced to reduce to about 100,000, whereas B would be entitled to retain 120,000, for which there appears to be no sort of justification. This is the absurd result that would be produced as regards effectives by Articles 1 and 2 of the Russian Draft.

Articles 3 and 4 are technical and merely define the categories of effectives to which the reduction is to apply and provide that reduction should apply not only to total effectives but proportionately to each category, i.e. regular army, militia, reserves, officers, non-commissioned officers, etc. An apparently needless complication is introduced by the provisions that a supplementary convention shall fix the new maximum limits to be imposed on each national army.

Article 5 claims to offer some means of limiting reserves, but I am bound to confess that I am quite unable to understand how it is intended to operate.

Chapter II, beginning with *Article 6*, deals with material. That article standardises for ever the models of arms in use on the 1st January, 1928, with the exception of tanks and long-range artillery, which I suppose are to be destroyed altogether, although this is not definitely indicated.

Article 7 enjoins the complete destruction of material for aerial and chemical warfare without giving any indication as to how this is to be done nor what is to be understood by material for aerial warfare.

Article 8 purports to limit the amount of material that may be retained, which it defines as being necessary for (*a*) the army in time of peace, and (*b*) the number of trained reservists, with a quite incomprehensible provision as to the number of these last.

Article 9 supplements, but does not in any way illumine, Article 8, and *Article 10* provides that a special convention shall be concluded in order to give effect to Articles 8 & 9, which would seem to confront the Conference with rather a difficult task.

Article 11 merely provides for the destruction of all surplus armament.

Article 12 and following deal with naval armaments on the same lines as land armaments, that is to say, countries are divided into (a) those having more than 200,000 tons, and (b) those having less than that figure. Class (a) are to be reduced by one-half, both as regards total tonnage and as regards the tonnage of each individual class. The classes specified are (1) capital ships, (2) surface vessels larger than 10,000 tons, (3) light vessels, (4) submarines. Class (b) are to be reduced by one-quarter. All aircraft carriers are to be transformed within six months of the entry into force of the convention so as to render them unsuitable for any purpose. Another special convention is to fix the maximum limits of naval armaments after the entry into force of the convention.

Articles 14–19 inclusive deal mainly with the destruction of surplus tonnage and the limitation of new construction, and certain tables are annexed. According to these tables, capital ships may not exceed 10,000 tons in displacement and may not carry guns more than 12″ in diameter. It is curious that these tables involve the division of cruisers into two classes, those over 7,000 tons carrying 8″ guns, and those under 7,000 tons carrying 6″ guns. There is a maximum tonnage for flotilla leaders and destroyers of 1,200 tons with 4″ guns and for submarines of 600 tons of 4″ guns. The amount of ammunition and torpedoes that may be carried is limited in proportion to the number of guns.

Articles 20–30 inclusive deal with the air forces and begin with the enunciation of the principle (in Article 20) that within a year from the entry into force of the convention all military aircraft, either heavier or lighter than air, must be disarmed and reduced to a condition which excludes the possibility of their utilisation for military purposes. Here again States are divided into three classes, (a) those having more than 200 aeroplanes in service, (b) those having between 200 and 100, and (c) those having less than 100. The first class reduce their numbers by one-half, the second by one-third, and the third by one-quarter. In addition, the horse power of every aeroplane must be reduced to 400.

The remaining articles of this chapter deal with the destruction of surplus aircraft, the prohibition of any design that might render them serviceable in war, the destruction of all stocks of bombs and the manufacture of further supplies, the reduction of air effectives in proportion to the number of aeroplanes left to each country, and the inevitable provision for a supplementary convention which shall fix the limits to be observed after the entry into force of the main convention.

Articles 31–33 inclusive deal with chemical warfare and will be just as effective in time of peace as any other agreement on this subject and just as ineffective in time of war.

Articles 34–36 deal with military budgets and propose a proportionate reduction on the same scale as is suggested for naval, military and air armaments. This reduction is just as arbitrary and just as inequitable as in the former cases.

Articles 37–38 fix the time-limits for the execution of the various provisions of the convention.

Articles 39–46 inclusive deal with the question of control. In regard to this chapter it is only necessary to observe that the permanent international commission of control proposed is formed of equal numbers of representatives of legislative bodies and trades unions and other workmen's organisations. Its duties appear to be as vague as its constitution.

The last chapter deals with the ratification and entry into force of the convention, and here, as in the case of the former Russian Draft Convention, there is no mention whatever of the League of Nations or of Geneva.

A. Cadogan

No. 335

Mr. Cazalet (Geneva) to Sir A. Chamberlain (Received March 24, 8 p.m.)
No. 54 L.N. Telegraphic [Telegrams 48/32]

GENEVA, *March 24, 1928, 6.20 p.m.*

Following from Mr. Steward[1] for Sir Arthur Willert:—

'We are issuing this afternoon the following message in the form of a communiqué. I suggest that it might be useful to form the basis of a wireless message to-night:—

' "It will be remembered that in the course of his speech at the meeting of the Preparatory Disarmament Commission on Tuesday last,[2] when dealing with proposed disarmament plan of Soviet Government, Lord Cushendun referred to the attitude of His Britannic Majesty's Government in regard to capital ships. In doing so he drew attention to a statement made by British delegation at Three-Power Naval Conference at Geneva suggesting further reduction in the size of capital ships and an increase in the accepted life of these vessels.

' "To-day Lord Cushendun has addressed a note to the representatives on the Preparatory Commission for Disarmament of United States of America, France, Japan and Italy, the signatory Powers to Washington Treaty,[3] in the course of which he states that he was compelled during his speech on Tuesday to refer in indefinite terms to these proposals, exact purport of which he proceeds to set forth in the note. He points out that the proposals of his Government are, first, that any battleship to be built in future shall be

---

[1] Mr. G. F. Steward of the News Department of the Foreign Office was a member of the British Delegation at Geneva.

[2] March 20, 1928: cf. No. 327.

[3] Lord Cushendun transmitted a copy of this note in Geneva despatch No. 19 L.N.C.C. of March 24 (neither preserved in Foreign Office archives): the text of this note as transmitted to Washington by Mr. Gibson is printed in *Papers relating to the Foreign Relations of the United States 1928*, vol. i, pp. 256–7.

reduced in size from the present limit of 35,000 tons displacement to something under 30,000 tons. Secondly, to reduce the size of guns in battleships from present limit of 16-inch guns to 13·5 inches, and thirdly to extend the accepted life of existing capital ships from twenty to twenty-six years, this involving a waiver by Powers of their full rights under the replacement tables agreed upon at Washington. Such an arrangement, it is pointed out, would naturally have to provide for some little elasticity on each side of that figure. The note adds that it would obviously be of advantage if such a step were agreed upon, that it should be taken in time to enable it to become effective before commencement of capital ship replacement programme provided for by Washington Convention.

'"Proposals outlined in note would represent a great step towards disarmament and a large measure of financial relief, both as regards initial cost and maintenance charges of all future vessels in this class."'

No. 336

Mr. Dormer (Tokyo) to Sir A. Chamberlain (Received March 27, 11.10 a.m.)
No. 49 Telegraphic [W 3039/28/98]

TOKYO, *March 27, 1928, 4.5 p.m.*

Japanese Minister of Marine is stated in the press as having expressed approval of British proposal for Japan's participation in new naval disarmament conference. Admiral Okada was doubtful about project for reduction of size of guns in view of superiority of Nelson and Rodney.[1]

Japan approves in principle reduction in size of battleships. There is no objection to extending life of battleships but question of extension to 26 years required further deliberation since if affects Japanese ship building industry. Japanese Minister of Marine qualified his statement by saying that no definite opinion could be given till official accounts of proceedings at Geneva were received.

[1] The 35,000-ton battleships *Nelson* and *Rodney*, laid down in October 1922, had 16-inch guns: cf. Volume III, No. 399.

No. 337

Sir E. Howard (Washington) to Sir A. Chamberlain
(Received March 28, 9 a.m.)
No. 109 Telegraphic [Telegrams 48/32]

WASHINGTON, *March 27, 1928, 4.15 p.m.*

My telegram No. 92.[1]
Submission to Preparatory Committee at Geneva of His Majesty's Government's proposals for reduction of size and extension of life of battleships has, as might have been expected, stimulated big-navy press into renewed activity.

[1] No. 303.

'Washington Post' dishes up all the old accusations of treaty violation, &c., and says that, if His Majesty's Government wished to be honest, they would at the same time propose scrapping 'Rodney' and 'Nelson', which give Great Britain a present supremacy. It concludes by saying that proposal is an insult to American intelligence, and, unless withdrawn, will stand as a bar against any naval agreement with Great Britain.

'Herald Tribune' has an article milder in tone but similar in meaning.

Proposal was, of course, bound to irritate extreme big-navy parties, but I feel it is not necessary to attach too much importance to this. On the contrary, it seems to me an advantage that these proposals should have been published a considerable time before the next Naval Conference so that they can sink into the public mind, to which their reasonableness will surely appeal.

No. 338

Sir E. Howard (Washington) to Sir A. Chamberlain
(Received March 28, 9 a.m.)
No. 108 Telegraphic [P 559/2/150]

WASHINGTON, March 27, 1928, 10.26 p.m.

My telegram No. 109.[1]

In the meantime it might perhaps be useful in view of renewed big navy press campaign here to issue communiqué to associated press and United press correspondents in London placing before the public here the actual facts regarding alleged superiority of British battleship fleet since Rodney and Nelson have been commissioned and showing that United States fleet are actually superior in sixteen inch guns.[2]

[1] No. 337.

[2] Foreign Office telegrams Nos. 137–8 of March 30 transmitted to Washington the text of a statement on the lines suggested above which had been handed that day to the representatives of the three principal American press agencies. In a letter of April 5 to Sir A. Willert, Mr. Fletcher wrote from the British Library of Information at New York that the British statement had received 'very little publicity in the United States. The whole naval aspect of Anglo-American relations seems from our angle to require complete overhauling. No one is so ready to admit as I am that we have been treated with gross unfairness in quarters which we ourselves usually regard as responsible. High naval officials, important sections of the Press and, I personally believe, some of those in the highest places in this country have not scrupled to distort both the facts and our statements of policy. At the same time, it is clear that there are large and responsible elements in the United States which have taken alarm at the growing irritation . . . are not mutual suspicions bound to increase if the present trend is not decisively altered? . . . I wonder sometimes if the situation might not yield to personal discussions such as were so successful in bringing about Locarno. In short, if the Secretary of State can cross the Channel why not the Atlantic?'

No. 339

Lord Cushendun to Sir A. Chamberlain
No. 21 L.N.C.C. [W 3343/28/98]

FOREIGN OFFICE, *April 2, 1928*

Sir:—

I endeavoured to keep you informed by telegram from Geneva of the proceedings from day to day of the Preparatory Committee for the Disarmament Conference during its session which opened on March 15th. I now have the honour to submit the following report in the hope that it may provide a more coherent account of those proceedings.

2. As you are aware, the Committee met under the very general impression that nothing effective could be done at the present session. It was faced, on the one hand, with the Soviet proposals for total and immediate disarmament. These proposals, the general purport of which had been announced by Monsieur Litvinoff[1] to the Committee at its previous session in December, had been elaborated into a detailed draft convention, the text of which was circulated to the members of the Committee towards the end of February. They proved to be of a quite fantastic nature—probably designed for no other than propagandist purposes. On the other hand, in the absence of a decision to the contrary, the Committee was committed to a 'second reading' of the draft convention evolved at its session of March and April last year.

3. Nearly all Delegates were agreed that the Soviet proposals must be rejected or at least pigeon-holed, though this would probably have to be done with some outward semblance of courtesy, and that the second reading of the draft convention could not suitably be undertaken at the present session as no effective progress had been made with the negotiations between governments for bridging the differences which had rendered agreement impossible on the former occasion.

4. It had occurred to me that both these objects might be attained by the reference of the Soviet proposals to a special sub-committee, whose duty it would be to see how far these proposals might be reconciled with and even perhaps incorporated in the work already done. If such reference were agreed to, the second reading of the draft convention would logically have to await the results of the sub-committee's work.

5. I submitted this suggestion to a number of my colleagues, who seemed disposed to view it favourably. As, however, there were obvious reasons against my taking the lead in disposing of the Soviet proposals, I had to make it clear that I was not inclined to be the mover of any resolution giving effect to this procedure. I had hoped that, in view of the conversation which you had had in Geneva with M. Briand on March 9th,[2] the French Delegate might be prepared to initiate something of the kind. This, however, proved not to be the case. Count Clauzel, it appeared, had no authority to undertake any

---

[1] Soviet Vice-Commissar for Foreign Affairs and delegate to the Preparatory Commission.
[2] See Nos. 304–5.

responsibility in the matter, and his instructions seemed to be merely in general terms to work with his British colleague, without laying down any definite policy or giving him any useful guidance as to the course which he was expected to pursue. Moreover, on thinking over my suggestion, my colleagues realised that it would involve at least one definite and immediate decision—as to the composition of the sub-committee to which the Soviet proposals would be referred. They all evinced so positive a disinclination to serve on this committee that they set out to find an alternative procedure which would conduce generally to the same end without involving them in any particular responsibility. They therefore evolved the idea that, without the necessity of setting up a special sub-committee, the 'Bureau' of the Committee might be instructed to study the Soviet proposals and, if practicable, to incorporate them in the 'synoptic text', i.e., the document in parallel columns embodying the British and French draft conventions, and proposals by other Delegations, which had formed the basis of the Committee's work last year, and of which portions at least had been fused into a single text. Thus encumbered, the 'synoptic text' would be submitted to the Committee for a 'second reading' at a later session. The work of incorporating the Soviet proposals would take some little time, and therefore adjournment of the second reading might not seem unreasonable. My colleagues evidently hoped to induce an unwilling President to make this proposal himself. When consulted, I agreed that their scheme seemed no less plausible than my own, and although it was impossible to be confident that the President would have the courage to propose it, there was a general hope and belief that events would turn out as intended.

6. Meanwhile, the Preparatory Committee met for its first sitting on the morning of March 15, at which it was occupied mainly with formalities. The President made a review of the work of the Security Committee (Item I on the agenda) and welcomed the Turkish Delegation on their first appearance. The Turkish representative (Munir Bey), in his reply, asked that discussion of the main topics be deferred until the 19th, by which time the Turkish Minister for Foreign Affairs would have arrived.

7. The sitting of the following day (March 16) was occupied with taking note of the work of the Security Committee. A draft resolution was submitted but gave rise to practically no comment, and a second adjournment after a short sitting—this time for three days—gave an impression of ineffectiveness which evoked almost audible comment from the public, and representatives of the press.

8. The Committee met for business again on Monday, March 19, and at once adopted the resolution referred to in the preceding paragraph. (Annex I).[3] It then turned to item II on the Agenda—the Soviet draft convention for total and immediate disarmament—and the Soviet Delegate was called upon to speak. Monsieur Litvinoff obliged with a fairly lengthy dissertation, following lines that could easily have been forecast. He attempted to ridicule

[3] Printed in *Documents of the Preparatory Commission for the Disarmament Conference*, Series VI, p. 237.

the work on disarmament already performed by the League, referring to the fact that, apart from the Assembly and the Council, not less than 14 League organs had devoted over 120 sessions to the question of disarmament, on which 111 resolutions had been passed by the Assembly and the Council alone. He maintained that the amount of real progress achieved was practically nil, and he plainly meant to infer that the Members of the League were not in earnest on this question. The Soviet Government, on the other hand, were now submitting a genuine practical proposal, combining completeness with simplicity: this would afford a test of the real intentions of the States represented on the Committee, and he concluded by demanding 'unequivocal and affirmative replies' to his two questions:— (1) Does the Committee agree to base its further labours on the principle of complete disarmament during the periods proposed in the Soviet scheme? (2) Is it prepared so to carry out the first stage of disarmament as to make the conduct of war, if not an absolute impossibility, of extreme difficulty in a year's time? He slyly expressed himself confident of receiving support at least from that government which had lately been openly advocating the abolition of war.

9. The German and Turkish Delegates followed with faint praise of the Soviet scheme, after which the President, for lack of speakers, adjourned the debate to the afternoon of the following day.

10. Geneva telegram No. 46 (LN)[4] of March 20, shows the difficulties experienced in getting the debate going that afternoon, owing to the reluctance of the Delegates to initiate criticism of the Soviet proposals, and how General de Marinis, my Italian colleague, saved the situation by opening with a blunt denunciation of the scheme and a motion for its simple rejection.

11. After the French Delegate had put in his word, I felt that I might speak on behalf of His Majesty's Government. You have, I believe, already received the text of my speech, and you will have observed that I felt justified in speaking with a certain frankness, and in examining the motives which had brought the Soviet Delegation to Geneva on this occasion. While subjecting their scheme to criticism, I was, however, careful to suggest that there might be elements in it that would repay careful examination, and to avoid proposing rejection outright.

12. Having been given a lead, the other Delegates were not backward in giving open expression to their views on the Soviet proposals, and the whole of the next day was occupied by a series of speakers who were unanimous in condemning them. The only point on which there seemed to be a difference of opinion was whether the proposals should be forthwith rejected, or whether any time should be given for their further study, either by a special subcommittee or by the governments. A summary rejection would have placed the Committee in this difficulty, that it would be harder for it to adjourn the second reading of the draft convention. The idea of combining the Soviet proposals with the synoptic text afforded a plausible pretext for delaying further proceedings in connexion with either: the dissociation of the two would make it necessary to find a separate excuse for adjourning the second reading.

4 No. 327.

The day's discussion, however, concluded with a useful speech by the Greek Delegate (Monsieur Politis), who proposed that the Soviet draft should be submitted to the governments for further study, adding the suggestion that no further date should be fixed for the second reading, the convening of the next session of the Preparatory Committee being left to the discretion of the President. Monsieur Politis, in thus dealing simultaneously with points II and III of the Agenda, introduced into the debate a certain confusion which caused temporary inconvenience later, but the Committee must remain indebted to him for having been the first to have the courage to mention publicly the possibility of adjournment and for having taken so bold a line on the question.

13. On the following afternoon Monsieur Litvinoff made a lengthy reply to his many critics. His retorts were framed in such a way as to be relished in quarters where they would be welcome and expected, but his arguments were so feeble as to be unlikely to carry weight in any quarter. The upshot of his remarks was that, if the Committee would accept the *principle* of total disarmament, he would be ready to co-operate in a further examination of his draft convention, which did not pretend to be perfect in all details. If, on the other hand, the principle were rejected, he himself would oppose the waste of further time on his own draft.

14. Monsieur Litvinoff was followed by the French Delegate, Count Clauzel, who this time came out strongly against the Soviet proposals as a whole, while at the same time supporting my suggestion that portions of them might be worthy of study. He then went on to endorse Monsieur Politis' suggestion for an adjournment of the second reading without fixed date for its initiation, but expressed the hope that this would be before the next meeting of the Assembly. As an additional reason for the adjournment, Count Clauzel referred to the possibility of a satisfactory conclusion, in the not too distant future, of negotiations between the Governments whose divergence of views had rendered impossible further progress last year. In a private conversation before the meeting, he had told me of his intention to make such a reference, and I had seen no objection to his doing so. I had gathered from your telegram No. 19,[5] of March 18, that there would be no objection to the French delegate, if he so wished, making allusion to the exchange of ideas which had taken place between experts in Paris, and between yourself and M. Briand at Geneva, but that I should avoid taking the initiative in mentioning them. In his speech to the Committee, Count Clauzel did not, perhaps handle the matter with great felicity. He said 'While we have been holding these very interesting political discussions, the technical experts of most of our delegations have had a certain amount of leisure which they have turned to good account. They have entered into or continued useful conversations dealing with the treatment of some of these delicate questions to which I have alluded and for which only partial solutions had been found; we hope that some final settlement will be reached as speedily as possible. One of the conditions of such settlement and one of the

[5] No. 322.

main conditions of success is an exchange of views, not only between technical experts but between Governments. I am glad to say that we are far advanced along this path and there is no occasion to anticipate any very long delay before we arrive at appreciable results.'[6] This statement, as will be seen, led later to some difficulty.

15. Items II and III of the Agenda were now in a fair way to becoming inextricably involved—a confusion which detracted from the dignity and good order of the proceedings, and which the Bureau attempted to remedy by the production on the following day of a resolution (Annex II)[7] dealing only with the Soviet proposals—item II. Monsieur Litvinoff protested against this resolution: he observed that the Governments represented on the Committee were evidently resolved not to accept the principle of total and immediate disarmament. Undeterred by this, however, the Soviet Government would continue to collaborate in any attempt to achieve a reasonable measure of disarmament. If the Committee were not prepared to accept total disarmament, he had ready for them a scheme of partial disarmament, which he undertook to circulate that evening. This only added to the existing confusion. The Chairman, in one of his rare moments of firmness, told Monsieur Litvinoff that in any case his alternative draft convention for partial disarmament could not be given even a first reading during the present session. This ruling, though in accordance with our ideas of Order, since M. Litvinoff's draft was not on the Agenda, or strictly relevant to any item in it, was not explained by the President, and therefore appeared to leave Monsieur Litvinoff with a justifiable grievance.

16. The French Delegate demanded that all consideration of this alternative draft convention should await the second reading of the Committee's own convention, and in urging the adjournment of the latter, he again referred to the conversations to which he had made allusion in his earlier speech. This brought the Italian Delegate to his feet with a declaration to the effect that he knew nothing of these alleged conversations, and that, whether they reached a successful conclusion or not as between the parties concerned, Italy had important reservations to which she would adhere. In view of this declaration, I felt it incumbent on me to rise and confirm my French colleague's statement.[8] I had hoped it would be unnecessary for me to say anything on the subject, but after the Italian Delegate had dissociated himself from what Count Clauzel had said, I felt that further silence on my part would be unfair to the latter in view of the loyal support I had received from him. Moreover, General de Marinis' speech might provoke further disavowals which might in any case, by a process of elimination, point to the

[6] This citation is included in the extract from Count Clauzel's speech on March 22 printed as item No. 12 in Cmd. 3211 of 1928.

[7] Printed in *Documents of the Preparatory Commission for the Disarmament Conference*, Series VI, p. 284. The minutes of the meetings of the Preparatory Commission on March 23 are printed *ibid.*, pp. 278–97.

[8] The relevant extract from Lord Cushendun's speech on March 23 is printed as item No. 15 in Cmd. 3211 of 1928. *V. ibid.*, items Nos. 13–14 for extracts from statements made that day by Mr. Hugh Gibson and General de Marinis respectively.

British and French Governments being the only participants in these conversations (though I was aware of there having also been conversations between French and American experts) and I therefore thought it better at once to associate myself with my French colleague. This would establish beyond doubt the fact that such conversations had been initiated—a fact to which importance was evidently attached by the Committee—and might put an end to further reference to this rather delicate matter.

17. All this served once more to confuse items II and III of the agenda, and in face of repeated suggestions for the adjournment of the second reading, the German Delegate felt compelled to make his usual protest. This done, he submitted a resolution (Annex III),[9] the effect of which would have been to eliminate the second reading altogether and to convoke a Disarmament Conference irrespective of the fact that no agreement had been reached as to the principles on which disarmament should be accomplished.

18. It was not, therefore, surprising that on the morning of the last day of its session the Committee met in a state of some doubt as to what it was expected to discuss. The Bureau had, no doubt with the best intentions, submitted a new resolution (Annex IV),[10] which dealt at one blow with (1) the Soviet scheme for total disarmament, (2) the German proposals for publicity in regard to armaments (C.P.D. 111),[11] which Count Bernstorff had wished to have discussed on point III of the agenda, (3) the new Soviet draft convention for partial disarmament and (4) the date of the second reading. The result was that Delegates began to roam over all these topics, and I felt impelled to ask the Chairman to keep the Committee to one particular point at a time, and to indicate what point exactly was before the Committee. In reply, the Chairman ruled that the Committee should first discuss the German resolution referred to in paragraph 17. In the event this discussion occupied the whole morning and even at the end of the sitting Count Bernstorff, in acknowledging defeat, announced that he would have a declaration to make on the resumption in the afternoon.

19. This declaration proved, as might have been expected, to be in the form of a lament at the failure of the League to make any effective progress towards disarmament, and ended with what was practically an appeal from the Preparatory Committee to the Assembly itself.

20. The Committee then turned to the discussion of the Bureau's draft resolution (C.P.D. 118),[10] which was adopted, with some amendments, after a debate that was shorter than might have been expected. On the proposal of the Polish Delegate the passage in the second paragraph of Section I 'while in harmony . . .'[12] said draft' was deleted. The United States Delegate proposed the omission of the last sentence of the resolution, but after some discussion it was amended to read 'The Commission expresses the hope that the

---

[9] Printed in *Documents of the Preparatory Commission for the Disarmament Conference*, Series VI, pp. 294–5.

[10] Annex IV (C.P.D. 118) is printed *ibid.*, p. 307. The minutes of the meetings of the Preparatory Commission on March 24 are printed *ibid.*, pp. 297–314.

[11] See No. 319, note 1.   [12] Punctuation as in original quotation.

new session may begin at the earliest suitable date, and if possible before the next session of the Assembly'.

21. Thus ended, rather ingloriously, the Fifth Session of the Preparatory Committee. The fantastic Soviet scheme of total and immediate disarmament was for all practical purposes rejected, and the second reading of the Committee's own convention stood adjourned more or less indefinitely. As regards the latter point, it is unnecessary for me to say that this does not settle the question of disarmament. We have gained a few months for reflection and negotiation, and I trust that they may be put to better use than the twelve months which have already elapsed since the Preparatory Committee did any effective work. It would be out of place in this despatch to suggest what the next step should be, but I should like to emphasise that in my opinion it will be impossible for the Committee, if and when it meets again, to resort to another adjournment without being able to report any actual progress. It was difficult enough on this occasion to secure an adjournment, and it is undeniable that the adjournment produced a bad effect and brought the Committee, and the League itself, into disrepute. The naval question remains the principal difficulty in the way of agreement, and I do therefore earnestly hope that definite steps may be taken in the near future to ascertain whether it is by any means possible to come to some agreement with the French, Italian, Japanese and United States Governments. If this proves impossible, and if no new and more acceptable scheme of disarmament can be devised, I see nothing for it but to let the Committee meet again for a second reading and face a definite breakdown and an abandonment of the work on the lines which it has been pursuing. The deliberations of the Committee will be considerably complicated by the presence of the Soviet Delegation. They have dropped their scheme of total disarmament; their alternative scheme for partial disarmament is on unacceptable lines and can fairly easily be shown to be inequitable and unworkable. When that in its turn is rejected, may they not perhaps produce another version—for example, a proposal for a 10% reduction all round—which will look plausible enough and be much more difficult to resist, however unequal and inconvenient might be its operation in practice? I feel bound to draw attention to these points, in order to urge the necessity, in my opinion, of losing no time in opening regular conversations with the other naval Powers, in the hope of arriving at a compromise that might be embodied in the second reading text. I would remind you that a considerable emphasis was laid on the fact that 'conversations' were proceeding, and that several speakers seized on this as the most weighty reason for adjourning. It seems, therefore, that we are rather committed to carrying those conversations to their logical conclusion, and testing without further delay the chances of success.

22. I desire, further, to remind you that for the purpose of obtaining an adjournment of the 'second reading' of the draft conventions, to give breathing space in which to arrive at agreement, I laid considerable stress in my speeches at Geneva on the necessity to submit the Russian proposals to governments for examination and comment. Paragraph II of the resolution

adopted by the Committee provides for this being done, and also refers to the governments Count Bernstorff's proposals for publicity. Both documents should, therefore, now be considered by the competent departments of His Majesty's Government and a full and effective reply to them should be prepared.

23. In conclusion, I would refer to the fact, already reported to you, that I took occasion, in the course of my speech on the Soviet scheme, to refer to the proposals of His Majesty's Government in regard to the size, calibre of guns and age of capital ships.[13] I subsequently handed to the United States, Japanese, French and Italian Delegates identic notes[14] giving the details of these proposals. You have already received a copy of that note. None of my colleagues made any comment in the Committee on these proposals.

I have, &c.,
CUSHENDUN

[13] See No. 281, note 3.　　　[14] See No. 335.

No. 340

Sir E. Howard (Washington) to Sir A. Chamberlain
(Received April 4, 9.30 a.m.)
No. 115 Telegraphic [A 2355/1/45]

WASHINGTON, April 3, 1928, 3.10 p.m.

Franco-American negotiations to renounce war.

I asked Secretary of State last night what he thought of the latest French note of March 30th[1] which was published here on April 1st. He said that apart from some unnecessary arguing about the past, he felt that there was nothing which need now prevent agreement. He could accept Monsieur Briand's views as to right of legitimate defence and as to other partners being automatically relieved of obligations of treaty with regard to any Power which contravened it. The only difficulty he still saw lay in French contention that new treaty should not be considered in force until all States had signed. This if insisted on might postpone all the virtue of the treaty for years. He would be quite willing to have all the Little Entente Powers and indeed any Powers that wished to sign it immediately after the six Great Powers had signed but he thought that these Great Powers should first agree amongst themselves to be bound by its provisions and he felt sure that then other Powers would at once associate themselves with them. It would be most unfortunate, however, if treaty should not be enforced because one or two secondary Powers refused to join. I asked 'What about Russia?' He replied at once that he would have no objection but quite the reverse to Russia signing. If she did not sign and attacked some Eastern European nation such nation would of course have the right of self defence and other signatories

[1] This note, dated March 26 and delivered March 30, is printed as enclosure 2 (vi) in item No. 1 in Cmd. 3109 of 1928.

could take such action as they deemed appropriate. He seemed to think that Senator Borah would heartily support the treaty on these lines and this is borne out by an interview with him published in the 'New York Times' of March 25th in which he says that multi-lateral treaty should be widened to include nations such for instance as Belgium which have been the victims of aggression in the past in which case attack on Belgium would ipso facto release other signatories and enable them to take such action as they considered advisable. He added 'Another important result of such a treaty would be to enlist support of United States in co-operative action against any nation which is guilty of flagrant violation of this outlawry agreement'.

After saying that United States government must reserve the right to decide for itself whether or no the treaty has been violated, he went on to say 'It is inconceivable that United States would stand idly by in case of grave breach of a multi-lateral treaty to which it is a party'.

Secretary of State went on to say that he thought exchange of notes with France might now cease and that government[s] of the six Great Powers ought to confer together but he had not yet made up his mind how this was to be done.

He is undoubtedly personally interested in seeing this treaty go through and was indignant because some French papers had accused him of simply playing politics in pushing it forward.

I found French Ambassador yesterday also hopeful and enthusiastic about reaching agreement which he described Monsieur Briand as desiring most heartily.

These conversations coupled with views of Senator Borah make me feel that the whole question has now become a practical issue which may have most important and far-reaching consequences.

No. 341

Revised Draft Treaty of Arbitration with the United States[1]
[A 2358/154/45]

April 4, 1928

His Majesty the King of Great Britain, Ireland and the British Dominions beyond the Seas, Emperor of India, and the President of the United States of America;

Eager by their example not only to demonstrate their condemnation of war as an instrument of national policy in their mutual relations, but also to hasten the time when the perfection of international arrangements for the pacific settlement of international disputes shall have eliminated for ever the possibility of war among any of the Powers of the World;

Desirous of re-affirming their adherence to the policy of submitting to

---

[1] This draft treaty had been drawn up by Sir C. Hurst in consultation with Mr. Malkin and the Procurator-General and Treasury Solicitor, Mr. Gwyer, and revised by the Lord Chancellor, Sir Douglas Hogg. It was circulated to the Cabinet as C.P. 117 (28).

impartial decision all controversies between them which are by their nature justiciable and of submitting all other controversies between them to investigation by an impartial conciliation commission;

Have decided to conclude a new treaty of arbitration to replace the Convention between them signed at Washington on April 14th, 1908, and for that purpose have appointed as their respective plenipotentiaries:—

His Majesty, &c.,[2]

for Great Britain &c.[2]
for the Dominion of Canada[2]
for the Commonwealth of Australia[2]
for the Dominion of New Zealand[2]
for the Union of South Africa[2]
for the Irish Free State[2]
for India[2]

The President of the United States of America
. . . .[2]

Who having communicated their full powers found in good and due form have agreed as follows:

Article 1

The High Contracting Parties recognise that peaceful and cordial relations between them are essential to the welfare of their peoples. They therefore declare that it is their firm intention to allow no question to arise between them for which a peaceful solution cannot be found by the adoption of the procedure laid down in the present treaty.

Article 2

All differences relating to international matters in which the High Contracting Parties are concerned by virtue of a claim of right made by or against the other under treaty or otherwise which it has not been possible to adjust by diplomacy and which are agreed to be justiciable in their nature by reason of being susceptible of decision by the application of a recognised rule of international law, shall be submitted to the Permanent Court of International Justice, or, if so agreed between them, to some other competent tribunal. A special agreement defining the question or questions at issue and settling the terms of reference and if necessary prescribing the rule of law to be applied shall be concluded in each case. The special agreement shall also, if need be, provide for the organisation of the tribunal, define its powers and settle the procedure.

The special agreement shall be made on the part of His Majesty the King in accordance with the constitutional laws of the part of his realms which may be concerned, and on the part of the United States by the President of the United States by and with the advice and consent of the Senate.

[2] Thus in original.

The special agreement shall in each case become binding only when confirmed by an exchange of notes.

Article 3

The provisions of article 2 shall not be invoked in respect of any dispute the subject matter of which:—

(a) is recognised by international law to be within the domestic jurisdiction of either of the High Contracting Parties;

(b) involves the interests of third parties;

(c) arises out of or involves the maintenance of the traditional attitude of either of the High Contracting Parties in relation to particular parts of the world where such party possesses special interests which are known to the other party;

(d) arises out of or involves the observance of the obligations of His Majesty the King under the Covenant of the League of Nations;

(e) arises out of events prior to the signature of the present treaty.

Article 4

All questions between the High Contracting Parties other than those which are settled by the normal processes of diplomacy or are referred for decision under article 2 shall be referred to the Permanent International Commission established by the treaty between the High Contracting Parties signed at Washington on September 15th, 1914. The provisions of that treaty are maintained in full force except that the International Commission therein provided for shall, in the case of any dispute between the United States on the one side and Canada, Australia, New Zealand, South Africa or the Irish Free State on the other, be composed of one member chosen from the United States by the Government thereof, one member chosen from the Dominion concerned by the Government thereof, one member chosen by the Government of the United States from some third country, one member chosen by the Government of the Dominion concerned from some third country and a fifth member chosen by agreement between the Governments of the United States and the Dominion concerned, it being understood that he shall not be a national of either of the High Contracting Parties.

Article 5

The present treaty shall not affect in any way the provisions of the treaty of January 11th, 1909,[3] relating to questions arising between the United States and Canada.

[3] This treaty between Great Britain and the United States relating to boundary waters and questions arising along the boundary between Canada and the United States and the establishment of an international commission is printed in *British and Foreign State Papers*, vol. 102, pp. 137–44.

No. 342

Sir A. Chamberlain to Sir E. Howard (Washington)
No. 500 [A 2372/1/45]

Secret   FOREIGN OFFICE, *April 5, 1928*

Sir,

With reference to my telegram No. 143 of April 2nd,[1] I transmit to Your Excellency herewith copy of a letter which I caused to be addressed to the Committee of Imperial Defence on March 8th regarding the Washington Treaty for the protection of the lives of neutrals and non-combatants at sea in time of war, and to prevent the use in war of noxious gases and chemicals.

2. Inasmuch as it is not possible to separate that portion of the above treaty which deals with submarine warfare from the portion dealing with chemical warfare, and as His Majesty's Government desire, in view of the attitude of other Powers in regard to the use of gas in war, to retain their freedom of action upon this important subject, they have decided to take no further action with a view to the ratification of the treaty in question.

3. I should be glad if you would regard this despatch and its enclosure as having been sent for your own information only.

I am, &c.,
(For the Secretary of State)
T. M. SNOW[2]

ENCLOSURE IN No. 342
Letter from the Foreign Office to the Committee of Imperial Defence

FOREIGN OFFICE, *March 8, 1928*

Sir,

I am directed by Secretary Sir Austen Chamberlain to inform you that Mr. Frank B. Kellogg, Secretary of State of the United States, has on more than one occasion recently informed His Majesty's Ambassador at Washington verbally that the United States Government would willingly negotiate treaties with foreign Powers for the total abolition of the submarine. Mr. Kellogg has also stated that he is in favour of the early ratification of the Washington Treaty for the protection of the lives of neutrals and non-combatants at sea in time of war and to prevent the use in war of noxious gases and chemicals, which has not yet come into force owing to its non-ratification by France.

2. In view of the importance attached by His Majesty's Government to any proposal which might advance the cause of submarine abolition, His Majesty's Ambassador at Washington was instructed on January 17th last to seize the opportunity provided by Mr. Kellogg's statements above-mentioned to suggest to him, as a first step towards the desired goal, that the United

[1] Not printed. This telegram requested Sir E. Howard to take no further action on No. 254.
[2] A senior member of the American and African Department of the Foreign Office.

States Government should now urge upon the French Government the advisability of ratifying the Treaty above-mentioned. Sir Esme Howard duly took action in this sense[3] and the United States Secretary of State informed him that he would do his best to persuade the French Government to ratify the Treaty in question. Mr. Kellogg added, however, that as regards the second part of this Treaty, which deals with poison gas, he could not mention this subject in any representations which he might cause to be made to the French Government, inasmuch as in 1925 France had signed, and subsequently ratified, the Geneva Protocol for the prohibition of the use in war of asphyxiating gases, etc.[4]

3. The following point has now arisen in connexion with this matter. When His Majesty's Ambassador at Washington was instructed to suggest to Mr. Kellogg that the United States Government should exert pressure on France for the ratification of the Washington Treaty previously referred to, Sir Esme Howard was not specifically told to exclude the poison gas clause of that Treaty from the scope of his remarks, since this clause is an integral part of that instrument. In this connexion, however, I am to invite reference to the extract from the minutes of the two hundred and fifteenth meeting of the Committee of Imperial Defence held on July 22nd, 1926, recording a discussion on the subject of the attitude to be adopted by His Majesty's Government regarding the ratification of the Geneva Protocol prohibiting the use of asphyxiating gases.[5] It will be remembered that, as a result of this discussion, it was decided that His Majesty's Government should adopt a neutral attitude until other Powers had signified their intentions, and that the Protocol should only be ratified by this country if other Powers had previously taken such action.

4. In the course of the discussion referred to in the preceding paragraph, a number of indefinite references were made to the Washington Treaty for the Protection of the Lives of Neutrals and non-Combatants in Time of War. No indication was given, however, of the views entertained by His Majesty's Government in regard to the ratification of this treaty. In view of the decision reached in regard to the Geneva Gas Protocol and of the presence in Washington Treaty No. 2 of Article V prohibiting the use of poisonous gases, I am to enquire whether it is now the opinion of the Committee of Imperial Defence that no further effort should be made to secure the ratification by France and the entry into force of this treaty. In this connexion the Committee will doubtless give full weight to the advantages which this country is likely to derive in time of war from the existence of an international convention regulating the uses to which submarines may be put. Should an enemy country resort to an unrestricted use of the submarine in defiance of

[3] Sir E. Howard had reported on this interview on February 13 in Washington telegram No. 65 of that date, not printed.

[4] This international protocol, signed on June 17, 1925, is printed in *British and Foreign State Papers*, vol. 126, pp. 324–5. Ratifications were deposited on behalf of France on May 9, 1926, and of the British Empire and India on April 9, 1930.

[5] The relevant extract from these minutes is untraced in Foreign Office archives.

such a convention, His Majesty's Government would, if the Convention were in existence, clearly be in a stronger moral position for resorting to reprisals against that country than would be the case if the convention remains unratified.

5. I am to add that while there is no indication that the present French Government have any intention of ratifying this treaty, it is conceivable that a change in political circumstances in France might result in the accession to office of a government who would be more disposed to take action in this sense and thereby bring the treaty into force.

6. The matter appears therefore to have more than an academic interest and Sir Austen Chamberlain would be grateful for an expression of the Committee's views on the point raised.[6]

I am, &c.,

R. L. CRAIGIE

[6] In a memorandum of March 28 referring to this paper, Field-Marshal Sir G. Milne, Chief of the Imperial General Staff, reminded the Committee of Imperial Defence that he had 'already warned them of the extensive preparations that the Russians are making for the employment of gas in war. . . . The most recent information in our possession leads me to conclude that training in chemical warfare in the Russian Army continues and is improving, that all their troops are in possession of gas masks (though not perhaps of the latest type), that credits for the manufacture of gas and anti-gas equipment have increased, and that large quantities of gas are being stored.'

No. 343

Sir A. Chamberlain to Sir E. Howard (Washington)

No. 503 [A 2280/133/45]

Secret   FOREIGN OFFICE, *April 5, 1928*

Sir,

His Majesty's Government have, as you are aware, been giving serious consideration for some time past to the question of the future exercise of Belligerent Rights at Sea, with particular reference to the capture of private property in time of war. The growth of the United States Navy, the evident determination of a large section of American public opinion that the British Empire must never again be permitted to exercise to the full the rights claimed and put into operation during the Great War, the use which is being made of this circumstance by the Big-Navy element to inflame American opinion against this country, and, finally, the knowledge that this question of Belligerent Rights constitutes the only apparent and, indeed, conceivable *casus belli* between the Empire and the United States, have led to the appointment of a special sub-committee of the Committee of Imperial Defence to examine the whole question and, in particular, to recommend whether or not it would be wise to make an attempt to reach an agreement with the United States on this matter.

2. The Committee have as yet reached no definite conclusion. There is general agreement that our needs as a belligerent must prevail over our

interests as a neutral. It would seem, too, that our position in the world requires us, even in the altered circumstances in which modern warfare and modern commerce are conducted, to maintain as heretofore belligerent rights at as high a level as possible, although some serious arguments can be adduced in favour of the opposite view. But the Committee have, as already stated, not yet reached a final decision on these points—still less on the desirability or otherwise of attempting to negotiate an agreement on this subject with the United States.

3. A close analysis and comparison of British and American practice in this matter has led to the conclusion that, while there is no great divergence in principle, an agreement, even if otherwise desirable, might be difficult of achievement in regard to the application to the conditions of modern warfare of those principles on which the two countries are agreed. On this point it seems unlikely that the Committee can make much further progress without some more authoritative knowledge than it possesses at present as to the probable disposition of the United States Government towards the idea of an agreement which would take into account the circumstance that the generally recognised practice in the matter of blockade and contraband no longer appears to give adequate effect to the fundamental principles on which that practice was based. Clearly much must depend on the spirit in which this or any future United States Government would be likely to enter upon discussions of this delicate question.

4. United States Presidential elections take place in November, and the Republican Convention will be held in June. The Committee realise that if it were thought desirable to take any action in this matter *vis-à-vis* the present United States Government, such action would have to be taken without delay, and that, otherwise, action will have to be deferred until the autumn of 1929—the earliest date at which the new Administration, entering upon office in March of that year, would be in a position to discuss any serious questions of foreign policy. His Majesty's Government recognise that certain risks are involved in leaving the question open for some eighteen months longer, since it may be used by hostile elements in the United States in such a way as to embitter the existing public controversy in regard to naval construction and generally to prejudice Anglo-American relations. Nevertheless, this is the course which His Majesty's Government think it would probably be best to follow, unless there were clear reason to believe that negotiations would lead to an early and satisfactory agreement. There is, however, a further aspect to this matter which requires immediate attention.

5. It is possible that discussion may be precipitated by events beyond our control. In the first place, Senator Borah has introduced into the Senate a resolution urging the importance of re-codifying, by means of an international agreement, 'the rules of war governing the conduct of belligerents and neutrals in war at sea.'[1] He suggests that this should be done before the meeting of the Naval Conference of 1931. The second event is a conclusion by the twenty-one States of the Pan-American Union, during the recent conference

[1] i.e. 70th Congress, 1st Session, S.Res. 157 of February 21, 1928.

at Havana, of a Convention on Maritime Neutrality. A first examination of this document has disclosed no departure from the generally recognised principles of international law bearing on the interception of private property at sea. There appears, indeed, at first sight, to be nothing in the Convention which would be inconsistent with the idea of an ultimate agreement on this subject between the Empire and the United States.

6. But the importance of these events lies in the proof which they afford that the minds of responsible authorities in the United States may be moving in the direction of a general international settlement of these problems. The possibility of an abrupt and spectacular summoning by the United States Government of an international conference on the whole question of Belligerent Rights is, unfortunately, too much in keeping with the recent American practice to be lightly dismissed. His Majesty's Government would view with grave anxiety the summoning of such an international conference unless the ground had been carefully prepared by diplomatic channels, and it had been shown that there was sufficient basis of agreement to render success at least probable. If, therefore, the United States Government are seriously contemplating any action of the kind, it is important to convey to them without delay the earnest hope of His Majesty's Government that, in the interests of ultimate agreement, the first step may be by unofficial and strictly confidential conversations. It should be clearly understood that His Majesty's Government do not wish to invite, or encourage the initiation of, such confidential conversations at the present moment. They realise, however, that the very worst thing would be another failure due to insufficient preparation, such as occurred at Geneva, and, if your Excellency sees serious reason to expect the issue of invitations to a conference, you should, without delay, bring the matter up in conversation with Mr. Kellogg. I leave it to your Excellency to decide whether it is preferable that a warning in this sense should be given in the first instance as from yourself, or whether you should inform Mr. Kellogg that you are speaking under instructions.

7. Assuming, however, that you have as yet no reason to suppose that a move in this direction is impending, it would, nevertheless, be of great interest to us to get a clearer idea than we at present possess of the trend of American official opinion both in the State Department and the Navy Department on these questions. There have been some speeches or writings which seem to suggest that a section at least of American naval opinion is coming round to the view that in the altered circumstances of to-day the interest of the United States lies rather in upholding than in scaling down the rights of a belligerent. You will consider whether the naval attaché should be instructed to be especially on the watch for any information in regard to this point. You will, of course, realise that no enquiries should be made which could possibly give the impression that His Majesty's Government are desirous of raising this issue or are unduly apprehensive in regard to it.

8. In view of the complexity and delicacy of these questions, I am sending this despatch by Mr. Craigie, who will place before you fully the conclusions

provisionally reached during the deliberations of the Committee on Belligerent Rights, and explain the various difficulties encountered by the Committee in its consideration of this subject. He will be able to give your Excellency an outline of the numerous and valuable documents submitted to the Committee in the course of its enquiries, which are either not suitable for textual transmission abroad or require for their full appreciation some account of the discussions out of which they arose or to which they gave rise. In the light of this information, your Excellency will be in a position to furnish him with a full expression of your own views for the benefit of the Committee. It was at first suggested that I should ask your Excellency to come home at once on some family pretext in order that the Committee might have the full benefit of your knowledge and experience, but we have thought it would be more convenient to you and on other grounds more prudent that you should take your leave at the time proposed by yourself and that I should send Mr. Craigie on a similar pretext to the States.

9. The ostensible purpose of Mr. Craigie's journey will, therefore, be to pay a visit to his relatives in Georgia, and he will himself make no enquiries while in Washington without your Excellency's full approval. It seems desirable, however, that, while in Washington, he should pay the usual calls of courtesy on the officials of the State Department, and if, during these interviews, the conversation turned, as it well might, to recent press controversies on the subject of belligerent rights at sea, he might be able to gain some impression of the general attitude of the Administration towards these questions. He would, of course, be careful to avoid any appearance of initiating a negotiation or of being the bearer of any communication from His Majesty's Government, and would make it plain in anything that he said that he was speaking in a private capacity and without any instructions. He will, in any case, first discuss the matter fully with your Excellency and abstain even from making such soundings as I have suggested above should your Excellency consider such action undesirable in present circumstances.

I am, &c.,
Austen Chamberlain

No. 344

Record by Sir W. Tyrrell of a conversation with Mr. Houghton
[A 2542/1/45]

FOREIGN OFFICE, April 13, 1928

The American Ambassador handed to me to-day the accompanying note[1] relating to the recent negotiations between the French and American Governments with regard to the question of possible renunciation of war.

His Excellency at the same time made the following communication which

---

[1] This note of April 13 with the enclosed draft treaties and Franco-American correspondence is printed as item No. 1 in Cmd. 3109 of 1928.

he desired that we should treat as a verbal aide-mémoire. His Excellency said:

'The text of this note and the text of the draft treaty will be given out in Washington for publication in the afternoon papers of Friday, April 13th, and copies will be made available to the London press for publication on Saturday morning, April 14th. As the contents of the seven enclosures listed have already been given to the press, no further release of these documents is necessary.

'In submitting this note and enclosures to you I am instructed by my Government to state that, in accordance with a request which has been received from M. Briand, the submission has been agreed to by M. Briand on the definite understanding, so far as France is concerned:

' "(a) That the United States is so proceeding upon its own responsibility.

' "(b) That no commitment on the part of France is in any way involved.

' "(c) That any further observations that France may deem necessary or appropriate, either at this time or later, will of course be addressed by France to the other interested Powers as well as to the United States, so that the entire situation may be fully explored by us all."

'The Secretary of State attaches the very greatest importance to the negotiations which are hereby being initiated among the six Powers, and in stating this to you I desire to express, on Mr. Kellogg's behalf, his very earnest hope that these efforts may be crowned with success after a common exploration of the problem by the six Powers, all of whom are equally interested in agreeing upon a practical method for the promotion of the cause of world peace.'

W. T.

No. 345

Sir E. Howard (Washington) to Sir A. Chamberlain
(Received April 13, 9.40 p.m.)
No. 120 Telegraphic [A 2553/1/45]

WASHINGTON, *April 13, 1928, 2.30 p.m.*

My telegram No. 118.[1]

I have received from Secretary of State copy of preliminary draft treaty for renunciation of war which has been communicated to governments of Great Britain, Germany, Italy and Japan by United States representatives in those countries. Secretary of State states that draft representations in general way form treaty which United States Government would be prepared to sign with France with above-mentioned countries and any others similarly disposed. Secretary of State informed Mr. Chilton last night that he saw no

[1] Not printed. This telegram of April 8 reported that on April 7 M. Claudel had informed Sir E. Howard of the likelihood of the American action reported below.

reason why governments concerned should not feel able to accept treaty and that he was confident that he could get it through Congress. He thought it would be useful if Monsieur Briand were to call conference of ministers for foreign affairs to discuss draft. If Monsieur Briand wished treaty to be signed in Paris he would like to go over himself to sign it.

APPENDIX

Foreign Office Memorandum

[*W 3961/2193/50*]*

FOREIGN OFFICE, *April 5, 1928*

THE FOREIGN POLICY OF HIS MAJESTY'S GOVERNMENT

(*In Continuation of and Supplementary to the Memorandum of April 1927.*)[1]

I. *Western Europe and Morocco*

MOROCCO

1. The Franco-Spanish conversations regarding Tangier terminated in the signature on the 3rd March, 1928, of an Agreement which provides for—

(1) an increase in the penalties for promoting conspiracy and rebellion against the established order in the three zones;

(2) the transfer to Tangier from Malaga of the Franco-Spanish Information Bureau, which will be under the charge of a Spanish Inspector-General; and

(3) the establishment of a gendarmerie under the command of a Spanish officer with a strength of 400 men, which will be reduced when the Tangier zone has been disarmed.[2]

A conference consisting of British, French, Spanish and Italian representatives is now sitting at Paris to discuss first the Franco-Spanish Agreement, and secondly the conditions on which the Italian Government are ready to accede to the Tangier Convention. The British representatives are insisting on a date being fixed for the reduction in the numbers of the gendarmerie, since a force of 400 men is too small to deal with a serious attack by tribesmen from the Spanish zone, and too large for ordinary police work, while the expense of maintenance even of 250 men will embarrass the Tangier financial system.

II. *Central Europe and the Balkans*

GERMANY

2. His Majesty's Government's commitments, in so far as Germany is concerned, remain the same to-day as in April 1927. On the other hand, the situation described under the heading 'Germany' on pages 10–12 of the memorandum on the foreign policy of His Majesty's Government, dated the 26th April, 1927,[3] has developed to a certain extent since then.

3. There are still Allied, including British, troops on the Rhine, though the numbers of those troops have now been reduced materially under the terms of an

---

[1] See Volume III, Appendix.
[2] For an official summary of this agreement, cf. *The Times*, March 5, 1928, p. 13.
[3] See Volume III, Appendix, pp. 789–90.

agreement concluded in September 1927, on British initiative, between the three occupying Powers. The German and French Foreign Ministers exchanged orations at the end of January 1928 in regard to the conditions (relating principally to security and finance) on which an evacuation of the Rhineland before the date contemplated by the Treaty of Versailles might be carried out. About the same time His Majesty's Government intimated in Parliament that they would welcome any agreement with that object which might be concluded between the interested Powers.[4] Belgium has also indicated her views in this connexion, but nothing concrete has occurred up to date to show that the various declarations which have been made are in process of execution, such practical steps as are needed to realise the contemplated curtailment of the occupation being necessarily deferred until after the French and German elections have taken place in May.

4. There have, since the memorandum of 1927 was written, been certain developments in the working of the Dawes Plan for the payment of German reparations which require a brief explanation. By the Treaty of Versailles, Germany undertook to make reparation for the loss and damage caused to the Allied Powers as a result of the war. In May 1921 the amount of that compensation was fixed by the Reparation Commission at 132 milliards of gold marks. Some payments on account were actually made, but apart from the fact that the discharge of a debt of such magnitude was, in the view of His Majesty's Government, incapable of realisation, the German economic and financial situation deteriorated to such an extent during the years 1920–23 that a complete default in reparation payments became inevitable. This led to the Franco-Belgian occupation of the Ruhr, and the pledges policy in the Rhineland. The whole position was, however, materially altered by the adoption by the interested Governments, including the German, of the Dawes Plan, and by its embodiment in the London Agreements of 1924.

5. The Dawes Plan fixed, with careful regard to Germany's capacity to pay, the amounts annually due from Germany in respect of reparation, and provided, by means of the functions of the Transfer Committee, a system of protection for the German exchange. It did not, however, fix the number of annuities which Germany would have to pay in total discharge of her reparation liability, the actual annuities specified in the Plan being insufficient to cover year by year the interest at 5 per cent. on less than half the total debt fixed by the Reparation Commission in 1921, which remains the *legal* amount due from Germany to the ex-Allies in respect of reparation.

6. The Dawes Plan came into force on the 1st September, 1924, and since that date the sums for which it provided have duly been paid into the reparation account. Up till now, however, only reduced payments have had to be made. The real strain will begin in September of this year, when the first full payments fall due. The problem at once arises as to how these full payments are to be converted into sterling and dollars without upsetting the stability of the German currency. Moreover, the dissipation of German resources and German credit through the over-spending and over-borrowing in recent months of the German public authorities has led the Agent-General for Reparation Payments (who represents at Berlin the interests of the creditor Governments and who is responsible for the administration of the Plan) to examine the working of the present system and to attempt to improve it. After certain unavailing appeals to the German authorities

[4] For the statement by Mr. Locker Lampson on February 9, see *Parl. Debs., 5th ser., H. of C.*, vol. 213, col. 262.

to exercise greater prudence in the matter of foreign borrowing and administrative extravagance, he recently declared publicly that the only satisfactory issue is 'to be found in the final determination of the German reparation liability on an absolute basis' (i.e., without reference to the question of Inter-Allied debts) 'that contemplates no measure of transfer protection.'[5] The issue thus publicly presented is an extremely important and difficult one, which loses none of its difficulty and importance from the fact that no settlement on the lines indicated will be possible without the active co-operation of the United States Government, which has always hitherto refused to recognise the inter-relation (accepted in Europe) of reparation and Inter-Allied debts. It is the policy of His Majesty's Government, however, to prevent the problem from becoming active as long as possible, and, at any rate, not until after March 1929, when the new President of the United States takes office. In the meantime, the fact that the Allied occupation of the Rhineland is technically a guarantee for the payment of reparations, makes it unlikely that the problem of a premature evacuation of the Rhineland can in present circumstances be dealt with otherwise than as part of a general financial settlement to include war debts and reparations.

7. As regards the general relations between the British and German Governments, these remain good, even cordial; a certain amount of dissatisfaction has, however, been expressed in Germany at the operation of the Safeguarding of Industries Act, &c., as incompatible with the terms of the Anglo-German Commercial Treaty of December 1924, which, according to a recent declaration by the Minister of Commerce, will be denounced at the earliest possible moment (not before 1930).

AUSTRIA

8. As regards the 'Anschluss' question, recent indications seem to show that Italy might be prepared to use this question as a bargaining counter with either Germany or France. It is therefore no longer safe to say (as was said in the memorandum of 1927) that she would in all circumstances fight to prevent having a common frontier with Germany.

HUNGARY

9. The statement made in last year's memorandum that the Locarno Treaty system showed signs of bearing fruit in Central and South-Eastern Europe cannot unfortunately be maintained. Recent overtures on these lines were made by M. Benes, but they met with a most adverse response from Count Bethlen himself. It must therefore be concluded that so long as Hungary maintains her present attitude both towards her neighbours and the Treaty of Trianon, the application of Locarno principles to the security problem of Central Europe is hardly a matter of practical politics.

10. Even under the wise and temperate leadership of Count Bethlen, Hungary makes no secret of her aim to secure a revision of her present frontiers, and Lord Rothermere's press campaign in Great Britain and America to this end, coupled with the discovery of a large consignment of war material in Hungarian territory in January 1928, has merely served to strengthen the Little *Entente* just at a moment when signs were not wanting that that alliance was becoming weakened and confused owing to the disintegrating effect of Italo-French rivalry in Central Europe.

[5] See the *Report of the Agent General for Reparation Payments, December 10, 1927*, p. 171.

11. While it is true that Hungary has signed commercial treaties with Yugo-slavia and Czechoslovakia,[6] it would be wrong to assume that there has been any material improvement in the political relations between Hungary and her nor-thern and southern neighbours. If anything, a deterioration has been noticeable in the case of Yugoslavia since April 1927, when Hungary signed a Treaty of Friendship with Italy.[7] Since that date no progress has been made in the negotia-tions with Yugoslavia for Hungary's access to the Adriatic Sea, which it was at one time hoped would lead to wider agreements between the two countries.

12. Hungary's relations with Roumania and Czechoslovakia have been poisoned by the bitter controversy over the property of Hungarian landowners in Tran-sylvania, which for the past year has occupied the close attention of the Council of the League of Nations and is not yet settled.

13. British policy is directed to endeavouring to make plain to Hungary that the Peace Treaty must be respected, and when [sic] neighbours that they are ill-advised to treat Hungary as a pariah, and generally that the true road to peace and prosperity is by way of mutual arrangements for non-aggression and conciliation on the model of the arbitration treaties signed at Locarno.

ITALY

14. As regards the problem of increased population mentioned in the 1927 memorandum, the following factors should be stressed: Although the chief pre-war outlet for Italian emigration, the United States of America, is now practically closed, Signor Mussolini has repeatedly announced his wish for a much greater population. France now takes the bulk of Italian emigrants, and large compact colonies have been formed in the South and South-Eastern Departments. Steps are also being taken by reclamation work to create more room in Italy itself. The Fascist policy discourages emigration to foreign countries and aims at securing land for colonisation. The existing Italian colonies in Africa are incapable of supporting a large white population, and Italy has recently been paying marked attention to Cilicia, where she is carrying out an intensive peaceful penetration. Should there be any reshuffling of mandates, Italy would advance strong claims to receive one.

15. Relations between Italy and France have continued strained. Unpleasant incidents have been frequent along the Franco-Italian frontier, whilst the large Italian emigration into the South of France is a cause of serious misgiving. In Tunis the new French nationality decrees of 1921 impose French nationality on all persons born in the colony one of whose parents was also so born. The Italian colony, which greatly outnumbers the French, enjoyed the right to retain their own nationality under the Franco-Italian Treaty of 1896, which, however, was denounced in 1918, and has since only been prolonged for three months at a time pending its replacement by another agreement. Thus the nationality of this large block of Italian settlers, whose 'Italianità' is continually stimulated by Fascism, hangs in the balance. In Tangier again France is held to be opposing Italian claims to adequate representation on the international régime. There is also a dispute regarding the southern boundary of Tripoli, which the Italians claim should be moved farther south. A turn for the better took place during the winter, when, as a result of discreet pressure by His Majesty's Government, the French and Italian

[6] These treaties of July 24, 1926, and May 31, 1927, respectively, are printed with attached documents in *British and Foreign State Papers*, vol. 125, pp. 815–47, and *League of Nations Treaty Series*, vol. lxv, pp. 61–299, respectively.

[7] Printed in *British and Foreign State Papers*, vol. 127, pp. 737–40.

Governments were finally induced to open conversations with a view to a settlement of the various points of friction between them. Signor Mussolini has disclaimed any intention of making exaggerated demands, whilst M. Briand has announced his readiness to make reasonable concessions to be followed up by a Treaty of Arbitration and Friendship.

16. As regards the continued strained relations between Italy and Yugoslavia, both His Majesty's Government and France have urged on Italy and Yugoslavia the desirability of threshing out their differences by means of direct conversations, but although the Yugoslav Minister in Rome has been cordially received by Signor Mussolini, the latter has steadily refused to be drawn into any discussion or explanation of his policy which would be likely to allay suspicion in Yugoslavia. In these unsatisfactory circumstances it was decided last January to extend until June next the period within which notice must be given of the renunciation or renewal of the ineffective Pact of Rome between Italy and Yugoslavia, which provides for mutual consultation and co-operation. Italo-Yugoslav relations are really now dependent on Franco-Italian relations, and unless the negotiations now initiated at Rome lead to a better Franco-Italian understanding, a more satisfactory relationship between Yugoslavia and Italy can hardly be expected.

17. Quite recently we have had an indication of improved relations between Italy and Turkey. It is reported that Signor Mussolini considers the opening for trade of more importance to Italy than the chance of some day carving a colony or mandated territory out of Asia Minor.

The Balkans

18. France has now signed the Treaty with Yugoslavia which, in the memorandum of 1927, was described as being in suspension. This treaty at once provoked Italy into still further tightening her hold on Albania, and within a few days of its signature she had concluded a twenty-years' defensive alliance with Albania, whereby each State agrees to devote all its resources to their reciprocal defence and protection against all aggression.

19. Yugoslavia sees in this move a further threat to her south-west frontier, which is not diminished by her conviction that certain elements of the present régime in Italy give countenance to the Macedonian Revolutionary Organisation in Bulgaria, whose avowed object is the restoration of Southern Serbia to the Bulgarian organ. Detailed memoranda on the system of treaties now in existence in Central Europe and on the Macedonian problem are available.[8]

20. It is the object of His Majesty's Government to strengthen the influence of the League of Nations in the Balkans, to inculcate as far as possible the principles laid down at Locarno, and to counsel moderation when difficult situations arise. It has been a source of encouragement that Serbian foreign policy has for the last year been under the direction of M. Marinkovitch, who has given ample proof of a statesmanlike outlook in dealing with the complex questions with which Yugoslavia, surrounded as she is by no less than seven neighbours, is confronted.

III. *Turkey and Middle East*

Turkey

21. During the past year Mustapha Kemal[9] has further consolidated his position as dictator, and has continued the process of the modernisation of Turkey. In

---

[8] Not printed.   [9] President of Turkey.

international relations there are signs that the attitude of suspicious isolation is yielding before a desire that Turkey should play a part in world politics, cf. the Turkish Minister for Foreign Affairs' wish to attend the Preparatory Disarmament Conference at Geneva, the necessary invitation to which was procured through the good offices of His Majesty's Government.

Turkish relations with this country are apparently improving from day to day.

THE STRAITS

22. There has been no change during the past year in the position indicated in paragraphs 73–75 of the memorandum dated the 26th April, 1927.

PERSIA

23. During the past year Persia has been able to reach a comprehensive settlement of all her outstanding disputes with Russia. A series of agreements, including a treaty of guarantee and neutrality, a commercial convention, and an agreement regarding Caspian Fisheries, was signed on the 1st October,[10] and has since been ratified and come into force.

24. The Persian Government's relations with His Majesty's Government during the year have not been so fortunate. In March they withdrew the permission given to Imperial Airways (Limited) to operate a commercial air service from Iraq to India along the shores of the Persian Gulf; no reason was given for their decision save the 'interests of the country,' the 'internal situation and frontier considerations,' but the probable reason for their attitude was a fear that the route might in time come to be considered as an important strategic air line of the British Empire. In May, again, they announced their intention of terminating in May 1928 the system of foreign Consular jurisdiction in Persia known as the Capitulations, and any other exceptional privileges to which foreigners were entitled. With this end in view they denounced at a year's notice all the treaties in which such rights and privileges had been embodied.[11] Although no British treaty was so denounced, the Persian action has made it necessary for His Majesty's Government to endeavour to negotiate a fresh treaty to safeguard the interests of British nationals in Persia.

25. After the settlement of their differences with Russia, the Persian Government professed a strong desire to reach a similar settlement with Great Britain of all outstanding questions, and on the 31st December the Shah expressed his wish that His Majesty's Minister at Tehran would enter into secret negotiations with his Minister of the Court on all the main questions still under discussion between the two Governments. These negotiations are still proceeding.

IRAQ

26. Since the memorandum for last year was prepared the position has been modified by the conclusion in December, 1927, of a new Anglo-Iraq Treaty.[12]

---

[10] The Soviet-Persian treaty of guarantee and neutrality and the agreement regarding the Caspian Fisheries are printed with attached documents in *British and Foreign State Papers*, vol. 126, pp. 943–59. For the Soviet-Persian exchange of notes regarding commercial relations see Jane Degras, *Soviet Documents on Foreign Policy*, vol. ii, pp. 255–66.

[11] See Volume III, No. 516.

[12] The text of this treaty of December 14, 1927, which was not ratified, is printed in Cmd. 2998 of 1927.

This treaty has not yet entered into force, and it is not proposed to ratify it until the revised Financial and Military Agreements envisaged in Articles XII and XIII have been concluded, and all three instruments approved by the Council of the League of Nations. Some time must, therefore, elapse before the new treaty and connected agreements can become operative. In the meantime, the relations between His Majesty's Government and the Iraq Government are governed by the Anglo-Iraq Treaty of the 10th October, 1922, and subsidiary agreements, and the subsequent treaty of the 13th January, 1926,[13] and the commitments of His Majesty's Government towards Iraq, remain as defined therein.

27. It may be useful, however, to consider the more important variations between the new treaty and the earlier instruments in so far as these may affect the commitments of His Majesty's Government. Whereas Article VII of the treaty of 1922 contained an implied undertaking to provide support and assistance to the armed forces of the King of Iraq, the corresponding article (Article XIII) of the new treaty contains no such undertaking. It merely provides that a separate agreement shall regulate the military relations between the high contracting parties.

28. Formal negotiations in regard to the revised Military Agreement have not yet opened. A draft has, however, been prepared, has been approved by the Cabinet, and has been forwarded to the High Commissioner for Iraq for communication to the Iraq Government. From past experience it would seem probable that the text of the draft will undergo substantial modification in the course of negotiation with the Iraq Government, and a detailed examination of the present text would not therefore serve any useful purpose; but certain articles, viz., Articles I, IV and IX, in the draft have already been definitely accepted both by His Majesty's Government and, on behalf of the Iraq Government, by King Faisal, and there is, therefore, good reason to suppose that these articles will be embodied in the final agreement in their present form.

29. *Article I* reads as follows:—

'The two Governments hereby recognise the principle that the Government of Iraq shall at the earliest possible date accept full responsibility, both for the maintenance of internal order and for the defence of Iraq from external aggression. They also recognise, however, that the resources of Iraq are at present insufficient for this purpose, and therefore His Britannic Majesty's Government in Great Britain will afford such support and assistance as they may consider necessary and decide upon from time to time.'

It will be seen that the qualifying clause in the corresponding article of the existing Military Agreement[14] (which committed the Iraq Government to the acceptance in 1928 of full responsibility for internal security and defence from external aggression) has been omitted from the new article, which now definitely recognises the present inability of the Iraq Government fully to accept this responsibility. The extent and nature of the military assistance to be afforded to the Iraq Government from time to time is, however, left entirely to the judgment of His Majesty's Government.

30. *Article IV* reads as follows:—

'His Britannic Majesty's Government in Great Britain agree to grant facilities

[13] The Anglo-Iraqi treaties of October 10, 1922, and January 13, 1926, are printed respectively in *British and Foreign State Papers*, vol. 119, pp. 389–94, and vol. 123, pp. 446–8.
[14] i.e. the Anglo-Iraqi military agreement of March 25, 1924, printed *op. cit.*, vol. 119, pp. 410–16.

in the following matters, the cost of which will be met by the Iraq Government:—

(1.) Military and aeronautical instruction of Iraq officers in Great Britain so far as this may be possible.

(2.) The provision in sufficient quantities of arms, ammunition, equipment and aeroplanes of the latest available pattern for the Iraq Army.

(3.) The provision of British officers (in such numbers as may be mutually agreed upon between the two Governments) for the purpose of ensuring efficient co-operation between the British forces in Iraq and the Iraq Army. Such officers shall be employed upon terms of service identical with those upon which British Military Officers are at present serving.'

The text of this article differs but little from that of Article II of the Military Agreement of the 25th March, 1924. The reference in the latter article to the presence in Iraq either of an Imperial Garrison or of local Forces maintained by His Britannic Majesty's Government finds no place in the new article, but it is proposed to deal with this in a separate article.

31. *Article IX* (an extract from which is given below) is of more importance.

'The Iraq Government shall be entitled to the assistance of any forces maintained or controlled in Iraq by His Britannic Majesty's Government in Great Britain against or for the suppression of any external aggression or any civil disturbance or armed rising, provided that it shall not, in the opinion of the High Commissioner, have been provoked or occasioned by action taken, or policy pursued, by the Iraq Government contrary to the express wishes or contrary to or without the advice of His Britannic Majesty's Government in Great Britain.'

Under the terms of the corresponding article (Article VIII) of the Military Agreement of the 25th March, 1924, it might have been argued that no definite obligation was placed upon His Majesty's Government to give assistance to the Iraq Government in the event of unprovoked attack. It was, however, held at the time that such an obligation was, in fact, implicit in the article. As will be seen any ambiguity on this score has been removed in the new article, which, in the circumstances stated, definitely entitles the Iraq Government to the assistance of any British forces in Iraq.

32. There is one other article in the principal treaty which calls for comment. Whereas Article VI of the Treaty of 1922 did not specify any definite date for the admission of Iraq to membership of the League of Nations, Article VIII of the new treaty, subject to certain provisos, commits His Majesty's Government to support the candidature of Iraq for admission to the League in 1932.

33. Article VIII of the 1922 Treaty, which provided that no territory in Iraq should be ceded, or leased, or in any way placed under the control of any foreign Power, finds no place in the new treaty.

PALESTINE AND TRANS-JORDAN

34. British commitments in regard to Palestine and Trans-Jordan are still covered by the Mandate,[15] Article 5 of which lays down the territorial guarantee

[15] The mandate for the administration of the former Turkish territory of Palestine as confirmed by the Council of the League of Nations on July 24, 1922, together with the note of September 23, 1922, by the Secretary-General of the League of Nations relating to its application to Transjordan, is printed *op. cit.*, vol. 116, pp. 842–50.

given by His Majesty's Government in respect of those countries. By the agreement between His Majesty and His Highness the Amir of Trans-Jordan, which was signed in February 1928,[16] but has not yet been ratified: (1) His Majesty is empowered to maintain armed forces in Trans-Jordan and to raise, organise and control in Trans-Jordan such armed forces as may, in his opinion be necessary for the defence of the country and to assist the Amir in the preservation of peace and order; and (2) the Amir agrees that he will not raise or maintain in Trans-Jordan or allow to be raised or maintained any military forces without the consent of His Britannic Majesty.

THE HEJAZ AND NEJD

35. The commitments of His Majesty's Government in regard to Nejd, deriving from the treaty concluded with Ibn Saud as Sultan of Nejd on the 26th December, 1915, have been extinguished by the conclusion on the 20th May, 1927, of the Treaty of Jeddah, signed by Ibn Saud as King of the Hejaz and Nejd and its Dependencies.[17] This instrument contains no commitments of any sort.

36. A crisis in the relations between His Majesty's Government and Ibn Saud arose at the end of 1927. Ibn Saud protested that the construction of an advanced intelligence post, some 75 miles from the Iraq–Nejd frontier, was contrary to the provisions of an agreement between himself and the King of Iraq regulating frontier tribal relations;[18] he added that it was causing apprehension and excitement among his tribes. In the opinion of His Majesty's Government there was no question of any infraction of the agreement, and the object of the fort was solely the prevention of tribal raids, against which Ibn Saud himself had complained to the High Commissioner at Bagdad. The fierce and fanatical Wahabis were, however, undoubtedly alarmed and excited, and on the 5th November they exterminated the small garrison. Thereafter they carried out several further raids against Iraq tribes in Iraq territory, and one against a Transjordanian tribe in Nejd territory. The protests of His Majesty's Government to Ibn Saud had no effect and it was accordingly decided to retaliate by air action against the raiders, where necessary pursuing them into Nejd territory. Ibn Saud was notified of this decision before action was taken. Having hitherto endeavoured to exculpate himself and his tribes by the allegation that Iraq had broken a treaty, as soon as aeroplanes had crossed his frontier in pursuit of parties of raiders he complained that this violation of his territory had destroyed his work of pacification, and admitted that he could no longer control the Wahabi. Possibly this was true. At any rate the three great Akhwan tribes, the Mutair, Ataibi and Ajman, were rumoured to have come out under their banners and to have proclaimed a Jihad[19] against all non-Wahabi. All possible measures were taken for the defence of Iraq, Transjordan and Koweit, but Ibn Saud was informed that if he could give certain assurances (which are hitherto not forthcoming), orders would be issued, in order to enable him to regain control, that no aircraft should cross the Nejd frontier except

[16] This agreement of February 20, 1928, with the Emir Abdullah of Transjordan is printed *op. cit.*, vol. 128, pp. 273–8.

[17] The treaties of 1915 and 1927 are printed respectively in C. U. Aitchison, *A Collection of Treaties, Engagements and Sanads relating to India and Neighbouring Countries* (5th ed., Calcutta, 1929), vol. xi, pp. 206–8, and *British and Foreign State Papers*, vol. 134, pp. 273–9.

[18] The reference was to the Boundary Protocol No. 1 signed at Uqair on December 2, 1922, printed *op. cit.*, vol. 133, pp. 648–9.

[19] Holy War.

in active pursuit of raiders. The latest reports, however, tend to discredit the earlier rumours of a Jihad, and to indicate that Ibn Saud has dissociated himself from any such movement and that he has been at least temporarily successful in detaching from it the important Ataibi tribe.

37. The underlying causes of this unfortunate situation are probably Ibn Saud's dislike and distrust of Feisal and Abdullah, which he extends to British officials in Iraq and Transjordan, together with the raiding propensities and religious fanaticism of the Wahabis. The latter form Ibn Saud's fighting force in case of need, but his control over them is precarious. Throughout the whole period he has not ceased to proclaim his friendship for His Majesty's Government and to appeal for their assistance in reaching a solution of the difficulties which he attributes to the policy of the Iraq Government. It has now been decided that Sir Gilbert Clayton,[20] who negotiated the Treaty of Jeddah with him, should be sent out to discuss the situation and to endeavour to reach a solution. Given the frontier conditions and tribal characteristics, this will be no easy task.

The Idrisi of Asir

38. There have been at least two missions from Ibn Saud to the Imam Yehia[21] during the past year to discuss outstanding issues, notably the Asir question, but, as far as is known, no result has been achieved. But neither ruler has shown any disposition to seek a solution by more forcible methods. A mission from the Imam has recently come to Mecca and has been received with great ceremony.

The Aden Protectorate and the Red Sea Area

39. The Imam was informed in March 1927 that, while His Majesty's Government were anxious to secure a friendly settlement of their differences with him, they could not recognise that he had any rights whatever within the Aden Protectorate, and they warned him that his continued occupation of parts of it would render him liable to retaliatory measures.[22] In spite of this communication, armed Zeidi[23] forces penetrated further into the Protectorate in September 1927, and only withdrew on being warned that air action would be taken against them. Warnings were then dropped on certain towns in the Yemen that, in the event of further incursions being made into the Protectorate, air action would be taken against them. On the 8th February last the Zeidis kidnapped the Alawi Sheikh and a relation of the Koteibi Sheikh, both of whom are entitled by treaty to the protection of His Majesty's Government. After forty-eight hours' notice, air action was taken against Kataba, in Yemen territory, which is understood to be the headquarters of those Zeidi forces directly responsible for the outrage.[24] In the circumstances, there is necessarily some degree of uncertainty as to the future. It must depend largely upon the effects produced by air action, which has been continued, and upon the extent to which the Zeidis are made to realise that they cannot raid the Aden Protectorate with impunity. His Majesty's Government

[20] Formerly Chief Secretary to the Government of Palestine.
[21] Of the Yemen.
[22] Cf. Volume III, No. 511, note 3.
[23] i.e. Yemeni. The Imams of the Yemen were leaders of the Zeidi sect of Islam.
[24] The preceding passage is a citation from the statement by Mr. Amery, Secretary of State for Dominion Affairs and for the Colonies, on March 12, printed in *Parl. Debs., 5th ser., H. of C.*, vol. 214, col. 1516.

have not, and never have had, the smallest desire to quarrel with the Imam. They are still anxious, as they always have been, to come to a settlement with him on honourable terms which will satisfy the just claims of both parties and place their future relations on a friendly and neighbourly basis, but no settlement could be acceptable to His Majesty's Government which did not take account of their obligations to the tribes of the Aden Protectorate.

IV. *Northern Europe and Afghanistan*

POLAND, THE BALTIC STATES AND SCANDINAVIA

40. Of these countries little need be said. Our general aim here, as elsewhere, is peace and stability. In the multilateral declaration of the 23rd April, 1908,[25] His Majesty's Government announced, jointly with the Danish, French, Dutch and Swedish Governments, their firm resolution to preserve intact and mutually to respect the sovereign rights at that time enjoyed by the parties concerned over their respective territories in the regions bordering on the North Sea, and to concert together 'such measures as they (the signatories) may consider it useful to take' in the event of any menace to the *status quo*. The original German participation in this declaration has lapsed in accordance with article 289 of the Treaty of Versailles. There is no such agreement relating to the Baltic, and, apart from obligations which may arise under the Covenant of the League, we should not be bound to resist any change such as the federation of the Baltic States, or even their reabsorption by Russia. In the dispute between Poland and Lithuania, His Majesty's Government, in pursuance of their general policy of ensuring peace and stability, have encouraged, and taken part in, action by the League of Nations to induce Lithuania to resume friendly relations with Poland, while avoiding anything unduly wounding to the former's *amour-propre*; but they have refused to join with other Powers in any attempt to impose a settlement by direct pressure.

RUSSIA

41. The examination by the police on the 12th May, 1927, of the premises of Arcos (Limited) and of the Russian Trade Delegation conclusively proved that both military espionage and subversive activities throughout the British Empire were directed and carried out from the premises of the above institutions. His Majesty's Government therefore informed the Soviet Chargé d'Affaires on the 26th May, 1927, that they regarded themselves as free from the obligations of the Trade Agreement of 1921, and could no longer maintain diplomatic relations with the Soviet Government, though they had no intention of interfering with the ordinary course of legitimate Anglo-Russian trade.[26] This step does not, of course, imply the withdrawal of our *de jure* recognition of the Soviet Government.

42. It seems most probable that Russia will not be in a position for many years to wage war on a considerable scale outside the boundaries of the Union of Soviet Socialist Republics. The action which is to be feared from her (apart from her persistent anti-British propaganda) is that of gradual extension of her influence in directions which affect British interests.

[25] Printed in *British and Foreign State Papers*, vol. 101, pp. 179–81.
[26] See Volume III, No. 215. The Anglo-Soviet Trade Agreement of March 16, 1921, is printed in *British and Foreign State Papers*, vol. 114, pp. 373–9.

43. From the more purely political point of view it can be stated that the conviction of the Soviet Government that His Majesty's Government foment opposition to them on every side is founded on a myth. Our attitude is purely defensive. The hostile propaganda of the Soviet Government has, indeed, led to a breach of diplomatic relations, but no reason is seen to anticipate naval or military action. Apart from our obligations under the Covenant of the League of Nations, we have no obligations to render military assistance to any foreign country in the event of Russian aggression. So far as attacks on our own territory are concerned, the point of interest is, of course, India, and Russian policy in Afghanistan and Chinese Turkestan demands our unremitting vigilance. That policy, if it succeeds at all, will take the shape of an extension of Russian influence and perhaps control, but any such development must be gradual, and any early effect on the requirements of British military preparedness will be indirect. The dangers to be feared are those of Soviet intrigues in Afghanistan, the fomentation of hostile activity among the frontier tribes of India, and subversive propaganda in India itself, rather than the debouching of Russian forces on to Indian territory.

AFGHANISTAN

44. There are no signs at present of any likelihood of acute trouble with Afghanistan, such as might lead to a repetition of the war of 1919. Unless and until Russia becomes more aggressive and aims at creating a breach, our responsibilities will probably be limited to ordinary watchfulness and the endeavour to prevent any undesirable extension of Russian influence.

45. We are under no obligation to the Afghan Government to defend any of their frontiers, but the Committee of Imperial Defence have recently reaffirmed, as a cardinal principle, that 'by our own plain interest, our obligations to guard the independence and integrity of Afghanistan are unimpaired, and the deliberate crossing of the Oxus or the occupation of Herat by Russia would be the violation of a frontier which we are bound to defend'; and that, in the last resort, 'Russian action of the kind indicated would be followed by a declaration of war against that Power.' The Committee of Imperial Defence have left for further consideration by His Majesty's Government and the Government of India the question of what steps can be taken to place the Army and Royal Air Force in India in the state of preparedness required by such a policy. The question of a public announcement of this policy has also been left for the decision of the Cabinet. If no announcement is made the policy will have no deterrent effect on the Union of Socialist Soviet Republics; if too categorical an announcement is made, the Afghan Government will imagine that they can adopt what policy they like towards the Soviet Government, and that whatever happens we shall be obliged to defend them. The formula suggested by the Committee is:—

'That Britain could never regard with indifference the interference by a foreign Power in the existing territory of a friendly Afghanistan, but that the exact steps which ought, in that event, to be taken must depend upon the circumstances of the moment.'

46. Conversations have taken place between King Amanulla and His Majesty's Secretary of State for Foreign Affairs in the course of His Majesty's visit to England, but these conversations have not resulted in any change in the situation.

V. *Egypt and Abyssinia*

EGYPT

47. During the autumn of 1927 a treaty was negotiated with the Egyptian Prime Minister which provided for an Anglo-Egyptian alliance, regularised the position of the British army of occupation, and, in effect, confined our obligation to intervene on behalf of foreign interests to cases likely to imperil good relations between Egypt and a foreign power, or to threaten the lives and property of foreigners in Egypt.[27] The draft treaty was, however, rejected by the Egyptian Government in March 1928, with the result that the Declaration of February 1922,[28] with its consequential commitments described above,[29] remains in force.

VI. *Far East*

CHINA

48. So far as treaty obligations are concerned, the position of Great Britain is determined by the treaties signed at the time of the Washington Conference for the Limitation of Armament in 1921–22.[30] In actual fact, however, the position has been modified by events arising out of the Chinese civil war.

49. The obligations created by the Washington Treaties are analysed in the memorandum submitted in 1926.[31] For convenience of reference that analysis is repeated here:—

'The two principal international instruments which at present govern the relations between the four great Pacific Powers (Great Britain, Japan, United States and France) and between the Powers enjoying treaty rights in China and China herself, are—

(*a*.) The Four-Power Treaty signed at Washington on the 13th December, 1921; and

(*b*.) The Nine-Power Treaty signed on the 6th February, 1922.

These two treaties are at once the result and the guarantee of the attitude of quiescence or policy of co-operation and non-interference in Chinese affairs, adopted by the Powers with good or ill grace after the war, and they are characteristic of the phase through which the relations of the Far Eastern Powers are still passing.

By the Four-Power Treaty the contracting parties (the United States, the British Empire, France and Japan) agreed to respect their rights in relation to their insular possessions and dominions in the region of the Pacific Ocean. Any controversies arising out of any specific question not satisfactorily settled

---

[27] This draft treaty is printed as the enclosure in item No. 6 in Cmd. 3050 of 1928, *Papers regarding Negotiations for a Treaty of Alliance with Egypt.*

[28] The declaration by H.M. Government to Egypt dated February 28, 1922, is printed as enclosure No. 2 in item No. 35 in Cmd. 1592 of 1922, *Correspondence respecting Affairs in Egypt.*

[29] The reference was presumably to the relevant passage of Section V of the Foreign Office memorandum of April 26, 1927, which was the same as that printed in Section V of the Appendix to Volume I.

[30] See Cmd. 1627 of 1922, *Conference on Limitation of Armament. Washington, 1921–22* (*Treaties, Resolutions, &c.*).

[31] See the Appendix to Volume I. The passage cited below comprises paragraphs 106–13 thereof.

by diplomacy are to be submitted for consideration to a joint conference; the contracting Powers are to communicate with one another in the event of aggressive action by any other Power threatening the said rights; the treaty is to be in force for ten years, and thereafter to continue in force subject to twelve months' notice by any contracting party; upon ratification of the treaty (i.e., the 17th August, 1923) the Anglo-Japanese Alliance Agreement had to terminate. A subsequent treaty (the 6th February, 1922) defined the term 'insular possessions and insular dominions' in its application to Japan as *not* to include the main islands of Japan.

On the 2nd February, 1922, His Majesty's Government gave an assurance to the Government of Portugal, and on the 4th February to the Government of the Netherlands, that, although these countries were not parties to the Four-Power Treaty, yet Great Britain was firmly determined to respect their rights in relation to their insular possessions in the region of the Pacific. Similar assurances were given by the United States of America, France and Japan.

By Article 19 of the Washington Treaty for the Limitation of Naval Armaments, signed on the 6th February, 1922, His Majesty's Government undertook to maintain the *status quo* with regard to fortifications and naval bases at Hong Kong, and in our insular possessions in the Pacific Ocean, east of 110° longitude, except (*a*) those adjacent to the coast of Canada; (*b*) the Commonwealth of Australia and its territories; and (*c*) New Zealand.

By the Nine-Power Treaty, the contracting Powers other than China (United States, Belgium, British Empire, France, Italy, Japan, Netherlands and Portugal) agreed (1) to respect the sovereignty, the independence and the territorial and administrative integrity of China; (2) to provide the fullest and most unembarrassed opportunity to China to develop and maintain for herself an effective and stable Government; (3) to use their influence for the purpose of effectually establishing and maintaining the principle of equal opportunity for the commerce and industry of all nations throughout the territory of China; (4) to refrain from taking advantage of conditions in China in order to seek special rights or privileges which would abridge the rights of subjects or citizens of friendly States and from countenancing action inimical to the security of such States.

They further agreed not to enter into any treaty or agreement contrary to these principles, and that in deference to the principle of the 'open door' or equality of opportunity in China they would not seek nor support their nationals in seeking: (*a*) any arrangement which might purport to establish in favour of their interests any general superiority of rights with respect to commercial or economic development in any designated region of China; (*b*) any such monopoly or preference as would deprive nationals of any other Power of the right of undertaking any legitimate trade or industry in China, or of participating with the Chinese Government or with any local authority in any category of public enterprise which, by reason of its scope, duration or geographical extent, is calculated to frustrate the practical application of the principle of equal opportunity.

Other articles of the treaty stipulate: (i) that there will be no attempt by the Powers concerned to create spheres of influence; (ii) that there will be no unfair discrimination on Chinese railways; (iii) that Chinese neutrality in future wars will be respected; (iv) that the Powers concerned will communicate frankly and freely between themselves in any future situation affecting the treaty;

(v) that other Powers, having treaty relations with China, shall be invited to adhere to the treaty; (vi) that the treaty shall come into force on the deposit of ratifications (i.e., the 5th August, 1925). No definite date is fixed for the duration of the treaty.

The following Powers have acceded to the treaty: Sweden, Norway, Denmark and Spain.'

50. At the present date, Great Britain is bound by the provisions of these treaties; but the somewhat passive rôle played by China in the international experiment at Washington has changed to one of disconcerting activity which necessitated a corresponding change in the policy of His Majesty's Government and an advance beyond the limits of the attitude of 'wait-and-see' benevolence, adopted at Washington. The civil war—as a struggle between North and South, between Liberal (Kuomintang) and Conservative groups, between rival military chieftains and civilian intriguers with apparently neither principles nor patriotism—has been endemic in China since 1911. But in 1925 this mild chaos was galvanised by a change which speeded up the march of events and profoundly altered the relations between China and foreign Powers. The immediate cause of this change is to be found in the shooting incidents at Shanghai, Canton and Hankow in the summer of 1925;[32] the ultimate cause in the widening and deepening of Nationalist sensibilities and in the active intervention of Russian agents and propaganda in the domestic affairs of China. From 1919 to 1925 no party in the Chinese civil war had been actively supported by any foreign Power. In 1925 Russia began actively to support the Kuominchun in North China and the Kuomintang in Canton. This intervention and assistance altered the balance of power between the rival factions; it introduced a spirit of determination and extremism which had hitherto been lacking, and it inspired a degree of enmity against Great Britain which in ordinary circumstances and in an ordinary country could only have led to war. The state of affairs produced by the Canton boycott of Hongkong can only be described as a kind of one-sided war in which Great Britain resolutely refused to pick up the challenge thrown down to her because she believed that in the amorphous state of China it was impossible to find a vital spot for a decisive blow, and that to have embarked on a desultory war in China would have been to play Russia's game both in the Far East and at home. Our inactivity, however, strengthened the prestige of the Canton Kuomintang and promoted its victorious advance from Canton to the Yangtse in the latter half of 1926.

51. The Kuomintang, however, was formed out of two irreconcilable elements —the Left Wing, allied to the Communists and the Russians, and the Right Wing, who were certainly anti-Communist and probably anti-Russian except in so far as they could get material help out of Russia. The Right Wing were not averse to friendly relations with Great Britain, and the Left Wing, aware of this, were determined to prevent any such tendency by inciting incidents. The first of these incidents was the mob attack on the British concession at Hankow. This incident led to the despatch of the defence force to Shanghai to prevent any similar incident in that city, but it was considered inexpedient to recapture the Hankow concession by force in view of His Majesty's Government's promise to China regarding the

[32] For a brief account of the incidents at Shanghai and Canton and the anti-British boycott in the territory of the Chinese Nationalist Government at Canton see the Appendix to Volume II, pp. 951–3: see also Cmd. 2636 of 1926, *Papers respecting the First Firing in the Shameen Affair of June 23, 1925*, and *Survey of International Affairs 1925*, vol. ii, pp. 381–8.

rendition of concessions (see below, paragraph 52). The second incident was the attack on British nationals (including the Consul-General) at Nanking by soldiers of the Kuomintang army when they captured that city.[33] American, Japanese, French and Italian subjects also suffered, and for a moment it looked as if united action would be taken by these Powers to punish the aggressors. But, as so often happens in China, the objective for retaliatory action faded away owing to the definite split in the Kuomintang which followed immediately on the outrages, the anti-Communist action taken by the Chinese themselves, the setting up of an entirely new Government (in no way personally responsible for the outrages) at Nanking, and the hesitation and divided counsels among the Powers concerned. The moment for the satisfactory settlement of the incident was therefore lost.

52. But besides the despatch of the defence force to Shanghai, His Majesty's Government's China policy had already undergone another important modification. This was also caused by the deliberate singling out of Great Britain for attack by the Chinese Nationalists in 1925 and also by the failure of the Peking Tariff Conference in 1925–26[34] to liquidate the promises made at Washington regarding the increase of China's tariff duties. The Tariff Conference came to an inconclusive end (1) because of the attitude of certain Powers, notably Japan and the United States, in their determination to get their unsecured debts secured on the additional customs revenues, and (2) because the course of the civil war made it impossible for the Chinese to present anything like a representative delegation. His Majesty's Government, however, considered that, in view of the lapse of time, it was impossible to hold up the Washington promises any longer, and therefore that, since it was impossible to impose conditions, the additional customs revenues should be levied at the various ports, unconditionally. This proposal was laid before the United States Government on the 28th May, 1926. A few months later the Canton Government proceeded to levy the additional revenues. His Majesty's Government joined in a *pro forma* protest, but that was all. On the 18th December, 1926, His Majesty's Government renewed their proposal in a memorandum communicated to the representatives (at Peking) of all the Washington Treaty Powers;[35] further, as the Extra-territoriality Commission had just reported,[36] His Majesty's Government added a suggestion that the Commission's recommendations should be carried into effect as soon as possible and that 'the Powers should make it clear that in their constructive policy they desired to go as far as possible towards meeting the legitimate aspirations of the Chinese nation.' This memorandum, which will undoubtedly be a landmark in the history of Anglo-Chinese relations, was followed by an offer of measures for treaty modification which His Majesty's Government were prepared to take if the Chinese authorities in North or South

[33] For brief accounts of the attack on the British Concession at Hankow in January 1927, the despatch of the British Defence Force to Shanghai, the agreements of February 19, 1927, respecting the British Concessions at Hankow and Kiukiang (the Chen–O'Malley agreement, text in Cmd. 2869 of 1927), and the incident at Nanking in March 1927 and its settlement see Second Series, Volume VIII, No. 1, pp. 9–11, and Volume XI, Appendix, pp. 560–1. For the Nanking incident see also Cmd. 2953 of 1927 and Cmd. 3188 of 1928.

[34] For a brief account of this conference see the Appendix to Volume II of this Series, pp. 951–2.

[35] The note of May 28, 1926, together with the memorandum of December 18, 1926, is printed in *Survey of International Affairs 1926*, pp. 488–94.

[36] For this commission cf. Second Series, Volume VIII, No. 1, p. 7. Its report dated September 16, 1926, is printed as Cmd. 2774 of 1926.

desired them to do so.[37] This offer deals with the recognition of the Chinese law courts and of a reasonable Chinese nationality law, the application of Chinese law in British courts, the payment of Chinese taxation by British subjects, the consideration of the application of the revised Chinese penal code, the modification of the municipal administration of British concessions, and the rights of British missionaries and their converts. The publication of this offer, which at the time the Chinese affected to disparage, has had an increasing influence in promoting a more friendly attitude towards Great Britain. It has taken the sting out of the attack on Great Britain as protagonist of the old treaty position, and it has placed the Chinese in a quandary, since when it comes to work out the details for modification, they find that practical difficulties are very great and that there was more to be said, even from their own point of view, in favour of the old arrangements than they could ever be brought to admit. At Hankow, for instance, the Chinese were singularly unsuccessful in their attempts to administer the recovered concession. At Tien-tsin, where a modifying agreement had been initialled,[38] demands for the return of the concession gradually faded away as the Chinese became less and less ready to acquire advantages which would also entail responsibility.

53. One more result of the Nanking outrages should also be mentioned, viz., the instructions sent by His Majesty's Admiralty to the Commander-in-Chief, China, on the 11th May, 1927. These instructions gave the Commander-in-Chief much wider powers than he had formerly possessed to take immediate retaliatory action in the event of outrages which (1) endangered the lives of British nationals, or (2) endangered British property when there was actual deliberate and wanton destruction of property. These instructions have, as a matter of fact, not been used except in cases of desultory firing by Chinese troops at British vessels.

54. To resume, the policy of His Majesty's Government in China is still based on the Washington Treaty; but this has been modified in two directions, which are not in fact so divergent as they seem at first sight. The first direction is towards the necessity for defending British lives and property, which led to the despatch of the defence force and to the issuing of the revised instructions to the Commander-in-Chief. The second direction is towards the necessity for proving indisputably to the Chinese people that His Majesty's Government are not reactionary or unfriendly towards their efforts (such as they are) to improve themselves, and their conditions, and their status in the world; this led to the memorandum of the 18th December, 1926, and the treaty modification offer of the 28th January, 1927.

55. It may be added that for the moment the Chinese, both North and South of the Yangtse, have become so exasperated with the Russians and their methods that Russian influence is practically non-existent, and that the Chinese Communist Party (which is almost entirely political rather than social in its activities) has been driven under ground. In the present exhausted and desperate state of China, however, it would be most unwise to predict that we had heard the last of either the Communistic or the Russian influence.

56. Our relations with the various Chinese Governments—at Peking, at Nanking, at Hankow, at Canton—are not unfriendly. The anti-British feeling of the last three years has abated. These are encouraging signs of the revival of British trade. So far as this country is concerned the prospects are better than they have

[37] This offer was presented to the Minister for Foreign Affairs of the Chinese Governments at Hankow and Peking on January 27 and 28, 1927, respectively, and is printed in *Survey of International Affairs 1926*, pp. 494–5.

[38] Cf. Second Series, Volume VIII, No. 1, p. 13.

been for a long time; but there are no signs of a peaceful settlement of the civil war, and so long as the civil war continues, China will be a danger area in international relations.

JAPAN

57. Our relations with Japan are governed by the same Washington Treaties which have been analysed in paragraph 49 above. The Four-Power Treaty, especially, has taken the place of the old Alliance Agreement, and, although friendly orators in both countries are fond of announcing that the spirit of the alliance still exists, as a matter of fact our relations are polite rather than intimate. The two factors which keep Japan and Great Britain united are (1) the fear of a common danger from China or from Russia threatening their respective interests, and (2) a genuine admiration on the part of the Japanese ruling classes for the kind of democratic monarchy which presides over the British Empire. The former of these two factors has led to a certain degree of co-operation between Japan and Great Britain in China, especially since the Nanking outrages proved that all foreign interests there must stand or fall together. It was after these outrages that the Japanese followed our example by despatching a defence force to Shantung Province; this force was, however, withdrawn after three or four months. But our policy in China is not really identical with that of Japan. We wish to see China united and prosperous and purchasing the maximum quantity of high-grade British goods; Japan does not desire too united or too prosperous a China. The present China, with low customs duties permitting a big sale of Japanese low-grade goods, suits Japan very well. Japan, too, would like to see rather less of British influence in China and a corresponding increase of Japanese influence. Further, there is Manchuria, where Japan wishes to expand in the face of Russian opposition and Chinese obstruction; this is a special Japanese problem, in which we have little or no concern. It may lead to increased friction between Japan and Russia; or it may lead to increased intimacy between the two countries for protection of their mutual interests.

58. The most striking evidence of Japanese appreciation of British life and institutions was the sending in 1925 of His Imperial Highness Prince Chichibu, the Emperor's brother, to finish his education in this country. In 1924—owing to the American Immigration Law[39] and to His Majesty's Government's decision to proceed with the Singapore naval base[40]—the popularity of Great Britain in Japan was at a low ebb; but since that date, partly owing to Prince Chichibu's visit and partly to the events in China, we seem to have become better appreciated.

59. The prestige of Japan has certainly suffered an almost catastrophic deflation since the days of her wartime prosperity. The economic slump, the discontinuation of the alliance, the great earthquake, and now, more recently, the financial crisis of 1927, have revealed Japan's weakness to the eyes of the world, and perhaps

[39] For an account of the background to and the effects of the Immigration Law signed on May 26, 1924, and printed in the United States Department of Justice, *Immigration and Nationality Laws and Regulations as of March 1, 1944* (Washington, 1944), pp. 39–61, see *Survey of International Affairs 1924*, pp. 86–103 and 127–60.

[40] For developments in connection with the proposals first put forward in 1921 to develop Singapore as the main base for British naval forces in the Far East and for the control of sea communications in the Indian Ocean and the Southern Pacific, see S. Woodburn Kirby, *The War Against Japan* (London, 1957), vol. i, pp. 1–9.

still more to the eyes of the Japanese. In 1925, Sir Charles Eliot[41] reported that he considered that Japan was now a weak Power. In 1926 Sir John Tilley wrote: 'I feel able to say that Japan should not be regarded as a menace to peace in any quarter, or as likely to be a protagonist in any great world movement; her rôle, I believe, will for many years yet be only secondary.' It should be remembered, however, that her geographical position renders her almost unattackable; and that her admirable army and navy are by far the strongest factor in the Far Eastern position if Japan should ever decide to make full use of them. It will be His Majesty's Government's policy to strive to retain the friendship of Japan, and so far as possible to co-ordinate our policy in China with the justifiable claims of Japan for special consideration. It is to be hoped that Japan will deal equally loyally and considerately by us, but that is more doubtful.

SIAM

60. By a declaration of the 15th January, 1896, Great Britain and France each bound themselves not to advance armed forces into Siam, except with the consent of the other, and not to acquire any special privilege or advantage which shall not be equally enjoyed by both countries. This was, however, without prejudice to any agreed action for the purpose of upholding the independence of Siam. Great Britain and France also engaged not to enter into separate agreements permitting a third Power to take any action from which, by the declaration in question, they themselves were bound to abstain.

61. A general treaty and a treaty of commerce and navigation between this country and Siam were signed on the 14th July, 1925, and ratifications have now been exchanged. These two treaties mark the opening of a new era in Anglo-Siamese relations. The general treaty gives Siam full jurisdictional autonomy, and the commercial treaty gives her fiscal autonomy. In both cases, however, there are certain safeguards. A protocol is annexed to the general treaty providing that, pending the enforcement of the Siamese codes, now in preparation, and for five years thereafter, His Majesty's diplomatic and consular officials may evoke any case pending in any Siamese court, except the Supreme Court, in which a British subject is involved and dispose of it themselves in accordance with English law. An article of the commercial treaty stipulates that the articles of principal interest to British trade with Siam, namely, cotton yarns, threads, fabrics, and all other manufactures of cotton, iron and steel, and manufactures thereof, and machinery and parts thereof, manufactured in any of His Majesty's territories to which the treaty applies, shall not, on importation into Siam, be subjected to any customs duty in excess of 5 per cent. *ad valorem* during the first ten years after the coming into force of the treaty.

62. Relations between the two countries are cordial. British trade with Siam has been longer established and is larger in volume than that of any other country, and more than 50,000 Indian British subjects are resident in Siam.[42]

[41] H.M. Ambassador at Tokyo from January 1920 to February 1926.

[42] The preceding three paragraphs are the same as paragraphs 132–4 in the Appendix to Volume I. The declaration of 1896 and the treaties and protocols of 1925 are printed in *British and Foreign State Papers*, vol. 88, pp. 13–17, and vol. 121, pp. 840–57, respectively.

VII. *North and South America*

UNITED STATES

NAVAL COMPETITION

63. The danger to good relations arising out of naval competition, which it was hoped had been to all intents and purposes removed by the conclusion of the Washington Naval Treaty, again became perceptible with the opening of 1927 owing to the intensive propaganda by 'Big Navy' and unfriendly elements in the United States for the construction of a large cruiser force alleged to be required for the purpose of obtaining 'parity' with this country. This danger was accentuated by the failure of the Geneva Naval Conference, which was held at the invitation of the United States Government for the purpose of further limiting naval armaments by the extension of the 5:5:3 ratio agreed upon at Washington in 1921 for capital ships so as to cover all classes of war vessels. It is not necessary here to go into the causes which led to the failure of this conference. It will suffice to say that it gave rise to considerable resentment in the United States, and may be regarded as responsible for the subsequent decision of the President to support the demands of the General Board of the United States Navy for a large building programme. While it appears likely that the Naval question will prove to be a problem of some difficulty during the next few years, the relative lack of success which has attended the efforts of interested parties in the United States to arouse any real wave of anti-British feeling on the subject, justifies a hope that the problem may not prove to be insoluble.

64. Nevertheless, it must be frankly admitted that, as long as the element of veiled naval competition exists, relations are unlikely to improve and may, indeed, gradually deteriorate. Commercial and financial competition is a necessary and a permanent evil, but its effects are only likely to become serious if an acute and determined naval competition is superimposed. The situation has certain analogies with that existing as between Great Britain and Germany before the war, and for this reason needs careful watching. But there are also certain fundamental differences, chief of which is the fact that the American people is, as a whole, pacific in its outlook. In the words of Admiral Rodgers, United States of America, 'the United States is peaceably and benevolently, although somewhat arrogantly, disposed towards the rest of the world.'

WAR CLAIMS AGREEMENT

65. If the failure of the Geneva Conference did nothing to improve Anglo-American relations, the conclusion on the 19th May, 1927, of an agreement with that country for the mutual liquidation of all claims originating during the war 1914–18 can only be described as most fortunate and useful. In 1925 it became apparent that the United States Government were contemplating the presentation of a large number of so-called claims against Great Britain arising from the detention of United States merchant vessels and cargoes during the blockade of Germany. Such an event would have been definitely detrimental to the good relations between the two countries, chiefly on account of the unfortunate effect which the presentation of these war claims would have had upon public opinion in Great Britain. In 1926, however, negotiations were carried on quietly and without any measure of publicity both in Washington and in London, which led to the removal of this

menace and the mutual settlement of many other claims, without either Government being called upon to make any actual payment to the other. It is satisfactory to be able to add that, since the agreement was concluded, the United States Government have shown every disposition to deal as rapidly as possible with certain minor British claims not included within its scope which have been pending for some time, and generally to live up to the spirit as well as to the letter of the agreement.

UNITED STATES POLICY IN THE CARIBBEAN AREA

66. According to information supplied in confidence to His Majesty's Chargé d'Affaires at Port-au-Prince, the United States Government either have concluded or are about to conclude a secret agreement with the Government of Hayti, under which the United States will be authorised to fortify certain selected points in Hayti, and the Haytian Government will establish a military force (recruited it is alleged by conscription) to be commanded by United States officers. This alleged secret agreement, however, only represents an extension of an already existing state of affairs. Under the Treaty of 1915 between Hayti and the United States,[43] the latter already exercise a large measure of control in Hayti, while American officers command the Haytian gendarmerie.

PAN-AMERICAN CONFERENCE AT HAVANA

67. The VIth International Conference of American States, otherwise known as the Pan-American Conference, opened in Havana, Cuba, on the 16th January and terminated on the 21st February last. Great importance was attached to this conference by the United States Government, who, for some time prior to its commencement, had not been able to conceal their apprehension over the spread of anti-Americanism in South America, as reflected by a distinct fall in the volume of their trade with their Latin-American neighbours. Consequently, not only was the conference inaugurated by President Coolidge in person, but a very strong United States delegation, headed by Mr. Charles E. Hughes, late Secretary of State, attended.

68. The conference resulted in a great personal triumph for Mr. Hughes, whose skilful diplomacy successfully prevented any extended discussion upon political matters reflecting upon the United States, such as the question of the right of one country to intervene in the internal affairs of another (Nicaragua). On more than one occasion, however, disagreeable wrangles were only avoided with the utmost difficulty, and in this connexion it is worthy of note that Dr. Pueyrredon, Argentine Ambassador at Washington and head of the Argentine delegation, caused some embarrassment to the United States delegation, not only in the matter of intervention, but also as regards the question of inter-American tariffs. Dr. Pueyrredon appears, indeed, to have exceeded his instructions, and the attitude which he adopted led eventually to his resigning not only his leadership of the Argentine delegation, but also his post at Washington.

69. One purpose of the United States Government was probably to show that they are not in any sense behind the League of Nations in their desire to promote peace by the preparation and conclusion of international conventions. Amongst the numerous draft conventions, resolutions, &c., approved by the conference, perhaps the most important was that dealing with maritime neutrality, and a

[43] This treaty, signed on September 16, 1915, is printed *op. cit.*, vol. 109, pp. 958–62.

resolution approving the principle of compulsory arbitration of international disputes and providing for a conference to be held in Washington within the next twelve months to consider how this may best be carried out, as well as to define the limits of arbitrable questions. The draft convention on maritime neutrality recognises the right of search on the high seas and establishes that commercial vessels may only be attacked in the event of their refusing, after having been stopped, to obey instructions, and may not be disabled until passengers and crew have been removed to a place of safety. The treaty also lays down certain rules regarding the provision of war material to belligerents, and finally classifies armed merchant vessels as ships of war. This classification was strongly objected to by the United States and Cuba, who agreed to the treaty with reservations.

70. According to information received, it may be said that while the successful manœuvring of the United States delegation has been received by their compatriots with a chorus of acclamation, there is little doubt but that the conference failed in its primary purpose, namely, the creation of better feeling towards the United States on the part of Latin America in general.

Dd 152386 K 14 8/71